BOOK THE TENTH

# THE SLIPPERY SLOPE

A SERIES OF UNFORTUNATE EVENTS

# A Series of Unfortunate Events

BOOK THE TENTH

# THE SLIPPERY SLOPE

by

*Lemony Snicket*

Illustrated by
BRETT HELQUIST

TED SMART

First published in the USA 2003
by HarperCollins Children's Books
First published in Great Britain 2004
by Egmont Books Limited
239 Kensington High Street, London W8 6SA
This edition published in Great Britain 2005
for The Book People Ltd
Hall Wood Avenue, Haydock, St Helens WA11 9UL

Published by arrangement
with HarperCollins Children's Books
a division of HarperCollins Publishers, Inc.
1350 Avenue of the Americas, New York,
New York 10019, USA

Text copyright © 2003 Lemony Snicket
Inside illustration copyright © 2003 Brett Helquist
Cover illustration copyright © 2004 Brett Helquist

The moral right of the cover illustrator
has been asserted

A CIP catalogue for this title is available from
the British Library

Printed and bound in Italy

For Beatrice –

When we met, you were pretty, and I was lonely.

Now, I am pretty lonely.

A man of my acquaintance once wrote a poem called "The Road Less Traveled," describing a journey he took through the woods along a path most travelers never used. The poet found that the road less traveled was peaceful but quite lonely, and he was probably a bit nervous as he went along, because if anything happened on the road less traveled, the other travelers would be on the road more frequently traveled and so couldn't hear him as he cried for help. Sure enough, that poet is now dead.

Like a dead poet, this book can be said to be on the road less traveled, because it begins with the three Baudelaire children on a path leading through the Mortmain Mountains, which is not a popular destination for travelers, and it ends in the churning waters of the Stricken Stream, which few travelers even go near. But this book is also on the road less traveled, because unlike books most people prefer, which provide comforting and entertaining tales about charming people and talking animals, the tale you are reading now is nothing but distressing and unnerving, and the people unfortunate enough to be in the story are far more desperate and frantic than charming, and I would prefer to not speak about the animals at all. For that reason, I can no more suggest the reading of this woeful book than I can recommend wandering around the woods by yourself, because like the road less traveled, this book is likely to make you feel lonely, miserable, and in need of help.

The Baudelaire orphans, however, had no choice but to be on the road less traveled. Violet and Klaus, the two elder Baudelaires, were in a caravan, traveling very quickly along the high mountain path. Neither Violet, who was fourteen, nor Klaus, who had recently turned thirteen, had ever thought they would find themselves on this road, except perhaps with their parents on a family vacation. But the Baudelaire parents were nowhere to be found after a terrible fire destroyed their home— although the children had reason to believe that one parent may not have died in the blaze after all—and the caravan was not heading up the Mortmain Mountains, toward a secret headquarters the siblings had heard about and were hoping to find. The caravan was heading down the Mortmain Mountains, very quickly, with no way to control or stop its journey, so Violet and Klaus felt more like fish in a stormy sea than travelers on a vacation.

But Sunny Baudelaire was in a situation that could be said to be even more desperate. Sunny was the youngest Baudelaire, still learning to speak in a way that everyone could understand, so she scarcely had words for how frightened she was. Sunny was traveling uphill, toward the headquarters in the Mortmain Mountains, in an automobile that was working perfectly, but the driver of the automobile was a man who was reason enough for being terrified. Some people called this man wicked. Some called him facinorous, which is a fancy word for "wicked." But everyone called him Count Olaf, unless he was wearing one of his ridiculous disguises and making people call him a false name. Count Olaf was an actor, but he had largely abandoned his theatrical career to try to steal the enormous fortune the Baudelaire parents had left behind. Olaf's schemes to get the fortune had been mean-spirited and particularly complicated, but nevertheless he had managed to attract a girlfriend, a villainous and stylish woman named Esmé Squalor, who was sitting next to Count Olaf in the car, cackling nastily and clutching Sunny on her lap. Also in the car were several employees of Olaf's, including a man with hooks instead of hands, two women who liked to wear white powder all over their faces, and three new comrades Olaf had recently recruited at Caligari Carnival. The Baudelaire children had been at the carnival, too, wearing disguises of their own, and had pretended to join Count Olaf in his treachery, but the villain had seen through their ruse, a phrase which here means "realized who they really were, and cut the knot attaching the caravan to the car, leaving Sunny in Olaf's clutches and her siblings tumbling toward their doom." Sunny sat in the car and felt Esmé's long fingernails scratch her shoulders, and worried about what would happen to her and what was happening to her older siblings, as she heard their screams getting fainter and fainter as the car drove farther and farther away.

"We have to stop this caravan!" Klaus screamed. Hurriedly, he put on his glasses, as if by improving his vision he might improve the situation. But even in perfect focus, he could see their predicament was dire. The caravan had served as a home for several performers at the carnival's House of Freaks before they defected—a word which here means "joined Count Olaf's band of revolting comrades"—and now the contents of this tiny home were rattling and crashing with each bump in the road. Klaus ducked to avoid a roasting pan, which Hugo the hunchback had used to prepare meals and which had toppled off a shelf in the commotion. He lifted his feet from the floor as a set of dominoes skittered by—a set that Colette the contortionist had liked to play with. And he squinted above him as a hammock swung violently overhead. An ambidextrous person named Kevin used to sleep in that hammock until he had joined Olaf's troupe, along with Hugo and Colette, and now it seemed like it might fall at any moment and trap the Baudelaires beneath it.

The only comforting thing that Klaus could see was his sister, who was looking around the caravan with a fierce and thoughtful expression and unbuttoning the shirt the two siblings were sharing as part of their disguise. "Help me get us out of these freakish pants we're both in," Violet said. "There's no use pretending we're a two-headed person anymore, and we both need to be as able-bodied as possible."

In moments, the two Baudelaires wriggled out of the oversized clothing they had taken from Count Olaf's disguise kit and were standing in regular clothes, trying to balance in the shaky caravan. Klaus quickly stepped out of the path of a falling potted plant, but he couldn't help smiling as he looked at his sister. Violet was tying her hair up in a ribbon to keep it out of her eyes, a sure sign that she was thinking up an invention. Violet's impressive mechanical skills had saved the Baudelaires' lives more times than they could count, and Klaus was certain that his sister could concoct something that could stop the caravan's perilous journey.

"Are you going to make a brake?" Klaus asked.

"Not yet," Violet said. "A brake interferes with the wheels of a vehicle, and this caravan's wheels are spinning too quickly for interference. I'm going to unhook these hammocks and use them as a drag chute."

"Drag chute?" Klaus said.

"Drag chutes are a little like parachutes attached to the back of a car," Violet explained hurriedly, as a coatrack clattered around her. She reached up to the hammock where she and Klaus had slept and quickly detached it from the wall. "Race drivers use them to help stop their cars when a race is over. If I dangle these hammocks out the caravan door, we should slow down considerably."

"What can I do?" Klaus said.

"Look in Hugo's pantry," Violet said, "and see if you can find anything sticky."

When someone tells you to do something unusual without an explanation, it is very difficult not to ask why, but Klaus had learned long ago to have faith in his sister's ideas, and quickly crossed to a large cupboard Hugo had used to store ingredients for the meals he prepared. The door of the cupboard was swinging back and forth as if a ghost were fighting with it, but most of the items were still rattling around inside. Klaus looked at the cupboard and thought of his baby sister, who was getting farther and farther away from him. Even though Sunny was still quite young, she had recently shown an interest in cooking, and Klaus remembered how she had made up her own hot chocolate recipe, and helped prepare a delicious soup the entire caravan had enjoyed. Klaus held the cupboard door open and peered inside, and hoped that his sister would survive to develop her culinary skills.

"*Klaus,*" Violet said firmly, taking down another hammock and tying it to the first one. "I don't mean to rush you, but we need to stop this caravan as soon as possible. Have you found anything sticky?"

Klaus blinked and returned to the task at

hand. A ceramic pitcher rolled around his feet as he pushed through the bottles and jars of cooking materials. "There's lots of sticky things here," he said. "I see blackstrap molasses, wild clover honey, corn syrup, aged balsamic vinegar, apple butter, strawberry jam, caramel sauce, maple syrup, butterscotch topping, maraschino liqueur, virgin and extra-virgin olive oil, lemon curd, dried apricots, mango chutney, *crema di noci*, tamarind paste, hot mustard, marshmallows, creamed corn, peanut butter, grape preserves, salt water taffy, condensed milk, pumpkin pie filling, and glue. I don't know why Hugo kept glue in the pantry, but never mind. Which items do you want?"

"All of them," Violet said firmly. "Find some way of mixing them, while I tie these hammocks together."

Klaus grabbed the pitcher from the floor and began to pour the ingredients into it, while Violet, sitting on the floor to make it easier to balance, gathered the cords of the hammocks in her lap and began twisting them into a knot. The caravan's journey grew rougher and rougher, and with each jolt, the Baudelaires felt a bit seasick, as if they were back on Lake Lachrymose, crossing its stormy waters to try and rescue one of their many unfortunate guardians. But despite the tumult around them, in moments Violet stood up with the hammocks gathered in her arms, all tied together in a mass of fabric, and Klaus looked at his sister and held up the pitcher, which was filled to the brim with a thick and colorful slime.

"When I say the word," Violet said, "I'm going to open the door and cast these hammocks out. I want you at the other end of the caravan, Klaus. Open that little window and pour that mixture all over the wheels. If the hammocks work as a drag chute and the sticky substance interferes with the wheels, the caravan should slow down enough to save us. I just need to tie the hammocks to the doorknob."

"Are you using the Devil's Tongue knot?" Klaus asked.

"The Devil's Tongue hasn't brought us the best luck," Violet said, referring to several previous rope-related escapades. "I'm using the Sumac, a knot I invented myself. I named it after a singer I admire. There—it feels secure. Are you ready to pour that mixture onto the wheels?"

Klaus crossed to the window and opened it. The wild clattering sound of the caravan's wheels grew louder, and the Baudelaires stared for a moment at the countryside racing by. The land was jagged and twisty, and it seemed that the caravan could tumble at any moment into a hole, or off the edge of one of the mountain's square peaks. "I guess I'm ready," Klaus said hesitantly. "Violet, before we try your invention, I want to tell you something."

"If we don't try it now," Violet said grimly, "you won't have the chance to tell me anything." She gave her knot one more tug and then turned back to Klaus. "Now!" she said, and threw open the caravan door.

It is often said that if you have a room with a view, you will feel peaceful and relaxed, but if the room is a caravan hurtling down a steep and twisted road, and the view is an eerie mountain range racing backward away from you, while chilly mountain winds sting your face and toss dust into your eyes, then you will not feel one bit of peace or relaxation. Instead you will feel the horror and panic that the Baudelaires felt when Violet opened the door. For a moment they could do nothing but stand still, feeling the wild tilting of the caravan, and looking up at the odd, square peaks of the Mortmain Mountains, and hearing the grinding of the caravan's wheels as they rolled over rocks and tree stumps. But then Violet shouted "Now!" once more, and both siblings snapped into action. Klaus leaned out the window and began to pour the mixture of blackstrap molasses, wild clover honey, corn syrup, aged balsamic vinegar, apple butter, strawberry jam, caramel sauce, maple syrup, butterscotch topping, maraschino liqueur, virgin and extra-virgin olive oil, lemon curd, dried apricots, mango chutney, *crema di noci*, tamarind paste, hot mustard, marshmallows, creamed corn, peanut butter, grape preserves, salt water taffy, condensed milk, pumpkin pie filling, and glue onto the closest wheels, while his sister tossed the hammocks out of the door, and if you have read anything of the Baudelaire orphans' lives—which I hope you have not—then you will not be surprised to read that Violet's invention worked perfectly. The hammocks immediately caught the rushing air and swelled out behind the caravan like enormous cloth balloons, which slowed the caravan down quite a bit, the way you would run much slower if you were dragging something behind you, like a knapsack or a sheriff. The sticky mixture fell on the spinning wheels, which immediately began to move with less ferocity, the way you would run with less ferocity if you suddenly found yourself running in quicksand or through lasagne. The caravan slowed down, and the wheels spun less wildly, and within moments the two Baudelaires were traveling at a much more comfortable pace.

"It's working!" Klaus cried.

"We're not done yet," Violet said, and walked over to a small table that had overturned in the confusion. When the Baudelaires were living at Caligari Carnival, the table had come in handy as a place to sit and make plans, but now in the Mortmain Mountains, it would come in handy for a different reason. Violet dragged the table over to the open door. "Now that the wheels are slowing down," she said, "we can use this as a brake."

Klaus dumped the last of the mixture out of the pitcher, and turned to his sister. "How?" he said, but Violet was already showing him how. Quickly she lay on the floor, and holding the table by its legs, dangled it out of the caravan so it dragged on the ground. Immediately there was a loud scraping sound, and the table began to shake roughly in Violet's hands. But she held fast, forcing the table to scrape against the rocky ground and slow the caravan down even more. The swaying of the caravan became gentler and gentler, and the fallen items owned by the carnival employees stopped crashing, and then with one last whine, the wheels stopped altogether, and everything was still. Violet leaned out of the door and stuck the table in front of one of the wheels so it couldn't start rolling again, and then stood up and looked at her brother.

"We did it," Violet said.

"*You* did it," Klaus said. "The entire plan was your idea." He put down the pitcher on the floor and wiped his hands on a fallen towel.

"Don't put down that pitcher," Violet said, looking around the wreckage of the caravan. "We should gather up as many useful things as possible. We'll need to get this caravan moving uphill if we want to rescue Sunny."

"And reach the headquarters," Klaus added.

"Count Olaf has the map we found, but I remember that the headquarters are in the Valley of Four Drafts, near the source of the Stricken Stream. It'll be very cold there."

"Well, there is plenty of clothing," Violet said, looking around. "Let's grab everything we can and organize it outside."

Klaus nodded in agreement, and picked up the pitcher again, along with several items of clothing that had fallen in a heap on top of a small hand mirror that belonged to Colette. Staggering from carrying so many things, he walked out of the caravan behind his sister, who was carrying a large bread knife, three heavy coats, and a ukulele that Hugo used to play sometimes on lazy afternoons. The floors of the caravan creaked as the Baudelaires stepped outside, into the misty and empty landscape, and realized how fortunate they had been.

The caravan had stopped right at the edge of one of the odd, square peaks of the mountain

range. The Mortmain Mountains looked like a
staircase, heading up into the clouds or down
into a veil of thick, gray mist, and if the caravan
had kept going in the same direction, the two
Baudelaires would have toppled over the peak
and fallen down through the mist to the next
stair, far, far below. But to one side of the caravan, the children could see the waters of the
Stricken Stream, which were an odd grayish
black color, and moved slowly and lazily downhill like a river of spilled oil. Had the caravan
swerved to one side, the children would have
been dumped into the dark and filthy waters.

"It looks like the brake worked just in time,"
Violet said quietly. "No matter where the caravan
would have gone, we would have been finished."

Klaus nodded in agreement and looked
around at the wilderness. "It will be difficult to
navigate the caravan out of here," Klaus said.
"You'll have to invent a steering device."

"And some sort of engine," Violet said.

"That will take some time."

"We don't have any time," Klaus said. "If we don't hurry, Count Olaf will be too far away and we'll never find Sunny."

"We'll find her," Violet said firmly, and put down the items she was carrying. "Let's go back into the caravan, and look for—"

But before Violet could say what to look for, she was interrupted by an unpleasant crackling noise. The caravan seemed to moan, and then slowly began to roll toward the edge of the peak. The Baudelaires looked down and saw that the wheels had smashed the small table, so there was nothing to stop the caravan from moving again. Slowly and awkwardly it pitched forward, dragging the hammocks behind it as it neared the very edge of the peak. Klaus leaned down to grab hold of a hammock, but Violet stopped him. "It's too heavy," she said. "We can't stop it."

"We can't let it fall off the peak!" Klaus cried.

"We'd be dragged down, too," Violet said.

Klaus knew his sister was right, but still he wanted to grab the drag chute Violet had constructed. It is difficult, when faced with a situation you cannot control, to admit that you can do nothing, and it was difficult for the Baudelaires to stand and watch the caravan roll over the edge of the peak. There was one last creak as the back wheels bumped against a mound of dirt, and then the caravan disappeared in absolute silence. The Baudelaires stepped forward and peered over the edge of the peak, but it was so misty that the caravan was only a ghostly rectangle, getting smaller and smaller as it faded away.

"Why isn't there a crash?" Klaus asked.

"The drag chute is slowing it down," Violet said. "Just wait."

The siblings waited, and after a moment there was a muffled *boom!* from below as the caravan met its fate. In the mist, the children could not see a thing, but they knew that the caravan and everything inside it were gone forever, and indeed I have never been able to find its remains, even after months of searching the area with only a lantern and a rhyming dictionary for company. It seems that even after countless nights of battling snow gnats and praying the batteries would not run out, it is my fate that some of my questions will never be answered.

Fate is like a strange, unpopular restaurant, filled with odd waiters who bring you things you never asked for and don't always like. When the Baudelaires were very young, they would have guessed that their fate was to grow up in happiness and contentment with their parents in the Baudelaire mansion, but now both the mansion and their parents were gone. When they were attending Prufrock Preparatory School, they had thought that their fate was to graduate alongside their friends the Quagmires, but they hadn't seen the academy or the two triplets in a very long time. And just moments ago, it had looked like Violet and Klaus's fate had been to fall off a peak or into a stream, but now they were alive and well, but far away from their sister and without a vehicle to help them find her again.

Violet and Klaus moved closer to one another, and felt the icy winds of the Mortmain Mountains blow down the road less traveled and give them goosebumps. They looked at the dark and swirling waters of the Stricken Stream, and they looked down from the edge of the peak into the mist, and then looked at one another and shivered, not only at the fates they had avoided, but at all the mysterious fates that lay ahead.

# CHAPTER TWO

*Violet* took one last look over the misty peak, and then reached down to put on one of the heavy coats she had taken from the caravan. "Take one of these coats," she said to her brother. "It's cold out here, and it's likely to get even colder. The headquarters are supposed to be very high up in the mountains. By the time we get there, we'll probably be wearing every stitch of this clothing."

"But how are we going to get there?" Klaus said. "We're nowhere near the Valley of Four Drafts, and the caravan is destroyed."

"Let's take a moment to see what we have,"

Violet said. "I might be able to construct something from the items we managed to take."

"I hope so," Klaus said. "Sunny is getting farther and farther away. We'll never catch up with her without some sort of vehicle."

Klaus spread out the items from the caravan, and put on one of the coats while Violet picked through her pile, but instantly the two Baudelaires saw that a vehicle was not in the realm of possibility, a phrase which here means "could not be made from a few small objects and some articles of clothing previously belonging to carnival employees." Violet tied her hair up in a ribbon again and frowned down on the few items they had managed to save. In Klaus's pile there was the pitcher, still sticky from the substance he had used to slow down the caravan wheels, as well as Colette's hand mirror, a wool poncho, and a sweatshirt that read CALIGARI CARNIVAL. In Violet's pile was the large bread knife, the ukulele, and one more coat. Even

Klaus, who was not as mechanically minded as his sister, knew that the materials gathered on the ground were not enough to make something that could take the two children through the Mortmain Mountains.

"I suppose I could make a spark by rubbing two rocks together," Violet said, looking around the misty countryside for additional inventing materials, "or we could play the ukulele and bang on the pitcher. A loud noise might attract some help."

"But who would hear it?" Klaus said, gazing at the gloomy mist. "We didn't see a sign of anyone else when we were in the caravan. The way through the Mortmain Mountains is like a poem I read once, about the road less traveled."

"Did the poem have a happy ending?" Violet asked.

"It was neither happy nor unhappy," Klaus said. "It was ambiguous. Well, let's gather up these materials and take them with us."

"Take them with us?" Violet said. "We don't know where to go, and we don't know how to get there."

"Sure we do," Klaus said. "The Stricken Stream starts at a source high in the mountains, and winds its way down through the Valley of Four Drafts, where the headquarters are. It's probably not the quickest or easiest way to get there, but if we follow the stream up the mountains, it'll take us where we want to go."

"But that could take days," Violet said. "We don't have a map, or any food or water for the journey, or tents or sleeping bags or any other camping equipment."

"We can use all this clothing as blankets," Klaus said, "and we can sleep in any shelter we find. There were quite a few caves on the map that animals use for hibernation."

The two Baudelaires looked at one another and shivered in the chilly breeze. The idea of hiking for hours in the mountains, only to sleep wrapped in someone else's clothing in a cave that might contain hibernating animals, was not a pleasant one, and the siblings wished they did not have to take the road less traveled, but instead could travel in a swift, well-heated vehicle and reach their sister in mere moments. But wishing, like sipping a glass of punch, or pulling aside a bearskin rug in order to access a hidden trapdoor in the floor, is merely a quiet way to spend one's time before the candles are extinguished on one's birthday cake, and the Baudelaires knew that it would be best to stop wishing and start their journey. Klaus put the hand mirror and the ukulele in his coat pockets and picked up the poncho and the pitcher, while Violet put the bread knife in her pocket and picked up the sweatshirt and the last coat, and then, with one last look at the tracks the caravan left behind as it toppled over the peak, the two children began to follow the Stricken Stream.

If you have ever traveled a long distance with a family member, then you know that there are times when you feel like talking and times when you feel like being quiet. This was one of the quiet times. Violet and Klaus walked up the slopes of the mountain toward the head-quarters they hoped to reach, and they heard the sound of the mountain winds, a low, tune-less moan like someone blowing across the top of an empty bottle, and the odd, rough sound of the stream's fish as they stuck their heads out of the dark, thick waters of the stream, but both travelers were in a quiet mood and did not say a word to one another, each lost in their own thoughts.

Violet let her mind wander to the time she had spent with her siblings in the Village of Fowl Devotees, when a mysterious man named Jacques Snicket was murdered, and the children were blamed for the crime. They had managed to escape from prison and rescue their friends Duncan and Isadora Quagmire from Count Olaf's clutches, but then had been separated at the last moment from the two triplets, who sailed away in a self-sustaining hot air mobile home built by a man named Hector. None of the Baudelaires had seen Hector or the two Quagmires since, and Violet wondered if they were safe and if they had managed to contact a secret organization they'd discovered. The organization was called V.F.D., and the Baudelaires had not yet learned exactly what the organization did, or even what all the letters stood for. The children thought that the headquarters at the Valley of Four Drafts might prove to be helpful, but now, as the eldest Baudelaire trudged alongside the Stricken Stream, she wondered if she would ever find the answers she was looking for.

Klaus was also thinking about the Quagmires, although he was thinking about when the Baudelaires first met them, at Prufrock Preparatory School. Many of the students at the school had been quite mean to the three siblings—particularly a very nasty girl named Carmelita Spats—but Isadora and Duncan had been very

kind, and soon the Baudelaires and the Quagmires had become inseparable, a word which
here means "close friends." One reason for their
friendship had been that both sets of children
had lost people who were close to them. The
Baudelaires had lost their parents, of course, and
the Quagmires had lost not only their parents
but their brother, the third Quagmire triplet,
whose name was Quigley. Klaus thought about
the Quagmires' tragedy, and felt a little guilty
that one of his own parents might be alive after
all. A document the Baudelaires had found contained a picture of their parents standing with
Jacques Snicket and another man, with a cap-
tion reading "Because of the evidence discussed
on page nine, experts now suspect that there
may in fact be one survivor of the fire, but the
survivor's whereabouts are unknown." Klaus
had this document in his pocket right now, along
with a few scraps of the Quagmires' notebooks
that they had managed to give him. Klaus

walked beside his older sister, thinking of the puzzle of V.F.D. and how kindly the Quagmires had tried to help them solve the mystery that surrounded them all. He was thinking so hard about these things that when Violet finally broke the silence, it was as if he were waking up from a long, confusing dream.

"Klaus," she said, "when we were in the caravan, you said you wanted to tell me something before we tried the invention, but I didn't let you. What was it?"

"I don't know," Klaus admitted. "I just wanted to say something, in case—well, in case the invention didn't work." He sighed, and looked up at the darkening sky. "I don't remember the last thing I said to Sunny," he said quietly. "It must have been when we were in Madame Lulu's tent, or maybe outside, just before we stepped into the caravan. Had I known that Count Olaf was going to take her away, I would have tried to say something special. I could have complimented her on the hot chocolate she made, or told her how skillful she was at staying in disguise."

"You can tell her those things," Violet said, "when we see her again."

"I hope so," Klaus said glumly, "but we're so far behind Olaf and his troupe."

"But we know where they're going," Violet said, "and we know that he won't harm a hair on her head. Count Olaf thinks we perished in the caravan, so he needs Sunny to get his hands on the fortune."

"She's probably unharmed," Klaus agreed, "but I'm sure she's very frightened. I just hope she knows we're coming after her."

"Me, too," Violet said, and walked in a silence for a while, interrupted only by the wind and the odd, gurgling noise of the fish.

"I think those fish are having trouble breathing," Klaus said, pointing into the stream. "Something in the water is making them cough."

"Maybe the Stricken Stream isn't always

that ugly color," Violet said. "What would turn normal water into grayish black slime?"

"Iron ore," Klaus said thoughtfully, trying to remember a book on high-altitude environmentalism he had read when he was ten. "Or perhaps a clay deposit, loosened by an earthquake or another geological event, or some sort of pollution. There might be an ink or licorice factory nearby."

"Maybe V.F.D. will tell us," Violet said, "when we reach the headquarters."

"Maybe one of our parents will tell us," Klaus said quietly.

"We shouldn't get our hopes up," Violet said. "Even if one of our parents really did survive the fire, and the V.F.D. headquarters really are at the Valley of Four Drafts, we still don't know that we will see them when we arrive."

"I don't see the harm in getting our hopes up," Klaus said. "We're walking along a damaged stream, toward a vicious villain, in an attempt to rescue our sister and find the headquarters of a secret organization. I could use a little bit of hope right now."

Violet stopped in her path. "I could use another layer of clothing," she said. "It's getting colder."

Klaus nodded in agreement, and held up the garment he was carrying. "Do you want the poncho," he asked, "or the sweatshirt?"

"The poncho, if you don't mind," Violet said. "After my experience in the House of Freaks, I don't wish to advertise the Caligari Carnival."

"Me neither," Klaus said, taking the lettered sweatshirt from his sister. "I think I'll wear it inside out."

Rather than take off their coats and expose themselves to the icy winds of the Mortmain Mountains, Klaus put on the inside-out sweatshirt over his coat, and Violet wore the poncho outside hers, where it hung awkwardly around her. The two elder Baudelaires looked at one another and had to smile at their ridiculous appearance.

"These are worse than the pinstripe suits Esmé Squalor gave us," Violet said.

"Or those itchy sweaters we wore when we stayed with Mr. Poe," Klaus said, referring to a banker who was in charge of the Baudelaire fortune, with whom they had lost touch. "But at least we'll keep warm. If it gets even colder, we can take turns wearing the extra coat."

"If one of our parents is at the headquarters," Violet said, "he or she might not recognize us underneath all this clothing. We'll look like two large lumps."

The two Baudelaires looked up at the snow-covered peaks above them and felt a bit dizzy, not only from the height of the Mortmain Mountains but from all the questions buzzing around their heads. Could they really reach the Valley of Four Drafts all by themselves? What would the headquarters look like? Would V.F.D.

be expecting the Baudelaires? Would Count Olaf have reached the headquarters ahead of them? Would they find Sunny? Would they find one of their parents? Violet and Klaus looked at one another in silence and shivered in their strange clothes, until finally Klaus broke the silence with one more question, which seemed the dizziest one of all.

"Which parent," he said, "do you think is the survivor?"

Violet opened her mouth to answer, but at that moment another question immediately occupied the minds of the elder Baudelaires. It is a dreadful question, and nearly everyone who has found themselves asking it has ended up wishing that they'd never brought up the subject. My brother asked the question once, and had nightmares about it for weeks. An associate of mine asked the question, and found himself falling through the air before he could hear the answer. It is a question I asked once, a very long time ago and in a very timid voice, and a woman replied by quickly putting a motorcycle helmet on her head and wrapping her body in a red silk cape. The question is, "What in the world is that ominous-looking cloud of tiny, white buzzing objects coming toward us?" and I'm sorry to tell you that the answer is "A swarm of well-organized, ill-tempered insects known as snow gnats, who live in cold mountain areas and enjoy stinging people for no reason whatsoever."

"What in the world," Violet said, "is that ominous-looking cloud of tiny, white buzzing objects coming toward us?"

Klaus looked in the direction his sister was pointing and frowned. "I remember reading something in a book on mountainous insect life," he said, "but I can't quite recall the details."

"Try to remember," Violet said, looking nervously at the approaching swarm. The ominous-looking cloud of tiny, white buzzing objects had appeared from around a rocky corner, and from a distance it looked a bit like the beginnings of a snowfall. But now the snowfall was organizing itself into the shape of an arrow, and moving toward the two children, buzzing louder and louder as if it were annoyed. "I think they might be snow gnats," Klaus said. "Snow gnats live in cold mountain areas and have been known to group themselves into well-defined shapes."

Violet looked from the approaching arrow to the waters of the stream and the steep edge of the mountain peak. "I'm glad gnats are harm-less," she said. "It doesn't look like there's any way to avoid them."

"There's something else about snow gnats," Klaus said, "that I'm not quite remembering."

The swarm drew quite close, with the tip of the fluttering white arrow just a few inches from the Baudelaires' noses, and then stopped in its path, buzzing angrily. The two siblings stood face-to-face with the snow gnats for a long, tense second, and the gnat at the very, very tip of the arrow flew daintily forward and stung Vio-let on the nose.

"Ow!" Violet said. The snow gnat flew back

to its place, and the eldest Baudelaire was left rubbing a tiny red mark on her nose. "That hurt," she said. "It feels like a pin stuck me."

"I remember now," Klaus said. "Snow gnats are ill-tempered and enjoy stinging people for no reason whatso—"

But Klaus did not get to finish his sentence, because the snow gnats interrupted and gave a ghastly demonstration of just what he was talking about. Curling lazily in the mountain winds, the arrow twisted and became a large buzzing circle, and the gnats began to spin around and around the two Baudelaires like a well-organized and ill-tempered hula hoop. Each gnat was so tiny that the children could not see any of its features, but they felt as if the insects were smiling nastily.

"Are the stings poisonous?" Violet asked.

"Mildly," Klaus said. "We'll be all right if we get stung a few times, but many stings could make us very ill. Ow!"

One of the gnats had flown up and stung

Klaus on the cheek, as if it were seeing if the middle Baudelaire was fun to hurt. "People always say that if you don't bother stinging insects, they won't bother you," Violet said nervously. "Ow!"

"That's scarcely ever true," Klaus said, "and it's certainly not true with snow gnats. Ow! Ow! *Ow!*"

"What should we—*Ow!*" Violet half asked.

"I don't—*Ow!*" Klaus half answered, but in moments the Baudelaires did not have time for even half a conversation. The circle of snow gnats began spinning faster and faster, and the insects spread themselves out so it looked as if the two siblings were in the middle of a tiny, white tornado. Then, in a series of manuevers that must have taken a great deal of rehearsal, the gnats began stinging the Baudelaires, first on one side and then on the other. Violet shrieked as several gnats stung her chin. Klaus shouted as a handful of gnats stung his left ear. And both Baudelaires cried out as they tried to wave the gnats away only to feel the stingers all over their waving hands. The snow gnats stung to the left, and stung to the right. They approached the Baudelaires from above, making the children duck, and then from below, making the children stand on tiptoe in an effort to avoid them. And all the while, the swarm buzzed louder and louder, as if wishing to remind the Baudelaires how much fun the insects were having. Violet and Klaus closed their eyes and stood together, too scared to walk blindly and find themselves falling off a mountain peak or sinking into the waters of the Stricken Stream.

"*Coat!*" Klaus managed to shout, then spit out a gnat that had flown into his open mouth in the hopes of stinging his tongue. Violet understood at once, and grabbed the extra coat in her hands and draped it over Klaus and herself like a large, limp umbrella of cloth. The snow gnats buzzed furiously, trying to get inside to continue stinging them, but had to settle for stinging the Baudelaires' hands as they held the coat in place.

Violet and Klaus looked at one another dimly underneath the coat, wincing as their fingers were stung, and tried to keep walking.

"We'll never reach the Valley of Four Drafts like this," Violet said, speaking louder than usual over the buzzing of the gnats. "How can we stop them, Klaus?"

"Fire drives them away," Klaus said. "In the book I read, the author said that even the smell of smoke can keep a whole swarm at bay. But we can't start a fire underneath a coat."

"Ow!" A snow gnat stung Violet's thumb on a spot that had already been stung, just as the Baudelaires rounded the rocky corner where the swarm had first appeared. Through a worn spot in the fabric, the Baudelaires could just make out a dark, circular hole in the side of the mountain.

"That must be an entrance to one of the caves," Klaus said. "Could we start a fire in there?"

"Maybe," Violet said. "And maybe we'd annoy a hibernating animal."

"We've already managed to annoy thousands of animals," Klaus said, almost dropping the pitcher as a gnat stung his wrist. "I don't think we have much choice. I think we have to head into the cave and take our chances."

Violet nodded in agreement, but looked nervously at the entrance to the cave. Taking one's chances is like taking a bath, because sometimes you end up feeling comfortable and warm, and sometimes there is something terrible lurking around that you cannot see until it is too late and you can do nothing else but scream and cling to a plastic duck. The two Baudelaires walked carefully toward the dark, circular hole, making sure to stay clear of the nearby edge of the peak and pulling the coat tightly around them so the snow gnats could not find a way inside, but what worried them most was not the height of the peak or the stingers of the gnats but the chances they were taking as they ducked inside the gloomy entrance of the cave.

The two Baudelaires had never been in this

cave before, of course, and as far as I have been able to ascertain, they were never in it again, even on their way back down the mountain, after they had been reunited with their baby sister and learned the secret of Verbal Fridge Dialogue. And yet, as Violet and Klaus took their chances and walked inside, they found two things with which they were familiar. The first was fire. As they stood inside the entrance to the cave, the siblings realized at once that there was no need to worry about the snow gnats any longer, because they could smell nearby smoke, and even see, at a great distance, small orange flames toward the back of the cave. Fire, of course, was very familiar to the children, from the ashen smell of the remains of the Baudelaire mansion to the scent of the flames that destroyed Caligari Carnival. But as the snow gnats formed an arrow and darted away from the cave and the Baudelaires took another step inside, Violet and Klaus found another familiar thing—a familiar person, to be exact, who they had thought they would never see again.

"Hey you cakesniffers!" said a voice from the back of the cave, and the sound was almost enough to make the two Baudelaires wish they had taken their chances someplace else.

CHAPTER

Three

*You* may well wonder why there has been no account of Sunny Baudelaire in the first two chapters of this book, but there are several reasons why this is so. For one thing, Sunny's journey in Count Olaf's car was much more difficult to research. The tracks made by the tires of the car have vanished long ago, and so many blizzards and avalanches have occurred in the Mortmain Mountains that even the road itself has largely disappeared. The few witnesses to Olaf's journey have mostly died under mysterious circumstances, or were too frightened to answer the letters, telegrams, and greeting cards I sent them requesting an interview. And even the litter that was thrown out the window of Olaf's car—the clearest sign that evil people have driven by—was picked up off the road long before my work began. The missing litter is a good sign, as it indicates that certain animals of the Mortmain Mountains have returned to their posts and are rebuilding their nests, but it has made it very hard for me to write a complete account of Sunny's travels.

But if you are interested in knowing how Sunny Baudelaire spent her time while her siblings stopped the caravan, followed the path of the Stricken Stream, and struggled against the snow gnats, there is another story you might read that describes more or less the same situation. The story concerns a person named Cinderella. Cinderella was a young person who was placed in the care of various wicked people who teased her and forced her to do all the chores. Eventually Cinderella was rescued by her fairy godmother, who magically created a special outfit for Cinderella to wear to a ball where she met a handsome prince, married him soon afterward, and lived happily ever after in a castle. If you substitute the name "Cinderella" with the name "Sunny Baudelaire," and eliminate the fairy godmother, the special outfit, the ball, the handsome prince, the marriage, and living happily ever after in a castle, you will have a clear idea of Sunny's predicament.

"I wish the baby orphan would stop that irritating crying," Count Olaf said, wrinkling his one eyebrow as the car made another violent turn. "Nothing spoils a nice car trip like a whiny kidnapping victim."

"I'm pinching her as often as I can," Esmé Squalor said, and gave Sunny another pinch with her stylish fingernails, "but she still won't shut up."

"Listen, toothy," Olaf said, taking his eyes off the road to glare at Sunny. "If you don't stop crying, I'll give you something to cry about."

Sunny gave a little whimper of annoyance, and wiped her eyes with her tiny hands. It was true that she had been crying for most of the day, thoroughout a long drive that even the most dedicated of researchers would be unable to trace, and now as the sun set, she still had not been able to stop herself. But at Count Olaf's words, she was almost more irritated than frightened. It is always tedious when someone says that if you don't stop crying, they will give you something to cry about, because if you are crying than you already have something to cry about, and so there is no reason for them to give you anything additional to cry about, thank you very much. Sunny Baudelaire certainly felt she had sufficient reason to weep. She was worried about her siblings, and wondered how they were going to stop the runaway caravan from hurtling them to their doom. She was frightened for herself, now that Count Olaf had discovered her disguise, torn off her beard, and trapped her on Esmé's lap. And she was in pain, from the constant pinching of the villain's girlfriend. "No pinch," she said to Esmé, but the wicked and stylish woman just frowned as if Sunny had spoken nonsense.

"When she's not crying," Esmé said, "the baby talks in some foreign language. I can't understand a thing she's saying."

"Kidnapped children are never any fun," said the hook-handed man, who was perhaps Sunny's least favorite of Olaf's troupe. "Remember when we had the Quagmires in our clutches, boss? They did nothing but complain. They complained when we put them in a cage. They complained when we trapped them inside a fountain. Complain, complain, complain—I was so sick of them I was almost glad when they escaped from our clutches."

"Glad?" Count Olaf said with a snarl. "We worked hard to steal the Quagmire fortune, and we didn't get a single sapphire. That was a real waste of time."

"Don't blame yourself, Olaf," said one of the white-faced women from the back seat. "Everybody makes mistakes."

"Not this time," Olaf said. "With the two orphans squashed someplace underneath a crashed caravan and the baby orphan on your lap, the Baudelaire fortune is mine. And once we reach the Valley of Four Drafts and find the headquarters, all our worries will be over."

"Why?" asked Hugo, the hunchbacked man who had previously been employed at the carnival.

"Yes, please explain," said Kevin, another former carnival worker. At Caligari Carnival, Kevin had been embarrassed to be ambidextrous, but Esmé had lured him into joining Olaf's troupe by tying Kevin's right hand behind his back, so no one would know it was as strong as his left. "Remember, boss, we're new to the troupe, so we don't always know what's going on."

"I remember when I first joined Olaf's troupe," the other white-faced woman said. "I'd never even heard of the Snicket file."

"Working for me is a hands-on learning

experience," Olaf said. "You can't rely on me to explain everything to you. I'm a very busy man."

"I'll explain it, boss," said the hook-handed man. "Count Olaf, like any good businessman, has committed a wide variety of crimes."

"But these stupid volunteers have gathered all sorts of evidence and filed it away," Esmé said. "I tried to explain that crime is very in right now, but apparently they weren't interested."

Sunny wiped another tear from her eye and sighed. The youngest Baudelaire thought she'd almost rather be pinched again than hear any more of Esmé Squalor's nonsense about what was in—the word that Esmé used for "fashion-able"—and what was out.

"We need to destroy those files, or Count Olaf could be arrested," the hook-handed man said. "We have reason to believe that some of the files are at V.F.D. headquarters."

"What does V.F.D. stand for?" The voice of Colette came from the floor of the automobile.

Count Olaf had ordered her to use her skills as a carnival contortionist to curl up at the feet of the other members of the troupe.

"That's top-secret information!" Olaf growled, to Sunny's disappointment. "I used to be a member of the organization myself, but I found it was more fun to be an individual practitioner."

"What does that mean?" asked the hook-handed man.

"It means a life of crime," Esmé replied. "It's very in right now."

"Wrong def." Sunny could not help speaking through her tears. By "wrong def" she meant something along the lines of, "An individual practitioner means someone who works alone, instead of with a group, and it has nothing to do with a life of crime," and it made her sad that there was no one around who could understand her.

"There you go, babbling away," Esmé said. "This is why I never want to have children.

Except as servants, of course."

"This journey is easier than I thought," Olaf said. "The map says we just have to pass a few more caves."

"Is there an in hotel near the headquarters?" Esmé asked.

"I'm afraid not, sweetheart," the villain replied, "but I have two tents in the trunk of the car. We'll be camping on Mount Fraught, the summit of the Mortmain Mountains."

"The summit?" Esmé said. "It'll be cold at the highest peak."

"It's true," Olaf admitted, "but False Spring is on its way, so before long it'll be a bit warmer."

"But what about tonight?" Esmé Squalor said. "It is definitely *not* in for me to set up tents in the freezing cold."

Count Olaf looked at his girlfriend and began to laugh, and Sunny could smell the foul breath of his nasty giggles. "Don't be silly," the villain said finally. "*You're* not going to set up the tents, Esmé. You're going to stay nice and toasty in the car. The bucktoothed baby will set up the tents for us."

Now Olaf's entire troupe laughed, and the car filled with the stench of so many villains' bad breath. Sunny felt a few more tears roll down her face, and turned to the window so no one would see. The car's windows were very dirty, but the youngest Baudelaire could see the strange, square peaks of the Mortmain Mountains and the dark waters of the Stricken Stream. By now the car had driven so high up in the mountains that the stream was mostly ice, and Sunny looked at the wide stripe of frozen blackness and wondered where her siblings were, and if they were coming to rescue her. She remembered the other time she had been in Count Olaf's clutches, when the villain had tied her up, locked her in a cage and dangled her outside his tower room as part of one of his schemes. It had been an absolutely terrifying experience for the youngest Baudelaire, and she often still had nightmares about the creaking of the cage and the distant sight of her two siblings looking up at her from Count Olaf's backyard. But Violet had built a grappling hook to rescue her, and Klaus had done some important legal research to defeat Olaf's scheme. As the car took Sunny farther and farther away from her siblings, and she stared out at the lonesome terrain, she knew that they could save her again.

"How long will we stay on Mount Fraught?" Hugo asked.

"Until I say so, of course," Count Olaf replied.

"You'll soon find out that much of this job involves a lot of waiting around," the hook-handed man said. "I usually keep something around to help pass the time, like a deck of cards or a large rock."

"It can be dull," admitted one of the white-faced women, "and it can be dangerous. Several of our comrades have recently suffered terrible fates."

"It was worth it," Count Olaf said noncha-
lantly, a word which here means "in a tone of
voice that indicated he didn't care one bit about
his deceased employees." "Sometimes a few
people need to die in fires or get eaten by lions,
if it's all for the greater good."

"What's the greater good?" asked Colette.

"Money!" Esmé cried in greedy glee.
"Money and personal satisfaction, and we're
going to get both of those things out of this
whimpering baby on my lap! Once we have our
hands on the Baudelaire fortune, we'll have
enough money to live a life of luxury and plan
several more treacherous schemes!"

The entire troupe cheered, and Count Olaf
gave Sunny a filthy grin, but did not say anything more as the car raced up a steep, bumpy
hill, and at last screeched to a halt, just as the
last rays of the sun faded into the evening sky.
"We're here at last," Count Olaf said, and
handed the car keys to Sunny. "Get out, baby

orphan. Unload everything from the trunk and
set up the tents."

"And bring us some potato chips," Esmé
said, "so we'll have something in to eat while
we wait."

Esmé opened the door of the car, placed
Sunny on the frozen ground, and slammed the
door shut again. Instantly, the chilly mountain
air surrounded the youngest Baudelaire and
made her shiver. It was so bitterly cold at the
highest peak of the Mortmain Mountains that
her tears froze in their tracks, forming a tiny
mask of ice all over her face. Unsteadily, Sunny
rose to her feet and walked to the back of the
car. She was tempted to keep walking, and
escape from Olaf while he waited in the car with
his troupe. But where could she go? Sunny
looked around at her surroundings and could
not see a place where a baby would be safe by
herself.

The summit of Mount Fraught was a small,

flat square, and as Sunny walked to the trunk of the car, she gazed off each edge of the square, feeling a bit dizzy from the great height. From three of the edges, she could see the square and misty peaks of some of the other mountains, most of which were covered in snow, and twisting through the peaks were the strange, black waters of the Stricken Stream, and the rocky path that the car had driven along. But from the fourth side of the square peak, Sunny saw something so strange it took her a moment to figure out what it was.

Extending from the highest peak in the Mortmain Mountains was a glittering white strip, like an enormous piece of shiny paper folded downward, or the wing of some tremendous bird. Sunny watched the very last rays of the sunset reflect off this enormous surface and slowly realized what it was: the source of the Stricken Stream. Like many streams, the Stricken Stream originated within the rocks of the mountains, and in the warmer season, Sunny could see that it

cascaded down from the highest peak in an enormous waterfall. But this was not a warm time of
year, and just as Sunny's tears had frozen on her
face, the waterfall had frozen solid, into a long,
slippery slope that disappeared into the darkness
below. It was such an eerie sight that it took
Sunny a moment to wonder why the ice was
white, instead of black like the waters of the
Stricken Stream.

*Honk!* A loud blast from Count Olaf's horn
made Sunny remember what she was supposed
to be doing, and she hurriedly opened the trunk
and found a bag of potato chips, which she
brought back to the car. "That took a very long
time, orphan," said Olaf, rather than "Thank
you." "Now go set up the tents, one for Esmé
and me and one for my troupe, so we can get
some sleep."

"Where is the baby going to stay?" asked the
hook-handed man. "I don't want her in my tent.
I hear that babies can creep up and steal your
breath while you're sleeping."

"Well, she's certainly not sleeping with me," Esmé said. "It's not in to have a baby in your tent."

"She's not going to sleep in either tent," Olaf decided. "There's a large covered casserole dish in the trunk. She can sleep in there."

"Will she be safe in a casserole dish?" Esmé said. "Remember, Olaf honey, if she dies then we can't get our hands on the fortune."

"There are a few holes in the top so she can breathe," Olaf said, "and the cover will protect her from the snow gnats."

"Snow gnats?" asked Hugo.

"Snow gnats are well-organized, ill-tempered insects," Count Olaf explained, "who live in cold mountain areas and enjoy stinging people for no reason whatsoever. I've always been fond of them."

"Nonat," Sunny said, which meant "I didn't notice any such insects outside," but no one paid any attention.

"Won't she run away if no one's watching her?" asked Kevin.

"She wouldn't dare," Count Olaf said, "and even if she tried to survive in the mountains by herself, we could see where she went. That's why we're staying here at the summit. We'll know if the brat escapes, or if anyone's coming after us, because we can see everything and everyone for miles and miles."

"Eureka," Sunny said, before she could stop herself. She meant something along the lines of, "I've just realized something," but she had not meant to say it out loud.

"Stop your babbling and get busy, you fanged brat!" Esmé Squalor said, and slammed the car door shut. Sunny could hear the laughing of the troupe and the crunching of potato chips as she walked slowly back to the trunk to find the tents.

It is often quite frustrating to arrange all of the cloth and the poles so that a tent works correctly, which is why I have always preferred to stay in hotels or rented castles, which also have the added attractions of solid walls and maid service. Sunny, of course, had the extra disadvantages of trying to do it herself, in the dark, when she was still fairly new at walking and was worried about her siblings. But the youngest Baudelaire had a history of performing Herculean tasks, a phrase which here means "managing to do incredibly difficult things." As I'm sure you know, if you are ever forced to do something very difficult, it often helps to think of something inspiring to keep you going. When Sunny had engaged in a sword-and-tooth fight at Lucky Smells Lumbermill, for instance, she thought of how much she cared for her siblings, and it helped her defeat the evil Dr. Orwell. When Sunny climbed up an elevator shaft at 667 Dark Avenue, she had concentrated on her friends the Quagmires, and how much she wanted to rescue them, and before too long she had reached the penthouse apartment. So, as

Sunny dug a hole in the frozen ground with her teeth so the tent poles would stay in place, she thought of something that inspired her, and oddly enough it was something that Count Olaf had said, about being able to see everything and everyone for miles and miles. As Sunny assembled the tents, and gazed down every so often at the slippery slope of the frozen waterfall, she decided that she would not try to sneak away from Olaf and his troupe. She would not to try to sneak anywhere. Because if you could see everything and everyone from Mount Fraught, that also meant everything and everyone, including Violet and Klaus Baudelaire, would be able to see her.

CHAPTER
# Four

*That* night was a dark day. Of course, all nights
are dark days, because night is simply a badly
lit version of day, due to the fact that the Earth
travels around and around the sun reminding
everyone that it is time to get out of bed and
start the day with a cup of coffee or a secret message folded up into a paper airplane that can sail
out the barred window
of a ranger station. But
in this case,

the phrase "a dark day" means "a sad time in the history of the Baudelaire children, V.F.D., and all kind, brave, and well-read people in the world." But Violet and Klaus Baudelaire, of course, had no idea of the catastrophe occurring high above them in the Valley of Four Drafts. All they knew was that they were hearing a voice they had hoped never to hear again.

"Go away, cakesniffers!" the voice said. "This is a private cave!"

"Who are you talking to, Carmelita?" asked another voice. This voice was much louder, and sounded like it belonged to a grown man.

"I can see two shadows in the entrance of the cave, Uncle Bruce," said the first voice, "and to me they look like cakesniffers."

The back of the cave echoed with giggling, and Violet and Klaus looked at one another in dismay. The familiar voice belonged to Carmelita Spats, the nasty little girl whom the Baudelaires had encountered at Prufrock Preparatory School. Carmelita had taken an instant

dislike to the three siblings, calling them unpleasant names and generally making life miserable at the academy. If you have ever been a
student, then you know that there is usually one
such person at every school and that once you
have graduated you hope never to see them
again. The two elder Baudelaires had enough
troubles in the Mortmain Mountains without
running into this unpleasant person, and at the
sound of her voice they almost turned around
and took their chances once more with the snow
gnats swarming outside.

"Two shadows?" asked the second voice.
"Identify yourselves, please."

"We're mountain travelers," Violet called
from the entrance. "We lost our way and ran into
a swarm of snow gnats. Please let us rest here
for a moment, while the smell of smoke scares
them away, and then we'll be on our way."

"Absolutely not!" replied Carmelita, who
sounded even nastier than usual. "This is where
the Snow Scouts are camping, on their way to

celebrate False Spring and crown me queen. We don't want any cakesniffers spoiling our fun."

"Now, now, Carmelita," said the voice of the grown man. "Snow Scouts are supposed to be accommodating, remember? It's part of the Snow Scout Alphabet Pledge. And it would be very accommodating of us to offer these strangers the shelter of our cave."

"I don't want to be accommodating," Carmelita said. "I'm the False Spring Queen, so I get to do whatever I want."

"You're not the False Spring Queen yet, Carmelita," came the patient voice of a young boy. "Not until we dance around the Springpole. Do come in, travelers, and sit by the fire. We're happy to accommodate you."

"That's the spirit, kid," said the voice of the grown man. "Come on, Snow Scouts, let's all say the Snow Scout Alphabet Pledge together."

Instantly the cave echoed with the sound of many voices speaking in perfect unison, a phrase which here means "reciting a list of very

odd words at the very same time." "Snow
Scouts," recited the Snow Scouts, "are accommodating, basic, calm, darling, emblematic, frisky,
grinning, human, innocent, jumping, kept, limited, meek, nap-loving, official, pretty, quarantined, recent, scheduled, tidy, understandable,
victorious, wholesome, xylophone, young, and
zippered—every morning, every afternoon, every
night, and all day long!"

The two Baudelaires looked at one another
in confusion. Like many pledges, the Snow
Scout Alphabet Pledge had not made much
sense, and Violet and Klaus tried to imagine
how a scout could be "calm" and "meek" at the
same time as being "frisky" and "jumping," or
how all these children could avoid being
"young" or "human," even if they wanted to.
They couldn't figure out why the pledge suggested being all these things "every morning,"
"every afternoon," and "every night," and then
added "all day long," or why the word "xylophone" appeared in the pledge at all. But they

did not have much time to wonder, because when the pledge was over, the Snow Scouts all took a big breath and made a long, airy sound, as if they were imitating the wind outside, and this seemed even more strange.

"That's my favorite part," said the voice of the grown man, when the sound faded away. "There's nothing like ending the Snow Scout Alphabet Pledge with a snowy sound. Now approach, travelers, so we can get a look at you."

"Let's keep the coat over our faces," Klaus whispered to his sister. "Carmelita might recognize us."

"And the other scouts have probably seen our pictures in *The Daily Punctilio*," Violet said, and ducked her head underneath the coat. *The Daily Punctilio* was a newspaper that had published a story blaming the three Baudelaires for Jacques Snicket's murder. The story was utter nonsense, of course, but it seemed that everyone in the world had believed it and was searching for the Baudelaires to put them in jail. As the two siblings walked toward the voices of the Snow Scouts, however, they realized that they weren't the only ones concealing their faces.

The back of the cave was like a large, circular room, with very high ceilings and craggy walls of rock that flickered in the orange light of the flames. Seated in a circle around the fire were fifteen or twenty people, all looking up at the two Baudelaires. Through the fabric of the coat, the children could see that one person was much taller than the others—this was probably Bruce—and was wearing an ugly plaid coat and holding a large cigar. On the opposite side of the circle was someone wearing a thick wool sweater with several large pockets, and the rest of the Snow Scouts were wearing bright white uniforms with enormous zippers down the front and emblems of snowflakes, in all different sizes and shapes, along the long, puffy sleeves. On the back of the uniforms, the Baudelaires could see the words of the Snow Scout Alphabet Pledge printed in large pink letters, and on the

top of everyone's heads were white headbands
with tiny plastic snowflakes sticking out of
the top in all directions and the word "Brr!"
written in icy script. But Violet and Klaus
weren't looking at the plastic flurries of snow on
the Snow Scouts' heads, or the accommodating,
basic, calm, darling, emblematic, frisky, grinning, human, innocent, jumping, kept, limited,
meek, nap-loving, official, pretty, quarantined,
recent, scheduled, tidy, understandable, victorious, wholesome, xylophone, young, and zippered uniforms that most everyone was wearing.
They were looking at the dark, round masks that
were covering the scouts' faces. The masks were
covered in tiny holes, much like masks worn for
fencing, a sport in which people swordfight for
fun rather than for honor or in order to rescue a
writer who has been taped to the wall. But in
the flickering light of the cave, the Baudelaires
could not see the holes, and it looked like
the faces of Bruce and the Snow Scouts had

vanished, leaving a dark and empty hole above their necks.

"You cakesniffers look ridiculous," said one of the scouts, and the Baudelaires knew at once which masked figure was Carmelita Spats. "Your faces are all covered up."

"We're meek," Violet said, thinking quickly. "In fact, we're so meek that we hardly ever show our faces."

"Then you'll fit in just fine," said Bruce from behind his mask. "The name's Bruce, but you can call me Uncle Bruce, although I'm almost certainly not your real uncle. Welcome to the Snow Scouts, travelers, where all of us are meek. In fact, we're accommodating, basic, calm . . ."

The other Snow Scouts all joined in the pledge, and the two elder Baudelaires stood through another rendition of the absurd list, while the scout in the sweater stood up and stepped toward them. "We have some spare masks over there," he murmured quietly, and gestured toward a large pile of equipment, stacked beside a very long wooden pole. "They'll keep the snow gnats away when you go back outside. Help yourself."

"Thank you," Violet replied, as the scouts promised to be kept, limited, and meek. She and her brother quickly grabbed masks and put them on underneath the coat, so that by the time the scouts vowed to be xylophone, young, and zippered, they looked as faceless as everyone else in the cave.

"That was fun, kids," said Bruce, as the snowy sound faded and the pledge was over. "Now why don't you two join the Snow Scouts? We're an organization for young people to have fun and learn new things. Right now we're on a Snow Scout Hike. We're going to hike all the way up to Mount Fraught in order to celebrate False Spring."

"What's False Spring?" Violet asked, sitting down between her brother and the sweatered scout.

"Anybody who's not a cakesniffer knows what False Spring is," Carmelita said in a scornful voice. "It's when the weather gets unusually warm before getting very cold again. We celebrate it with a fancy dance where we spin around and around the Springpole." She pointed to the wooden pole, and the Baudelaires noticed that the Snow Scouts all wore bright white mittens, each emblazoned with an S. "When the dance is over, we choose the best Snow Scout and crown her the False Spring Queen. This time, it's me. In fact, it's always me."

"That's because Uncle Bruce is really your uncle," said one of the other Snow Scouts.

"No, it's not," Carmelita insisted. "It's because I'm the most accommodating, basic, calm, darling, emblematic, frisky, grinning, human, innocent, jumping, kept, limited, meek, nap-loving, official, pretty, quarantined, recent, scheduled, tidy, understandable, victorious, wholesome, xylophone, young, and zippered."

"How can anyone be 'xylophone'?" Klaus

couldn't help asking. "'Xylophone' isn't even an adjective."

"Uncle Bruce couldn't think of another word that began with X," explained the sweatered Snow Scout, in a tone of voice indicating that he thought this wasn't a very good excuse.

"How about 'xenial'?" Klaus suggested. "It's a word that means—"

"You can't change the words of the Snow Scout Alphabet Pledge," Bruce interrupted, moving his cigar toward his face as if he were going to try to smoke it through the mask. "The whole point of the Snow Scouts is that you do the same thing over and over. We celebrate False Spring over and over, on Mount Fraught, at the source of the Stricken Stream. My niece Carmelita Spats is False Spring Queen, over and over. And over and over, we stop here in this cave for Snow Scout Story Time."

"I read that the caves of the Mortmain Mountains contained hibernating animals," Klaus said. "Are you sure it's safe to stop here?"

The Snow Scout who was wearing a sweater instead of a uniform turned his head quickly to the Baudelaires, as if he was going to speak, but Bruce answered first. "It's safe now, kid," he said. "Years ago, apparently these mountains were crawling with bears. The bears were so intelligent that they were trained as soldiers. But they disappeared and no one knows why."

"Not bears," the scout in the sweater said, so quietly that the two Baudelaires had to lean in to hear him. "Lions lived in these caves. And they weren't soldiers. The lions were detectives—volunteer feline detectives." He turned so his mask was facing the two siblings, and the children knew he must be staring at them through the holes. "Volunteer Feline Detectives," he said again, and the Baudelaires almost gasped.

"Did you say—" Violet said, but the sweatered Snow Scout shook his head as if it was not safe to talk. Violet looked at her brother and then at the scout, wishing she could see both of their faces behind their masks. The initials of "Volunteer Feline Detectives," of course, spelled "V.F.D.," the name of the organization they were looking for. But were these initials a coincidence, as they had seemed to be so many times? Or was this mysterious scout giving them some sort of signal?

"I don't know what you kids are muttering about," Bruce said, "but stop it this instant. It's not time for conversation. It's Snow Scout Story Time, when one Snow Scout tells a story to the other Snow Scouts. Then we'll all eat marshmallows until we feel sick and go to sleep on a heap of blankets, just like we do every year. Why don't our new scouts tell the first story?"

"I should tell the first story," whined Carmelita. "After all, I'm the False Spring Queen."

"But I'm sure the travelers will have a wonderful story to tell," the sweatered scout said. "I'd love to hear a Very Fascinating Drama."

Klaus saw his sister raise her hands to her

head and smiled. He knew Violet had instinctively begun to tie her hair up in a ribbon to help
her think, but it was impossible to do so with a
mask on. Both the Baudelaire minds were racing to figure out a way to communicate with this
mysterious scout, and the children were so lost
in thought that they scarcely heard Carmelita
Spats insulting them.

"Stop sitting around, cakesniffers," Carmelita
said. "If you're going to tell us a story, get started."

"I'm sorry for the delay," Violet said, choosing her words as carefully as she could. "We
haven't had a Very Fun Day, so it's difficult to
think of a good story."

"I didn't realize this was a sad occasion,"
said the sweatered scout.

"Oh, yes," Klaus said. "We've had nothing
to eat all day except for some Vinegar-Flavored
Doughnuts."

"And then there were the snow gnats," Violet said. "They behaved like Violent Frozen
Dragonflies."

"When they form an arrow," Klaus said, "they're more like a Voracious Fierce Dragon."

"Or a Vain Fat Dictator, I imagine," the scout in the sweater said, and gave the Baudelaires a masked nod as if he had received their message.

"This is the most boring story I have ever heard," Carmelita Spats said. "Uncle Bruce, tell these two that they're both cakesniffers."

"Well, it wouldn't be very accommodating to say so," Bruce said, "but I must admit that the story you were telling was a little dull, kids. When Snow Scouts tell stories, they skip everything boring and only tell the interesting parts. That way, the story can be as accommodating, basic, calm, darling, emblematic, frisky, grinning, human, innocent, jumping, kept, limited, meek, nap-loving, official, pretty, quarantined, recent, scheduled, tidy, understandable, victorious, wholesome, xylophone, young, and zippered as possible."

"I'll show these cakesniffers how to tell an

interesting story," Carmelita said. "Once upon a time, I woke up and looked in the mirror, and there I saw the prettiest, smartest, most darling girl in the whole wide world. I put on a lovely pink dress to make myself look even prettier, and I skipped off to school where my teacher told me I looked more adorable than anyone she had ever seen in her entire life, and she gave me a lollipop as a special present . . ."

At this point, I will take a page from someone's book, a phrase which here means "adopt an idea used by somebody else." If, for instance, a man told you that the best way to write thank-you notes is to reward yourself with a cookie every time you finished one, you might take a page from his book, and have a plate of cookies nearby after your birthday or some other gift-giving occasion. If a girl told you that the best way to sneak out of the house late at night is to make sure everyone else is sound asleep, you might take a page from her book and mix a sleeping potion into everyone else's after-dinner coffee before climbing down the ivy that grows outside your bedroom window. And if you have been reading this miserable story, then the next time you find yourself in a similar situation, you might take a page from *The Slippery Slope* and use a combination of sticky substances and a drag chute to slow down a racing caravan, and then retrieve several articles of heavy clothing in order to protect yourself from the cold, and find a cave full of Snow Scouts gathered around a fire when the snow gnats begin to swarm.

But I will be taking a page from Bruce's book, when he suggested that a storyteller only tell the interesting parts of the story and skip everything boring. Certainly the two elder Baudelaires wished they could skip this boring part of their own story, as they were very eager to leave the cave and resume their search for their sister. But Violet and Klaus knew that they shouldn't leave the cave until they could talk to the mysterious boy in the sweater, and that they couldn't talk to the mysterious boy in the sweater in front of Bruce and the other Snow Scouts, and so they sat by the fire as Carmelita Spats talked on and on about how pretty and smart and darling she was and how everyone she met told her that she was unbelievably adorable. Although the Baudelaires had to sit through these tedious portions of their story, there is no reason for you to do so, and so I will skip ahead, past the tiresome details of Carmelita's endless story, and the senseless pledge that Bruce made everyone say several more times, and the all-marshmallow meal that the scouts shared with the two siblings. I will skip how irksome it was for Violet and Klaus to turn away from the scouts, quickly lift their masks, and pop marsh-mallows into their mouths before covering their faces again so they would not be recognized. After their long, tiring journey, the children would have preferred a more substantial supper and a less complicated way of eating it, but the siblings could not skip these parts of their story,

so they had to wait for the evening to pass and
for all the other Snow Scouts to feel sick and
arrange blankets into a large heap beside the
Springpole. Even when Bruce led the Snow
Scouts in one more alphabet pledge as a way of
saying good night, Violet and Klaus dared not
get up and talk to the sweatered scout for fear
of being overheard, and they had to wait for
hours, too curious and anxious to sleep, as the
fire died down and the cave echoed with the
sounds of Snow Scout snoring. But I will take a
page from the book of the Snow Scout leader,
and skip ahead to the next interesting thing that
happened, which was very, very late at night,
when so many interesting parts of stories happen and so many people miss them because
they are asleep in their beds, or hiding in the
broom closet of a mustard factory, disguised as
a dustpan to fool the night watchwoman.

It was very late at night—in fact one might
say that it was the darkest part of this dark day—
and it was so late that the Baudelaires had

almost given up on staying awake, particularly after such an exhausting day, but just as the two siblings were beginning to fall asleep, they each felt a hand touch them on the shoulder, and they quickly sat up and found themselves looking into the masked face of the sweatered scout.

"Come with me, Baudelaires," the boy said in a very quiet voice. "I know a shortcut to the headquarters," and this was an interesting part of the story indeed.

# CHAPTER

# Five

When you have many questions on your mind, and you suddenly have an opportunity to ask them, the questions tend to crowd together and trip over one another, much like passengers on a crowded train when it reaches a popular station. With Bruce and the Snow Scouts asleep, the two elder Baudelaires finally had an opportunity to talk with the mysterious scout in the sweater, but everything they wanted to ask seemed hopelessly entangled.

"How—" Violet started, but the question "How did you know we were the Baudelaires?" stumbled against the question "Who are you?" and fell back against the questions "Are you a member of V.F.D.?" and "What does V.F.D. stand for?"

"Do—" Klaus said, but the question "Do you know where our sister is?" tripped over the question "Do you know if one of our parents is alive?" which was already struggling with "How can we get to the headquarters?" and "Will my sisters and I ever find a safe place to live without constantly being threatened by Count Olaf and his troupe as they hatch plan after plan to steal the Baudelaire fortune?" although the middle Baudelaire knew that his last question was unlikely to be answered at all.

"I'm sure you have lots of questions," the boy whispered, "but we can't talk here. Bruce is a light sleeper, and he's caused V.F.D. enough trouble already without learning another of our secrets. I promise all your questions will be answered, but first we've got to get to the head-quarters. Come with me."

Without another word, the sweatered scout turned around, and the Baudelaires saw he was wearing a backpack inscribed with an insignia they had seen at Caligari Carnival. At first glance, this insignia merely appeared to be an eye, but the children had discovered that if you looked closely you could see the initials V.F.D. cleverly hidden in the drawing. The scout began to walk, and the two siblings got out of their blankets as quietly as they could and followed him. To their surprise, he did not lead them toward the cave entrance, but to the back of the cave, where the Snow Scouts' fire had been. Now it was nothing more than a pile of gray ashes, although it was still very warm, and the smell of smoke was still in the air. The sweatered scout reached into his pocket and brought out a flashlight. "I had to wait for the fire to die down before I showed you," he said, and with a nervous glance at the sleeping scouts, turned the flashlight on and shone it above them. "Look."

Violet and Klaus looked, and saw that there was a hole in the ceiling, big enough for a person to crawl through. The last wisps of smoke from the fire were floating up into the hole. "A chimney," Klaus murmured. "I was wondering why the fire didn't fill the cave with smoke."

"The official name is Vertical Flame Diversion," the scout whispered. "It serves as a chimney and as a secret passageway. It runs from this cave to the Valley of Four Drafts. If we climb up there, we can reach headquarters within hours, instead of hiking all the way up the mountain. Years ago, there was a metal pole that ran down the center of the hole, so people could slide down and hide in this cave in case of an emergency. The pole is gone now, but there should be carved toeholds in the sides to climb all the way up." He shone the flashlight on the cave wall, and sure enough, the Baudelaires could see two rows of small carved holes, perfect for sticking one's feet and hands into.

"How do you know all this?" Violet asked.

The scout looked at her for a moment, and it seemed to the Baudelaires that he was smiling behind his mask. "I read it," he said, "in a book called *Remarkable Phenomena of the Mortmain Mountains.*"

"That sounds familiar," Klaus said.

"It should," the scout replied. "I borrowed it from Dr. Montgomery's library."

Dr. Montgomery was one of the Baudelaires' first guardians, and at the mention of his name Violet and Klaus found they had several more questions they wanted to ask.

"When—" Violet started.

"Why—" Klaus started.

"Carm—" Another voice startled the Baudelaires and the scout—the voice of Bruce, waking up halfway at the sound of the conversation. All three children froze for a moment, as Bruce turned over on his blanket, and with a long sigh, went back to sleep.

"We'll talk when we reach the headquarters," the scout whispered. "The Vertical Flame Diversion is very echoey, so we'll have to be absolutely silent as we climb, or the echoing noise will alert Bruce and the Snow Scouts. It'll be very dark inside, so you'll have to feel against the wall for the footholds, and the air will be smoky, but if you keep your masks on they'll filter the air and make it easier to breathe. I'll go first and lead the way. Are you ready?"

Violet and Klaus turned toward one another. Even though they could not see each other's faces through the masks, both siblings knew that they were not at all ready. Following a complete stranger into a secret passageway through the center of the mountains, toward a headquarters they could not even be sure existed, did not seem like a very safe thing to do. The last time they had agreed to take a risky journey, their baby sister had been snatched away from them. What would happen this time, when they were all alone with a mysterious masked figure in a dark and smoky hole?

"I know it must be hard to trust me, Baude-laires," said the sweatered scout, "after so many people have done you wrong."

"Can you give us a reason to trust you?" Violet said.

The scout looked down for a moment, and then turned his mask to face both Baudelaires. "One of you mentioned the word 'xenial,'" he said, "when you were talking with Bruce about that silly pledge. 'Xenial' is a word which refers to the giving of gifts to a stranger."

"He's right," Klaus murmured to his sister.

"I know that having a good vocabulary doesn't guarantee that I'm a good person," the boy said. "But it does mean I've read a great deal. And in my experience, well-read people are less likely to be evil."

Violet and Klaus looked at one another through their masks. Neither of them were entirely convinced by what the masked scout had said. There are, of course, plenty of evil people who have read a great many books, and plenty of very kind people who seem to have found some other method of spending their time. But the Baudelaires knew that there was a kind of truth to the boy's statement, and they had to admit that they preferred to take their chances with a stranger who knew what the word "xenial" meant, rather than exiting the cave and trying to find the headquarters all by themselves. So the siblings turned back to the scout, nodded their masks, and followed him to the footholds in the wall, making sure they still had all the items from the caravan with them. The footholds were surprisingly easy to use, and in a short time the Baudelaires were following the mysterious scout into the dark and smoky entrance of the passageway.

The Vertical Flame Diversion that connected the Mortmain Mountain headquarters to this particular Volunteer Feline Detectives cave was once one of the most heavily guarded secrets in the world. Anyone who wanted to use it had to correctly answer a series of questions concerning the force of gravity, the habits of carnivorous beasts, and the central themes of Russian novels, so very few people even knew the passageway's exact whereabouts. Until the two Baudelaires' journey, the passageway had not been used for many years, ever since one of my comrades removed the pole in order to use it in the construction of a submarine. So it would be accurate to say that the Vertical Flame Diversion was a road less traveled—even less traveled than the path through the Mortmain Mountains on which this book began.

While the elder Baudelaires had a very good reason to be on the road less traveled, as they were in a great hurry to reach the headquarters and rescue their sister from the clutches of Count Olaf, there is no reason whatsoever why you should be on the road less traveled and choose to read the rest of this woeful chapter, which describes their dark and smoky journey.

The ashen air from the Snow Scouts' fire was difficult to breathe, even through the masks, and Violet and Klaus had to struggle not to cough, knowing that the coughing sound would echo down the passageway and wake up Bruce, but there is no reason for you to struggle through my dismal description of this problem. A number of spiders had noticed the footholds were not being used lately, and had moved in and converted them into spider condominiums, but you are under no obligation to read what happens when spiders are suddenly woken up by the sudden appearance of a climbing foot in their new homes. And as the Baudelaires followed the scout farther and farther up, the strong freezing winds from the top of the mountain would rush through the passageway, and all three youngsters would cling to the footholds with their very lives, hoping that the wind would not blow them back down to the cave floor, but although the Baudelaires found it necessary to keep climbing through the rest of

the dark day so they could reach the headquarters as quickly as possible, and I find it necessary to finish describing it, so my account of the
Baudelaire case is as accurate and as complete
as possible, it is not necessary for you to finish
reading the rest of this chapter, so you can be
as miserable as possible. My description of the
Baudelaires' journey up through the road less
traveled begins on the next page, but I beg you
not to travel along with them. Instead, you may
take a page from Bruce's book, and skip ahead
to Chapter Six, and find my report on Sunny
Baudelaire's tribulations—a word which here
means "opportunities to eavesdrop while cooking for a theater troupe"—with Count Olaf, or
you may skip ahead to Chapter Seven, when
the elder Baudelaires arrive at the site of the
V.F.D. headquarters and unmask the stranger
who led them there, or you may take the road
very frequently traveled and skip away from
this book altogether, and find something better

to do with your time besides finishing this unhappy tale and becoming a weary, weeping, and well-read person.

The Baudelaires' journey up the Vertical Flame Diversion was so dark and treacherous that it is not enough to write "The Baudelaires' journey up the Vertical Flame Diversion was so dark and treacherous that it is not enough to write 'The Baudelaires' journey up the Vertical Flame Diversion was so dark and treacherous that it is not enough to write "The Baudelaires' journey up the Vertical Flame Diversion was so dark and treacherous that it is not enough to write 'The Baudelaires' journey up the Vertical Flame Diversion was so dark and treacherous that it is not enough to write "*My dear sister,*

I am taking a great risk in hiding a letter to you inside one of my books, but I am certain that even the most melancholy and well-read people in the world have found my account of the lives of the three Baudelaire children even more wretched than I had promised, and so this book will stay on the shelves of libraries, utterly ignored, waiting for you to open it and find this message. As an additional precaution, I placed a warning that the rest of this chapter contains a description of the Baudelaires' miserable journey up the Vertical Flame Diversion, so anyone who has the courage to read such a description is probably brave enough to read my letter to you.

I have at last learned the whereabouts of the evidence that will exonerate me, a phrase which here means "prove to the authorities that it is Count Olaf, and not me, who has started so many fires." Your suggestion, so many years ago at that picnic, that a tea set would be a handy place to hide anything important and small in the event of a dark day, has turned out to be correct. (Incidentally, your other picnic suggestion, that a simple combination of sliced mango, black beans, and chopped celery mixed with black pepper, lime juice, and olive oil would make a delicious chilled salad also turned out to be correct.)

I am on my way now to the Valley of Four Drafts, in order to continue my research on the Baudelaire case. I hope also to retrieve the aforementioned evidence at last. It is too late to restore my happiness, of course, but at least I can clear my name. From the site of V.F.D. headquarters, I will head straight for the Hotel Denouement. I should arrive by—well, it wouldn't be wise to type the date, but it should be easy for you to remember Beatrice's birthday. Meet me at the hotel. Try to get us a room without ugly curtains.

*With all due respect,*
*Lemony Snicket*
Lemony Snicket

P.S. If you substitute the chopped celery with hearts of palm, it is equally delicious.

# CHAPTER

## Six

*In* the very early hours of the morning, while the two elder Baudelaires struggled to find their footing as they climbed up the Vertical Flame Diversion—and I sincerely hope that you did not read the description of that journey—the youngest Baudelaire found herself struggling with a different sort of footing altogether. Sunny had not enjoyed the long, cold night on Mount Fraught. If you have ever slept in a covered casserole dish on the highest peak of a mountain range, then you know that it is an uncomfortable place to lay one's head, even if you find a dishtowel inside it that can serve as a blanket. All night long, the chilly mountain winds blew through the tiny holes inside the top of the cover, making it so cold inside the dish that Sunny's enormous teeth chattered all night, giving her tiny cuts on her lips and making such a loud noise that it was impossible to sleep. Finally, when the first rays of the morning sun shone through the holes and made it warm enough to doze, Count Olaf left his tent and kicked open the cover of the dish to begin ordering Sunny around. "Wake up, you dentist's nightmare!" he cried. Sunny opened one exhausted eye and found herself staring at the villain's footing, particularly the tattoo on Olaf's left ankle, a sight that was enough to make her wish her eyes were still closed.

Tattooed on Olaf's ankle was the image of an eye, and it seemed to Sunny that this eye had been watching the Baudelaires throughout all of their troubles, from the day on Briny Beach when they learned of the terrible fire that destroyed their home. Time after time, Count Olaf had tried to hide this eye so the authorities would not recognize him, so the children were always uncovering it from behind his ridiculous disguises, and the Baudelaires had begun seeing the eye in other places, such as at the office of an evil hypnotist, on the side of a carnival tent, on Esmé Squalor's purse, and on a necklace owned by a mysterious fortune-teller. It was almost as if this eye had replaced the eyes of their parents, but instead of keeping watch over the children and making sure that they were safe from harm, this eye merely gave them a blank stare, as if it did not care about the children's troubles, or could do nothing about them. If you looked very closely, you could find the letters V.F.D. half-hidden in the eye, and this reminded Sunny of all the sinister secrets that surrounded the three siblings, and how far they were from understanding the web of mystery in which they found themselves. But it is hard to think about mysteries and secrets first thing in the morning, particularly if someone is yelling at you, and Sunny turned her attention to what her captor was saying.

"You'll be doing all the cooking and cleaning for us, orphan," Count Olaf said, "and you can start by making us breakfast. We have a big day ahead of us, and a good breakfast will give me and my troupe the energy we need to perform unspeakable crimes."

"Plakna?" Sunny asked, which meant "How am I supposed to cook breakfast on the top of a freezing mountain?" but Count Olaf just gave her a nasty smile.

"Too bad your brain isn't as big as your teeth, you little monkey," he said. "You're talking nonsense, as usual."

Sunny sighed, frustrated that there was no one on top of the Mortmain Mountains who understood what she was trying to say. "Translo," she said, which meant "Just because you don't understand something doesn't mean that it's nonsense."

"There you go, babbling again," Olaf said,

and tossed Sunny the car keys. "Get the groceries out of the trunk of the car and get to work."

Sunny suddenly thought of something that might cheer her up a little bit. "Sneakitawc," she said, which was her way of saying "Of course, because you don't understand me, I can say anything I want to you, and you'll have no idea what I'm talking about."

"I'm getting quite tired of your ridiculous speech impediment," Count Olaf said.

"Brummel," Sunny said, which meant "In my opinion, you desperately need a bath, and your clothing is a shambles."

"Be quiet this instant," Olaf ordered.

"Busheney," Sunny said, which meant something along the lines of, "You're an evil man with no concern whatsoever for other people."

"Shut up!" Count Olaf roared. "Shut up and get cooking!"

Sunny got out of the casserole dish and stood up, looking down at the snowy ground so the villain would not see she was smiling. It is not nice to tease people, of course, but the youngest Baudelaire felt that it was all right to enjoy a joke at the expense of such a murderous and evil man, and she walked to Olaf's car with a spring in her step, a phrase which here means "in a surprisingly cheerful manner considering she was in the clutches of a ruthless villain on top of a mountain so cold that even the nearby waterfall was frozen solid."

But when Sunny Baudelaire opened the trunk of the car her smile faded. Under normal circumstances, it is not safe to keep groceries in the trunk of a car for an extended period of time, because some foods will spoil without being refrigerated. But Sunny saw that the temperatures of the Mortmain Mountains had caused the groceries to become over-refrigerated. A thin layer of frost covered every item, and Sunny had to crawl inside and wipe the frost off with her bare hands to see what she might make for the troupe. There was a variety of well-chilled food that Olaf had stolen from the carnival, but none of it seemed like the makings of a good breakfast. There was a bag of coffee beans beneath a harpoon gun and a frozen hunk of spinach, but there was no way to grind the beans into tiny pieces to make coffee. Near a picnic basket and a large bag of mushrooms was a jug of orange juice, but it had been close to one of the bullet holes in the trunk, and so had frozen completely solid in the cold. And after Sunny moved aside three chunks of cold cheese, a large can of water chestnuts, and an eggplant as big as herself, she finally found a small jar of boysenberry jam, and a loaf of bread she could use to make toast, although it was so cold it felt more like a log than a breakfast ingredient.

"Wake up!" Sunny peeked out of the trunk and saw Count Olaf calling through the door of one of the tents she had assembled. "Wake up and get dressed for breakfast!"

"Can't we sleep ten minutes more?" asked the whiny voice of the hook-handed man. "I was having a lovely dream about sneezing without covering my nose and mouth, and giving everybody germs."

"Absolutely not!" Olaf replied. "I have lots of work for you to do."

"But Olaf," said Esmé Squalor, emerging from the tent she had shared with Count Olaf. Her hair was in curlers and she was wearing a long robe and a pair of fuzzy slippers. "I need a little while to choose what I'm going to wear. It's not in to burn down a headquarters without wearing a fashionable outfit."

Sunny gasped in the trunk. She had known that Olaf was eager to reach the V.F.D. head-quarters as soon as possible, in order to get his hands on the rest of some crucial evidence, but it had not occurred to her that he would combine this evidence-grabbing with his usual pyro-mania, a word which here means "a love of fire, usually the product of a deranged mind."

"I can't imagine why you need all this time,"

was Count Olaf's grumpy reply to his girlfriend. "After all, I wear the same outfit for weeks at a time, except when I'm in disguise, and I look almost unbearably handsome. Well, I suppose you have a few minutes before breakfast is ready. Slow service is one of the disadvantages of having infants for slaves." Olaf strode over to the car and peered in at Sunny, who was still clutching the loaf of bread.

"Hurry up, bigmouth," he growled at Sunny. "I need a nice hot meal to take the chill out of the morning."

"Unfeasi!" Sunny cried. By "Unfeasi" she meant "To make a hot meal without any electricity, I'd need a fire, and expecting a baby to start a fire all by herself on top of a snowy mountain is cruelly impossible and impossibly cruel," but Olaf merely frowned.

"Your baby talk is really beginning to annoy me," he said.

"Hygiene," Sunny said, to make herself feel

better. She meant something along the lines of, "Additionally, you ought to be ashamed of yourself for wearing the same outfit for weeks at a time without washing," but Olaf merely scowled at her and walked back into his tent.

Sunny looked at the cold ingredients and tried to think. Even if she had been old enough to start a fire by herself, Sunny had been nervous around flames since the fire that had destroyed the Baudelaire mansion. But as she thought of the fire that destroyed her own home, she remembered something her mother had told her once. They had both been busy in the kitchen—Sunny's mother was busy preparing for a fancy luncheon, and Sunny was busy dropping a fork on the floor over and over again to see what sort of sound it made. The luncheon was due to start any minute, and Sunny's mother was quickly mixing up a salad of sliced mango, black beans, and chopped celery mixed with black pepper, lime juice, and olive oil.

"This isn't a very complicated recipe, Sunny," her mother had said, "but if I arrange the salad very nicely on fancy plates, people will think I've been cooking all day. Often, when cooking, the presentation of the food can be as important as the food itself." Thinking of what her mother had said, she opened the picnic basket in Olaf's trunk and found that it contained a set of elegant plates, each emblazoned with the familiar eye insignia, and a small tea set. Then she rolled up her sleeves—an expression which here means "focused very hard on the task at hand, but did not actually roll up her sleeves, because it was very cold on the highest peak of the Mortmain Mountains"—and got to work as Count Olaf and his comrades started their day.

"I'll use these blankets for a tablecloth," Sunny heard Olaf say in the tent, over the sound her own teeth were making.

"Good idea," she heard Esmé reply. "It's very in to dine *al fresco*."

"What does that mean?" Olaf asked.

"It means 'outside,' of course," Esmé explained. "It's fashionable to eat your meals in the fresh air."

"I knew what it meant," Count Olaf replied. "I was just testing you."

"Hey boss," Hugo called from the next tent. "Colette won't share the dental floss."

"There's no reason to use dental floss," Count Olaf said, "unless you're trying to strangle someone with a very weak neck."

"Kevin, would you do me a favor?" the hook-handed man asked, as Sunny struggled to open the jug of juice. "Will you help me comb my hair? These hooks can make it difficult sometimes."

"I'm jealous of your hooks," Kevin replied. "Having no hands is better than having two equally strong hands."

"Don't be ridiculous," one of the white-faced women replied. "Having a white face is worse than both of your situations."

"But you have a white face because you put makeup on," Colette said, as Sunny climbed back out of the trunk and knelt down in the snow. "You're putting powder on your face right now."

"Must you bicker every single morning?" Count Olaf asked, and stomped back out of his tent carrying a blanket covered in images of eyes. "Somebody take this blanket and set the table over there on that flat rock."

Hugo walked out of the tent and smiled at his new boss. "I'd be happy to," he said.

Esmé stepped outside, having changed into a bright red snowsuit, and put her arm around Olaf. "Fold the blanket into a large triangle," she said to Hugo. "That's the in way to do it."

"Yes ma'am," Hugo said, "and, if you don't mind my saying so, that's a very handsome snowsuit you are wearing."

The villainous girlfriend turned all the way around to show off her outfit from every angle. Sunny looked up from her cooking and noticed that the letter B was sewn onto the back of it, along with the eye insignia. "I'm glad you like it, Hugo," Esmé said. "It's stolen."

Count Olaf glanced at Sunny and quickly stepped in front of his girlfriend. "What are you staring at, toothy?" he asked. "Are you done making breakfast?"

"Almost," Sunny replied.

"That infant never makes any sense," Hugo said. "No wonder she fooled us into thinking she was a carnival freak."

Sunny sighed, but no one heard her over the scornful laughter of Olaf's troupe. One by one, the villain's wretched employees emerged from the tent and strolled over to the flat rock where Hugo was laying out the blanket. One of the white-faced women glanced at Sunny and gave her a small smile, but nobody offered to help her finish with the breakfast preparations, or even to set the table with the eye-patterned dishes. Instead, they gathered around the rock talking and laughing until Sunny carefully carried the breakfast over to them, arranged on a large eye-shaped tray that she'd found in the bottom of the picnic basket. Although she was still frightened to be in Olaf's clutches and worried about her siblings, Sunny could not help but be a little proud as Count Olaf and his comrades looked at the meal she had prepared.

Sunny had kept in mind what her mother had said about presentation being as important as the food itself, and managed to put together a lovely breakfast despite the difficult circumstances. First, she had opened the jug of frozen orange juice and used a small spoon to chip away at the ice until she had a large heap of juice shavings, which she arranged into tiny piles on each plate to make orange granita, a cold and delicious concoction that is often served at fancy dinner parties and masked balls. Then, Sunny had rinsed her mouth out with melted snow so it would be as clean as possible, and chopped some of the coffee beans with her teeth. She placed a bit of the ground coffee inside each cup and combined it with more snow she had melted in her own hands to make iced coffee, a delicious beverage I first enjoyed when visiting Thailand to interview a taxi driver. Meanwhile, the youngest Baudelaire had put the chilled bread underneath her shirt to warm it up, and when it was warm enough to eat she put one slice on each plate, and using a small spoon, spread some boysenberry jam on each piece of bread. She did her best to spread the jam in the shape of an eye, to please the villains who would be eating it, and as a finishing touch she found a bouquet of ivy, which Count Olaf had given his girlfriend not so long ago, and placed it in the small pitcher of the tea set used for cream. There was no cream, but the ivy would help the presentation of the food by serving as a centerpiece, a word which here means "a decoration placed in the middle of a table, often used to distract people from the food." Of course, orange granita and iced coffee are not often served at *al fresco* breakfasts on cold mountain peaks, and bread with jam is more traditionally prepared as toast, but without a source of heat or any other cooking equipment, Sunny had done the best she could, and she hoped that Olaf and his troupe might appreciate her efforts.

"Caffefredde, sorbet, toast tartar," she announced.

"What is this?" Count Olaf said suspiciously, peering into his coffee cup. "It looks like coffee, but it's freezing cold!"

"And what is this orange stuff?" Esmé asked suspiciously. "I want fashionable, in food, not a handful of ice!"

Colette picked up a piece of the bread and stared at it suspiciously. "This toast feels raw," she said. "Is it safe to eat raw toast?"

"Of course not," Hugo said. "I bet that baby is trying to poison us."

"Actually, the coffee isn't bad," one of the white-faced women said, "even if it is a little bitter. Could someone pass the sugar, please?"

"*Sugar?*" shrieked Count Olaf, erupting in

anger. He stood up, grabbed one end of the blanket, and pulled as hard as he could, scattering all of Sunny's hard work. Food, beverages, and dishes fell everywhere, and Sunny had to duck to avoid getting hit on the head with a flying fork. "All the sugar in the world couldn't save this terrible breakfast!" he roared, and then leaned down so that his shiny, shiny eyes stared right into Sunny's. "I told you to make a nice, hot breakfast, and you gave me cold, disgusting nonsense!" he said, his smelly breath making a cloud in the chilly air. "Don't you see how high up we are, you sabertoothed papoose? If I threw you off Mount Fraught, you'd never survive!"

"Olaf!" Esmé said. "I'm surprised at you! Surely you remember that we'll never get the Baudelaire fortune if we toss Sunny off the mountain. We have to keep Sunny alive for the greater good."

"Yes, yes," Count Olaf said. "I remember. I'm not going to throw the orphan off the mountain. I just wanted to terrify her." He gave Sunny a cruel smirk, and then turned to the hook-handed man. "Walk over to that frozen water-fall," he said, "and crack a hole in the ice with your hook. The stream is full of Stricken Salmon. Catch enough for all of us, and we'll have the baby prepare us a proper meal."

"Good idea, Olaf," the hook-handed man said, standing up and walking toward the icy slope. "You're as smart as you are intelligent."

"Sakesushi," Sunny said quietly, which meant "I don't think you'll enjoy salmon if it's not cooked."

"Stop your baby talk and wash these dishes," Olaf ordered. "They're covered in lousy food."

"You know, Olaf," said the white-faced woman who had asked for sugar, "it's none of my business, but we might put someone else in charge of cooking. It was probably difficult for a baby to prepare a hot breakfast without a fire."

"But there is a fire," said a deep, low voice, and everyone turned around to see who had arrived.

Having an aura of menace is like having a pet weasel, because you rarely meet someone who has one, and when you do it makes you want to hide under the coffee table. An aura of menace is simply a distinct feeling of evil that accompanies the arrival of certain people, and very few individuals are evil enough to produce an aura of menace that is very strong. Count Olaf, for example, had an aura of menace that the three Baudelaires had felt the moment they met him, but a number of other people never seemed to sense that a villain was in their midst, even when Olaf was standing right next to them with an evil gleam in his eye. But when two visitors arrived at the highest peak of the Mortmain Mountains, their aura of menace was unmistakable. Sunny gasped when she saw them. Esmé Squalor shuddered in her snowsuit. The members of Olaf's troupe—all except the hook-handed man, who was busy fishing for salmon and so was lucky enough to miss the visitors' arrival—gazed down at the snowy ground rather than take a further look at them. Count Olaf himself looked a bit nervous as the man, the woman, and their aura of menace drew closer and closer. And even I, after all this time, can feel their aura of menace so strongly, just by writing about these two people, that I dare not say their names, and will instead refer to them the way everyone who dares refer to them refers to them, as "the man with a beard, but no hair" and "the woman with hair, but no beard."

"It's good to see you, Olaf," continued the deep voice, and Sunny realized that the voice belonged to the sinister-looking woman. She was dressed in a suit made of a strange blue fabric that was very shiny, decorated with two large pads, one on each shoulder. She was dragging a wooden toboggan—a word which here means "a sled big enough to hold several people," which made an eerie scraping sound against the cold ground. "I was worried that the authorities might have captured you."

"You look well," said the man with a beard

but no hair. He was dressed identically to the woman with hair but no beard, but his voice was very hoarse, as if he had been screaming for hours and could hardly talk. "It's been a long time since we've laid eyes on one another." The man gave Olaf a grin that made it seem even colder on the mountain peak, and then stopped and helped the woman lean the toboggan against the rock where Sunny had served breakfast. The youngest Baudelaire saw that the toboggan was painted with the familiar eye insignia, and had a few long leather straps, presumably used for steering.

Count Olaf coughed lightly into his hand, which is something people often do when they cannot think of what to say. "Hello," he said, a bit nervously. "Did I hear you say something about a fire?"

The man with a beard but no hair and the woman with hair but no beard looked at one another and shared a laugh that made Sunny cover her ears with her hands. "Haven't you noticed," the woman said, "that there are no snow gnats around?"

"We had noticed that," Esmé said. "I thought maybe snow gnats were no longer in."

"Don't be ridiculous, Esmé," said the man with a beard but no hair. He reached out and kissed Esmé's hand, which Sunny could see was trembling. "The gnats aren't around because they can smell the smoke."

"I don't smell anything," said Hugo.

"Well, if you were a tiny insect, you'd smell something," replied the woman with hair but no beard. "If you were a snow gnat, you'd smell the smoke from the V.F.D. headquarters."

"We did you a favor, Olaf," the man said. "We burned the entire place down."

"No!" Sunny cried, before she could stop herself. By "No!" she meant "I certainly hope that isn't true, because my siblings and I hoped to reach V.F.D. headquarters, solve the mysteries that surround us, and perhaps find one of our parents," but she had not planned to say it out

loud. The two visitors looked down at the youngest Baudelaire, casting their aura of menace in
her direction.

"What is that?" asked the man with a beard
but no hair.

"That's the youngest Baudelaire," replied
Esmé. "We've eliminated the other two, but
we're keeping this one around to do our bidding
until we can finally steal the fortune."

The woman with hair but no beard nodded.
"Infant servants are so troublesome," she said.
"I had an infant servant once—a long time ago,
before the schism."

"Before the schism?" Olaf said, and Sunny
wished Klaus were with her, because the baby
did not know what the word "schism" meant.
"That *is* a long time ago. That infant must be
all grown up by now."

"Not necessarily," the woman said, and
laughed again, while her companion leaned down
to gaze at Sunny. Sunny could not bear to look
into the eyes of the man with a beard but no hair,

and instead looked down at his shiny shoes.

"So this is Sunny Baudelaire," he said in his strange, hoarse voice. "Well, well, well. I've heard so much about this little orphan. She's caused almost as many problems as her parents did." He stood up again and looked around at Olaf and his troupe. "But we know how to solve problems, don't we? Fire can solve any problem in the world."

He began to laugh, and the woman with hair but no beard laughed along with him. Nervously, Count Olaf began to laugh, too, and then glared at his troupe until they laughed along with him, and Sunny found herself surrounded by tall, laughing villains. "Oh, it was wonderful," said the woman with hair but no beard. "First we burned down the kitchen. Then we burned down the dining room. Then we burned down the parlor, and then the disguise center, the movie room, and the stables. Then we moved on to the gymnasium and the training center, and the garage and all six of the laboratories. We burned down the dormitories and schoolrooms, the lounge, the theater, and the music room, as well as the museum and the ice cream shop. Then we burned down the rehearsal studios and the testing centers and the swimming pool, which was very hard to burn down. Then we burned down all the bathrooms, and then finally, we burned down the V.F.D. library last night. That was my favorite part— books and books and books, all turned to ashes so no one could read them. You should have been there, Olaf! Every morning we lit fires and every evening we celebrated with a bottle of wine and some finger puppets. We've been wearing these fireproof suits for almost a month. It's been a marvelous time."

"Why did you burn it down gradually?" Count Olaf asked. "Whenever I burn something down, I do it all at once."

"We couldn't have burned down the entire headquarters at once," said the man with a beard but no hair. "Someone would have spotted us.

Remember, where there's smoke there's fire."

"But if you burned the headquarters down room by room," Esmé said, "didn't all of the volunteers escape?"

"They were gone already," said the man, and scratched his head where his hair might have been. "The entire headquarters were deserted. It was as if they knew we were coming. Oh well, you can't win them all."

"Maybe we'll find some of them when we burn down the carnival," said the woman, in her deep, deep voice.

"Carnival?" Olaf asked nervously.

"Yes," the woman said, and scratched the place where her beard would have been, if she had one. "There's an important piece of evidence that V.F.D. has hidden in a figurine sold at Caligari Carnival, so we need to go burn it down."

"I burned it down already," Count Olaf said.

"The whole place?" the woman said in surprise.

"The whole place," Olaf said, giving her a nervous smile.

"Congratulations," she said, in a deep purr. "You're better than I thought, Olaf."

Count Olaf looked relieved, as if he had not been sure whether the woman was going to compliment him or kick him. "Well, it's all for the greater good," he said.

"As a reward," the woman said, "I have a gift for you, Olaf." Sunny watched as the woman reached into the pocket of her shiny suit and drew out a stack of paper, tied together with thick rope. The paper looked very old and worn, as if it had been passed around to a variety of different people, hidden in a number of secret compartments, and perhaps even divided into different piles, driven around a city in horse-drawn carriages, and then put back together at midnight in the back room of a bookstore disguised as a café disguised as a sporting goods store. Count Olaf's eyes grew very wide and very shiny, and he reached his filthy hands toward it as if it were the Baudelaire fortune itself.

"The Snicket file!" he said, in a hushed whisper.

"It's all here," the woman said. "Every chart, every map and every photograph from the only file that could put us all in jail."

"It's complete except for page thirteen, of course," the man said. "We understand that the Baudelaires managed to steal that page from Heimlich Hospital."

The two visitors glared down at Sunny Baudelaire, who couldn't help whimpering in fear. "Surchmi," she said. She meant something along the lines of, "I don't have it—my siblings do," but she did not need a translator.

"The older orphans have it," Olaf said, "but I'm fairly certain they're dead."

"Then all of our problems have gone up in smoke," said the woman with hair but no beard.

Count Olaf grabbed the file and held it to his chest as if it were a newborn baby, although he was not the sort of person to treat a newborn baby very kindly. "This is the most wonderful gift in the world," he said. "I'm going to go read it right now."

"We'll all read it together," said the woman with hair but no beard. "It contains secrets we all ought to know."

"But first," said the man with a beard but no hair, "I have a gift for your girlfriend, Olaf."

"For me?" Esmé asked.

"I found these in one of the rooms of headquarters," the man said. "I've never seen one before, but it has been quite some time since I was a volunteer." With a sly smile, he reached into his pocket and took out a small green tube.

"What's that?" Esmé asked.

"I think it's a cigarette," the man said.

"A cigarette!" Esmé said, with a smile as big as Olaf's. "How in!"

"I thought you'd enjoy them," the man said. "Here, try it. I happen to have quite a few matches right here."

The man with a beard but no hair struck a

match, lit the end of the green tube, and offered it to the wicked girlfriend, who grabbed it and held it to her mouth. A bitter smell, like that of burning vegetables, filled the air, and Esmé Squalor began to cough.

"What's the matter?" asked the woman in her deep voice. "I thought you liked things that are in."

"I do," Esmé said, and then coughed quite a bit more. Sunny was reminded of Mr. Poe, who was always coughing into a handkerchief, as Esmé coughed and coughed and finally dropped the green tube to the ground where it spewed out a dark green smoke. "I love cigarettes," she explained to the man with a beard but no hair, "but I prefer to smoke them with a long holder because I don't like the smell or taste and because they're very bad for you."

"Never mind that now," Count Olaf said impatiently. "Let's go into my tent and read the file." He started to walk toward the tent but stopped and glared at his comrades, who were beginning to follow him. "The rest of you stay out here," he said. "There are secrets in this file that I do not want you to know."

The two sinister visitors began to laugh, and followed Count Olaf and Esmé into the tent, closing the flap behind them. Sunny stood with Hugo, Colette, Kevin, and the two white-faced women and stared after them in silence, waiting for the aura of menace to disappear.

"Who were those people?" asked the hook-handed man, and everyone turned to see that he had returned from his fishing expedition. Four salmon hung from each of his hooks, dripping with the waters of the Stricken Stream.

"I don't know," said one of the white-faced women, "but they made me very nervous."

"If they're friends of Count Olaf's," Kevin said, "how bad could they be?"

The members of the troupe looked at one another, but no one answered the ambidextrous person's question. "What did that man mean when he said 'Where there's smoke there's fire'?" Hugo asked.

"I don't know," Colette said. A chilly wind blew, and Sunny watched her contort her body in the breeze until it looked almost as curvy as the smoke from the green tube Esmé had dropped.

"Forget those questions," the hook-handed man said. "My question is, how are you going to prepare this salmon, orphan?"

Olaf's henchman was looking down at Sunny, but the youngest Baudelaire did not answer for a moment. Sunny was thinking, and her siblings would have been proud of her for the way she was thinking. Klaus would have been proud, because she was thinking about the phrase "Where there's smoke there's fire," and what it might mean. And Violet would have been proud, because she was thinking about the salmon that the hook-handed man was holding, and what she might invent that would help her.

Sunny stared at the hook-handed man and thought as hard as she could, and she felt almost as if both siblings were with her, Klaus helping her think about a phrase and Violet helping her think about an invention.

"Answer me, baby," the hook-handed man growled. "What are you going to make for us out of this salmon?"

"Lox!" Sunny said, but it was as if all three of the Baudelaires had answered the question.

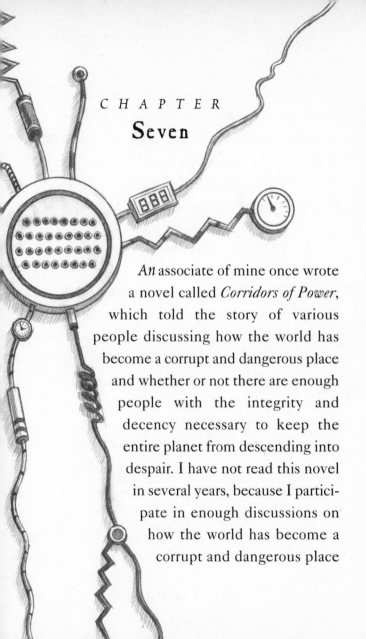

CHAPTER
**Seven**

*An* associate of mine once wrote a novel called *Corridors of Power*, which told the story of various people discussing how the world has become a corrupt and dangerous place and whether or not there are enough people with the integrity and decency necessary to keep the entire planet from descending into despair. I have not read this novel in several years, because I participate in enough discussions on how the world has become a corrupt and dangerous place and whether or not there are enough people with the integrity and decency necessary to keep the entire planet from descending into despair without reading about it in my leisure time, but nevertheless the phrase "corridors of power" has come to mean the hushed and often secret places where important matters are discussed. Whether or not they are actual corridors, the corridors of power tend to feel quiet and mysterious. If you have ever walked inside an important building, such as the main branch of a library or the office of a dentist who has agreed to disguise your teeth, then you may have experienced this feeling that accompanies the corridors of power, and Violet and Klaus Baudelaire experienced it as they reached the end of the Vertical Flame Diversion, and followed the mysterious sweatered scout as he climbed out of the secret passageway. Even through their masks, the two siblings could sense that they were in an important place, even though it was nothing more than a dim, curved hallway with a small grate on the ceiling where the morning light was shining through.

"That's where the smoke escapes from the Snow Scouts' fire," whispered the mysterious scout, pointing up at the ceiling. "That leads to the very center of the Valley of Four Drafts, so the smoke is scattered to the four winds. V.F.D. doesn't want anyone to see the smoke."

"Where there's smoke," Violet said, "there's fire."

"Exactly," the scout said. "Anyone who saw smoke coming from this high up in the mountains might become suspicious and investigate. In fact, I found a device that works exactly according to this principle." He reached into his backpack and drew out a small rectangular box filled with small green tubes, exactly like the one that Sunny had seen the man with a beard but no hair give to Esmé Squalor.

"No thank you," Violet said. "I don't smoke."

"I don't, either," the scout said, "but these aren't cigarettes. These are Verdant Flammable

Devices. Verdant means 'green,' so when you light one, it gives out a dark green smoke, so another volunteer will know where you are."

Klaus took the box from the scout and squinted at it in the dim light. "I've seen a box like this before," he said, "in my father's desk, when I was looking for a letter opener. I remember thinking it was strange to find them, because he didn't smoke."

"He must have been hiding them," Violet said. "Why was he keeping them a secret?"

"The entire organization is a secret," the scout said. "It was very difficult for me to learn the secret location of the headquarters."

"It was difficult for us, too," Klaus said. "We found it in a coded map."

"I had to draw my own map," the scout said, and reached into a pocket in his sweater. He turned on the flashlight, and the two Baudelaires could see he was holding a notebook with a dark purple cover.

"What's that?" Violet asked.

"It's a commonplace book," the scout said. "Whenever I find something that seems important or interesting, I write it down. That way, all my important information is in one place."

"I should start one," Klaus said. "My pockets are bulging with scraps of paper."

"From information I read in Dr. Montgomery's book, and a few others," the scout said, "I managed to draw a map of where to go from here." He opened the purple notebook and flipped a few pages until he reached a small but elegant rendering of the cave, the Vertical Flame Diversion, and the hallway in which they were standing now. "As you can see," he said, running his finger along the hallway, "the passageway branches off in two directions."

"This is a very well-drawn map," Violet said.

"Thank you," the scout replied. "I've been interested in cartography for quite some time. See, if we go to the left, there's a small area used for sled and snowsuit storage, at least according to a newspaper article I found. But if we go

right, we'll arrive at the Vernacularly Fastened
Door, which should open onto the headquarters'
kitchen. We might walk in on the entire organization having breakfast."

The two Baudelaires looked at one another
through their masks, and Violet put a hand on
her brother's shoulder. They did not dare to say
out loud their hope that one of their parents
might be just around the corner. "Let's go,"
Violet whispered.

The scout nodded silently in agreement,
and led the Baudelaires down the hallway,
which seemed to get colder and colder with
every step. By now they were so far from Bruce
and the Snow Scouts that there was no need to
whisper, but all three children kept quiet as
they walked down the dim, curved hallway,
hushed by the feeling of the corridors of power.
At last they reached a large metal door with a
strange device where the doorknob should have
been. The device looked a bit like a spider, with
curly wires spreading out in all directions, but

where the head of the spider might have been was the keyboard of a typewriter. Even in her excitement to see the headquarters, Violet's inventing mind was interested in such a device, and she leaned closer to see what it was.

"Wait," the sweatered scout said, reaching his arm out to stop her. "This is a coded lock. If we don't operate it properly, we won't be able to get into the headquarters."

"How does it work?" Violet said, shivering slightly in the cold.

"I'm not sure," the scout admitted, and took out his commonplace book again. "It's called the Vernacularly Fastened Door, so—"

"So it operates on language," Klaus finished. "Vernacular is a word for 'a local language or dialect.'"

"Of course," Violet said. "See how the wires are curled around the hinges of the door? They're locked in place, unless you type in the right sequence of letters on that keyboard. There are more letters than numbers, so it would be more difficult for someone to guess the combination of the lock."

"That's what I read," the scout confirmed, looking at a page in his notebook. "You're supposed to type in three specific phrases in a row. The phrases change every season, so volunteers need to have a lot of information at their fingertips to use this door. The first is the name of the scientist most widely credited with the discovery of gravity."

"That's easy," Violet said, and typed in S-I-R-I-S-A-A-C-N-E-W-T-O-N, the name of a physicist she had always admired. When she was finished, there was a muted clicking sound from the typewriter keyboard, as if the device was warming up.

"The second is the Latin name for the Volunteer Feline Detectives," the scout said. "I found the answer in *Remarkable Phenomena of the Mortmain Mountains*. It's *Panthera leo*." He leaned forward and typed in P-A-N-T-H-E-R-A-L-E-O. There was a very quiet buzzing sound, and the children saw that the wires near the hinges were shaking very slightly.

"It's beginning to unlock," Violet said. "I hope I get a chance to study this invention."

"Let's get to the headquarters first," Klaus said. "What's the third phrase?"

The scout sighed, and turned a page in the commonplace book. "I'm not sure," he admitted. "Another volunteer told me that it's the central theme of Leo Tolstoy's novel *Anna Karenina*, but I haven't had a chance to read it yet."

Violet knew that her brother was smiling, even though she could not see his face through the mask. She was remembering one summer, very long ago, when Klaus was very young and Sunny was not even conceived. Every summer, the Baudelaires' mother would read a very long book, joking that lifting a large novel was the only exercise she liked to get during the hot months. During the time Violet was thinking of, Mrs. Baudelaire chose *Anna Karenina* for her summer reading, and Klaus would sit on his mother's lap for hours at a time while she read. The middle Baudelaire had not been reading very long, but their mother helped him with the big words and would occasionally stop reading to explain what had happened in the story, and in this way Klaus and his mother read the story of Ms. Karenina, whose boyfriend treats her so poorly that she throws herself under a train. Violet had spent most of that summer studying the laws of thermodynamics and building a miniature helicopter out of an eggbeater and some old copper wiring, but she knew that Klaus must remember the central theme of the book he read on his mother's lap.

"The central theme of *Anna Karenina*," he said, "is that a rural life of moral simplicity, despite its monotony, is the preferable personal narrative to a daring life of impulsive passion, which only leads to tragedy."

"That's a very long theme," the scout said.

"It's a very long book," Klaus replied. "But I can work quickly. My sisters and I once tapped out a long telegram in no time at all."

"Too bad that telegram never arrived," the scout said quietly, but the middle Baudelaire was already pressing the keys on the Vernacularly Fastened Door. As Klaus typed the words "a rural life," a phrase which here means "living in the country," the wires began to curl and uncurl very quickly, like worms on a sidewalk after it has rained, and by the time Klaus was typing "the preferable personal narrative," a phrase which here means "the way to live your life," the entire door was quivering as if it were as nervous as the Baudelaires. Finally, Klaus typed "T-R-A-G-E-D-Y," and the three children stepped back, but instead of opening, the door stopped shaking and the wires stopped moving, and the passageway was dead quiet.

"It's not opening," Violet said. "Maybe that isn't the central theme of Leo Tolstoy's *Anna Karenina*."

"It seemed like it was working until the last word," the scout said.

"Maybe the mechanism is a little stuck," Violet said.

"Or maybe a daring life of impulsive passion only leads to something else," the scout said, and in some cases this mysterious person was right. A daring life of impulsive passion is an expression which refers to people who follow what is in their hearts, and like people who prefer to follow their head, or follow the advice of other people, or follow a mysterious man in a dark blue raincoat, people who lead a daring life of impulsive passion end up doing all sorts of things. For instance, if you ever find yourself reading a book entitled The Bible, you would find the story of Adam and Eve, whose daring life of impulsive passion led to them putting on clothing for the first time in their lives, in order to leave the snake-infested garden where they had been living. Bonnie and Clyde, another famous couple who lived a daring life of impulsive passion, found that it led them to a successful if short career in bank robbery. And in my own case, in the few moments where I have led a daring life of impulsive passion, it has led to all sorts of trouble, from false accusations of arson to a broken cuff link I can never have repaired. But in this case, as the Baudelaires stood at the Vernacularly Fastened Door, hoping to reach the V.F.D. headquarters, rescue their sister, and see if one of their parents was indeed alive, it was not the sweatered scout but the two Baudelaires who were right, because in Leo Tolstoy's *Anna Karenina*, a daring life of impulsive passion leads only to tragedy, as Klaus said, and as Violet said, the mechanism was a little stuck, and after a few seconds, the door swung open with a slow and eerie creak. The children stepped through the door, blinking in the sudden light, and stood frozen in their steps. If you have read this far in the Baudelaires' woeful story, then you will not be surprised to learn that the V.F.D. headquarters in the Valley of Four Drafts in the Mortmain Mountains was no more, but Violet and

Klaus, of course, were not reading their own story. They were in their own story, and this was the part of their story where they were sick with shock at what they saw.

The Vernacularly Fastened Door did not open onto a kitchen, not anymore. When the Baudelaires followed the mysterious scout through the doorway, they found themselves standing in what at first seemed to be a large field, growing a black and ruined harvest in a valley as cold and drafty as its name. But slowly, they saw the charred remains of the grand and impressive building that had stood where the three children were standing. Nearby was a handful of silverware that had survived the blaze, scattered in front of the remnants of a stove, and a refrigerator stood to one side, as if it were guarding the ashen remains of the rest of the kitchen. To one side was a pile of burnt wood that had probably once been a large dining table, with a half-melted candelabra sticking out of the top like a baby tree. Farther away, they could see the mysterious shapes of other objects that had survived the fire—a trombone, the pendulum of a grandfather clock, what looked like a periscope, or perhaps a spyglass, an ice cream scoop, lying forlornly in a pile of ashes encrusted with burnt sugar, and an iron archway emblazoned with the words "V.F.D. Library," but there was nothing beyond the archway but piles and piles of blackened remains. It was a devastating sight, and it made Violet and Klaus feel as if they were all alone in a world that had been completely ruined. The only thing they could see that seemed untouched by the fire was a sheer, white wall, beyond the refrigerator, that rose up as far as two siblings could see. It took the Baudelaires a few moments to realize that it was a frozen waterfall, rising up in a slippery slope toward the source of the Stricken Stream on Mount Fraught, so shiny and white that it made the ruined headquarters look even darker.

"It must have been beautiful," the sweatered scout said, in a quivering voice. He walked toward the waterfall, his feet churning up black dust with every step. "I read that there was a large window," he said, moving his gloved hand in the air as if it were still there. "When it was your turn to cook, you could look out at the waterfall while you were chopping vegetables or simmering a sauce. It was supposed to be very peaceful. And there was a mechanism just outside the window that turned some of the water from the pool into steam. The steam rose up and covered the headquarters, so it couldn't be seen through the blanket of mist."

The Baudelaires walked to where the scout was standing, and looked into the frozen pool at the bottom of the waterfall. The pool branched off into two tributaries, a word which here means "divisions of a river or stream, each twisting off in a different direction past the ruins of the head-quarters, and curving around the Mortmain Mountains until they disappeared from view." Violet and Klaus gazed sadly at the icy swirls of black and gray they had noticed when they were walking alongside the Stricken Stream. "It was ashes," Klaus said quietly. "Ashes from the fire fell into the pool at the bottom of the waterfall, and the stream carried them down the river."

Violet found that it was easier to discuss a small, specific matter than think about her immense disappointment. "But the pool is frozen solid," she said. "The stream couldn't have carried the ashes anywhere."

"It wouldn't have been frozen when it happened," Klaus replied. "The heat from the fire would have thawed the pool."

"It must have been awful to see," the sweatered scout said. Violet and Klaus stood with him, imagining the inferno, a word which here means "enormous fire that destroyed a secret headquarters high in the mountains." They could almost hear the shattering of glass as the windows fell away, and the crackle of the fire as it consumed everything it could. They could almost smell the thick smoke as it floated upward and blackened the sky, and they could almost see the books in the library, falling from the burning shelves and tumbling into ashes. The only thing they could not picture was who might have been at the headquarters when the fire began, running out into the freezing cold to avoid the flames.

"Do you think," Violet said, "any of the volunteers . . ."

"There's no sign that anyone was here," the scout said quickly.

"But how can we know for sure?" Klaus asked. "There could be a survivor someplace right now."

"*Hello?*" Violet called, looking around her at the rubble. "*Hello?*" She found that her eyes were filling with tears, as she called out for the people she knew in her heart were nowhere nearby. The eldest Baudelaire felt as if she had been calling for these people since that terrible day on the beach, and that if she called them enough they might appear before her. She thought of all the times she had called them, back when she lived with her siblings in the Baudelaire mansion.

Sometimes she called them when she wanted them to see something she had invented. Sometimes she called them when she wanted them to know she had arrived home. And sometimes she called them just because she wanted to know where they were. Sometimes Violet just wanted to see them, and feel that she was safe as long as they were around. *"Mother!"* Violet Baudelaire called. *"Father!"*

There was no answer.

*"Mom!"* Klaus called. *"Dad!"*

The Baudelaires heard nothing but the rush of all four of the valley's drafts, and a long creak as the Vernacularly Fastened Door blew shut. They saw that the door had been made to look just like the side of the mountain, so that they could scarcely see where they had come from, or the way to get back. Now they were truly alone.

"I know we were all hoping to find people at the headquarters," the sweatered scout said gently, "but I don't think anyone is here. I think we're all by ourselves."

"That's *impossible*!" Klaus cried, and Violet could hear that he was crying. He reached through his layers of clothing until he found his pocket, and pulled out page thirteen from the Snicket file, which he had been carrying with him since the Baudelaires had found it at Heimlich Hospital. The page had a photograph of their parents, standing with Jacques Snicket and another man the Baudelaires had been unable to identify, and above the photograph was a sentence Klaus had memorized from reading it so many times. "'Because of the evidence discussed on page nine,'" he recited tearfully, "'experts now suspect that there may in fact be one survivor of the fire, but the survivor's whereabouts are unknown.'" He walked up to the scout and shook the page in his face. "We thought the survivor would be here," he said.

"I think the survivor *is* here," the scout said quietly, and removed his mask to reveal his face at last. "I'm Quigley Quagmire," he said, "I survived the fire that destroyed my home, and I was hoping to find my brother and sister."

# CHAPTER Eight

*It* is one of the peculiar truths of life that people often say things that they know full well are ridiculous. If someone asks you how you are, for example, you might automatically say "Fine, thank you," when in fact you have just failed an examination or been trampled by an ox. A friend might tell you, "I've looked every-where in the world for my keys," when you know that they have actually only looked in a few places in the immediate area. Once I said to a woman I loved very much, "I'm sure that this trouble will end soon, and you and I will spend the rest of our lives together in happiness and bliss," when I actually suspected that things were about to get much worse. And so it was with the two elder Baudelaires, when they stood face-to-face with Quigley Quagmire and found themselves to be saying things they knew were absurd.

"You're dead," Violet said, and took off her mask to make sure she was seeing things clearly. But there was no mistaking Quigley, even though the Baudelaires had never seen him before. He looked so much like Duncan and Isadora that he could only be the third Quagmire triplet.

"You perished in a fire along with your parents," Klaus said, but as he took off his mask he knew this wasn't so. Quigley was even giving the two Baudelaires a small smile that looked exactly like his siblings'.

"No," Quigley said. "I survived, and I've been looking for my siblings ever since."

"But how did you survive?" Violet asked.

"Duncan and Isadora said that the house burned to the ground."

"It did," Quigley said sadly. He looked out at the frozen waterfall and sighed deeply. "I suppose I should start at the beginning. I was in my family's library, studying a map of the Finite Forest, when I heard a shattering of glass, and people shouting. My mother ran into the room and said there was a fire. We tried to go out the front door but the main hall was filled with smoke, so she took me back into the library and lifted a corner of the rug. There was a secret door underneath. She told me to wait down below while she fetched my siblings, and she left me there in the dark. I remember hearing the house falling to pieces above me, and the sound of frantic footsteps, and my siblings screaming." Quigley put his mask down on the ground and looked at the two Baudelaires. "But she never came back," he said. "Nobody came back, and when I tried to open the door, something had fallen on top of it and it wouldn't budge."

"How did you get out?" Klaus asked.

"I walked," Quigley said. "When it became clear that no one was going to rescue me, I felt around in the dark and realized I was in a sort of passageway. There was nowhere else to go, so I started walking. I've never been so frightened in my life, walking alone in some dark passageway my parents had kept secret. I couldn't imagine where it would lead."

The two Baudelaires looked at one another. They were thinking about the secret passageway they had discovered underneath their home, which they had discovered when they were under the care of Esmé Squalor and her husband. "And where did it lead?" Violet said.

"To the house of a herpetologist," Quigley said. "At the end of the passageway was a secret door that opened into an enormous room, made entirely of glass. The room was filled with empty cages, but it was clear that the room had once housed an enormous collection of reptiles."

"We've been there!" Klaus cried in amazement. "That's Uncle Monty's house! He was our guardian until Count Olaf arrived, disguised as—"

"As a lab assistant," Quigley finished. "I know. His suitcase was still there."

"There was a secret passageway under our house, too," Violet said, "but we didn't discover it until we lived with Esmé Squalor."

"There are secrets everywhere," Quigley said. "I think everyone's parents have secrets. You just have to know where to look for them."

"But why would our parents, and yours, have tunnels underneath their homes leading to a fancy apartment building and a herpetologist's home?" Klaus said. "It doesn't make any sense."

Quigley sighed, and put his backpack on the ashen ground, next to his mask. "There's a lot that doesn't make sense," he said. "I was hoping to find the answers here, but now I don't know if I'll ever find them." He took out his purple notebook and opened it to the first page.

"All I can tell you is what I have here in this commonplace book."

Klaus gave Quigley a small smile, and reached into his pockets to retrieve all of the papers he had stored there. "You tell us what you know," he said, "and we'll tell you what we know. Perhaps together we can answer our own questions."

Quigley nodded in agreement, and the three children sat in a circle on what was once the kitchen floor. Quigley opened his backpack and took out a bag of salted almonds, which he passed around. "You must be hungry from the climb up the Vertical Flame Diversion," he said. "I know I am. Let's see, where was I?"

"In the Reptile Room," Violet said, "at the end of the passageway."

"Well, nothing happened for a while," Quigley said. "On the doorstep of the house was a copy of *The Daily Punctilio*, which had an article about the fire. That's how I learned that my parents were dead. I spent days and days there, all by myself. I was so sad, and so scared, and I didn't know what else to do. I suppose I was waiting for the herpetologist to show up for work, and see if he was a friend of my parents and might be of some assistance. The kitchen was filled with food, so I had enough to eat, and every night I slept at the bottom of the stairs, so I could hear if anyone came in."

The Baudelaires nodded sympathetically, and Violet put a comforting hand on Quigley's shoulder. "We were the same way," Violet said, "right when we heard the news about our parents. I scarcely remember what we did and what we said."

"But didn't anyone come looking for you?" Klaus asked.

"*The Daily Punctilio* said that I died in the fire, too," Quigley said. "The article said that my sister and brother were sent off to Prufrock Preparatory School, and that my parents' estate was under the care of the city's sixth most important financial advisor."

"*Esmé Squalor*," Violet and Klaus said simultaneously, a word which here means "in a disgusted voice, and at the exact same time."

"Right," Quigley said, "but I wasn't interested in that part of the story. I was determined to go to the school and find my siblings again. I found an atlas in Dr. Montgomery's library, and studied it until I found Prufrock Preparatory School. It wasn't too far, so I started to gather whatever supplies I could find around his house."

"Didn't you think of calling the authorities?" Klaus asked.

"I guess I wasn't thinking very clearly," Quigley admitted. "All I could think of was finding my siblings."

"Of course," Violet said. "So what happened then?"

"I was interrupted," Quigley said. "Someone walked in just as I was putting the atlas in a totebag I found. It was Jacques Snicket, although I didn't know who he was, of course. But he knew who I was, and was overjoyed that

I was alive after all."

"How did you know you could trust him?" Klaus asked.

"Well, he knew about the secret passage-way," Quigley said. "In fact, he knew quite a bit about my family, even though he hadn't seen my parents in years. And . . ."

"And?" Violet said.

Quigley gave her a small smile. "And he was very well-read," he said. "In fact, he was at Dr. Montgomery's house to do a bit more reading. He said there was an important file that was hidden someplace on the premises, and he had to stay for a few days to try and complete his investigation."

"So he didn't take you to the school?" Violet asked.

"He said it wasn't safe for me to be seen," Quigley said. "He explained that he was part of a secret organization, and that my parents had been a part of it, too."

"V.F.D.," Klaus said, and Quigley nodded in agreement.

"Duncan and Isadora tried to tell us about V.F.D.," Violet said, "but they never got the chance. We don't even know what it stands for."

"It seems to stand for many things," Quigley said, flipping pages in his notebook. "Nearly everything the organization uses, from the Volunteer Feline Detectives to the Vernacularly Fastened Door, has the same initials."

"But what is the organization?" Violet asked. "What is V.F.D.?"

"Jacques wouldn't tell me," Quigley said, "but I think the letters stand for Volunteer Fire Department."

"Volunteer Fire Department," Violet repeated, and looked at her brother. "What does that mean?"

"In some communities," Klaus said, "there's no official fire department, and so they rely on volunteers to extinguish fires."

"I know that," Violet said, "but what does that have to do with our parents, or Count Olaf, or anything that has happened to us? I always thought that knowing what the letters stood for would solve the mystery, but I'm as mystified as I ever was."

"Do you think our parents were secretly fighting fires?" Klaus asked.

"But why would they keep it a secret?" Violet asked. "And why would they have a secret passageway underneath the house?"

"Jacques said that the passageways were built by members of the organization," Quigley said. "In the case of an emergency, they could escape to a safe place."

"But the tunnel we found connects our house to the home of Esmé Squalor," Klaus said. "That's not a safe place."

"Something happened," Quigley said. "Something that changed everything." He flipped through a few pages of his commonplace book until he found what he was looking for. "Jacques Snicket called it a 'schism,'" he said, "but I don't know what that word means."

"A schism," Klaus said, "is a division of a

previously united group of people into two or more oppositional parties. It's like a big argument, with everybody choosing sides."

"That makes sense," Quigley said. "The way Jacques talked, it sounded like the entire organization was in chaos. Volunteers who were once working together are now enemies. Places that were once safe are now dangerous. Both sides are using the same codes, and the same disguises. Even the V.F.D. insignia used to represent the noble ideals everyone shared, but now it's all gone up in smoke."

"But how did the schism start?" Violet asked. "What was everyone fighting over?"

"I don't know," Quigley said. "Jacques didn't have much time to explain things to me."

"What was he doing?" Klaus asked.

"He was looking for you," Quigley replied. "He showed me a picture of all three of you, waiting at the dock on some lake, and asked me if I'd seen you anywhere. He knew that you'd been placed in Count Olaf's care, and all the terrible things that had happened there. He knew that you had gone to live with Dr. Montgomery. He even knew about some of the inventions you made, Violet, and the research you did, Klaus, and some of Sunny's tooth-related exploits. He wanted to find you before it was too late."

"Too late for what?" Violet said.

"I don't know," Quigley said with a sigh. "Jacques spent a long time at Dr. Montgomery's house, but he was too busy conducting his investigation to explain everything to me. He would stay up all night reading and copying information into his notebook, and then sleep all day, or disappear for hours at a time. And then one day, he said he had to go interview someone in the town of Paltryville, but he never came back. I waited weeks and weeks for him to return. I read books in Dr. Montgomery's library, and started a commonplace book of my own. At first it was difficult to find any information on V.F.D., but I took notes on anything I could find. I must have read hundreds of books, but Jacques never returned. Finally, one morning, two things happened that made me decide not to wait any longer. The first was an article in *The Daily Punctilio* saying that my siblings had been kidnapped from the school. I knew I had to do something. I couldn't wait for Jacques Snicket or for anyone else."

The Baudelaires nodded in solemn agreement. "What was the second thing?" Violet asked.

Quigley was silent for a moment, and he reached down to the ground and scooped up a handful of ashes, letting them fall from his gloved hands. "I smelled smoke," he said, "and when I opened the door of the Reptile Room, I saw that someone had thrown a torch through the glass of the ceiling, starting a fire in the library. Within minutes, the entire house was in flames."

"Oh," Violet said quietly. "Oh" is a word which usually means something along the lines

of, "I heard you, and I'm not particularly interested," but in this case, of course, the eldest
Baudelaire meant something entirely different,
and it is something that is difficult to define. She
meant "I am sad to hear that Uncle Monty's
house burned down," but that is not all. By "Oh,"
Violet was also trying to describe her sadness
about all of the fires that had brought Quigley
and Klaus and herself here to the Mortmain
Mountains, to huddle in a circle and try to solve
the mystery that surrounded them. When Violet
said "Oh," she was not only thinking of the fire
in the Reptile Room, but the fires that had
destroyed the Baudelaire home, and the Quagmire home, and Heimlich Hospital, and Caligari
Carnival, and the V.F.D. headquarters, where the
smell of smoke still lingered around where the
children were sitting. Thinking of all those fires
made Violet feel as if the entire world were going
up in flames, and that she and her siblings and
all the other decent people in the world might

never find a place that was truly safe.

"Another fire," Klaus murmured, and Violet knew he was thinking the same thing. "Where could you go, Quigley?"

"The only place I could think of was Paltry-ville," Quigley said. "The last time I saw Jacques, he'd said he was going there. I thought if I went there I might find him again, and see if he could help me rescue Duncan and Isadora. Dr. Mont-gomery's atlas showed me how to get there, but I had to go on foot, because I was afraid that anyone who might offer me a ride would be an enemy. It was a long time before I finally arrived, but as soon as I stepped into town I saw a large building that matched the tattoo on Jacques Snicket's ankle. I thought it might be a safe place to go."

"Dr. Orwell's office!" Klaus cried. "That's not a safe place to go!"

"Klaus was hypnotized there," Violet ex-plained, "and Count Olaf was disguised as—"

"As a receptionist," Quigley finished. "I know. His fake nameplate was still on the desk. The office was deserted, but I could tell that Jacques had been there, because there were some notes in his handwriting that he'd left on the desk. With those notes, and the information I'd read in Dr. Montgomery's library, I learned about the V.F.D. headquarters. So instead of waiting for Jacques again, I set out to find the organization. I thought they were my best hope of rescuing my siblings."

"So you set off to the Mortmain Mountains by yourself?" Violet asked.

"Not quite by myself," Quigley said. "I had this backpack that Jacques left behind, with the Verdant Flammable Devices and a few other items, and I had my commonplace book. And eventually, I ran into the Snow Scouts, and realized that hiding among them would be the quickest way to reach Mount Fraught." He turned a page in his commonplace book and examined his notes. "*Remarkable Phenomena of the Mortmain Mountains*, which I read in Dr. Montgomery's library, had a hidden chapter that told me all about the Vertical Flame Diversion and the Vernacularly Fastened Door."

Klaus looked over Quigley's shoulder to read his notes. "I should have read that book when I had the chance," he said, shaking his head. "If we had known about V.F.D. when we were living with Uncle Monty, we might have avoided all the trouble that followed."

"When we were living with Uncle Monty," Violet reminded him, "we were too busy trying to escape Count Olaf's clutches to do any additional research."

"I've had plenty of time to do research," Quigley said, "but I still haven't found all the answers I'm looking for. I still haven't found Duncan and Isadora, and I still don't know where Jacques Snicket is."

"He's dead," Klaus said, very quietly. "Count Olaf murdered him."

"I thought you might say that," Quigley said. "I knew something was very wrong when he didn't return. But what about my siblings? Do you know what happened to them?"

"They're safe, Quigley," Violet said. "We think they're safe. We rescued them from Olaf's clutches, and they escaped with a man named Hector."

"Escaped?" Quigley repeated. "Where did they go?"

"We don't know," Klaus admitted. "Hector built a self-sustaining hot air mobile home. It was like a flying house, kept in the air by a bunch of balloons, and Hector said it could stay up in the sky forever."

"We tried to climb aboard," Violet said, "but Count Olaf managed to stop us."

"So you don't know where they are?" Quigley asked.

"I'm afraid not," Violet said, and patted his hand. "But Duncan and Isadora are intrepid people, Quigley. They survived for quite some time in Olaf's clutches, taking notes on his schemes and trying to pass on the information to us."

"Violet's right," Klaus said. "I'm sure that wherever they are, they're continuing their research. Eventually, they'll find out you're alive, and they'll come looking for you, just like you went looking for them."

The two Baudelaires looked at one another and shivered. They had been talking about Quigley's family, of course, but they felt as if they were talking about their own. "I'm sure that if your parents are alive, they're looking for you, too," Quigley said, as if he'd read their minds. "And Sunny, too. Do you know where she is?"

"Someplace nearby," Violet said. "She's with Count Olaf, and Olaf wanted to find the headquarters, too."

"Maybe Olaf has already been here," Quigley said, looking around at the wreckage. "Maybe he's the one who burned this place down."

"I don't think so," Klaus said. "He wouldn't have had time to burn this whole place down. We were right on his trail. Plus, I don't think this place burned down all at once."

"Why not?" Quigley said.

"It's too big," Klaus replied. "If the whole headquarters were burning, the sky would be covered in smoke."

"That's true," Violet said. "That much smoke would arouse too much suspicion."

"Where there's smoke," Quigley said, "there's fire."

Violet and Klaus turned to their friend to agree, but Quigley was not looking at the two Baudelaires. He was looking past them, toward the frozen pool and the two frozen tributaries, where the enormous windows of the V.F.D. kitchen had once stood, and where I once chopped broccoli while the woman I loved mixed up a spicy peanut sauce to go with it, and he was pointing up toward the sky, where my associates and I used to watch the volunteer eagles who could spot smoke from a very great distance.

That afternoon, there were no eagles in the skies over the Mortmain Mountains, but as Violet and Klaus stood up and looked in the direction Quigley was pointing, there was something in the sky that caught their attention. Because when Quigley Quagmire said, "Where there's smoke, there's fire," he was not referring to Klaus's theory about the destruction of V.F.D. headquarters. He was talking about the sight of green smoke, wafting up into the sky from the peak of Mount Fraught, at the top of the slippery slope.

# CHAPTER Nine

*The* two elder Baudelaires stood
for a moment with Quigley, gazing up at the small plume, a word
which here means "mysterious
cloud of green smoke." After the
long, strange story he had told
them about surviving the fire and
what he had learned about V.F.D.,
they could scarcely believe that
they were confronting another
mystery.

"It's a Verdant Flammable
Device," Quigley said. "There's
someone at the top of the waterfall, sending a signal."

"Yes," Violet said, "but who?"

"Maybe it's a volunteer, who escaped from the fire," Klaus said. "They're signaling to see if there are any other volunteers nearby."

"Or it could be a trap," Quigley said. "They could be luring volunteers up to the peak in order to ambush them. Remember, the codes of V.F.D. are used by both sides of the schism."

"It hardly seems like a code," Violet said. "We know that someone is communicating, but we don't have the faintest idea who they are, or what they're saying."

"This is what it must be like," Klaus said thoughtfully, "when Sunny talks to people who don't know her very well."

At the mention of Sunny's name, the Baudelaires were reminded of how much they missed her. "Whether it's a volunteer or a trap," Violet said, "it might be our only chance to find our sister."

"Or my sister and brother," Quigley said.

"Let's signal back," Klaus said. "Do you

still have those Verdant Flammable Devices, Quigley?"

"Of course," Quigley said, taking the box of green tubes out of his backpack, "but Bruce saw my matches and confiscated them, because children shouldn't play with matches."

"Confiscated them?" Klaus said. "Do you think he's an enemy of V.F.D.?"

"If everyone who said that children shouldn't play with matches was an enemy of V.F.D.," Violet said with a smile, "then we wouldn't have a chance of survival."

"But how are we going to light these without matches?" Quigley asked.

Violet reached into her pocket. It was a bit tricky to tie her hair up in a ribbon, as all four drafts in the Valley of Four Drafts were blowing hard, but at last her hair was out of her eyes, and the gears and levers of her inventing mind began to move as she gazed up at the mysterious signal.

But of course this signal was neither a volunteer nor a trap. It was a baby, with unusually large teeth and a way of talking that some people found confusing. When Sunny Baudelaire had said "lox," for example, the members of Count Olaf's troupe had assumed she was simply babbling, rather than explaining how she was going to cook the salmon that the hook-handed man had caught. "Lox" is a word which refers to smoked salmon, and it is a delicious way to enjoy freshly caught fish, particularly if one has the appropriate accoutrements, a phrase which here means "bagels, cream cheese, sliced cucumber, black pepper, and capers, which can be eaten along with the lox for an enjoyable meal." Lox also has an additional benefit of producing quite a bit of smoke as it is prepared, and this is the reason Sunny chose this method of preparing salmon, as opposed to gravlax, which is salmon marinated for several days in a mixture of spices, or sashimi, which is salmon cut into pleasing shapes and simply served raw. Remembering what Count Olaf had said about being able to see everything and everyone from

the peak where he had brought her, the
youngest Baudelaire realized that the phrase
"where there's smoke there's fire" might be
able to help her. As Violet and Klaus heard
Quigley's extraordinary tale at the bottom of the
frozen waterfall, Sunny hurried to prepare lox
and send a signal to her siblings, who she hoped
were nearby. First, she nudged the Verdant
Flammable Device—which she, like everyone
at the peak, believed was a cigarette—into a
small patch of weeds, in order to increase the
smoke. Then she dragged over the covered
casserole dish that she had been using as a
makeshift bed, and placed the salmon inside it.
In no time at all, the fish caught by the hook-
handed man were absorbing the heat and smoke
from the simmering green tube, and a large
plume of green smoke was floating up into the
sky above Mount Fraught. Sunny gazed up at
the signal she made and couldn't help smiling.
The last time she had been separated from her
siblings, she had simply waited in the birdcage

for them to come and rescue her, but she had grown since then, and was able to take an active part in defeating Count Olaf and his troupe, while still having time to prepare a seafood dish.

"Something smells delicious," said one of the white-faced women, walking by the casserole dish. "I must admit, I had some doubts that an infant should be in charge of the cooking, but your salmon recipe seems like it will be very tasty indeed."

"There's a word for the way she's preparing the fish," the hook-handed man said, "but I can't remember what it is."

"*Lox*," Sunny said, but no one heard her over the sound of Count Olaf storming out of his tent, followed by Esmé and the two sinister visitors. Olaf was clutching the Snicket file and glaring down at Sunny with his shiny, shiny eyes.

"Put that smoke out *at once*!" he ordered. "I thought you were a terrified orphan prisoner, but I'm beginning to think you're a spy!"

"What do you mean, Olaf?" asked the other white-faced woman. "She's using Esmé's cigarette to cook us some fish."

"Someone might see the smoke," Esmé snarled, as if she had not been smoking herself just moments ago. "Where there's smoke, there's fire."

The man with a beard but no hair picked up a handful of snow and threw it onto the weeds, extinguishing the Verdant Flammable Device. "Who are you signaling to, baby?" he asked, in his strange, hoarse voice. "If you're a spy, we're going to toss you off this mountain."

"Goo goo," Sunny said, which meant something along the lines of "I'm going to pretend I'm a helpless baby, instead of answering your question."

"You see?" the white-faced woman said, looking nervously at the man with a beard but no hair. "She's just a helpless baby."

"Perhaps you're right," said the woman with

hair but no beard. "Besides, there's no reason to toss a baby off a mountain unless you absolutely have to."

"Babies can come in handy," Count Olaf agreed. "In fact, I've been thinking about recruiting more young people into my troupe. They're less likely to complain about doing my bidding."

"But we never complain," the hook-handed man said. "I try to be as accommodating as possible."

"Enough chitchat," said the man with a beard but no hair. "We have a lot of scheming to do, Olaf. I have some information that might help you with your recruiting idea, and according to the Snicket file, there's one more safe place for the volunteers to gather."

"The last safe place," said the sinister woman. "We have to find it and burn it down."

"And once we do," Count Olaf said, "the last evidence of our plans will be completely destroyed. We'll never have to worry about the authorities again."

"Where is this last safe place?" asked Kevin.

Olaf opened his mouth to answer, but the woman with hair but no beard stopped him with a quick gesture and a suspicious glance down at Sunny. "Not in front of the toothy orphan," she said, in her deep, deep voice. "If she learned what we were up to, she'd never sleep again, and you need your infant servant full of energy. Send her away, and we'll make our plans."

"Of course," Olaf said, smiling nervously at the sinister visitors. "Orphan, go to my car and remove all of the potato chip crumbs from the interior by blowing as hard as you can."

"Futil," Sunny said, which meant something like, "That is an absolutely impossible chore," but she walked unsteadily toward the car while Olaf's troupe laughed and gathered around the flat rock to hear the new scheme. Passing the extinguished fire and the covered casserole dish where she would sleep that night, Sunny sighed sadly, thinking that her signal plan must have failed. But when she reached Olaf's car and gazed down at the frozen waterfall, she saw something that lightened her spirits, a phrase which here means "an identical plume of green smoke, coming from the very bottom of the slope." The youngest Baudelaire looked down at the smoke and smiled. "Sibling," she said to herself. Sunny, of course, could not be certain that it was Violet and Klaus who were signaling to her, but she could hope it was so, and hope was enough to cheer her up as she opened the door of the car and began blowing at the crumbs Olaf and his troupe had scattered all over the upholstery.

But at the bottom of the frozen waterfall, the two elder Baudelaires did not feel nearly as hopeful as they stood with Quigley and watched the green smoke disappear from the highest peak.

"Someone put out the Verdant Flammable Device," Quigley said, holding the green tube to one side so he wouldn't smell the smoke. "What do you think that means?"

"I don't know," Violet said, and sighed. "This isn't working."

"Of course it's working," Klaus said. "It's working perfectly. You noticed that the afternoon sun was reflecting off the frozen waterfall, and it gave you the idea to use the scientific principles of the convergence and refraction of light—just like you did on Lake Lachrymose, when we were battling the leeches. So you used Colette's hand mirror to catch the sun's rays and reflect them onto the end of the Verdant Flammable Device, so we could light it and send a signal."

"Klaus is right," Quigley said. "It couldn't have worked better."

"Thank you," Violet said, "but that's not what I mean. I mean this code isn't working. We still don't know who's up on the peak, or why they were signaling us, and now the signal has stopped, but we still don't know what it means."

"Maybe we should extinguish our Verdant

Flammable Device, too," Klaus said.

"Maybe," Violet agreed, "or maybe we should go up to the top of the waterfall and see for ourselves who is there."

Quigley frowned, and took out his commonplace book. "The only way up to the highest peak," he said, "is the path that the Snow Scouts are taking. We'd have to go back through the Vernacularly Fastened Door, back down the Vertical Flame Diversion, back into the Volunteer Feline Detective cave, rejoin the scouts and hike for a long time."

"That's not the only way up to the peak," Violet said with a smile.

"Yes, it is," Quigley insisted. "Look at the map."

"Look at the waterfall," Violet replied, and all three children looked up at the shiny slope.

"Do you mean," Klaus said, "that you think you can invent something which can get us up a frozen waterfall?"

But Violet was already tying her hair out of

her eyes again, and looking around at the ruins of the V.F.D. headquarters. "I'll need that ukulele that you took from the caravan," she said to Klaus, "and that half-melted candelabra over there by the dining room table."

Klaus took the ukulele from his coat pocket and handed it to his sister, and then walked over to the table to retrieve the strange, melted object. "Unless you need any further assistance," he said, "I think I might go examine the wreckage of the library and see if any documents have survived. We might as well learn as much from this headquarters as we can."

"Good idea," Quigley said, and reached into his backpack. He brought out a notebook much like his own, except it had a dark blue cover. "I have a spare notebook," he said. "You might be interested in starting a commonplace book of your own."

"That's very kind of you," Klaus said. "I'll write down anything I find. Do you want to join the search?"

"I think I'll stay here," Quigley said, looking at Violet. "I've heard quite a bit about Violet Baudelaire's marvelous inventions, and I'd like to see her at work."

Klaus nodded, and walked off to the iron archway marking the entrance of the ruined library, while Violet blushed and leaned down to pick up one of the forks that had survived the fire.

It is one of the great sadnesses of the Baude-laire case that Violet never got to meet a man named C. M. Kornbluth, an associate of mine who spent most of his life living and working in the Valley of Four Drafts as a mechanical instruc-tor at the V.F.D. headquarters. Mr. Kornbluth was a quiet and secretive man, so secretive that no one ever knew who he was, where he came from, or even what the C or the M stood for, and he spent much of his time holed up in his dor-mitory room writing strange stories, or gazing sadly out the windows of the kitchen. The one thing that put Mr. Kornbluth in a good mood would be a particularly promising mechanical student. If a young man showed an interest in deep sea radar, Mr. Kornbluth would take off his glasses and smile. If a young woman brought him a staple gun she had built, Mr. Kornbluth would clap his hands in excitement. And if a pair of twins asked him how to properly reroute some copper wiring, he would take a paper bag out of his pocket and offer some pistachio nuts to anyone who happened to be around. So, when I think of Violet Baudelaire standing in the wreckage of the V.F.D. headquarters, carefully taking the strings off the ukulele and bending some of the forks in half, I can imagine Mr. Kornbluth, even though he and his pistachios are long gone, turning from the window, smiling at the Baudelaire inventor, and saying, "Beatrice, come over here! Look at what this girl is making!"

"What are you making?" Quigley asked.

"Something that will get us up that waterfall," Violet replied. "I only wish that Sunny were here. Her teeth would be perfect to slice these ukulele strings into halves."

"I might have something that could help," Quigley said, looking through his backpack. "When I was in Dr. Orwell's office, I found these fake fingernails. They're a horrible shade of pink, but they're quite sharp."

Violet took a fingernail from Quigley and looked at it carefully. "I think Count Olaf was wearing these," she said, "as part of his receptionist disguise. It's so strange that you have been following in our footsteps all this time, and yet we never even knew you were alive."

"I knew you were alive," Quigley said. "Jacques Snicket told me all about you, Klaus, Sunny, and even your parents. He knew them quite well before you were born."

"I thought so," Violet said, cutting the ukulele strings. "In the photograph we found, my parents are standing with Jacques Snicket and another man."

"He's probably Jacques's brother," Quigley

said. "Jacques told me that he was working closely with his two siblings on an important file."

"The Snicket file," Violet said. "We were hoping to find it here."

Quigley looked up at the frozen waterfall. "Maybe whoever signaled us will know where it is," he said.

"We'll find out soon enough," Violet said. "Please take off your shoes."

"My shoes?" Quigley asked.

"The waterfall will be very slippery," Violet explained, "so I'm using the ukulele strings to tie these bent forks to the toe area, to make fork-assisted climbing shoes. We'll hold two more forks in our hands. Tines of the forks are almost as sharp as Sunny's teeth, so the fork-assisted climbing shoes will easily dig into the ice with each step, and enable us to keep our balance."

"But what's the candelabra for?" Quigley asked, unlacing his shoes.

"I'm going to use it as an ice tester," Violet

said. "A moving body of water, such as a water-fall, is rarely completely frozen. There are probably places on that slope where there is only a thin layer of ice, particularly with False Spring on its way. If we stuck our forks through the ice and hit water, we'd lose our grip and fall. So I'll tap on the ice with the candelabra before each step, to find the solid places we should climb."

"It sounds like a difficult journey," Quigley said.

"No more difficult than climbing up the Vertical Flame Diversion," Violet said, tying a fork onto Quigley's shoe. "I'm using the Sumac knot, so it should hold tight. Now, all we need is Klaus's shoes, and—"

"I'm sorry to interrupt, but I think this might be important," Klaus said, and Violet turned to see that her brother had returned. He was holding the dark blue notebook in one hand and a small, burnt piece of paper in the other. "I found this scrap of paper in a pile of ashes," he said. "It's from some kind of code book."

"What does it say?" Violet asked.

"'In the e          flagration resulting in the destruction of a sanc    ,'" Klaus read, "'    teers should avail themselves of Verbal Fri    Dialogue, which is concealed accordingly.'"

"That doesn't make any sense," Quigley said. "Do you think it's in code?"

"Sort of," Klaus said. "Parts of the sentence are burned away, so you have to figure the sentence out as if it's encoded. 'Flagration' is probably the last part of the word 'conflagration,' a fancy word for fire, and 'sanc' is probably the beginning of the word 'sanctuary,' which means a safe place. So the sentence probably began something like, 'In the event of a conflagration resulting in the destruction of a sanctuary.'"

Violet stood up and looked over his shoulder. "'Teers,'" she said, "is probably 'volunteers,' but I don't know what 'avail themselves' means."

"It means 'to make use of,'" Klaus said, "like you're availing yourself of the ukulele and those forks. Don't you see? This says that in case a safe place burns down, they'll leave some sort of message—'Verbal Fri    Dialogue.'"

"But what could 'Verbal Fri      Dialogue' be?" Quigley asked. "Friends? Frisky?"

"Frilly?" Violet guessed. "Frightening?"

"But it says that it's concealed accordingly," Klaus pointed out. "That means that the dialogue is hidden in a logical way. If it were Verbal Waterfall Dialogue, it would be hidden in the waterfall. So none of those words can be right. Where would someone leave a message where fire couldn't destroy it?"

"But fire destroys everything," Violet said. "Look at the headquarters. Nothing is left standing except the library entrance, and . . ."

". . . and the refrigerator," Klaus finished. "Or, we might say, the fridge."

"Verbal Fridge Dialogue!" Quigley said.

"The volunteers left a message," said Klaus, who was already halfway to the refrigerator, "in the only place they knew wouldn't be affected by the fire."

"And the one place their enemies wouldn't think of looking," Quigley said. "After all, there's never anything terribly important in the refrigerator."

What Quigley said, of course, is not entirely true. Like an envelope, a hollow figurine, and a coffin, a refrigerator can hold all sorts of things, and they may turn out to be very important depending on what kind of day you are having. A refrigerator may hold an icepack, for example, which would be important if you had been wounded. A refrigerator may hold a bottle of water, which would be important if you were dying of thirst. And a refrigerator may hold a basket of strawberries, which would be important if a maniac said to you, "If you don't give me a basket of strawberries right now, I'm going to poke you with this large stick." But when the two elder Baudelaires and Quigley Quagmire opened the refrigerator, they found nothing that would help someone who was wounded, dying of thirst, or being threatened by a strawberry-crazed, stick-carrying maniac, or anything that looked important at all. The fridge was mostly empty, with just a few of the usual things people keep in their refrigerators and rarely use, including a jar of mustard, a container of olives, three jars of different kinds of jam, a bottle of lemon juice, and one lonely pickle in a small glass jug.

"There's nothing here," Violet said.

"Look in the crisper," Quigley said, pointing to a drawer in the refrigerator traditionally used for storing fruits and vegetables. Klaus opened the drawer and pulled out a few strands of a green plant with tiny, skinny leaves.

"It smells like dill," Klaus said, "and it's quite crisp, as if it were picked yesterday."

"Very Fresh Dill," Quigley said.

"Another mystery," Violet said, and tears filled her eyes. "We have nothing but mysteries. We don't know where Sunny is. We don't know where Count Olaf is. We don't know who's signaling to us at the top of the waterfall, or what they're trying to say, and now there's a mysterious message in a mysterious code in a mysterious refrigerator, and a bunch of mysterious herbs in the crisper. I'm tired of mysteries. I want someone to help us."

"We can help each other," Klaus said. "We have your inventions, and Quigley's maps, and my research."

"And we're all very well-read," Quigley said. "That should be enough to solve any mystery."

Violet sighed, and kicked at something that lay on the ashen ground. It was the small shell of a pistachio nut, blackened from the fire that destroyed the headquarters. "It's like we're members of V.F.D. already," she said. "We're sending signals, and breaking codes, and finding secrets in the ruins of a fire."

"Do you think our parents would be proud of us," Klaus asked, "for following in their footsteps?"

"I don't know," Violet said. "After all, they kept V.F.D. a secret."

"Maybe they were going to tell us later," Klaus said.

"Or maybe they hoped we would never find out," Violet said.

"I keep wondering the same thing," Quigley said. "If I could travel back in time to the moment my mother showed me the secret passageway under the library, I would ask her why she was keeping these secrets."

"That's one more mystery," Violet said sadly, and looked up at the slippery slope. It was getting later and later in the afternoon, and the frozen waterfall looked less and less shiny in the fading sunlight, as if time were running out to climb to the top and see who had been signaling to them. "We should each investigate the mystery we're most likely to solve," she said. "I'll climb up the waterfall, and solve the mystery of the Verdant Flammable Device by learning who's up there, and what they want. You should stay down here, Klaus, and solve the mystery of the Verbal Fridge Dialogue, by learning the code and discovering what the message is."

"And I'll help you both," Quigley said, taking out his purple notebook. "I'll leave my commonplace book with Klaus, in case it's any help with the codes. And I'll climb up the waterfall with you, Violet, in case you need my help."

"Are you sure?" Violet asked. "You've already taken us this far, Quigley. You don't have to risk your life any further."

"We'll understand," Klaus said, "if you want to leave and search for your siblings."

"Don't be absurd," Quigley said. "We're all part of this mystery, whatever it is. Of course I'm going to help you."

The two Baudelaires looked at one another and smiled. It is so rare in this world to meet a trustworthy person who truly wants to help you, and finding such a person can make you feel warm and safe, even if you are in the middle of a windy valley high up in the mountains. For a moment, as their friend smiled back at them, it seemed as if all the mysteries had been solved already, even with Sunny still separated from them, and Count Olaf still at large, and the abandoned V.F.D. headquarters still in ashes around them. Just knowing that they had found a person like Quigley Quagmire made Violet and Klaus feel as if every code made sense, and every signal was clear.

Violet stepped forward, her fork-assisted climbing shoes making small, determined noises on the ground, and took Quigley's hand. "Thank you," she said, "for volunteering."

# CHAPTER Ten

*Violet* and Quigley walked carefully across the frozen pool until they reached the bottom of the waterfall. "Good luck!" Klaus called, from the archway of the ruined library. He was polishing his glasses, as he often did before embarking on serious research.

"Good luck to you!" Violet replied, shouting over the rush of the mountain winds, and as she looked back at her brother, she remembered when the two siblings were trying to stop the caravan as it hurtled down the mountain. Klaus had wanted to say something to her, in case the drag chute and the mixture of sticky substances hadn't worked. Violet had the same feeling now, as she prepared to climb the frozen waterfall and leave her brother behind at the ashy remains of the V.F.D. headquarters. "Klaus—" she said.

Klaus put his glasses on and gave his sister his bravest smile. "Whatever you're thinking of saying," he said, "say it when you return."

Violet nodded, and tapped the candelabra against a spot on the ice. She heard a deep *thunk!*, as if she were tapping something very solid. "We'll start here," she said to Quigley. "Brace yourself."

The expression "brace yourself," as I'm sure you know, does not mean to take some metal

wiring and rivets and other orthodontic materials and apply them to your own teeth in order
to straighten them. The expression simply
means "get ready for something that will probably be difficult,"and it was indeed very difficult to climb a frozen waterfall in the middle of
a windswept valley with nothing but a candelabra and a few well-placed forks to aid the two
children in their climb. It took a few moments
for Violet and Quigley to work her invention
properly, and push the forks into the ice just far
enough to hold them there, but not so far that
they would be permanently stuck, and once
both of them were in position, Violet had to
reach up as far as she could and tap the candelabra on the ice above them to find the next
solid place to climb. For the first few steps, it
seemed like ascending the icy slope in this manner would be impossible, but as time went on,
and the two volunteers grew more and more
skillful with the fork-tipped climbing shoes and

the candelabra ice-tester, it became clear that once again Violet's inventing skills would carry the day, a phrase which here means "enable Violet Baudelaire and Quigley Quagmire to climb up a frozen waterfall after bracing themselves for the difficult journey."

"Your invention is working," Quigley called up to Violet. "These fork-assisted climbing shoes are marvelous."

"They do seem to be working," Violet agreed, "but let's not celebrate just yet. We have a long way to go."

"My sister wrote a couplet about that very thing," Quigley said, and recited Isadora's poem:

*"Celebrate when you're half-done,*
*And the finish won't be half as fun."*

Violet smiled, and reached up to test the ice above her. "Isadora is a good poet," Violet said, "and her poems have come in handy more than once. When we were at the Village of Fowl

Devotees, she led us to her location by hiding a secret message in a series of couplets."

"I wonder if that's a code she learned from V.F.D.," Quigley said, "or if she made it up herself."

"I don't know," Violet said thoughtfully. "She and Duncan were the first to tell us about V.F.D., but it never occurred to me that they might already be members. When I think about it, however, the code she used was similar to one that our Aunt Josephine used. They both hid a secret location within a note, and waited for us to discover the hidden message. Maybe they were all volunteers." She removed her left fork-assisted climbing shoe from the ice, and kicked it back in a few inches up to further her climb. "Maybe all our guardians have been members of V.F.D., on one side or the other of the schism."

"It's hard to believe," Quigley said, "that we've always been surrounded by people carrying out secret errands, and never known it."

"It's hard to believe that we're climbing a

frozen waterfall in the Mortmain Mountains,"
Violet replied, "and yet, here we are. There,
Quigley, do you see the ledge where my left
fork is? It's solid enough for both of us to sit for
a moment and catch our breath."

"Good," Quigley said. "I have a small bag of
carrots in my backpack we can eat to regain our
energy." The triplet climbed up to where Violet
was sitting, on a small ledge scarcely the size of
a sofa, and slid so he was sitting next to her. The
two climbers could see that they had traveled
farther than they'd thought. Far below them
were the blackened ruins of the headquarters,
and Klaus was only a small speck near a tiny iron
archway. Quigley handed Violet a carrot, and she
bit down on it thoughtfully.

"Sunny loves raw carrots," Violet said. "I
hope that she's eating well, wherever she is."

"I hope my siblings are eating well, too,"
Quigley said. "My father always used to say that
a good meal can cheer one up considerably."

"My father always said the same thing," Violet said, looking at Quigley curiously. "Do you think *that* was a code, too?"

Quigley shrugged and sighed. Small bits of ice from the waterfall fell from the ends of forks and blew away in the wind. "It's like we never really knew our parents," he said.

"We knew them," Violet said. "They just had a few secrets, that's all. Everyone should keep a few secrets."

"I suppose so," Quigley said, "but they might have mentioned that they were in a secret organization with a headquarters hidden in the Mortmain Mountains."

"Maybe they didn't want us to find out about such a dangerous place," Violet said, peering off the ledge, "although if you have to hide a headquarters, it's a beautiful place to do it. Aside from the remains of the fire, this is a very lovely view."

"Very lovely indeed," Quigley said, but he

was not looking at the view beneath him. He was looking beside him, where Violet Baudelaire was sitting.

Many things have been taken from the three Baudelaires. Their parents were taken, of course, and their home was taken from them, by a terrible fire. Their various guardians were taken from them, because they were murdered by Count Olaf or were simply miserable guardians who soon lost interest in three young children with nowhere to go. The Baudelaires' dignity was taken from them, on the occasions when the siblings were forced to wear absurd disguises, and recently they had been taken from one another, with the kidnapped Sunny doing chores at the top of the frozen waterfall while Violet and Klaus learned the secrets of V.F.D. at the bottom. But one thing that was taken from the Baudelaires that is not often discussed is their privacy, a word which here means "time by oneself, without anyone watching or interfering." Unless you are a hermit or half of a pair of

Siamese twins, you probably enjoy taking the occasional break from members of your family to enjoy some privacy, perhaps with a friend or companion, in your room or in a railway car you have managed to sneak aboard. But since that dreadful day at Briny Beach, when Mr. Poe arrived to tell the Baudelaires that their parents had perished, the three children had scarcely had any privacy at all. From the small, dark bedroom where they slept at Count Olaf's house, to the crowded caravan at Caligari Carnival, and all of the other woeful places in between, the Baudelaires' situation was always so desperate and cramped that they were rarely able to spare a moment for a bit of private time.

So, as Violet and Quigley rest for a few minutes more on a ledge halfway up the frozen waterfall, I will take this opportunity to give them a bit of privacy, by not writing down anything more of what happened between these two friends on that chilly afternoon. Certainly there are aspects of my own personal life that I

will never write down, however precious they are to me, and I will offer the eldest Baudelaire the same courtesy. I will tell you that the two young people resumed their climb, and that the afternoon slowly turned to evening and that both Violet and Quigley had small secret smiles on their faces as the candelabra ice-tester and the fork-assisted climbing shoes helped them both get closer and closer to the mountains' highest peak, but there has been so little privacy in the life of Violet Baudelaire that I will allow her to keep a few important moments to herself, rather than sharing them with my distressed and weeping readers.

"We're almost there," Violet said. "It's difficult to see with the sun going down, but I believe we're just about at the top of the peak."

"I can't believe we've been climbing all afternoon," Quigley said.

"Not *all* afternoon," she reminded him with a shy smile. "I guess this waterfall is about as high as 667 Dark Avenue. It took a very long time to go up and down that elevator shaft, trying to rescue your siblings. I hope this is a more successful journey."

"Me, too," Quigley said. "What do you think we will find at the top?"

"Set!" came the reply.

"I couldn't hear you over the wind," Quigley said. "What did you say?"

"I didn't say anything," Violet said. She squinted above her, trying to see in the last of the sunset, and scarcely daring to hope that she had heard correctly.

Out of all the words in the English language, the word "set" has the most definitions, and if you open a good dictionary and read the word's long, long entry, you will begin to think that "set" is scarcely a word at all, only a sound that means something different depending on who is saying it. If a group of jazz musicians says "set," for instance, they are probably referring to the songs they are planning to play at a club that evening, assuming it doesn't burn down. If the owner of a restaurant uses the word "set," they might mean a group of matching wineglasses, or a bunch of waitresses who look exactly alike. A librarian will say "set" to refer to a collection of books that are all by the same author or about the same subject, and an Egyptologist will use the word "set" to refer to the ancient god of evil, although he does not come up very often in conversation. But when Violet heard the word "set" from the top of Mount Fraught, she did not think there was a group of jazz musicians, a restaurant owner, a librarian, or an Egyptologist talking about jazz tunes, wineglasses, waitresses, thematically linked books, or a black, immoral aardvark who is the sworn enemy of the god Osiris. She reached her fork as high as she could so she could climb closer, and saw the rays of the sunset reflect off a large tooth, and Violet knew that this time, the definition of "set" was "I knew you would find me!" and the speaker was Sunny Baudelaire.

"Set!" Sunny said again.

"Sunny!" Violet cried.

"Sssh!" Sunny said.

"What is going on?" Quigley asked, several forksteps behind Violet.

"It's Sunny," Violet said, and hoisted herself onto the peak to see her baby sister, standing next to Count Olaf's car and grinning from ear to ear. Without another word, the two Baudelaire sisters hugged fiercely, Violet taking care not to poke Sunny with one of the forks she was holding. By the time Quigley reached the top of the peak and pulled himself up to lean against one of the car's tires, the two Baudelaires were smiling at each other with tears in their eyes.

"I knew we'd see you again, Sunny," Violet said. "I just knew it."

"Klaus?" Sunny asked.

"He's safe and nearby," Violet said. "He knew we could find you, too."

"Set," Sunny agreed, but then she noticed Quigley and her eyes grew wide. "Quagmire?" she asked in amazement.

"Yes," Violet said. "This is Quigley Quag-mire, Sunny. He survived the fire after all." Sunny walked unsteadily over to Quigley and shook his hand. "He led us to the headquarters, Sunny, with a map he drew himself."

"Arigato," Sunny said, which meant some-thing like, "I appreciate your help, Quigley."

"Was it you who signaled us?" Quigley asked.

"Yep," Sunny said. "Lox."

"Count Olaf's been making you do the cooking?" Violet asked in amazement.

"Vaccurum," Sunny said.

"Olaf even made her clean crumbs out of the car," Violet translated to Quigley, "by blow-ing as hard as she could."

"That's ridiculous!" Quigley said.

"Cinderella," Sunny said. She meant some-thing along the lines of, "I've had to do all of the chores, while being humiliated at every turn," but Violet had no time to translate over the sound of Count Olaf's scratchy voice.

"Where are you, Babylaire?" he asked, adding

an absurd nickname to his list of insults. "I've thought of more tasks for you to perform."

The three children looked at one another in panic. "Hide," Sunny whispered, and there was no need for translation. Violet and Quigley looked around the desolate landscape of the peak for a place to hide, but there was only one place to go.

"Under the car," Violet said, and she and Quigley wriggled underneath the long, black automobile, which was as dirty and smelly as its owner. As an inventor, the eldest Baudelaire had stared closely at automotive machinery plenty of times, but she had never seen such an extreme state of disrepair, a phrase which here means "an underside of an automobile in such bad shape that it was dripping oil on her and her companion." But Violet and Quigley didn't have a moment to waste thinking of their discomfort. They had no sooner moved their fork-assisted climbing shoes out of view when Count Olaf and his companions arrived. From underneath the car, the two volunteers could see only the villain's tattoo on the filthy ankle above his left shoe, and a pair of very stylish pumps, decorated with glitter and tiny paintings of eyes, that could only belong to Esmé Squalor.

"All we've had to eat all day is that smoked salmon, and it's almost dinnertime," Count Olaf said. "You'd better get cooking, orphan."

"Tomorrow is False Spring," Esmé said, "and it would be very in to have a False Spring dinner."

"Did you hear that, toothy?" Olaf asked. "My girlfriend wants a stylish dinner. Get to work."

"Olaf, we need you," said a very deep voice, and Violet and Quigley saw two pairs of sinister black shoes appear behind the villain and his girlfriend, whose shoes twitched nervously at the sight of them. All of a sudden, it seemed much colder underneath the car, and Violet had to push her legs against the tires, so they would not shiver against the mechanics of the underside and be heard.

"Yes, Olaf," agreed the hoarse voice of the man with a beard but no hair, although Violet and Quigley could not see him. "Our recruitment plan will happen first thing in the morning, so we need you to help spread the net out on the ground."

"Can't you ask one of our employees?" asked Esmé. "There's the hook-handed man, the two white-faced women, and the three freaks we picked up at the carnival. That's eight people, if you include yourselves, to spread out the net. Why should we do it?"

The four black shoes stepped toward Esme's stylish pumps and Olaf's tattoo. "You'll do it," said the woman with hair but no beard, "because I say so."

There was a long, ominous pause, and then Count Olaf gave a little high-pitched laugh. "That's a good point," he said. "Come on, Esmé. We've bossed around the baby, so there's nothing else to do around here anyway."

"That's true," Esmé agreed. "In fact, I was

thinking about taking up smoking again, because I'm bored. Do you have any more of those green cigarettes?"

"I'm afraid not," replied the man with a beard but no hair, leading the villains away from the car. "That's the only one I found."

"That's too bad," Esmé said. "I don't like the taste or the smell, and they're very bad for you, but cigarettes are very in and I'd like to smoke another one."

"Maybe there's another one in the ruins of headquarters," said the woman with hair but no beard. "It's hard to find everything in all those ashes. We searched for days and couldn't find the sugar bowl."

"Not in front of the baby," Olaf said quickly, and the four pairs of shoes walked away. Violet and Quigley stayed underneath the car until Sunny said "Coastkleer," which meant something like, "It's safe to come out now."

"Those were terrible people," Quigley said with a shudder, brushing oil and grime off his coat. "They made me feel cold all over."

"They certainly had an aura of menace," Violet agreed in a whisper. "The feet with the tattoo were Count Olaf, and those glittery shoes were Esmé Squalor, but who were the other two, Sunny?"

"Unno Narsonist," Sunny murmured. She meant something along the lines of "I don't know, but they burned down V.F.D. headquarters," and Violet was quick to explain this to Quigley.

"Klaus has found an important message that survived the fire," Violet said. "By the time we take you down the waterfall, I'm sure he'll have decoded the message. Come on."

"Nogo," Sunny said, which meant "I don't think I ought to accompany you."

"Why on earth not?" Violet asked.

"Unasanc," Sunny said.

"Sunny says that the villains have mentioned one more safe place for volunteers to gather," Violet explained to Quigley.

"Do you know where it is?" Quigley asked.

Sunny shook her head. "Olafile," she said.

"But if Count Olaf has the Snicket file," Violet said, "how are you going to find out where this safe place is?"

"Matahari," she said, which meant something like, "If I stay, I can spy on them and find out."

"Absolutely not," Violet said, after she had translated. "It's not safe for you to stay here, Sunny. It's bad enough that Olaf has made you do the cooking."

"Lox," Sunny pointed out.

"But what are you going to make for a False Spring dinner?" Violet asked.

Sunny gave her sister a smile, and walked over to the trunk of the car. Violet and Quigley heard her rummaging around among the remaining groceries, but stayed put so Olaf or any of his associates wouldn't spot them. When Sunny returned, she had a triumphant smile on her face, and the frozen hunk of spinach, the large bag of mushrooms, the can of water chestnuts, and the enormous eggplant in her arms. "False spring rolls!" she said, which meant something like, "An assortment of vegetables wrapped in spinach leaves, prepared in honor of False Spring."

"I'm surprised you can even carry that eggplant, let alone prepare it," Violet said. "It must weigh as much as you do."

"Suppertunity," Sunny said. She meant something like, "Serving the troupe dinner will be a perfect chance to listen to their conversation," and Violet reluctantly translated.

"It sounds dangerous," Quigley said.

"Of course it's dangerous," Violet said. "If she's caught spying, who knows what they'll do?"

"Ga ga goo goo," Sunny said, which meant "I won't be caught, because they think I'm only a helpless baby."

"I think your sister is right," Quigley said. "It wouldn't be safe to carry her down the waterfall, anyway. We need our hands and feet for the climb. Let Sunny investigate the mystery she's most likely to solve, while we work on an escape plan."

Violet shook her head. "I don't want to leave my sister behind," she said. "The Baudelaires should never be separated."

"Separate Klaus," Sunny pointed out.

"If there's another place where volunteers are gathering," Quigley said, "we need to know where it is. Sunny can find out for us, but only if she stays here."

"I'm not going to leave my baby sister on top of a mountain," Violet said.

Sunny dropped her vegetables on the ground and walked over to her sister and smiled. "I'm not a baby," Sunny said, and hugged her. It was the longest sentence the youngest Baudelaire had ever said, and as Violet looked down at her sister, she saw how true it was. Sunny was not really a baby, not anymore. She was a young girl with unusually sharp teeth, some impressive cooking skills, and an opportunity to spy on a group of villains and discover a piece of crucial information. Sometime, during the unfortunate events that had befallen the three orphans, Sunny had grown out of her babyhood, and although it made Violet a bit sad to think about it, it made her proud, too, and she gave her sister a smile.

"I guess you're right," Violet said. "You're not a baby. But be careful, Sunny. You're a young girl, but it's still quite dangerous for a young girl to spy on villains. And remember, we're right at the bottom of the slope, Sunny. If you need us, just signal again."

Sunny opened her mouth to reply, but before she could utter a sound, the three children heard a long, lazy hissing noise from underneath Olaf's car, as if one of Dr. Montgomery's snakes were hiding there. The car shifted lightly, and Violet pointed to one of Olaf's tires, which had gone flat. "I must have punctured it," Violet said, "with my fork-assisted climbing shoes."

"I suppose that's not a nice thing to do,"

Quigley said, "but I can't say I'm sorry."

"How's dinner coming along, toothface?" called Count Olaf's cruel voice over the sound of the wind.

"I guess we'd better leave before we're discovered," Violet said, giving her sister one more hug and a kiss on the top of her head. "We'll see you soon, Sunny."

"Good-bye, Sunny," Quigley said. "I'm so glad we finally met in person. And thank you very much for helping us find the last safe place."

Sunny Baudelaire looked up at Quigley, and then at her older sister, and gave them both a big, happy smile that showed all of her impressive teeth. After spending so much time in the company of villains, she was happy to be with some people who respected her skills, appreciated her work, and understood her way of speaking. Even with Klaus still at the bottom of the waterfall, Sunny felt as if she had already been happily reunited with her family, and that her time in the Mortmain Mountains would have a happy ending. She was wrong about that, of course, but for now the youngest Baudelaire smiled up at these two people who cared about her, one she had just met and one she had known her entire life, and felt as if she were growing taller at that very moment.

"Happy," said the young girl, and everyone who heard her knew what she was talking about.

*If* you ever look at a picture of someone who has just had an idea, you might notice a drawing of a lightbulb over the person's head. Of course, there is not usually a lightbulb hovering in the air when someone has an idea, but the image of a lightbulb over someone's head has become a sort of symbol for thinking, just as the image of an eye, sadly, has become a symbol for crime and devious behavior rather

than integrity, the prevention of fire, and being well-read.

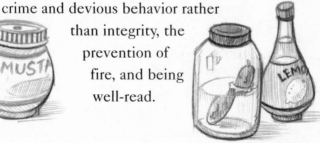

As Violet and Quigley climbed back down the slippery slope of the frozen waterfall, their fork-assisted climbing shoes poking into the ice with each step, they looked down and saw, by the last light of the setting sun, the figure of Klaus. He was holding a flashlight over his head to help the two climbers find their way down, but it looked as if he'd just had an idea.

"He must have found a flashlight in the wreckage," Quigley said. "It looks like the one Jacques gave me."

"I hope he found enough information to decode Verbal Fridge Dialogue," Violet said, and tapped the candelabra below her feet. "Be careful here, Quigley. The ice feels thin. We'll have to climb around it."

"The ice has been less solid on our way down," Quigley said.

"That's not surprising," Violet said. "We've poked a great deal of it with forks. By the time False Spring arrives, this whole slope will probably only be half frozen."

"By the time False Spring arrives," Quigley said, "I hope we'll be on our way to the last safe place."

"Me, too," Violet said quietly, and the two climbers said no more until they reached the bottom of the waterfall and walked carefully across the frozen pool along the path Klaus shone with his flashlight.

"I'm so glad you returned in one piece," Klaus said, shining his flashlight in the direction of the dining room remains. "It looked like a very slippery journey. It's getting cold, but if we sit behind the library entrance, we'll be away from much of the wind."

But Violet was so eager to tell her brother who they had found at the top of the peak that she could not wait another moment. "It's Sunny," she said. "Sunny's at the top. It was her who was signaling us."

"Sunny?" Klaus said, his eyes as wide as his smile. "How did she get up there? Is she safe? Why didn't you bring her back?"

"She's safe," Violet said. "She's with Count Olaf, but she's safe."

"Has he harmed her?" Klaus asked.

Violet shook her head. "No," she said. "He's making her do all the cooking and cleaning."

"But she's a baby!" Klaus said.

"Not anymore," Violet said. "We haven't noticed, Klaus, but she's grown up quite a bit. She's really too young to be in charge of all the chores, of course, but sometime, during all the hardship we've been through, she stopped being a baby."

"She's old enough to eavesdrop," Quigley said. "She's already discovered who burned down the V.F.D. headquarters."

"They're two terrible people, a man and a woman, who have quite an aura of menace," Violet said. "Even Count Olaf is a little afraid of them."

"What are they all doing up there?" Klaus asked.

"They're having some sort of villainous

meeting," Quigley said. "We heard them mention something about a recruitment plan, and a large net."

"That doesn't sound pleasant," Klaus said.

"There's more, Klaus," Violet said. "Count Olaf has the Snicket file, and he found out about some secret location—the last safe place where the V.F.D. can gather. That's why Sunny stayed up there. If she overhears where the place is, we'll know where to go to meet up with the rest of the volunteers."

"I hope she manages to find out," Klaus said. "Without that piece of information, all that I've discovered is useless."

"What have you discovered?" Quigley asked.

"I'll show you," Klaus said, and led the way to the ruins of the library, where Violet could see he'd been working. His dark blue notebook was open, and she could see that several pages were filled with notes. Nearby were several half-burnt scraps of paper, stacked underneath a burnt teacup Klaus was using for a paperweight, and all of the contents of the refrigerator were laid out in a careful half circle: the jar of mustard, the container of olives, three jars of jam, and the very fresh dill. The small glass jug, containing one pickle, and the bottle of lemon juice were off to one side. "This is some of the most difficult research I've ever done," Klaus said, sitting down next to his notebook. "Justice Strauss's legal library was confusing, and Aunt Josephine's grammatical library was dull, but the ruined V.F.D. library is a much bigger challenge. Even if I know what book I'm looking for, it may be nothing but ashes."

"Did you find anything about Verbal Fridge Dialogue?" Quigley asked, sitting beside him.

"Not at first," Klaus said. "The scrap of paper that led us to the refrigerator was in a large pile of ashes, and it took awhile to sift through it. But I finally found one page that was probably from the same book." He reached for his notebook and held up his flashlight so he could see the pages. "The page was so delicate," he said, "that

I immediately copied it into my commonplace book. It explains how the whole code works."

"Read it to us," Violet said, and Klaus complied, a word which here means "followed Violet's suggestion and read a very complicated paragraph out loud, explaining it as he went along."

"'Verbal Fridge Dialogue,'" he read, "'is an emergency communication system that avails itself of the more esoteric products in a refrigerator. Volunteers will know such a code is being used by the presence of very fr—'" He looked up from his notebook. "The sentence ends there," he said, "but I assume that 'very fr' is the beginning of 'very fresh dill.' If very fresh dill is in the refrigerator, that means there's a message there, too."

"I understand that part," Violet said, "but what does 'esoteric' mean?"

"In this case," Klaus said, "I think it refers to things that aren't used very much—the things that stay in the refrigerator for a long time."

"Like mustard and jam and things like that," Violet said. "I understand."

"'The receiver of the message should find his or her initials, as noted by one of our poet volunteers, as follows,'" Klaus continued. "And then there's a short poem:

*"The darkest of the jams of three
contains within the addressee."*

"That's a couplet," Quigley said, "like my sister writes."

"I don't think your sister wrote that particular poem," Violet said. "This code was probably invented before your sister was born."

"That's what I thought," Klaus said, "but it made me wonder who taught Isadora about couplets. They might have been a volunteer."

"She had a poetry teacher when we were young," Quigley said, "but I never met him. I always had cartography class."

"And your mapmaking skills," Violet said,

"led us to the headquarters."

"And your inventing skills," Klaus said, "allowed you to climb up to Mount Fraught."

"And your researching skills are helping us now," Violet said. "It's as if we were being trained for all this, and we didn't even know it."

"I never thought of learning about maps as training," Quigley said. "I just liked it."

"Well, I haven't had much training in poetry," Klaus said, "but the couplet seems to say that inside the darkest jar of jam is the name of the person who's supposed to get the message."

Violet looked down at the three jars of jam. "There's apricot, strawberry, and boysenberry," she said. "Boysenberry's the darkest."

Klaus nodded, and unscrewed the cap from the jar of boysenberry jam. "Look inside," he said, and shined the flashlight so Violet and Quigley could see. Someone had taken a knife and written two letters in the surface of the jam: J and S.

"J.S.," Quigley said. "Jacques Snicket."

"The message can't be for Jacques Snicket," Violet said. "He's dead."

"Maybe whoever wrote this message doesn't know that," Klaus said, and continued to read from the commonplace book. "'If necessary, the dialogue uses a cured, fruit-based calendar for days of the week in order to announce a gathering. Sunday is represented by a lone—' Here it's cut off again, but I think that means that these olives are an encoded way of communicating which day of the week a gathering will take place, with Sunday being one olive, Monday being two, and so on."

"How many olives are in that container?" Quigley asked.

"Five," Klaus said, wrinkling his nose. "I didn't like counting them. Ever since the Squalors fixed us aqueous martinis, the taste of olives hasn't really appealed to me."

"Five olives means Thursday," Violet said.

"Today's Friday," Quigley said. "The gathering of the volunteers is less than a week away."

The two Baudelaires nodded in agreement, and Klaus opened his notebook again. "'Any spice-based condiment,'" he read, "'should have a coded label referring volunteers to encoded poems.'"

"I don't think I understand," Quigley said.

Klaus sighed, and reached for the jar of mustard. "This is where it really gets complicated. Mustard is a spice-based condiment, and according to the code, it should refer us to a poem of some sort."

"How can mustard refer us to a poem?" Violet asked.

Klaus smiled. "I was puzzled for a long time," he said, "but I finally thought to look at the list of ingredients. Listen to this: 'Vinegar, mustard seed, salt, tumeric, the final quatrain of the eleventh stanza of "The Garden of Proserpine," by Algernon Charles Swinburne, and calcium disodium, an allegedly natural preservative.' A quatrain is four lines of a poem, and a stanza is another word for a verse. They hid a reference to a poem in the list of ingredients."

"It's the perfect place to hide something," Violet said. "No one ever reads those lists very carefully. But did you find the poem?"

Klaus frowned, and lifted the teacup. "Under a burnt wooden sign marked 'Poetry,' I found a pile of papers that were burned practically beyond recognition," he said, "but here's the one surviving scrap, and it's the last quatrain of the eleventh stanza of 'The Garden of Proserpine,' by Algernon Charles Swinburne."

"That's convenient," Quigley said.

"A little *too* convenient," Klaus said. "The entire library was destroyed, and the one poem that survived is the one we need. It can't be a coincidence." He held out the scrap of paper so Violet and Quigley could see it. "It's as if someone knew we'd be looking for this."

"What does the quatrain say?" Violet asked.

"It's not very cheerful," Klaus said, and tilted the flashlight so he could read it:

*"That no life lives forever;*
*That dead men rise up never;*
*That even the weariest river*
*Winds somewhere safe to sea."*

The children shivered, and moved so they were sitting even closer together on the ground. It had grown darker, and Klaus's flashlight was pratically the only thing they could see. If you have ever found yourself sitting in darkness with a flashlight, you may have experienced the feeling that something is lurking just beyond the circle of light that a flashlight makes, and reading a poem about dead men is not a good way to make yourself feel better.

"I wish Isadora were here," Quigley said. "She could tell us what that poem means."

*"Even the weariest river winds somewhere safe to sea,"* Violet repeated. "Do you think that refers to the last safe place?"

"I don't know," Klaus said. "I couldn't find

anything else that would help us."

"What about the lemon juice?" Violet asked. "And the pickle?"

Klaus shook his head, although his sister could scarcely see him in the dark. "There might be more to the message," he said, "but it's all gone up in smoke. I couldn't find anything more in the library that seemed helpful."

Violet took the scrap of paper from her brother and looked at the quatrain. "There's something very faint here," she said. "Something written in pencil, but it's too faint to read."

Quigley reached into his backpack. "I forgot we have two flashlights," he said, and shone a second light onto the paper. Sure enough, there was one word, written very faintly in pencil beside the last four lines of the poem's eleventh stanza. Violet, Klaus, and Quigley leaned in as far as they could to see what it was. The night winds rustled the fragile paper, and made the children shiver, shaking the flashlights, but at last the light shone on the quatrain and they could see what words were there.

"Sugar bowl," they said in unison, and looked at one another.

"What could that mean?" Klaus asked.

Violet sighed. "When we were hiding underneath the car," she said to Quigley, "one of those villains said something about searching for a sugar bowl, remember?"

Quigley nodded, and took out his purple notebook. "Jacques Snicket mentioned a sugar bowl once," he said, "when we were in Dr. Montgomery's library. He said it was very important to find it. I wrote it down on the top of a page in my commonplace book, so I could add any information I learned about its whereabouts." He held up the page so the two Baudelaires could see that it was blank. "I never learned anything more," he said.

Klaus sighed. "It seems that the more we learn, the more mysteries we find. We reached V.F.D. headquarters and decoded a message, and all we know is that there's one last safe place, and volunteers are gathering there on Thursday."

"That might be enough," Violet said, "if Sunny finds out where the safe place is."

"But how are we going to get Sunny away from Count Olaf?" Klaus asked.

"With your fork-assisted climbing shoes," Quigley said. "We can climb up there again, and sneak away with Sunny."

Violet shook her head. "The moment they noticed Sunny was gone," she said, "they would find us. From Mount Fraught, they can see everything and everyone for miles and miles, and we're hopelessly outnumbered."

"That's true," Quigley admitted. "There are ten villains up there, and only four of us. Then how are we going to rescue her?"

"Olaf has someone we love," Klaus said thoughtfully. "If we had something he loves, we could trade it for Sunny's return. What does Count Olaf love?"

"Money," Violet said.

"Fire," Quigley said.

"We don't have any money," Klaus said, "and Olaf won't trade Sunny for a fire. There must be something he really loves—something that makes him happy, and would make him very unhappy if it were taken away."

Violet and Quigley looked at one another and smiled. "Count Olaf loves Esmé Squalor," Violet said. "If we were holding Esmé prisoner, we could arrange a trade."

"That's true," Klaus said, "but we're not holding Esmé prisoner."

"We could take her prisoner," Quigley said, and everyone was quiet. Taking someone prisoner, of course, is a villainous thing to do, and when you think of doing a villainous thing— even if you have a very good reason for thinking of doing it—it can make you feel like a villain, too. Lately, the Baudelaires had been doing things like wearing disguises and helping burn down a carnival, and were beginning to feel more and more like villains themselves. But

Violet and Klaus had never done anything as villainous as taking somebody prisoner, and as
they looked at Quigley they could tell that he
felt just as uncomfortable, sitting in the dark
and thinking up a villainous plan.

"How would we do it?" Klaus asked quietly.

"We could lure her to us," Violet said, "and
trap her."

Quigley wrote something down in his commonplace book. "We could use the Verdant
Flammable Devices," he said. "Esmé thinks
they're cigarettes, and she thinks cigarettes are
in. If we lit some of them, she might smell the
smoke and come down here."

"But then what?" Klaus asked.

Violet shivered in the cold, and reached
into her pocket. Her fingers bumped up
against the large bread knife, which she had
almost forgotten was there, and then found
what she was looking for. She took the ribbon
out of her pocket and tied her hair up, to keep it
out of her eyes. The eldest Baudelaire could

scarcely believe she was using her inventing skills to think up a trap. "The easiest trap to build," she said, "is a pit. We could dig a deep hole, and cover it up with some of this half-burned wood so Esmé couldn't see it. The wood has been weakened by the fire, so when she steps on it . . ."

Violet did not finish her sentence, but by the glow of the flashlights, she could see that Klaus and Quigley were both nodding. "Hunters have used traps like that for centuries," Klaus said, "to capture wild animals."

"That doesn't make me feel any better," Violet said.

"How could we dig such a pit?" Quigley said.

"Well," Violet said, "we don't really have any tools, so we probably have to use our hands. As the pit got deeper, we'd have to use something to carry the dirt away."

"I still have that pitcher," Klaus said.

"And we'd need a way to make sure that we wouldn't get trapped ourselves," Violet said.

"I have a rope," Quigley said, "in my back-pack. We could tie one end to the archway, and use it to climb out."

Violet reached her hand down to the ground. The dirt was very cold, but quite loose, and she saw that they could dig a pit without too much trouble. "Is this the right thing to do?" Violet asked. "Do you think this is what our parents would do?"

"Our parents aren't here," Klaus said. "They might have been here once, but they're not here now."

The children were quiet again, and tried to think as best they could in the cold and the dark. Deciding on the right thing to do in a situation is a bit like deciding on the right thing to wear to a party. It is easy to decide on what is wrong to wear to a party, such as deep-sea diving equipment or a pair of large pillows, but deciding what is right is much trickier. It might seem right to wear a navy blue suit, for instance, but when you arrive there could be several other people wearing the same thing, and you could end up being hand-cuffed due to a case of mistaken identity. It might seem right to wear your favorite pair of shoes, but there could be a sudden flood at the party, and your shoes would be ruined. And it might seem right to wear a suit of armor to the party, but there could be several other people wearing the same thing, and you could end up being caught in a flood due to a case of mistaken identity, and find yourself drifting out to sea wishing that you were wearing deep-sea diving equipment after all. The truth is that you can never be sure if you have decided on the right thing until the party is over, and by then it is too late to go back and change your mind, which is why the world is filled with people doing terrible things and wearing ugly clothing, and so few volunteers who are able to stop them.

"I don't know if it's the right thing to do," Violet said, "but Count Olaf captured Sunny, and we might have to capture someone our-selves, in order to stop him."

Klaus nodded solemnly. "We'll fight fire," he said, "with fire."

"Then we'd better get started," Quigley said, and stood up. "When the sun rises, we can light the Verdant Flammable Devices with the mirror again, like we did when we were signaling Sunny."

"If we want the pit to be ready by dawn," Violet said, "we'll have to dig all night."

"Where shall we put the pit?" Klaus asked.

"In front of the entrance," Violet decided. "Then we can hide behind the arch when Esmé approaches."

"How will we know when she's fallen in," Quigley asked, "if we can't see her?"

"We'll hear it," Violet replied. "We'll hear the breaking of the wood, and Esmé might scream."

Klaus shuddered. "That's not going to be a pleasant sound."

"We're not in a pleasant situation," Violet said, and the eldest Baudelaire was right. It was not pleasant to kneel down in front of the ruined library entrance, and dig through the ashes and dirt with their bare hands by the light of two flash-lights, as all four drafts of the valley blew around them. It was not pleasant for Violet and her brother to carry the dirt away in the pitcher, while Quigley tied his rope to the iron archway, so they could climb in and out as the pit grew bigger and deeper, like an enormous dark mouth opening wider and wider to swallow them whole. It was not even pleasant to pause and eat a carrot to keep up their energy, or to gaze at the shiny white shape of the frozen waterfall as it glinted in the moonlight, imagining Esmé Squalor, lured by the smoke of the Verdant Flammable Devices, approaching the ruined headquarters to become their prisoner. But the least pleasant part of the situation wasn't the cold dirt, or the freezing winds, or even their own exhaustion as it grew later and later and the children dug deeper and deeper. The least pleasant part was the idea, shared by the two Baudelaires and their new friend, that they might be doing a villainous thing.

The siblings were not sure if digging a deep pit to trap someone, in order to trade prisoners with a villain, was something that their parents or any other volunteers would do, but with so many of the V.F.D. secrets lost in the ashes, it was impossible to know for sure, and this uncertainty haunted them with every pitcherful of dirt, and every climb up the rope, and every piece of weakened wood they laid on top of the pit to hide it from view.

As the first rays of the morning sun appeared on the misty horizon, the elder Baudelaires gazed up at the waterfall. At the summit of the Mortmain Mountains, they knew, was a group of villains, from whom Sunny was hopefully learning the location of the last safe place. But as Violet and Klaus lowered their gaze to their own handiwork, and looked at the dark, deep pit Quigley had helped them dig, they could not help wondering if there were also a group of villains at the bottom of the slippery slope. As they looked at the villainous thing they had made, the three volunteers could not help wondering if they were villains, too, and this was the least pleasant feeling in the world.

*Not* too long ago, in the Swedish city of Stockholm, a group of bank robbers took a few prisoners during the course of their work. For several days, the bank robbers and the prisoners lived together in close proximity, a word which here means "while the police gathered outside and eventually managed to arrest the robbers and take them to jail." When the prisoners were finally freed, however, the authorities discovered that they had become friends with the bank robbers, and since that time the expression "Stockholm Syndrome" has been used to describe a situation in which someone becomes friendly with the people who are holding them prisoner.

There is another expression, however, which describes a situation that is far more common, when a prisoner does not become friends with such people, but instead regards them as villains, and despises them more and more with each passing moment, waiting desperately for an opportunity to escape. The expression is "Mount Fraught Syndrome," and Sunny Baudelaire was experiencing it as she stood at the top of Mount Fraught, gazing down at the frozen waterfall and thinking about her circumstances.

The young girl had spent another sleepless
night in the covered casserole dish, after washing
the salmon out of it with a few handfuls of
melted snow. It was chilly, of course, with the
winds of the Mortmain Mountains blowing
through the holes in the lid, and it was painful,
because once again her teeth were chattering in
the cold and giving her tiny cuts on her lips, but
there was another reason Sunny did not sleep
well, which is that she was frustrated. Despite
her best spying attempts, the youngest Baudelaire had been unable to eavesdrop on the villains' conversation and learn the location of the
last safe place where V.F.D. would be gathering,
or learn any more about the dreadful recruitment scheme planned by the man with a beard
but no hair and the woman with hair but no
beard. When the troupe gathered around the
flat rock for dinner, they discussed these things,
but every time Sunny tried to get close enough
to hear what they were saying, they glared at her
and quickly changed the subject. It seemed to

Sunny that the only thing she had accomplished all evening was preparing a meal that the troupe enjoyed. When she had presented her platter of False Spring Rolls, no one had complained, and every single villainous person had taken second helpings.

But something crucial had escaped the attention of Count Olaf and his comrades during the meal, and for that Sunny was very grateful. As she had told her siblings, the youngest Baudelaire had prepared an assortment of vegetables wrapped in spinach leaves, in honor of False Spring. Her recipe had required the bag of mushrooms, the can of water chestnuts, and the frozen hunk of spinach, which she had thawed by holding it underneath her shirt, as she had when preparing toast tartar. But Sunny had decided at the last minute that she would not use the enormous eggplant. When Violet mentioned that the eggplant must weigh as much as Sunny did, the youngest Baudelaire had an idea, and rather than chopping the eggplant into small strips with her teeth, she hid it behind the flat tire of Count Olaf's car, and now, as the sun rose and the group of villains began their usual morning bickering, she was retrieving the eggplant and rolling it to the casserole dish. As she rolled it past the automobile, Sunny looked down at the frozen waterfall, which was looking less and less frozen in the morning sun. She knew her siblings were at the bottom with Quigley, and although she couldn't see them, it made her feel better knowing they were relatively nearby and that, if her plan worked out, she would soon be joining them.

"What are you doing, baby?" Sunny had just slipped the eggplant under the cover of the casserole dish when she heard the voice of one of Olaf's comrades. The two white-faced women were standing just outside their tent and stretching in the morning sun.

"Aubergine," Sunny replied, which meant "I've concocted a plan involving this eggplant, and it doesn't matter if I tell you about it because you never understand a single word I say."

"More babytalk," said the other white-faced woman with a sigh. "I'm beginning to think that Sunny is only a helpless baby, and not a spy."

"Goo goo ga—" Sunny began, but the flap of Count Olaf's tent opened before she could utter the last "ga." The villain and his girlfriend stood in the morning sun, and it was clear that they expected the new day—Saturday—to be an important one, because they were dressed for the occasion, a phrase which here means "wearing such strange clothing that the youngest Baudelaire was too surprised to say the final 'ga' she had been planning." Amazingly, it appeared that Count Olaf had washed his face, and he was wearing a brand-new suit made out of material that at first seemed to be covered in tiny polka dots. But when Sunny took a closer look, she saw that each dot was a small eye, matching Olaf's tattoo and the V.F.D. insignia and all of the other eyes that had plagued the Baudelaires since that terrible day on the beach, so that looking at Count Olaf in his new suit felt like looking at a crowd of villains, all staring at Sunny Baudelaire. But no matter how unnerving Olaf's fashion choice was, Esmé Squalor's outfit was worse to behold. Sunny could not remember when she had ever seen a dress so enormous, and was surprised that such an article of clothing could have fit in the tent and still leave room for villains to sleep. The dress was made of layers upon layers of shiny cloth, in different shades of yellow, orange, and red, all cut in fierce triangular shapes so that each layer seemed to cut into the next, and rising from the shoulders of the dress were enormous piles of black lace, sticking up into the air in strange curves. For a moment, the dress was so huge and odd that Sunny could not imagine why anyone would wear it, but as the wicked girlfriend stepped farther out of the tent, it became horribly clear. Esmé Squalor was dressed to look like an enormous fire.

"What a wonderful morning!" Count Olaf

crowed. "Just think, by the end of the day I'll have more new members of my troupe than ever before!"

"And we'll need them," Esmé agreed. "We're all going to have to work together for the greater good—burning down the last safe place!"

"Just the idea of the Hotel Denouement in flames makes me so excited, I'm going to open a bottle of wine!" Count Olaf announced, and Sunny covered her mouth with her hands so the villains would not hear her gasp. The Hotel Denouement, she realized, must be the last safe place for volunteers to gather, and Olaf was so excited that he had uttered the name inadvertently, a word which here means "where the youngest Baudelaire could hear it."

"The idea of all those eagles filling the sky makes me so excited, I'm going to smoke one of those in green cigarettes!" Esmé announced, and then frowned. "Except I don't have one. Drat."

"Beg your pardon, your Esméship," said one of the white-faced women, "but I see some of that green smoke down at the bottom of the waterfall."

"Really?" Esmé asked eagerly, and looked in the direction Olaf's employee was pointing. Sunny looked, too, and saw a familiar plume of green smoke at the very bottom of the slope, getting bigger and bigger as the sun continued to rise. The youngest Baudelaire wondered why her siblings were signaling her, and what they were trying to say.

"That's strange," Olaf said. "You'd think there'd be nothing left of the headquarters to burn."

"Look how much smoke there is," Esmé said greedily. "There must be a whole pack of cigarettes down there. This day is getting even better!"

Count Olaf smiled, and then looked away from the waterfall and noticed Sunny for the first time. "I'll have the baby go down and get them for you," Count Olaf said.

"Yessir!" Sunny said eagerly.

"The baby would probably steal all the cigarettes for herself," Esmé said, glaring at the
young girl. "I'll go."

"But climbing down there will take hours,"
Olaf said. "Don't you want to be here for the
recruitment scheme? I just love springing traps
on people."

"Me, too," Esmé agreed, "but don't worry,
Olaf. I'll be back in moments. I'm not going to
climb. I'll take one of the toboggans and sled
down the waterfall before anyone else even
notices I'm gone."

"Drat!" Sunny couldn't help saying. She
meant something along the lines of, "That is
exactly what I was planning on doing," but once
again no one understood.

"Shut up, toothy," Esmé said, "and get out
of my way." She flounced past the youngest
Baudelaire, and Sunny realized that there was
something sewn to the bottom of the dress that
made it make a crackling noise as she walked,
so that the wicked girlfriend sounded as much

like a fire as she looked like one. Blowing a kiss to Count Olaf, she grabbed the toboggan belonging to sinister villains.

"I'll be right back, darling," Esmé said. "Tell that baby to take a nap so she won't see what we're up to."

"Esmé's right," Olaf said, giving Sunny a cruel smile. "Get in the casserole dish. You're such an ugly, helpless creature, I can scarcely stand to look at you."

"You said it, handsome," Esmé said, and chuckled meanly as she sat at the top of the waterfall. The two white-faced women scurried to help, and gave the toboggan a big push as Sunny did as she was told, and disappeared from Olaf's sight.

As you may imagine, the sight of a grown woman in an enormous flame-imitating dress tobogganing down from the source of the Stricken Stream to the two tributaries and the half-frozen pool at the bottom of the waterfall is not the sort of thing to pass unnoticed, even from far away. Violet was the first to see the colorful blur heading quickly down the slope, and she lowered Colette's hand mirror, which she had used once again to catch the rays of the rising sun and reflect them onto the Verdant Flammable Devices, which she had put in a pile in front of the pit. Wrinkling her nose from the bitter smell of the smoke, she turned to Klaus and Quigley, who were putting one last piece of weakened wood across the pit, so their trap would be hidden from view.

"Look," Violet said, and pointed to the descending shape.

"Do you think it's Esmé?" Klaus asked.

Violet squinted up at the tobogganing figure. "I think so," she said. "Nobody but Esmé Squalor would wear an outfit like that."

"We'd better hide behind the archway," Quigley said, "before she spots us."

The two Baudelaires nodded in agreement, and walked carefully to the library entrance, making sure to step around the hole they had dug.

"I'm happy that we can't see the pit any-more," Klaus said. "Looking into that blackness reminded me of that terrible passageway at 667 Dark Avenue."

"First Esmé trapped your siblings there," Violet said to Quigley, "and then she trapped us."

"And now we're fighting fire with fire, and trapping her," Quigley said uncomfortably.

"It's best not to think about it," Violet said, although she had not stopped thinking about the trap since the first handful of ashes and earth. "Soon we'll have Sunny back, and that's what's important."

"Maybe this is important, too," Klaus said, and pointed up at the archway. "I never noticed it until now."

Violet and Quigley looked up to see what he was referring to, and saw four tiny words etched over their heads, right underneath the large let-ters spelling "V.F.D. Library."

"'The world is quiet here,'" Quigley read. "What do you think it means?"

"It looks like a motto," Klaus said. "At Prufrock Preparatory School, they had a motto carved near the entrance, so everyone would remember it when they entered the academy."

Violet shook her head. "That's not what I'm thinking of," she said. "I'm remembering something about that phrase, but just barely."

"The world certainly feels quiet around here," Klaus said. "We haven't heard a single snow gnat since we arrived."

"The smell of smoke scares them away, remember?" Quigley asked.

"Of course," Klaus said, and peered around the archway to check on Esmé's progress. The colorful blur was about halfway down the waterfall, heading straight for the trap they had built. "There's been so much smoke here at headquarters, the gnats might never come back."

"Without snow gnats," Quigley said, "the salmon of the Stricken Stream will go hungry. They feed on snow gnats." He reached into his pocket and opened his commonplace book.

"And without salmon," he said, "the Mortmain Mountain eagles will go hungry. The destruction of V.F.D. headquarters has caused even more damage than I thought."

Klaus nodded in agreement. "When we were walking along the Stricken Stream," he said, "the fish were coughing from all the ashes in the water. Remember, Violet?"

He turned to his sister, but Violet was only half listening. She was still gazing at the words on the archway, and trying to remember where she heard them before. "I can just hear those words," she said. *"The world is quiet here."* She closed her eyes. "I think it was a very long time ago, before you were born, Klaus."

"Maybe someone said them to you," Quigley said.

Violet tried to remember as far back as she could, but everything seemed as misty as it did in the mountains. She could see the face of her mother, and her father standing behind her, wearing a suit as black as the ashes of V.F.D.

headquarters. Their mouths were open, but Violet could not remember what they were saying. No matter how hard she tried, the memory was as silent as the grave. "Nobody said them to me," she said finally. "Someone *sang* them. I think my parents sang the words 'the world is quiet here' a long time ago, but I don't know why." She opened her eyes and faced her brother and her friend. "I think we might be doing the wrong thing," she said.

"But we agreed," Quigley said, "to fight fire with fire."

Violet nodded, and stuck her hands in her pocket, bumping up against the bread knife again. She thought of the darkness of the pit, and the scream Esmé would make as she fell into it. "I know we agreed," Violet said, "but if V.F.D. really stands for Volunteer Fire Department, then they're an organization that stops fire. If everyone fought fire with fire, the entire world would go up in smoke."

"I see what you mean," Quigley said. "If the V.F.D. motto is 'The world is quiet here,' we ought to be doing something less noisy and violent than trapping someone, no matter how wicked they are."

"When I was looking into the pit," Klaus said quietly, "I was remembering something I read in a book by a famous philosopher. He said, 'Whoever fights monsters should see to it that in the process he does not become a monster. And when you look long into an abyss, the abyss also looks into you.'" Klaus looked at his sister, and then at the sight of Esmé approaching, and then at the weakened wood that the three children had placed on the ground. "'Abyss' is a fancy word for 'pit,'" he said. "We built an abyss for Esmé to fall into. That's something a monster might do."

Quigley was copying Klaus's words into his commonplace book. "What happened to that philosopher?" he asked.

"He's dead," Klaus replied. "I think you're right, Violet. We don't want to be as villainous and monstrous as Count Olaf."

"But what are we going to do?" Quigley asked. "Sunny is still Olaf's prisoner, and Esmé will be here at any moment. If we don't think of the right thing right now, it'll be too late."

As soon as the triplet finished his sentence, however, the three children heard something that made them realize it might already be too late. From behind the archway, Violet, Klaus, and Quigley heard a rough, scraping sound as the toboggan reached the bottom of the waterfall and slid to a halt, and then a triumphant giggle from the mouth of Esmé Squalor. The three volunteers peeked around the archway and saw the treacherous girlfriend step off the toboggan with a greedy smile on her face. But when Esmé adjusted her enormous flame-imitating dress and took a step toward the smoking Verdant Flammable Devices, Violet was not looking at her any more. Violet was looking down at the ground, just

a few steps from where she was standing. Three
dark, round masks were sitting in a pile, where
Violet, Klaus, and Quigley had left them upon
arriving at the ruins of headquarters. They had
assumed that they would not need them again,
but the eldest Baudelaire realized they had been
wrong. As Esmé took another step closer to the
trap, Violet dashed over to the masks, put one on
and stepped out of her hiding place as her brother
and her friend looked on.

"Stop, Esmé!" she cried. "It's a trap!"

Esmé stopped in her tracks and gave Violet
a curious look. "Who are you?" she asked. "You
shouldn't sneak up on people like that. It's a villainous thing to do."

"I'm a volunteer," Violet said.

Esmé's mouth, heavy with orange lipstick
that matched her dress, curled into a sneer.
"There are no volunteers here," she said. "The
entire headquarters are destroyed!"

Klaus was the next to grab a mask and confront Olaf's treacherous romantic companion.

"Our headquarters might be destroyed," he said, "but the V.F.D. is as strong as ever!"

Esmé frowned at the two siblings as if she couldn't decide whether to be frightened or not. "You may be strong," she said nervously, "but you're also very short." Her dress crackled as she started to take another step toward the pit. "When I get my hands on you—"

"No!" Quigley cried, and stepped out from the arch wearing his mask, taking care not to fall into his own trap. "Don't come any closer, Esmé. If you take another step, you'll fall into our trap."

"You're making that up," Esmé said, but she did not move any closer. "You're trying to keep all the cigarettes for yourself."

"They're not cigarettes," Klaus said, "and we're not liars. Underneath the wood you're about to step on is a very deep pit."

Esmé looked at them suspiciously. Gingerly—a word which here means "without falling into a very deep hole"—she leaned down and moved a piece of wood aside, and stared down into the trap the children had built. "Well, well, well," she said. "You *did* build a trap. I never would have fallen for it, of course, but I must admit you dug quite a pit."

"We wanted to trap you," Violet said, "so we could trade you for the safe return of Sunny Baudelaire. But—"

"But you didn't have the courage to go through with it," Esmé said with a mocking smile. "You volunteers are never brave enough to do something for the greater good."

"Throwing people into pits isn't the greater good!" Quigley cried. "It's villainous treachery!"

"If you weren't such an idiot," Esmé said, "you'd realize that those things are more or less the same."

"He is not an idiot," Violet said fiercely. She knew, of course, that it was not worthwhile to get upset over insults from such a ridiculous person, but she liked Quigley too much to hear him called names. "He led us here to the headquarters using a map he drew himself."

"He's very well-read," Klaus said.

At Klaus's words, Esmé threw back her head and laughed, shaking the crackling layers of her enormous dress. *"Well-read!"* she repeated in a particularly nasty tone of voice. "Being well-read won't help you in this world. Many years ago, I was supposed to waste my entire summer reading *Anna Karenina*, but I knew that silly book would never help me, so I threw it into the fireplace." She reached down and picked up a few more pieces of wood, which she tossed aside with a snicker. "Look at your precious headquarters, volunteers! It's as ruined as my book. And look at *me*! I'm beautiful, fashionable, and I smoke cigarettes!" She laughed again, and pointed at the children with a scornful finger. "If you didn't spend all your time with your heads stuck in books, you'd have that precious baby back."

"We're going to get her back," Violet said firmly.

"Really?" Esmé said mockingly. "And how do you propose to do that?"

"I'm going to talk to Count Olaf," Violet said, "and he's going to give her back to me."

Esmé threw back her head and started to laugh, but not with as much enthusiasm as before. "What do you mean?" she said.

"Just what I said," Violet said.

"Hmmm," Esmé said suspiciously. "Let me think for a moment." The evil girlfriend began to pace back and forth on the frozen pond, her enormous dress crackling with every step.

Klaus leaned in to whisper to his sister. "What are you doing?" he asked. "Do you honestly think that we can get Sunny back from Count Olaf with a simple conversation?"

"I don't know," Violet whispered back, "but it's better than luring someone into a trap."

"It was wrong to dig that pit," Quigley agreed, "but I'm not sure that walking straight into Olaf's clutches is the right thing to do, either."

"It'll take a while to reach Mount Fraught again," Violet said. "We'll think of something during the climb."

"I hope so," Klaus said, "but if we can't think of something—"

Klaus did not get a chance to say what might happen if they couldn't think of something, because Esmé clapped her hands together to get the children's attention.

"If you really want to talk to my boyfriend," she said, "I suppose I can take you to where he is. If you weren't so stupid, you'd know that he's very nearby."

"We know where he is, Esmé," Klaus said. "He's at the top of the waterfall, at the source of the Stricken Stream."

"Then I suppose you know how we can get there," Esmé said, and looked a little foolish. "The toboggan doesn't go uphill, so I actually have no idea how we can reach the peak."

"She will invent a way," Quigley said, pointing at Violet.

Violet smiled at her friend, grateful for his support, and closed her eyes underneath her mask. Once more, she was thinking of something she had heard sung to her, when she was a very little girl. She had already thought of the way that the three children could take Esmé with them when they ascended the hill, but thinking of their journey made her think of a song she had not thought of for many years. Perhaps when you were very young, someone sang this song to you, perhaps to lull you to sleep, or to entertain you on a long car trip, or in order to teach you a secret code. The song is called "The Itsy Bitsy Spider," and it is one of the saddest songs ever composed. It tells the story of a small spider who is trying to climb up a water spout, but every time its climb is half over, there is a great burst of water, either due to rain or somebody turning the spout on, and at the end of the song, the spider has decided to try one more time, and will likely be washed away once again.

Violet Baudelaire could not help feeling like this poor spider as she ascended the waterfall for the last time, with Quigley and Klaus beside her and Esmé Squalor on her toboggan behind them. After attaching the last two forks to Klaus's shoes, she had told her companions to tie the leather straps of the toboggan around their waists, so they could drag the villainous girlfriend behind them as they climbed. It was exhausting to approach the peak of Mount Fraught in this manner, particularly after staying up all night digging a pit, and it seemed like they might get washed back down by the dripping water of the Stricken Stream, like the spider Violet had heard about when she was a little girl. The ice on the slope was weakening, after two fork-assisted climbs, a toboggan ride, and the increasing temperatures of False Spring, and with each step of Violet's invention, the ice would shift slightly. It was clear that the slippery slope was almost as exhausted as they were, and soon the ice would vanish completely.

"Mush!" Esmé called from the toboggan. She was using an expression that arctic explorers shouted to their sled dogs, and it certainly did not make the journey any easier.

"I wish she'd stop saying that," Violet murmured from behind her mask. She tapped the
candelabra on the ice ahead of her, and a small
piece detached from the waterfall and fell to the
ruins of headquarters. She watched it disappear
below her and sighed. She would never see the
V.F.D. headquarters in all its glory. None of the
Baudelaires would. Violet would never know
how it felt to cook in the kitchen and gaze at the
two tributaries of the Stricken Stream, while
chatting with the other volunteers. Klaus would
never know how it felt to relax in the library and
learn all of the secrets of V.F.D. in the comfort
of one of the library's chairs, with his feet up on
one of the matching V.F.D. footstools. Sunny
would never operate the projector in the movie
room, or practice the art of the fake mustache in
the disguise center, or sit in the parlor at tea time
and eat the almond cookies made from my grand-
mother's recipe. Violet would never study chemical composition in one of the six laboratories, and
Klaus would never use the balance beams at the

gymnasium, and Sunny would never stand behind the counter at the ice cream shop and prepare butterscotch sundaes for the swimming coaches when it was her turn. And none of the Baudelaires would ever meet some of the organization's most beloved volunteers, including the mechanical instructor C. M. Kornbluth, and Dr. Isaac Anwhistle, whom everyone called Ike, and the brave volunteer who tossed the sugar bowl out the kitchen window so it would not be destroyed in the blaze, and watched it float away on one of the tributaries of the Stricken Stream. The Baudelaires would never do any of these things, any more than I will ever see my beloved Beatrice again, or retrieve my pickle from the refrigerator in which I left it, and return it to its rightful place in an important coded sandwich. Violet, of course, was not aware of everything she would never do, but as she gazed down at the vast, ashen remains of the headquarters, she felt as if her whole journey in the Mortmain Mountains had been as useless as the journey of a tiny arachnid in a song she had never liked to hear.

"Mush!" Esmé cried again, with a cruel chuckle.

"Please stop saying that, Esmé," Violet called down impatiently. "That *mush* nonsense is slowing our climb."

"A slow climb might be to our advantage," Klaus murmured to his sister. "The longer it takes us to reach the summit, the longer we have to think up what we're going to say to Count Olaf."

"We could tell him that he's surrounded," Quigley said, "and that there are volunteers everywhere ready to arrest him if he doesn't let Sunny go free."

Violet shook her mask. "He won't believe that," she said, sticking a fork-assisted shoe into the waterfall. "He can see everything and everyone from Mount Fraught. He'll know we're the only volunteers in the area."

"There must be something we can do," Klaus said. "We didn't make this journey into the mountains for nothing."

"Of course not," Quigley said. "We found each other, and we solved some of the mysteries that were haunting us."

"Will that be enough," Violet asked, "to defeat all those villains on the peak?"

Violet's question was a difficult one, and neither Klaus nor Quigley had the answer, and so rather than hazard a guess—a phrase which here means "continue to expend their energy by discussing the matter"—they decided to hazard their climb, a phrase which here means "continue their difficult journey in silence, until they arrived at last at the source of the Stricken Stream." Hoisting themselves up onto the flat peak, they sat on the edge and pulled the leather straps as hard as they could. It was such a difficult task to drag Esmé Squalor and the toboggan over the edge of the slope and onto Mount Fraught that the children did not notice who was nearby until they heard a familiar scratchy voice right behind them.

"Who goes there?" Count Olaf demanded.

Breathless from the climb, the three children turned around to see the villain standing with his two sinister cohorts near his long, black automobile, glaring suspiciously at the masked volunteers.

"We thought you'd get here by taking the path," said the man with a beard but no hair, "not by climbing up the waterfall."

"No, no, no," Esmé said quickly. "These aren't the people we're expecting. These are some volunteers I found at headquarters."

"Volunteers?" said the woman with hair but no beard, but her voice did not sound as deep as it usually did. The villains gave the children the same confused frown they had seen from Esmé, as if they were unsure whether to be scared or scornful, and the hook-handed man, the two white-faced women, and the three former carnival employees gathered around to see what had made their villainous boss fall silent. Although they were exhausted, the two Baudelaires hurriedly untied the straps of the toboggan from their waists and stood with Quigley to face their enemies. The orphans were very scared, of course, but they found that with their faces concealed they could speak their minds, a phrase which here means "confront Count Olaf and his companions as if they weren't one bit frightened."

"We built a trap to capture your girlfriend, Olaf," Violet said, "but we didn't want to become a monster like you."

"They're idiotic *liars*!" Esmé cried. "I found them hogging the cigarettes, so I captured them myself and made them drag me up the waterfall like sled dogs."

The middle Baudelaire ignored the wicked girlfriend's nonsense. "We're here for Sunny Baudelaire," Klaus said, "and we're not leaving without her."

Count Olaf frowned, and peered at them with his shiny, shiny eyes as if he were trying to see through their masks. "And what makes you

so certain," he said, "that I'll give you my prisoner just because you say so?"

Violet thought furiously, looking around at
her surroundings for anything that might give
her an idea of what to do. Count Olaf clearly
believed that the three masked people in front
of him were members of V.F.D., and she felt that
if she could just find the right words to say, she
could defeat him without becoming as villainous as her enemies. But she could not find the
words, and neither could her brother nor her
friend, who stood beside her in silence. The
winds of the Mortmain Mountains blew against
them, and Violet stuck her hands in her pockets, bumping one finger against the long bread
knife. She began to think that perhaps trapping
Esmé had been the right thing to do after all.
Count Olaf's frown began to fade, and his
mouth started to curl upward in a triumphant
smile, but just as he opened his mouth to
speak, Violet saw two things that gave her hope

once more. The first was the sight of two note-books, one a deep shade of purple and the other dark blue, sticking out of the pockets of her companions—commonplace books, where Klaus and Quigley had written down all of the information they had found in the ruined library of V.F.D. headquarters. And the other was a collection of dishes spread out on the flat rock that Olaf's troupe had been using for a table. Sunny had been forced to wash these dishes, using handfuls of melted snow, and she had laid them out to dry in the sunshine of False Spring. Violet could see a stack of plates, each emblazoned with the familiar image of an eye, as well as a row of teacups and a small pitcher for cream. But there was something missing from the tea set, and it made Violet smile behind her mask as she turned to face Count Olaf again.

"You will give us Sunny," she said, "because we know where the sugar bowl is."

*Count* Olaf gasped, and raised his one eyebrow very high as he gazed at the two Baudelaires and their companion, his eyes shinier than they had ever seen them. *"Where is it?"* he said, in a terrible, wheezing whisper. *"Give it to me!"*

Violet shook her head, grateful that her face was still hidden behind a mask. "Not until you give us Sunny Baudelaire," she said.

*"Never!"* the villain replied. "Without that big-toothed brat, I'll never capture the Baudelaire fortune. You give me the sugar bowl this instant, or I'll throw all of you off this mountain!"

"If you throw us off the mountain," Klaus said, "you'll never know where the sugar bowl

is." He did not add, of course, that the Baudelaires had no idea where the sugar bowl was, or
why in the world it was so important.

Esmé Squalor took a sinister step toward her
boyfriend, her flame-imitating dress crackling
against the cold ground. "We must have that
sugar bowl," she snarled. "Let the baby go. We'll
cook up another scheme to steal the fortune."

"But stealing the fortune is the greater good,"
Count Olaf said. "We can't let the baby go."

"Getting the sugar bowl is the greater
good," Esmé said, with a frown.

"Stealing the fortune," Olaf insisted.

"Getting the sugar bowl," Esmé replied.

"Fortune!"

"Sugar bowl!"

*"Fortune!"*

*"Sugar bowl!"*

"That's enough!" ordered the man with a
beard but no hair. "Our recruitment scheme is
about to be put into action. We can't have you
arguing all day long."

"We wouldn't have argued all day long," Count Olaf said timidly. "After a few hours—"

"We said *that's enough*!" ordered the woman with hair but no beard. "Bring the baby over here!"

"Bring the baby at once!" Count Olaf ordered the two white-faced women. "She's napping in her casserole dish."

The two white-faced women sighed, but hurried over to the casserole dish and lifted it together, as if they were cooks removing something from the oven instead of villainous employees bringing over a prisoner, while the two sinister visitors reached down the necks of their shirts and retrieved something that was hanging around their necks. Violet and Klaus were surprised to see two shiny silver whistles, like the one Count Olaf had used as part of his disguise at Prufrock Preparatory School, when he was pretending to be a coach.

"Watch this, volunteers," said the sinister man in his hoarse voice, and the two mysterious villains blew their whistles. Instantly, the children heard an enormous rustling sound over their heads, as if the Mortmain Mountain winds were as frightened as the youngsters, and it suddenly grew very dim, as if the morning sun had also put on a mask. But when they looked up, Violet, Klaus, and Quigley saw that the reason for the noisy sky and the fading light was perhaps more strange than frightened winds and a masked sun.

The sky above Mount Fraught was swarming with eagles. There were hundreds and hundreds of them, flying in silent circles high above the two sinister villains. They must have been nesting nearby to have arrived so quickly, and they must have been very thoroughly trained to be so eerily silent. Some of them looked very old, old enough to have been in the skies when the Baudelaire parents were children themselves. Some of them looked quite young, as if they had only recently emerged from the egg and were already obeying the shrill sound of a whistle. But all of them looked exhausted, as if they would rather be anywhere else but the summit of the Mortmain Mountains, doing absolutely anything rather than following the orders of such wretched people.

"Look at these creatures!" cried the woman with hair but no beard. "When the schism occurred, you may have won the carrier crows, volunteers, and you may have won the trained reptiles."

"Not anymore," Count Olaf said. "All of the reptiles except one—"

"Don't interrupt," the sinister woman interrupted. "You may have the carrier crows, but we have the two most powerful mammals in the world to do our bidding—the lions and eagles!"

"Eagles aren't *mammals*," Klaus cried out in frustration. "They're *birds*!"

"They're *slaves*," said the man with a beard but no hair, and the two villains reached into the pockets of their suits and drew out two long, wicked-looking whips. Violet and Klaus could see at once that they were similar to the whip

Olaf had used when bossing around the lions at Caligari Carnival. With matching, sinister sneers, the two mysterious villains cracked their whips in the air, and four eagles swooped down from the sky, landing on the strange thick pads that the villains had on their shoulders.

"These beasts will do anything we tell them to do," the woman said. "And today they're going to help us with our greatest triumph." She uncurled the whip and gestured to the ground around her, and the children noticed for the first time an enormous net on the ground, spread out over almost the entire peak and just stopping at their fork-assisted climbing shoes. "On my signal, these eagles will lift this net from the ground and carry it into the sky, capturing a group of young people who think they're here to celebrate False Spring."

"The Snow Scouts," Violet said in astonishment.

"We'll capture every one of those uniformed

brats," the villainous man bragged, "and each one of them will be offered the exciting opportunity to join us."

"They'll never join you," Klaus said.

"Of course they will," said the sinister woman, in her deep, deep voice. "They'll either be recruited, or they'll be our prisoners. But one thing is for certain—we'll burn down every single one of their parents' homes."

The two Baudelaires shuddered, and even Count Olaf looked a bit uneasy. "Of course," he said quickly, "the main reason we're doing all this is to get our hands on all those fortunes."

"Of course," Esmé said with a nervous snicker. "We'll have the Spats fortune, the Kornbluth fortune, the Winnipeg fortune, and many others. I'll be able to afford the penthouse apartment of every single building that isn't on fire!"

"Once you tell us where the sugar bowl is," said the man with a beard but no hair, "you can leave, volunteers, and take your baby friend with you. But wouldn't you rather join us?"

"No, thank you," Quigley said. "We're not interested."

"It doesn't matter if you're interested or not," said the woman with hair but no beard. "Look around you. You're hopelessly outnumbered. Wherever we go, we find new comrades who are eager to assist us in our work."

"We have comrades, too," Violet said bravely. "As soon as we rescue Sunny, we're going to meet up with the other volunteers at the last safe place, and tell them about your terrible scheme!"

"It's too late for that, volunteers," said Count Olaf in triumph. "Here come my new recruits!"

With a horrible laugh, the villain pointed in the direction of the rocky path, and the elder Baudelaires could see, past the covered casserole dish still held by the white-faced women, the arrival of the uniformed Snow Scouts, walking in two neat lines, more like eggs in a carton than young people on a hike. Apparently, the scouts had realized that the snow gnats were absent from this part of the Mortmain Mountains and had removed their masks, so Violet and Klaus could instantly spot Carmelita Spats, standing at the front of one of the lines with a tiara on her head—"tiara" is a word which here means "small crown given to a nasty little girl for no good reason"—and a large smirk on her face. Beside her, at the head of the other line, stood Bruce, holding the Springpole in one hand and a big cigar in the other. There was something about his face that Violet and Klaus found familiar, but they were too concerned about the villainous recruitment plan to give it much thought.

"What are all you cakesniffers doing here?" demanded Carmelita, in an obnoxious voice the two siblings found equally familiar. "I'm the False Spring Queen, and I order you to go away!"

"Now, now, Carmelita," Bruce said. "I'm sure these people are here to help celebrate your special day. Let's try to be accommodating. In fact, we should try to be accommodating, basic, calm, darling—"

The scouts had begun to say the ridiculous pledge along with Bruce, but the two Baudelaires knew they could not wait for the entire alphabetical list to be recited. "Bruce," Violet interrupted quickly, "these people are not here to help you celebrate False Spring. They're here to kidnap all of the Snow Scouts."

"What?" Bruce asked with a smile, as if the eldest Baudelaire might have been joking.

"It's a trap," Klaus said. "Please, turn around and lead the scouts away from here."

"Pay no attention to these three masked idiots," Count Olaf said quickly. "The mountain air has gone to their heads. Just take a few steps closer and we'll all join in a special celebration."

"We're happy to accommodate," Bruce said.

"After all, we're accommodating, basic—"

"No!" Violet cried. "Don't you see the net on the ground? Don't you see the eagles in the sky?"

"The net is decoration," Esmé said, with a smile as false as the Spring, "and the eagles are wildlife."

"Please listen to us!" Klaus said. "You're in terrible danger!"

Carmelita glared at the two Baudelaires, and adjusted her tiara. "Why should I listen to cakesniffing strangers like you?" she asked. "You're so stupid that you've still got your masks on, even though there aren't any snow gnats around here."

Violet and Klaus looked at one another through their masks. Carmelita's response had been quite rude, but the two siblings had to admit she had a point. The Baudelaires were unlikely to convince anyone that they were telling the truth while their faces were unnecessarily covered. They did not want to sacrifice

their disguises and reveal their true identities
to Count Olaf and his troupe, but they couldn't
risk the kidnapping of all the Snow Scouts, even
to save their sister. The two Baudelaires nodded at one another, and then turned to see that
Quigley was nodding, too, and the three children reached up and took off their masks for the
greater good.

Count Olaf's mouth dropped open in surprise. "You're dead!" he said to the eldest Baudelaire, saying something that he knew full well was
ridiculous. "You perished in the caravan, along
with Klaus!"

Esmé stared at Klaus, looking just as astonished as her boyfriend. "You're dead, too!" she
cried. "You fell off a mountain!"

"And you're one of those twins!" Olaf said
to Quigley. "You died a long time ago!"

"I'm not a twin," Quigley said, "and I'm not
dead."

"And," Count Olaf said with a sneer, "you're
not a volunteer. None of you are members of

V.F.D. You're just a bunch of orphan brats."

"In that case," said the woman with hair but no beard, in her deep, deep voice, "there's no reason to worry about that stupid baby any longer."

"That's true," Olaf said, and turned to the white-faced women. "Throw the baby off the mountain!" he ordered.

Violet and Klaus cried out in horror, but the two white-faced women merely looked at the covered casserole dish they were holding, and then at one another. Then, slowly, they looked at Count Olaf, but neither of them moved an inch.

"Didn't you hear me?" Olaf asked. "Throw that baby off this mountain!"

"No," said one of the white-faced women, and the two Baudelaires turned to them in relief.

"*No?*" asked Esmé Squalor in an astonished voice. "What do you mean, *no?*"

"We mean no," said the white-faced woman,

and her companion nodded. Together they put the covered casserole dish down on the ground in front of them. Violet and Klaus were surprised to see that the dish did not move, and assumed that their sister must have been too scared to come out.

"We don't want to participate in your schemes anymore," said the other white-faced woman, and sighed. "For a while, it was fun to fight fire with fire, but we've seen enough flames and smoke to last our whole lives."

"We don't think that it was a coincidence that our home burned to the ground," said the first woman. "We lost a sibling in that fire, Olaf."

Count Olaf pointed at the two women with a long, bony finger. "Obey my orders this *instant*!" he screamed, but his two former accomplices merely shook their heads, turned away from the villain, and began to walk away. Everyone on the square peak watched in silence as the two white-faced women walked past Count Olaf, past Esmé Squalor, past the two sinister villains with eagles on their shoulders, past the two Baudelaires and Quigley Quagmire, past the hook-handed man and the former employees of the carnival, and finally past Bruce and Carmelita Spats and the rest of the Snow Scouts, until they reached the rocky path and began to walk away from Mount Fraught altogether.

Count Olaf opened his mouth and let out a terrible roar, and jumped up and down on the net. "You can't walk away from me, you pasty-faced women!" he cried. "I'll find you and destroy you myself! In fact, I can do anything myself! I'm an individual practitioner, and I don't need anybody's help to throw this baby off the mountain!" With a nasty chuckle, he picked up the covered casserole dish, staggering slightly, and walked to the edge of the half-frozen waterfall.

"*No!*" Violet cried.

"*Sunny!*" Klaus screamed.

"Say good-bye to your baby sister, Baudelaires!" Count Olaf said, with a triumphant smile that showed all of his filthy teeth.

"I'm not a baby!" cried a familiar voice from under the villain's long, black automobile, and the two elder Baudelaires watched with pride and relief as Sunny emerged from behind the tire Violet had punctured, and ran to hug her siblings. Klaus had to take his glasses off to wipe the tears from his eyes as he was finally reunited with the young girl who was his sister. "I'm not a baby!" Sunny said again, turning to Olaf in triumph.

"How could this be?" Count Olaf said, but when he removed the cover from the casserole dish, he saw how this could be, because the object inside, which was about the same size and weight as the youngest Baudelaire, wasn't a baby either.

"Babganoush!" Sunny cried, which meant something along the lines of, "I concocted an escape plan with the eggplant that turned out to be even handier than I thought," but there was no need for anyone to translate, as the large vegetable slid out of the casserole dish and landed with a *plop!* at Olaf's feet.

"Nothing is going right for me today!" cried the villain. "I'm beginning to think that washing my face was a complete waste of time!"

"Don't upset yourself, boss," said Colette, contorting herself in concern. "I'm sure that Sunny will cook us something delicious with the eggplant."

"That's true," the hook-handed man said. "She's becoming quite a cook. The False Spring Rolls were quite tasty, and the lox was delicious."

"It could have used a little dill, in my opinion," Hugo said, but the three reunited Baudelaires turned away from this ridiculous conversation to face the Snow Scouts.

"Now do you believe us?" Violet asked Bruce. "Can't you see that this man is a terrible villain who is trying to do you harm?"

"Don't you remember us?" Klaus asked Carmelita Spats. "Count Olaf had a terrible scheme at Prufrock Prep, and he has a terrible scheme now!"

"Of course I remember you," Carmelita said. "You're those cakesniffing orphans who caused Vice Principal Nero all that trouble. And now you're trying to ruin my very special day! Give me that Springpole, Uncle Bruce!"

"Now, now, Carmelita," Bruce said, but Carmelita had already grabbed the long pole from Bruce's hands and was marching across the net toward the source of the Stricken Stream. The man with a beard but no hair and the woman with hair but no beard clasped their wicked whips and raised their shiny whistles to their sinister mouths, but the Baudelaires could see they were waiting to spring their trap until the rest of the scouts stepped forward, so they would be inside the net when the eagles lifted it from the ground.

"I crown myself False Spring Queen!" Carmelita announced, when she reached the very edge of Mount Fraught. With a nasty laugh of triumph, she elbowed the Baudelaires aside and drove the Springpole into the half-frozen top of the waterfall. There was a slow, loud shattering sound, and the Baudelaires looked down the slope and saw that an enormous crack was slowly making its way down the center of the waterfall, toward the pool and the two tributaries of the Stricken Stream. The Baudelaires gasped in horror. Although it was only the ice that was cracking, it looked as if the mountain were beginning to split in half, and that soon an enormous schism would divide the entire world.

"What are you looking at?" Carmelita asked scornfully. "Everybody's supposed to be doing a dance in my honor."

"That's right," Count Olaf said, "why doesn't everybody step forward and do a dance in honor of this darling little girl?"

"Sounds good to me," Kevin said, leading his fellow employees onto the net. "After all, I have two equally strong feet."

"And we should try to be accommodating," the hook-handed man said. "Isn't that what you said, Uncle Bruce?"

"Absolutely," Bruce agreed, with a puff on his cigar. He looked a bit relieved that all the arguing had ceased, and that the scouts finally had an opportunity to do the same thing they did every year. "Come on, Snow Scouts, let's recite the Snow Scout Alphabet Pledge as we dance around the Springpole."

The scouts cheered and followed Bruce onto the net. "Snow Scouts," the Snow Scouts said, "are accommodating, basic, calm, darling, emblematic, frisky, grinning, human, innocent, jumping, kept, limited, meek, nap-loving, official, pretty, quarantined, recent, scheduled, tidy, understandable, victorious, wholesome, xylophone, young, and zippered, every morning, every afternoon, every night, and all day long!"

There is nothing wrong, of course, with having a pledge, and putting into words what you might feel is important in your life as a reminder to yourself as you make your way in the world. If you feel, for instance, that well-read people are less likely to be evil, and a world full of people sitting quietly with good books in their hands is preferable to a world filled with schisms and sirens and other noisy and troublesome things, then every time you enter a library you might say to yourself, "The world is quiet here," as a sort of pledge proclaiming reading to be the greater good. If you feel that well-read people ought to be lit on fire and their fortunes stolen, you might adopt the saying "Fight fire with fire!" as your pledge, whenever you ordered one of your comrades around. But whatever words you might choose to describe your own life, there are two basic guidelines for composing a good pledge. One guideline is that the pledge make good sense, so that if your pledge contains the word "xylophone," for example, you mean that a percussion instrument played with mallets is very important to you, and not that you simply couldn't think of a good word that begins with the letter X. The other guideline is that the pledge be relatively short, so if a group of villains is luring you into a trap with a net and a group of exhausted trained eagles, you'll have more time to escape.

The Snow Scout Alphabet Pledge, sadly, did not follow either of these guidelines. As the Snow Scouts promised to be "xylophone," the man with a beard but no hair cracked his whip in the air, and the eagles sitting on both villains' shoulders began to flap their wings and, digging their claws into the thick pads, lifted the two sinister people high in the air, and when the pledge neared its end, and the Snow Scouts were all taking a big breath to make the snowy sound, the woman with hair but no beard blew her whistle, making a loud shriek the Baudelaires remembered from running laps as part of Olaf's scheme at Prufrock Prep. The three siblings stood with Quigley and watched as the rest of the eagles quickly dove to the ground, picked up the net, and, their wings trembling with the effort, lifted everyone who was standing on it into the air, the way you might remove all the dinner dishes from the table by lifting all the corners of the tablecloth. If you were to try such an unusual method of clearing the table, you would likely be sent to your room or chased out of the restaurant, and the results on Mount Fraught were equally disastrous. In moments, all of the Snow Scouts and Olaf's henchfolk were in an aerial heap, struggling together inside the net that the eagles were holding. The only person who escaped recruitment—besides the Baudelaires and Quigley Quagmire, of course—was Carmelita Spats, standing next to Count Olaf and his girlfriend.

"What's going on?" Bruce asked Count Olaf from inside the net. "What have you done?"

"I've triumphed," Count Olaf said, "*again*. A long time ago, I tricked you out of a reptile collection that I needed for my own use." The Baudelaires looked at one another in astonishment, suddenly realizing when they had met Bruce before. "And now, I've tricked you out of a collection of children!"

"What's going to happen to us?" asked one of the Snow Scouts fearfully.

"I don't care," said another Snow Scout, who seemed to be afflicted with Stockholm Syndrome already. "Every year we hike up to Mount Fraught and do the same thing. At least this year is a little different!"

"Why are you recruiting me, too?" asked the hook-handed man, and the Baudelaires could see one of his hooks frantically sticking out of the net. "I already work for you."

"Don't worry, hooky," Esmé replied mockingly. "It's all for the greater good!"

"Mush!" cried the man with a beard but no hair, cracking his whip in the air. Squawking in fear, the eagles began to drag the net across the sky, away from Mount Fraught.

"You get the sugar bowl from those bratty orphans, Olaf," ordered the woman with hair but no beard, "and we'll all meet up at the last safe place!"

"With these eagles at our disposal," the sinister man said in his hoarse voice, "we can finally catch up to that self-sustaining hot air mobile home and destroy those volunteers!"

The Baudelaires gasped, and shared an astonished look with Quigley. The villain was surely talking about the device that Hector had built at the Village of Fowl Devotees, in which Duncan and Isadora had escaped.

"We'll fight fire with fire!" the woman with hair but no beard cried in triumph, and the eagles carried her away. Count Olaf muttered something to himself and then turned and began creeping toward the Baudelaires. "I only need one of you to learn where the sugar bowl is," he said, his eyes shining brightly, "and to get my hands on the fortune. But which one should it be?"

"That's a difficult decision," Esmé said. "On one hand, it's been enjoyable having an infant servant. But it would be a lot of fun to smash Klaus's glasses and watch him bump into things."

"But Violet has the longest hair," Carmelita volunteered, as the Baudelaires backed toward the cracked waterfall with Quigley right behind them. "You could yank on it all the time, and tie it to things when you were bored."

"Those are both excellent ideas," Count Olaf said. "I'd forgotten what an adorable little girl you are. Why don't you join us?"

"Join you?" Carmelita asked.

"Look at my stylish dress," Esmé said to Carmelita. "If you joined us, I'd buy you all sorts of in outfits."

Carmelita looked thoughtful, gazing first at the children, and then at the two villains standing next to her and smiling. The three Baudelaires shared a look of horrified disappointment with Quigley. The siblings remembered how monstrous Carmelita had been at school, but it had never occurred to them that she would be interested in joining up with even more monstrous people.

"Don't believe them, Carmelita," Quigley said, and took his purple notebook out of his pocket. "They'll burn your parents' house down.

I have the evidence right here, in my common-place book."

"What are you going to believe, Carmelita?" Count Olaf asked. "A silly book, or something an adult tells you?"

"Look at us, you adorable little girl," Esmé said, her yellow, orange, and red dress crackling on the ground. "Do we look like the sort of people who like to burn down houses?"

"Carmelita!" Violet cried. "Don't listen to them!"

"Carmelita!" Klaus cried. "Don't join them!"

"Carmelita!" Sunny cried, which meant something like, "You're making a monstrous decision!"

"Carmelita," Count Olaf said, in a sickeningly sweet voice. "Why don't you choose one orphan to live, and push the others off the cliff, and then we'll all go to a nice hotel together."

"You'll be like the daughter we never had," Esmé said, stroking her tiara.

"Or something," added Olaf, who looked

like he would prefer having another employee rather than a daughter.

Carmelita glanced once more at the Baudelaires, and then smiled up at the two villains. "Do you really think I'm adorable?" she asked.

"I think you're adorable, beautiful, cute, dainty, eye-pleasing, flawless, gorgeous, harmonious, impeccable, jaw-droppingly adorable, keen, luscious, magnificent, nifty, obviously adorable, photogenic, quite adorable, ravishing, splendid, thin, undeformed, very adorable, well-proportioned, xylophone, yummy, and zestfully adorable," Esmé pledged, "every morning, every afternoon, every night, and all day long!"

"Don't listen to her!" Quigley pleaded. "A person can't be 'xylophone'!"

"I don't care!" Carmelita said. "I'm going to push these cakesniffers off the mountain, and start an exciting and fashionable new life!"

The Baudelaires took another step back,

and Quigley followed, giving the children a pan-
icked look. Above them they could hear the
squawking of the eagles as they took the villains' new recruits farther and farther away.
Behind them they could feel the four drafts of
the valley below, where the headquarters had
been destroyed by people the children's parents had devoted their lives to stopping. Violet
reached in her pocket for her ribbon, trying to
imagine what she could invent that could get
them away from such villainous people, and
journeying toward their fellow volunteers at the
last safe place. Her fingers brushed against the
bread knife, and she wondered if she should
remove the weapon from her pocket and use it
to threaten the villains with violence, or
whether this, too, would make her as villainous
as the man who was staring at her now.

"Poor Baudelaires," Count Olaf said mockingly. "You might as well give up. You're hopelessly outnumbered."

"We're not outnumbered at all," Klaus said. "There are four of us, and only three of you."

"I count triple because I'm the False Spring Queen," Carmelita said, "so you *are* outnumbered, cakesniffers."

This, of course, was more utter nonsense from the mouth of this cruel girl, but even if it weren't nonsense, it does not always matter if one is outnumbered or not. When Violet and Klaus were hiking toward the Valley of Four Drafts, for instance, they were outnumbered by the swarm of snow gnats, but they managed to find Quigley Quagmire, climb up the Vertical Flame Diversion to the headquarters, and find the message hidden in the refrigerator. Sunny had been outnumbered by all of the villains on top of Mount Fraught, and had still managed to survive the experience, discover the location of the last safe place, and concoct a few recipes that were as easy as they were delicious. And the members of V.F.D. have always been outnumbered, because the number of greedy and

wicked people always seems to be increasing,
while more and more libraries go up in smoke,
but the volunteers have managed to endure, a
word which here means "meet in secret, communicate in code, and gather crucial evidence
to foil the schemes of their enemies." It does
not always matter whether there are more
people on your side of the schism than there
are on the opposite side, and as the Baudelaires
stood with Quigley and took one more step
back, they knew what was more important.

"Rosebud!" Sunny cried, which meant "In
some situations, the location of a certain object
can be much more important than being outnumbered," and it was true. As the villains
gasped in astonishment, Violet sat down in the
toboggan, grabbing the leather straps. Quigley
sat down behind her and put his arms around
her waist, and Klaus sat down next, and put his
arms around Quigley's, and there was just
enough room in back for a young girl, so Sunny
sat behind her brother and hung on tight as

Violet pushed off from the peak of Mount Fraught and sent the four children hurtling down the slope. It did not matter that they were outnumbered. It only mattered that they could escape from a monstrous end by racing down the last of the slippery slope, just as it only matters for you to escape from a monstrous end by putting down the last of *The Slippery Slope*, and reading a book in which villains do not roar at children who are trying to escape.

"We'll be right behind you, Baudelaires!" Count Olaf roared, as the toboggan raced toward the Valley of Four Drafts, bumping and splashing against the cracked and melting ice.

"He won't be right behind us," Violet said. "My shoes punctured his tire, remember?"

Quigley nodded. "And he'll have to take that path," he said. "A car can't go down a waterfall."

"We'll have a head start," Violet said. "Maybe we can reach the last safe place before he does."

"Overhear!" Sunny cried. "Hotel Denouement!"

"Good work, Sunny!" Violet said proudly, pulling on the leather straps to steer the toboggan away from the large crack. "I knew you'd be a good spy."

"Hotel Denouement," Quigley said. "I think I have that in one of my maps. I'll check my commonplace book when we get to the bottom."

"Bruce!" Sunny cried.

"That's another thing to write down in our commonplace books," Klaus agreed. "That man Bruce was at Dr. Montgomery's house at the end of our stay. He said he was packing up Monty's reptile collection for the herpetological society."

"Do you think he's really a member of V.F.D.?" Violet asked.

"We can't be sure," Quigley said. "We've managed to investigate so many mysteries, and yet there's still so much we don't know." He sighed thoughtfully, and gazed down at the ruins of headquarters rushing toward them. "My siblings—"

But the Baudelaires never got to hear any more about Quigley's siblings, because at that moment the toboggan, despite Violet's efforts with the leather straps, slipped against a melted section of the waterfall, and the large sled began to spin. The children screamed, and Violet grabbed the straps as hard as she could, only to have them break in her hands. "The steering mechanism is broken!" she yelled. "Dragging Esmé Squalor up the slope must have weakened the straps!"

"Uh-oh!" Sunny cried, which meant something along the lines of, "That doesn't sound like good news."

"At this velocity," Violet said, using a scientific word for speed, "the toboggan won't stop when we reach the frozen pool. If we don't slow down, we'll fall right into the pit we dug."

Klaus was getting dizzy from all the spinning, and closed his eyes behind his glasses. "What can we do?" he asked.

"Drag your shoes against the ice!" Violet cried. "The forks should slow us down!"

Quickly, the two elder Baudelaires stretched out their legs and dragged the forks of their shoes against the last of the ice on the slope. Quigley followed suit, but Sunny, who of course was not wearing fork-assisted climbing shoes, could do nothing but listen to the scraping and splashing of the forks against the thawing ice of the stream as the toboggan slowed ever so slightly.

"It's not enough!" Klaus cried. As the toboggan continued to spin, he caught brief glimpses of the pit they had dug, covered with a thin layer of weakened wood, getting closer and closer as the four children hurtled toward the bottom of the waterfall.

"Bicuspid?" Sunny asked, which meant something like "Should I drag my teeth against the ice, too?"

"It's worth a try," Klaus said, but as soon as the youngest Baudelaire leaned down and dragged her teeth along the thawing waterfall, the Baudelaires could see at once that it was not really worth a try at all, as the toboggan kept spinning and racing toward the bottom.

"That's not enough, either," Violet said, and focused her inventing mind as hard as she could, remembering how she had stopped the caravan, when she and her brother were hurtling away from Count Olaf's automobile. There was nothing large enough to use as a drag chute, and the eldest Baudelaire found herself wishing that Esmé Squalor were on board with them, so she could stop the toboggan with her enormous, flame-imitating dress. She knew there was no blackstrap molasses, wild clover honey, corn syrup, aged balsamic vinegar, apple butter, strawberry jam, caramel sauce, maple syrup, butterscotch topping, maraschino liqueur, virgin and extra-virgin olive oil, lemon curd, dried apricots, mango chutney, *crema di noci*, tamarind paste, hot mustard, marshmallows, creamed corn, peanut butter, grape preserves, salt water taffy, condensed milk, pumpkin pie filling, or glue on board, or any other sticky substance, for that matter. But then she remembered the small table she had used to drag on the ground, behind the caravan, and she reached into her pocket and knew what she could do.

"Hang on!" Violet cried, but she did not hang on herself. Dropping the broken straps of the toboggan, she grabbed the long bread knife and took it out of her pocket at last. It had only been several days, but it felt like a very long time since she had taken the knife from the caravan, and it seemed that every few minutes she had felt its jagged blade in her pocket as she tried to defeat the villains high above her, without becoming a villain herself. But now, at last, there was something she could do with the knife that might save them all, without hurting anyone. Gritting her teeth, Violet leaned out of the spinning toboggan and thrust the knife as hard as she could into the ice of the slippery slope.

The tip of the blade hit the crack caused by

Carmelita's Springpole, and then the entire knife sank into the slope just as the toboggan reached the bottom. There was a sound the likes of which the Baudelaires had never heard, like a combination of an enormous window shattering and the deep, booming sound of someone firing a cannon. The knife had widened the crack, and in one tremendous crash, the last of the ice fell to pieces and all of the forks, sunlight, teeth, and tobogganing finally took their toll on the waterfall. In one enormous *whoosh!*, the waters of the Stricken Stream came rushing down the slope, and in a moment the Baudelaires were no longer on a frozen pool at the bottom of a strange curve of ice, but simply at the bottom of a rushing waterfall, with gallons and gallons of water pouring down on them. The orphans had just enough time to take a deep breath before the toboggan was forced underwater. The three siblings hung on tight, but the eldest Baudelaire felt a pair of hands slip from her waist, and when the wooden toboggan bobbed to the surface again, she called out the name of her lost friend.

"*Quigley!*" she screamed.

"*Violet!*" The Baudelaires heard the triplet's voice as the toboggan began to float down one of the tributaries. Klaus pointed, and through the rush of the waterfall the children could see a glimpse of their friend. He had managed to grab onto a piece of wood from the ruins of headquarters, something that looked a bit like a banister, such as one might need to walk up a narrow staircase leading to an astronomical observatory. The rush of the water was dragging the wood, and Quigley, down the opposite tributary of the Stricken Stream.

"*Quigley!*" Violet screamed again.

"*Violet!*" Quigley shouted, over the roar of the water. The siblings could see he had removed his commonplace book from his pocket and was desperately waving it at them. "*Wait for me! Wait for me at—*"

But the Baudelaires heard no more. The

Stricken Stream, in its sudden thaw from the arrival of False Spring, whisked the banister and the toboggan away from one another, down the two separate tributaries. The siblings had one last glimpse of the notebook's dark purple cover before Quigley rushed around one twist in the stream, and the Baudelaires rushed around another, and the triplet was gone from their sight.

"*Quigley!*" Violet called, one more time, and tears sprung in her eyes.

"He's alive," Klaus said, and held Violet's shoulder to help her balance on the bobbing toboggan. She could not tell if the middle Baudelaire was crying, too, or if his face was just wet from the waterfall. "He's alive, and that's the important thing."

"Intrepid," Sunny said, which meant something like, "Quigley Quagmire was brave and resourceful enough to survive the fire that destroyed his home, and I'm sure he'll survive this, too."

Violet could not bear that her friend was

rushing away from her, so soon after first making his acquaintance. "But we're supposed to wait for him," she said, "and we don't know where."

"Maybe he's going to try to reach his siblings before the eagles do," Klaus said, "but we don't know where they are."

"Hotel Denouement?" Sunny guessed. "V.F.D.?"

"Klaus," Violet said, "you saw some of Quigley's research. Do you know if these two tributaries ever meet up again?"

Klaus shook his head. "I don't know," he said. "Quigley's the cartographer."

"Godot," Sunny said, which meant "We don't know where to go, and we don't know how to get there."

"We know some things," Klaus said. "We know that someone sent a message to J.S."

"Jacques," Sunny said.

Klaus nodded. "And we know that the message said to meet on Thursday at the last safe place."

"Matahari," Sunny said, and Klaus smiled, and pulled Sunny toward him so she wouldn't fall off the floating toboggan. She was no longer a baby, but the youngest Baudelaire was still young enough to sit on her brother's lap.

"Yes," Klaus agreed. "Thanks to you, we know that the last safe place is the Hotel Denouement."

"But we don't know where that is," Violet said. "We don't know where to find these volunteers, or if indeed there are any more surviving members of V.F.D. We can't even be certain what V.F.D. stands for, or if our parents are truly dead. Quigley was right. We've managed to investigate so many mysteries, and yet there's still so much we don't know."

Her siblings nodded sadly, and if I had been there at that moment, instead of arriving far too late to see the Baudelaires, I would have nodded, too. Even for an author like myself, who has dedicated his entire life to investigating the mysteries that surround the Baudelaire case, there is still much I have been unable to discover. I do not know, for instance, what happened to the two white-faced women who decided to quit Olaf's troupe and walk away, all by themselves, down the Mortmain Mountains. There are some who say that they still paint their faces white, and can be seen singing sad songs in some of the gloomiest music halls in the city. There are some who say that they live together in the hinterlands, attempting to grow rhubarb in the dry and barren ground. And there are those who say that they did not survive the trip down from Mount Fraught, and that their bones can be found in one of the many caves in the odd, square peaks. But although I have sat through song after dreary song, and tasted some of the worst rhubarb in my life, and brought bone after bone to a skeleton expert until she told me that I was making her so miserable that I should never return, I have not been able to discover what truly happened to the two women. I do not know where the remains of the caravan are, as I have told you, and as I reach the end of the rhyming dictionary, and read the short list of words that rhyme with "zucchini," I am beginning to think I should stop my search for the destroyed vehicle and give up that particular part of my research. And I have not tracked down the refrigerator in which the Baudelaires found the Verbal Fridge Dialogue, despite stories that it is also in one of the Mortmain Mountain caves, or performing in some of the gloomiest music halls in the city.

But even though there is much I do not know, there are a few mysteries that I have solved for certain, and one thing I am sure about is where the Baudelaire orphans went next, as the ashen waters of the Stricken Stream hurried their toboggan out of the Mortmain Mountains, just as the sugar bowl was hurried along, after the volunteer tossed it into the stream to save it from the fire. But although I know exactly where the Baudelaires went, and can even trace their path on a map drawn by one of the most promising young cartographers of our time, I am not the writer who can describe it best. The writer who can most accurately and elegantly describe the path of the three orphans was an associate of mine who, like the man who wrote "The Road Less Traveled," is now dead. Before he died, however, he was widely regarded as a very good poet, although some people think his writings about religion were a little too mean-spirited. His name was Algernon Charles Swinburne, and the last quatrain of the eleventh stanza of his poem "The Garden of Proserpine" perfectly describes what the children found as this chapter in their story drew to an end, and the next one began. The first half of the quatrain reads,

> *That no life lives forever;*
> *That dead men rise up never;*

and indeed, the grown men in the Baudelaires' lives who were dead, such as Jacques Snicket, or the children's father, were never going to rise up. And the second half of the quatrain reads,

*That even the weariest river*
*Winds somewhere safe to sea.*

This part is a bit trickier, because some poems are a bit like secret codes, in that you must study them carefully in order to discover their meaning. A poet such as Quigley Quagmire's sister, Isadora, of course, would know at once what those two lines mean, but it took me quite some time before I decoded them. Eventually, however, it became clear that "the weariest river" refers to the Stricken Stream, which indeed seemed weary from carrying away all of the ashes from the destruction of V.F.D. headquarters, and that "winds somewhere safe to sea" refers to the last safe place where all the volunteers, including Quigley Quagmire, could gather. As Sunny said, she and her siblings did not know where to go, and they didn't know how to get there, but the Baudelaire orphans were winding there anyway, and that is one thing I know for certain.

Until recently, Lemony Snicket was presumed to be 'presumed dead'. Instead, this 'presumed' presumption wasn't disproved not to be incorrect. As he continues with his investigation, interest in the Baudelaire case has increased. So has his horror.

www.unfortunateevents.com

Brett Helquist was born in Ganado, Arizona, grew up in Orem, Utah and now lives in Brooklyn, New York. He earned a bachelor's degree in fine arts from Brigham Young University and has been illustrating ever since. His work deciphering the evidence provided by Lemony Snicket into pictures often leaves him so distraught that he is awake late into the night.

To My Kind Editor –

I apologize for the watery quality of this letter, but I'm afraid the ink I am using has become diluted, a word which here means "soaked with salt water from the ocean and from the author's own tears." It is difficult to conduct my investigation on the damaged submarine where the Baudelaires lived during this episode of their lives, and I can only hope that the rest of this letter will not wash away.

The Grim Gr

Ecology and Management of
# Atlantic Salmon

A salmon, on its way upstream, leaps 3.5 m to clear the Orrin Falls situated a few kilometres downstream of the Orrin Dam in Ross-shire, Scotland. (Photo by Derek Mills.)

# Ecology and Management of
# Atlantic Salmon

## DEREK MILLS

*Department of Forestry and Natural Resources*
*University of Edinburgh*

London   New York
CHAPMAN AND HALL

First published in 1989 by
Chapman and Hall Ltd
11 New Fetter Lane, London EC4P 4EE

Published in the USA by
Chapman and Hall
29 West 35th Street, New York, NY 10001

Typeset in 10 on 12 pt Photina by
Cotswold Typesetting Ltd, Gloucester
Printed in Great Britain at
the University Press, Cambridge

ISBN 0 412 32140 8

British Library Cataloguing in Publication Data

Mills, D. H. (Derek Henry), 1928–
Ecology and management of Atlantic salmon
1. Atlantic Ocean. Salmon
I. Title
597'.55
ISBN 0–412–32140–8


Library of Congress Cataloging in Publication Data

Mills, D. H. (Derek Henry), 1928–
Ecology and management of Atlantic salmon/Derek Mills.
    p.      cm.
Bibliography: p.
Includes index.
ISBN 0–412–32140–8
1. Atlantic salmon—Ecology. 2. Fishery management.
3. Fishes—Ecology. I. Title.
QL638.S2M48 1989
597'.55—dc19
88-25641 CIP

# Salar the Salmon

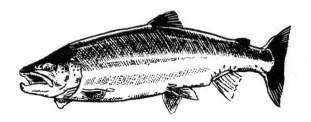

# Contents

# Preface

Since I wrote *Salmon and Trout: A Resource, its Ecology, Conservation and Management* (Oliver and Boyd and St. Martin's Press) some eighteen years ago the literature relating to these two species has grown exponentially. When asked by Croom Helm (now under the Chapman and Hall imprint) to revise the book I realized that it was just not possible. Besides, I felt that the trout deserved a book of its own and hoped someone might feel up to the task of writing it. Even writing a dissertation on the Atlantic salmon, a fish with which I am more familiar, although enjoyable, has not been easy.

Over the last twenty years the salmon scene has changed almost beyond recognition. In 1970, the Greenland high seas salmon fishery was still escalating and the long-line fishery north of the Faroes had not begun. International co-operation over salmon exploitation on the open seas was still some way off and quotas had not been considered as a means of controlling salmon catches, although in the final chapter of my book (p. 293) I had suggested the possibility of a quota system. The two major salmon conservation bodies, the Atlantic Salmon Trust and the Atlantic Salmon Federation, which have played such an important role in salmon affairs in recent years, were still in their infancy, and the North Atlantic Salmon Conservation Organisation (NASCO) was not to appear for fourteen years.

The regulation of fisheries in home waters (the future of which was discussed on p. 294 of my book) is now becoming a possibility in some directions with the buying-out of commercial fisheries, the banning of monofilament drift nets by some countries and the control of illegal fishing through sophisticated means of surveillance and restrictions on salmon sales through carcass tagging and dealer licensing. At the same time, though, we have seen a marked increase in exploitation in some inshore fisheries, such as those of north-east England and north-west Ireland.

On the environmental scene the effects of afforestation and acidification were only just beginning to be felt and acid rain was rarely, if ever, mentioned. Changes in farming methods over the last two decades, too, have allowed silage effluent and farm slurry to influence water quality. In 1970, no one gave any thought to the possible environmental and biological effects of salmon farming, and only clever crystal-ball gazing could have resulted in a forecast of the problems we are facing today in this field.

Salmon farming was still at the research and development stage in 1970 and I doubt whether many visualized the exponential growth of the salmon farming industry, with Norwegian and Faroese fjords and Scottish sea and freshwater lochs becoming crammed with cages. The threats to wild salmon stocks were, however, concerning some people, and I quoted (p. 297) Dr Rasmusson from Sweden who, in considering the population-genetic aspects of salmon culture, warned of a relaxation of selection during the young stages and how heavy fishing and international rivalries on the high seas may lead to an unwanted change in the selection of fish that are captured when returning to their native rivers and used for breeding purposes.

In rewriting my earlier book and confining myself to the Atlantic salmon, I have tried to cover all these changes and make it a useful reference for those with varying interests in salmon including anglers, students, fishery managers, biologists, conservationists, administrators and politicians. This work is not as comprehensive as I would have liked due to the necessary word limitation imposed on me. For this reason I hope that those whose work has not been mentioned will understand.

I am greatly indebted to Dr Margaret Brown, Dr Tom Cross and Mr Gerry Hadoke for so kindly taking the time to read some of the chapters and for making a number of most valuable comments and suggestions.

Discussions with friends and colleagues have been most helpful and stimulating at all times and I should like to thank particularly: Mr Thor Gudjonsson, one-time director of the Freshwater Fisheries Research Institute, Reykjavik; Professor Tony Hawkins, director of the Marine Laboratory, Aberdeen; Mr Gerry Hadoke, one-time director of the Atlantic Salmon Trust; Dr Lars Hansen, Fish Research Division of the Directorate for Nature Management, Trondheim; Dr Gersham Kennedy, director of the Fisheries Research Laboratory, Coleraine; Dr David Piggins, director of the Salmon Research Trust for Ireland, Inc.; Dr Dick Shelton, officer-in-charge of the Freshwater Fisheries Laboratory, Pitlochry; Mr Willie Shearer and Dr John Thorpe, also of the Freshwater Fisheries Laboratory, Pitlochry; Miss Eileen Twomey of the Fisheries Research Centre, Abbotstown; and Mr Robert Williamson, Inspector of Salmon and Freshwater Fisheries for Scotland.

It gives me great pleasure to thank Mr Ted Hughes, the Poet Laureate, for the privilege of using a number of verses from his poem *The Best Worker in Europe* as introductions to Chapters 2, 3 and 4, and verses from an unpublished poem for Chapters 8 and 11. I am also most grateful to the artist Mr Charles Jardine for producing the cover illustration.

I greatly appreciate the time Mr David Haswell of the Department of Forestry and Natural Resources in this university put into preparing some of the artwork, including Figs 1.3 and 3.2.

My acknowledgements are due also to the following for so kindly allowing me to reproduce some of their material: Mr I. R. H. Allan (Tables 1.3 and 1.4); British Gas PLC (Fig. 9.3); Dr Margaret Brown (Fig. 1.1); Mr R. Buck and Dr D.

Hay (Fig. 8.4); *Canadian Journal of Fisheries and Aquatic Sciences* (Figs 3.7 and
4.5); Dr E. M. Chadwick (Fig. 8.6); Controller of Her Majesty's Stationery Office
(Figs 4.6, 8.14 and 9.2); Professor Beverley Cook (Fig. 6.2); Fisheagle Trading
Co., Lechlade (Fig. 8.15); Fisheries Society of the British Isles (Figs 1.6 and
8.4); Dr P. E. Fredriksen (Figs 4.8 and 4.9); Dr L. Hansen (Tables 5.2, 5.5 and
11.1); Professor A. Hawkins (Table 4.1); Drs T. G. Heggberget and B. O.
Johnsen (Figs 4.8 and 4.9); International Council for the Exploration of the Sea
(Fig. 7.3); Dr G. J. A. Kennedy (Fig. 2.1 and Table 3.1); Mr T. Kirkwood (Fig.
5.2); Dr F. Lugmayr (Fig. 12.1); Dr J. H. Martin (Fig. 3.7); Mr C. Mylne (Fig.
15.5); NASCO (Fig. 14.1 and Appendix A); North of Scotland Hydro-electric
Board (Fig. 9.1); Dr D. J. Piggins (Tables 4.4 and 4.5); Dr G. Power (Fig. 4.5);
Dr D. G. Reddin (Figs 3.3–3.6); The Salmon Net Fishing Association (Figs 3.7
and 5.1); Dr I. H. Sevaldrud (Fig. 11.2); Mr W. M. Shearer (Fig. 1.5, Tables 5.3
and 5.4); and Dr R. G. Shelton (Fig. 8.13).

Derek Mills
*Edinburgh*
*September 1988*

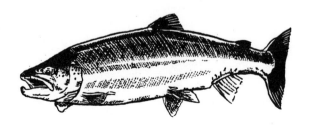

# Ecology

# CHAPTER ONE

# General biology

*The salmon is accounted the king of freshwater fish, and is ever bred in rivers relating to the sea, yet so high, or far from it, as admits of no tincture of salt, or brackishness.*

Izaak Walton, 1653

## 1.1  CLASSIFICATION

The Atlantic salmon (*Salmo salar*) is a member of one of the most primitive superorders of the Teleosts or bony fishes, namely the Protacanthopterygii, which includes the Salmonoids and a few genera of deep-sea fish. The family Salmonidae includes the Atlantic and Pacific salmon, the trout and the charr – classified as the Salmoninae – and the grayling (Thymallinae) and whitefishes (Coregoninae) (Fig. 1.1).

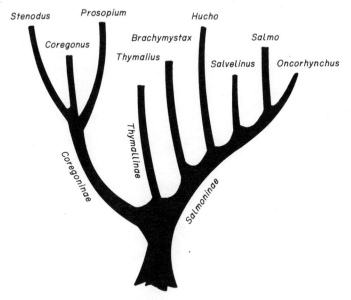

**Fig. 1.1**   The hypothetical phylogeny of the Salmonid fishes (after Norden, 1961).

Frost and Brown (1967) point out the anatomical features that separate the genera *Salmo* and *Oncorhynchus* (the salmon and trout) from the genus *Salvelinus* (the charr). In the two former genera the teeth form a double or zigzag series over the whole of the vomer bone (in the roof of the mouth), which is flat and not boat-shaped, while in the latter the teeth are restricted to the head (front) of a boat-shaped vomer. In the genus *Salmo* there is only a small gap between the vomerine and palatine teeth but this gap is wide in adult *Oncorhynchus*. An interesting specialization occurring in *Oncorhynchus* and not in *Salmo* is the simultaneous ripening of all the germ cells (i.e. sperm and ova) so that these fish can spawn only once.

There are a number of anatomical features which help in the identification of the various species of *Salmo* and *Oncorhynchus* (Fig. 1.2). Those used by taxonomists include scale and fin ray counts and the number and shape of the gill rakers on the first arch. Almost certainly the most reliable features that help in identifying the genus *Oncorhynchus* are the larger number of anal fin rays and gill rakers, while the scale count between the base of the adipose fin and the lateral line and the length of the upper jaw bone or maxilla in relation to the eye are two of the most reliable features for distinguishing *Salmo salar* Linnaeus from *S. trutta* Linnaeus (Table 1.1 and Fig. 1.3).

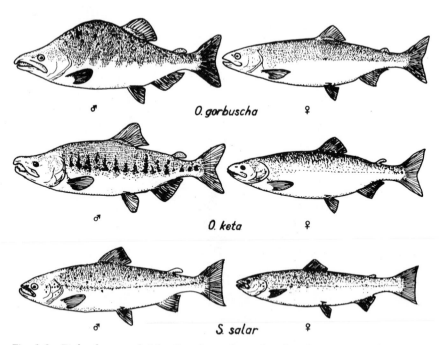

**Fig. 1.2**  Pink, chum and Atlantic salmon (reproduced with permission from Berg, 1961).

## 1.2 DISTRIBUTION

The Atlantic salmon originally occurred in every country whose rivers flowed into the North Atlantic Ocean and Baltic Sea. In some instances the country has no coastline bordering either of these waters, for example Czechoslovakia, Luxembourg and Switzerland, and the salmon had to undergo long upstream migrations up such rivers as the Vltava (Czechoslovakia) and the Rhine (Luxembourg and Switzerland). Salmon have now disappeared from the rivers of these countries due to the erection of navigation locks, the construction of dams and pollution. MacCrimmon and Gots (1979) have produced a comprehensive review of the past and present distribution of the Atlantic salmon and include an exhaustive account of the history of introductions, both successful and unsuccessful, of this species to countries in the Northern and Southern Hemispheres. Table 1.2 summarizes the present status in Europe.

Detailed accounts have been produced of the recent distribution of salmon in the rivers of Iceland (Stewart, 1950; Gudjonsson and Mills, 1982), France (Brittany and Lower Normandy) (Phélipot, 1982), northern Norway (Berg, 1964), Quebec (Tetreault, 1967), Newfoundland (Porter, Riche and Traverse, 1974), Scotland (Mills and Graesser, 1981) and Spain (Léaniz et al., 1987). Earlier descriptions of the salmon rivers of Scotland, England, Wales and Ireland were given by Calderwood (1909, 1921) and Grimble (1902, 1903, 1904 and 1913) and an early account of the salmon rivers of Newfoundland was written by Palmer (1928).

## 1.3 GENERAL LIFE HISTORY

Hector Boece (1527) gave a correct outline of the life history of the Atlantic salmon, while a sixteenth-century priest, Peder Clausson Friis (1595–1614) surmised that salmon bred in fresh water, that the young fish spent a period in the river before migrating to sea, and that, once there, they grew rapidly and carried out extensive migrations. It is interesting to note that Ray and Willughby refer to the first description of the salmon in an old Latin folio *Salmo omnium autorum* (North, 1840), and Pliny the Elder writes of salmon in *Historia Naturalis* in the first century AD. There was, nonetheless, for some considerable time a misunderstanding about the juvenile life of the salmon, which arose because the parr is similar to a small brown trout and quite unlike the next stage in the life cycle, the smolt which, having silvery scales in preparation for its journey to sea, resembles a salmon. Indeed, the famous naturalist Agassiz considered the parr to be a variety of trout. However, some male salmon parr develop functional testes, a phenomenon known as paedogenesis. The parr was therefore considered a separate species and was

**Table 1.2**   History and present status of *Salmo salar* in Europe*

| Country | Stock |
|---|---|
| Belgium | Sea (native) |
| | Lake (from USA, 1898) |
| Czechoslovakia | Sea (native) |
| Cyprus | Sea (from UK, 1971) |
| Denmark: | |
|   Mainland | Sea (native) |
|   Faroes | Sea (from Iceland, 1947) |
|   Greenland | Sea (native, also from Norway and Canada) |
| Finland | Sea (native) |
| | Lake (native) |
| France | Sea (native, also from Scotland, 1970s) |
| Germany (BRD and DDR) | Sea (native) |
| | Lake (from USA, 1881) |
| Iceland | Sea (native) |
| Italy | Sea (from Scotland, 1885) |
| | Lake (from USA, 1897) |
| Ireland (Republic of) | Sea (native, also from Iceland and Norway, 1980s) |
| | Lake (from Quebec, 1908) |
| Luxembourg | Sea (native) |
| Netherlands | Sea (native) |
| Norway | Sea (native, also from Iceland and Sweden, 1970s, 1980s) |
| Poland | Sea (native) |
| Portugal | Sea (native) |
| Spain | Sea (native, also from Scotland, 1980s) |
| Sweden | Sea (native) |
| | Lake (native) |
| Switzerland | Sea (native) |
| United Kingdom: | |
|   England | Sea (native) |
| | Lake (Canada, 1870s; USA, 1880s) |
|   Wales | Sea (native) |
| | Lake (USA, 1902) |
|   Scotland | Sea (native; Norway, 1980s) |
| | Lake (USA, 1884) |
|   Northern Ireland | Sea (native) |
| USSR | Sea (native) |
| | Lake (native) |

given the specific name *Salmo salmulus*, while the smolt was considered to be the fry of the salmon which went to sea in its first year of life.

The recognition of the parr as a separate species was promulgated for well over 150 years by such eminent naturalists as Ray and Willughby (1686), Pennant (1761), Davy (1832), Yarrell (1836) and Parnell (1840). It was not until Shaw (1836, 1840) carried out experiments and observations in ponds at Drumlanrig by the River Nith that it was confirmed that the parr was the young of the salmon. This fact was previously suspected by the angler Thomas Stoddart in *The Scottish Angler* in 1831. Even so, the famous ichthyologist Yarrell (1839) was not prepared to accept these findings. Although Andrew Young (1843) and Sir William Jardine corroborated Shaw's observations, the controversy was still raging in the 1860s and was well documented by Flowerdew (1871). One wonders whether opinions would have differed had any of these naturalists learnt of the existence of mature female parr. These are said to exist in Spanish rivers (Léaniz and Martinez, 1988) and have recently been recorded in the River Ason by Léaniz (personal communication, 1988). They have also been found in the River Elorn in France, and a large mature female parr measuring 22.5 cm and weighing 150 g caught in this river produced 256 viable ova (Prouzet, 1981).

Unfamiliarity with the salmon's life cycle also led to old male salmon being given the specific name *S. hamatus* (Cuvier, 1829) and kelts the name *S. argenteus* (Gunther, 1866).

Agreement over the salmon's life cycle seems to have been reached in the late 1860s, and successive definitive works on its life history were produced over the next 100 years by Gunther (1864), Day (1887), Calderwood (1907), Malloch (1910), Hutton (1924), Menzies (1931), Jones (1959) and Mills (1971). A revised terminology and list of definitions and terms designating the different life stages of the Atlantic salmon was produced in 1975 by Allan and Ritter (Table 1.3).

With rare exceptions, the salmon depends on two distinct environments for the successful fulfilment of its life history: (a) a freshwater environment in which the reproductive and nursery phase of its life cycle can occur and (b) a marine environment for its main feeding phase, during which rapid growth is achieved. For these reasons it is termed 'anadromous'.

The salmon enters the rivers at all times of the year and if it has spent two, three or four years at sea before returning to fresh water it is known as a 'salmon' and, depending on the time of year at which it returns, is called either a spring, summer or autumn fish. If the salmon has spent only a little over a year at sea before returning it is termed a 'grilse'. A third, but rare, category of salmon is the jack salmon. This fish spends only one summer at sea before first spawning. It has been recorded in Little Codroy River (Murray, 1968), Western Arm Brook (Chadwick, 1982a) and in rivers of Ungava Bay (Robitaille *et al.*, 1986). Quite often there is little difference in the size of grilse and salmon, but their age can be determined by examining their scales, which lay down rings in a seasonal pattern. On approaching fresh water the salmon stops feeding and will not feed again until it returns to salt water as a spent fish or kelt, which may be six months to a year or more later. Fortunately this phenomenon makes little difference to the angler as salmon, for some

**Table 1.3**    Revised terminology list* for Atlantic salmon (*Salmo salar* L.)

| Stage | Term† | Definition |
|---|---|---|
| 1 | Alevin | Stage from hatching to end of dependence on yolk sac as primary source of nutrition |
| 2 | Fry | Stage from independence on yolk sac as primary source of nutrition to dispersal from the redd |
| 3 | Parr | Stage from dispersal from redd to migration as a smolt: 0+parr, parr less than 1 year old (parr of the year's hatch); 1+ parr, parr 1 year or over but less than 2 years; 2+ parr, parr 2 years or over but less than 3 years; 3+ parr, parr 3 years or over but less than 4 years; precocious parr, male parr fully ripened or matured in fresh water; partially-silvered parr, parr that are partially silvered and migrating downstream prior to the normal smolt run |
| 4 | Smolt | Fully-silvered juvenile salmon migrating to the sea |
| 5 | Post-smolt | Stage from departure from river until onset of wide annulus formation at the end of the first winter in the sea: 'pre-grilse', post-smolt stage returning to fresh water to spawn in year of smolt migration |
| 6 | Salmon | All fish after onset of wide annulus formation at the end of the first winter in the sea: (a) 1-sea-winter salmon, salmon which has spent one winter at sea ('grilse' when maturing to spawn); (b) 2-sea-winter salmon, salmon which has spent two winters at sea; (c) 3-sea-winter salmon, salmon which has spent three winters at sea; (d) 4-sea-winter salmon, salmon which has spent four winters at sea; (e) previous spawner, salmon which has spawned on previous occasion(s) |
| 7 | Kelt | Spent or spawned-out salmon until it enters salt water |

*Source: Allan and Ritter (1975).*
†*The national terminologies collated by these two authors are given in Table 1.4.*

inexplicable reason, take anglers' lures into their mouths although not feeding. Once in fresh water the salmon will migrate upstream at varying speeds depending on the time of year, water temperature and stream flow.

[Spawning, or egg laying, starts in the late autumn. Some fish will lay their eggs in November, but those that have entered the river late in the season may not deposit theirs until January or February. By the time spawning commences salmon will have occupied suitable spawning grounds, which consist of silt-free gravel in areas extending from the upper reaches of the watershed down to tidal level. The salmon does not lay many eggs, relatively speaking, and how many depends on its size. The number ranges between 2000 and 15 000. A high fecundity is not essential because the eggs are well protected in nests or

| France | Iceland | Spain | United Kingdom |
|---|---|---|---|
| vin vésiculé | Kvidpokaseidi, Pokasei-di | Alevin | Alevin |
| vin | Seidi (Sumargamalt seidi- =0+parr) | Jaramugo | Fry |
| on (=Tocan) | | Pinto y Añal | Parr<br>Precocious parr |
| on (=Tocan) de escente monneau | Gönguseidi | Esguin y Pinto | Smolt |
| | Smálax | | Post-smolt, Pre-grilse |
| mon | Lax | Salmón | Salmon |
| deleineau astillon erbillot | Smálax | Añal | 1-sea-winter salmon (Grilse) |
| mon de rintemps | Lax Millilax | Salmón temprano or vernal pequeño<br>Salmón estival or serondo pequeño | 2-sea-winters salmon |
| mon d'été | Stórlax | Salmón temprano or vernal grande<br>Salmón estival or serondo grande | 3-sea-winters salmon |
| mon d'hiver | | Salmón temprano or vernal muy grande | 4-sea-winters salmon |
| mon mature | | | Repeat spawner 2nd(3rd)-time spawner<br>Previous spawner |
| rognard | Nidurgöngulax Hoplax | Zancado | Kelt |

rce: Allan and Ritter (1975).
    Table 1.3.
málaks of Baltic Sea commercial catches.
laks of Baltic Sea commercial catches.

Land-locked salmon also occur in the USSR in Lake Ladoga and in Norway in Lake Byglandsfjord. There are also land-locked Atlantic salmon in South Island, New Zealand. The majority of the salmon originally planted in the New Zealand rivers running into Lake Te Anau descend only to the lake and, after feeding there, return to the head rivers to spawn. Their passage to the sea is not barred as the River Waiau flows out of this lake.

In Dalmatia a fish bearing a strong resemblance to a salmon parr lives in the rivers and is called *Salmothymus obtusirostris* (Heckel). It has a smaller mouth than a salmon parr and more numerous gill rakers. *Salmothymus obtusirostris* may be derived from a colony of salmon parr established in glacial times when salmon might have entered the Mediterranean.

Berg (1953) gives an interesting account of a relict salmon called 'smablank' from the River Namsen in Norway. These look very like salmon parr. This land-locked form remains in the rivers and does not migrate to a lake. According to Berg, 'It is very abundant in the river higher up than the fall Fiskemoss where the salmon from the sea stop.'

## 1.4   THE SCALE AS AN INDICATOR OF LIFE HISTORY

The salmon scale, like the scales of many other fish, appears under a microscope to consist of a number of ridges, rings or **circuli** formed successively around a small unringed centre or nucleus or focus. The actual histology of the scale is very elaborate and reference should be made to the work of Wallin (1957) who has described in detail the growth structure and developmental physiology of the scale. Here it is sufficient to say that the scale is a growing part of the body and the spacing of the ridges or rings on it is an indicator of the rate of its former growth in the period when the rings were being formed. The growth rings seen on the salmon (and trout) scale are of two types: (a) widely spaced rings characteristic of fast growth (summer growth) and (b) less widely spaced and less numerous rings indicative of slow or winter growth. From an examination of the scale, therefore, it is possible to tell how old the fish is (by counting the bands of winter rings or **annuli**), how much time it has spent in fresh water and, if an adult, how much of its time was spent in the sea (Fig. 1.5). If the length of the fish at capture is known it is possible to calculate its length at the end of each of its previous years of life. It is also possible to tell if it has spawned before, due to the presence of a spawning mark brought about by scale erosion, and how long ago, and how old and how large it was when it left the river as a smolt. However, White and Medcof (1968) have shown that scale readings alone do not give a dependable estimate of the number of times a salmon has spawned if it has spawned two or more times because of extensive scale erosion.

The use of salmon scales as a means for ascertaining the age and other biological conditions of the fish was almost certainly due to Mr H. W. Johnston who wrote an account in the *23rd Annual Report of the Fishery Board for Scotland* in 1904 describing the technique. A popular article on the subject appeared in the *Dundee Advertiser* on 6 July 1909. Since that date a large amount of literature has been published on salmon scale investigations. Other early investigators include Hutton (1909, 1910 and 1924), Dahl (1910),

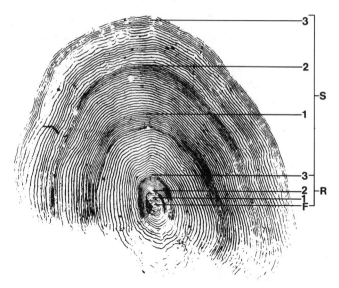

**Fig. 1.5** A scale from an Atlantic salmon from New Brunswick, Canada. The salmon is seen to have spent three years in the river (R) and three years at sea (S). F is the focus or nucleus of the scale. The end of each year of life is clearly defined as a band (annulus) of closely spaced rings (circuli). (Reproduced with permission from *Atlantic Salmon Scale Reading*, Report of the Atlantic Salmon Scale Reading Workshop, 1984, under the auspices of the International Council for the Exploration of the Sea.)

Hoek (1910), Malloch (1910) and Masterman (1913). An interesting report on the studies of the scale of juvenile salmon was written some years later by Jones (1949).

A recent report on Atlantic salmon scale reading published by the International Council for the Exploration of the Sea (Anon, 1985a) updates scale reading procedures.

## 1.5   ORIGIN

There has been much debate as to whether the Atlantic salmon had its origins in the sea or fresh water. Day (1887) and Regan (1911, 1914) considered that the Salmonidae had a marine origin with an ancestor similar to the Argentinidae (Argentines), which are entirely marine and, like the salmonids and smelts (Osmeridae), bear an adipose fin. However, Tchernavin (1939) considered the salmonids to have a freshwater origin, supporting his case by suggesting that as the group had both freshwater-resident and migratory forms within the species there had been recent divergence and as there were no entirely marine forms among modern salmonids they could not have had a marine origin. Thorpe (1981) considered that this implied that *Salmo*, being least marine, was more primitive than *Oncorhynchus*. Tchernavin further suggested that distribution routes had been by fresh water and that marine migration had only developed since the glacial period. Neave (1958) also considered that the genus *Salmo* had a freshwater origin and put forward the view that it had entered the Pacific coastal drainage system by a freshwater route through North America. He considered that *Oncorhynchus* was derived from this invading *Salmo* by isolation in an enclosed brackish sea in the Sea of Japan region during a lowering of sea level in the Pleistocene within the last million years. When the sea level rose, the newly-evolved genus adapted to full seawater life and invaded the rest of the North Pacific seaboard. Neave, in putting forward his views, agreed with Tchernavin that *Salmo* was more primitive than *Oncorhynchus* and that land-locked forms were relicts. Perhaps we have evidence for this in the behaviour of *Salmo salar* when introduced to Lake Te Anau in South Island, New Zealand.

However, Thorpe (1981, 1988b), in a comprehensive and thought-provoking consideration of life-history strategy and origins of the salmonids, feels it is appropriate to view the Salmonidae as relatively primitive teleosts of probable marine pelagic origin, whose specializations are associated with reproduction and early development in fresh water. Thorpe (1981, 1984) points out that Balon's hypothesis (1968) of the evolution of salmonid life-history strategies through penetration of fresh water by a pelagic marine fish, and progressive restrictions of life history to the freshwater habitat, demands the acquisition of adaptations permitting survival, growth and reproduction there. Thorpe (1981, 1988b) shows that the salmonid genera show several ranges of evolutionary progression in this direction, with generally greater flexibility among *Salmo* and *Salvelinus* than among *Oncorhynchus* species (Table 1.5).

Evidence for this evolutionary progression is perhaps even greater if one starts the sequence with the Argentinidae or Argentines and the Osmeridae or smelts. These are small relations of the salmonoids and possess the adipose fin characteristic of the salmon family. They are basically marine coastal fishes. Some enter the rivers to breed, some live in fresh water continuously, while others such as the capelin (*Mallotus villosus* (Müller)) spawn in the gravel of the seashore. The spawning capelin ride up the shore on the waves, lay and fertilize their eggs in the gravel and are swept back on succeeding waves. Like the Salmonidae, they bury their eggs in the gravel.

## 1.6 GEOGRAPHIC VARIATION AND STOCK DISCRIMINATION

From the work of Nyman (1966) Møller (1970a), Wilkins (1971), Payne, Child and Forrest (1971), Nyman and Pippy (1972), Cross and Healy (1983),

**Table 1.5** Examples of flexibility of life-history patterns in salmonid genera: anadromy implies emigration from fresh water as juveniles, and return as adults; non-anadromy implies a completion of the life-cycle without leaving fresh water, although this may involve migration between a river and a lake habitat*

| | Species | | |
| --- | --- | --- | --- |
| *Genus* | *Anadromous only* | *Both* | *Non-anadromous only* |
| *Oncorhynchus* | *gorbuscha* (pink salmon) | *nerka* (sockeye salmon) | none |
| *Parasalmo*† | none | *gairdneri* (rainbow trout) | *aguabonita* |
| *Salmo* | none | *salar* (Atlantic salmon) | *ischchan* |
| *Salvelinus* | none | *alpinus* (Arctic charr) | *namaycush* (lake charr) |
| *Hucho* | none | *perryi* | *hucho* (Danube salmon) |
| *Salmothymus* | none | none | *obtusirostris* |
| *Brachymystax* | none | none | *lenok* |

*(Reproduced with permission from Thorpe, 1988b).*
†*Thorpe places the rainbow trout (*Salmo gairdneri*) into the genus* Parasalmo.

and Verspoor (1986) it has been concluded that the Atlantic salmon can be divided genetically into a North American race and a European race; neither race is homogenous, both consisting of subsidiary stocks. Within North America these stocks are related clinally to each other. In Europe there exist at least two races, the 'celtic' and the 'boreal'. The Baltic salmon constitute a third distinct European race (Wilkins, 1985).

The Swedish scientist Lennart Nyman was the first to provide the genetic evidence, based on electrophoretic studies of proteins in the blood serum of salmon, that North American and European salmon were different races. Using the protein differences, he could calculate the proportions of North American and European fish in the West Greenland and Labrador fisheries (Nyman, 1966; Nyman, 1967; Nyman and Pippy, 1972).

Payne *et al.* (1971) investigated transferrin polymorphism in Atlantic salmon by an analysis by starch gel electrophoresis of the serum transferrin phenotypes of 4492 fish collected at several locations in Great Britain, Ireland and the Gulf of St Lawrence in Canada. Three transferrin phenotypes, TF1, TF1/TF2 and TF2 were observed in Atlantic salmon populations sampled in Great Britain and Ireland. In the Canadian samples the TF1 transferrin phenotype was present but neither the TF1/TF2 nor the TF2 was observed. However, four other phenotypes were identified in the Canadian fish, TF1/TF3, TF1/TF4, TF3/TF4 and TF4. The authors concluded that the most satisfactory explanation for the observed transferrin polymorphism is that the transferrin phenotype is determined by four co-dominant allelomorphic genes TF1, TF2, TF3 and TF4. It would seem that the TF2 allele is restricted to European salmon and the TF3 and TF4 alleles are exclusively North American. The authors therefore suggested that, as gene exchange between Atlantic salmon from European and North American rivers is negligible or non-existent and this isolation has been maintained for a period sufficient to permit genetic divergence, *Salmo salar* L. should be split into two subspecific taxa: *S. salar americanus* and *S. salar europaeus*.

Gruchy (1971) was critical of these authors' conclusions and suggested that the European stock must become the nominate subspecies and therefore should bear the name *Salmo salar*, Linnaeus, 1758. The nomination of the North American stock was more difficult as a number of older names were available, including *S. immaculatus* Storer 1950, *S. sebago* Girard 1854, *S. gloveri* Girard 1856 and *S. ouananiche* McCarthy, 1894, any one of which should take precedence over *S. salar americanus*. Ståhl (1987) also had doubts, although in his studies of the genetic population structure of Atlantic salmon the differentiation he observed between the Western Atlantic and European populations agreed qualitatively with the results of Payne *et al.* (1971). He considered that the average genetic distance between these two groups (i.e. 'boreal' and 'celtic' races) lies well within the range found between conspecific populations of other salmonids and that the limited divergence over all loci indicated by his data supported Behnke's (1972) contention that subspecific recognition on the basis of the single locus coding for transferrin is unjustified.

Nyman and Pippy (1972) used differences in the electrophoretograms produced by serum proteins and liver esterases to identify North American and European salmon caught at sea. Division of salmon according to continent of origin was supported by mean river age, mean fork length and the abundance of two parasites *Anisakis simplex* and *Eubothrium crassum*. The authors considered that consistent differences in the electrophoretic behaviour of serum proteins and liver esterases in salmon from the two continents supported the suggestion that salmon from North America and Europe represent different subspecies.

Not only did Payne *et al.* (1971) postulate that there were two subspecies but they also produced evidence for the existence of two races in the European subspecies. The two races identified were a northern 'boreal' race and a south-western 'celtic' race (Fig. 1.6). Further work on the existence of two races of Atlantic salmon in the British Isles was carried out by Child, Burnell and Wilkins (1976) and from the combined data of almost 10 000 individual salmon they concluded that the hypothesis that at least two races of salmon occur in the British Isles was valid. Payne *et al.* (1971) described in detail the possible mechanism for the formation of races which involved the southward movement of the salmon population of the British Isles during the last interglacial period as climatic conditions deteriorated with the advance of the

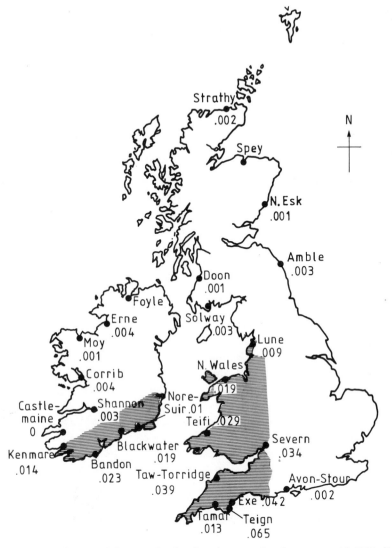

**Fig. 1.6.** Sketch map of the British Isles showing sampling locations with TF2 allele frequencies: shaded area shows range of 'celtic' race (reproduced with permission from Child *et al.*, 1976).

Würm I ice cap and the subsequent northerly and southerly movements between the recession and advance of further Würm ice caps. Such a phenomenon, the authors maintain, would have led to these two races being isolated genetically for at least 15 000 years. However, both Cross and Healy (1983) and Ståhl (1987) have failed to demonstrate any differences between these groups using enzyme loci. When Ståhl (1987) lumped TF with over 40 enzyme loci the difference between 'celtic' and 'boreal' races was minimal and insufficient for them to be considered separate races.

The use of scale characteristics and discriminant function analysis to discriminate between Atlantic salmon of North American and European origin caught off West Greenland has also proved very successful. Early work in this field was carried out by Lear (1972a) and Lear and Sandeman (1974) and was continued by Reddin (1982) and Reddin and Burfitt (1983), using new discriminant analysis techniques. Lear (1972a) concluded that there were five scale characters that could be valuable in discriminating between salmon of European and North American origin:

1. The width of the second river zone measured through the largest anterior radius;
2. The number of circuli in the second river zone;
3. The width of the first sea zone measured through the largest anterior radius;
4. The number of circuli in the first sea zone;
5. The river age of the fish.

Shearer (1983) considered that there were considerable difficulties in using discriminant functions for establishing a reference standard for a national stock of salmon. However, Pontual and Prouzet (1987) found that stock discrimination by scale-shape analysis using scale features (shape factors, moment invariants and elliptic Fourier descriptors) produced sufficiently promising results to merit further research.

MacCrimmon and Claytor (1986) looked at the possible use of taxonomic characters to identify Newfoundland and Scottish salmon stocks. Using a pooled sample of 367 juvenile salmon from eight geographically distinct home rivers, they found that stocks from Scotland and Newfoundland can be distinguished by meristic and morphometric character sets using discriminant analysis procedures. Reduced character sets required meristic counts of pectoral fin rays, dorsal fin rays, gill rakers and vertebrae, and morphometric measurements of standard length, pectoral and pelvic fin lengths, body depth and gape width. Regional differences based on these morphometric and meristic sets were substantiated electrophoretically by monomorphism at each MDH (malate dehydrogenase) locus in Scottish fish in contrast to polymorphism at the MDH-1 and MDH-3 loci in Newfoundland fish. The authors concluded that these findings for juvenile fish indicate that, while meristic, morphometric and electrophoretic criteria provide a likely means for distinguishing regional fish stocks, morphometric character sets would seem to offer the best possibility for identifying home-river origins of adult salmon in mixed fisheries.

## 1.7 HYBRIDIZATION

Early work on salmon hybrids has been described by Alm (1955). More recently hybrids between salmon and sea trout have been produced in Ireland (Piggins, 1961, 1962, 1963, 1964 and 1965a, b). The hybrids described by Piggins were the result of a single experimental cross between a small female grilse (1.6 kg) and a male sea trout (1.4 kg). The resulting progeny were found to have a much better growth rate than salmon or sea trout had under the same hatchery conditions. At the end of 2 years these hybrids averaged about 30.5 cm in length. In the autumn of their second year the growth rate began to decline when both sexes became sexually mature, but they continued to grow at a reduced rate and at $4\frac{1}{2}$ years their average size was 44.4 cm and 1.4 kg. Some of the F1 hybrids were released into a lake and one was caught at 7 + years and weighed almost 3.2 kg. The hybrids were found to be hardy and disease resistant. Further experiments continued after the initial trials over the period 1960–63.

Piggins (1965a) found it possible to breed from the F1 generation. He also successfully back-crossed male and female hybrids with the opposite sex of both salmon and sea trout; the resulting offspring were reared. The progeny of his hybrids back-crossed to salmon showed a strengthening of the salmon-like characters while the back-crosses to sea trout resembled the trout more closely. It would seem, therefore, that this hybrid strain possessed considerable plasticity in its ability to breed both *inter se* and with either parent stock. The F2 generation hybrids were reared for two years in a hatchery and released in a land-locked lake and their subsequent growth rate was much above normal for trout in the area.

For many years there has been some controversy regarding hybrids between salmon and sea trout, particularly in the Tay and Tweed where both large salmon and sea trout occur and where confusion sometimes arises over their identity. These questionable fish have been referred to as 'bull trout'. Calderwood (1904) produced evidence that the bull trout of the Tay is a salmon which has spawned previously, while the bull trout of the Tweed is a sea trout. The bull trout (salmon) of the Tay has a lot of spots on the shoulder, sometimes extending along the back and below the lateral line, and it has a lot of maggots in its gills although recently in from the sea. The bull trout (sea trout) of the Tweed has a round (convex) tail and has long been known as the 'round tail' because of its stunted and rounded caudal fin, a feature which gradually develops as the fish advances in years. Nall (1930) and Hynd (1964) have examined the scales of these large sea trout and have found that they grow very fast and spawn only once or twice – characteristics which, as Nall states, bring them more nearly into line with salmon. However, Nall considers that hybrids between salmon and sea trout are very rare and justifies his statement with an account (Nall, 1930) of the examination of the scales taken from fish which might be regarded as hybrids caught in the Berwick nets at the mouth of the Tweed. However, recent investigations, which are still in progress, suggest that the incidence of hybridization between salmon and sea trout on the Tweed is much higher than Nall believed.

Nyman (1970), too, considered that, despite similar demands for spawning grounds and overlapping spawning periods, natural hybridization between salmon and trout is extremely rare. This seems to be borne out by the work of Payne, Child and Forrest (1972) who, by electrophoretic analysis of serum samples, found that the percentage of hybrids in a sample of 4431 salmon was only 0.4%, although no salmon from the Tay or Tweed were included in their sample, nor any large sea trout! It is interesting to note that they considered that in rivers where there is a large population of trout and a small salmon run the fertilization of salmon ova by trout milt may be a major contributory factor to the extinction of salmon, especially when conditions in a river become more favourable to non-anadromous or facultatively anadromous salmonids. Walker (1988) reviews the question of hybridization between salmon and sea trout in an article describing the true identification of a 12.93 kg sea trout, the largest recorded in Scotland.

Verspoor (in press) found a higher frequency of hybrids in Newfoundland, where brown trout have been introduced, than has been observed in the British Isles and Scandinavia. However, in 1987 Léaniz and Verspoor (in press) detected Atlantic salmon and brown trout hybrids in two (the Asón and Pas) of four watersheds studied in northern Spain. The proportions of hybrids in samples of 'salmon' ranged from 0.0% to 7.7%, resulting in a mean hybridization rate of 2.3%. This is the highest rate of natural hybridization reported so far. Léaniz and Verspoor discuss the probable reasons for this high hybridization rate. They consider that reproductive isolation between the two species may have been decreased as a consequence of the introduction to the rivers of salmon populations from foreign hatcheries.

# CHAPTER TWO

# Juvenile phase

*He comes out of a heap of stones*
*Like some old-fashioned elf.*
*And all he asks is plain water,*
*Such as you drink yourself, my dears,*
*Such as you drink yourself.*
*Two years toiling secretly*
*He fits his craft, without a sigh*
*To rest his head or close his eye.*

Ted Hughes, 1985
from *The Best Worker in Europe*

## 2.1   SPAWNING

Salmon spawn throughout the river system wherever there is a suitable substrate of clean, silt-free, adequately aerated gravel in which to 'cut' or dig their nests or redds. Spawning therefore tends to be in the riffles or faster-flowing areas at the head and tail of pools. The greatest proportion of this type of substrate occurs in the upper reaches of the rivers and their tributaries where the flow is more turbulent, but spawning can also occur in the main river channel immediately above tide level (Mills and Graesser, 1981, p. 150). The most detailed accounts of the spawning behaviour of Atlantic salmon are given by Jones and King (1949) and Jones (1959).

A wide range of stone or gravel size can be used for egg deposition and no size preference is known for certainty, although probably very small gravel is normally avoided. Rantz (1964), in his list of criteria for favourable spawning conditions for king salmon, gives the optimum stream-bed composition in terms of the weight fraction of silt and the sand and stone size; the majority of stones measured were between 2.5 and 15.3 cm in diameter. Peterson (1978) measured the physical characteristics of gravel used by spawning salmon in New Brunswick streams. Size distribution of gravel varied widely but percentage sand (0.06–2.2 mm) appeared to be critical: more than 20% caused a very low permeability. A permeability of more than 1 m/h appeared to be necessary for successful emergence of fry and corresponded to a sand content of 12–15%. Gravel composition was also considered to be a critical factor.

Spawning salmon do seem to prefer certain water velocities and depths. According to Beland, Jordan and Meister (1982), female Atlantic salmon in the USA constructed redds in water with a mean depth of 38 cm, and the mean water velocity 12 cm above the substrate was $93 \pm 1.3$ cm/s. Mills (1973) found that the main factor limiting spawning by salmon in certain tributaries of the Tweed was gradient, with gradients of less than 3% being favourable. Sea trout were found to spawn in streams with gradients of up to 4%. There is probably some overlap in the spawning requirements of salmon and sea trout, which may result in some competition between these two species for available spawning areas.

Spawning usually takes place from late October to December but in some rivers, where late runs of fish occur, spawning may not be completed until the end of January or even later. Unfortunately, few detailed observations of spawning salmon have been made in the wild. Once the net fishing and angling season is over, the salmon river becomes a closed book to all but the most dedicated biologist. Chapman (1924) attempted such a study on the River North Tyne, but it was too anthropomorphic to be of any real value. Biologists and fisheries organizations carry out redd counts at spawning time: these are of value in providing some assessment of spawning escapement (the number of fish that have escaped capture by nets and rods and are available to spawn) (Fox, 1982; Hay, 1984; Prouzet and Dumas, 1988) and potential egg deposition (Elson and Tuomi, 1975; Gudjonsson, 1988) because the fecundity of salmon is known within certain limits (Pope, Mills and Shearer, 1961). However, while their smaller size makes it possible to distinguish redds made by smaller fish or grilse from those made by the larger salmon, there is no easy method of determining the distribution of redds of early-running (spring) and late-running (autumn) salmon. There has been a lot of speculation over the spawning distribution of various age classes in a river system, but the phenomenon requires further attention, as does the degree of spawning among fish from the spring, summer and autumn components of the stock.

Observations made by Berg, Abrahamsen and Berg (1986) of spawning by uninjured and injured salmon indicated that uninjured fish usually spawned in the outlets or inlets of pools and on coarse sediments, whereas injured females frequently spawned in very shallow water with a slow current and on a bed of sand or fine gravel.

In a study of the fecundity of salmon in Scottish rivers, Pope et al. (1961) showed that there is a relationship between the length of the salmon and the number of eggs produced. Although the year-to-year variations in this relationship are not significant, there are significant variations in this relationship between fish from different rivers. The average egg counts corresponding to a fish length of 70 cm (the average length of all salmon handled in the study) on each of the six rivers studied are: Lyon, 4943; Blackwater, 5117; Garry, 5370; Dee, 5495; Conon, 5572; Meig, 6067.

As egg number does not increase linearly with fork length ($L$, in cm), the classification of different rivers by reference to the number of eggs per unit fish length is not possible. However, as the power of $L$ in the following relationships is constant from river to river, then fish of the same length from different rivers may correctly be compared:

| Lyon | $\log_{10}N = 2.3345 \log_{10}L - 0.622$ |
| Blackwater | $\log_{10}N = 2.3345 \log_{10}L - 0.607$ |
| Garry | $\log_{10}N = 2.3345 \log_{10}L - 0.586$ |
| Dee | $\log_{10}N = 2.3345 \log_{10}L - 0.576$ |
| Conon | $\log_{10}N = 2.3345 \log_{10}L - 0.570$ |
| Meig | $\log_{10}N = 2.3345 \log_{10}L - 0.533$ |

Of the six rivers studied, three (the Blackwater, Conon and Meig) are tributaries of the one river system. The differences among these tributaries are of interest in the light of the findings of Heggberget *et al.* (1986) who found genetically differentiated populations within the River Alta.

To assess the order of magnitude of the potential egg deposition on any river, if great accuracy in the final figure is not essential, it may be sufficient to employ the average equation for the above six rivers, namely:

$$\log_{10}N = 2.3345 \log_{10}L - 0.582$$

where $N$ = number of eggs and $L$ = length in cm.

However, Thorpe, Miles and Keay (1984) found among 111 mature females of three river-year and two sea-year age groups from the River Almond that egg number increased linearly with each age grouping. Those that had developed more rapidly in fresh water produced more but smaller eggs at any given body size than slower developers.

It has been assumed that a female salmon makes only one redd and that therefore one redd denotes two salmon – one female and one male (Elson and Tuomi, 1975; Gudjonsson, 1988). However, recent investigations in the Girnock Burn, Aberdeenshire, on spawning salmon marked with acoustic tags have shown that a female salmon may 'cut' as many as six redds and that male salmon may spawn with more than one female (A. D. Hawkins, personal communication).

There appear to be certain limiting factors to spawning which, while not documented for every Atlantic-salmon-producing country, have been recorded in Iceland (Einarsson, 1987) and Greenland (Jonas, 1974) where water temperature and stability of the river bed seem to limit spawning and affect the survival of egg, alevin and fry.

## 2.2 EGG AND FRY SURVIVAL

The eggs deposited in the redds may be under 15–30 cm of gravel and the time required for their hatching ranges from 70 to 160 days depending on water temperature. On hatching, the fish, which is about 2 cm long, is called an alevin and possesses a large yolk sac on its ventral surface. The alevins move about in the gravel as a result of photokinesis and geo- and rheotaxes (L. Dill, 1969; P. Dill, 1977; Brannon, 1965, 1972; Mason, 1976). At first they move obliquely downwards but after a few days the direction of this movement changes and they move obliquely upwards. By the time the fish have emerged from the gravel the yolk sac has been absorbed: they are ready to start feeding and are known as fry. Thorpe *et al.* (1984) found that large eggs gave rise to large first-feeding fry, but that this size advantage was not maintained through the first year of growth. The fry have now entered an environment subject to wide ranges of light intensity and water velocity. Positive thigmotaxis ensures contact with the substrate and aided by positive rheotaxis they are able to avoid immediate displacement downstream by the current.

Water temperature seems to be the most important factor limiting the successful survival of salmon in fresh water. Power (1969) speculates that for northern Canada the survival of salmon may be reduced when there are fewer than 100 days in a year with a mean air temperature of at least 10 °C. In Iceland, salmon only thrive where water temperatures exceed 10 °C for about three months each year. Low water temperatures inhibit the development of the egg and result in a late hatch of alevins. In some Icelandic and Finnish rivers (Niemela, McComas and Niemela, 1985) alevins do not emerge from the gravel until July, giving them a very short time to feed and grow before temperatures drop to a level at which feeding stops. In countries further south, this is only likely to occur in high-altitude streams and probably the factors more likely to limit egg survival are low pH values and high concentrations of suspended solids. In Newfoundland, Chadwick (1982a, b) found that survival from the egg to fry stage was correlated with water temperature and stream discharge. He considered that the present recommended egg deposition of 2.4 eggs/$m^2$ of parr-rearing habitat is inadequate for Newfoundland rivers, yet Chadwick (1985b) refers to a fixed egg deposition rate of 2.4 eggs/$m^2$ being used in all assessments (Marshall, 1984; Randall, 1984) in Canada. However, Elson and Tuomi (1975) estimate the egg deposition for the River Foyle in Ireland to be 1.68 eggs/$m^2$ while Buck and Hay (1984), working on the Girnock Burn in Aberdeenshire, suggest a maximum deposition of 3.4 eggs/$m^2$. On the Girnock Burn, this level of deposition gave an average production of 4000 juvenile migrants (0.07 fish/$m^2$) each season. Symons (1979) suggests modifying egg deposition estimates according to the age of the smolts produced.

After emergence the fry disperse over the 'nursery' area and their survival depends upon availability of space and food (Kalleberg, 1958; Dymond, 1961). During the first few weeks, there is usually a high mortality due to starvation, predation and competition for territories, which together set the 'carrying capacity' of the stream. Studies of fry survival in Scottish streams (Mills, 1964,

1965b, 1969a, 1969b; Egglishaw and Shackley, 1977, 1980) have enabled useful recommendations to be drawn up for the stocking of streams with eggs and fry (Egglishaw *et al.*, 1984). Fish remain in the fry stage for a varying period, but at a length of about 6.5–7.0 cm they develop dark blotches along their sides, known as parr marks, and are now referred to as parr. Allan and Ritter (1975) in their revised salmonid terminology consider that the fry stage ends after dispersal from the redd.

## 2.3   DENSITIES OF FRY AND PARR

Young salmon are territorial and this behaviour has been closely observed by Kalleberg (1958), Keenleyside and Yamomoto (1962) and Leániz (1988). The density and standing crop of salmon fry and parr in a stream depends on this territoriality, and to some extent on water temperature and the gross production of the stream, and also on the presence of other fish species and other environmental conditions such as stream bed stability, water velocity and water depth. Egglishaw and Shackley (1982, 1985) for example, showed that water depth, or some factor associated with water depth, can determine the suitability of a stream habitat for juvenile Atlantic salmon as can type of substrate, food resources, competition and recruitment. Egglishaw and Shackley (1982) found the highest densities of 0+ age salmon in those sections of stream with a high proportion of shallow water. Brown trout (*Salmo trutta*) of 1+ age on the other hand were found in their highest densities where there was a high proportion of deeper water.

Differences in densities of salmon within streams with widely varying physical characteristics can be as great as those between streams. Such differences may be due to food availability, river bed stability or water temperature. For example, on the Laxa í Kjos river system in Iceland, the density of fry and parr in an upstream section of a tributary, the Bugda, immediately below a lake (Meddelfelsvatn) outfall, was several times greater than that in a downstream section of the same tributary a few hundred metres below its confluence with a cold-water tributary. While the resulting lower water temperature in the lower section would have some effect, the additional factor favouring the higher density of fry and parr in the upper section was a rich food supply of larval simuliids feeding on organic drift from the lake (Einarsson, 1987). Elsewhere, the differences may be influenced more by low spawning escapement, bird predation, pollution, land drainage, stream channel excavation or afforestation.

The densities of fry and parr in some Scottish streams have been recorded by Mills (1964, 1969a, 1969b), Mills, Griffiths and Parfitt (1978), Mills and Tomison (1985) and Egglishaw and Shackley (1977). Fry and parr densities have also been recorded for salmon rivers in Iceland (Einarsson, 1987),

**Table 2.1** The mean population densities and standing crops of juvenile salmon in six areas of the Tweed river system, 1984*

| River system | No. of sampling sites | Density (no./m$^2$) Mean range | Standing crop (g/m$^2$) Mean range |
|---|---|---|---|
| Upper Tweed | 42 | 0.25 (0.01–1.7) | 2.3 (0.02–10.6) |
| Middle Tweed | 9 | 0.14 (0.1–0.4) | 2.5 (0.07–6.4) |
| Ettrick | 10 | 0.59 (0.03–1.5) | 4.8 (0.4–12.0) |
| Teviot | 5 | 0.29 (0.01–0.7) | 3.1 (0.04–8.0) |
| Lower Tweed | 8 | 0.02 (0.002–0.1) | 0.9 (0.01–3.2) |
| Till | 5 | 0.08 (0.03–0.2) | 1.1 (0.5–3.6) |

*Source: Mills and Tomison (1985).*

**Table 2.2** Densities of salmon fry and parr in Ireland, Scotland, England and Wales obtained from electro-fishing surveys*

| Details | Mean salmon densities per 100 m$^2$ (maxima in parentheses) | |
|---|---|---|
| **Northern Ireland** | 0+ | 1+ |
| R. Bush | 32.5 (231.3) | 7.1 (24.5) |
| R. Foyle and tributaries | 13.9 (49.0) | 8.2 (46.0) |
| L. Neagh catchment | 56.2 (236.0) | 29.8 (92.0) |
| R. Camowen (pre-drainage) | 78.3 (169.8) | 12.9 (32.8) |
| L. Erne tributaries | 20.6 (71.0) | 11.5 (39.0) |
| **Republic of Ireland** | | |
| Corrib system | 153.8 (730.0) | 20.6 (121.0) |
| R. Erriff | 42.9 (68.0) | 16.6 (25.0) |
| R. Suir | 21.6 (77.8) | 16.6 (46.2) |
| L. Currane catchment | 30.3 (78.0) | 8.4 (15.0) |
| **Scotland** | | |
| R. Tummel | 56.0 (107.0) | 27.8 (36.0) |
| Shelligan burn | 206.2 (309.0) | 33.4 (97.0) |
| **Wales** | | |
| R. Wye | 94.6 (197.2) | 9.5 (20.2) |
| **England** | | |
| R. Exe tributaries | 15.6 (30.1) | 3.3 (6.3) |
| R. Lune | 27.6 (391.6) | 7.5 (70.4) |
| R. Esk (Yorkshire) | 3.6 (15.3) | 2.7 (8.8) |

*Source: Kennedy (1988).*

Finland (Niemela *et al.*, 1985), Wales (Jones, 1970; Gee *et al.*, 1978), England (Nott and Bielby, 1966), Republic of Ireland (Elson and Tuomi, 1975; Browne and Gallagher, 1981, 1987), Northern Ireland (Kennedy and Strange, 1980; Kennedy *et al.*, 1983) and Spain (Ventura, 1988). Table 2.1 shows the variation in the density and standing crop of juvenile salmon in the Tweed river system in Great Britain. Table 2.2 gives the mean fry and parr densities for a number of river systems in Great Britain and Ireland.

Egglishaw and Shackley (1977) showed that over a 10-year period in one Scottish stream the length of salmon fry at the end of the growing season was inversely related to their population density. In another stream, over 8 years, they found that the weight of salmon fry was inversely correlated both to their population density and to the biomass of $1 +$ salmon parr present (Egglishaw and Shackley, 1980). Prouzet (1978) found that in a stream with a steep gradient, growth of salmon fry was density dependent, but in another stream with a lower gradient the biomass was regulated by emigration. In the Miramichi River, New Brunswick, growth of salmon fry was inversely correlated with population density but growth of parr was not (Randall, 1982; Randall and Paim, 1982).

## 2.4   HABITAT SELECTION

Juvenile rearing habitat has been defined as any part of a river accessible to adult salmon which contains a combination of gravel, rubble, cobble or boulder substrate (Elson, 1975) or where at least 10% of the substrate is of particle size greater than 10 cm (Gray, Cameron and Jefferson, 1986). Kennedy (1984a) considered that the physical requirements of juvenile salmon include streams of moderate size. Ideally most of the stream should be taken up by riffles over which the water flows fairly fast. The substrate should be varied with gravel and stones of varied sizes; this ensures a range of current conditions near the bottom and provides obstructions to vision between each salmon parr and its neighbour, thus reducing territorial aggression.

The habitat preference of juvenile salmon tends to show a seasonal change. In the summer months shallow, riffle habitat is preferred while in the colder months, when feeding activity is reduced or stops, the fish move into the deeper water of pools. Allen (1940, 1941) observed this behaviour in the rivers Eden and Thurso, with the movement from shallow to deeper water occurring when water temperatures fell below 7 °C. Gardiner and Geddes (1980) also recorded a change in the habitat of young salmon in the Shelligan Burn (Scotland), finding few young salmon in the stream when temperatures fell below 5 °C. Fish reappeared once water temperature rose above 6–7 °C. However, on the Matamek River in Quebec, Gibson (1978) noticed that parr went into hiding when water temperatures dropped to 10 °C and similar observations were

made by Rimmer, Paim and Saunders (1984) on a small river in New
Brunswick. Rimmer *et al.* (1984) also observed that in summer the stream-bed
stones most closely associated with the individual positions of the juvenile fish
of all ages were always less than 20 cm, and mostly (84–92%) less than
10 cm, in diameter. In autumn, all ages were associated with 'home' stones
(i.e. within their territory) up to 40 cm in diameter, with 65–83% of the stones
exceeding 20 cm; the size of 'home' stones selected increased with fish age in
autumn. Young salmon of all age classes occupied a wide range of water
depths during summer, but were concentrated mainly in depths of 24–36 cm.
In autumn, they occurred in this range almost exclusively. The preference for
certain water velocities was also recorded by these authors. Summer focal
water velocity (velocity at the fish's snout) was predominantly 10–30 cm/s for
0+ fish, 10–40 cm/s for 1+ and 30–50 cm s for 2+ salmon, but during the
autumn it was almost always less than 10 cm/s for all ages. As a result of these
observations, the authors consider substrate size followed by water depth to be
the primary features influencing stream suitability for juvenile salmon in the
autumn.

In very cold rivers, such as those on the western and northern coasts of
Norway, where water temperatures may never exceed 10 °C (Jensen and
Johnsen, 1986) salmon do not react to river temperatures in the same way as,
for example, salmon in the Matamek River, and in some of those Norwegian
rivers (e.g. Saltdaselva and Strygnselva) the lower temperature limit for
growth of salmon is not fixed.

## 2.5  FEEDING BEHAVIOUR AND INTERSPECIFIC COMPETITION

### Feeding behaviour

In a study of the fry and parr in the River Eden, England, Allen (1940, 1941)
has shown that growth takes place from early April until late October but does
not occur during the winter months. This growth can be divided into two
parts, an early period of rapid growth lasting until mid-August in the first year
and mid-July in the second year, and a later period of slow growth. This change
during the summer from rapid to slow growth he felt may be caused either by
the high water temperature or some other external cause, or possibly by
changes within the fish. The former factor governs the availability of the food,
the latter the degree of selection, which tends to increase as the stomach
becomes fuller. In a study of the food, growth and population structure of
young salmon and trout in two Scottish highland streams Egglishaw (1967)
found that the variation in the kind and amount of food in the stomachs of
salmon and trout is very large. A great deal of this variation, and the apparent
selection of food by some fish, can probably be attributed to the distribution or

behaviour of certain benthic organisms and the type of habitat in which the fish are feeding. Egglishaw (1967) found, for instance, that salmon parr feeding in pools in the River Almond contained significantly more emerging Chironomidae and terrestrial organisms than salmon feeding in riffle areas. Both Egglishaw (1967) and Mills (1964) found that brown trout tend to eat more terrestrial organisms than salmon parr. This difference in diet of these two species was also observed by Gibson and Cunjak (1986) in Newfoundland rivers.

Wankowski and Thorpe (1979) used scuba diving techniques in a study of the spatial distribution and feeding of juvenile salmon in rivers of the Central Highlands of Scotland and found that juvenile salmon distribution was closely related to the maximum local current velocity. Drift feeding was the predominant method of acquisition, although foraging on substrate-associated prey also took place where fish themselves were closely associated with the substrate. Swimming and capture forays extended the feeding range to a distance of several fish body lengths from the position being held. The authors also observed that a fish-size-dependent swimming ability was also responsible for segregating different size groups into effectively different microhabitats: larger fish maintained position in faster currents, thus fulfilling to some extent their increased food requirements.

Further underwater observations on the feeding behaviour of salmon parr were made by Stradmeyer and Thorpe (1987) in the River Tilt in Scotland. They found that territories comprised one or more preferred stations on or just above the substrate, from which the fish intercepted drifting particles (75% of feeding) or foraged on the substrate (25%). Drift feeding occurred at the surface (36%), in mid-water (35%) and the remainder at the feeding station. About one-third of the prey particles were attacked directly from the feeding station, and about two-thirds indirectly after preliminary inspection, sometimes involving a drift downstream by the fish. The larger parr (12–15 cm) fed more frequently at the surface, while fish of about 10 cm fed in mid-water or at their stations. It was noticed that surface feeding decreased proportionately during rainfall, and the frequency of feeding increased with temperature. Feeding was depressed in the presence of large brown trout and adult salmon.

The seasonal changes in feeding motivation of parr have been studied by Metcalfe, Huntingford and Thorpe (1986). In a study under experimental tank conditions of the lower modal group of parr (i.e. the smaller of the two size categories occurring in the first autumn of life) it was found that feeding motivation declined through the season, regardless of water temperature, competition or food supply. Fish also reduced the distances over which they would travel to intercept food, thus minimizing the costs of obtaining a maintenance ration.

In a further study Metcalfe *et al.* (1987) investigated the influence of predation risk on feeding motivation and foraging strategy. It was observed that after a brief exposure to a model trout predator, parr changed their foraging strategy markedly in ways that reduced their conspicuousness and hence risk of being preyed upon. After seeing the predator, the salmon were less likely to orientate to passing food particles, and having orientated, were less likely to attack them. They also reduced the extent of their movements by attacking only those particles that came close to them.

### Interspecific competition

There have been a number of investigations of competitive interactions between juvenile salmon and other stream-dwelling fish species, such as brown trout (*Salmo trutta*) and brook trout (*Salvelinus fontinalis* Mitchill).

MacCrimmon, Dickson and Gibson (1983) in a study of interspecific competition between brook trout and young salmon observed a depression in the growth of the salmon in an unproductive cool stream. However, where food was abundant in experimental stream tanks brook trout had no effect on the growth of salmon. In a large river, where there was a diversity of habitat, growth of fry and 1 + salmon parr was not affected by brook trout, but growth of older (2 +) parr was negatively affected by trout (Gibson and Dickson, 1984). These authors concluded from their study that in areas of rapids, generally considered the preferred juvenile salmon habitat, intraspecific competition within year classes of salmon is more severe than interspecific competition from brook trout. In a study of the interactions between young salmon and brown trout in Newfoundland rivers Gibson and Cunjak (1986) found that the two species were spatially segregated: brown trout older than the fry stage occurred in deeper, slower water than salmon. They concluded that the two species apparently are ecologically compatible and competition appears to be minimized by habitat segregation related mainly to water velocity and depth. Within the limitations of the study they found no evidence of negative effects of brown trout on juvenile salmon. However, there is evidence to suggest that there is marked interspecific competition when salmon fry reared in a hatchery are released into the wild. Kennedy and Strange (1980) found that stocked salmon fry had poorer growth and survival when older salmon and brown trout were present. Egglishaw (1983), too, found that salmon fry planted in streams in the Tummel Valley where densities of brown trout were low survived much better than salmon fry in streams with higher densities of trout.

## 2.6   PRECOCIOUS MALE PARR

A varying proportion of male parr attain sexual maturity, and Jones (1959) described their presence on spawning ground in large numbers in November and December. From observations of the spawning behaviour of adult salmon and ripe male parr Jones (1959) concluded that the presence of ripe male parr was an adaptation to ensure fertilization of the eggs in case of inadequate fertilization by adult males. Hutchings and Myers (1985) and Myers and Hutchings (1987) also noted that the sexually mature male parr will successfully fertilize eggs of females in the absence of anadromous (adult) males. They found that no significant differences occurred in the proportion of eggs which can be fertilized by mature male parr and adult males. One of the demographic consequences (Myers, 1984) of these observations is that an increased fishery could eventually completely eliminate anadromous migration in males. However, Myers (1983) also pointed out that increases in the proportion of male parr that mature could be an evolutionary response to fishing pressure.

Parr have two main periods of movement, in spring and autumn/early winter. The autumn movement frequently consists mainly of ripe males (Pyefinch and Mills, 1963). It has been thought that these fish might be the forerunners of the next year's smolt migration, or fish destined for the sea that autumn. Some ripe male parr were tagged at a trap on the River Meig in Scotland, and one was caught two years later at the trap as a grilse, thus indicating that at least some parr were forerunners of the coming year's smolt migration. Shearer (1972) records an autumn seaward movement of parr on the River North Esk, and Saunders and Bailey (1980) interpret downstream movement of parr in autumn as stock-specific behaviour developed to ensure timely arrival at sea the following spring.

It is suspected that not all ripe male parr go to sea, and probably many die while still in fresh water. The mortality rate among mature male parr has been shown to be higher than in immature parr (Österdahl, 1969; Mitans, 1973; Myers, 1984), possibly partly because of reduced lipid levels in the mature parr (Saunders and Sreedharan, 1977). In Newfoundland (Dalley, Andrews and Green, 1983) the incidence of sexual precocity in male salmon was examined in selected rivers from 1974 to 1977. The incidence was variable (12.3–100%), but generally high, particularly in eastern rivers (mean overall incidence was 72.7%). From smolt rivers examined, it appears that too few precocious parr migrate as smolts to contribute to the grilse population. As a result of high mortality associated with maturation in fresh water, rivers with a high percentage of sexually precocious males tend to have a correspondingly high percentage of adult females. Myers (1984) estimated that 60% of potential sea-run male production of one Newfoundland river was lost in this way.

## 2.7  SMOLT MIGRATION

The length of time that salmon parr spend in fresh water before going to sea as smolts in spring varies with the location of the river. In the Hampshire Avon, over 90% of the smolts are yearlings. The age at smolt migration increases towards the north of the salmon's range. In northern Norway Dahl (1910) and Sømme (1941) found the highest smolt ages in the extreme north where smolts of up to 7 years of age occurred. In some rivers draining from glaciers in western Norway the mean smolt age is above 5 years (Jensen and Johnsen, 1986). On the west side of the Atlantic the anadromous Atlantic salmon has its northern range in rivers draining into Ungava Bay in Canada and in the Kapisigdlit River in Greenland. Smolt ages are high in the Ungava Bay region ranging from 4 years to 8 years and with a mean of 5 years. In Iceland smolts go to sea in their third, fourth and fifth year of life. At the time of their seaward migration in Scotland, smolts are entering their third and fourth years (i.e. 2 + and 3 + years), with a few in their fifth year. On some rivers there is a big variation in the age composition of smolts, with older smolts tending to occur in greater proportions in the upper reaches of the river system (Table 2.3). Symons (1979) points out that, with the exception of the Ungava rivers, average smolt age in any particular river can be estimated from the number of days each year on which the temperature reaches or exceeds 7 °C.

**Table 2.3**   Age composition of salmon parr in the Tweed river system in 1984*

| River system† | No. in sample | Percentage of parr in their 2nd, 3rd and 4th year of life and destined to become smolts in the next year | | |
|---|---|---|---|---|
| | | 1+ | 2+ | 3+ |
| Upper Tweed | 60 | 53 | 41 | 6 |
| Ettrick and Yarrow | 65 | 75 | 25 | 0 |
| Middle Tweed | 50 | 85 | 12 | 3 |
| Teviot | 90 | 90 | 10 | 0 |
| Lower Tweed | 45 | 97.5 | 2.5 | 0 |
| Till | 20 | 100 | 0 | 0 |

*Source: Mills and Tomison (1985).
†Listed in order of distance from sea.

The transformation from parr to smolt involves a number of morphological, physiological and behavioural changes which pre-adapt young salmon for life in the sea while they are still in fresh water (Hoar, 1976). In spring, during transformation of the parr to the smolt stage, or smoltification as the process is called, the length–weight relationship of the fish changes, a subcutaneous deposit of guanin is laid down, concealing the parr markings, and the pectoral and caudal fins turn black. Allen (1944) determined the degree of smolt development on the Thurso River, Caithness and found that the average rate of development was about 0.08 per day on a colour scale where 4.0 represents full development.

Elson (1957) presented evidence from both sides of the Atlantic to show that, as a general rule, parr that have reached a certain size (10 cm) towards the end of one growing season are likely to become smolts at the next season of smolt descent. Saunders and Sreedharan (1977) considered that photoperiod is the environmental cue that acts through the endocrine system and affects these changes, resulting in smoltification. In addition to the associated changes in appearance, smolt development consists of the development of susceptibility to migration-producing stimuli. A number of attempts have been made to correlate the onset of the main migrations with various environmental factors such as rainfall, solar radiation and water temperature. The timing appears to be influenced mostly by water temperature (Berry, 1932, 1933; Mills, 1964; Solomon, 1978; Einarsson, 1987), with the run starting in earnest once the water temperature remains above 10 °C. However, in Norway, Jonsson and Ruud-Hansen (1985) found that the start of the smolt migration was not triggered by a specific water temperature or by a specific number of degree-days, but was controlled by a combination of temperature increase and temperature level in the river during spring. They found no significant correlation between smolt descent and water flow, turbidity or lunar cycle. It is possible that there are stock-specific responses to the environmental cue for smolting and to those for triggering migratory behaviour.

It has been found that during the early (April and early May) part of the smolt migration smolt movement is during the hours of darkness but later on (late May and early June) movement occurs during the middle part of the day (Munro, 1965a). It is likely that smolts drop downstream tail first, although in a lake they almost certainly swim actively downstream. At natural falls, traps and screens the fish I have observed have always been heading upstream against the current. The average speed at which they migrate downstream varies between 0.46 and 1.80 km/day (Mills, 1964), the speed varying with the nature of the river; migration through a lake is usually slower (Table 2.4).

Thorpe and Morgan (1978) briefly reviewed behavioural and physiological mechanisms for the control of downstream migration of smolts. They concluded that although these mechanisms imply passive displacement as the primary means of migration, it is likely that active components must also exist, as the rates of travel of smolts through loch systems are only slightly slower than those recorded for river systems.

## 2.8 SMOLT PRODUCTION

Annual smolt production has been estimated in a number of river systems. In Scotland, through an intensive tagging programme on the River North Esk, Shearer (1984a) was able to estimate both annual smolt production and the number of adults surviving to return to home waters. His estimates of natural

**Table 2.4**   Rate of passage of smolts*

| River system | Reach | Distance (km) | Rate of travel Max. (km/day) | Av. (km/day) |
|---|---|---|---|---|
| Thurso | Sleach – Water – Loch Beg (loch) | 2.4 | 0.6 | 0.2 |
| | Dalnaha – Loch Beg (loch) | 4.0 | 4.0 | 0.4 |
| | Dalganachan – Dalnaha (river) | 8.5 | 4.25 | 1.2 |
| Bran | 1961: Achanalt Pass – | | | |
| | L. Luichart (loch) | 11.6 | 0.97 | 0.46 |
| | Caiseachan – L. | | | |
| | Achanalt (river) | 5.2 | 1.73 | 1.04 |
| | 1962: Achanalt Pass – L. | | | |
| | Luichart (loch) | 11.6 | 1.29 | 1.06 |
| | Allt a'Chomair – | | | |
| | Caiseachan (river) | 3.6 | 4.11 | 1.80 |
| Tummel | Dunalastair – Clunie (river and loch) | 16.0 | 5.3 | 0.92 |
| Loire–Allier | | — | 70.0 | 20.0 |

*Authorities: Thurso, Allan (1944); Bran, Mills (1964); Tummel, Struthers, in Thorpe and Morgan (1978); Loire–Allier, Cuinat (1988).*

mortality suggest that smolt survival may be relatively high, with a total return rate between 16% and 46%. Mills (1964) estimated that the annual smolt production from releases of hatchery-reared unfed fry into the River Bran, in which no natural spawning occurred, was in the order of 18 000 smolts. This estimate implied a smolt-rearing capacity of approximately 4.2 per 100 m². In Canada, Symons (1979) estimated the average maximum production of smolts per 100 m² as approximately five for 2 + smolts, two for 3 + smolts and one for 4 + smolts. The minimum egg depositions recommended for the production of these numbers of smolts are 220 per 100 m², 165–200 per 100 m² and 80 per 100 m² for each age of smolt respectively. Assuming that smolt production is equivalent to the numbers of juvenile salmon surviving to two years of age, Gee, Milner and Hemsworth (1978) recorded a maximum smolt production on the River Wye in Wales of 0.043 per m² (95% confidence interval 0.019–0.097). This is estimated to be attained from a fry density on 1 June of 0.75 per m². Symons considered that the likely range of smolt production on both sides of the Atlantic was spread over a wide range from about 1–10 smolts per 100 m², depending on a number of biotic and abiotic factors.

   In estimating smolt production it is not sufficient just to assess the area of the river when calculating rearing habitat. Parr are known to occupy lakes extensively in Newfoundland (Pepper, 1976; Chadwick, 1982a) and in some river systems in Newfoundland 70% of smolt production occurs in lakes (Chadwick, 1985a). A significant smolt production in some Icelandic lakes has

**Table 2.5** Densities of salmon smolts recorded for various river systems

| River system | Density (no. per 100 m²) | Authority |
|---|---|---|
| CANADA | | |
| Miramichi | 4.7 | Elson (1975) |
| Pollet | 6.0 | Elson (1975) |
| Big Salmon | 3.9 | Jessop (1975) |
| Matamek | 2.6 | Gibson and Côté (1982) |
| IRELAND | | |
| Foyle | 8.4 | Elson and Tuomi (1975) |
| NORWAY | | |
| Orkla | 4.1 | Garnås and Hvidsten (1985) |
| Vardnes | 2.9 | Berg (1977a) |
| SCOTLAND | | |
| Bran | 3.5 | Mills (1964) |
| Shelligan | 10.0–22.0 | Egglishaw (1970) |
| Tweed | 11.6 | Mills *et al.* (1978) |
| Girnock Burn | 7.0 | Buck and Hay (1984) |
| SWEDEN | | |
| Ricklea | 1.9 | Østerdahl (1969) |
| USA | | |
| Cove Brook | 3.6 | Meister (1962) |
| WALES | | |
| Wye | 4.3 | Gee *et al.* (1978) |

also been recorded by Einarsson (1987). Densities of smolts recorded for various river systems are shown in Table 2.5.

It seems likely that smolts need some time to become acclimatized to saline conditions. Calderwood (1906a) and others have noticed that smolts may remain in the estuary for a short time for this purpose before entering the sea. There are many rivers that have no estuary, such as those on the north-west coast of Scotland, and here the smolts go straight from fresh to salt water, although as there must be some mixing of fresh and salt water at the river mouth, the transition will not be abrupt. Huntsman and Hoar (1939) observed smolts at the mouth of the Margaree River, Cape Breton Island, Canada, lying completely inactive for a time after entering the sea. Tytler, Thorpe and Shearer (1978) tracked the movements of smolts in the estuaries of two Scottish rivers by using ultrasonic tags. They found that salinities hyperosmotic to smolt blood did not appear to present a significant barrier to the migration of smolts in the Eden estuary. They concluded that the patterns of

movement through tidal reaches will be related to the characteristics of the
estuary of each river system. In the partially-mixed-wedge-flow estuary, the
pattern is likely to be strongly influenced by the tidal changes in the direction
and velocity of water flow. It is also likely that smolts will tend to leave the
estuary on an ebb tide, with no apparent retardation due to increasing salinity.
In a two-layer-flow type estuary where there is a continuous downstream flow
in the freshwater layer independent of the tidal cycle, the pattern of movement
may be a continuation of that found in the upper reaches of the river.

In northern Canadian rivers very low water temperatures in the estuary
may delay the July smolt migration (Power, 1969) at this point until August
when sea surface temperatures finally reach 2–4 °C in Ungava Bay (Dunbar,
1958). Many smolts remain in the estuary all summer and are still there in
September and October, at which time they have attained lengths of 30–35 cm
and weights of 500 g. At this time the differential between river and sea
temperatures disappears, or is reversed, and most smolts have left Ungava Bay.

Chadwick (1988) has shown that the sea age of Atlantic salmon can be at
least partly determined from an examination of the state of development of the
smolt ovaries. It was found, for example, that smolts from one-sea winter
parents had more than 10% stage 5 and 6 oocytes in their ovaries, while
smolts from three-sea-winter parents had none.

## 2.9   PREDATION AND SURVIVAL

### Predation

During the juvenile phase there has been a considerable reduction in the
numbers of the adults' progeny, firstly through density-dependent mechanisms as territories are occupied and those unable to establish such living
quarters are displaced and die from starvation and predation. Predation
continues throughout the parr and smolt stages. Older parr and trout will eat
fry; brown trout, burbot (*Lota lota*) and pike (*Esox lucius*) will consume the parr
and smolts and at times can be serious predators. For example, it was estimated
that 10% of the smolt run on the River Bran, Ross-shire, in 1959 and 1961
was eaten by pike (Mills, 1964). Birds, too, particularly the sawbill ducks
(*Mergus merganser* and *M. serrator*) and the cormorant (*Phalacrocorax carbo*),
can cause serious inroads into the parr and smolt populations (Mills, 1962 and
1965a).

White (1957) basing his calculations on an average weight of salmon parr
of 9 g, estimated that rearing a single American merganser (*Mergus merganser
americanus*) to full growth took 32 kg of fish, of which 46% or 15 kg are young
salmon; the 15 kg is equivalent to 1584 salmon parr. He also estimated that

1200 mergansers shot on the Miramichi River represent an annual consumption of over 1 900 000 salmon parr.

A detailed experiment on the value of merganser control was carried out on the Pollett River, New Brunswick, by Elson (1962). Hatchery-reared Atlantic salmon underyearlings were planted annually for 9 years in a 16 km stretch of the river and the smolt production from each planting was measured by counting descending migrants at a trap at the lower end of the experimental area. The average annual smolt production from the first five annual plantings of between 16 000 and 250 000 underyearlings was 3000. American mergansers and belted kingfishers (*Megaceryle alcyon*) were then controlled, and the average annual smolt production, from the final four plantings of 250 000 underyearlings annually, was nearly 20 000 (13 600–24 300). Control of these birds had thus made possible at least a fivefold increase in average smolt production. However, Lack (1966) felt that, while these birds ate many fish, their ultimate influence on the size of the fish population was not established by Elson, since there was effectively only 1 year of comparable observations before the birds were controlled and the low densities of fish before bird control might have been due to some other factor. Although it is true that in only one year prior to control were 250 000 underyearlings planted, while in the 4 years of control 250 000 were planted annually, Elson stated that the initial plantings (i.e. before bird control) used about 16 000 underyearlings in order to permit maximum survival rates without waste due to overstocking. Later, heavier plantings were used to measure the total capacity of the area to produce smolts. From this study, Elson was able to produce a rule-of-thumb for successful merganser control. The average population density of American mergansers on these streams was about 10 birds per 24 km of stream of 9 m width (about 1 bird per 2 ha) but the effect of control was slight until the population density was reduced to 3 birds per 24 km at 9 m width (about 1 bird per 7 ha). Reduction of the merganser population below this level, however, had an increasingly advantageous effect on smolt production down to a population density of 1 bird per 24 km at 9 m width (about 1 bird per 22 ha). Any further reduction had little effect. This rule-of-thumb was used by Mills (1962) to assess the effect of goosander (*Mergus merganser*) predation on smolts in salmon rivers in northern Scotland. With the increased spread in the distribution of goosanders in Scotland and into north-west England and Wales, considerable concern has been raised regarding goosanders and further studies are in progress. More recently in Canada, Anderson (1986) assessed the impact of merganser predation on Atlantic salmon stocks in the Restigouche river system. He considered that as a direct consequence of the merganser control programme over 3 years about 170 000 smolts and 8400 adults were conserved. However, he found it difficult to find unequivocal correlations between presumed merganser-control-induced smolt increases and returning adults.

More recently Shearer *et al.* (1987) produced a model to assess the effect of predation by sawbill ducks on the salmon stock of the River North Esk. They calculated that the greatest benefit that might be expected by controlling sawbill predation is a 35% increase in the number of adult salmon returning to the river. The authors, however, consider the benefit is likely to be lower than this if only because it is unlikely that all predation by sawbills could be eliminated.

The cormorant (*Phalacrocorax carbo*) has also been shown to prey heavily on smolts and Kennedy and Greer (1988) estimated that total daily predation rates of cormorants, feeding on the River Bush in Northern Ireland, were 1083–2023 wild smolts, 176–382 hatchery smolts and 691–1285 brown trout.

### Survival rates

The survival rates from the egg to the smolt stage are summarized in Table 2.6. Kennedy (1988) produced a model (Fig. 2.1) for the potential production of 2 + smolts based on a range of published annual survival rates per 100 0 + summer fry (summerlings). The summerling stage is that at which the initial high fry mortality has already occurred.

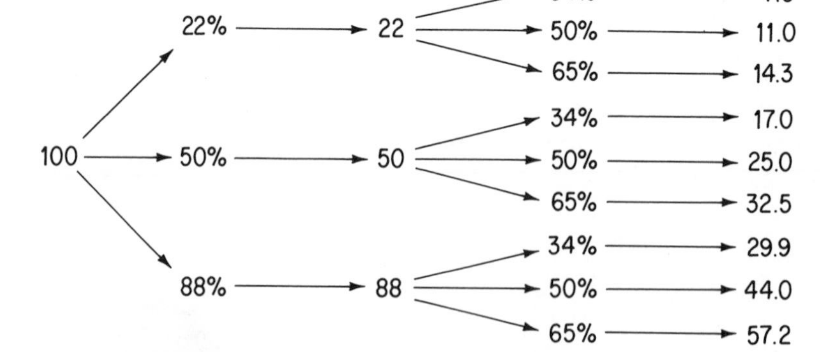

| No. 0+ summer fry | Annual fry survival rate | No. surviving 1+ parr | Annual parr survival rate | No. 2+ smolts produced annually |
|---|---|---|---|---|
| | | | 34% | 7.5 |
| | 22% | 22 | 50% | 11.0 |
| | | | 65% | 14.3 |
| | | | 34% | 17.0 |
| 100 | 50% | 50 | 50% | 25.0 |
| | | | 65% | 32.5 |
| | | | 34% | 29.9 |
| | 88% | 88 | 50% | 44.0 |
| | | | 65% | 57.2 |

**Fig. 2.1** Potential 2 + smolt production from the range of published annual survival rates per 100 0 + summer fry (Kennedy, personal communication).

**Table 2.6** Survival rates at various stages in the life cycle of the salmon*

| Stage | No. of individuals | % Survival Mean | Range |
|-------|--------------------|-----------------|-------|
| Egg | 5000 | – | – |
| Alevin/Fry | 4700 | 94 | – |
| Fry at end of 1st year‡ | 360 | 8 | 5–14 |
| Parr (1+ years old)§ | 140 | 43 | 28–53 |
| Parr (2+ years old)§ | 77 = 52 smolts† | 57 | 44–67 |
| Parr (3+ years old)§ | 39 | 55 | 47–65 |

*Compiled from the work of Hay and Piggins.*
†*Mean survival rate from egg to smolt stage is 1.0%.*
‡*88% of total mortality occurs between March and July.*
§*A proportion of these migrate to sea as smolts.*

The smolts now go to sea and so starts the salmon's ocean life, a phase about which we know relatively little. Much of what we do know is based on conjecture, which is not surprising as it is barely three decades ago that the salmon's sea-feeding areas were first discovered.

# CHAPTER THREE

# Ocean life

*He hauls his trawl from Scilly Isles*
*To the Subarctic shore.*
*No overheads, no crew to pay*
*Whose wives will cry for more, my dears,*
*Wives always cry for more.*
*Through storm and freeze, with cheerful grin,*
*Candelfish and Capelin,*
*He crams the Ocean's goodness in.*

Ted Hughes, 1985
from *The Best Worker in Europe*

## 3.1   POST SMOLTS

Once the smolts have entered the sea little is known of their movements. Reddin (1988) considers that they must move away from their natal streams fairly rapidly because they are infrequently caught in inshore areas. Smolts from northern Swedish rivers have been caught in the Gulf of Bothnia and have been recorded taking insects blown off the land (Lindroth, 1961; Jutila and Toivonen, 1985). Tagged smolts released in these northern Swedish rivers are later recaptured as adults in the southern Baltic by fishermen from a number of Baltic countries (Fig. 3.1). Here the picture of the salmon's migrations is fairly complete, but of smolts entering the North Sea and Atlantic from the rivers of the British Isles, Canada, France, Ireland, Spain and the United States little is known. There are, however, a few interesting records of the capture of post smolts. A considerable number (259), originally tagged as smolts in Maine, have been caught off Nova Scotia, Newfoundland and Labrador (Meister, 1984), and some have been caught off the Kintyre Peninsula in south-west Scotland by pair trawling at night in the surface 10 m (Morgan, Greenstreet and Thorpe, 1986). No doubt the capture of more post smolts will be recorded as salmon research work at sea is extended. It is to be hoped that they do not in future form the basis of a fishery.

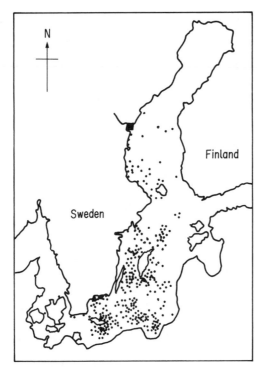

**Fig. 3.1** Map showing recaptures (black dots) from a smolt-tagging experiment in the River Indalsalven (black square) in May 1961 (reproduced with permission from Carlin, 1969).

## 3.2 EARLY RECORDS

Prior to the development of the Greenland and Faroese salmon fisheries the general picture of the salmon's life at sea was pieced together from isolated records. Balmain and Shearer (1956) summarized the records of salmon and sea trout caught at sea. Over the period 1888–1954 there are only 78 Scottish records of salmon taken at sea and these describe the capture of approximately 90 'clean' salmon, ten salmon kelts, five grilse and three pre-grilse. It is perhaps the capture of pre-grilse that was the most interesting as it provides a clue to their distribution during the first year of their life at sea. Salmon captured at sea have been taken in drift nets, trawls and nets set for garfish and prawns.

Between 1954 and 1970 records of incidental captures at sea increased. Many of these records were collected as a result of the examination of the stomachs of other fish. One of the more interesting records was of a pre-grilse taken off the Greenland coast. This fish was probably one of the native stock that breed in Greenland's only salmon river, the Kapisigdlit near Nuuk (Gothab).

Other early records of salmon caught at sea are of (a) a fish taken by the weather ship *Weather Surveyor* when on station 'India' (59°00′N, 19°00′W) in June, (b) four salmon caught by the Danish research vessel *Dana* during drift netting experiments in the Irminger Sea at the end of June 1966 (Jensen, 1967) along the 62°00′N latitude and (c) two fish tagged as kelts in the River Polly on the west coast of Scotland and one fish tagged as a smolt in the River Meig, in north-east Scotland, caught by Faroese line vessels north of the Faroes (Munro, 1969).

## 3.3   DISTRIBUTION

Since the advent of the high-seas fisheries off west Greenland in 1957 and off the Faroes and in the Norwegian Sea some years later, much more is known about the salmon's ocean life. This increased knowledge is due not only to the recapture in some or all of these fisheries of tagged smolts and previously-spawned adults or kelts from Canada, England, France, Iceland, Ireland, Norway, Scotland, Sweden and the United States, but also to the subsequent recapture in home waters of adult salmon tagged in some of the high-seas fisheries. The capture of salmon off the Greenland coast during the autumn months, together with the recapture of a large number of fish which had been tagged in rivers on both sides of the Atlantic supports Menzies' hypothesis (1949) that the feeding ground of Scottish salmon lies in the vicinity of Greenland and that it is shared with salmon from elsewhere in northern Europe and from the Atlantic seaboard of North America. The development of the salmon floating long-line fishery north of the Faroes and in the Norwegian Sea also confirms the views of Carlin (1969) who gave a very interesting account of the migration of salmon from Swedish west coast rivers. He suggested that while the waters off west Greenland may be the main feeding grounds for all the European as well as for the North American Atlantic salmon, there was also some indication of feeding grounds for salmon in the eastern part of the Atlantic, as Swedish fish had been recaptured off the coast of northern Norway far away from what could be expected to be the normal route from Greenland to Sweden. Furthermore, although large numbers of smolts had been tagged in Norway none had been recovered off Greenland, and also Soviet scientists reported catches of young feeding salmon in the open sea far off the Norwegian coast. The recapture of large numbers of tagged Norwegian and Swedish salmon in the Faroese fishery confirmed Carlin's supposition. However, fish tagged as smolts in the rivers of France, Iceland, the Republic of Ireland and the United Kingdom have also been regularly caught in this fishery. Fish from Canada and the USSR have also been recorded in this fishery (Fig. 3.2).

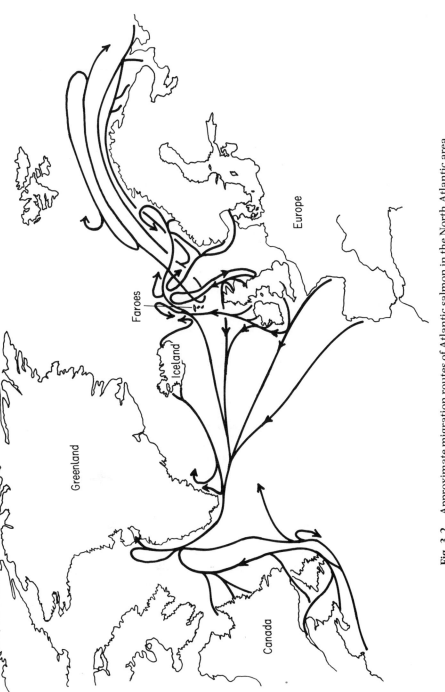

**Fig. 3.2** Approximate migration routes of Atlantic salmon in the North Atlantic area.

Furthermore, recent studies of tagged Atlantic salmon have revealed their inter-continental migrations, with salmon tagged in the United Kingdom being recaptured in North America and salmon tagged in North America being recovered off Norway and the Faroes (Reddin, Shearer and Burfitt, 1984). Recently, a new feeding area for salmon was found to the east of the Newfoundland continental shelf (Reddin and Burfitt, 1984). The sea age composition of the catch and the conditions of the gonads indicated that some of these fish would have matured as grilse. This is the first record of grilse being caught at sea other than in coastal fisheries. Salmon caught off Greenland are destined to return as multi-sea-winter salmon.

Further information on the movements and distribution of salmon in the North Atlantic, particularly in the north-east Atlantic, will be obtained gradually from independent or joint international research cruises by interested countries. Such an experimental cruise at east Greenland (Thorsteinsson and Gudjonsson, 1986) resulted in a number of findings regarding the characteristics of the local salmon fishery and the capture of fish tagged as smolts in Iceland, Ireland and Norway.

Reddin and Shearer (1987) have summarized the results of research vessel surveys over 20 years (1965–85) in the north-west Atlantic from latitude 43° to 70°. They used data from research surveys up to 1972 reported by May (1973), combined with studies in the area of the Grand Bank of Newfoundland (Reddin and Burfitt, 1984; Reddin, 1985) and Irminger Sea (Møller Jensen and Lear, 1980) (Fig. 3.3). Salmon were found in the spring in surface water of the north-west Atlantic from the southern edge of the Grand Bank to slightly south of Cape Farewell, Greenland. The most westerly position where salmon were caught closely follows the edge of the Arctic pack ice in spring (May, 1973). Reddin (1988) refers to two locations where salmon have been found in abundance during spring. One of them is located 500 km east of the Strait of Belle Isle. The other is located slightly to the east of the 200 m depth contour along the eastern edge of the Grand Bank (Fig. 3.4). In late summer and autumn, non-maturing salmon are concentrated along the west Greenland coast from the inner coastal fjords to between 45 and 60 km offshore.

Information on salmon distribution in the north-east Atlantic has been obtained from the Faroese floating long-line fishery. Jákupsstovu *et al.* (1985) noticed that multi-sea-winter salmon were present in higher concentrations in the colder northern part of the Norwegian Sea compared to the area to the south, where younger fish were present.

## 3.4   MIGRATIONS AND MOVEMENTS

The mystery of how the salmon find their way in the ocean and eventually back to their parent rivers still needs to be solved. It is suspected that they may

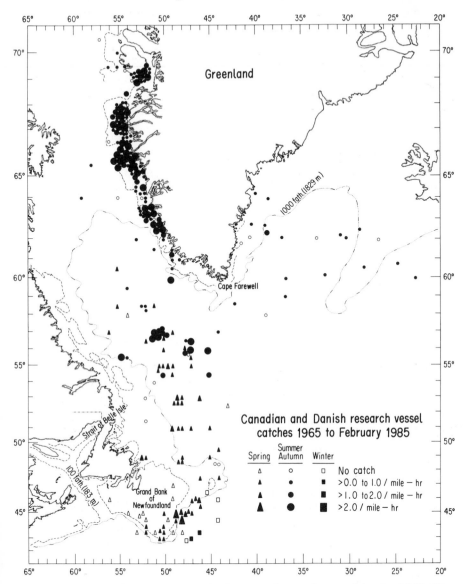

**Fig. 3.3** Research vessel catches of salmon in the north-west Atlantic, 1965–85 (reproduced with permission from Reddin, 1988).

be able to sense the gradient in electric potential generated by the movement of an ocean current in the earth's magnetic field (Rommel and McLeave, 1973; Stasko, Sutterlin, Rommel and Elson, 1973). Sensitivities close to that required have already been demonstrated in this species. Stewart (1978) put forward a

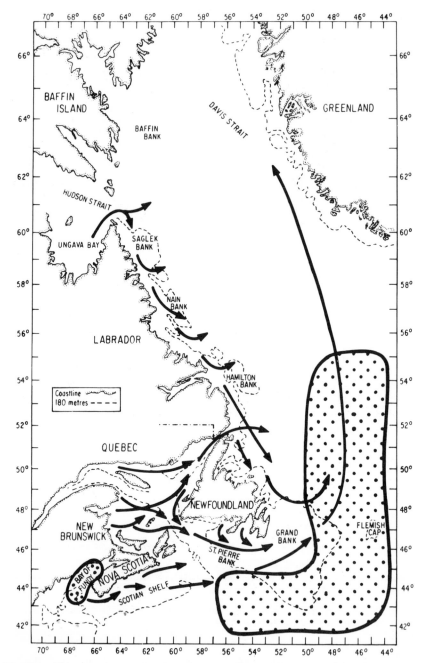

**Fig. 3.4** The migration routes for salmon smolts away from coastal areas showing possible overwintering areas and movement of multi-sea-winter salmon into the West Greenland area (reproduced with permission from Reddin, 1988). Arrows indicate the path of movement of the salmon, and dotted area indicates the overwintering area.

theory involving gyres or rotating ocean currents. Stewart suggested that when a smolt leaves coastal waters it will come within the influence of an oceanic gyre in which it will drift along. At certain times it may leave and rejoin it or even transfer to other associated gyres. The ultimate result, if it were to keep within its original gyre, would be its return to the point at which it embarked as a smolt. The lack of oceanic gyres owing to the absence of integral land masses is the explanation Stewart gives for the failure of Atlantic salmon to establish sea-going populations when introduced into the Southern Hemisphere. Certainly there are a number of current systems in the North Atlantic (Fig. 3.5) and Reddin (1988) refers to salmon being found concentrated in the Labrador Sea gyre throughout the year.

Reddin (1988) has been able to describe the migration routes of North American salmon very fully as a result of many ocean surveys and tagging experiments:

'The salmon stocks in the Northwest Atlantic consist primarily of two components: one that will mature as grilse and the other that will mature as two sea-winter (2SW) or older salmon. At the time of smolt migration salmon of North American origin that will mature as 2SW or older salmon enter the surface waters of the Northwest Atlantic from the Connecticut River, USA, in the south to the Kapisigdlit River, Greenland, in the north. The immature post-smolts from rivers south of Labrador migrate northward throughout the summer, away from the warmer areas to the south up into the cooler waters of the Labrador Sea (e.g. as has been shown for Maine and Quebec salmon stocks by Meister, 1984 and Caron, 1983). These salmon spend much of their time feeding in water temperatures suitable for growth on the abundant food resources in the eddy system bounded by the Labrador, North Atlantic, Irminger and West Greenland currents.

'During their second summer in the sea some of these non-maturing one sea-winter (1SW) salmon move northwards to an area extending from the northern Labrador Sea up into the Davis Strait and Irminger Sea. There are also non-maturing 1SW salmon caught in the Newfoundland–Labrador fishery. In most years, if coastal water temperatures are suitable, they will move close into the fjords along the coast of West Greenland.

'In the autumn, salmon move south either through the Labrador Sea or along the Labrador coast (Reddin and Dempson, 1986) to occupy an area in winter and spring about 480 km east of the Strait of Belle Isle.' (Fig. 3.6).

Martin and Mitchell (1985) proposed an interesting hypothesis that the temperature of the Subarctic influences the migratory pattern and that fish travel further into the Arctic/Subarctic only during those years when the minimum temperature remains above 2 °C.

The question is often raised whether or not salmon shoal while feeding at sea. From detailed monitoring of salmon long-line haulbacks and analysis of

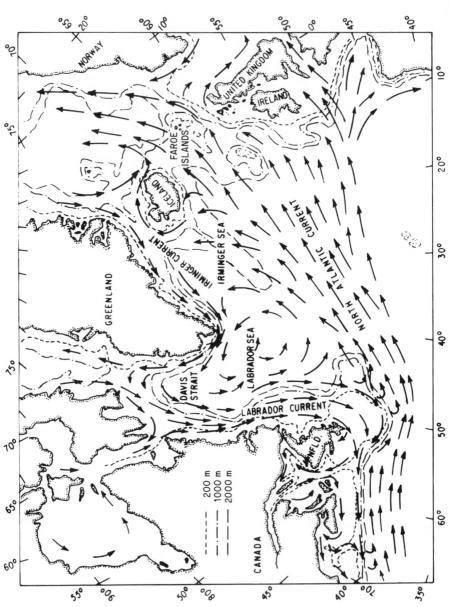

**Fig. 3.5** The main surface currents in the northern part of the North Atlantic (adapted from Templeman, 1967, and Stasko *et al.*, 1973:

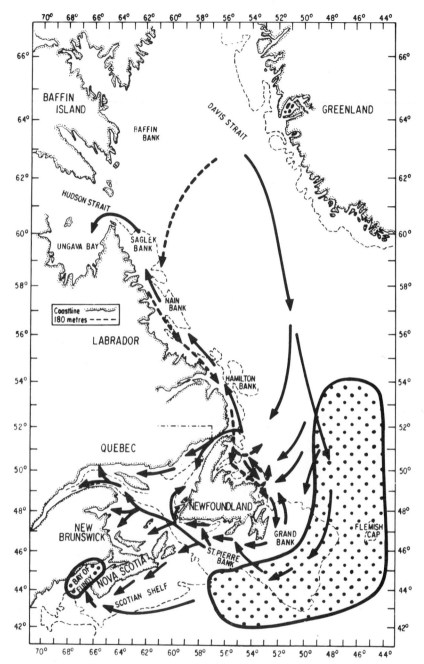

**Fig. 3.6** The migration routes for salmon from West Greenland and overwintering areas on return routes to rivers in North America (reproduced with permission from Reddin, 1988). Solid arrows indicate migration in mid-summer and earlier; broken arrows indicate movement in late summer and autumn; dotted areas are the wintering areas.

recapture data on salmon tagged as smolts Jákupsstovu *et al.* (1985) concluded that: (a) salmon do not appear in large shoals while feeding and (b) salmon from the same smolt groups (tagged and released the same day) do not remain in a single shoal throughout their sea-going phase.

The vertical and horizontal movements of salmon at sea have been investigated to a limited extent by Jákupsstovu (1988). Depth-sensitive tags were used to obtain the vertical movements of three fish. After release all salmon dived very rapidly to a depth of more than 100 m, most probably due to stress from the handling and tagging. One of the fish, after the deep dive, ascended slowly and reached the top 10 m surface layer 4 hours after release. One of the other salmon was tracked for $5\frac{1}{2}$ days. After the initial deep dive this fish ascended to a depth of approximately 40 m where it stayed for the next 50 hours, interrupted only by irregular visits to the surface. Following this, the salmon stayed at the surface for 2 days. During the last $1\frac{1}{2}$ days it made some very rapid dives to more than 150 m (the limit of the depth sensitivity of the tag), and after some time made equally rapid ascents to the surface.

The horizontal movements of the two salmon tracked were apparently directional – one towards the west at an average speed of half a knot (1.9 m/s) and the other towards the north-east. The swimming speeds over ground of two of the tracked salmon indicated periods of high activity mostly during daytime and low activity during the evening and night.

## 3.5  ENVIRONMENTAL CONDITIONS AND ABUNDANCE

Cushing (1983) and Dunbar (1981) have shown that climatic changes can affect the distribution and abundance of many species of marine fish. Changes in the climate may affect the sea surface water temperature, the strength of the ocean currents and, through increase in the amount of melting ice, the salinity. Any of these factors can influence food availability, survival, growth, maturation and activity. Dunbar and Thomson (1979) attributed the presence and absence of salmon at west Greenland to climatic change. Reddin and Murray (1985) and Reddin and Shearer (1987) also showed that the abundance of salmon at west Greenland is affected by environmental conditions in January and August in the north-west Atlantic and the cold water (less than 3–4 °C) can act as a barrier to salmon migration. In colder years fewer salmon move into the west Greenland area from the Labrador Sea than in warmer years. Reddin and Murray (1985) considered that the low catches at west Greenland in 1983 and 1984 can be partly attributed to colder-than-normal water temperatures.

Reddin (1988), from the results of analysis of sea surface and air surface temperature in the north-west Atlantic in January and March, suggested that environmental conditions in this region during the winter may have some influence on total salmon production. This is also the situation in the north-east Atlantic. In this region, Scarnecchia (1984a) obtained significant correlations between the variations in climate and hydrography with declines in primary production, standing crop of zooplankton and with reduced abundance and altered distribution of pelagic forage fishes and salmon catches.

Temperature may also be linked to sea age at maturity (Saunders, Henderson, Glebe and Loudenslager, 1983), and Martin and Mitchell (1985) found that an increase in temperature in the Subarctic (Grimsey Island, Iceland) is associated with large numbers of older (multi-sea-winter) salmon and fewer young salmon (grilse) returning to the Aberdeenshire Dee in Scotland (Fig. 3.7). They also observed a 4-year periodicity in the grilse catch data. Reddin (1988) found that this change in the proportion of multi-sea-winter salmon and grilse coincided with recent events in Canada where grilse: salmon ratios have decreased coincidental with a colder marine climate. Scarnecchia (1984b) also found for Icelandic salmon runs highly significant relationships between mean June–July sea temperatures and the catch of salmon in the following year.

## 3.6 FEEDING

The sea food of salmon consists chiefly of fish such as capelin and sand eels and large zooplankton organisms, particularly euphausids and amphipods. There were a few early records of the food of salmon caught at sea but most information on the sea diet of salmon has been acquired since the advent of the fisheries off west Greenland, at the Faroes and in the Norwegian Sea. Pyefinch (1952) records the following organisms from a pre-grilse caught off the Faroes – amphipods (*Themisto gracilipes*), euphausids (*Thysanoessa longicaudata*) and sand eels. Other early records come from salmon caught in the Irminger Sea and off west Greenland. Fish in the Irminger Sea had been feeding on amphipods (*Themisto gaudichaudi*) and squid (*Brachioteuthis riisei*), while off west Greenland fish had been taking mainly (86%) capelin (*Mallotus villosus*) (Shearer and Balmain, 1967).

Reddin (1988) refers to salmon off west Greenland feeding on capelin and sand eels (sand lance) in coastal waters, while in the Labrador Sea herring, barracudina (*Paralepis coregonides borealis*), amphipods, euphausids and squid make up the major portion of the diet (Templeman, 1968; Lear, 1972b; Lear and Christensen, 1980). Reddin (1988) reported that salmon caught over the Grand Bank were feeding on capelin and sand lance; while over oceanic depths to the east of the Grand Bank salmon were feeding on barracudina, black smelts and amphipods. In the coastal waters of Newfoundland salmon feed mainly on herring, capelin and sand eels, while in Labrador pteropods, sand

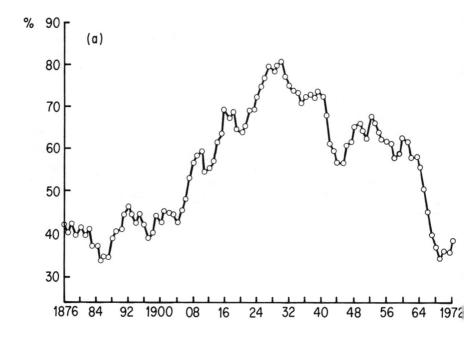

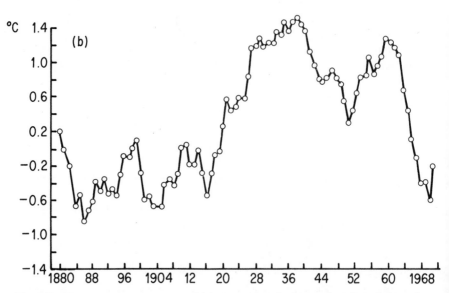

Fig. 3.7   Five-year running means of (a) percentage of salmon in total catch from the same smolt year (Aberdeen Harbour Board data) and (b) annual sea surface temperature anomaly at Grimsey Island, Iceland (reproduced with permission from Martin and Mitchell, 1985).

eels, young cod and capelin are the main food (Lear, 1972b). Reddin (1988) concludes from this wide variety of prey species that adult salmon are opportunistic feeders and prey on whatever organisms are present.

The same conclusion can be reached for salmon feeding in the north-east Atlantic. Struthers (1970, 1971) examined the stomach contents of 272 salmon caught by long-line baited with sprats. The overall picture given by the two years of results is that amphipods and euphausids were the main food items. Hislop and Youngson (1984) in a more recent study of the diet of 48 salmon taken in the Faroese long-line fishery found that the main food organisms were amphipods (*Parathemisto* spp.) euphausids, Myctophidae (lantern fish), capelin and *Maurolicus muelleri* (pearlsides). The difference between the diet of the salmon examined by Struthers and that of the fish examined by Hislop and Youngson probably exists because, although all the fish were caught at the same time of the year, the fish taken by Hislop and Youngson came from grounds considerably to the north.

A much larger number (1145) of stomachs from salmon caught in northern Norwegian waters were examined by Hansen and Pethon (1985). The fish were caught off the shelf of Helgeland/Trøndelag, and in the oceanic waters off Andenes. The most important food items found in fish caught in the Helgeland/Trøndelag area were euphausids and hyperid amphipods, while the myctophid *Benthosema glaciale*, the squid *Gonatus fabricii* and euphausids were found most frequently in the salmon caught off Andenes. Most salmon had preyed on only one species and few stomachs contained three or more prey species.

Some information is available on the food of salmon caught in Scottish inshore waters (Fraser, 1987). The food of Scottish drift-net-caught salmon included polychaete worms (*Nereis* spp.), amphipods, euphausids (*Meganyctiphanes norvegica*) and herring, sprats, whiting and sand eels. Fraser (1987) refers to the presence of sand eels (*Ammodytes marinus*) in the stomachs of a proportion of salmon caught in bag nets set off the west coast of Scotland and suggests that either there is a local feeding stock of salmon or fish feed during migration from distant waters.

Thurow (1968), in a study of the food, behaviour and population mechanism of Baltic salmon, estimated that a 'clean' salmon more than 60 cm long consumes not less than 50 g of food a day. He also estimated that more than 16 000 tons (14 545 tonnes) of sprats are eaten by the exploitable part of the Baltic salmon stock in a year. He considered that the growth rate of adult salmon is determined largely by the amount of food available during the first few months in the sea. This is a particularly important point to which Thorpe (1984) refers when considering food available to smolts during the apparently critical period of the first 30–40 days at sea. In experiments with young Atlantic salmon Wankowski and Thorpe (1979) found that this species was very precise in its choice of size of food item and that it grew successfully only when eating particles of this preferred size. That size was defined by the maximum width of the prey animal, and throughout the 2-year period of freshwater growth salmon selected prey with a width equivalent to 2.2–2.6% of their own body length. Since the jaw size, mouth gape, and gill-raker spacing maintained the same proportional relationships to body size during the sea phase as they had done in fresh water, it seemed reasonable to them to predict that in the ocean the optimal prey size would remain at 2.2–2.6% of fish body size.

On the basis of this Browne *et al.* (1983) examined the probable vulnerability of several fish species whose juveniles have been reported as present in the stomachs of salmon taken at sea. Species such as sprat (*Sprattus sprattus*) apparently grow fast enough to be at risk for a relatively brief period (Fig. 3.8) whereas 0 + herring (*Clupea harengus*) are an almost ideal size as prey for salmon throughout their first 12 months at sea (Fig. 3.9). This prediction seems to be confirmed by Morgan, Greenstreet and Thorpe (1986) who found that post smolts (16.7–20.0 cm long), caught off the Kintyre Peninsula during

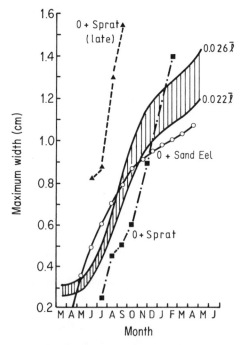

**Fig. 3.8** Width growth of potential prey species of juvenile Atlantic salmon at sea (sprat and sand eels). The hatched area indicates 0.022–0.026 times the mean length ($\bar{l}$) of salmon growing at sea, and represents the range of optimal prey widths to achieve that growth (after Browne *et al.*, 1983, and Morgan *et al.*, 1986).

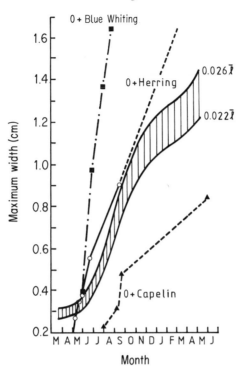

**Fig. 3.9** As Fig. 3.8 but for herring, capelin and blue whiting (after Browne *et al.*, 1983, and Morgan *et al.*, 1986).

June by pair-trawling at night in the surface 10 m, were feeding chiefly on 2–6 cm sand eels.

However, large zooplankton organisms form a significant part of the diet of salmon so a total reliance by post smolts on fish is probably unlikely particularly in the light of evidence on the feeding of post smolts in the Baltic. However, there has been some concern over the effects of industrial fishing for small species of fish such as young herring, blue whiting, myctophids and sand eels on the populations of these species; any significant reduction in their numbers could conceivably affect the survival and growth of salmon in certain areas (Mills, 1987a).

Reddin and Carscadden (1982) looked at the possible interactions of salmon and capelin in relation to their ecology. Adult capelin are important, but not exclusive, components of the diet of adult salmon. Possible relationships between salmon and abundance of capelin on which they might have been feeding were tested by correlation analysis, but none was significant. The authors could not attribute the poor sea survival of the 1977 smolt class from

Canadian rivers to the recent decline of capelin through poor recruitment. However, since the prey species for post-smolt salmon are unknown and mortality on the 1977 smolt class may have occurred during the post-smolt stage, low capelin abundance could not be completely eliminated as a factor contributing to the failure of the 1977 smolt class.

## 3.7   PREDATION

There is very little information on predation on salmon in the sea. Salmon have been found in the stomachs of large fish such as the skate (*Raia batis*), halibut (*Hippoglossus vulgaris*), ling (*Molva molva*), cod (*Gadus morrhua*), porbeagle shark (*Lamna cornubica*) and Greenland shark (*Somniosus microcephalus*). Two salmon recovered from one porbeagle shark weighed 2.5 kg and 3.6 kg respectively, while those taken by cod ranged from 15 to 45 cm in length. The smallest of these fish were little more than smolts and Piggins (1959) has recorded another member of the cod family, the pollack or lythe (*G. pollachius*), taking smolts. It has been suggested that squid could be serious predators of adult salmon and they have been observed in appreciable numbers in the salmon feeding grounds north of the Faroes in some years. Bass (*Dicentrarchus labrax*), too, have been recorded taking smolts in Irish estuary waters (Kennedy, 1954). Probably predation is most serious at the post-smolt stage and once salmon assume larger proportions the number of species of animal able to eat them decreases. Wheeler and Gardner (1974) made a survey of the literature and compiled an account of recorded fish predators on salmon and from this it would seem that sharks are the most important predator. However, investigations on mortality from predation at the post-smolt stage are likely to be of greatest importance.

To this end Morgan *et al.* (1986) examined the stomachs of 763 dogfish (*Squalus acanthias*) caught off the Kintyre Peninsula during June, shortly after emigration of smolts from the local rivers, but found that none had eaten smolts. An extensive study of predation on post smolts by cod, saithe (*Gadus virens*) and sea trout in Norwegian fjords was undertaken by Hvidsten and Møkkelgjerd (1987). Cod, which are thought to assemble in the Surna estuary in the spring, were found to prey heavily on smolts, and a total mortality of up to 24.8% was found in a small restricted area.

Predation on post smolts in the Baltic Sea has been investigated by Valle (1985) who found that Caspian terns (*Hydroprogne tschegrava*) and various species of gull were the main predators.

It has been said that porpoises and dolphins could be predators of salmon, but there is no record of these marine mammals having taken them. However Lindroth (1950, 1965a), in attempting to explain the fluctuations in Swedish salmon catches, tried to correlate degree of ice cover on the Baltic with salmon catch. He considered that in winters when there was complete ice cover on the Baltic there would be no predation on salmon by porpoises and consequently more salmon would survive.

One marine mammal that is an important salmon predator is the grey seal (*Halichoerus grypus*). Rae (1960) gives a very full account of the distribution of both the grey seal and the common seal (*Phoca vitulina*) and their relation to the Scottish fisheries. It was found that there was considerable damage to fish, nets and fishing power and probably the seals also diverted fish from the nets. Rae and Shearer (1965), on the basis of the number of seals seen by fishermen in the vicinity of the nets when they are being fished, estimated that 147 888 · salmonids had been killed by seals on the Scottish east coast from 1959 to 1963. Although grey seals are protected in Scottish waters they can be shot when in the vicinity of coastal salmon nets. Up until recently there was an annual cull of grey seal pups on the breeding grounds, but this caused so much concern to 'conservationists' and animal-rights followers that the practice was discontinued. A recent government report on the grey seal in Scotland suggested that salmon were not an important component of the animals' diet which it alleged consisted chiefly of sand eels.

## 3.8   SEA AGE AND TIME OF RETURN TO HOME WATERS

Several authors have noticed a possible relationship between the river age at smoltification and the subsequent sea age at the return to fresh water. Calderwood (1925) commented that the oldest smolts tended to return soonest to fresh water. Hutton (1937) reached a similar conclusion and propounded what he called 'the inverse ratio theory of river and sea life', which supposes that the total age (smolt age + sea age) at maturity tends to be constant. There has been much work tending both to support and to refute this theory and the subject is competently reviewed by Gardner (1976).

More recently, Shearer (1984b) has shown that on the North Esk there is a correlation between the calendar date when a fish returns to fresh water within its own sea age group and its river age, irrespective of whether the fish returns as a one-sea-winter or multi-sea-winter (MSW) fish. The longer the fish has spent in fresh water, the earlier it is likely to return within its own sea age group. Thus, few MSW fish derived from one-year-old smolts are caught before May and few grilse derived from one-year-old smolts are caught before July. In general, the monthly average smolt age of each sea age group decreases throughout its migrating season. Over the last 20 years there has been a general decline in average smolt age. Shearer (1984b) found that the relationship between sea age and time of return is less well defined. However, few one-sea-winter fish are caught before June and few three-sea-winter fish are caught after June. In his review of factors which may influence the sea age and maturation of Atlantic salmon, Gardner (1976) considers the evidence that this timing is under either genetic or environmental control. The whole subject is still confused and much more work is required to unravel its complexity.

## 3.9   COASTAL MOVEMENTS

A wealth of literature exists on the coastal movements of adult salmon that have been caught and tagged off shore. The results of the Scottish tagging operations have been summarized by Calderwood (1940). Similar experiments have been conducted off the coasts of Norway and Canada and in the Baltic. The results of many of these experiments have been summarized by Menzies (1949) and Carlin (1969). Other tagging experiments have been performed off the east coast of Scotland and the Irish coast. Most of the results of the Irish investigations have been reviewed by Went (1964a).

The value of these tagging operations has been to provide data on the coastal movements of adult salmon, the general direction of these movements and the rate of migration. Pyefinch and Woodward (1955) suggest that the proportion of fish recaptured in their experiment off the Scottish east coast gives some indication of the proportion of catchable stock removed along a heavily-netted section of coast and that the rate of recapture gives some idea of the rate at which salmon penetrate the barrage of coastal and estuarine nets.

The coastal movements of individual returning Atlantic salmon have been studied by Hawkins, Urquhart and Shearer (1979) who tagged six grilse with ultrasonic transmitters and tracked them by means of directional hydrophones mounted beneath two small boats. In the open sea, the fish generally moved with the tidal currents. In the vicinity of the river, the behaviour changed and the fish swam against the current, eventually entering the river mouth. The transition from full sea water to fresh water was rapid and without any period of adaption. In reaching the river mouth, the salmon often passed through lines of bag and stake nets demonstrating that these nets are rather inefficient.

Ikonen (1986) found that the spawning migration of salmon in the coastal waters of the Gulf of Bothnia is guided at least partly by thermal fields in the surface layer of the sea. This dependence on a water temperature gradient may well be an important factor in influencing the movement of fish into fresh water. Ikonen's findings confirm those of Westerberg (1984) who also suggested that salmon orientate at least partly by following the thermal field. It is interesting to note Ikonen's views concerning the efficiency of coastal nets in the context of the findings of Hawkins *et al.* (1979), as Ikonen suggests that if salmon bag nets were placed across the temperature field along which salmon migrate, they might be very effective.

**Table 3.1** Estimates of survival of salmon at sea for two rates of smolt mortality and two rates of monthly marine mortality for (Ireland) a predominantly grilse (1SW) stock and (Scotland) a stock composed of approximately 60% 2SW fish*

| No. of smolts | Smolt mortality | No. of surviving post smolts | Monthly marine mortality† | No. surviving to feeding grounds | No. of adult salmon surviving to return to home waters‡ | | | | |
|---|---|---|---|---|---|---|---|---|---|
| | | | | | Ireland (1SW:2SW ratio approx. 9:1) | | Scotland (1SW:2SW ratio approx. 4:6) | | | |
| | | | | | 1SW | 2SW | (1SW:2SW ratio approx. 4:6) 1SW | 2SW | |
| 100 | 0.50 | 50 | 0.02 | 40 | 32 | 4 | 13 | 20 |
| 100 | 0.50 | 50 | 0.01 | 45 | 39 | 4 | 16 | 25 |
| 100 | 0.25 | 75 | 0.02 | 60 | 49 | 5 | 20 | 30 |
| 100 | 0.25 | 75 | 0.01 | 68 | 58 | 6 | 25 | 38 |

*Source: Kennedy (personal communication).
†Marine mortality was assumed to have acted for approximately 10 months to the feeding grounds, approximately 14 months for 1SW return to home waters and approximately 24 months for 2SW return to home waters.
‡No estimates for exploitation on the feeding grounds have been incorporated in this model.

*Ocean life*

## 3.10  SURVIVAL RATES

Kennedy (personal communication) assumes that, in the absence of firm data, the natural mortality during the smolt and post-smolt phase is normally within the range 25–50%. A lack of information on accurate values for the natural marine mortality rate after the post-smolt stage has led to these being estimated by the North Atlantic Salmon Working Group at between 0.01 and 0.02 per month (Anon., 1987a). Using these values, Kennedy calculated how many adult salmon would be expected to return to home waters if there was no exploitation on the feeding grounds at Faroes and Greenland (Table 3.1). The figures were calculated separately for two stocks representing the predominantly grilse stock found in home water catches off Ireland and the majority multi-sea-winter stock found in Scottish home water catches.

# CHAPTER FOUR

# Return to the river

*Then in from Ocean's curve he brings*
*His National Gross Achievement*
*Even the miracle of two fishes*
*Cries: ''Tis past believement, my dears,*
*'Tis simply past believement!'*
*Nobody's had to lift a hand!*
*No prayer, no contract, no command,*
*And he could feed the entire land!*

Ted Hughes, 1985
from *The Best Worker in Europe*

## 4.1 HOMING INSTINCT

Probably one of the most intriguing aspects of the salmon's life history is its homing instinct. A Scottish priest, Hector Boece, in his *History of Scotland*, published in Latin in 1527 and translated into Scots by John Bellenden in 1536 as the *History and Croniklis of Scotland*, refers to adult salmon returning to the place where they were born:

They have a fervent desire and apetite to return to the places where they were born. Because many of the Waters of Scotland are full of waterfalls, as soon as they come to a fall they leap. Those that are strong or leap well, get up through the fall, and return to the place where they were bred, and remain there until their breeding season.

A Norwegian priest, Peder Clausson Friis, wrote in 1595 of the habit of salmon returning to their birthplace. However, Professor Hawkins of Aberdeen considers it possible that the behaviour of the salmon was well known at that time to most men of the church, perhaps either through some earlier ecclesiastical text or from local hearsay.

According to Izaak Walton, the return of the salmon to its parent river had already been established by 1653 by 'tying a riband or some known tape or thread in the tail of smolts and catching them again when they came back to the same place usually six months after'. Russel (1864, p. 54) refers to smolt-marking experiments on the Tay in 1854, 1855 and 1856. The marking was by fin mutilation, and while a small number of adult salmon were subsequently recaptured bearing marks on the fins that could have been due to this earlier fin-clipping, the results were considered inconclusive. The tagging experiments carried out on the River Tay in 1905 and 1906 by P. D. H. Malloch of Perth were among the first serious marking investigations carried out anywhere in the world (Malloch, 1910). About 1.7% of the marked smolts were recaptured in the Tay as adult fish, thus demonstrating their return to their parent river. Some marked fish were, however, caught in other rivers which shows that the homing instinct is not always 100%. Since these early experiments many smolt-marking investigations have been carried out in Scotland, England, Canada, Ireland, Norway and Sweden, and all have demonstrated this homing instinct.

Many theories have been put forward to explain the way in which salmon find their way back to their parent river. Calderwood (1903a, b) believed temperature was an important factor determining the choice of tributary or main stream. Others considered that current, temperature, quality of water and the amount and direction of light were all important factors influencing migration. Some workers suggested that the salmon on its return is responding to the carbon dioxide gradient of a fresh–salt water gradient while others believe that migratory fish follow a salinity gradient as they move upstream and that spawning takes place near the point where the salt content of the water is at a minimum. Probably the theory which has most acceptance is one derived from the work of Hasler and Wisby (1951), Hasler (1954) and Groves, Collins and Trefethen (1968) which demonstrates the importance of stream odours in the orientation of fish and dependence upon the intact function of the olfactory organ. This implies that the fish are guided by odour trails back to their spawning grounds. The substances responsible for these trails have been suggested to emanate from the plants and minerals characteristic of the home-stream water (Hasler, 1966; Scholz *et al.*, 1976; Hasler, Scholz and Horrall, 1978). However, this theory is not new and more than a hundred years ago Buckland (1880) suggested that salmon were assisted by their power of smell to find their way in the ocean and also to find their parent river. Døving, Jonsson and Hansen (1984) demonstrated from studies of the effect of anosmia on the migration of smolts in fresh water that the olfactory sense is not essential for smolt navigation through rivers and lakes.

Huntsman (1952) considers that salmon return to their breeding grounds by a wandering mechanism rather than a homing mechanism. Huntsman tagged migrating smolts from two branches of the Moser River in Nova Scotia. On return as adults, the marked fish of both kinds ascended both branches but on average 80% of the fish did ascend the home rather than the foreign branch. In the sea, the marked Moser salmon were taken mostly in the Moser outflow, but they were also taken in the outflows of certain neighbouring rivers in both directions along the Nova Scotian coast, which they would readily reach in wandering. However, they were not taken in one neighbouring river, the St Mary River, which drains country very different geologically and agriculturally from that drained by the Moser River and other neighbouring rivers. Huntsman considers that these facts indicate that in the sea Moser salmon avoid very foreign water, but not water sufficiently similar to the home water. He also found that the smolt tagging showed that many foreign fish, presumably from neighbouring rivers, also ascended the Moser River above the head of tide, sometimes exceeding the native fish in numbers. Otterström (1938) found that the salmon in the West Jutland rivers were partly of local and partly of foreign origin. Huntsman considered that home water does not direct the fish home but may stop the wandering and that very foreign water may actually be avoided by the fish. Other evidence of straying has been produced by Pyefinch and Mills (1963), Mills (1966, 1968) and Carlin (1969).

Another interesting aspect of homing instinct is that fish reared in one river or in a hatchery fed by one river, and then released in another river, sometimes very far away and often under such conditions that they will leave this second river almost immediately, have returned to the river in which they were released. This suggests that the memory of the smell of the home water is not imprinted during their early river life, but during a few days before entering the sea or on their downstream migration. This phenomenon has been observed from the release of Scottish hatchery-reared fish and by Carlin (1969).

Carlin points out that the effect of this imprinting at the moment of leaving the river is, however, not confined to the last stage of the return migration, which is the wandering at the coast trying to locate the mouth of the native river. The migration in the sea also seems to be determined by events in connection with the smolts leaving the river. Carlin illustrates this well from the following example: salmon eggs were taken from the Angermanälven and the young salmon were reared for two years in a hatchery in southern Sweden. The smolts were transported to a hatchery at the River Ume älv and kept there for a month. After that they were transported to the River Lule älv and kept there for a week, during which time they were tagged. Half the fish were then released in the Lule älv, and the other half in the Kalix älv, 64 km to the north-east. Of those released in the Kalix älv three were taken in the Torne älv 48 km east of the Kalix älv, 74 in the Kalix älv and three in the Lule älv. Of the fish released in the Lule älv, one went to the Kalix älv, 150 to the Lule älv and six to the Ume älv. In this case, in spite of the very complicated origin, the fish returned mainly to the rivers of release. They are not very far apart, so this could have been explained if all the fish had returned to the same coastal area and then sorted out the rivers according to the smell. But this was not the case, as can be seen from Fig. 4.1. The two batches of fish were quite well separated already when approaching the coast.

In 1960 some salmon ova from the River Indalsälven were sent to Poland

*Return to the river*

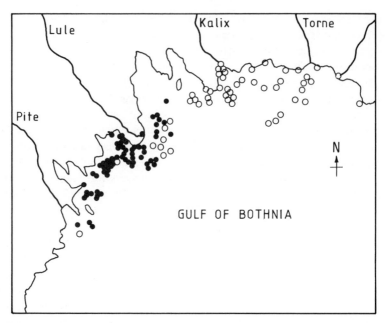

**Fig. 4.1** Recaptures of salmon tagged as smolts in the R. Lule (blackdots) and R. Kalix (circles) (reproduced with permission from Carlin, 1969).

and the resulting smolts were released in the River Vistula. A few fish went as far north as the Gulf of Bothnia, but none were taken near the Indalsälven. On the other hand 15 were taken in the Vistula or its estuary. They had therefore migrated south instead of going north, which they should have done had their migration been guided only by an inherited kind of reaction to whatever stimulus guides their sea migrations.

Carlin (1969) concludes also that the migration at sea must in some way be determined by the circumstances at the release, but, as he says, 'it is still quite impossible to imagine how fish distributed over a vast area of open sea and moving about in it for a couple of years, still can converge towards the place where they first entered sea water.'

Solomon (1973) presents evidence which indicates that the homing of adult salmon may be largely dependent on the presence of other individuals in the river. He suggests that the presence of young salmon in a river might render it attractive to migrating adults in the first instance, and that a metabolic product of a discrete population could be the odour to which adults home. Nordeng (1971, 1977) put forward evidence to indicate that the homing of a migratory population of charr (*Salvelinus alpinus* Linnaeus) was influenced by pheromones and suggested that the attractant might be secreted in the mucus of their young progeny in the river. This explanation for homing in adult salmonids had been raised many years before by Chidester (1924), but he concluded from his limited evidence that it was rather unlikely. However, the results of Selset and Døving (1980) support the 'pheromone hypothesis' presented by Nordeng (1971, 1977). The results of Selset and Døving (1980) do not exclude an olfactory 'imprinting', but make it likely that the possible imprinting would be to substances emanating from the fishes themselves and not from vegetation or minerals.

The imprinting hypothesis of Hasler and Wisby (1951) was extended by Harden Jones (1968) who suggested that salmon were sequentially imprinted during smolt migration. He proposed that salmon have to experience the outward migration as smolts, and postulated that sequential imprinting of the migrating smolts and post smolts was needed for the successful return as adults. Hansen, Døving and Jonsson (1987) produced evidence to support this theory in their study of the migration of farmed adult salmon with and without olfactory sense, released on the Norwegian coast. In this study three groups of fish aged 4 years of the River Imsa stock, therefore having the genetic link needed to recognize their home river, were released in coastal waters off south-western Norway: one group, with functional olfactory organs, was released at a fish farm 4 km away from the River Imsa: two other groups, one with transected olfactory nerves and the other with functional olfactory organs, were released in the sea 90 km from the River Imsa. To compare them with the migration pattern of reared, large smolts of the Imsa stock, a group of 3 + smolts was released in the River Imsa. The adults of the fish released as 3-year-old smolts homed with high precision to the River Imsa. The 4-year-olds released in the sea were recaptured in the fjord and in the coastal current, the majority north of the places of release. Immatures migrated to feeding areas in the North Atlantic. Mature fish seemed to enter rivers at random when ready to spawn. There was no difference in migration pattern between anosmics and controls. The olfactory sense was found not to be mandatory for entering fresh water. This would certainly seem to suggest that the homing behaviour of the smolts is not a direct consequence of a single imprinting of the smolts, and that there is not a direct genetic link for return to a particular river.

Additional work by Hansen, Jonsson and Andersen (1988) was undertaken to test the single-imprinting, sequential-imprinting and pheromone hypotheses for homeward migration of salmon by transplantation experiments. The results were based on adult tag returns of smolts from different stocks released in the River Imsa, in the sea and in a small stream with no salmon. The authors concluded that their results cannot be explained by Nordeng's pheromone hypothesis as, when released as smolts in the ocean and foreign rivers, the returning adults did not enter their river of origin. When released in rivers, the adults returned independent of stock origin, even when released in an area in southern Norway where salmon are absent due to acidification. They also concluded that salmon do not require a 'smolt trail' to navigate from distant feeding areas to rivers, as suggested by Nordeng (1977). Salmon are also able to return independent of the presence of juveniles in the stream. Neither could the results be explained by the single-imprinting hypothesis (Hasler and Wisby, 1951; Carlin, 1969). When the smolts were exposed to water from different rivers and released in the ocean, they failed to return to particular rivers. Even smolts of the River Imsa stock transported in water from the River Imsa and released in the sea failed to return to the Imsa. On the basis of the present experiments the authors cannot reject the sequential-imprinting hypothesis of Harden Jones as, when released in fresh water, the salmon returned to the river of release. When released in the ocean and thus deprived of parts of the smolt migration, the salmon did not return to a particular river. Hansen, Jonsson and Andersen (1988) review the various theories on homing behaviour and conclude that their data give support to the sequential-imprinting hypothesis, indicating that the homing behaviour is a composite phenomenon requiring a continuous set of cues during smolt migration.

The subject of homing and olfaction in salmonids in general and with special reference to Atlantic salmon is reviewed by Stabell (1984).

## 4.2   FACTORS AFFECTING UPSTREAM MIGRATION

Many factors are claimed to be responsible for the time of entry of salmon into rivers and their subsequent upstream migration. The importance of any one of these factors probably changes as the fish move upstream. Hayes (1953) found that fish move out of tidal waters into fresh water at dusk, and light change may be the controlling factor. He also had evidence that fairly strong onshore winds approaching 32 km/h induce salmon to concentrate in the river estuary and eventually to ascend. Peaks in the tidal cycles representing daily increasing differences between high and low tides seem to be effective in concentrating salmon on the coast, and indicate the probability of a run into fresh water. Hayes (1953) showed that large natural freshets can indicate a major run of fish into the river, provided the winds and tides are favourable. In cases where these two other factors were not favourable, no run occurred.

The movements of salmon in estuaries have been studied by Stasko *et al.*, (1973) and Stasko (1975) by ultrasonic tracking. It was noticed that there was drifting with the tidal currents, and holding position relative to land. Fish that achieved overall upstream progress did so by drifting with flood tidal currents and by stemming the ebb currents. Fish that did not achieve upstream progress also drifted with flood tidal currents, but these fish did not stem the ebb currents and dropped back downstream during ebb tides. There were no apparent movement patterns for different times of day or wind condition.

Menzies (1931) describes how in dry weather grilse which are held up in tidal waters moved up the estuary just ahead of the tide and fell back with the tide as it ebbed; but during a spate, tidal movements were ignored and fish entered the estuary and moved directly and rapidly upstream. Almost 100 years earlier Williamson (1843) writes:

It is well known that salmon do not travel in dry weather. Before they ascend a river they require a 'leading water'. They persist in hovering about the estuary, ascending with the tide but, unless there be a fresh in the river, returning with it and, what is very strange, however low the river may have sunk, no sooner does it become quietened by a heavy fall of rain, than they rush up in shoals, run up with great vivacity, and are taken many miles from the sea in the course of a few hours. It is evident, therefore, that a dry summer, though fatal to fishes above high water mark, is eminently favourable to those below it; and the more so, the closer the approximation to the sea.

Jackson and Howie (1967) discovered from an analysis of the draft net catches in the Erne estuary (Republic of Ireland) that of the total season's catch the majority (76% and 87% in two consecutive years) were taken on the flood tide, particularly during the first two hours of the flood. They also showed that only 16% of the catch in one year and 5% of the catch in the next were taken between sunset and sunrise (Fig. 4.2).

Menzies (1931) has shown that water temperature is of great importance to

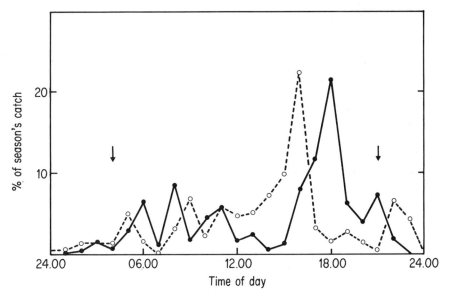

**Fig. 4.2** The total catch by the nets in the Erne estuary for each of the seasons 1959 (broken curve) and 1960 (solid curve), summated in hours of the day; arrows denote approximate times of sunrise and sunset (reproduced from Jackson and Howie, 1967).

fish movement in the spring, and until the water temperature reaches 5.5 °C there is little upstream movement of fish over obstacles. Mills and Graesser (1981) refer to the upstream movement of salmon on the River Cassley in the spring being governed by water temperature and point out that fish do not jump some formidable falls on the river until the water temperature exceeds 11 °C. Stewart (1973) observed that salmon migrate upstream most frequently when air temperature is lower than that of river water. A review of the literature on the upstream migration of adult salmonids has been made by Banks (1969).

Lindroth (1952) estimated that the average rate of travel upstream by adult fish ascending the River Indalsälven in Sweden was 10–20 km/day. It also seemed to him as if the salmon which entered the river last travelled furthest upstream. More detailed observations on the upstream movements of salmon in the Aberdeenshire Dee were made by Hawkins and Smith (1986) using radio-tracking methods. They noticed that the passage of fish through the estuary and lower reaches of the river was rapid. The fish then moved further up river in phases of active swimming interspersed with stationary periods. Those fish tracked for several months eventually slowed their rate of upstream movement and settled at particular locations. Later the fish moved short distances upstream from these sites to the spawning grounds. In recent work, Hawkins (1988) noticed that those fish entering the River Dee early in the year travelled further upstream than those coming into the river late in the season. He also noticed that upstream movement did not appear to be related to river flow. In summer when the freshwater temperatures might exceed 20 °C fish often remained in the sea.

Hawkins and Smith also confirmed Lindroth's estimation of the swimming speed of salmon. They found that upstream progress was initially quite fast, above 10 km/day. Actual swimming speeds were considerably faster for short periods even against quite high river flow rates, speeds of more than 20 km/day being common (Table 4.1).

Slower rates of progress have been recorded by other investigators. Smirnov (1971) reported that the rates of upstream movement for salmon of Lake Onega (USSR) were seldom more than 4 km/day, and salmon ascending a 64 km stretch of the north-west Miramichi River were moving at a rate of about 4.3 km/day (Hayes, 1953). However, fish moving upstream through the Miramichi estuary have shown rates of progress of between 3.45 and 12 km/day (Stasko, 1975).

Upstream migration is undoubtedly associated with thyroid activity as the salmon becomes sexually mature and Fontaine (1951) has suggested that the alternating periods of activity and torpor which characterize the behaviour of ascending salmon may be due to variations in the activity of the thyroid gland. As the season advances and the thyroid activity increases one might expect to see an increase in the urgency of upstream movement. Mills (1968) found that

**Table 4.1** Calculations of swimming speeds over ground for seven salmon during the initial phase of upstream migration: because the fish may have been stemming currents, their speed relative to the water may have been higher*

| Fork length of fish (cm) | Swimming speeds (km/day) | (m/s) | (body lengths/s) | Prevailing flow rates (m³/s) |
|---|---|---|---|---|
| 72 | 21.30 | 0.27 | 0.34 | 124.85 |
| 69 | 19.08 | 0.22 | 0.32 | 40.14 |
| | 14.53 | 0.17 | 0.24 | 43.85 |
| | 29.81 | 0.35 | 0.50 | 22.04 |
| 75 | 20.74 | 0.24 | 0.32 | 24.04 |
| | 25.10 | 0.29 | 0.39 | 26.03 |
| | 25.07 | 0.29 | 0.39 | 29.42 |
| 56 | 21.49 | 0.25 | 0.45 | 23.75 |
| 62 | 33.44 | 0.39 | 0.63 | 31.35 |
| | 22.13 | 0.26 | 0.42 | 31.01 |
| 58 | 36.98 | 0.43 | 0.74 | 32.16 |
| 65 | 25.17 | 0.29 | 0.45 | 48.27 |

*Source: Hawkins and Smith (1986).*

adult fish released downstream from a trap they had just entered reappeared in the trap several times and that there was an increase in the persistence of this upstream movement as the season progressed.

Hawkins and Smith (1986) found that fish started to move at dusk and Dunkley and Shearer (1983), using an electronic fish counter on the River North Esk, also recorded ascending fish moving upstream after sunset, while Kristinsson and Alexandersdottir (1978) found that salmon in the Ellidaar in Iceland migrate in dense runs during the night.

However, Hawkins and Smith (1986) stress that salmon are quite flexible and variable in their behaviour and that fish may well move during the day in turbid water and when close to maturity. There are also many recorded observations of fish moving during the day both in clear and low water conditions (Allan, 1965; Mills, 1968; Hellawell, 1973) and Hellawell (1976) concludes that the primary factor in salmonid migration is season. This may be an oversimplification of a complicated phenomenon which is more likely governed by water temperature.

## 4.3   TIME OF ENTRY

The time of entry of the main runs of fish varies from river to river. In Scotland, some rivers such as the Aberdeenshire Dee, Tay, Tweed, Spey, Helmsdale, Naver and Brora have early (spring) runs of multi-sea-winter fish, while in others, such as those on the west coast, there are usually very few spring fish and here the first large runs of both grilse and multi-sea-winter fish only start to enter the rivers in June and July (Mills and Graesser, 1981). There are also rivers such as the Annan, Nith and Tweed in Scotland and the Taw and Torridge in England, which have a large run of fish in the late autumn and even early winter. In some of these rivers fish come in from the sea in every month of the year. In other countries, however, the season in which salmon return to the rivers is much more contracted. In Iceland, for example, salmon enter the rivers between early June and early September.

The length of the river may be partly responsible for the time of year at which fish return. It is tempting to suggest that fish returning to short rivers need not return as early in the season as those entering long river systems. However, on the large river systems of the Spey, Tweed and Tay in Scotland salmon enter in significant numbers both early and late in the season. The Tweed, which is 154 km long, has a very late (October–November) run of fish some of which move into the upper reaches of the system before spawning in December and early January. On the other hand, it is interesting to note that on the Loire–Allier system the length of river presently available to salmon is some 860 km (Cuinat, 1988). It is therefore perhaps not surprising that fish enter the 30-km-long estuary of this river system at intervals from October up to the end of the spring, a period of 6–8 months, before spawning in the following November. Cuinat (1988) points out that by comparison with other French rivers, where the distance from the sea to the spawning grounds is relatively short (less than 42 km for practically all other salmon rivers in France), the life cycle of the Loire–Allier salmon is lengthy, although the freshwater stage is short (more than 80% are 1+ smolts compared with 50–60% in other river systems). This is due primarily to the long period of growth in the sea (24% two summers, 73% three summers and occasionally 0.5% four summers) compared with other river systems whose salmon spend 1 or 2 years in the sea (sometimes 3 years in the Gave d'Oleron), and secondly to the very lengthy adult phase in fresh water: from 6 to 14 months compared with 2–10 months in other river systems.

In a number of Scottish rivers, an increasing proportion of the run currently takes places outside the legal netting season, which on most rivers extends from mid-February to the end of August. Shelton (1984) considers that the reasons may be linked with the decline in smolt age noted on the North Esk (Dunkley, 1986). Gardner (1976) suggested that, where the stocks are heavily exploited, natural selection would tend to favour winter-running fish which enter the river during the annual close time. Hansen (1988) pointed out that in several Norwegian rivers salmon now ascend later in the season compared with earlier years and that this might be a result of selective fishing, but stock enhancement using late-running fish as broodstock might also contribute to this phenomenon. There is little direct evidence that selective fishing has changed the genetic frequency in Norwegian salmon populations. There is evidence from the Tweed to suggest that this change from early-running to late-running stocks, and also in the alternating dominance of salmon and grilse is cyclical (Figs 4.3, 4.4) (Mills, 1986).

Power (1981), in considering temperature constraints on salmon movement in northern Canadian rivers shows that Atlantic salmon migrate only within certain ranges of temperature. This is particularly critical for salmon in nothern Arctic Canada and governs the time of their river entry. He records (1976) the return migration of Atlantic salmon to the estuaries being coincidental with the attainment of suitable temperatures in Ungava Bay. Time of arrival of these fish varies from year to year depending on ice and wind conditions. Two-sea-winter salmon, 70% female, arrive on average 7–10 days ahead of one-sea-winter fish, 85% of which are male. About 5% of the females and 85% of the males have immature gonads. Mature fish spawn in the autumn when they enter the rivers; the remainder stay in fresh water for more than 12 months before their gonads ripen. This mechanism is an adaptation to late arrival of fish at the river mouth, which is controlled by sea temperature, and to a short period of temperatures suitable for migration and maturation once the fish enter the rivers. Power (1981) illustrates this schematically (Fig. 4.5) and shows how constraints on movement vary with latitude.

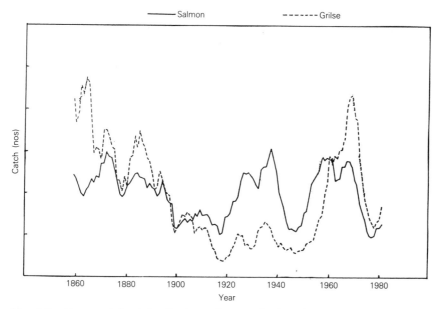

**Fig. 4.3** Commercial catch of salmon (————— line) and grilse (– – – – – line) by Berwick Salmon Fisheries Company, presented as five-year rolling averages (reproduced from Mills, 1986).

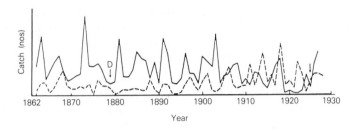

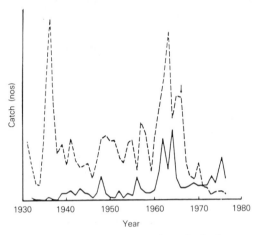

**Fig. 4.4**    Annual spring and autumn rod catch of salmon on a lower beat of the River Tweed: broken curve, spring fish (Feb.–May); solid curve, autumn fish (Oct.–Nov.); arrows denote outbreaks of disease; data unavailable for autumn 1928 to autumn 1930 and for autumn 1931 (reproduced from Mills, 1987a).

There is sufficient evidence, given in both this and the preceding chapter, to conclude that both differences between sea and river temperatures at any point in time and, similarly, between river and air temperatures are the basic factors controlling salmon migration. This is a subject that was given considerable space in *The Life of the Salmon* by Calderwood as long ago as 1907.

## 4.4    BEHAVIOUR AT NATURAL OBSTACLES

Stuart (1962) carried out a study of the leaping behaviour of salmon and trout at falls and obstructions. The stimulus to leap was found to be closely related to the presence of a standing wave, or hydraulic jump, and the distance of the standing wave from the obstacle influences the success of the leap. Thus, in shallow fall pools and pools below sloping weirs the standing wave becomes located too far downstream for the fish to strike the crest of the fall on the

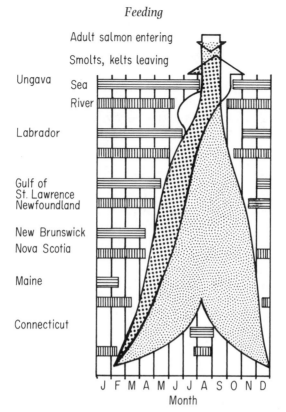

**Fig. 4.5** Constraints to movement of Atlantic salmon imposed by sea and river temperatures. Horizontal shading, unsuitable sea temperatures; vertical shading, unsuitable river temperatures; fine stippling, suitable river temperatures; heavy stippling, suitable sea temperatures. Note that in Ungava there is a very short period for free movement when both sea and river temperatures are favourable. In the south, summer temperatures begin to affect movement and there is selection for early and late-running stocks. Maine and Connecticut stocks, 12 000 and 15 000 years ago, would have been subject to restraints similar to those experienced by Ungava and Labrador stocks today (reproduced with permission from Power, 1981).

upward arc of its trajectory. If the fish strikes the falling water on the downward arc it is immediately swept downstream. Salmon have been observed leaping at and surmounting vertical falls of up to 3.5 m in height, such as those on the River Orrin in Ross-shire, Scotland (frontispiece).

## 4.5   FEEDING

It is common knowledge that adult salmon do not feed in fresh water and over the years the stomachs of many thousands of salmon examined have been found to be empty. Calderwood (1907) refers to Hoek examining 2000 salmon in the lower Rhine and finding food remains in only seven, which were taken in March and April, and Ruesch at Basle, 800 km up the river, examined 2162 salmon in four years and found food in only two male kelts. Grey and Tosh (1894) examined 1694 salmon from the Tweed, 1236 being taken in the nets at the river mouth at Berwick. Of these Berwick fish, 156 (12.6%) contained food (Table 4.2) which consisted chiefly of herring, sand eels, whiting, haddock and amphipods. The greatest proportion of fish with food in their stomachs occurred in March and April.

**Table 4.2**  Details of the examination of salmon from the nets of the Berwick Salmon Fisheries Company at the mouth of the River Tweed*

| Month | No. examined | No. with food | % with food |
|-------|-------------|---------------|-------------|
| February | 7 | 1 | 14.3 |
| March | 46 | 20 | 43.5 |
| April | 133 | 53 | 39.8 |
| May | 215 | 36 | 16.7 |
| June | 236 | 31 | 13.1 |
| July | 283 | 5 | 1.8 |
| August | 210 | 8 | 3.8 |
| September | 106 | 2 | 1.9 |
| Total | 1236 | 156 | |

*Source: Grey and Tosh (1894).*

Very occasionally salmon parr have been recorded in the stomachs of adult male salmon at spawning time. These were probably precocious male parr that were in the immediate vicinity of spawning fish. Kelts, too, have been recorded taking smolts and abrasions and teeth marks on smolts have been attributed to attacks by kelts.

In a histological study of the digestive tracts in kelts Barton (1902) produced evidence of feeding having recently taken place, although no food was present in their stomachs at the time of examination.

## 4.6  MORTALITY

### Disease

The salmon is subject to a number of diseases, some of which can be responsible for very high mortalities. The diseases include furunculosis, Dee disease, kidney disease, salmon disease, ulcerative dermal necrosis, 'columnaris', vibriosis and cataracts.

*Furunculosis.* This is a well-known disease of salmonids and is caused by the bacterium *Aeromonas salmonicida.* The bacterium is short, non-motile, Gram-negative and non-spore-forming. Salmon that are suffering from furunculosis show a variety of external symptoms including congestion of the fins, haemorrhage at the vent and furuncles. At times the only external symptoms may be congestion of the fins and at other times there may be no external symptoms.

The disease has been recognized for over 55 years as a cause of death during the summer, especially when the rivers are low and the water temperature rises to 12.7 °C. Serious outbreaks have been recorded when there have been large concentrations of fish assembled below falls and in pools during low water conditions. However, Smith (1960, 1962) reported a high incidence of furunculosis in kelts in some Scottish rivers in the winter of 1958–59 and 1960–61 and a lower incidence in 1959–60. A high incidence was also found in kelts in some English and Welsh rivers in 1958–59, but a very low one in Irish rivers in 1960–61 and 1961–62 (Hewetson, 1962a, b).

An interesting feature of the disease in kelts is that many of the fish suffering from it are less likely to develop external symptoms than unspent fish. Smith (1962) showed that of 194 unspent fish with the disease, 142 (73.2%) showed some external sign while only 51 (29.7%) of 172 kelts with furunculosis showed external symptoms. Smith also showed that over the period October to December, i.e. the period when most of the dead kelts are found, only 43% of the unspent fish showed external symptoms, a proportion much closer to that found for kelts. Thus, as Smith states:

The possibility of an unspent fish developing external symptoms is much greater in the summer months, though any unspent fish is more likely to develop such symptoms than a kelt. This does not agree with the observations that at higher temperatures during the summer, fish are more likely to die from an acute infection of furunculosis (in which there are no external symptoms), than from a chronic infection (where furuncles are present). It might, however, explain why the incidence of furunculosis in kelts has hitherto gone unnoticed.

Smith noticed that male kelts seem to be more susceptible to furunculosis than unspent males. She rightly points out that as some or most of the kelts that die are suffering from furunculosis, their importance as sources of infection should be borne in mind. It was found that the bacteria are viable for as long as three to six months under certain conditions and as most of the kelts die soon after spawning there is the possibility of direct infection of unspent salmon entering the river during the winter. Some smolts were also recorded as dying from furunculosis and their infection was attributed to the presence of diseased kelts. Investigations have shown that the viability of *A. salmonicida* in sea water is not negligible, so its survival in the tissues of a host adapted to sea water seems a distinct possibility. Therefore, *A. salmonicida* may not only pass from one adult host to another, it may also pass from an adult host to a juvenile host and survive a period in the sea, with the consequence that at least part of the returning migrants are infected before they reach fresh water.

There has been a certain amount of confusion over the classification of '*Bacterium salmonicida*'. As the systematic position of this organism was in doubt, 42 strains of '*Bacterium salmonicida*', six of a non-pigmented fish pathogen and 42 *Aeromonas* strains were compared morphologically, culturally, biochemically and metabolically by Smith (1963). The results showed a distinct difference between '*B. salmonicida*' and the *Aeromonas* species. On the grounds of this variation in morphology, culture and biochemistry, Smith suggested that '*B. salmonicida*' be removed from the genus *Aeromonas* and given a generic place in the family Pseudomonadaceae. The name *Necromonas salmonicida* was suggested as an alternative to '*B. salmonicida*'. However, in a paper on the pathogenicity of '*Bacterium salmonicida*' in sea and brackish waters Scott (1968) uses the name *Aeromonas salmonicida* (Griffin) and this remains the accepted name (Smith, pers. comm.).

*Dee disease.* This disease is so called because it was first described in salmon from the Aberdeenshire Dee in 1930, and first recorded in the *Second Interim Report* of the UK government's Furunculosis Committee (1933). The fish were found to have small necrotic lesions on their spleens. From these lesions a small Gram-positive bacillus could be demonstrated but could not be grown successfully on culture media.

Fish suffering from this disease may show congestion of the fins, haemorrhage at the vent and, in a very few cases, haemorrhagic spots on the muscle. As Smith (1964) points out, such symptoms are found in other fish diseases so they are of little value in the diagnosis of Dee disease. Internally the salmon shows very characteristic lesions, the most prevalent one being petechial haemorrhage of the muscle lining the peritoneum. The organ next most often affected is the kidney which, instead of its normal uniform reddish-brown colour, develops greyish-brown areas which, if the disease is more advanced, develop an almost cyst-like appearance. The spleen is the next in order. On its surface develop a number of creamy-white lesions, which vary in size from pin-head to about 4 mm in diameter. The number of such lesions varies from fish to fish, ranging from a very few to a large number which give the spleen a peppered appearance. The liver exhibits similar pathological changes but here the number of lesions is often smaller, and as a whole the liver is less often affected in this manner. Occasionally the swim bladder is covered with petechial haemorrhages. The above symptoms are those most often found in Dee disease, but early in the year the pathology of the disease is somewhat different. At this time the spleen, liver, gonads and even the swim bladder and peritoneal muscle are partially or completely covered with a white membrane. This membrane is not firmly attached to any of these organs but can be peeled off leaving the surface of the organ apparently unharmed. In this type of infection, the pericardial sac is occasionally filled with a milky fluid consisting of tissue cells and the Gram-positive bacilli.

There is no sharp boundary between the two forms and so in some salmon both the necrotic lesions and the white membrane are manifested. The second clinical picture was thought to represent a chronic infection so the water temperature of the river was studied to see if there was any correlation between type of symptom and water temperature. Salmon that had white membranes on their spleen or liver were nearly all found dead when the water temperature ranged from 1.5 °C to 9.4 °C; those with both white membranes and necrotic lesions were found from 7.2 °C to 10.5 °C; and those having only necrotic lesions were found from 7.2 °C to 17.2 ° C (Fig. 4.6).

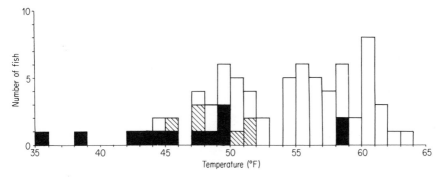

**Fig. 4.6** The relationship between water temperature and the symptoms developed by salmon suffering from Dee disease: black columns, white membrane; hatched columns, white membrane and necrosis; white columns, necrosis (reproduced with permission from Smith, 1964).

Smith (1964) considered that the organism most probably belongs to the *Corynebacteria* spp. She also concluded that Dee disease is very similar to or identical with kidney disease which has been described in Pacific salmon by Earp, Ellis and Ordal (1953) and in *Salvelinus fontinalis*, *Salmo trutta* and *Salmo gairdneri* by Snieszko and Griffin (1955). Smith (1964) gives a summary of the pathological symptoms recorded by these workers together with those recorded for Atlantic salmon.

*Salmon disease.* Salmon disease was noticed originally in the spring and autumn of 1877 in the Border Esk and Nith. It soon spread to the Eden and neighbouring rivers and in the spring of 1879 it was observed in the Tweed. It had spread to other rivers in the south-west of Scotland in 1880 and by 1882 had spread to North Wales and to the Tay and North Esk in Scotland.

The first symptom of this disease was the appearance of small greyish or ashy discoloration of the skin, usually upon those parts of the body that are devoid of scales, such as the top and sides of the head, the adipose fin and the soft skin at the base of other fins. A detailed description of the symptoms of the disease appears in the *21st Annual Report (for the year 1881) of the Inspector of [Salmon] Fisheries (England and Wales)*:

When a patch of diseased skin has once appeared it rapidly increases in size and runs into any other patches which may have appeared in its neighbourhood. The marginal zone, constantly extending into the healthy surrounding skin, retains its previous characters, while the ashy central part changes. It assumes the consistency of wet paper and can be detached in flakes, like a slough, from the skin which it covers. If the subjacent surface is now examined it will be found that the epidermis has disappeared and that the surface of the vascular and sensitive derma beneath is exposed. As the diseased area extends, the papyraceous coat more and more completely takes the place of the epidermis until, in extremely bad cases, it may invest the back and sides of a large salmon from snout to tail.

The affection, however, is not confined to the epidermis. As the patch acquires larger and larger dimensions, the derma in its centre becomes subject to a process of ulceration, and thus a deep bleeding sore is formed, which eats down to the bones of the head and sends off burrowing passages, or sinuses, from its margins.

Huxley (1882) believed that salmon disease was caused by the fungus *Saprolegnia ferax*. However, Patterson (1903) established the fact that *S. ferax* did not constitute in itself the active agent in the disease. He considered that salmon disease was due 'to the invasion of the tissues of the fish by a special bacillus *Bacillus salmonis pestis*'. The bacillus was said to gain access through abrasions or ulceration of the skin, and the disease was apparently not contracted when the skin of the fish was in a healthy state. Patterson (1903) also found that: (1) *B. salmonis pestis* can be transmitted from dead diseased fish to other dead fish in the water; (2) the disease can be transmitted from dead fish to living fish in the same water; (3) the fact that the bacillus grows profusely when placed in a freezing mixture of ice and salt, while a temperature of 37 °C soon destroys it, shows that the cold season is more favourable to its growth.

In the *22nd Annual Report (for the year 1882) of the Inspector of [Salmon] Fisheries (England and Wales)* it was said:

What is known of the history of the 'salmon disease' brings out the curious fact that the epidemic, starting apparently from a centre near the Solway, and extending thence to the Scottish rivers both east and west of this point, has spread to nearly all the English and Welsh rivers on the west coast in pretty regular rotation, from Cumberland to Herefordshire; while, on the east, it has spread only very slightly, if at all, south of the Tweed, notwithstanding the fact that larger numbers of diseased fish have been found in the Tweed than in the Eden, the first and worst affected of all English rivers.

Over 6000 diseased salmon were taken out of the Eden between 1878 and 1883 (up to 31 May).

The report also commented on the fact that, in the rivers in which the disease had been most virulent, the salmon harvest had increased rather than diminished.

*Ulcerative dermal necrosis.* There are many reasons for believing that ulcerative dermal necrosis, or UDN as it is popularly called, is the same disease as the 'salmon disease' which occurred at the end of last century. The pattern of the spread of the disease is similar, the symptoms are remarkably alike, even to some authorities (Stuart and Fuller, 1968) believing that *Saprolegnia* spp. may be the causative organism, and there is a direct relationship between the prevalence of the disease and low water temperature (Elson, 1968a) (Fig. 4.7).

UDN was first observed in epidemic proportions in a number of rivers in south-west Ireland during 1964–65 and full details of this are given in reports prepared by the Fisheries Division of the Department of Agriculture and Fisheries of Ireland in August 1966 and April and May 1967 and which were also published in *Salmon Net* (Anon., 1967). During 1966 the disease spread to the Lancashire, Cumberland and Solway river systems. By the end of 1967 the disease had spread to all east coast rivers from the Tweed to the Nairn with the exception of the Forth and Tay and, on the west coast, from the Solway Firth to the River Ayr. In 1968 cases appeared in the Forth, Tay, Ness and Conon river systems. The progress of the disease up the east coast of Scotland resembled that in Ireland, in that for no apparent reason, one river might remain clear of the disease while its immediate neighbours were seriously affected. Elson (1968a) suggests that it is possible that sea trout may have contributed to the spread of the disease as these fish may move from estuary to estuary. In the rivers Deveron and Spey sea trout were seriously affected for almost two weeks before any diseased salmon were observed.

Pyefinch and Elson (1967) describe the symptoms of the disease in some detail:

The first signs of this disease are the appearance of small bleached areas of the skin, on the head, back and near the dorsal fin and on the tail. As the disease progresses areas of a bluish-grey, slimy growth develop over these bleached areas, making the fish very conspicuous in the water. The appearance of the fish at this stage has been likened to that of a fish heavily infected with fungus but, if the fish is taken out of the water, the affected patches show none of the woolly or fuzzy appearance which characterises a fungal infection; instead

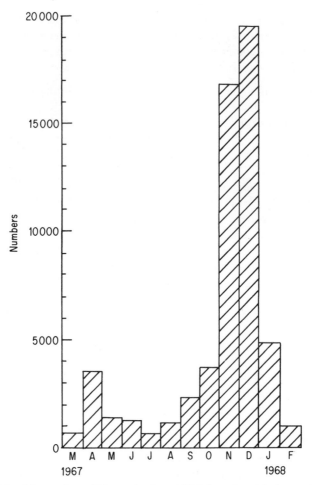

**Fig. 4.7**  Monthly numbers of diseased salmonid fish from Scottish rivers where UDN is suspected of being the major contributory cause of disease (reproduced with permission from Elson, 1968a).

they resemble masses of sodden blue-grey blotting paper. Further, these slimy masses can readily be pulled away, exposing inflammation or shallow ulceration of the underlying skin.

As the disease progresses, more patches appear and the others spread, so that considerable areas over the head, back and the 'wrist' of the tail are affected and, at this stage, the head may be so badly affected that it seems largely covered by raw, reddish areas. As often happens when the skin of a fish is damaged, fungus may infect these exposed areas but it is important to recognise that this fungal growth is a secondary effect, consequent upon primary infection, and not a primary symptom. Once established, however, the fungus spreads and, in the most advanced stages of the disease, the head and tail regions of the fish may be largely covered with fungus.

Elson (1968a) also mentions that the gall bladder is commonly affected. In fish showing the early stages of the disease the gall bladder is enlarged but in the more seriously affected fish it is often found to be empty. Certain actions such as aquaplaning and jumping with an agitated flapping movement have been described as characteristic of infected fish. It was found that there was a marked depletion of serum protein in diseased fish. Adult salmon appear to be much more susceptible to the disease than juveniles and relatively few infected parr and smolts have been recorded.

The report prepared by the Fisheries Division of the Department of Agriculture and Fisheries of Ireland in August 1966 mentioned that Dr Jensen suggested that the disease was 'columnaris', but he was insistent that this diagnosis would have to be proved by the isolation and culture of *Chondrococcus* (*Cytophaga*) *columnaris* and the subsequent reproduction of the disease in healthy salmon by infection with bacteria thus cultured. Dr Snieszko examined more diseased salmon and isolated *Aeromonas liquefaciens* and a *Pseudomonas* species. While these are well-known fish pathogens in Europe, Dr Snieszko was not convinced of their significance in this disease.

Further examination of diseased salmon showed the presence of 'columnaris' organisms and fungi of the *Saprolegnia* type and attempts were made to conduct small-scale infectivity experiments. A number of these experiments were conducted with all of the above bacteria using both injection and water infectivity processes. While it was repeatedly possible to kill fish and isolate the specific organisms used from the infected tissues, thereby demonstrating their pathogenicity, the true lesions of UDN were not reproduced.

The lack of knowledge of the surface bacterial populations of healthy salmon made it necessary for a study to be made of the normal skin flora of salmon in marine, estuarine and river environments in which no disease had been encountered. One of the things that emerged from this survey was that 'columnaris' type bacteria could be isolated from the skin of 36.5% of all fish examined from non-affected areas.

Elson (1968a) describes examining fresh-run infected salmon within five minutes of their capture in nets in the tidal reaches of the Tweed. These fish exhibited the typical ulcerated areas on the head but no fungus. Salmon heavily infested with sea lice but showing shallow ulcerations of the head have also been taken in coastal nets off the north-east of Scotland (Elson, 1968b), which suggests that some fish are infected with UDN before they reach fresh water. In some Scottish west coast rivers fish bearing the characteristic UDN ulcerations and fungus have been noticed shortly after entering fresh water in the warm summer months of July and August. From an examination of the salmon from the tidal reaches of the Tweed Elson found that bacteria were neither culturable nor demonstrable, but microscopical preparations of liver and kidney impression smears revealed the presence of inclusions within the cells which indicated a possible virus infection. Carberry and Strickland (1968) in Ireland claim to have produced the disease in apparently healthy fish with the use of bacteria-free and fungus-free filtrates of infected fish tissues and this could indicate a virus involvement. It was also found that the ætiological agent of UDN was resistant to antibiotics and was smaller than 0.2 $\mu$m in size. Roberts (1969) considered that the microscopical appearance of the early lesions suggests that a virus is responsible but that it is only the harbinger of the initial skin damage which allows both loss of body proteins and attack on unprotected tissue by fungi. No abnormalities were detected in any organs other than the skin. Roberts, Shearer and Elson (1969) found no definite evidence to suggest a primary virus ætiology, but the lesions resembled those produced in the virus disease of cattle known as mucosal disease, where secondary infection is again a common occurrence.

While the work to isolate the causative organism of UDN went on, the numbers of infected salmon in Scottish rivers rose and from March 1967 to 25 February 1968 a total of 41 234 infected salmon and grilse were removed from Scottish rivers. This total is 12.6% of the provisional Scottish catch of salmon and grilse for 1967 by all methods of fishing.

However, a note of hope was sounded by Elson (1968a):

During the last decades of the nineteenth century, a disease characterised by clinical symptoms similar to those of UDN occurred in many Scottish rivers. This took some time to die out, e.g. the River Tweed was seriously affected over the fifteen-year period from 1879 to 1893, and though there are now methods for treating bacterial fish disease which were not available seventy or eighty years ago, these are economically impracticable in an open river system and recovery must still, presumably, depend upon a balance taking place between the host and the pathogen by the process of natural selection. In this context, a certain number of kelts have been observed to show repair tissue, and experiments carried out in Ireland have indicated that the progeny of diseased salmon were apparently healthy and showed no evidence of UDN.

Munro (1970) points out that many high annual catches were made over the period of the outbreak in the late nineteenth century, indicating that the species was never in danger of extinction; indeed the disease may have occurred as a result of an exceedingly large population. Munro considers that similar factors may have operated to start the present outbreak, though available information is too meagre to draw such a conclusion.

Roberts (1978) pointed out in a review of the investigations into the causes of UDN that the ætiology of the disease has never been resolved. Attempts at virus isolation in a wide range of tissue cultures have all proved unsuccessful.

He suggests that it is possible that a virus infection of the central nervous system or peripheral ganglia serving the sites of the lesions may result in so-called trophic skin ulceration. Bullock and Roberts (1979) showed that UDN-like lesions could be induced in salmonid fish by exposure to UV-A (ultraviolet) light. They considered that in view of the great number of phototoxic compounds known to exist in the marine environment and the complete absence of evidence for any other possible causes of the disease, the possibility of a phototoxic contribution to its ætiology must be considered. It is interesting to note that Calderwood (1906b) attributed white lesions on the head recorded in fish congregating near the mouth of rivers as being due to injury by sunlight.

Johansson, Svensson and Fridberg (1982) investigating the pathology of UDN in Swedish salmon found no substantial evidence for the presence of a virus at any stage of the disease and concluded that the disease is a squames (an infection of the squamous cells) and the fungus appears as an opportunist which causes the eventual death of the fish.

Since the pandemic of UDN in Scottish rivers in the late 1960s and 1970s the disease has tended to wane, although every year there are isolated outbreaks varying in their severity. However, more recently salmon in Spanish rivers have been seriously affected by a disease with symptoms similar to UDN and during 1986 a total of 1889 salmon were recorded with symptoms of disease; Ventura (1988) gives records of the proportion of diseased fish in five rivers (Table 4.3).

**Table 4.3**   Incidence of diseased salmon in Spanish rivers*

| River | Total catch | Diseased fish | % |
|---|---|---|---|
| Sella | 2737 | 1646 | 60.13 |
| Esva | 807 | 191 | 23.67 |
| Cares | 686 | 49 | 7.14 |
| Narcea | 537 | 3 | 0.56 |
| Eo | 667 | 0 | 0 |

*Source: Ventura (1988).

*Vibriosis.* The causative organism of this disease is the common marine bacterium *Vibrio anguillarum* which is a Gram-negative, motile, curved rod. This organism is also pathogenic to sea trout, eels, perch, plaice (*Pleuronectes platessa*) and saithe (*Gadus virens*).

The symptoms of the disease are haemorrhagic spots on the body, particularly on the belly. Internal organs often show signs of degeneration. Because it is a marine bacterium salmon in salt and brackish water are often affected, but it also occurs on salmon in most rivers. Infected fish showing signs of vibriosis are often believed to be suffering from furunculosis which has similar symptoms. For this reason a bacteriological examination is necessary before the disease can be diagnosed.

*Cataracts.* Another affliction which has been recorded in recent years in adult salmon at sea is the incidence of cataracts in the eyes. The damage was first observed at Achiltibuie on the west coast of Scotland in the summer of 1984. It has also been recorded in salmon caught in the Faroese fishery. Incidence as high as 40% has been reported.

### Mass mortality

Mortalities of adult salmon in the river may also from time to time result from causes other than disease. One such example was a mass mortality on the River Wye involving at least 426 adult salmon. This was caused by high water temperature (maximum 27.6 °C), low flow conditions and the accelerated decay of aquatic macrophytes (*Ranunculus fluitans*) which resulted in severe deoxygenation (Brooker, Morris and Hemsworth, 1977). Elsewhere, Huntsman (1942) recorded the deaths of adult salmon in the Moser River, Nova Scotia, which he attributed to high water temperatures during very low water conditions. He found that freshly-run grilse died at about 29.5 °C and acclimatized grilse at about 30.5 °C. During low flow conditions one summer on the River Tweed Waddington (1957) recorded the deaths of large numbers of salmon and trout. These were caused by low dissolved oxygen concentrations and low pH levels at night as a result of massive growths of *Cladophora glomerata*. The growth of this alga had been stimulated by nutrients contained in sewage and textile effluents discharged further upstream.

## 4.7   PARASITES

The parasites of salmon which are best known are the ecto- or external parasites. There are those which attack the fish in the sea and those which attack the fish when it enters brackish or fresh water.

### Invertebrates

The marine invertebrate parasite most well known is *Lepeophtheirus salmonis* or the sea louse as it is called by fishermen. It survives for a short time in fresh water and its presence on salmon in fresh water is therefore a good indication that the salmon is only recently in from the sea. The female sea lice, which often have long egg sacs or 'streamers', are most conspicuous. Hutton (1923) has found sea lice on salmon in the River Wye 193 km upstream and believes that they may survive in fresh water for over a week when the water temperature is low.

White (1940) describes the damage caused by 'lice' and mentions the capture of a grilse so heavily infested that its body colours from above were obscured by the brown parasites.

White believed that the death of a number of salmon in the Moser River in August 1939 was partly due to areas of abrasion caused by the lice. Practically all the salmon running during July and early August were very badly infested with the parasites and the later ones showed white patches over the frontal region, on the opercula, along the occipital region and extending posteriorly along the nape. White felt that these abrasions were not severe enough of themselves to cause death. However, some days later dead fish were found with the skin over part of the head sloughed away exposing the muscle beneath. White found that on many of the fish which were severely infested the skin was loose over the same areas. It was also noticed that when the 'lice' were scraped off, the skin readily came away exposing the flesh beneath. Before the skin sloughs off there is a distinct white area over these infected regions and White believes that this condition is the same as that described by Calderwood (1906b) as 'white spot disease'. Calderwood also recorded it from salmon under the same conditions as those in which the infected salmon on the Moser River were existing, namely in very low water when the fish were prevented from ascending the streams and were congregated near the mouths. Calderwood attributed the injury to sunlight.

The life history of *Lepeophtheirus* was later described by White (1942) and he records finding bits of fish skin with melanophores in the digestive tracts of the sea lice; he also observed them taking into their mouths minute pieces of chopped skin which had been fed to them. This parasite is now a serious problem to salmon farmers, and fish being reared in sea cages are badly afflicted by this parasite and have to be treated regularly to rid them of the infestation (Wooten, Smith and Needham, 1982).

The most well-known freshwater parasite of salmon is the gill maggot *Salmincola salmonea*. This organism, like *Lepeophtheirus*, is a parasitic copepod but is not free-living and bears little resemblance to *Lepeophtheirus*. Its life history and ecology have been fully described by Friend (1941). Salmon are infected by this parasite in fresh water. The free-swimming larva attaches itself to the gills of a salmon while it is in fresh water. On becoming attached to the gills it eventually moults twice and becomes either a mature male or a first-stage female, both of which can move about on the gills. After copulation the male dies; the female develops an attachment organ and becomes fixed. About six months after copulation eggs are produced. A moult follows and the eggs are extruded; two further sets of eggs may be extruded by the female before the salmon returns to the sea. If the kelt returns to the sea before these later generations of eggs have been extruded reproduction is inhibited in the sea and will not be resumed until the fish returns to fresh water. Then the parasite lays its eggs and drops off the gills; the fish is then liable to reinfection. The epizootic significance of the parasite is comparatively slight: it causes some injury to the ends of the gill lamellae to which it is attached. The salmon shows definite seasonal variations in its susceptibility to infection. In the pre-spawning period infection intensity averages 11.2 copepods per fish; in November it increases to 20.8, and in December to February, up to 53.7 copepods per fish.

An attempt was made to establish the life span of the copepod. If the salmon remains in the sea for only one summer on its second visit to that environment and re-enters the river in the autumn to spawn a second time, the copepod probably lives about 1 year. The cycle in this case is – infection in the river in late autumn or winter, maturation in fresh water for six months, growth in the sea in the summer, reproduction in the river and death in the spring. However, in cases where the salmon spends 1 year or more in the sea before returning to spawn a second time, some of the copepods remain alive and continue to grow until they are two to three times larger than usual.

The leech *Piscicola geometra* is parasitic on salmon, as well as other fish, and is adapted to life in cool, well-aerated water. It is found in fast-flowing streams and on the wave-washed shores of eutrophic lakes and occurs most frequently in hard waters.

In February 1967 these leeches were found on salmon taken from the Tweed at Kelso, Roxburghshire. Most of the salmon were kelts and according to reports about 50% of the kelts seen were infected. Although the leeches were found on all parts of the fish they occurred mainly around the dorsal and pectoral fins, the flanks and caudal peduncle. The number of specimens per fish varied from one to 15 (Mills, 1967).

This leech is a little over 2.5 cm long and is olive brown in colour. The body, which is cylindrical, is divided into numerous small annuli and along the lateral margins are pulsating vesicles. There are powerful suckers at the anterior and posterior ends of the organism and the anterior one forms a conspicuous dilation on the head region.

A skin parasite, *Gyrodactylus salaris*, probably introduced to Norwegian salmon farms from resistant farm stock in Sweden (Johnsen, 1978; Johnels, 1984), has subsequently spread to wild salmon stocks in Norwegian rivers.

*Gyrodactylus salaris* is a monogenetic trematode. It is an external parasite infesting the skin and fins of juvenile salmon (Figs 4.8, 4.9). The adult parasite is about 0.5 mm long and feeds by taking pieces out of the fish's skin. As a result of the meals taken by the parasite, a collection of small holes appear and these in turn become liable to infection by bacteria and fungi. Often an additional layer of mucus covers the skin and the parasitic fungus *Saprolegnia* develops. *G. salaris* does not lay eggs but produces live young. As a result it is able to multiply very rapidly and it is said that one single individual can develop into 4 million in the space of 40 days (Haukbø, 1983).

**Fig. 4.8** Salmon parr infected with *Gyrodactylus salaris*. Fish 1 and 2 are heavily attacked: note the formation of fungus at fins and the extra mucoid layer. Fish 3 (top) is lightly attacked. Fish 4 is not attacked. Scale in cm (photo by P. E. Fredriksen, reproduced with permission from Heggberget and Johnsen, 1982).

Infestations in Norwegian rivers have been characterized by violent outbreaks, often with thousands of parasites on a single fish which, combined with fungus attacks, has resulted in the mass death of salmon parr (Heggberget and Johnsen, 1982; Johnsen and Jensen, 1986). As a result the parasite has considerably reduced the stocks of juvenile salmon in many rivers with a consequent reduction in the numbers of returning adults estimated at $1.144–2.464 \times 10^6$ kg (Johnsen and Jensen, 1986; Dolmen, 1987).

Fortunately this species of *Gyrodactylus* does not occur in other salmon

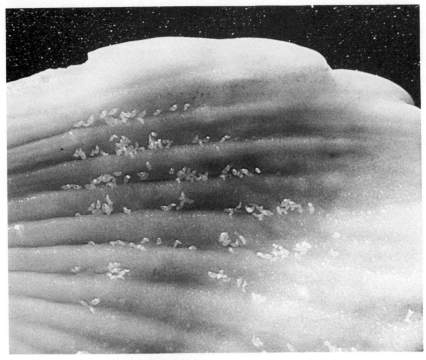

**Fig. 4.9** *Gyrodactylus salaris* sited at the pectoral fin of a salmon parr (photo by P. E. Fredriksen, reproduced with permission from Heggberget and Johnsen, 1982).

producing countries as yet. However, there is a connection in the distribution of the parasite with transport of eyed ova from infested hatcheries (Johnsen and Jensen, 1986; Dolmen, 1987). As 2.4 million Norwegian salmon ova and a similar number from Sweden were introduced into Scotland in 1986, and 100 000 ova were exported from Norway to Ireland in the same year, this might be one way in which the parasite might be expected to be introduced. A further pathway might be via rainbow trout, as observations indicate that brown trout and rainbow trout may be carriers of *G. salaris.*

The only known method of eradicating the parasite is with rotenone which, being a fish poison, kills the host. Successful attempts have been carried out on one Norwegian river to date. Infested hatcheries have been successfully disinfected by drying them out.

A number of internal parasites occur in the juvenile and adult stages of the salmon and include representatives of the trematodes (flukes), cestodes (tapeworms), acanthocephalans (spiny-headed worms) and nematodes (round worms). One of the largest of these is the tapeworm *Eubothrium crassum* which, in its adult stage, may measure between 12 and 60 cm in length and occurs in the pyloric cæca. The intermediate hosts of this parasite are copepods (e.g. *Cyclops strenuus*) and the perch (*Perca fluviatilis*). A list of the parasites infecting the Atlantic salmon is given by Hoffman (1967).

Ecological studies of the parasites of the salmon have been made by Heitz (1918) and Dogiel and Petrushevski (1935). Heitz, in a work devoted to the salmon of the Rhine, described the gradual reduction of the parasitic fauna with the progress of the fish upstream. Dogiel and Petrushevski succeeded in obtaining a full picture of the changes in the parasite fauna of the salmon throughout its entire life cycle, having collected data not only on the adult fish, but also on the young inhabiting the upper reaches of the rivers. Data were collected from the Rivers Onega, Vyg and tributaries of the North Dvina. The freshwater parasite fauna of the young fish was found to be composed of 12 species. The young fish acquires this fauna gradually with the progress of growth, this slow build-up lending support to the rule of the age dynamics of parasite fauna. It was found that a considerable proportion of the three-to-four-months-old fish were completely free of parasites. Almost all the fish of the 1 + group were infested; the 4-year-old fish retained the same number of parasitic species as the 2 + and 3 + group fish, but their incidence and the intensity of infestation became higher.

The process of this gradual development of the parasite fauna in small salmon may be expressed by the mean number of parasitic species in infested fish of various ages. For the three-to-four-months-old fish this number is 1.0, for the 1 + group it is 1.3, for the 2 + and 3 + it is 2.3 and for the 4 + it is 2.7 parasite species.

Once in the sea the salmon frees itself completely of its freshwater parasites and acquires parasites of marine origin. The parasite fauna of 15 species found in the salmon on its return to fresh water included only three freshwater parasites. Even these few freshwater parasites, however, were not survivors of the salmon's original parasite fauna but were newly acquired by it during its ascent of the river. All the marine species accompany the salmon on entering fresh water. Once in fresh water the salmon begins to lose its marine parasite fauna. The first to go are the ectoparasites, subjected to the direct influence of fresh water. For example, all salmon caught in Belomorsk on the White Sea (mouth of the River Vyg) were infested with *Lepeophtheirus*. The salmon caught about 10 km up the river from that town were only 25% infested, while further upstream they were completely free of *Lepeophtheirus*. The loss of ectoparasites is followed by the gradual loss of the marine intestinal parasites, the decrease in the number of species and the intensity of infestation being inversely proportional to the length of time spent by the host in fresh water.

The parasites of the body cavity, not exposed to the direct influences of fresh water and unable to leave their habitat, are only little affected by the migration of the host. This is shown by the larvae of the nematode *Terranova decipiens*, which were equally abundant in both salmon that had recently entered fresh water from the sea and in those that had been in fresh water for a few months.

The small number of freshwater parasites acquired by the salmon in its ascent of rivers is due to the behaviour of the fish at this stage of its life history. The salmon does not feed during its upstream journey, so one of the main paths of infection, the gut, remains closed.

### Vertebrates

Without doubt the most important vertebrate parasite of salmon is the sea lamprey *Petromyzon marinus*. Unfortunately there is little information on its effects on Atlantic salmon stocks. Malloch (1910) describes them being caught in the salmon fishers' nets on the Tay when they are ascending the rivers in May and June to spawn. They are present in a number of Scottish rivers and can be seen at spawning time carrying stones in their sucker-like mouths to build their 'nests' in which the eggs are deposited. In June and July recently-formed depressions or 'clean' areas of gravel may be noticed in streams and these may be due to the spawning activities of lampreys.

## 4.8   SPAWNING

The adult male and female change in appearance after entering fresh water and as spawning time approaches. Some of the bones of the salmon grow substantially and there appears a new set of breeding teeth. The bones that increase their size and acquire new material include the main bones of the jaws; this is particularly noticeable in the male which develops a hooked lower jaw or kype. The parts of the skull growing at the breeding period require a large amount of material, mostly calcium (Tchernvin, 1938). As the salmon does not feed during the time it is in fresh water (as a result of which it may lose about 25% of its body weight) the only material available is from other parts of the body. Comparing the enormous growth of the jaw bones and of the teeth with the relatively small absorption of the bones of the gill covers there would appear to be insufficient calcium to supply all the growing elements with necessary material. However, there is also considerable erosion or absorption of the scales and Crichton (1935) and van Someren (1937) suggest that the calcium from this source is also used by the growing bones and teeth. In the case of the scale, as a result of this erosion, all that remains of the scale becomes deeply embedded in the spongy dermis.

The most detailed account of the spawning behaviour of salmon is that given by Belding (1934a), Jones and King (1949) and Jones (1959) and readers should refer to these works for a complete description of spawning.

*Do like breed like?* As has been mentioned earlier, particular rivers, or even tributaries of a river, may be characterized by the time of year when salmon enter them and by the proportions among them of grilse and salmon. These facts have commonly been interpreted as meaning that there are more-or-less-distinct races in the various rivers, characterized by such behaviour and also by certain body proportions and other details of structure. This conception has been generally accepted and in the past a great deal of work was done in describing the characteristics of salmon of individual rivers from the results of studies of their scales. As White and Huntsman (1938) state:

Even for one river the salmon may come in from the sea at quite different seasons and these 'runs' may differ considerably in character, such as size and body proportions. The theory has been extended to fit these facts by the supposition that there are more or less distinct early-running and late-running races in the one river.

The early-running and large fish are of most value to the fishermen, and White and Huntsman go on to say:

It has been natural, therefore, that the fishermen have wished to have the theory of races put to practical use in two ways: first, by having the early and large fish used in fish cultural practice so that their numbers might be maintained and increased, and, second, by having the young from rivers with early-running and large salmon planted in those rivers where the local fish are late-running and small. To secure the early and large fish and to hold them until spawning time, was therefore, undertaken by the Fish Culture Branch of the Department of Fisheries of Canada, and proved to be a difficult and costly business. This made it desirable to ascertain whether the practice had any real justification.

There were conflicting views over whether local behaviour was heritable. To start with, late-running fish in the Miramichi River, New Brunswick, were tagged and liberated after spawning. Of those recaptured in the river after one or two years, and presumably ready to spawn again, six out of 16 were taken early in the summer. This raised doubts as to the distinctness of the early-running and late-running habits in individual fish. Calderwood (1930), however, has argued that the seasonal habit persists in individual fish, making use of the fact that of all the grilse (which run in summer) marked in Scotland, not one when recaptured as a salmon was taken in the spring. He also argued that the heavy netting of the salmon in summer and autumn on many parts of the coast of Scotland has caused the late-running grilse to decline and the spring salmon to increase, and that large catches of salmon in the summer and autumn in the Tweed district resulted in the Tweed changing in 25 years from a late river into an early river. He states: 'If we do not accept the premise (the existence of early and late runs as separate local races of salmon) I am unable to account for the spring run in the Tweed in any other way.' At the present time the Tweed again has a late run of autumn fish and in the opinion of some the spring run is declining; it would be interesting to know how Calderwood would have explained this situation, as the autumn fish enter the river after the netting season has closed. However, the spring fish are heavily exploited throughout the season by both nets and rods and their decline could be attributed to overexploitation on these stocks, thus favouring the lightly exploited autumn stocks. Huntsman would probably not have agreed, as he concluded (1931) for the Miramichi River 'that man's experiment lasting for more than 80 years in restricting fishing to the early run and encouraging reproduction of the late run has succeeded neither in materially reducing the early run nor in materially increasing the late run.'

It was apparent to White that a test was necessary in order to determine whether or not such peculiarity in behaviour is inherited. To carry out this test, fry hatched from eggs of salmon in Chaleur Bay, near the mouth of the Restigouche River, New Brunswick, where salmon enter early in the summer as two-sea-year and three-sea-year fish, were planted in 1932 in the East Branch (without salmon) of the Apple River at the head of the Bay of Fundy. In this region the local salmon enter only in the autumn and nearly all as grilse. The Restigouche fish, as parr, grew more rapidly than the local fish, corresponding with the less-crowded conditions in the East Branch. The smolts were marked by removal of the adipose fin when descending to sea in 1934. Traps were placed on both branches in 1935 and in the autumn 92 marked grilse entered the East Branch and six the South Branch. In 1936 five marked two-sea-year salmon entered the East Branch in the autumn and one entered the South Branch. No difference in appearance or behaviour was observable between the fish in the East Branch (from Restigouche parents) and the local salmon of the South Branch.

In summing up the results of the Apple River experiment White (1936) says:

The outcome of this experiment is quite clear. The Restigouche fish remained only two years in the Apple River instead of the three years characteristic of their native stream. Also they returned from the sea predominantly (95%) as grilse instead of as two sea-year and three sea-year fish, the behaviour in their native region. Finally, while in the Restigouche River a large number of the fish return as early-run fish and ascend the river as such, those introduced into the Apple River did not, on return, ascend as early-run fish, but were found both early and late in the estuary in common with the native stock. Water conditions in the river were probably not suitable for an early ascent, but later in the summer when there was sufficient water they did not ascend. Except in rate of growth in the river, for which obvious reasons have been given (i.e. less crowded conditions), the Restigouche salmon introduced into Apple River could not be distinguished by their behaviour from the indigenous salmon, and hence failed to show any evidence of a 'Restigouche' inheritance. Although the failure is definite as to any racial distinction between Restigouche and Apple River salmon, the possibility of there being such distinctions in other places is not excluded. The significant point is that, in this instance, there has been a demonstration that environmental conditions, acting on the individual from the fry stage on, make the full observed difference in behaviour between Restigouche and Apple River salmon almost as great a difference as is to be found in the salmon in Canadian waters.

More recently the Salmon Research Trust of Ireland has undertaken the rearing of fish of known ancestry and their subsequent tagging, release and recapture and the question of whether the sea-absence period of maiden salmon was governed by heredity or was due solely to the influence of the environment was one of the primary objectives of its work. Piggins (1974) found that: (1) within the region of the Trust's operations the major proportion of the returns from reared smolts has occurred as grilse, irrespective of parentage; (2) smolts of two-sea-winter fish parentage types have produced a greater proportion of two-sea-winter fish in the returns than have grilse-parentage smolts and (3) 1-year-old smolts of both parentage types have produced more two-sea-winter fish than have 2-year-old smolts of comparable parentage (Tables 4.4, 4.5).

Wilkins (1985) stated that '"like" does not always "breed like" where characters like "growth rate", "age at first maturity" or "time of return to the river" are concerned'. He considered that there is abundant evidence from wild fish and from hatchery experiments to show that inheritance is a significant determinant of age at first maturity in the salmon. What these studies show is that quantitative traits are governed by genes at a number of loci and that the effects of these are modified by environmental factors. Wilkins (1985) explains

**Table 4.4** Data on the numbers of smolts of known parentage reared and released at the Burrishoole Fishery, Ireland, and their subsequent time of return*

| Smolt type and age | No. of smolts released | No. of smolts recaptured† | No. recaptured as grilse‡ | No. recaptured as spring fish‡ |
|---|---|---|---|---|
| Spring fish (1 + smolts) | 6 351 | 30 (0.5) | 21 (70) | 9 (30) |
| Spring fish (2 + smolts) | 23 344 | 180 (0.8) | 162 (90) | 18 (10) |
| Grilse (1 + smolts) | 27 390 | 543 (2.0) | 523 (96) | 20 (4) |
| Grilse (2 + smolts) | 63 953 | 1 790 (2.8) | 1 767 (99) | 23 (1) |
| Spring fish × grilse (1 +) | 1 032 | 10 (1.0) | 9 (90) | 1 (10) |
| Spring fish × grilse (2 +) | 5 100 | 143 (2.8) | 138 (96) | 5 (4) |

*Source: Piggins (1974).*
†*Figures in parentheses denote percentages of no. released.*
‡*Figures in parentheses are percentages of no. recaptured.*

**Table 4.5**   Details of time of return of fish of known ancestry reared and released as smolts at the Burrishoole Fishery, Ireland*

| Smolt parentage | No. and percentage recaptured as: | | |
| --- | --- | --- | --- |
| | Grilse | 2SW fish | Pre-grilse |
| 2SW | 409 (86.1%) | 66 (13.9%) | 0 |
| (Spring and summer fish) | | | |
| Grilse | 6346 (98.6%) | 90 (1.4%) | 9 (0.14%) |
| 2SW × Grilse | 147 (96.1%) | 6 (3.9%) | 0 |

*Source: Piggins (1986).*

at length how this occurs and concludes by saying: 'the complexity of the "age at first maturity" phenotype and other quantitative traits depend on genotype and environment, but we do not always know the relative importance of each at any particular time or in any particular stock.'

## 4.9   KELTS

After spawning, both male and female fish are known as kelts. The death rate after spawning is high, especially among male fish. According to Taylor (1968, p. 97), the fish suddenly develops Cushing's disease caused by an increased output of the hormone ACTH. Apparently the salmon contains some internal 'clockwork mechanism' which turns up its pituitary controls at the time of migration, and the over-stimulated pituitary causes the excessive output of ACTH.

However, Belding (1934b) considers that the cause of the high mortality in salmon after spawning is a severe reduction in body weight. Physiologists have found that death occurs in animals during starvation when the body weight is reduced approximately 40%. The loss of between 31% and 44% in weight, according to the length of stay in the rivers, brings the salmon close to the line of physiological death. As a result it is so weak on its return to the ocean that it is unable to undergo normal recuperation. Salmon that are spawning for a second time are recruited from the more vigorous individuals which manage to recover their strength before being subjected to a hostile environment.

Some information on the proportion of the upstream run of spawners returning downstream as kelts has been collected at two points on the Conon River system in Ross-shire. On the River Meig the proportion of fish returning downstream as kelts over 4 years from an average upstream run of 333 fish was 14.4% ranging from 10.2% to 24.6%. Unfortunately this information is incomplete, as the trap at which the information was collected was flooded at times during the winter months. However, at Torr Achilty dam on the River

Conon, where little spilling occurs, the proportion was much higher and, with an average upstream run over 6 years of 2300 fish, the proportion descending was on average 26%, ranging from 20% to 36%.

The proportion of previously spawned fish in the rivers of various countries is very similar on average and is in the region of 3–6%. However, there are some short-course rivers, such as those in the west of Scotland and parts of eastern Canada, where the proportion of previously spawned fish may be as high as 34%. Nall (1933) has recorded a salmon caught in Loch Maree on the west coast of Scotland which had spawned four times. It was 13 years old and is probably the oldest recorded Scottish salmon. However, salmon have been known to spawn as many as five or six times in the wild (White and Medcof, 1968; Ducharme, 1969). Observations show that there are two main periods when the downstream movement of kelts occurs, one being in November and December and the other in April and May. However, these records of kelt descent have been made at, or a short distance below, hydroelectric installations where delay in descent is known to occur, and therefore the time of descent in an uncontrolled river may be different.

Although fish liberated as kelts may at times tend to stay in the estuary or in the sea within the influence of the river, kelts do undergo long-distance migrations. Menzies and Shearer (1957) give details of a kelt tagged at Loch na Croic on the River Blackwater, Ross-shire, which was recaptured 1730 miles (2784 km) away on the west coast of Greenland. Went and Piggins (1965) also record kelts tagged in rivers in the west of Ireland being captured off the west coast of Greenland.

The absence periods or lengths of time salmon spend in the sea between spawnings have been classified by Jones (1959).

1.  Short period: a few months' duration, i.e. when a kelt goes down in spring and comes up the following autumn to spawn again;
2.  Long period: about 1 year, i.e. a whole summer and winter spent in the sea;
3.  Very long period: a stay in the sea of about 18 months.

Since the beginning of the century over 22 000 kelts have been marked in the Republic of Ireland and of these 490 have been recaptured in the river as clean fish and 486 or 99.2% of these recaptures were made in the river in which marking was done or in the estuary thereof. This indicates a marked homing instinct in the previously spawned fish.

*The kelt and its value.* There has been some controversy over the value of the kelt to the commercial and rod fisheries, and opinions differ from country to country. In Canada, for example, there is a rod fishery in the spring for kelts or 'black salmon' on the Miramichi. Kerswill (1955a), in his conclusions on the assessment of the effects of black salmon angling on Miramichi salmon stocks, states:

Although the Miramichi black salmon fishery takes some of the early-run stock of salmon, there is a small chance that these would become available again to fishermen even though they were spared. Less than 10% of Miramichi salmon have come into fresh water previously for spawning. Recent tagging of incoming salmon throughout the season has shown that the proportion of the late-run fish taken by black salmon anglers in the following spring is greater than the proportion taken of the early-run fish. The black salmon fishery appears to be a worthwhile use for the late-run stock which is quite plentiful in the Miramichi area. In weighing the merits and disadvantages of black salmon angling these points must be considered carefully, as well as the financial benefits derived from this popular sport fishing. Wanton destruction of black salmon is to be avoided, of course, since some of the largest early-run salmon in future years will be survivors of the earlier spawning.

Harriman (1960) describes the 'black salmon controversy' and quotes the opinions given him by a number of salmon experts from different countries. Two only will be quoted here, one from 'each side of the house' as it were. The first one is from Menzies' *Report on the present position of the Atlantic salmon fisheries of Canada* (Atlantic Salmon Association Document No. 17, 1951):

Like drift netting in the sea, black salmon angling, in plain language, "kelt fishing", has become an established practice on the Miramichi River, and is engaged in to a lesser extent on two or three other rivers. It is a queer form of sport but, apparently some people enjoy it, though one cannot imagine anyone enjoying the eating of a kelt; the justification appears to be that the anglers provide employment and bring money into the area which otherwise, at that time, would not have the benefit.
Expediency, or financial gain, seem poor excuses for this departure from the law and from normal sporting standards, even if harm done to the stock is small. I recommend that the law should be strictly enforced in the other rivers, and serious and immediate consideration should be given to taking the same step on the Miramichi.

In a letter to the Narraguagus Salmon Association (31 October 1959) Menzies says:

Scale reading shows that the previously spawned fish constitute in our (Scottish) rivers between 3 and 5% of the total stock. Consequently, in a normal river, if the entire kelt population were destroyed, the stock would be reduced by no more than 5%, although necessarily this would have a cumulative effect. This last point, the cumulative effect, is, I think, important, especially since nearly all the kelts which survive until the spring and are then caught are females.

In Scotland and throughout Great Britain, the taking and killing of kelts has been illegal for all time.

Carlin is of the opposite opinion and in his letter to the Narraguagus Salmon Association (23 January 1960) says:

The regulation of kelt fishing is different in different parts of Sweden. In the rivers of the northern part of our east coast, the closed season is usually from September 1st to December 31st, although in some cases the salmon fishing is closed until May to protect the kelts. A very rough estimation, founded on tagging experiments, gave the results that, if the kelts are spared, about one third of them would be taken later as mended fish, and the individual fish would have increased about three times in value.

My personal opinion is that the salmon fishing could be free after the spawning season unless the salmon population is so low that the kelts are urgently needed to increase the salmon population.

Harriman (1960) in his conclusion says:

In light of overwhelming evidence and opinion as to the wisdom of legalising black-salmon angling, it is submitted that the Maine Sea-Run Salmon Commission should not only reverse its decision with respect to the Narraguagus but should outlaw black-salmon angling on all Maine streams until such time as it becomes evident that additions to the spawning stock are in excess of requirements.

It is interesting to note that at the present time 25% of the total number of salmon retained in the New Brunswick salmon sport fishery are kelts (Marshall, 1988).

Probably the best evidence put forward for conserving kelts, in Ireland at least, is that given by Went (1964a):

In Irish waters it has been obvious that the returned kelts may make fairly substantial contributions to the stocks of salmon. In the Shannon the proportion of previous spawners has varied considerably from year to year. In the year 1941, for example, by weight the previous spawners amounted to 7.3% of the total. From other investigations we know that of the previous spawners at least four out of five are females, so we can assume that female previous spawners in 1941 represented 5.8% of the total stock by weight. In the maiden fish, as far as we can ascertain in this river the sexes are more or less equally abundant.

Now the number of eggs spawned by a female is roughly proportional to her weight and if we take 500 eggs per lb of body weight as a round figure then 100 pounds of spawning fish in the Shannon might be expected to yield the following eggs:

| Previous spawners | Females | 5.8 lb = | $5.8 \times 500 =$ | 2 900 |
|---|---|---|---|---|
| | Males | 1.5 lb | Nil | |
| Maiden or unspawned fish | Females | 46.35 lb = | $46.35 \times 500 =$ | 23 175 |
| Total | | | | 26 075 |

On that basis in the Shannon the previous spawners would have accounted for 11.1% of all the eggs deposited or, say, 1 in 9, certainly a worthwhile contribution.

Chadwick (1988) considers that repeat or previous spawners are important in mitigating the effects of variation in sea survival. Unfortunately, he showed that previous spawners are less common in Canada than they used to be.

Probably for these reasons the Canadian Department of Fisheries and Oceans is now reconditioning kelts artificially using a moist pellet diet. It has been found that the feeding response and growth of kelts was highest when salinities were maintained at 28% during winter and 16% during summer. Two-sea-winter kelts reconditioned at a slower rate than one-sea-winter kelts. Kelt survival was 93.1% the first year and 82.7% the second year (Gray, Cameron and McLennan, 1987).

It is stated in the *Report of the Committee on Salmon and Freshwater Fisheries* (the Bledisloe Report) in 1961 (Cmnd. 1350) (Anon., 1961) under Section 89:

In England and Wales only about 5% of the salmon entering our rivers survive to spawn a second time, so if a fisherman takes a kelt there is a large chance that it would have died anyway and therefore that it would not have contributed to the future stock. If, indeed, a river is so short of fish that it depends on the maintenance of the population of fish which have spawned before, then clearly it is being overfished and the effective remedy is a reduction of fishing by means of an increased annual or weekly close time, reduction of netting, or even by restriction of angling.

Some adult fish, generally females, may not spawn due either to some physical abnormality or to absence of one of the opposite sex. These fish are known as baggots or rawners and return to the sea with eggs or milt unshed.

There are a number of physical differences which are supposed to distinguish a previous spawner from a virgin fish. These are:

1. Previous spawners are not truly silvery, but have a golden sheen on their scales (but apparently some late-running virgin fish may also have this golden sheen!);
2. Previous spawners generally have many more spots, especially on the back and gill covers;
3. Previous spawners invariably have gill maggots (*Salmincola salmonea*) on their gills;
4. The scales of previous spawners show a spawning mark.

I would be reluctant to use the first two characteristics and I would qualify the third by saying that fresh-run previous spawners will have gill maggots but fresh-run virgin fish will not; after virgin fish have been in the river for some time they also will carry gill maggots. Kelts also have gill maggots; I have witnessed many arguments among anglers as to whether a certain fish which had been killed was a kelt or a previous spawner, and I have generally been brought in to decide with a scale examination. However, it is usually possible to recognize a fresh-run previous spawner from a kelt by its general appearance, although the reasons one gives would not necessarily stand up to expert cross-examination.

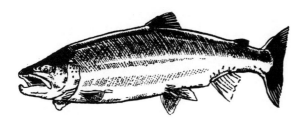

# PART TWO

# Exploitation

# CHAPTER FIVE

# Exploitation of the salmon resource

The Atlantic salmon is exploited throughout its whole geographical range. Some countries have allocated the resource to total (Spain and the United States) or almost total (Iceland) exploitation by the sport fishermen, while other countries have both commercial and recreational fisheries.

## 5.1   COMMERCIAL FISHERY

The main commercial fisheries are centred on the eastern seaboard of North America, the west coast of Greenland, Ireland, the United Kingdom, France, Norway, the USSR, Sweden and Denmark and, to a lesser extent, other countries bordering the Baltic Sea, including Finland and Poland. In addition, a major high seas fishery exists north of the Faroes. Although in some countries there is offshore fishing for salmon using drift nets (e.g. Greenland, Canada, Ireland and north-east England) or floating long lines (Faroes, Denmark and Poland), the majority of the salmon fisheries are concentrated along the coasts and estuaries in order to catch the fish returning to their parent rivers to spawn. Fish moving along the coast are caught in a variety of fixed nets (or fixed engines) set out from the shore, while those ascending the rivers are taken at weirs or cruives, in beach seines or draft nets, or by a variety of nets and traps peculiar to particular countries.

*Scotland.* In Scotland the principal fixed engines are the bag net and the fly net which were first used in the 1800s. The bag net (Fig. 5.1) is commonly used on rocky coasts and consists essentially of a trap made of netting to which fish are directed by a leader, that is a line of netting placed across the route the salmon usually follow as they move along the coast. The salmon swim towards the leader but cannot get through and instinctively turn seawards. They swim along the leader and are led into the mouth of the net and through a succession of compartments into a final chamber or fish court (Fig. 5.1).

A good description of the history, construction and operation of the bag net is given by Hector (1966). In describing the operation of fishing this type of net he says:

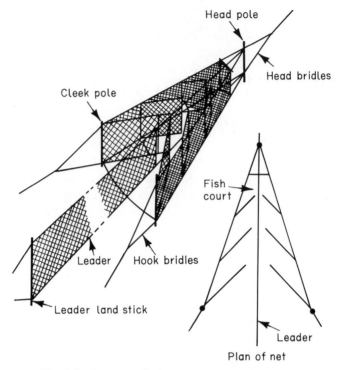

**Fig. 5.1** Diagram of a bag net (from Hector, 1966).

The best time to fish a net is either at high water or low water when the tide is on the turn, and therefore at its slackest. The boat approaches the side from which the tide is flowing. The head pole is seized by means of a boat hook, and the rope untied at the top. This removes the rigidity of the net and the bottom floats towards the surface and the net now lies along the side of the boat. The crew grasp the net and by means of two ropes the bottom is brought to meet the top rope. The boat now crosses the net by the man grasping the meshes of the cover and the bottom. As a result of the flowing tide the netting forms a bulge and the salmon are imprisoned in this section. At the centre of the side is a lacing, which, when undone, allow the salmon to be removed and killed. The net is put in fishing order again by fixing the head pole in its original position, restoring the rigidity of the net. Once a week each net is replaced by a clean one to allow it to be repaired and the sea growth removed by exposure to the sun.

This method of obtaining fish must necessitate relatively calm seas and such a net is very susceptible to storm damage. A recent development has been the use of a double-headed bag net where the leader runs into two bag nets set opposite each other at the seaward end (Smart, 1986).

Stake nets, known as fly nets or 'jumpers' depending on their construction, are used on sandy shores and consist of walls of netting erected on stakes in the sea-bed which act as leaders to approaching salmon. At intervals pockets or traps are inserted to take the fish that are directed along the leader. Unlike bag nets, they are not floating but are fixed to the ground throughout their length. Fish taken by these nets and the bag net are trapped, and not caught in the meshes, and are usually alive when removed (Fig. 5.2).

The bag nets and stake nets have benefited in recent years from being constructed of synthetic materials such as nylon, courlene, polypropylene and fibrefilm rather than tarred cotton as they were in the past. Smart (1986) refers to improvements in the operation of these nets with the advent of mechanization which has inevitably led to a reduction in manpower.

Another type of fixed net used in Scotland is the poke net. Poke nets are used exclusively on the Scottish side of the Solway Firth. They are mounted in lines on rows of poles and consist of a series of pockets of net in which fish are trapped and enmeshed.

Two other types of net used for catching salmon in the Solway Firth are the haaf net and the whammel net. Haaf nets are mounted on a wooden frame

**Fig. 5.2** Stake net set in Montrose Bay on the east coast of Scotland. The entrance to the trap is in the centre of the picture immediately below the long-handled net used to remove the fish. (Photo by T. Kirkwood.)

(about 5 m by 1.25 m) with a handle in the middle of the long side. The fisherman stands in the tide with the middle stick over his shoulder and the net streaming behind him. When he feels a fish strike he lifts the lower lip to prevent its escape. The fisherman must place himself within a few yards of the probable course of moving fish. It is customary for a number of men to fish together. They stand side by side facing the current of the tide and as the tide rises the outermost man in turn transfers himself to the inner end. The procedure is repeated in the reverse order as the tide recedes. A whammel net is a small type of drift net used only to a limited extent, but from the decision of a Scottish court in 1962 it appears that the use of whammel nets on the Scottish side of the main channel in the Solway Firth is illegal.

The net and coble is the only method of net fishing that is legal inside estuary limits throughout Scotland. The net is loaded on the coble and attached to it is a rope held by a fisherman on the shore who, once the operation begins, must keep the rope in motion by his own exertions. The coble moves across the estuary or river, shooting the net as it goes. Its course is roughly a semicircle finishing on the shore from which the boat started out. The ends of the net are then hauled in and the fish removed. It is an essential part of net and coble fishing that the net is hauled through the water continuously and kept in motion by the exertions of the fishermen, who are in some areas assisted by powered winches. The net must not be allowed to remain stationary or drift with the tide, as the fish taken in the net are guided to the landing ground but not enmeshed. The central and deeper part of the net is generally bag-shaped and the fishermen drive the fish towards the bag by splashing the ropes as the net is being pulled in.

Among other catching devices at one time used in the rivers, but now illegal, were cruives, stell nets and cairn nets. Cruives consisted of weirs in which were incorporated boxes or traps. These are still present on some rivers (e.g. the Conon and Beauly) but are no longer operational.

The stell net is rowed into the river in a semi-circular shape. A rope attached to one end of it is held by the fishermen on the shore, and to the other end is attached an anchor, which is cast and secured to the bed of the river. The fishermen in the boat then go near to the centre of the net on the outside of it, and take hold of it, and when they either feel fish strike against the net or see them approach within its reach they warn the men on the shore, and while the latter haul in their end of the net, the men in the boat hoist the anchor, release the net, and bring it to the shore.

A cairn net was a short net fastened to the outer end of a short pier known as a cairn or putt which ran out two or three yards into the river, particularly the Tweed, causing an eddy or backwater. The net was allowed to swing down with the stream, so forming a barrier parallel to the bank between the eddy and the main current, and leaving a good chance of intercepting all fish that turned out to pass outwards from their resting place. Cairn and stell nets were made illegal by the *Tweed Act* of 1857.

One type of trap still in operation is the yair net, unique to the Galloway Dee. A yair consists of two converging fences or leaders made of stakes interwoven with saplings to form a coarse wickerwork. In the apex of the V formed by the converging leaders is a rectangular opening, across the top of which is a platform on which the fisherman sits on a box. The actual net is a deep bag. The fisherman lowers it into the opening so that the water flows through it, and he sits holding a system of lines leading from the end of the bag. If a fish touches the end of the bag, he feels the impact through the lines and immediately hauls up the mouth of the net, thus securing it.

An interesting type of moving net was the shoulder net used on the Galloway Dee and described by King-Webster (1969):

Shoulder nets were used in small pools among the rocks, some of which were reached by a system of wooden catwalks. The gear consisted of a 7.5 m shaft with a 2 m wooden cross-piece at the end, kept square by two rope stays. The triangle formed by cross-piece and stays supported the mouth of a deep bag of netting. Before making a cast, the fisherman flaked the net on top of the shaft, and rested the shaft on a wooden shoe fitted to his shoulder. The cast was made by shooting the net forward, so that the shaft slid over the shoe and the net fell beyond the fish. The net was then drawn in through the pool, the shaft sliding back over the shoe. Shoulder netting required great strength and skill, as fishing was done only at night, and the stance was often precarious and slippery.

Brief mention should also be made of a drift-net fishery which developed off the east coast of Scotland in 1960. This drift-net fishing was a new technique which had no parallel in Scotland and until the Prohibition Order became effective on 15 September 1962, drift net fishing for salmon was lawful outside the three-mile (4.8 km) limit. The development and description of this fishery is given more fully in the First Report of the Hunter Committee, *Scottish Salmon and Trout Fisheries* (Anon., 1963). The drift nets consisted of sections of hemp netting about 10 feet (2.62 m) in depth suspended from a corked head rope and were weighted at the bottom either not at all or only very lightly. Each section of net measured about 100 m in length. The sections were divided into two fleets, each consisting of about 1000 m of netting. The nets were shot by casting them over the side a few feet at a time in a straight line. Some skippers joined their two fleets of nets together and lay at one end of them; others preferred to let each fleet drift independently with the boat taking up station between them. The best results were obtained at night in breezy weather from wind force 3 to wind force 5 when the surface of water was disturbed.

Hemp nets were replaced by monofilament nets in the late 1960s. These nets are less visible to fish and can be used effectively during the day and in calm weather which makes this method of fishing now much safer for fishermen, but more lethal to fish.

These monofilament nets also made illegal fishing operations both off the Scottish coast and in estuaries and rivers much more efficient and the extent of illegal fishing increased dramatically in the 1970s and 80s after the advent and availability of monofilament netting. In 1985, 2365 illegal nets – from a few metres to more than 1000 m in length – were removed from the salt and freshwater areas of the River Tweed district on the borders of Scotland and England (Fig. 5.3). In the sea, alone, 67 nets were seized in 1984. However, with an increase in air surveillance using helicopters, and the imposition of severe penalties on those prosecuted, illegal netting at sea declined dramatically, and in 1986 there were no offences recorded (Fig. 5.4).

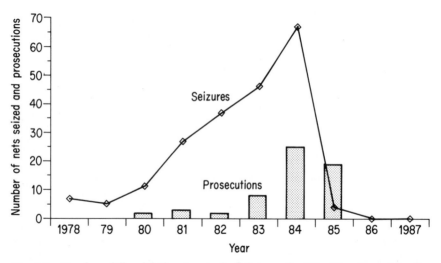

**Fig. 5.3** Number of illegal drift nets seized off the mouth of the River Tweed, by the River Tweed Commissioners and the Fishery Protection Service, 1978–87 and the number of prosecutions resulting from their seizure (reproduced with permission from the River Tweed Commissioners).

*England and Wales.* Fixed engines, which are the principal method of sea fishing for salmon in Scotland, are with a few exceptions forbidden in England and Wales. One type of fixed engine used on the Northumberland coast is the T net which is very similar to the Norwegian kilenot. Its advantage over the Scottish stake and bag nets is its portability and frequently the net is moved inshore as the tide advances. Salmon are also taken with seine, draft or draw

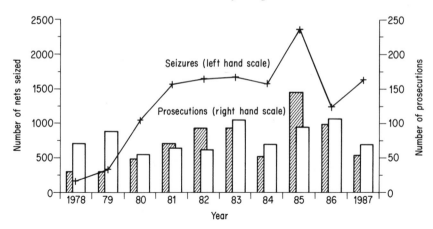

**Fig. 5.4** Number of illegal river and beach nets seized in the River Tweed and from the beach at the mouth of the River Tweed, by the River Tweed Commissioners, 1978–87 and the number of subsequent prosecutions: hatched columns, lower river and beach nets; white columns upper river nets (reproduced with permission from the River Tweed Commissioners).

nets. Most of these are operated from a boat but in Carmarthen Bay and Norfolk a boat is not used and the net is shot by a man wading into the water while his companion holds the shore end.

Another common method of fishing in England and Wales is by drift nets. They consist of a wall of netting (approximately 8 m deep) shot from a boat across the current and allowed to drift freely. One end of the net is attached to a floating buoy and the other remains fixed to the boat. The head rope is corked and the foot rope leaded to keep the net upright. These nets are used in the Bristol Channel, the Ribble and the Lune estuaries, the Solway, and off the north-east coast from Filey to Berwick-on-Tweed\*. These drift nets gill the fish, that is, their heads pass through the meshes of netting. The mesh sizes vary according to the size of fish expected to be caught. The salmon are generally meshed on the south side of the nets, and the best catches are made in the top ten meshes. Before 1960 most of the drift netting was carried out using J nets, which were not true drift nets (Iremonger, 1981).

With the advent of monofilament in about 1969, which replaced the old hemp nets, the drift-net fishery off the north-east coast of England escalated (Fig. 5.5), with part-time fishermen helping to increase fishing effort. The number of licences was controlled in 1972, but the catches were still much

\* The actual limit is south of the legal mouth of the Tweed as defined in Section 4 of the *Tweed Fisheries Amendment Act, 1859* (i.e. 7 miles (11 km) south of Berwick).

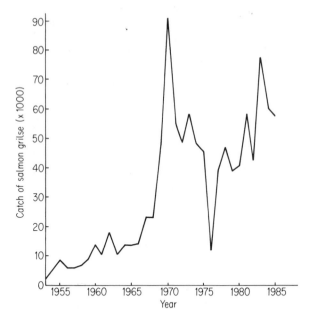

**Fig. 5.5**  Northumbrian and Yorkshire drift-net catch, 1953–85.

higher than before 1969 (Fig. 5.6). This is due to the better fish-catching properties of monofilament.

In the estuary of the Cheshire Dee, the drift nets are trammels. Trammels consist of either two or three sheets of netting. One sheet, the middle one if there are three, is of a standard mesh and is sometimes called the lint. The others are of much bigger mesh and are known as armouring. A fish striking the lint may be gilled as it drives a pocket of this netting through a mesh of the armouring and is trapped.

The Welsh coracle net is used as a drift net and has one sheet of armouring. Coracle netting differs from drift netting, however, in that two coracles are used with the net between them, travelling downstream, armoured side foremost.

Other methods for catching salmon in England and Wales include: (1) types of landing nets going under the name of bow or click nets (Humber area), lave nets (Severn) and haaf or heave nets (between the Lune and Eden); (2) nets operated from a boat anchored across the current and known as stop nets (Wye) or compass nets (Cleddau); (3) fixed weirs situated between tide marks, which may be of stone or of stone surmounted by netting or of stakes and wattles, and which consist of two arms set to form a V pointing in the direction of the ebbing tide; (4) putchers, which consist of a wooden framework into which are inserted tiers of trumpet-shaped basket traps, and which are used in

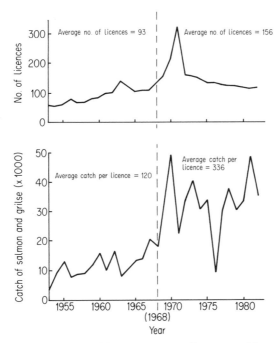

**Fig. 5.6** Northumbrian drift-net fishery, 1953–82, illustrating fishing effort. Vertical dashed line denotes the changeover, after 1968, to monofilament.

the estuaries of the Severn, Wye, Parrett and the Bristol Channel; (5) crib or coop, which is essentially a weir with a gap in it: gratings are set at an angle pointing upstream from each of the downstream corners of the gap, so set that the space between the gratings is only just sufficient to allow a salmon to pass through; the rush of water through the gap entices salmon to pass between these gratings, but their egress to the river above the weir is stopped by another grating set across the gap and they are trapped.

*Ireland.* The methods which are or have been used for catching salmon in Ireland have been admirably described by Went (1964b). He divides the methods into four categories: (A) man-power engines (other than nets) which include spears or leisters, strokehauls, gaffs, snares and tailers; (B) fixed engines such as head weirs, stake nets, bag nets, riverine weirs, cudjail nets, and baskets for smolts; (C) nets (other than fixed engines) which are numerous and include draft nets, drift nets, snap, pole and hoop nets; (D) other methods such as poisoning and explosives.

The methods in the first category are common to many countries and salmon spearing or leistering was a method used in Scotland and eastern Canada and abolished in both countries around 1857.

The head weirs, under (B), are similar to those used in England, while the riverine weirs have cruives as their counterpart in Scotland. Cudjail nets consisted of a stout wire frame to which netting was attached. The net was fixed in gaps in the navigation weirs on the River Barrow and the salmon moving upstream were trapped and eventually drowned. Went says that there is no documentary evidence that baskets for smolts were used in Ireland but there is much local tradition on the subject. Any suitable gap in an artificial or natural obstruction would be useful for this purpose and during the smolt run would provide quantities of small fish.

The beach seine, or draft net, is fished in the same way as in the United Kingdom and at one time accounted for more salmon in Ireland than all the other methods put together.

Drift nets as used in Ireland are of two types: (1) estuarine or bag drift nets and (2) open-sea drift nets. The latter used to be shot just before dark and in the biggest boats were normally only hauled at dawn. The smaller boats, with comparatively small nets, usually hauled the nets several times a night. This was because with hemp nets the most favourable weather conditions were dark stormy nights, for on calm nights the fish did not enmesh themselves, just as was the case in the Scottish and north-east England drift-net fisheries. However, with the advent of monofilament and multifilament nylon (which is the material used in the Irish drift-net fisheries) the nets are less visible and fish also enmesh themselves in calm bright weather, thus making fishery operations that much easier. Went found that generally salmon swim near the water surface and they normally become enmeshed in the upper metre of the net. A survey of the open-sea drift-net fishery for the years 1925 to 1954 has been described by Went (1956). However, since that time the open-sea drift-net fishery has increased alarmingly and there is now an illegal as well as a legal drift-net fishery off the west coast of Ireland extending many miles out to sea.

The proportion of the total catch of salmon taken in the Republic of Ireland by drift nets has risen from 16% in 1961 to 83% in 1983 (Table 5.1). As can be seen from this table, other more traditional methods of catching salmon, such as draft nets, are rapidly declining.

One of the traditional methods of taking salmon in Ireland is with the snap net. Snap nets require two boats, often called cots, to operate them. The net is suspended between the two cots which then drift downstream. The net is therefore fished in much the same way as in the Welsh coracle fishery, although the snap net is a single sheet of netting in which the fish is trapped rather than enmeshed. Two other types of net are used in Ireland. The pole net is a type of landing net with which fish were actively hunted when they showed themselves at weirs or falls or in pools. The other net is the Swilly 'loop' net which is of unusual design to overcome fishing in the deep soft muddy conditions occurring in the River Swilly estuary.

**Table 5.1** Proportion of annual catch taken by various engines*

| Year | Drift nets (%) | Draft nets (%) | Other nets (%) | Rod and line (%) |
|---|---|---|---|---|
| 1951 | 20 | 56 | 15 | 9 |
| 1952 | 23 | 45 | 20 | 12 |
| 1953 | 20 | 48 | 20 | 12 |
| 1954 | 24 | 47 | 14 | 15 |
| 1955 | 19 | 48 | 14 | 19 |
| 1956 | 17 | 50 | 15 | 18 |
| 1957 | 17 | 56 | 10 | 17 |
| 1958 | 17 | 47 | 13 | 23 |
| 1959 | 22 | 53 | 9 | 16 |
| 1960 | 19 | 51 | 13 | 17 |
| 1961 | 16 | 55 | 14 | 15 |
| 1962 | 21 | 57 | 13 | 9 |
| 1963 | 24 | 49 | 15 | 12 |
| 1964 | 25 | 50 | 12 | 13 |
| 1965 | 28 | 44 | 14 | 14 |
| 1966 | 32 | 41 | 14 | 13 |
| 1967 | 37 | 39 | 14 | 10 |
| 1968 | 38 | 39 | 13 | 10 |
| 1969 | 49 | 35 | 10 | 6 |
| 1970 | 49 | 36 | 11 | 4 |
| 1971 | 50 | 36 | 10 | 4 |
| 1972 | 64 | 24 | 7 | 5 |
| 1973 | 66 | 23 | 6 | 5 |
| 1974 | 72 | 20 | 5 | 3 |
| 1975 | 68 | 24 | 6 | 2 |
| 1976 | 70 | 20 | 7 | 3 |
| 1977 | 75 | 17 | 5 | 3 |
| 1978 | 71 | 22 | 4 | 3 |
| 1979 | 82 | 12 | 2 | 4 |
| 1980 | 72 | 19 | 5 | 4 |
| 1981 | 75 | 12 | 7 | 6 |
| 1982 | 76 | 15 | 5 | 4 |
| 1983 | 83 | 11 | 3 | 3 |

*Source: Department of Fisheries and Forestry, Dublin.

Detailed statistics on quantity of salmon taken by instruments of capture and total value of catch, the percentage of catch by various instruments, the average salmon catch per licence and the number of salmon fishing licences are given in the *Report of the Salmon Review Group* (Anon., 1987c)

*Norway.* In Norway salmon are caught along the coast with drift nets, bag nets (kilenots), bend nets, stationary lift nets and stake nets. In the rivers, nets and traps are used. Up until the late 1960s the bag net or kilenot was the most important gear for taking salmon in the sea and this type of net had been in use in northern Norway for over a hundred years. In the 1960s about 88% of the salmon in north Norway were caught in the sea, mostly in bag nets. Although drift-net fishing has been carried on for at least 80 years offshore drift netting using long nets only began in 1960. As in Ireland, so in Norway the number of drift nets has increased rapidly since that date (Table 5.2). Unlike the nets in Ireland, which are made of multifilament, the Norwegian drift nets have been made of monofilament; so too have the bend nets, while the bag nets and lift nets are made of spun nylon. A ban on the use of monofilament came into force in 1988. A total ban on drift-net fishing came into force in 1989.

**Table 5.2**   Number of fishing gears used in the Norwegian home water salmon fishery, 1966–83*

| Year | Seine net | Set net | Bag net | Bend net | Stationed lift net | Drift net |
|------|-----------|---------|---------|----------|--------------------|-----------|
| 1966 | – | – | 7101 | – | 55 | – |
| 1967 | – | 4607 | 7106 | 2827 | 48 | 11 498† |
| 1968 | 345 | 4817 | 6588 | 2613 | 36 | 9 149 |
| 1969 | 307 | 3959 | 6012 | 2756 | 32 | 8 956 |
| 1970 | 309 | 4006 | 5476 | 2548 | 32 | 7 932 |
| 1971 | 288 | 3980 | 4608 | 2421 | 26 | 8 976 |
| 1972 | 436 | 4798 | 4215 | 2367 | 24 | 13 448 |
| 1973 | 477 | 5443 | 4047 | 2996 | 32 | 18 616 |
| 1974 | 409 | 5616 | 3382 | 3342 | 29 | 14 078 |
| 1975 | 349 | 5877 | 3150 | 3549 | 25 | 15 968 |
| 1976 | 260 | 4775 | 2569 | 3890 | 22 | 17 794 |
| 1977 | 303 | 4074 | 2680 | 4047 | 26 | 30 201 |
| 1978 | 301 | 4433 | 1980 | 3976 | 12 | 23 301 |
| 1979 | – | – | 1835 | 5001 | 17 | 23 989‡ |
| 1980 | – | – | 2118 | 4922 | 20 | 25 652‡ |
| 1981 | – | – | 2060 | 5546 | 19 | 24 081‡ |
| 1982 | – | – | 1843 | 5217 | 27 | 22 520‡ |
| 1983 | – | – | 1735 | 5428 | 21 | 21 813‡ |

*Source: Hansen (1986a).
†Inclusive of seine nets.
‡Number of drift nets at start of the season.

*Canada.* Inshore drift nets are used in the Ungava fishery in northern Canada, while offshore drift nets, which must not be made of monofilament, are used in the Maritime Provinces where drift-net fisheries are centred on Port aux Basques (Newfoundland), Escuminac (New Brunswick) and the upper part of the Bay of Fundy and Nova Scotia. Trap or shore nets are used on the coast of the Gaspé Peninsula and on the north shore of the St Lawrence. Along the coast of New Brunswick gill nets, trap nets, pound nets and weirs are also used.

Indian fisheries operate in some of the rivers of New Brunswick and Quebec (Hazell, 1988).

*France and Spain.* Commercial salmon fishing in France is carried out mainly with seine and draft nets, while in Spain all nets have been banned from salmon rivers and their estuaries since 1942. Spain is the only country to have handed over the salmon resource entirely to the sport fisherman.

*Iceland.* With one exception, the Andakilsa, netting is only carried out in the lower reaches of the three largest glacial rivers – the Olfusa–Hvita and Thjorsa in the south and Hvita in the west. About 40% of the annual salmon catch of 250 tonnes is taken by these fixed gill nets which number about 100 (Fig. 5.7). The only other commercial netting for salmon, apart from that carried out in the lakes by the farmers, is at three points near Borgarnes and two points in Hvaldfjordur near Akranes. These coastal nets account for only 1% of the total catch and were permitted to continue after all other sea netting was banned in 1932 because the farms involved had a traditional income from salmon fishing.

*USSR.* According to Kozhin (1964), the Atlantic salmon is taken in the USSR with drift nets, bag nets and seines. In inland waters harvesting is carried

**Fig. 5.7**  Fixed salmon gill net set in the glacial River Thjorsa, Iceland. (Photo by Derek Mills.)

out only at the fish-counting points (blocking stations) in the Pechora, Volonga and Indiga rivers and in other rivers chosen by scientific institutions in conformity with fishery conservation authorities of the Ministry of Fisheries of the USSR. Fishing may be carried out by a limited number of stow seines in the straight between the White Sea and the Barents Sea by special permission of fishery conservation authorities.

Sport fishing is prohibited in all areas with the exception of strictly limited licensed fishing in three rivers of the Kola Peninsula.

*Greenland.* The Greenland salmon fishery is operated using drift nets and fixed hang nets. The latter are fished close inshore and in the fjords. Sometimes one end of the net is attached to the shore. Boats fishing drift nets are allowed to fish up to 40 miles (64 km) from the coast.

Size and type of vessels used in the Greenland salmon fishery are now related to the partitioning of the quota into two allocations. By far the largest fraction of the quota is open to all boats of up to 150 gross registered tonnes. Vessels fishing under this section of the quota range in size up to that maximum in the case of Greenland-registered multi-capability offshore trawlers. However, the majority of the vessels fishing this fraction of the quota are usually smaller, ranging in length from 10.8 m to 15.4 m. They are, for the most part, of a traditional northern European double-ended design, wooden hulled and decked, and are almost always equipped with hull plating along and below the water line for protection against ice. With high bows, foremast with winch and boom, and a large, open work area in front of the wheelhouse, they permit untroublesome rigging-over to shrimp or cod fishing when the brief salmon season ends. These boats may carry from five to 12 crew, and when rigged for drift netting will carry a tubular frame enclosure mounted on the stern. This item, termed a net pound, holds the drift net for storage and while shooting or paying out; it is usually lined with a tough polyethylene tarpaulin distinctive for its bright colour, orange or blue.

In the small-boat category, less than 8 m, there is predictably a wide variety of craft used. Some, the larger of the group, are scaled-down versions of the larger boats. However, many are essentially open boats, with only a small shelter, or cuddy, forward. The requirement of storing a net on board consumes much space, together with a plan for working the net. The smaller craft are, therefore, very limited in their ice and fish storage capacity. As with all larger drifters, some of these vessels are diesel powered and radio equipped; those with enough space usually carry several radar units. These vessels also are recognizable by their stern-mounted net pounds and bright tarpaulins. Some of the very smallest boats used are open fibreglass hulls powered by outboard motors and cannot stay at sea more than a day (larger vessels may stay out from two to five days at a time).

The standard fishing gear is a light-coloured nylon monofilament gill net, with a stretched mesh size of 130–140 mm (distance knot to knot on a side 65–70 mm). Such a mesh size catches salmon from 1 kg to 15 kg weight with most falling in the intermediate range, and requires a floating or float-equipped head rope and a weighted foot rope. Styrofoam or plastic floats are fixed every 2 m, and the average distance, head rope to foot rope, of a net is 3–4 m. Flagged buoys with radar reflectors mark intervals along a net. A drift net comprises a number of standard units linked together with swivels to prevent twisting. On a large vessel with the storage capacity for it, a drift net may contain over 100 such units. Two to three miles (3.2–4.8 km) is normally the maximum length; in contrast, fixed nets having one end anchored to a shore point are seldom longer than five or six units, or 250 m. Mesh size of salmon drift nets is carefully regulated and it is illegal to import undersized nets.

In other than the smallest drift netters, which must use *ad hoc* arrangements, the standard method of shooting or paying out a net uses one or two men, standing over the wake of the vessel in small crow's-nest-type baskets welded to the net pound framework. A centre-mounted fixed hub guides the net out of the pound and as the vessel slowly steams ahead, the netsmen watch the setting. When the net is to be hauled, a forward gunwale-mounted hauler or gurdy is used; this is a simple powered hub around which several turns of foot rope are taken. The net is passed along one side of the work area inboard, where crewmen remove the catch and fouling. At the end of the work area, a funnel-equipped pipe of approximately 30 cm diameter guides the collapsed net alongside the wheel-house to emerge over the net pound on the stern. Netsmen in their baskets stow the net or pay it out again.

The net fishes near the surface, but depending on its specific gravity as determined by floats and fouling, may fish as much as 2 m below the surface. The presence of currents causes nets to hang away from the vertical and reduces the effective working depth. Ice is a serious hazard to drift nets, although they can be used underneath very light ice. Nets are shot throughout the day, an advantage of the practically invisible monofilament. Earlier nets had to be fished at night, as otherwise they were too easily avoided by fish. For a variety of reasons, some undoubtedly unscientific but including poor visibility of nets, drift nets fish better in poor weather. They are seldom left in the water for longer than a few hours due to the deterioration of the catch and potential losses to predators (seals and scavenging shrimp-like amphipods). In the case of bad weather preventing the hauling of nets, much of the catch may drop out or be damaged. While some nets are set far up in fjords, most are set offshore, seldom more than 20 miles (32 km) off, and more commonly less than 15 miles (24 km) out.

In the case of fixed nets, they are normally inspected by small open boats and hand-picked using a boat hook to lift part of the net. Weather plays a far more crucial role in the fixed-net fishery, for if a net cannot be regularly tended, it will lose most of its catch to predators or deterioration (there are substantial differences in price for various grades and sizes of salmon). As a result most fixed nets are deployed in sheltered locations, near harbours, and often in close proximity to one another. This is in contrast to the drift-net fishery, where there are seldom more than one or two boats visible on the horizon. A comprehensive account of the organization and administration of the salmon fishery is given by Kreiberg (1981).

*Faroes.* The Faroese fishery developed some years after the Greenland fishery and it was not until 1979 that the salmon catch rose significantly from a previous high of 51 tonnes to 194 tonnes (Fig. 5.8). Unlike the Greenland fishery which is operated with gill nets, the Faroese fish are taken on floating long lines, although gill nets had been tried but were not very successful.

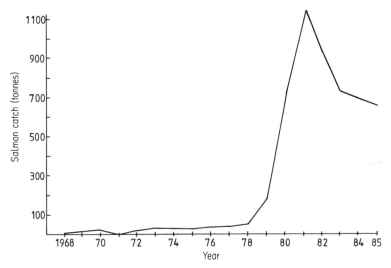

**Fig. 5.8**  Growth of the long-line fishery off the Faroe Islands, 1968–85 (data from ICES Working Group on North Atlantic salmon, Copenhagen, 18–26 March 1985 and 17–26 March 1986; reproduced with permission from Spencer, 1988).

The earlier evidence that a salmon fishery off the Faroes was not viable due to the number of small fish was misleading (Mills and Smart, 1982). This was probably because the earlier voyages were centred chiefly close to the islands and in the south, while in recent years the fishing has been centred on an area 160 km north of the islands in the region of 63°N and 64°30′N. Between April and May the fishing extends further north and is in an area approximately between 4°W and 4°E, and 70°N and 71°30′N. In May the area is approximately between 3°W and 2°E and 67°N and 69°N.

Some of the larger vessels are steel-hulled long-line vessels and multi-capability offshore trawlers with side-gallows of up to 285 gross registered tonnes (Fig. 5.9(a)). The smaller ships are line boats of 15 m overall length and are of the traditional northern European design, wooden-hulled and decked with a gross-registered tonnage of 49 or less. Most of the ships are capable of staying at sea for 7–10 days and are equipped with radar and direction-finding equipment. The size of the crew ranges from four to nine men. Only one or two ships have refrigeration plants; the majority store their catch in ice. Ships with no freezing facilities are not allowed to be at sea for salmon fishing more than 9 days including the days the ship leaves and enters harbour.

The floating long lines are made up of pins, each of 80 hooks; one line consists of ten pins or 800 hooks. The hooks are no. 3/0 Mustad hollow-point. They are tied to a 4.5 m length of monofilament nylon known as a snood. The snood, which is attached to the main line by means of a swivel, is weighted at its mid-point by a barrel lead incorporating another swivel. The gauge of the nylon snood from the main line, which is made of ulstron, to the barrel lead is 0.5–0.6 mm and between the barrel lead and the hook it is 0.3–0.4 mm. The snoods are mounted 18.2 m apart, with yellow 6.3 m plastic floats being positioned on the main line at the mid-point between two snoods. Radio-transmitting 'Dhan' buoys are attached at intervals along the line (Fig. 5.9(b)). These are often spaced 4 km apart. As many as 25 pins may on occasions be joined together. These will extend over a distance of 28.9 km. The whole length of line is often referred to as a set.

The bait consists of sprats which are hooked behind the eyes so that they hang 'tail down'. Catches tend to be best in rough weather and at dawn and dusk. Fishing success can also be affected by squid which eat the bait and any fish already hooked.

The line is shot, usually at night, from the quarter of the vessel as it steams slowly along. The hooks are baited while the line is being shot. The line is retrieved by hand and all fish are lifted out with a long-handled net. It takes 4–5 hours to shoot one set of 32 km and 10–12 hours to haul the same. If the line is cut or broken, which it frequently is, it can be found by picking up the radio transmissions from one of the Dhan buoys.

The fish, on being brought aboard, are placed belly-up on an inverted-V board in which a notch is cut at 60 cm. Those that are above 60 cm in length are retained. They are cut open from vent to the pectoral fins and the gut, gonads, kidney and heart are removed. The fish are then thrown into boxes and later, when the crew has time, are stored away in ice, or frozen if there is a refrigeration unit on board. Salmon will remain fresh for a week if not frozen. Full details of the administration of the salmon fishery are described by Mills and Smart (1982).

*The Baltic Countries.* The countries bordering the Baltic, particularly Denmark, Poland and Sweden, fish for salmon in the open sea with drift nets

**Fig. 5.9(a)**   A steel-hulled long-liner at Nordtoftir, Bordoy, Faroes. (Photo by Derek Mills.)

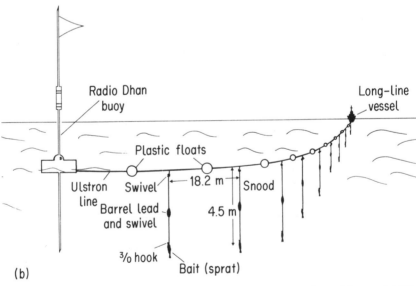

**Fig. 5.9(b)**   A salmon floating long-line (reproduced from Mills and Smart, 1982).

and floating long lines known as 'drift hooks' baited with herring. The lines are similar to those used in the Faroese fishery.

The Swedish coastal fishery employs fixed engines similar to the Scottish stake nets. There are also sweep- or seine-net fisheries in the large northern rivers. One type of trap in use in the rivers, particularly the Torn älv, the river separating Sweden from Finland, is the karsinapatorna. In some of the rivers in southern Sweden, such as the Murramsö, traps used to be set to catch seaward-migrating smolts for feeding to pigs: this is of course now illegal.

## 5.2   SPORT

When fish are sought for sport they are fished or angled for with the aid of a rod and line. Sport fishing is an ancient pastime. Archaeologists have found fish-hooks believed to be 5000 years old and the earliest known picture of a rod fisherman dates from about 2000 BC. There is a record from Roman writing that anglers were fishing with artificial flies more than seventeen centuries ago (Radcliffe, 1921).

The main ways of luring salmon are with artificial flies and fish, or with natural bait such as live earthworms or preserved fish and prawns. The development of fishing tackle has increased rapidly in recent years. In the past salmon rods were long (up to 6.1 m) and heavy, being built of greenheart or split cane, and reels were of brass, making them heavy and cumbersome. The lures were of a size in keeping with the rod, and flies were heavily dressed on large hooks or 'irons'. In recent years the rods have become shorter and split cane is being replaced by fibreglass, carbon fibre and boron.

Brass has been replaced by light alloys in reel manufacture and the development of the fixed-spool and multiplier spinning reels has produced an efficient piece of equipment which enables the novice to achieve a high standard of casting in a very short time. Synthetic fibres such as nylon and Terylene have replaced the more expensive plaited silk lines. This development has not stopped at rods, reels and lines but is seen also among the flies and lures. The flies tend to be smaller and hair has to some extent replaced the more expensive and exotic feathers used in fly dressing in the past. Artificial minnows are giving way to pieces of metal called spoons. The trend has been towards less elaborate tackle and more efficient methods of fishing. With increasing affluence and leisure, fishing is becoming more and more accessible to everyone. However, salmon angling remains on the whole an expensive sport because of the high rents salmon rivers can demand and sport fishing is a valuable asset to many salmon countries.

The sport fishery is a valuable resource and has been well developed as a tourist attraction, although in some areas it is for commercial gain and the catch is sent direct to the market. The popularity of salmon angling is difficult to assess, particularly in Scotland where no licence is required. However, in countries where licences are issued this is possible. Went (1964b) indicated the present attraction of salmon angling in Ireland when he revealed that in 26 of the 32 counties in Ireland in 1961 the total number of licences issued for salmon rods was 9820. In countries such as Canada, Norway and Scotland many of the salmon rivers run through sparsely populated country and the sport fishery centred on them helps to bring employment and money into remote areas. Because of their sporting value salmon have also been introduced to other countries such as New Zealand.

In Scotland, Iceland and Norway, many of the better salmon rivers are only available to the more wealthy anglers who can afford to pay the large rents demanded when they are fortunate enough to get the opportunity of obtaining a lease. In Scotland, high prices have been paid for the better beats of the first-class salmon rivers. Rivers such as the Findhorn, Tweed, Tay, Spey and Aberdeenshire Dee have only small stretches upon which the angler of moderate means can fish. These stretches are usually leased from large estates as a concession to the local angling clubs or associations. These bodies then manage the rented water and make it available to the local and visiting angler on a ticket basis. In some districts there are some very good stretches of water running through towns such as Grantown-on-Spey, Inverness, Peebles and Perth which are available to the public at a nominal fee. However, this results in the rivers being overcrowded during the best parts of the season and anglers may frequently be seen fishing practically shoulder to shoulder. Other rivers, particularly in the north and west of Scotland, are frequently owned or rented by hotels who keep their fishing for guests. When some of the better stretches of rivers come on the market nowadays, they are bought and then resold on a time-share basis. In this arrangement a purchaser buys the salmon-fishing rights for a named week or month in perpetuity. Other arrangements include syndication, that is a syndicate of anglers may lease a stretch of river on either an annual or longer-term basis from a salmon proprietor. The arrangement may be either for part of the season or part of the week. These latter arrangements virtually exclude the occasional or visiting angler from a large proportion of the better salmon fishing. Fishing can also be rented from sporting agents, some of whom specialize in salmon and sea trout fishing leases. Lastly, mention should be made of fishing-instruction holidays. These are held at a few angling resorts on good salmon rivers and do give the novice angler access to some good salmon fishing.

Salmon rivers are frequently divided into beats. All of the bigger rivers have their pools named and some of these pools have become famous because of the number of salmon taken from them. Mills and Graesser (1981) in their book *The Salmon Rivers of Scotland* give maps of some of the major salmon rivers with all the beats and pools named.

The position in Ireland is similar to that in Scotland and many hotels own or rent fisheries on some of the famous rivers such as the Bandon, Laune and Newport, while the more private fishing is to be found on the Boyne, Slaney, Moy and Cork Blackwater. However, cheaper fishing is available on the Liffey almost in the centre of Dublin and the Central Fisheries Board leases excellent fishing on the River Erriff.

The exclusive and expensive nature of salmon angling is common to many countries. In England this is particularly true on rivers such as the Hampshire Avon, Eden, Lune and Wye. In Norway the bigger the purse the better the fishing. Even so, there is a shortage of available fishing places on the famous Norwegian rivers like the Lærdalselve, Namsen and Aurlandsalve. Cheaper fishing is, however, available on rivers such as the Rauma, Driva and Gula. Berg (1964), in his book on north Norwegian salmon rivers, mentions rod fishing in north Norway for the 'man in the street'. In Finnmark fishing licences may be bought for most of the rivers, while in Nordland and Troms many rivers are private.

Netboy (1968) reviews the history of angling in Norway and refers to the rapid rise in the value of the Norwegian salmon sport fishery:

In the first decade of the twentieth century 80 rivers were leased wholly or in part to sportsmen, with rentals totalling 300 000 kroner. In 1951 rentals aggregated 450 000 kroner; ten years later they had more than doubled: some 94 rivers were leased for a total of 1 150 000 kroner. In 1964 one river, the Alta, was leased to an American millionaire for 250 000 kroner ($35 000) for the period June 24 to July 24. No doubt rents are even higher now.

Salmon fishing in eastern Canada is a very popular, albeit rather exclusive, sport in the provinces of Quebec and New Brunswick. In New Brunswick it attracts annually some four or five thousand non-residents, almost exclusively from the United States. Many of these have formed angling clubs on the main salmon rivers such as the Miramichi, Restigouche and Tobique. Some others own their own luxury camps on the rivers. Most, however, use accommodation offered by 'outfitters' and self-employed guides licensed by the Province. Several hundred people find employment for a part of the year as outfitters, guides and camp helpers. A few companies own fishing lodges to entertain their guests and executives.

In New Brunswick, inland waters can be divided into four groups from the viewpoint of ownership and accessibility for anglers: (1) private waters belonging to individuals or organizations who possess exclusive angling rights, subject to protective regulations limiting the amount of the catch; (2) public waters leased for 10 years to individuals or organizations by public auction, subject to protective regulations; (3) Crown reserved waters, available to a limited number of licensed anglers per day; (4) the major part of public waters, open to all for angling, subject to usual protective restrictions.

In Quebec most of the fishing is run by licensed clubs which are incorporated and kept up without pecuniary gain for salmon fishing in areas leased from the Province. Other methods of exploitation take the form of private fishing grounds where salmon are fished for pleasure by the owners; licensed outfitters, who exploit for profit an area leased from the Province, and Crown salmon preserves, organized and operated by the Department of Leisure, Game and Fisheries. Quebec rivers such as the St Jean, Grand Cascapedia and Little Cascapedia are very exclusive, while on the Matane River there are no restrictions on the number of anglers who may fish and no exclusive areas are reserved. Carter (1964) and Tetreault (1967) give good accounts of the position in Quebec salmon rivers.

In Nova Scotia and Newfoundland, in contrast to Quebec and New Brunswick, there are no private angling clubs and no privately owned or leased waters. Consequently all salmon rivers and streams are open to the public during the fishing season. However, a very great deal of the angling is done without guides, while in New Brunswick non-residents are almost without exception required to employ guides. The principal river systems of Nova Scotia are described by Morse (1965).

Salmon angling has only become popular among the people of Iceland since the Second World War. Prior to that few Icelanders fished for sport and it was chiefly visiting anglers from the United Kingdom who came north for the excellent salmon fishing, as is recorded by Stewart (1949, 1950) and Mills (1981, 1983). Eighty of the 250 rivers in Iceland hold salmon. The owners of the salmon fishing, who are usually farmers, have formed fishing associations. These associations manage the fishing and are responsible for local conservation. Each association has a guard or a bailiff. Between 40 and 50 of these associations have representatives on the River Owners' Association. The angling administration and regulations are fully described by Gudjonsson and Mills (1982). Salmon fishing in Iceland is now extremely expensive and booked up almost a year in advance and increasingly so by local anglers.

In Spain the salmon fishing is under the control of the government and accommodation has been built to attract anglers. Three of the best rivers, the Eo, Narcea and Deva–Cares, were designated as national fishing preserves managed by the State Tourist Bureau. The rivers are divided into restricted zones called 'cotos', and free areas or 'libres zones'. In the latter anybody can fish during the season; on the cotos one must have a special permit specifying the dates on which fishing is permitted. Salmon angling in Spain is described in detail by Léaniz et al. (1987).

One country in which salmon angling has developed very recently is the Faroes. This has been due to the importation of salmon eggs from Iceland and the subsequent release of fry. Until 1957 no salmon were recorded in the rivers of the Faroe Islands. Salmon have now become established in five rivers and salmon angling is administered by the Faroes Sport Fishing Association.

## 5.3 EXPLOITATION RATES

It is of considerable value to obtain some idea of the level of exploitation of the stocks by various types of fishing gear in both the commercial and recreational fisheries. These levels of exploitation are frequently referred to as exploitation rates. One method of estimating exploitation rates is from the recapture rates of fish that have been tagged, released and subsequently recaptured. The exploitation rate is therefore taken to mean the proportion of the assumed available tagged fish which are removed by various methods of fishing. Shearer (1986a) calculated the rate of exploitation by different types of fishing gear by two methods: (A) assuming that all tagged fish were available equally to all fishing methods; (B) assuming that fish caught by bag nets and stake nets were unavailable to net and coble and anglers, and those caught by bag nets and stake nets and net and coble were unavailable to anglers.

Table 5.3 gives the exploitation rates calculated by method (A) for multi-sea-winter fish tagged at Scottish coastal netting stations and Table 5.4 lists the exploitation rates on one-sea-winter and multi-sea-winter fish by the River North Esk net and coble fishery.

Jensen (1979, 1981) and Rosseland (1979) presented exploitation rates on the stocks of salmon of the River Eira and River Lærdalselve. The exploitation rate of salmon in the Lærdalselve was calculated by combining the autumn counts of spawning salmon with the number of salmon caught in the same year. This rate was combined with the official statistics of salmon catches in the rivers and in the sea in the neighbouring district to estimate the total rate of exploitation of the Lærdalselve's salmon stock. The same method, but based on salmon catches and redd counts, was used for the River Eira salmon. For both stocks the total rates of exploitation were very high (0.80–0.97).

**Table 5.3** Exploitation rates (U) on multi-sea-winter salmon tagged at Scottish coastal netting stations in 1952–83, expressed as percentages and calculated by method (A)*†

| Area | Year | Number tagged | Fixed engine | | Net and coble | | All nets | | Rod and line | | All methods | |
|---|---|---|---|---|---|---|---|---|---|---|---|---|
| | | | U | CL | U | CL | U | CL | U | CL | U | CL |
| Moray Firth | 1983 | 191 | 8± | 4 | 6± | 3 | 13± | 5 | 3 | – | 17± | 6 |
| East coast | 1952 | 127 | 29± | 8 | 11± | 5 | 40± | 9 | 5 | – | 45± | 9 |
| | 1954 | 209 | 24± | 6 | 28± | 6 | 52± | 7 | 2 | – | 54± | 7 |
| | 1955 | 96 | 32± | 9 | 17± | 7 | 49±10 | | – | – | 49±10 | |
| | 1978 | 49 | 27±12 | | 20±11 | | 47±14 | | – | – | 47±14 | |
| | Overall | 481 | 27± | 4 | 20± | 4 | 48± | 4 | 2±1 | | 50± | 4 |

*Reproduced with permission from Shearer (1986a).
†CL denotes 95% confidence limits (%).

**Table 5.4** Exploitation rates by North Esk net and coble fishery during the commercial netting season, expressed as percentages*

| Year | One-sea-winter | Multi-sea-winter |
|------|----------------|------------------|
| 1976 | 52 | 55 |
| 1977 | 51 | 43 |
| 1978 | 44 | 51 |
| 1979 | 42 | 45 |
| 1980 | 39 | 39 |
| 1981 | 50 | 57 |
| 1982 | 50 | 63 |
| 1983 | 53 | 39 |

*Reproduced with permission from Shearer (1986a).*

Hansen (1988) refers to the exploitation rates of River Imsa salmon (Anon., 1985b) and the following assumptions and approximations were made:

1. Tagged fish escaping home-water fisheries return to the River Imsa;
2. The monthly instantaneous mortality rate was taken to be 0.01;
3. Tagged and untagged fish were equally vulnerable to the gear;
4. Non-catch fishing mortality was taken to be negligible;
5. The mean dates of capture in the Norwegian Sea, Norwegian home waters and the River Imsa trap were taken to be 15 March, 15 July and 15 September respectively;
6. Tag reporting efficiency was assumed to range between 50% and 70% in Norwegian home waters, and was estimated to be 75% in the Norwegian Sea.

Table 5.5 gives estimates of 1SW and 2SW salmon of the River Imsa stock available to the Norwegian Sea fishery and the Norwegian home-water fishery and the estimated exploitation rates in these fisheries. The exploitation rates in home waters for both age classes of fish were very high, being 0.66 to 0.98 for 1SW and 0.89 to 1.00 for 2SW fish. On the Norwegian river Drammenselv, Hansen, Naesje and Garnås (1986) give exploitation rates by anglers of 0.04 above the salmon ladder and 0.33 below. They consider that this relatively low exploitation rate is probably one of the main factors responsible for the rapid increase in the salmon population of this river.

The exploitation rates of salmon in Icelandic rivers by rod and line have been assessed by using the rod catch and either redd counts or an estimate of the total run by either (a) direct counts or mechanical and resistivity fish counters or (b) tag and recapture (Gudjonsson, 1988). Table 5.6 lists the exploitation rates by rod and line for the Ellidaar, Ulfarsa, Blanda and Nordura.

Exploitation rates by rod and line on the Burrishoole River system, western

**Table 5.5** Estimated number of one-sea-winter and two-sea-winter salmon of the River Imsa stock available to the Norwegian home-water fishery*, and estimated exploitation rates†‡

| | | | One-sea-winter | | | | | Two-sea-winter | | | | |
| | | | Norwegian Sea | | Norwegian home waters | | | Norwegian Sea | | Norwegian home waters | | |
| | Smolt type | No. tagged | No. of fish available | Expl. rate | No. of fish available | Expl. rate | No. in trap | No. of fish available | Expl. rate | No. of fish available | Expl. rate | No. in trap |
|---|---|---|---|---|---|---|---|---|---|---|---|---|
| Released 1981 | R. Imsa wild | 3214 | 592 | 0.00 | 416 | 0.84 | 66 | 142 | 0.32 | 93 | 0.90 | 9 |
| | R. Imsa 2+ | 5819 | 596 | 0.01 | 452 | 0.74 | 114 | 105 | 0.46 | 55 | 0.89 | 6 |
| Released 1982 | R. Imsa wild | 736 | 48 | 0.00 | 29 | 0.83 | 5 | 16 | 0.56 | 7 | 0.86 | 1 |
| | R. Imsa 1+ | 5581 | 98 | 0.00 | 52 | 0.98 | 1 | 39 | 0.41 | 22 | 0.95 | 1 |
| | R. Imsa 2+ | 8501 | 549 | 0.04 | 382 | 0.93 | 25 | 115 | 0.63 | 40 | 0.90 | 4 |
| Released 1983 | R. Imsa wild | 1287 | 163 | 0.00 | 133 | 0.76 | 31 | 22 | 0.41 | 12 | 0.92 | 1 |
| | R. Imsa 1+ | 5861 | 20 | 0.00 | 17 | 0.94 | 1 | 2 | 0.50 | 1 | 1.00 | 0 |
| | R. Imsa 2+ | 6052 | 154 | 0.03 | 126 | 0.90 | 12 | 16 | 0.56 | 7 | 1.00 | 0 |
| Released 1984 | R. Imsa wild | 936 | 94 | 0.00 | 90 | 0.66 | 30 | | | | | |
| | R. Imsa 1+ | 1863 | 17 | 0.00 | 16 | 0.69 | 5 | | | | | |
| | R. Imsa 2+ | 7445 | 272 | 0.06 | 245 | 0.80 | 48 | | | | | |

*Estimates are based on 75% and 70% tag reporting rates in the Norwegian Sea and Norwegian home waters respectively.
†The number of salmon caught in the trap in River Imsa is considered to be the total river escapement.
‡Reproduced with permission from Hansen (1988).

**Table 5.6**   Exploitation rates by rod and line in four Icelandic rivers*

| River | No. of observations (years) | Exploitation rate (%) Mean | Range |
|---|---|---|---|
| Ellidaar | 42 | 34.6 | 23.0–58.0 |
| Ulfarsa | 6 | 28.6 | 14.1–46.2 |
| Blanda | 4 | 64.9 | 55.0–82.0 |
| Nordura | 13 | 25.3 | 10.9–81.6 |

*Sources: Gudbergsson and Gudjonsson (1986); Gudjonsson (1988).*

Ireland, varied from 6% to 20%, the average over the period 1970–81 being 12% (Mills, Mahon and Piggins, 1986).

Overall exploitation rates by rod fishing on the River Wye were estimated to be 25% in the period 1925–34 (*c.* 200 licences issued) and 47% over the period 1965–74 (*c.* 1300 licences issued) (Gee and Milner, 1980). These authors also noted that exploitation rates increased as fish size increased, and salmon over 9.1 kg could suffer angler exploitation rates of 1.0.

In Canada, Chadwick (1982c) calculated the exploitation rate by anglers in ten rivers in insular Newfoundland. The exploitation rate ($E$) was equal to the ratio of the recreational harvest to total escapement or $E = RH/(RH + FC)$ where $RH$ is the recreational harvest and $FC$ fishway counts. Mean exploitation rates ranged from 0.16 (Salmon River) to 0.38 (Northeast Placentia). Chadwick noticed that exploitation rates are influenced by changes in catchability in the recreational fishery and he presumed (1982d) that in years of low discharge catchability is increased.

Some information is available on the average catch of salmon per angler-hour for a number of rivers and this is given in Table 5.7.

Elson (1974) gives details of angling pressure and catch of Atlantic salmon, including grilse, on tributaries of the Miramichi system. The river is conveniently divided into the areas above and below a counting fence. Data for catch per rod-day on the Northwest Miramichi, above and below the fence, for the years 1971–73 are given in Table 5.8.

## 5.4   REGULATIONS

Exploitation of the resource can be controlled by:

1. Limiting entry to the fishery;
2. Regulating the season and time during which the resource can be cropped and also the area in which fishing can take place;
3. Placing a limit on the level of fishing effort;

**Table 5.7** Details of catch of salmon per angler-hour for a number of rivers

| River | Av. catch per angler-hour | Range | Authority |
|-------|--------------------------|-------|-----------|
| Wye | 0.039* | – | Gee (1980) |
|  | 0.045† | ±0.022 | |
| 6 Welsh rivers | n.d. | 0.025– | South West Wales |
|  | | 0.053 | River Authority (1968) |
| Little Main Restigouche | n.d. | 0.03–0.05 | Peppar (1977) |
| Miramichi (tributary) | 0.08 | n.d. | Peppar and Pickard (1978) |
| Foyle | 0.09 | n.d. | Hadoke (1967) |

*Overall.
†Mean of 10 fisheries.
n.d. no data.

**Table 5.8** Catch of salmon per rod-day on the Northwest Miramichi, 1971–73*

| Area | 1971 | 1972 | 1973 |
|------|------|------|------|
| Above fence | 0.31 | 0.71 | 0.46 |
| Below fence | 0.55 | 0.66 | 0.32 |

*Source: Elson (1974).

4. Putting restrictions on the type, quality and quantity of fishing gear used.
5. Imposing a limit on the amount of the total catch;
6. Requiring an accurate return of catch data.

Most of these regulations have to be legally enforced by imposing penalties on those who fail to observe them. In certain instances there is a flagrant violation of these regulations, while in other cases they are strictly and conscientiously observed.

*Limited entry.* One way to implement this is by allowing only certain social groups in the community entry. For example, only fishermen, seal hunters and sheep farmers are allowed to fish for salmon in Greenland; authorization is not given to incorporated bodies or forms of shared ownerships, only to an individual. In Norway, the drift-net fishery was only open to persons with fishing or the combination of fishing and farming as their main source of living. Similarly the Northumberland and Yorkshire drift-net fisheries are now operated by full-time fishermen only, as are the drift-net fisheries in both Ireland and Canada.

Another way is to issue only a fixed number of licences. In Greenland, no commercial salmon fishing is allowed without a licence and the fishing industries are not allowed to buy salmon except from fishermen with a licence. The fishing vessels in the Faroese long-line salmon fishery have to be licensed by the Fishermen's Association. In addition, the Home Government department (Føroya Gjaldstova) charges a certain amount per kilogram landed weight of salmon. This fee has to be paid separately for each fishing trip and the levy goes towards the cost of smolt production in the Faroese hatcheries.

The Northumberland and Yorkshire drift-net fisheries are restricted to a fixed number of licence holders, the number being set by Net Licence Limitation Orders. In the Irish and Canadian drift-net fisheries similar regulations apply. In 1984 licences were restricted to 1000 Irish fishermen.

In the sport fisheries too, similar licence restrictions apply in some countries. For example, in England and Wales a salmon angler must have a licence issued by the appropriate water authority in whose area he or she wishes to fish, but this does not give the angler the right to fish without prior consent from the owner of the salmon fishery. In Scotland no licence to fish is required but prior permission must be obtained from the salmon proprietor. No licence is required in Iceland but permission to fish is needed. The number of anglers permitted to fish on Icelandic rivers is strictly controlled, with only a limited number of anglers being allowed to fish on any one river on any one day for a given time (i.e. 12 hours a day). A licence is required to fish for salmon with rod and line in France and Spain and in the three rivers in the USSR where angling is permitted. In France licences are referred to as 'salmon stamps'.

*Season, time and area limits.* The season and time during which fishing is permitted varies from country to country and even within the same country, and nowhere is this more so than Scotland, where there are 108 fishery districts with varying annual close times both for net fishing and rod fishing. In Greenland and Faroes the fishing season, unlike those in British waters, is not linked to the spawning season during which there is no commercial or sport fishing. However, in Greenland the fishing season usually starts in early August and then varies depending on how quickly the quota is achieved. In the Faroes the fishery is operated over the winter and early spring, except for the sport fishery where the close season is from 1 September to 1 April.

In addition to an annual close season there is also a weekly close season and this applies particularly to inshore and river fisheries, commercial and sport. In Scotland there is a weekly close season for nets from 18.00 on Friday to 06.00 on Monday; at the moment the length of this weekly close time is under review. No salmon angling is allowed in Scotland on a Sunday. The Irish drift-net fishery is restricted to four days a week and a weekly close season also operates in the north-east England drift-net fishery. In Iceland netting is only permitted for half of the week, from 10.00 on Tuesday to 22.00 on Friday.

In the Foyle area the netting season of about 26 days is spread over six weeks from late June to early August (Crawford, 1988).

Fishing may also be limited to a certain time in the 24 hours. Fishing is not permitted during the hours of darkness (20.00–04.00) in the north-east England drift-net fishery and in Iceland angling is only permitted from 07.00 to 13.00 and 16.00 to 22.00. In Spain, fishing can take place from one hour before sunrise to one hour after sunset.

The area in which fishing is allowed also varies. On the high seas no fishing for salmon is permitted beyond 12 miles (19 km) from the coast, except in the cases of Greenland, where fishing is allowed out to 40 miles (65 km) from the shore, and the Faroes, where all vessels must fish within the 200-mile (320 km) fisheries zone. In some fisheries the permitted distance from the shore may be less than 12 miles (19 km). In the north-east England drift-net fishery it is only 6 miles (9.6 km). Fishing in Icelandic coastal waters is prohibited, as it is in Spain.

Within the permitted fishing zone there are sometimes designated areas or 'boxes' in which fishing is prohibited. For example, there is a 'box' off the mouth of the Tyne in which the north-east England drift-net fishery cannot operate, and there were similar 'boxes' in the Norwegian Sea where the Norwegian long-line fishery could not operate. Similarly, certain areas off Newfoundland are closed to salmon fishing and in recent years certain eastern Canadian coastal salmon fisheries, and even some small rivers, have been closed to fishing altogether (Marshall, 1988).

*Fishing effort.* Fishing effort can be controlled by limiting the number of fishermen entering the fishery by restricting the number of licences issued, as in the north-east England and Irish fisheries, but this has to be reinforced by limiting the amount of gear (e.g. number and size of nets) a licence holder can use. In the Greenland fishery, restrictions on fishing effort include size of vessel that can participate, with only vessels up to 150 gross registered tonnes being allowed to fish. A recent restriction on fishing effort has been imposed on the Faroese fishery. This limits the fishery to a fishing fleet of 26 vessels with a total fishing effort in any one year of no more than 1600 days.

*Gear restrictions.* Gear restrictions usually involve limiting the type of gear permitted in a commercial fishery or the type of lure allowed in a sport fishery. Certain types of fishing gear may be prohibited, such as drift nets have now (1989) been in Norway, or may be permitted only if made of certain materials. Monofilament is banned in Norway and drift nets must not be made of monofilament in the New Brunswick fishery. The length of the nets may be restricted (e.g. 370–550 m in the north-east England drift-net fishery, 1234 m in the New Brunswick drift-net fishery, and 731 m in the Irish fishery except along the Donegal coast where nets 1371 m long are permitted) and sometimes the depth (e.g. 30 m in Ireland). In Newfoundland, full-time fishermen are limited to 200 fathoms (366 m) of net and part-time fishermen to 50–100 fathoms (91–183 m). The size of mesh is also legally set (for drift nets – 127 mm stretched mesh in Canada and Ireland and 140 mm in Greenland).

In the Irish drift-net fishery all nets must bear a tag on which is inscribed the licence number, and the boat used for fishing the gear must also bear the licence number.

Mesh size to some extent regulates the size of the fish caught by allowing small fish to pass, or struggle, through the mesh. In gear where there is no netting, such as long lines, other methods are needed to regulate the size of the fish caught. The size of the hook (no. 3/0 Mustad) used on long lines in the Faroese fishery may to some extent select the size of the fish caught, but this is not sufficiently effective, so a minimum size (60 cm long) of fish that can be retained is set (p. 121) as in the Baltic long-line fishery. In the Canadian sport fishery in the Maritime Provinces and Newfoundland (excluding Labrador) all multi-sea-winter salmon (63 cm and greater in length) hooked by anglers must be released immediately.

*Quotas.* While the allocation of quotas is common practice in marine fisheries, a quota system for commercial salmon fishing is less usual and at present is only used in the Greenland and Faroese high-seas salmon fisheries; one was used in the commercial trap-net and drift-net fisheries of New Brunswick until their closure in 1984 (Cook and McGaw, 1988). In the first two fisheries if the quota is taken before the season ends, as is sometimes the case, then the season naturally closes. A check on the extent of fishing may be important in this respect and information on the position of fishing vessels, as well as other surface and underwater craft, is collected by satellites and AWAC aircraft. This information may be unclassified and could be made available.

Although quotas tend to be exclusive to commercial fisheries, a similar system, known as a 'bag limit', is adopted in some sport fisheries. In Canada, the seasonal bag limit, the number of salmon an angler is allowed to be in possession of at one time and the daily bag limit are respectively ten, six and two salmon in New Brunswick and Nova Scotia and five, one and one in Prince Edward Island. All fish retained must be grilse, all multi-sea-winter fish (more than 63 cm in length) being returned immediately. A 15-fish seasonal bag limit was introduced in the Newfoundland and Labrador recreational fishery in 1986. The daily and seasonal bag limits did not include any salmon that are hooked and subsequently released. However, on a daily basis, anglers had to stop fishing for salmon once they had retained the daily limit or had released a maximum number of fish equal to twice the daily limit. In Spain, a catch of three salmon per day per coto is allowed; in other sectors, the free or unrestricted zones, one salmon per day per angler is permitted. In France an annual rod quota of five salmon is to be introduced shortly.

*Catch records.* It is a statutory requirement in most countries for both commercial and recreational fishermen to submit a note of their catches to the appropriate authorities at the end of each season or more frequently. For example, in the Faroese long-line fishery the master of a fishing vessel has to inform the Fishermen's Association every Monday of the number and weight of salmon caught. In addition, he has to keep a log book and enter into it daily the number of salmon taken and where they were caught. When the catch is unloaded and classified the master sends a note of the weight to the Fishermen's Association. In the Norwegian drift-net fishery catch record books had to be kept and sent to the Central Bureau of Statistics at the end of the season. The Greenland salmon fishery is also strictly controlled and all places of purchase of salmon are responsible for reporting catch statistics to the Governor's Office.

Mandatory tagging of all salmon caught commercially and by anglers in eastern Canada enables a reliable collection of catch statistics to be made. Spain, too, requires all rod-caught salmon to be tagged and certificates to be issued to the anglers. This system of tags and certificates facilitates the collection of catch statistics and, as in Canada, restricts the trade in illegally caught fish. France has also introduced a compulsory tagging scheme for salmon.

Catch statistics in some countries or some fisheries are still unreliable (Harris, 1988) even though accurate catch returns are a statutory requirement and, for official purposes, a category referred to as 'unreported catch' has to be estimated (Williamson, 1988). The International Council for the Exploration of the Sea gave a figure of 3000 tonnes in the 'unreported' catch category for 1987 (Mills, 1988).

# CHAPTER SIX

# The economic evaluation of the commercial and sport fisheries

A great deal of importance is now, quite understandably, being attached to the economic value of salmon, and particularly to the relative values of salmon caught by the angler and the commercial fisherman. As the 'nets versus rods' controversy rages in the salmon world, more and more reliable figures are being sought to determine who has the most right to harvest the resource. Perhaps put more objectively, which method of harvesting brings in most revenue to the community and therefore who should have access to the resource, or if continued exploitation is possible what shares should be allocated to each sector?

## 6.1    VALUE OF ANGLING

Various methods have been developed which assign a monetary value to a resource, particularly to one involving recreation. The techniques used to assign monetary values to recreation include (a) the direct method which involves interviews and surveys to test the participants' willingness to pay for angling services and (b) the same techniques to simulate a system of prices and attendance on the basis of travel costs incurred by anglers coming from various distances to fish a river – this is known as the indirect method. The economic value of the commercial fishery can be based on a costs and earnings survey. There are various methods within (a) and (b) above to assess the value of angling and these have been reviewed by Sewell and Rostron (1970). They include:

*Cost method.* This assumes that the value of any angling facility is equal to the costs involved in its development.

*Expenditure method.* This attempts to measure both the value of angling to the angler and the value of angling to the local area in terms of the total amount spent on angling by the angler. It is based on two assumptions: (a) the value of angling is worth at least as much as the angler's total expenditures associated with angling; (b) the amount spent on angling is determined by free choice over other alternatives to spend or save the same sum of money. This method only indicates minimum values placed on angling; it does not indicate total values including the provision of the goods and services purchased by the anglers.

*Gross national product method.* Attempts have been made to measure the contribution of angling to GNP, assuming angling as a factor of production or something which stimulates production (Lerner, 1962). This approach rests on the contention that the value of a day spent in angling can be assumed to be (on the average) equal to the GNP divided by the product of the total population and the number of days in the year.

*Value added method.* In this method the aim is to determine the value added in a given area because of angling. The method is based on the gross expenditure method, but recognizes that all the money received from the anglers does not fall into the category of profit but is only part of gross income, which must in turn be divided into operating expenses and profits. This method indicates the volume of business within a local area. However, this expenditure is not for the provision of the angling opportunity, but for the provision of other services connected with the use of the angling opportunity.. This method is sometimes referred to as the 'net output' method. It takes account of leakages (the import content of goods and services) and of 'multiplier' effects (income generated indirectly as a result of anglers' expenditure working its way through the economy). Net output is a measure which can be applied to both the recreational and commercial salmon fisheries.

*Travel costs and consumer surplus methods.* This is one of the most popular methods and relies on the travel costs incurred by anglers coming from various distances and the frequency of visits from those distances (Scott, 1965). Clawson (1959) made additional suggestions for measuring recreational values. She proposed the derivation of a demand schedule for the total recreation experience by plotting the relationship of the number of visits per 100 000 population to a recreation site and the travel costs per visit. She assumed that the visit to the recreational site was the main purpose of the trip and therefore had to bear all costs of the trip, allocating to other activities on the trip only those costs additional to the main trip. By assuming that various prices were to be charged for entry to the recreation site she constructed a series of demand curves to show the effects that those prices would have on attendance and revenue that might be expected (Fig. 6.1). This is accomplished by assuming that the differences in the rates of use between various

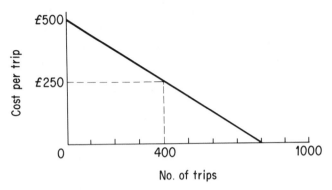

**Fig. 6.1**  Theoretical demand curve (after Clawson, 1959 and Radford, 1984). The theory being that as a fishing trip becomes more expensive fewer anglers will go fishing. So at a cost of £500 per trip no angler will go fishing, but as the cost per trip is reduced (say to £250) 400 visits will be made. So one can relate 400 trips to a value at least equal to £250. At zero cost 800 trips are made.

distance zones are caused by differences in the money costs of visiting the site (Copes and Knetsch, 1981).

*Willingness to pay method.* The methods outlined so far are related to the indirect approach to recreation evaluation. The direct approach differs in that it involves asking the recreationists how much they would be willing to pay for the right to participate in the activity.

Sewell and Rostron (1970) give a further method which attempts to measure the benefits of recreational salt-water fishing for Pacific salmon and steelhead (*Salmo gairdneri*). This method included distance and income and Brown, Singh and Castle (1964) found that income exerted a positive effect on the number of angler days spent fishing.

Crutchfield and MacFarlane (1968) in their economic valuation of the salt-water salmon angling in Washington chose to measure value on the basis of gross expenditures by sport fishermen, their contribution to incomes in the State and the net benefits generated by the sport fisheries. They state that:

For comparison with other water uses and as a basis for more rational division of the salmon catch between sport and commercial fishermen, the net economic benefit concept is of primary importance. The net economic value of sport fishing relates to the value of the recreation experience, and cannot be inferred directly from data now available. It is, therefore, necessary to simulate a demand function measuring the number of user-days that would be forthcoming if the right to participate in sport salmon fishing were priced at different levels, with other factors determining the satisfaction derived from sport fishing (such as income, population, and quality of fishing), taken as given. It would then be possible to determine the combination of price and user days that produces the largest net benefit that the fishery can yield in recreational usage, or expressed in other terms, the true net loss to the economy if the fishery were to be eliminated.

The values of landings of Atlantic salmon for four selected countries are given in Table 6.1. While these national fisheries give a true picture in terms of direct value to each country, in most instances the figures do not represent the actual value. For example, in Canada, as in other countries with a large sport fishery for salmon, the benefit to income and employment of a rod-caught salmon is much greater than is represented by the price which the fish fetches when sold. Good salmon angling can command a high rent, a fact that is of importance to those owners of estates who are also proprietors of salmon fisheries, and to local authorities. The availability of salmon angling contributes directly to the revenue of the tourist industry. In Scotland, for example, hotels in some parts of the country rely on anglers, particularly in the early spring and late autumn when other sectors of the tourist trade are not so busy. A few may rely on anglers to such an extent that they would have to seek an entirely new type of customer if angling declined, while others, but for angling, would have a shorter season and offer a shorter period of employment to most of their staff. This example of value of rod-caught salmon being worth more than the price which the fish fetches when sold is further borne out by Maheux (1956). Maheux showed that the combined rod and net fishery for salmon in Quebec brought each year to the residents of the Province, in personal income, $2 085 850 or 80% of the total received from the salmon resource. Of this sum, the 12 000 fish caught by rod and line (less than one-fifth of the commercial catch) contributed nearly 75%.

**Table 6.1** Value of landings of Atlantic salmon in four countries, expressed in national currency*

|  | 1983 | | 1984 | | 1985 | | 1986 | |
|---|---|---|---|---|---|---|---|---|
|  | W† | F† | W | F | W | F | W | F |
| Canada (millions of dollars) | 3.13 | –‡ | 3.53 | – | 4.68 | – | N/A‡ | N/A |
| Ireland (millions of punts) | 6.67 | 1.04 | 4.61 | 1.80 | 7.73 | 3.15 | N/A | N/A |
| Sweden (millions of kronor) | N/A | N/A | 2.13 | – | 3.08 | – | 2.48 | – |
| Greenland (millions of kroner) | N/A | – | N/A | – | 3.23 | – | N/A | – |

*Source: Review of Fisheries, OECD.*
†W. wild; F, farmed.
‡N/A, not available; —, no farmed salmon.

## 6.2   VALUE OF SALMON

Methods used for the economic evaluation of Atlantic salmon have varied widely between countries and no standard method has been adopted. This is not surprising bearing in mind the variety of techniques that exist (Stabler, 1982). However, if comparisons are to be made between the values of salmon in various countries some standardized approach will have to be adopted. A review of the various studies and methods of evaluation in a number of countries follows.

*Canada.* The first detailed studies of the economic value of the Atlantic salmon were made in Canada for the Provinces of Quebec, New Brunswick and Nova Scotia by Maheux (1956), Grasberg (1956) and Morse (1965) respectively. In the surveys by Maheux and Grasberg emphasis was placed on studies of the economic aspects or revenue channels of salmon fishing which was divided into sport fishing, commercial fishing, federal expenditure and personal income of residents. Each source of revenue was reviewed, then the elements composing each source were analysed. The studies are too large to permit a satisfactory summary and the reader is advised to refer to the original works. One paragraph of interest in the survey by Maheux is that concerning the cost of salmon angling to licensed clubs in Quebec:

If we compare the $1 245 000 and the 7000 salmon caught by the club members and their guests, we realize that the salmon is truly a luxury fish. Each salmon would come to about $175.00; and as the average weight of each fish is not far from 12 pounds, the price per pound of salmon would be $14.60. This is proof that we are dealing with a sport, that is to say a pastime, which has no price tag attached to it. It is also proof that, in this Province, the clubs constitute an important economic factor, since goods, for which the commercial fisherman received 40 cents, have, in the hands of the angler, a value 36 times as great. The net result of the activity of the clubs is to obtain higher incomes for a greater number of people. Salmon angling is thus becoming an appreciable element of prosperity in those regions favoured by this fish, as well as an important factor of conservation.

It was impossible in Nova Scotia for Morse to estimate the values as has been done in Quebec and New Brunswick owing to the institutional arrangements in the Province and to the open and diffuse nature of the sport fishery. However, by using questionnaires Morse found that the average expenditure per salmon angler in Nova Scotia in 1964 was between $100 and $160 and the expenditures of 959 anglers who responded to the questionnaire was $376 368. On an assumption (based on a list of known anglers) that there was a total of 3000 anglers the estimated minimum and maximum level of aggregated expenditures was $300 000 and $480 000. The landed value of the commercial fishery was $164 300.

More recently, studies of Canada's Atlantic salmon recreational fisheries have been undertaken by Tuomi (1980, 1986). Tuomi (1986), using mail surveys, estimated that 54 000 anglers fished for salmon in the five Atlantic seaboard provinces. This was based on preliminary Canada-wide sport-fishing results for 1985. These anglers spent $39 M to go fishing and also made major purchases and investments totalling $72 M of which $45 M was chargeable to salmon angling. A comparison between the commercial and recreational fisheries showed that anglers accounted for 93% of the combined total of economic activity generated while taking only 29% of the catch. It also estimated that anglers' expenditures create 2090 person years of employment compared with 160 by the commercial fishery. The public cost of salmon supply rose from about $11 a fish in 1980 to $47 in 1985. Tuomi considered that if these costs were charged to it, the effect on the economically marginal Atlantic salmon commercial fishery would be prohibitive.

Cook and McGaw (1988) determined the economic value of the Atlantic salmon commercial fisheries in the New Brunswick rivers, the Restigouche, the Miramichi and the Saint John, using a costs and earnings survey of 92 (out of 225) fishery enterprises for the 1983 season. This fishery was closed for 9 years and only reopened in 1981 in which year an extensive review of that season was conducted by Meagher (1981). The fishery is operated using trap nets and gill nets. Revenue, variable and fixed costs and economic profit were obtained for the two methods. It was found that when fixed costs are considered the average drift net lost $336 while the average trap net earned $1210. Drift nets had revenues that were some 10% higher than trap nets but the higher labour and operating costs of drift nets resulted in net revenues that were less than half those of trap nets. The levels of viability of the two methods were also gained by estimating the cost functions. These indicate (Fig. 6.2) that the drift net outperforms the trap net only at very low levels of output and it was found that the trap net acquires a cost advantage at 49 salmon caught. Table 6.2 shows the average cost per salmon at selected output levels.

From the survey by Cook and McGaw, the average landed value per salmon was $29.50 for trap nets (due to a higher price for Restigouche salmon) and $26.70 for drift nets. From the estimated cost functions, the break-even level of output for a trap net is 79 salmon on the Restigouche and 109 salmon on the Miramichi and for a drift net, 185 salmon (Fig. 6.2). The authors expected that, even without intervention, the commercial salmon fishery would continue its decline in the number of active licences and a buy-back programme would be acceptable to a large number of licence holders. This was borne out by the acceptance of annual compensation not to fish in 1984, 1985 and 1986 by a large number of licence holders.

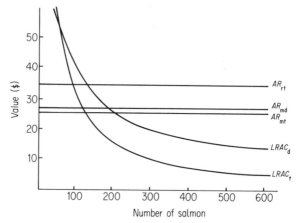

**Fig. 6.2** Average-cost and average-revenue curves for trap nets and drift nets. Horizontal lines are average revenue for Restigouche trap nets $(AR_{rt})$, Miramichi drift nets $(AR_{md})$, and Miramichi trap nets $(AR_{mt})$; curves depict long-range average costs for drift nets $(LRAC_d)$ and trap nets $(LRAC_t)$. Values are in Canadian dollars (reproduced with permission from Cook and McGaw, 1988).

**Table 6.2** Average cost per salmon by fishing method*

| No. of salmon | Trap net | Drift net |
|---|---|---|
| 50 | $53.60 | $54.40 |
| 100 | 27.60 | 37.30 |
| 200 | 14.20 | 25.60 |
| 300 | 9.60 | 20.50 |
| 400 | 7.30 | 17.60 |
| 500 | 5.90 | 15.50 |
| 600 | 5.10 | 14.10 |

*Source: Cook and McGaw (1988).*

*Ireland.* An interesting comparison of the relative value of salmon angling and netting was made by Hadoke (1972) in an economic evaluation of the salmon fisheries of the Foyle area. The relative cost/value of rod and net caught salmon in the Foyle area in 1968 is given in Table 6.3.

This Table shows that far more anglers than commercial fishermen were involved in the actual process of fishing for salmon and that the anglers spent more money on catching a salmon than the commercial fishermen received as gross income for each fish they caught.

O'Connor, Whelan and McCashin (1973–74) and O'Connor (1983) estimated the value of salmon fishing in the Republic of Ireland by calculating the gross output of the industry and from this they deducted costs incurred in

**Table 6.3** Relative cost/value of rod and net caught salmon from the Foyle, Northern Ireland, 1968*

| Class of engine | No. of persons involved | Expenses (£) | Net income (£) | Catch (fish) | Catch: gross income Cost of each fish (£) |
|---|---|---|---|---|---|
| Rod | 2344 | 58 600 | – | 3 005 | 19.5† |
| Draft net | 180 | 15 899 | 33 649 | 28 126 | 1.76 |
| Drift net | 71 | 14 366 | 41 507 | 31 856 | 1.75 |
| Londonderry fishery | 49 | 17 619 | 23 413 | 18 072 | 2.27 |
| Private | 4 | 1 637 | 2 408 | 2 312 | 1.75 |

*Source: Hadoke (1972).
†This value catch: expenses.

producing goods and services to obtain the net output. The commercial salmon catch in 1982 was 862.8 tonnes valued at £3.81 M and if the anglers' expenditure is added to the gross output of the industry the total gross output is £9.53 M, a drop of about £1.7 M compared with a gross output in 1970 of £11.19 M at 1982 prices.

In order to estimate the net output of salmon fishing in 1982 O'Connor (1983) assumed that the average import content of both Irish and visiting anglers' expenditure in 1982 was the same as that of other tourists (26.6%) and that the average import content of the commercial salmon output was equal on average to the import content of all exports from the fishing industry in 1982 (25%). The import contents were calculated on this basis and deducted from gross outputs to get a net output of £2.66 M for sales to visiting anglers, £1.54 M for sale to Irish anglers and £2.86 M for sales of salmon by commercial fishermen. The total net output or value added by salmon fishing in 1982 was thus estimated at £7.06 M. The corresponding figure for 1970 at 1982 prices was £9.13 M made up of £2.06 M for visiting anglers, £1.22 M for Irish anglers and £5.85 M for the commercial fishermen. O'Connor applied a multiplier of 1.3 to allow for second and further round spending effects; the estimates obtained of value added for salmon fishing in Ireland in 1970 and 1982 appear in Table 6.4.

Whelan and Whelan (1987) used a model for an earlier study (O'Connor, Whelan and McCashin, 1973–74) which was based on the issue that if 1000 extra salmon were available, to which sector should they be allocated. The basic conclusion of the earlier analysis was that the 1000 salmon, if allowed upriver, will result in an angling catch of 200. This would give rise to an expenditure of £2800. If the 1000 fish were caught commercially, they would have a gross value of £2400. So each additional salmon which is allocated to recreational exploitation is worth £2.81 compared to £2.45 commercially.

**Table 6.4**  Estimates of value (£M) added for
salmon fishing in Ireland in 1970 and 1982*

|  | 1970† | 1982 |
|---|---|---|
| Visiting anglers | 2.68 | 3.46 |
| Irish anglers | 1.22 | 1.54 |
| Commercial fisher-men | 7.61 | 3.72 |
| Total | 11.51 | 8.72 |

*Source: O'Connor (1983).
†Entries are corrected to 1982 prices: see text.

This gave a margin in favour of recreational exploitation of 15%. Re-estimating this model based on 1982 data Whelan and Whelan (1987) found the resulting values to be £18.02 for recreational use and £13.05 for commercial exploitation. The margin in favour of angling had thus widened to 38%.

*Scotland.* Little detailed information is available on the economic value of salmon angling in Scotland. However, a study of three areas – the lower Tay, the middle Spey, and the Kyle of Sutherland – was undertaken by the Tourism and Recreation Unit of the University of Edinburgh between 1981 and 1982 (1984). The study was seen as a pilot exercise (a) to indicate the average pattern and amount of expenditure by salmon anglers in three selected areas, (b) to compare patterns of amounts of expenditure in these different areas, and (c) if feasible, to indicate the range of total expenditure of salmon anglers in Scotland. A survey of salmon anglers was undertaken on selected fishing beats to establish the level of expenditure for the whole fishing trip, differentiating that which was spent locally from that which was spent outside the study area. Secondly, a survey of proprietors of salmon fisheries in Scotland was carried out to establish the total number of rod days let for salmon fishing. Data were collected by both a direct interview with the angler using a standardized questionnaire and the completion of a questionnaire by the anglers themselves. Estimates of total annual expenditures were derived by multiplying the number of rod days calculated from a survey by the Department of Agriculture and Fisheries for Scotland by the average expenditure per rod day from the anglers' survey. The overall expenditure by anglers, including expenditure outside the local area, was estimated to be £34 M and was likely to be between £22 M and £46 M.

*Wales.* Gee and Edwards (1982), using the results of a questionnaire survey, estimated the total expenditure on salmon angling in the River Wye as being in excess of £800 per salmon, compared with a commercial value of only £36.

Radford (1984) looked at the economics and value of four recreational salmon fisheries in Wales and England. These were the Wye and Mawddach in Wales and the Tamar and Lune in England. The author obtained his statistics from the mailing of a considerable number of questionnaires both to the anglers on these four rivers and to the owners of the fishing rights. An economic evaluation of the net value was obtained by considering the travel cost method, the economic rent and angler expenditure. The total net economic value of the four fisheries is given in Table 6.5.

**Table 6.5** Total net economic value (1984 prices) of four recreational salmon fisheries in England and Wales*

| River | Value (£M) |
| --- | --- |
| Wye | 28.72 |
| Mawddach | 4.91 |
| Tamar | 15.89 |
| Lune | 2.40 |

*Source: Radford (1984).*

*England.* Mitchell (1985), working on the published catches and fish prices appearing in articles written by the drift netters, showed that in 1981 the average gross income per net licence in the Northumbrian and Yorkshire drift net fishery was £6325 and £3150 respectively. These average gross incomes, prior to deductions for boats, fuel, gear, boxes, transport and licence and market dues, cannot be described as an important part of the livelihood of even the licence holder, far less the crew. However, this assumes that the 'reported' catch represents the 'actual' catch.

*Iceland.* No detailed economic evaluation of the salmon resource in Iceland is available but the estimated value of the Icelandic salmon resource for 1986 is given in Table 6.6.

The average rental price of 21 Icelandic rivers for 1985 was 2.83 million Icelandic kronur (£1.00 = 51 Is kr., 1985 exchange rate). The rental price ranged from 300 000 Is kr. for the Saemundará to 12.3 M Is kr. for the Laxa ín Kjos. The rental price is the actual sum the landowners (farmers) are paid for the fishing rights in each river and does not include any other expenses the anglers have to pay, such as travel and hotel costs and the hire of guides. The average price of each rod-caught salmon in 1985 was 5300 Is kr. (£103.92).

**Table 6.6**    Estimated value of the salmon resource in Iceland, 1986*

| Source | Icelandic kronur (Is kr.)† (million) |
|---|---|
| Commercial netting and ocean ranching | 45 |
| Angling | 170 |
| Fish farming (culture of salmon fry, parr and smolts) | 200 |
| Fish farming (cage rearing of salmon) | 66 |
| Total value | 481 |

*Source: Einar Hanneson, Institute of Freshwater Fisheries, Reykjavik.*
†*£1.00 sterling is equivalent to 60 Is kr. (1986 exchange rate).*

## 6.3    ANGLING VERSUS NETTING

It would seem, from this review of the studies undertaken, that a salmon caught with rod and line is of more value than a salmon taken commercially (Table 6.7) although in some instances (e.g. Ireland) only marginally more. However, the Canadian studies suggest that the commercial fishery is so economically inefficient that its permanent closure is justified. The Hunter Committee (Anon., 1965), in considering the future of the Scottish salmon fisheries, states (para. 56):

. . . As, however, a salmon caught or available for catching by rod and line generally contributes more to the Scottish economy than a salmon caught for

**Table 6.7**    Comparative values of salmon angling and commercial fishing based on either the value of a salmon or the person years of employment

| Country | Year | Angling | Commercial fishing | Authority |
|---|---|---|---|---|
| Canada (Quebec) | 1956 | $158 | $6.80 | Maheux (1956) |
| Canada (New Brunswick) | 1966 | $214 | $6.63 | Carter (1985) |
| Canada (5 eastern seaboard provinces) | 1985 | 2090* | 160* | Tuomi (1986) |
| Ireland | 1970 | £2.81 | £2.45 | O'Connor, Whelan and McCashin (1973–74) |
| Ireland | 1982 | £18.02 | £13.05 | Whelan and Whelan (1987) |
| Wales | 1980 | >£800 | £36.00 | Gee and Edwards (1981) |

*Person years of employment.*

commercial purposes, and as the commercial fishing effort is applied before the fish reach the main angling areas, the commercial catch should be so regulated as to allow attractive and reasonably successful angling.

The Bledisloe Committee (Anon., 1961), reviewing the English fisheries, were of the opposite opinion (para. 5):

The figures . . . moreover suggest that the reduction or cessation of netting does not always result in strikingly better angling and we think that to abolish commercial fishing altogether would result in a substantial loss of good food without countervailing advantage to the angler.

Hadoke (1972) from his study of the Foyle salmon fisheries considered that there were strong grounds for accepting the findings of the Bledisloe Committee as the most appropriate to the Foyle area:

Firstly, it must be realized, and accepted, that commercial salmon netting gives employment to persons in addition to their normal occupation, or, in many cases to unemployed persons. This factor must be considered of more benefit to the community than the provision of sporting facilities to generally employed persons, even if it is accepted that the provision of sporting facilities is a necessity in modern times; on the question of priority the commercial netting must take first place. Secondly, by offering even a limited amount of employment to unemployed persons the two Governments are thereby saved the expense of providing National Assistance benefits to such persons at no additional investment or cost other than the initial expenditure on the purchase of the Fishery in 1952.

This reasoning does not necessarily hold for every salmon-producing nation and in eastern Canada, in supporting a permanent closure of the commercial salmon fisheries, economists argue that the commercial salmon fishermen engage in any case in other, more productive forms of fishing, such as for herring, cod, lobster and crab. It has been suggested in Ireland that unemployed commercial salmon fishermen could be directed into related industries such as salmon farming and salmon ranching.

In Scotland, one of the main functions of the Atlantic Salmon Conservation Trust (Scotland), recently established, is to purchase commercial fishing rights as they come on the market, thus reducing or eliminating netting on some salmon rivers. In this way more of the resource is being allocated for angling, although the Trust stresses that limited netting may be reintroduced when there is evidence to show that salmon stocks have increased and reached a 'healthy' level for renewed commercial exploitation. However, there may be some disadvantages in a 'sport-fishing-only' policy. As the salmon stocks increased and there were more fish in the rivers there would be increased poaching in the rivers, and most certainly more illegal fishing at sea as a result of no surveillance by the then-absent legal netsmen. There would be an increased demand for the improved rod fishing, resulting in increases in prices and rents. In Scotland, increased catches and the absence of funds arising from commercial fishing rates would lead to increased rate (tax) assessments for the salmon proprietors and anglers leasing waters. This happened on the River Tweed in 1985, where an agreed late start to the netting season led to higher rate assessments for the rod fisheries. The Tweed netting stations have traditionally provided around 40% of the revenue required through annual assessments and if the Trust brings commercial fishing to an end the costs will have to be transferred exclusively to the owners of the rod fishing beats. In 1986 the rods experienced a 23% increase in assessments due, as in 1985, to a late start to the netting season. As HRH the Prince of Wales warned in his address to the Second International Atlantic Salmon Symposium in Edinburgh in 1978, angling could become too commercialized. There is evidence for this on some Scottish rivers where syndication and time sharing tend to restrict access.

Lord Thurso in a debate on salmon conservation in the House of Lords (Hansard (House of Lords) 20 January 1988) observed that in 1986 when the spring catch by the rods was 9485 fish, the spring catch by the estuary nets was only 4453 fish and the spring catch by the fixed engines was 2795 fish. He then suggested to Lord Sanderson of Bowden, Minister of State for Scotland, that if he wanted to improve the runs of spring salmon what he should have done was to stop the anglers fishing, then there would have been more salmon running up the rivers.

Before finally leaving this topic it is worth briefly considering the economics of a Scottish salmon rod fishery from the point of view of the 'poor' fishing proprietor. Semple (1967) in discussing the 'mythical profits of the fishing proprietors' says:

It is in assessing the precise value of these latter factors (i.e. salmon rod fishing) that difficulties arise. Returns of catches on individual rivers are confidential to the Secretary of State for Scotland and rod rents can vary tremendously . . . Certainly high rents are charged in certain areas at peak periods of the year, and a legendary American tourist is said to have offered £700 for a week of high grade fishing . . .

This difficulty in obtaining precise information, the knowledge that high rents are sometimes charged, and the fact that demand has probably never been greater have all combined to perpetuate a myth that the landed gentry are making a great deal of money out of their fishing stretches . . .

Indications are, however, that this is far from the truth . . .'

Not a penny is taken from the national purse to support this most prolific part of a national asset. The owners pick up the whole tab and, despite the myth, they are making little or no money from their sporting fisheries.

Last year a typical mid-river salmon rod fishery, representing a stretch of two and half miles on each side of the river (Tweed) drew £1866 in rents. As Table 6.8 – an extract of audited accounts – shows, the profit was marginal. It was fortunate that no unusual expenditure was incurred, but last year repairs to a cauld cost £300 and the fishery account showed a loss . . .

Naturally, the relevant 1987 figures are far in excess of these. For example, the price for a week's salmon fishing for one rod on a top-grade beat can be as much as £1500 or even more. The figure of £700 given by Semple was probably the then price for the lease of the beat for two or three rods. The letting price of a good beat now is based on a value of £200 per salmon. On the River Tweed the assessment is presently £20 per rod-caught salmon and the local authority (county) rate is £10 per fish. Need one say more.

**Table 6.8** Extracts from audited accounts of a typical mid-river salmon rod fishery on the River Tweed in 1966, showing a profit of £113

| Income (£) | | Expenditure (£) | |
| --- | --- | --- | --- |
| Rents | 1866 | Wages | 737 |
| | | Rates on houses | 82 |
| | | Fishermen's perks | 73 |
| | | Upkeep of boats | 47 |
| | | Telephone | 24 |
| | | Tweed assessment | 172 |
| | | County rate | 518 |
| | | Miscellaneous | 100 |
| | 1866 | | 1753 |

Exemption of certain Scottish salmon fishings from local authority rates has arisen as a result of recent legislation. Under paragraph 6 of Part II of Schedule 12 to the *Local Government Finance Act 1988*, a new section (22A) has been added to the *Valuation and Rating (Scotland) Act 1954*.

This provides for exemption of certain salmon fishing rights from local authority rates. The rights to be exempted are those which are entered separately in the valuation roll and are situated in a salmon fishery district for which there is a district salmon fishery board immediately before April 1st each year. For the River Tweed there will be exemption from local authority rates of salmon fishing rights on both Scottish and English parts of the river.

# CHAPTER SEVEN

# Problems and solutions in the management of open seas fisheries for Atlantic salmon

## 7.1 INTRODUCTION

Up until the late 1950s the Atlantic salmon stocks of each salmon-producing nation were almost completely under the control of their country of origin. Exploitation and management of the stocks was the exclusive concern of the nations to which they belonged. The salmon feeding areas in the North Atlantic Ocean had not been located and so there was no exploitation of stocks prior to their return migration. The only exception to this stable situation was the southern Baltic long-line and drift-net fishery for salmon originating mainly from northern Swedish rivers and exploited principally by Denmark. A few other small open seas fisheries were already in existence and these do intercept some salmon returning to more distant home waters. These fisheries are confined to offshore areas 10–19 km off the coast and are operated, using drift nets, by nations having their own salmon stocks. They occur along the west coast of Ireland, the north-east coast of England, and parts of the New Brunswick and Nova Scotia coasts of Canada's eastern seaboard.

In 1956, the capture of a tagged Scottish salmon kelt at a small inshore fishery off the west coast of Greenland was the signal for a new chapter in the history of salmon management. The subsequent capture off the west coast of Greenland of other salmon tagged in Canada, England, France, Ireland, Scotland, Sweden, the USA and Wales confirmed beyond doubt the importance of the Davis Strait as a major feeding area for the Atlantic salmon. Probably as a result of the advent of nylon monofilament net and the availability of local processing plants the West Greenland fishery developed rapidly from this time into an efficient high seas operation, with well-equipped foreign vessels using up to 32 km of drift net to increasingly exploit salmon stocks from North American and European rivers. The phasing out of foreign-vessel participation in 1976 and the fixing of a quota and regulations on Greenland fishermen fishing within 64 km of the coast has helped to control this fishery.

Another high seas salmon fishery using floating long lines was developing almost simultaneously off the north-west Norwegian coast at about the latitude of the Lofoten Islands, and an inshore drift-net fishery became established off the Norwegian coast in 1965. More recently a floating long-line fishery was established north of the Faroe Islands, and this too has been taking fish tagged in Canada, England, France, Iceland, Ireland, Scotland, Norway and Sweden.

The salmon resource therefore rapidly became an international one requiring international negotiations for its effective management. In addition the problems of management at a national level became more complex. The replacement of drift nets made of natural fibre by the rot-proof and less visible nylon monofilament net has attracted more effort into the open seas fisheries in home waters; it has also encouraged the development of an illegal fishery off the Scottish coast and some breach in the regulations controlling the drift-net fishing off the west coast of Ireland.

The future overall management of some of these open seas fisheries is receiving considerable attention from the North Atlantic Salmon Conservation Organisation (NASCO) and the governments of a number of salmon-producing nations before other such fisheries develop in salmon feeding areas not yet located.

## 7.2   THE RATIONALE OF THE OPEN SEAS FISHERIES

### Biological

It can be very convincingly argued that there should be no open seas fisheries for Atlantic salmon and, on biological grounds, there are very sound reasons against harvesting an anadromous species either on its feeding grounds or during the course of its return migration to spawn in its natal streams. The fisheries taking place on the salmon's feeding grounds, such as off West Greenland, to the north of the Faroes and until recently in the Norwegian Sea, are harvesting fish which are still in the process of putting on substantial weight. Fish allowed to return to their parent rivers probably gain a great deal in net harvestable weight and suffer relatively small marginal loss to natural mortality although, as Crutchfield (1979) points out, there is as yet little empirical verification of this point. Generally speaking then, salmon of maximum weight may be harvested at least cost per unit of effort in coastal waters. The first bone of contention now appears, because when speaking of 'least cost per unit of effort' one is assuming that the same nation is involved in both fisheries – the open seas and the coastal. This is true for the Pacific salmon fisheries (Crutchfield, 1979; Copes, 1977), but not for the Atlantic salmon fisheries.

However, the second line of argument concerns the probable random exploitation of the stocks in the open seas. Salmon stocks become mixed on their feeding grounds, with fish of European and North American origin being taken off West Greenland in relatively equal proportions. There is therefore no precise way of achieving the goal of regulating the exploitation of stocks destined for each country, let alone each river (Thorpe and Mitchell, 1981). Only by conducting all harvesting in the rivers or near the river mouths can selective escapement be regulated to achieve maximum runs. This would appear to be an important biological reason for confining salmon harvesting to the relevant coastal states.

Those fisheries closer to the states of origin, the interceptory fisheries, may be considered to be even more damaging to the stocks. They are exploiting fish which have almost ceased feeding, have survived the various sources of mortality and are on direct course to their spawning rivers. The Irish west coast fishery has now been recorded as taking fish destined for rivers in Scotland, England and Wales, while in the Northumberland and Yorkshire fisheries tagging experiments revealed that 80% and 61% respectively of the salmon are *en route* for Scottish rivers, with some estimates (Potter and Swain, 1982) indicating that 94% of the fish in this north-east England fishery are of Scottish origin. A similar situation occurs in Canada, with the Newfoundland fisheries intercepting salmon travelling to rivers in the Maritime Provinces and the New England states of the USA. As salmon move into coastal waters they are arriving in what might be considered to be collecting grounds from which they will disperse to rivers along the coast, and for that reason should be protected at this point on their migration.

It is generally agreed that in optimum stock management the regulation of spawning escapement up the rivers is important. Each river and spawning tributary has a particular capacity for spawning and for accommodation of juvenile fish. The maximum number of fish required is difficult to assess and exploitation rates by inshore commercial fisheries and anglers have only been fully investigated on a few river systems (Elson and Tuomi, 1975). It is on this subject that there tends to be a division of opinion over the numbers of salmon required to maintain a stock both for survival and for exploitation of the species. Fish are very resilient to overfishing: it has been said that large broods do not appear to depend on large numbers of adult spawners, and this lends support to the belief that certain fish populations are entirely unaffected by man (Gordon, 1954). It is interesting to note that many Faroese fishermen found it hard to understand why there should be so much concern over the amount of salmon they are taking, as they say that the numbers of salmon they see while hauling their lines are countless (Mills and Smart, 1982).

Shelton (1986) gives the current estimates of home water losses in tonnes for every tonne intercepted, subject to the limitations imposed by the estimation of input parameters, as: (a) North-east England, 1 t; (b) Greenland 1.29–1.75 t (Europe), 1.47–2.00 t (North America), combined 1.37–1.85 t; (c) Faroes, 1.59 t.

The estimate of home water loss for the Northumbrian fishery assumes that no natural mortality takes place between the site of this fishery and those of fisheries in home waters.

The catches in the interceptory fisheries off Faroes and Greenland and the estimated consequent losses to home water stocks are given in Table 7.1. It can be seen that the 1985 catches in the interceptory fisheries of 1523 t resulted in a loss to home water stocks of 2436 t which represents 42% of the total catch of the home water fisheries throughout the North Atlantic. The loss to the Community's home water stocks accounts for 55% of that total loss. Spencer (1988) states that in the Community's view these fisheries are still being conducted at an unacceptably high level and constitute a considerable burden on North Atlantic salmon stocks.

**Table 7.1**  Catches (tonnes) in the interceptory fisheries and consequent losses to home water stocks 1980–85*

|  | *1980* | *1981* | *1982* | *1983* | *1984* | *1985* | *Total 1980–85* |
|---|---|---|---|---|---|---|---|
| Faroese catches | 718 | 1125 | 960 | 783 | 697 | 672 | 4 925 |
| Greenland catches | 1194 | 1264 | 1077 | 310 | 297 | 851 | 4 993 |
| Total | 1912 | 2389 | 2037 | 1063 | 994 | 1523 | 9 918 |
| Loss to home water stock | 3060 | 3822 | 3260 | 1700 | 1590 | 2436 | 15 868 |
| EEC share of loss | 1640 | 2090 | 1768 | 970 | 910 | 1330 | 8 708 |

*Source: ICES working group reports on North Atlantic salmon 1985 and 1986.*

What effect a total ban on the interceptory fisheries in the North Atlantic and North Sea would have on home water fisheries has not been estimated. However, Larsson (1984) estimated that a total ban on the Baltic offshore fishery would mean a sixfold increase in the catch value for home water fisheries, and a total value twice that in the then current situation with the current seasonal mean weights of salmon.

Before one can state categorically that the salmon resource is experiencing serious depletion one has to consider whether or not the declines in any one stock are related to some environmental factor such as climate (Reddin, 1988). There is considerable controversy concerning the weight to attach to human predation, in contrast to natural factors, in explaining both short-term and long-term fluctuations in the vitality of salmon stocks (Gulland, 1970). It should not surprise us that fish stocks respond to climatic factors and to climatic changes although they live their lives within the weight of water. Their migration circuits are tied to hydrodynamic structures, and reproductive isolation is obtained by the capacity of fish to join or leave current systems as they will. Perturbations of a migration circuit with an unsuspected advection will spill fish outside their normal range where they either establish a new spawning group or die, for they do not return (Cushing, 1983).

### Social and economic

Hardin (1968) pointed out that a tragedy in fisheries occurs when there is a rapid increase in the number of fishermen and the average success of the fishermen declines. However, he went on to divide the tragedy into two aspects, (a) environmental – when the biomass of the resources reaches such a low level that it is threatened with extinction and (b) human – when the participants harvesting a resource obtain less and less of it. This situation can occur when the biomass of a resource is decreasing at a faster rate than the number of participants.

With the open seas fisheries the participants are in direct competition with those harvesting the resource at its predictable point of return. On social or economic grounds how can one decide who has more right to what is a common-property resource? Commercial fishermen in traditional and long-established fisheries as well as sport fishermen have shown some resentment to these open seas fisheries, feeling that the harvest becomes divided further with a consequent reduction in their share. For example, the Hunter Committee in its first report in 1963 (Anon., 1963), reviewing the recently developed drift-net fishery off the Scottish east coast, obtained evidence that competition from drift-net fishermen had already exerted some effects on the structure of the salmon industry. The success of the drift-net fishermen was a threat to their employment. The appearance of the Scottish drift-net fishery, which was quickly banned, may have been a sign that other fisheries had declined. Inshore Scottish fishermen who had traditionally fished for white fish (e.g. cod, haddock, plaice) claimed that this was indeed the reason for their having to switch to salmon in order to pay off the loans for purchasing their vessels.

In Greenland, the salmon fishery developed at a time when Denmark was investing large sums of money in the country as part of a vast programme of modernization with a view to bringing up the Greenlanders' standard of living to the level of the Danes'. Modern fish-processing plants gave the Greenlanders an opportunity of disposing of their salmon catch (Fig. 7.1) and the fishery was a welcome additional source of employment for a rapidly expanding population (Mills, 1980a) which was finding the seal and cod stocks declining. While it may be only a seasonal occupation for many, the domestic importance of the Greenland fishing industry, including salmon, renders unsuitable the principle of paying compensation to salmon fishermen for not fishing, as

**Fig. 7.1** Salmon ready for freezing at a processing plant in Nuuk, Greenland. (Photo by Derek Mills.)

happened in the New Brunswick salmon fishery (Ritter and Porter, 1980). Aside from the socially undesirable effects of such a tactic, due in part to an absence of alternative employment of any nature, there would be serious ripple effects on the entire fishing resource industry, of which fishermen form only one, albeit vital, part. The loss of a source of income at a time when many younger people, students and unskilled labourers, are looking to the fishery ashore and afloat for a significant portion of their yearly needs would have the potential to create social friction and much dissatisfaction with international influences on Greenland's fisheries (Kreiberg, 1981). The Greenlanders' own resentment of salmon sport fishermen, who have in the past demanded the closure of this fishery, is seen when they refer to them as 'hobby fishermen' who should do something to reduce pollution in their own rivers. The Greenlanders of course feel they have a right to a share of the catch of a fish which spends a significant part of its time in their waters – 'you rear the smolts, we rear the adults'. They do receive a share in the form of a grazing fee (p. 159).

The Faroese fishery could arguably be justified on the same grounds. The fishing industry is of great importance to the Faroes (Fig. 7.2). In 1977 about one-third of the gross factor income stemmed from fishing and 95% of exports consisted of fish or fish products (Mills and Smart, 1982). With the collapse of the herring fishery in the late 1960s and the reduction in the cod stocks, the

**Fig. 7.2**    The fishing industry is of great importance to the Faroes. Frozen salmon being off-loaded at Torshavn. (Photo by Derek Mills.)

salmon is a valuable substitute. The Faroese have a strong desire to see other salmon-producing nations also regulating their fisheries more effectively, and rightly criticize the illegal Scottish drift-net fishery and the infringements for which the Irish drift-net fishery is so renowned (Mills, 1982). Regulations are made to be observed, but all too often the proposed regulations have conflicted so strongly with basic social and cultural features of fishing communities that they have been massively resisted. It has been argued that opposition to fisheries regulations will be minimized if such regulations are congruent with the social and economic system (Acheson, 1975).

## 7.3    AN ASSESSMENT OF PRESENT REGULATIONS

Present regulations can be basically divided into two groups: those that use a quota system to limit the actual amount of fish taken and those that restrict and control the type of fishing effort applied to ensure some escapement of fish without limiting the fishermen to a fixed amount of the resource.

In the West Greenland fishery the quota is divided into a 'free' component open to all licensed fishermen and a 'local' component allocated to all communities within the fishery area. The allocation of a quota to the fishery as a whole has its drawbacks in that, providing fish are relatively abundant, the quota can be achieved in a short space of time and the fish-processing plants become overloaded at a time when other species are also being accepted. This tends to be the position in the West Greenland fishery where in 1980 the quota was achieved in under three weeks and some poor-quality salmon were being landed. The processing plants at that time were also having to deal with landings of shrimp and cod. A 'race' to achieve the quota results in lack of selection for fish condition and ends in an uneven distribution of fish among vessels. One Danish salmon smoke-house finds the quality of Faroese cage-reared salmon to be superior to Greenland drift-net-caught fish, probably because of the poor-quality of salmon being landed.

The allocation of individual and non-transferable quotas to licensed vessels, as in the Faroese fishery, appears more logical. Here each vessel is aware of its target and can adjust its effort and be more selective. Each vessel on achieving its quota can then transfer to other types of fishing; there is no competition among fishermen. There can be more selection of salmon in the Faroese long-line fishery, as most discards (i.e. fish below the agreed size for retention) can be returned to the sea alive; in the Greenland drift-net fishery discarded, poor-condition fish would be dead and there would be a consequent wastage. One is only too aware of the practice of dumping catches of mackerel at sea if their quality is poor or the market unfavourable (see footnote at the end of this chapter).

It is also of value to link the quota system both to a season and to fishing-effort limitation. Fish taken early in the year may be too small or in poor condition. Seasons should always be under review and be adjusted to cater for any changes in stock distribution and size composition. For example, the opening date for the West Greenland fishery was changed in 1981 with the aim of catching larger fish (the mesh size of the drift nets was also increased) so enabling a slightly larger quota to be permitted without a greater number of fish being taken. According to one report the expected result did not in fact materialize and, unexpectedly, many more small fish were caught.

However, at present the Greenland quota, set at 850 tonnes with a season opening date of 1 August, can be adjusted so that there is a permitted increase linked to a later opening date. For example, Fig. 7.3 depicts two curves (produced in 1982 when the quota was 1190 t) for seasons starting on 10 August. The upper curve refers to gill nets of mesh size 140 mm, which is the target mesh size (measured diagonally, knot to knot) at West Greenland. In 1986 and 1987 the curves were used to adjust the quota for a season starting after 1 August. In 1987 the quota was set at 850 t but, as the season opening was delayed, an increase in the quota was permitted and 920 t of salmon were landed (see footnote at the end of this chapter).

The present regulations controlling the open seas drift-net fisheries (other than that off Greenland) within 6 to 12 miles (9.6–19.3 km) of the coast put no

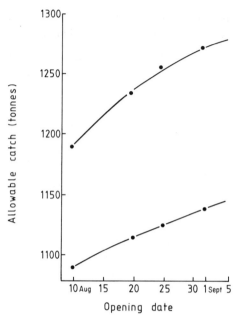

**Fig. 7.3**    Allowable catch levels for the West Greenland salmon fishery in relation to season (opening date 10 August = day 1) for mesh sizes of 134 mm (lower curve) and 140 mm (upper curve) (reproduced with permission from ICES C.M. 1982/Assess: 19).

limits on the catch but simply restrict the fishermen's catching power. Much of the enforcement of these regulations must take place at sea using patrol vessels and aircraft. As there is no limit to the amount a fisherman may land he is in a position of being bribed to land the catch of a non-licensed vessel. In the illegal Scottish drift-net fishery some fish are passed to legal inshore commercial fisheries for dispatch to market, while others are landed and distributed undetected.

A licensing system which is now in force in all these fisheries does control illegal fishing if points of landing can be monitored effectively. However, one reason for discarding suggestions for a quota system for some of these fisheries has been the difficulty of checking on amounts landed. Nevertheless, the recent salmon-tagging scheme originally introduced in New Brunswick (Anon., 1982b; National Water Council, 1983) and now adopted in Nova Scotia, Maine, France and Spain, has much to commend it, as each salmon has to have a numbered coloured tag attached immediately it is caught. In North America the colour of tag depends on whether the fish has been caught commercially or by angling.

All salmon fishing beyond the 12-mile limits has now been banned with the exception of the Greenland and Faroese fisheries. Drift netting off the

Norwegian coast has also been prohibited, while the Norwegian Sea fishery has been closed. There have been numerous demands to have the open sea drift-net fisheries off north-east England and the west coast of Ireland also banned. The resistance to this is great and has become as much of a political issue as has the demand to close the fisheries off Greenland and the Faroes.

## 7.4 FISHERIES CONFLICTS AND THE FUTURE

The open seas fisheries off Greenland and the Faroes and in the Norwegian Sea have been a contentious issue since they first began. The International Commission for the North-West Atlantic Fisheries (ICNAF) had a limited effect on reducing the extent of the Greenland fishery; only the threat of an embargo on Danish imports by the USA was immediately effective in restricting this fishery. Other high seas fisheries have been less of a problem. A voluntary reduction in the quota by the Faroese met with general approval and has enabled co-operation among scientists to investigate the salmon stocks in the fishery; the Norwegian Sea fishery has been closed.

There have in the past been a number of controversies over high seas fisheries that have put severe strains on major alliances vital to the political and economic stability of the Free World. The threat of embargo is probably more intolerable than the actual embargo. An embargo on trade might result in the opening up of a new outlet more profitable than the first and having serious repercussions on the country imposing the embargo (Fisher, 1969). Before making threats, a government should look ahead to a situation in which the threat has failed to exert the desired influence. Retaliatory restrictions on international trade can develop further and lead to denial of strategic bases for the NATO countries. This situation was close to occurring during the Anglo–Icelandic 'cod war' of 1972–73 (Hart, 1976; Gilchrist, 1977), when the future of Keflavik as a NATO base was in some doubt. Greenland and the Faroes are also of immense strategic value to the western alliance (Bertram and Holst, 1977). Many observers believe that deep-seated sensitivities about security constitute serious barriers to co-ordinated resource management at the international level.

The future of the Greenland fishery, at least, would not appear to be in doubt although the quota may have to be more flexible. It is interesting to note that in 1983 and 1984 the quotas were not achieved even though boats continued fishing until December. The quota has a 'grazing fee' component incorporated. The theory behind such a 'fee' is that the salmon are using a common property resource and remove part of the biological potential of the ocean which will not be available to feed other commercial fish species in the same area. If state-of-origin ownership of the salmon is conceded and protected then there has to be reciprocal recognition that the owners of the salmon pay for the value of the pasturage enjoyed at the expense of the community in whose waters they are grazing, the payment being in the form of an accepted amount of salmon. A similar 'grazing fee' could be negotiated for Faroese waters. The quotas for both these fisheries are now negotiated through the appropriate commissions in the North Atlantic Salmon Conservation Organisation (NASCO).

The negotiations are sometimes only completed after prolonged discussions and often it is then only a compromise that is agreed. In 1987 the Faroese asked for a quota of 750 tonnes and the EEC demanded that it should be reduced from the existing 625 t to 550 t. It was eventually agreed that the quota should be 1790 t (i.e. 597 t/year) over a 3 year trial period with allowance for a 5% overrun on the annual average catch. Linked to this agreement was one for effort limitation where (a) there could be a closure of areas at short notice to prevent the catch of undersized fish, (b) there would be a fishing fleet of 26 vessels with a total fishing effort in any one year of no more than 1600 days, and (c) there would be a reduction of the fishing season to 15 January–30 April and 1 November–15 December.

In discussions with both the Greenland and Faroese authorities frequent reference has been made to the Scottish, English and Irish drift-net fisheries. The accusing finger is pointed particularly at the illegal Scottish drift-net fishery and the unknown amount of fish it catches. Unless solutions are found to the problem centred around these national fisheries one cannot expect the fullest co-operation internationally. The saying 'to put one's own house in order' is regularly uttered, and the question frequently asked is 'why have you no quota?' When attention was drawn to an overrun of 51 t on Greenland's 1986 quota of 909 t at the 1987 meeting of NASCO, one delegate wondered what the fuss was all about when the estimated unreported catch (partly by illegal fishing) in home waters was put at 3500 t.

In a draft report to the European Parliament's Committee on Agriculture in 1983, Mr Brøndlund Nielsen of Denmark stated in his conclusions that the maintenance of regulation of the Faroese fishery will be dependent in the longer term on proper controls of salmon fishing by Community fishermen. He went on to say:

The Faroese have shown a co-operative and even generous attitude towards the scientists in negotiations to fish the present quota. This attitude will not be maintained if illegal drift-net fishing continues in Scottish, English and Irish waters. Effective action must be taken by the Community to regulate salmon fishing by means of quotas, licences and effective inspection, if we are to expect the Faroese to co-operate in future talks as they have in these.

According to Atli Dam (1988), Prime Minister of the Faroes, the Faroese point of view is basically that the well-being of the salmon stocks must be seen throughout their whole migratory range and that it is therefore illogical and unbalanced that NASCO can only regulate the fishery for salmon when a salmon is fished in a fisheries zone different from the one from which it originates.

More rigorous enforcement of existing legislation could have more impact on the Scottish illegal drift-nets while the introduction of a licensing and/or a tagging system for the legal commercial and sports fisheries would go a long way to eliminate illegal fishing entirely and also make the collection of catch statistics more reliable. However, such arrangements are opposed by certain organizations in Scotland, and tagging was dismissed by those government departments dealing with fisheries in Scotland, England and Wales as being inappropriate due to the problems regarding (a) imported farmed salmon from Norway, (b) the tagging of Scottish farmed salmon and (c) the likely black market in salmon tags. This proposal to introduce carcass tagging was also rejected by NASCO in 1987 as a result of the statement made by the EEC representative, who supported the conclusions reached by the United Kingdom government. Furthermore, such a tagging scheme was not included in the 1986 *Salmon Act*, but powers to introduce a dealer-licensing system under the *Civic Government (Scotland) Act*, 1982, have been incorporated.

The issue has now become a political one which no one is prepared to attend to at present. Politics, too, prevent the north-east England fishery from being banned, and MPs are not prepared to lose the support of the fishermen in these constituencies, probably because if the fishery was closed there would be further unemployment. The Irish drift-net fishery has the same problem: politicians are not anxious to see existing regulations more rigorously enforced, but are prepared to pass laws enabling their drift-net fishermen to fish with longer nets and in coastal areas previously regarded as sanctuaries, although it has been suggested that the fishery could be phased out and the fishermen employed in salmon farming and ranching. The name of the game is no longer 'resource management' but political 'snakes and ladders', with the Danes and Faroese as spectators. Unless the Scottish illegal fishery is more effectively banned and the north-east England drift-net fishery further controlled, at least initially, by reduced fishing effort and possibly a quota, the traditional Scottish salmon netting industry, already being affected by the effects of increased numbers of farmed salmon on the falling fish price, could go out of business. Much of the money to finance Scottish salmon district fishery boards comes from the boards' rates levied on these commercial firms, who also do much to see that the coastal areas are 'policed' and the rivers well managed.

While many would prefer to see traditional coastal netting banned as in Iceland, and all catching of salmon in rivers left to sport fishermen as has been proposed (Mills and Piggins, 1988, p. 577), it is unlikely that the salmon resource would in fact be adequately exploited if this 'anglers only' policy was adopted (Mills, 1988). Efforts are being made to buy back commercial fishing rights both in Canada (Marshall, 1988; Rolland, 1987) and in Scotland. The

Atlantic Salmon Conservation Trust (Scotland) has bought up a number of netting stations in both north-east and south-east Scotland with a view to managing the rivers more carefully, and while it involves the present curtailment of commercial fishing on these rivers, for which the Trust has been strongly criticized, it is only a temporary measure until it is felt that salmon stocks have 'recovered' sufficiently to stand commercial exploitation. Such a decision of course does imply that there should be a greater understanding of the problems involved in deriving reliable stock-recruitment relationships.

**Footnote**

At its annual meeting in June, 1988, NASCO adopted the proposed quota of its West Greenland Commission. This set a TAC of 2520 t for the calendar years 1988, 1989 and 1990. However, in any given year the annual catch shall not exceed the annual average (840 t) by more than 10%. Thus, in any one year, the maximum catch would be 924 t (840 + 84). These quantities are based on the fishery opening on August 1st. If, however, the season is opened at a later date the above quantities would be adjusted in accordance with the calculations set by the ICES Working Group (Fig. 7.3). The quota system will now be operated on an individual boat basis, in which each boat has its own set quota, as in the Faroese salmon fishery.

# CHAPTER EIGHT

# Stock assessment

*The Salmophile's uneasy laugh*
*Betrays his religious disposition*
*His eye, that nervous diagnostician*
*Of the parr-pulation graph,*
*Knows that falling points express,*
*The growth of human wretchedness.*

Ted Hughes, 1985
*(unpublished)*

The subject of stock assessment is all-embracing and many manuals have been written on the topic. It includes more than just the various methods to estimate the stocks of either juvenile or adult fish. It covers also the relationship between stock and recruitment, mortality, rate of exploitation, fishing effort and assessment of long-term catch data. These estimates require reliable data and many of them have to be based on either (a) catch statistics, the collection of which can be affected in a number of ways over a period of years (Browne, 1986; Shearer, 1986b; 1988), by changes in fishing effort for example, or (b) actual counts using various counting facilities or (c) indirect methods of abundance estimation. Sometimes the term 'stock' is more limited in its meaning and is defined as 'a group of fish spawning in a particular location at a particular time so that they do not substantially interbreed with another group.' This is a biological definition and relies on spatial and/or temporal reproductive isolation; 'substantially' is to be emphasized. It is very similar to the term 'population' but the fishery manager may have for convenience to group many stocks together in his attempt to assess the size of the total salmon population in the river. So by the term 'stock assessment' one often means 'population assessment'.

## 8.1 METHODS FOR ESTIMATING STOCK OR POPULATION SIZE

### Direct evaluation

Various methods of direct evaluation have been described by Mills (1978) and Prouzet and Dumas (1988). These include:

## Capture

This may be achieved by trapping and electrofishing. Traps or counting fences range from sizeable structures the size of weirs and cruives to small boxes or cages for sampling fry. The most effective trap for sampling migratory fish is the Wolf trap. This consists of a horizontal framework covered with wire mesh or a wooden grid. The water flows through this horizontal screen leaving a small film of water to flow into a trough attached to the downstream side of the screen. Downstream-migrating fish are 'sieved' out of the water, drop into the trough and swim down it to a holding pool (Fig. 8.1). Wolf traps can be of various sizes, from only a few metres wide, built on small nursery streams, to large structures built across a river 20 m or more wide. Ascending fish are usually caught in a subsidiary, adjoining trap which consists of a small confined pool into which the fish swim through a V-shaped entrance (Fig. 8.1).

Another type of trap, which is a useful sampling device, is the box trap (Fig. 8.2). This consists of a square wooden box-shaped frame, covered with small-meshed netting, with a V-entrance and an inclined ramp. The fish can be led into and up the 'funnel entrance' by means of a leader. These traps are useful in small streams and fish passes where they can be temporarily erected for sampling seasonal movements of fish.

Many traps used for migratory fish are known as counting fences and consist of vertical screens with box traps sited along them (Fig. 8.3). In recent years there has been some criticism of them in that they may cause some delay to both ascending and descending fish (Ruggles, 1974).

### Visual counts

Fish may be counted at fish passes, particularly those sited at hydroelectric dams, or at other selected points as they move upstream at which manual or photographic enumeration may be used. Their numbers may also be noted underwater by divers, or from the air using photography. In addition, an estimate of numbers may be obtained from redd counts (Gudjonsson, 1988), although these are not always reliable: their value is discussed by Hay (1984).

### Automatic counts

Electronic counters may be used, sometimes in association with closed-circuit television (Trefethen and Collins, 1974), and of these, resistivity counters appear to be the most reliable and have been used for instance by Hellawell (1973), Lawson (1974), McGrath (1975), Dunkley and Shearer (1982, 1983), Mann *et al.* (1983) and Struthers and Stewart (1984, 1985). Sonar counters have been used less widely for Atlantic salmon. Unlike the resistivity counter, which operates when a fish passing over a weak electric field created by submerged electrodes unbalances a Wheatstone bridge, so producing a signal which is amplified and processed, the sonar counter picks up an echo

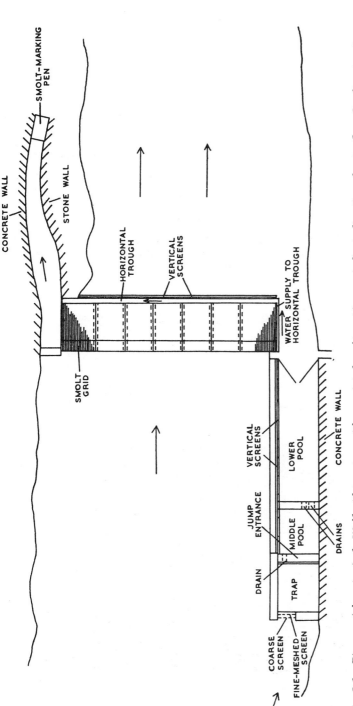

**Fig. 8.1** Diagram (plan view) of a Wolf grid-type trap with associated pool trap. Arrows indicate direction of water flow. Smolts migrating downstream pass over a grid (only partly shown) into a trough and swim into the smolt-marking pen. Fish swimming upstream are diverted through a V-shaped entrance into a series of pools, the last of which is a trap: they cannot jump out of it (reproduced with permission from Pyefinch and Mills, 1963).

**Fig. 8.2** Box trap, designed for collecting fish migrating downstream. A 'leader' is attached: the fish are thereby encouraged to swim into the narrowing entrance and up the ramp into the box (note smolts tend to move downstream tail first) (reproduced from Mills, 1971).

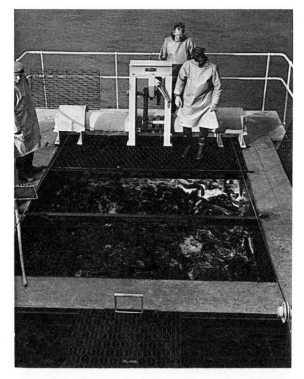

**Fig 8.3** Collecting adult salmon for the hatchery at a permanent trap at Loch na Croic on the River Blackwater, Ross-shire, Scotland. (Photo by Derek Mills.)

produced by the fish as it passes through a vertical ultrasonic beam coming from a transmitter placed on the river bed. The resistivity counter can detect fish of various size ranges and whether they are passing up- or downstream, and can be sited in fish passes and on weirs. The sonar counter does not operate reliably in turbulent water and for this reason suitable sites for its efficient operation are more difficult to select.

Another method of fish stock assessment in this category is the use of hydroacoustic instrumentation techniques (Templeton, 1987) and is mentioned briefly in the above paragraph when referring to sonar counters. The operation of a sonar system is by the generation of sound in discrete pulses, and after each pulse the system waits for a certain period to receive echoes from any targets in the insonified volume of water (Burczynski, 1979). Alaskan Fish and Game Department biologists are using side-scan salmon counters, together with an artificial substrate, to assess the upstream adult migration as well as the downstream migration of smolts.

## Indirect evaluation

Indirect methods of evaluation include:

### Use of catch per unit of effort (CPUE)

Prouzet and Dumas (1988) point out that CPUE is used to measure the comparative abundance of stock. This comparative abundance rating makes it possible to follow the fluctuations in the size of a fish population, on condition that certain assumptions are met. The expression of the catch ($C$) as defined by Gulland (1969) is:

$$C = qf \, N/A$$

where  $q$ = the constant expressing the stock capture potential or vulnerability,
$f$ = fishing effort per operating unit,
$N$ = average abundance of stock produced,
$A$ = area inhabited by stock produced.

The size of the catch is dependent on the parameters: density of stock $N/A$, the fishing effort deployed and the capture potential of the stock. Taking CPUE as the comparative abundance rating one is independent of the variation in effort from one year to the next but not of yearly fluctuations in vulnerability.

Prouzet and Dumas (1988) point out that Atlantic salmon rod-fishing catches are used for the parental abundance rating as described by Dempson (1980), working from the theory that fishing effort does not vary from one year to another. Prouzet and Dumas point out that this seems to be confirmed because a reasonable balance between rod-fishing catches and stock abundance has been observed by Elson (1974), Pomerleau, Côté and Migneault (1980) and Chadwick (1982b). However, Piggins (1976) found only a slight correlation between catch and stock in Lough Feeagh in Ireland and Mills, Mahon and Piggins (1986) found that the most important single determinant of catch was fishing effort. The relationship between catch and stock was weaker.

Shearer (1983), while not referring to rod catches *per se*, also stressed that even in the short term, the use of catch figures to compare the strength of spawning stocks between years could give misleading results because the proportion of the total stock entering fresh water before the end of the net fishing season can vary significantly from one year to another. He also pointed out that the lack of reliable data describing the effort put into catching salmon is another difficulty in attempting to relate catches to abundance.

### Mark-recapture estimates

Methods for estimating populations are numerous. One of the most commonly used is the Peterson estimate or Lincoln index which has been modified by Bailey (1951). Bailey derived the formula:

$$N = M(n+1)/(m+1)$$

where $N$ = total population size,
$M$ = number taken in first sample, marked and released,
$n$ = number taken in second sample,
$m$ = number of marked individuals recaptured in second sample.

The accuracy of the estimates depends on a homogeneous distribution of the marked fish, identical vulnerability of the marked fish, and constancy in the balance between the marked and unmarked individuals during the recapture period. For these reasons this method is usually only used for abundance estimates on big rivers where no other method can be used satisfactorily (Cousens *et al.*, 1982). It has been used for Atlantic salmon to determine the production rate of a fishery in the Miramichi River (Ruggles and Turner, 1973). The estimation of population size by marking experiments is fully reviewed by Schaefer (1951).

### Leslie matrices

Browne (1988) describes the use of Leslie matrices (Leslie, 1945) as a useful tool in the preliminary investigations of populations where some good data are available but data on some parts of the life history are lacking. Existing data, he points out, can be tested in the model and areas where further data are required can be pin-pointed. The advantage of this method is that simulation also provides a method of investigating the effects of proposed management changes. Browne used a ten-by-ten matrix so that he could investigate the survival of ova to 1, 2 and 3-year-old smolts and the number of each age group of one-sea-winter and two-sea-winter spawners.

## 8.2  POPULATION ESTIMATES OF JUVENILE SALMON

There have been countless studies of the densities of juvenile salmon and most have involved electrofishing surveys. The reliability of these surveys is very variable and depends on the efficiency of the electrofishing apparatus and the characteristics of the environment in which it is used, including conductivity, turbidity, water velocity and water depth. It is not always possible therefore to make valid comparisons between rivers. However, these population estimates are of value to the fishery manager in providing an assessment of the juvenile stock and whether or not it is increasing, remaining steady or declining. Browne and Gallagher (1987), for example, concluded from population estimates of juvenile salmon in the Corrib system in Ireland over the period 1982–84 that the system was adequately stocked with young salmon. Mills and Tomison (1985), on the other hand, decided from a comparison of the results of River Tweed surveys carried out at roughly 5-year intervals that the juvenile salmon populations in some tributaries had declined and that action to remedy the situation was needed.

Density has an important effect on mortality in juvenile salmon, particularly when there is competition for territories during the post-dispersal phase (Mills, 1964, 1969b; Egglishaw, 1970). Gee *et al.* (1978) studied this relationship in some detail on some River Wye tributaries and found that, within each site studied, the instantaneous mortality rate remained remarkably constant over the period of study and the mortality rate at each site was directly related to the estimated density of fry on 1 June. Thus, with an estimate of the fry density on 1 June, it was possible to predict the in-site survivorship of juvenile salmon.

Estimates of smolt production can be made from the data on fry and parr densities. Gee *et al.* (1978) estimated a maximum smolt production of 0.043 fish/m$^2$ (95% confidence interval 0.019–0.097) in the upper Wye catchment from a fry density on 1 June of 0.75 fish/m$^2$, assuming the smolt production was equivalent to the numbers of juvenile salmon surviving to 2 years of age. Mills (1964), using a similar method of estimation, obtained a smolt production figure for the River Bran, Ross-shire, Scotland, of some 18 000 smolts. This estimate was confirmed by mark and recapture experiments in 1961 and 1962 of smolts trapped on the Bran and subsequently recaptured some distance downstream.

Elson and Tuomi (1975) used data on salmon catch and redd counts from the River Foyle in Ireland to estimate numbers of migrant smolts and produced a stock–recruitment relationship.

More recent studies of smolt production, from which stock–recruitment relationships were derived, have been made at traps or counting fences in Scotland (Buck and Hay, 1984) and Newfoundland (Chadwick, 1982a, 1985c). Browne (1988) estimated the entire smolt run on the Corrib using trap data and micro-tagging and adult recapture results and the formula suggested by Pearson (1982):

$$S = S_t N_c / N_t$$

where  $S$ = the number of smolts migrating,
   $S_t$ = the number of smolts tagged,
   $N_t$ = the number of returning adults caught with tags,
   $N_c$ = the number of returning adults caught at the trap without tags.

the variance ($N$) is given by:

$$N = S_t N_c (S_t - N_c) (N_t + N_c) / N_t$$

The average number of smolts migrating over the years 1980–84 was estimated to be 116 000.

Potter (1982) estimates the total annual smolt production for the Atlantic to be about 30 M smolts. He obtains this estimate from the figure for the total home water catches for the North Atlantic of 7000 t ($= 1.75 \times 10^6$ salmon of mean weight 4 kg) and by assuming a return rate of 15% and an exploitation rate of 40% or:

$$(1.75 \times 10^6)/(0.15)(0.4) = 3 \times 10^7 \text{ smolts.}$$

## 8.3   STOCK–RECRUITMENT

The expression 'stock–recruitment relationship' is used to refer to the relationship between the spawning stock and the subsequent recruitment.

The ability to predict recruitment from numbers of spawners is an important management tool (Jones, 1985). However, estimating the numbers of spawners can be difficult. Ideally one would like to have actual counts of adult fish. The more fortunate fishery managers can obtain these directly through the use of various counting facilities such as traps, fish passes and electronic counters.

Chadwick (1982c) used the recreational catch as an index of salmon spawning escapement on some Newfoundland rivers. He found that on eight rivers with fishways and counting weirs there was a significant correlation between recreational catch and river escapement. Further use of recreational catches has been made by Chadwick and Randall (1986) who obtained a stock–recruitment relationship for salmon in the Miramichi River, New Brunswick, using angling catches of kelts or 'black salmon' as an indication of spawning stock, and densities of small parr determined from electrofishing surveys as an index of recruitment.

Chadwick (1985c) provides an equation to determine the number of spawners required for optimal yield:

$$S = AE/F$$

where $A$ is the surface area of juvenile rearing habitat, E is a fixed deposition rate and $F$ is the average fecundity per spawner. The fixed egg deposition rate (E) of 2.4 eggs/m$^2$ is used in all assessments (Marshall, 1984).

Buck and Hay (1984), working on the Girnock Burn in Aberdeenshire, were able to obtain a good stock–recruitment relationship through the use of trap counts of ascending spawners and descending juvenile migrants (Fig. 8.4).

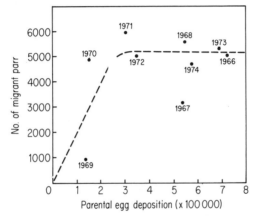

**Fig. 8.4**  Relationship obtained on the Girnock Burn, Aberdeenshire, between number of eggs laid and number of migrating parr produced, 1966–74. The line is fitted by eye (reproduced with permission from Buck and Hay, 1984).

Although there were large variations in the number of female adult salmon spawning in the Girnock Burn each year (range 28–127) they resulted in only small variations in the number of juvenile migrants (range 900–5600). The relative constancy of the parr migrations was achieved by changes in their age composition. It was interesting to note that large numbers of deposited ova (up to 12.5 eggs/m$^2$) did not decrease the number of juvenile migrants, although there may be no advantage in allowing ova deposition to exceed 3.4 eggs/m$^2$. The flat-topped recruitment curve obtained by Buck and Hay is contrary to the findings of Elson and Tuomi (1975) using data on salmon catches and redd counts from the River Foyle, Ireland (Fig. 8.5), and of Gee *et al.* (1978) working on the River Wye in Wales, who both obtained a dome-shaped stock–recruitment curve above an optimum egg deposition level. Chadwick (1985b, c), on

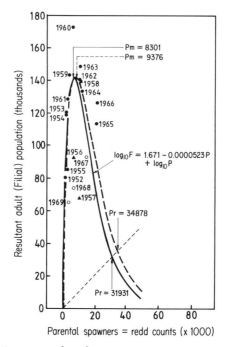

**Fig. 8.5** Reproduction curves based on restructuring regression equations to give relationship between redd counts and resultant adult population (including local coastal catch) for the River Foyle, Ireland, parent years 1952–69. Diagonal line indicates equality. Solid line is the functional regression and broken line the predictive regression. Pm is the number of spawners which on average would give the maximum number of resultant adults (i.e. the filial population). Pr is the number of spawners which just reproduces a filial population equal to its own numbers (32 000). The reproduction from the Pm number value of 8301 spawners works out at 143 000 fish. This rate of reproduction is about 17 fish per spawner.

The points shown as open circles are years in which some returning adult (filial) fish had to pass through more intensive drift-net fisheries than occurred in previous years. Points shown as solid triangles represent adult populations in which the young were exposed to drought in 1958 and to extensive river drainage operations in 1957, 1958 and 1959 (reproduced with permission from Elson and Tuomi, 1975).

the other hand, like Buck and Hay, obtained a flat-topped stock–recruitment curve in Western Arm Brook, Newfoundland (Fig. 8.6). However, as Chadwick mentions, it is possible that spawning requirements may be different for each geographical area, so it might be necessary to calculate a unique stock–recruitment relationship for each area. However, the general consensus of opinion at the moment is that the flat-topped recruitment curve is the most appropriate for salmon stock assessment work.

Solomon (1985) discusses the anomalies of stock–recruitment curves and reviews the evidence for 'dome-shaped' and 'flat-topped' curves. He considers

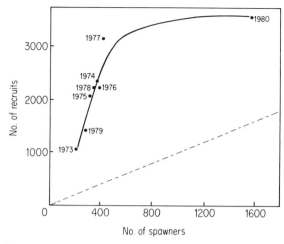

**Fig. 8.6** Stock recruitment curve for Atlantic salmon in Western Arm Brook, Newfoundland, year classes 1973–80. Dashed line, Ricker's replacement line (Ricker, 1954b) (reproduced with permission from Chadwick, 1985c).

the role of density-dependent and density-independent mortality and points out that density-independent mortality acting upon eggs and fry prior to density-dependent factors would, in many years or streams, leave insufficient young to fully populate the available area when the initial numbers had been only just sufficient. His major conclusion is that natural reproduction at low stock densities is a very efficient process, and that management of spawning escapement should be a most effective means of enhancement of depleted stocks. At higher stock levels improvements to stream carrying capacity might be most effective.

In leaving this subject it is important to stress the need for index rivers, on which it is necessary to count all upstream and downstream migrants without large errors, otherwise, as Ludwig and Walters (1981) warn, stock–recruitment relationships may be obscured.

## 8.4   STOCK ESTIMATES OF ADULT SALMON AT SEA

Salmon stock assessment in the open seas is fraught with difficulties and these have been clearly pointed out by Potter (1982). For example, unlike many marine fish species: (a) the Atlantic salmon population comprises many hundred well-isolated spawning stocks; (b) recruitment is generally measured at the smolt stage when the fish may be between 1 year and 7 years old; (c) the salmon may enter mixed stock fisheries within 6 months; (d) several different fisheries may exploit distinguishable parts of each stock; (e) these fisheries operate, in most cases, once on each smolt year class and (f) the incidence of multiple spawning can be ignored. Lassen (1978) proposed a model for the assessment of Baltic salmon stocks which is not entirely applicable for the North Atlantic. The basic 'general' equation describes the change in stock size in a given area in a set time period:

$$
\begin{aligned}
\text{Stock in area A} &= \text{Stock in area A} \\
\text{at time } t+1 \qquad & \quad \text{at time } t \\
& \quad + \text{growth} \\
& \quad + \text{recruitment} \\
& \quad + \text{immigration into area A} \quad \left.\begin{array}{c}\\\\\\\end{array}\right\} \quad \text{in time} \\
& \quad - \text{emigration from area A} \qquad \text{interval} \\
& \quad - \text{fishing mortality in area A} \\
& \quad - \text{natural mortality}
\end{aligned}
$$

Potter points out that stock–recruitment relationships are not so important in the Baltic salmon fishery where 70% of the annual smolt production of 4 M 'artificial smolt units' originates from hatcheries. The 'artificial smolt unit' (a.s.u.) compensates for the low survival rates of hatchery-reared smolts compared with wild smolts (100 a.s.u. = 100 hatchery smolts aged 2 years or 200 hatchery smolts aged 1 year or 50 wild smolts).

In addition the Baltic salmon stock is effectively a closed system and relatively little is known about the migration patterns of salmon in the North Atlantic, while the migrations of Baltic salmon are well documented. However, Hoydal (1988) feels that in principle it should be possible to treat the Baltic and Atlantic systems in the same way.

An estimate of the number of salmon present in the West Greenland fishery has been made by Andersen *et al.* (1980). From mark-recapture data and the model of Ricker (1975), suitably modified, the estimated rate of exploitation in 1972 was 33% at the beginning of the season and based on a catch of 585 000 fish the estimated number present was 1.75 M.

## 8.5   ASSESSMENT OF LONG-TERM CATCH DATA

There are a number of salmon fisheries in which the catches have shown downward trends. Usually in any fishery after a 'period of abundance' there is a downward trend but this usually levels off with rational exploitation. However, in some fisheries where there has been either over-exploitation or change in the river regime due to barriers or pollution, the trend has continued downwards to a point where the fishery is eliminated, as occurred on a number of major rivers in Europe and the USA.

In some cases the trend in the fisheries may be upward and many would consider this a good sign when in fact it might be the opposite. The actual amount of fish landed in a year is a poor guide to what is happening to any particular fishery. The real test is not the total intake of fish, which is called the 'total yield', but the average catch per unit of fishing effort, that is, per net, per trap or per rod, in a given time, say per week, per day or per hour. This is called the 'density' of the catch, and the first sign of a real decline in the supply of fish will be shown not by the total yield but in the density. The total yield could still go on rising while the density is declining.

A trend in the fishery may also be due to changes in fishing methods or in legislation. Ritchie (1920) shows the 'extraordinary decline' of the salmon and trout catches at the mouth of the River Tweed by the Berwick Salmon Fisheries Company (Fig. 8.7). He accepts that part of this decline, from an average of 110 000 salmon and trout in the period 1842–46 to less than 40 000 in the 1870s is 'no doubt due to restrictive legislation controlling the size of mesh of salmon nets'. It is most unlikely that the slight change in mesh size could be responsible for a large change in the average catch in this instance; the decline was more likely due, in greater part, to pollution which was very severe in some areas of the Tweed watershed at this time, and catches declined even further. In recent years the salmon catches on the Tweed have shown expected fluctuations between years and in the mid-1970s reached the level of the catches in the 1870s, but have never risen to the very high levels of the early nineteenth century. Part of the reason for not doing so could be due to the marked reduction in fishing effort by the Berwick Salmon Fisheries Company

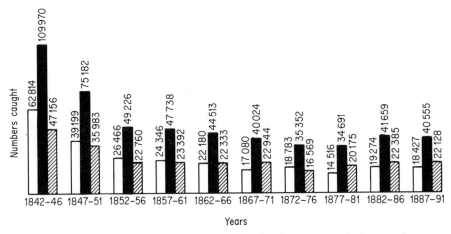

**Fig. 8.7** The decline of Tweed fisheries, as shown by the statistics of salmon and trout caught during 50 years. Each column indicates the average annual catch in a period of 5 years: white columns, number of trout caught; hatched columns, salmon; black columns total catch of salmon and trout (reproduced with permission from Ritchie, 1920).

over the last few decades. Historical records for other Scottish rivers have been described by George (1982) and Shearer (1985).

In addition to definite trends there are also fluctuations which may be long-term or short-term or, as Lindroth (1965) calls them, primary and secondary fluctuations. The short-term fluctuations are the expected variations in the size of the catches from year to year and some of these fluctuations of course could result from differences in the numbers of nets or traps used. In a study of the salmon catches in northern Sweden for the period 1860–1950 Lindroth (1950, 1965) found that fluctuations were remarkably synchronized not only for these rivers but for the Baltic countries as a whole. The trend of the catches in most of them was found to be similar, irrespective of whether the rivers were polluted or unpolluted, with or without power dams or with or without accessory artificial propagation. As the 'curves of capture' for almost every river running to the Baltic show a rather uniform appearance Lindroth speaks of a 'salmon curve' (Fig. 8.8). Similar fluctuations have been recorded for the Baltic in more recent years by Lind (1981). Comparable long-term fluctuations in catches are apparent for the river Tweed (Figs 4.4, 8.9) and for the total Scottish salmon catch (Fig. 8.10) but not for the same periods of time as the Baltic. The biological explanation of the long-term swings in catches is still obscure and Lindroth concludes that 'the main factors must be sought in changes in the biological balance induced by climatic factors'.

A clear periodicity of 8–11 years was also shown to occur in salmon in the north of the USSR, Norway and Canada by Berg (1935). Nikolsky (1969, p. 129) points out that the periodicity coincides with that of the aurora borealis, from which Berg concluded that the factors governing the size of the year classes act during the river period of life.

Menzies (1949) discusses at length some possible causes for the annual or

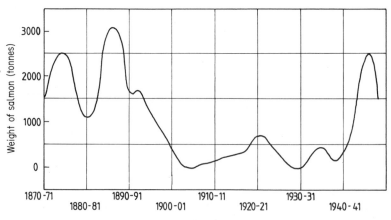

**Fig. 8.8**   The 'salmon curve' (reproduced with permission from Lindroth, 1950).

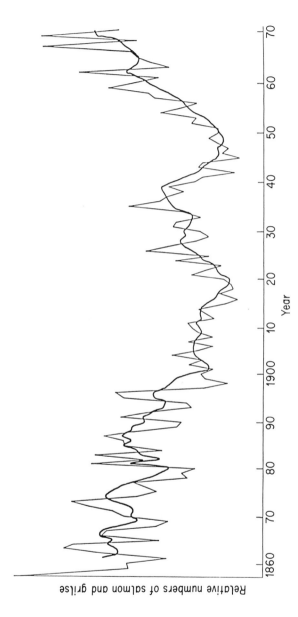

**Fig. 8.9** Relative numbers of salmon and grilse taken by the Berwick Salmon Fisheries Company. 1857–1970. Smooth curve is 5 year running mean (reproduced from Mills, 1987a).

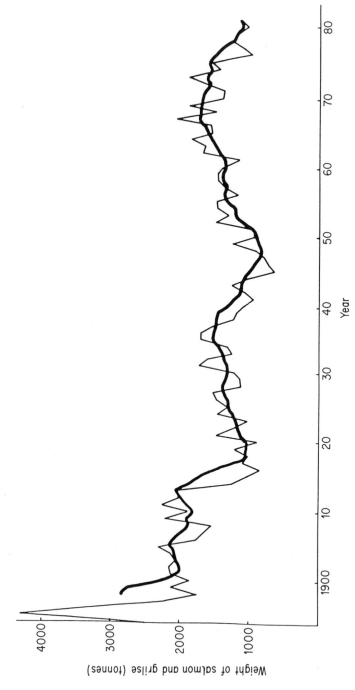

**Fig. 8.10** Combined annual catch by all methods, 1894–1981, of Scottish salmon and grilse. Jagged curve, combined catch; smooth curve, 5 year running mean; data from Annual Reports of the Fishery Board for Scotland (reproduced from Mills, 1987a).

short-term fluctuations in the stock of Scottish salmon. He suggests that the reasons for the fluctuations in the stock may be spread over the whole field of the life history of the fish in both fresh and salt water. They may be linked with weather conditions on land or with usual or unusual movements of great bodies of water and seasonal or exceptional changes in the temperature and currents in the ocean.

In 1947 Hutton published a series of graphs showing salmon statistics for different parts of the British Isles from 1906 to 1945. The commercial landings for Ireland, Scotland, England and Wales handled at Billingsgate market, the Billingsgate total and the total catch by rods and nets on the River Wye for the 30-year period 1911–40 had been averaged separately. Then the annual figures from each of the five sources for the 40-year period were plotted as percentages above and below the averages. This gave five graphs all to the same scale, which permitted comparison of the relative time of abundance and scarcity in each area. In the same way, Kerswill (1955b) calculated the total Canadian commercial landings in the Maritime Provinces for the same period. A striking similarity (Fig. 8.11) was found to exist between the Canadian commercial production and the landings in the British Isles. Kerswill concluded that these graphs indicate that the availability of salmon on both sides of the North Atlantic was affected by common environmental conditions which were most likely to occur in the sea. It is interesting to note that the period of salmon scarcity in the late 1940s also extended to southern Norway and Iceland (Menzies, 1949). Using the same method for the catch data over the period 1960–81 for Scotland, England and Wales, Republic of Ireland, Canada, Norway and Iceland, Mills (1987a) noticed that a similar pattern in

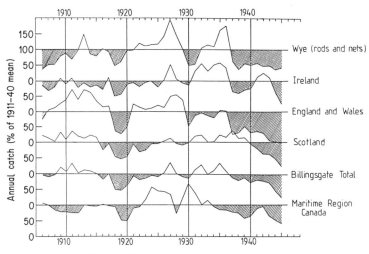

**Fig. 8.11** Salmon catches in the British Isles and Canada as percentages of 30-year averages, 1911–40, see text (reproduced from Kerswill, 1955b).

the timing of periods of abundance and scarcity was just discernible
(Fig. 8.12).

The geographical ranges inhabited by most fish species and or major long-
term changes in their abundance have generally been attributed to the effects
of climatic change (Shepherd *et al.*, 1982). Reddin and Shearer (1987) and
Reddin (1988) have shown that the abundance of salmon at West Greenland
is affected by environmental conditions in January and August in the north-
west Atlantic and that cold water (less than 3–4 °C) can act as a barrier to

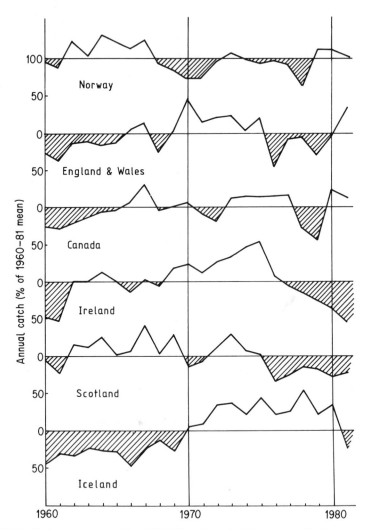

**Fig. 8.12**   Salmon catches in the British Isles, Canada, Norway, and Iceland, expressed
as percentages of their 1960–81 (22-year) means (reproduced from Mills, 1987a).

salmon migration. Recent events in the Icelandic area have also shown that variations in climate and hydrography have been correlated with changes in primary production and salmon catches (Scarnecchia, 1984a, b). Gee and Milner (1980), in an analysis of 70-year catch statistics for salmon in the River Wye, refer to the findings of Hutton and Kerswill and consider that it may be significant that the fluctuations noted by them have a roughly 10-year periodicity. A computer simulation of the life history of the salmon incorporating a stock-dependent parr mortality model (Gee *et al.*, 1978) suggests that the abundance of returning migrants (of mixed sea age) may also follow an approximate 10-year cycle. However, the probability that this is likely to be synchronous throughout the range of the salmon in the North Atlantic must be very low.

Bielak and Power (1988) warn that 'historical catch records should rarely, if ever, be taken simply at face value, nor should any undue significance be accorded to short or medium-term records as indicators of absolute or irreversible changes in salmon stocks'. They go on to say that

If interpreted by investigators with some familiarity with both the animal and fishery in question, and an understanding of the limitations of the data, we believe historical records can ultimately be of major significance, not only as indicators of past and present stock and fishing characteristics, but also as indicators of potential future production.

## 8.6   MARKING AND TAGGING

Marking fish is an important technique in the study of fish populations and fish movement and migration. Marks such as fin clips, tattoos, dyes and tags are used to study (a) the various population parameters such as density and mortality rate, (b) movements and migrations, (c) growth and age and (d) behaviour. An ideal fish mark should have some of the following characteristics:

1. It should be retained in an essentially unaltered condition for the lifetime of the fish;
2. It should have no effect on the fish's behaviour, reproduction, life span, growth, feeding, movement or vulnerability to predation, angling and other external factors;
3. It should not entangle in vegetation or nets;
4. It should be inexpensive;
5. It should be easy to apply to fish in the field without the need for anaesthetic, although most fishery managers prefer to anaesthetize their fish;
6. It should be easily detected in the field by untrained personnel or the public;

7. There should be enough possible variations of the mark so that many individuals or small groups can be identified separately;
8. The mark should not cause adverse public relations by spoiling edible parts of the fish.

The most commonly used tags on the salmon during various stages of its life history are depicted in Fig. 8.13: of these the micro-tag is the one used most frequently on smolts and its ease and speed of application enable many thousands of fish to be given an individually recognizable mark. The micro-tag, which is essentially a small segment of binary-coded ferromagnetic wire inserted into the nose of the fish by means of a semi-automatic device (Fig. 8.14), is described in detail by Jefferts *et al.* (1963). It is usual practice to excise the adipose fin when the fish is micro-tagged. This enables easy identification of a tagged fish in commercial catches. The presence of a tag can then be confirmed with the use of a magnetometer or coil detector. If the presence of a tag is registered it can then be removed from the fish's head. However, refinements now permit a reliable reading of the coded wire by X-ray without its removal from the fish. There are limitations with X-ray detection as the coding cannot be so detailed and is best suited for batch identification of fish

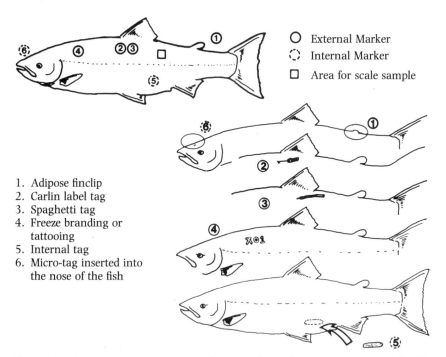

O    External Marker
◌    Internal Marker
□    Area for scale sample

1. Adipose finclip
2. Carlin label tag
3. Spaghetti tag
4. Freeze branding or tattooing
5. Internal tag
6. Micro-tag inserted into the nose of the fish

**Fig. 8.13**   The tags most commonly used on the salmon during various stages of its life history.

**Fig. 8.14** A binary-coded micro-tag being applied to a smolt by means of a semi-automatic device (reproduced with permission from HMSO).

from geographic areas either by country or river, rather than identification of individual fish. The new non-fading colour coded wire tags will help recognition.

One wonders what effect a magnetic wire tag in the nose of the fish has on its ability to orientate in the sea. Taylor (1986) obtained experimental evidence which suggests that some salmon can detect the earth's magnetic field. Is this power of detection confused by a piece of magnetic wire? Anaesthetics (usually MS 222) are also used in conjunction with tagging with coded-wire and Taylor (1988) suggests that if these fish are released shortly after treatment they may not remember the release site. Similarly, he points out that the use of anaesthetics during the insertion of transmitters may affect the subsequent behaviour of the fish during tracking studies.

A tag of particular value to sophisticated individual fish recognition and where fish are required to be recognized on passing through sensors fitted in fish passes is the Passive Integrated Transported (PIT) Tag made by ID Devices, Inc., USA. It is small (1.0 cm × 0.2 cm), about the size of a grain of rice and glass encapsulated. It is implanted by means of a veterinary needle into the body cavity of the fish. There are 34 billion separate unique codes, so that no two tags have the same code. The recognition distance is up to 4 cm by the handwand method or readable in or out of water through 30 cm tube detectors. Recognition systems can be linked direct or via memory in a portable detector (1300 code memory) to a computer. Pacific salmon down to 2.5 g have been tagged with 95% retention. Tagging of 8 g fish has shown 100% retention.

PIT tags are ideal for any study where fish are expected or organized to be reviewed regularly with minimum handling and stress. For example, they are in use in a major study of downstream smolt migration on the Columbia and Snake rivers where there is automatic recording of juvenile and, later, adult salmon movements through the Bonnington Power Authority dams. The sole distributor of this tag is the Fisheagle Trading Co.

Another recently designed tag, developed by the company Fisheagle Trading Co., Lechlade, England, is the VI (Visible Implant) tag attached to the fish by means of a tag injector (Fig. 8.15). This is a small readable label

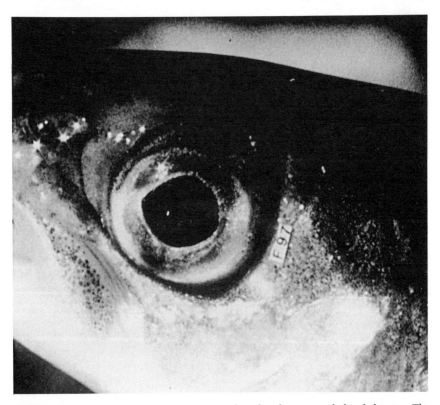

**Fig. 8.15**   A visible implant (VI) tag inserted in the clear tissue behind the eye. The number – F97 – is quite legible (photo courtesy of Fisheagle Trading Co.).

implanted into living transparent tissue. The VI tag is made of biologically compatible material and is designed to eliminate the various pathological and other failure modes associated with all fish tags attached through the skin. Because the VI tag is internal its use is dependent upon a window of clear tissue. The concept involves implanting the tag and allowing the healing process to permanently seal in the information for subsequent identification. Transparent tissue is found around the eyes of various migratory fish and extends to the postocular (i.e. behind the eye) region.

A reward scheme to encourage the return of tags and information on recapture, implemented by many government laboratories, is an incentive to captors of tagged fish. Lotteries, implying greater rewards, might, if implemented, encourage those more reluctant to submit tag returns.

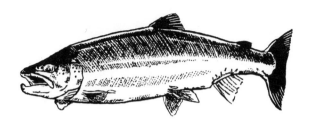

# PART THREE

# Environmental and biological hazards and their control

# CHAPTER NINE

# Hydroelectric development and pipeline construction

Over the years many fast-flowing rivers in mountainous areas of high rainfall have been progressively harnessed to produce energy from the stored water power. These hydroelectric schemes have proliferated in many Atlantic-salmon-producing countries including Canada, France, Iceland, Ireland, Norway, Scotland, Sweden and the USA. The very presence of a hydroelectric scheme on a migratory-fish river will result in some interference, however small, to the successful life cycle of these fish. An understanding of the type of installations involved and how they can affect the fish will help us to devise ways of overcoming some of these effects.

Hydroelectric installations are of four main types: (1) a simple dam or barrage which diverts water for use in an adjoining watercourse or in another catchment area; (2) a simple dam, normally larger than the diversion dam, which impounds water which is piped to a power station some distance downstream of the dam and, after passing through the turbines in the station, is returned to the river; these first two types are sometimes known as 'run-of-the-river' schemes and often the generating station is built into the dam; (3) a type involving a storage reservoir some distance from, and usually at a much higher level than, the power station, thus providing a greater 'head' of water so that less water is required to produce the same or greater amount of electricity as in type (2); (4) a pumped-storage scheme involving two reservoirs at different levels (e.g. Loch Awe and Loch Cruachan), so that during the day at periods of peak demand, water is released from the upper to the lower reservoir via a high-head power station, whereas at night, when there is spare cheap power, water is pumped back up to the top reservoir.

## 9.1   ADVERSE EFFECTS OF POWER DEVELOPMENTS

### Obstructions to fish migration

#### Ascent of upstream migrants

During periods of low discharge the ascent of fish from the estuary may be delayed and fish in the river may be deterred from moving upstream. As Brett

(1957) points out, the question which arises is how long can delay in salt water or fresh water occur without affecting the ability to move upstream and to spawn effectively. There may be a change in the quality of the fresh water because of reduced flow, increased temperature and perhaps even pollution. For example, McGrath and Murphy (1965) attribute a high mortality of adult salmon in the River Lee, Ireland, partly to a change in the quality of the water discharged from Inischarra Dam as the dissolved oxygen in the deeper parts of the reservoir had reached a dangerously low level. This was a transitory condition and arose because of the decay of organic matter in the reservoir basin following the first flooding with water; the situation had been aggravated by the fact that the turbines had not gone into operation for some time after the reservoir was filled, which permitted the quality of the water to deteriorate. It has been shown that the deterioration of the water quality in the Saint John River, New Brunswick, has been exacerbated both by increased pollution loads and by a reduction in the biological assimilative capacity of the river as a result of hydro-power developments on the river. Fish have been killed below Mactaquac Dam on the Saint John as a result of gas bubble disease caused by exposure to water supersaturated with dissolved nitrogen gas.

Dams will, initially at least, obstruct the ascent of adults. Most dams on migratory-fish rivers have fish passes of one sort or another, but the problems associated with such structures involve the question whether the fish can find the entrance to the pass and, when they have found it, whether they will ascend readily. Fish not immediately finding the pass may attempt to 'fight' the spill water and even to ascend the dam spillway, while others are occasionally injured by entering badly-screened turbine draft tubes. However readily the fish ascend there must always be some delay there.

With diversion of water from one river to another there may be some 'straying' of fish that home to 'home waters' being discharged down another river channel. This may result in fish merely moving up a 'foreign' river or may result in their reaching an impassable source such as a power station. Pyefinch and Mills (1963) and Mills (1965b) refer to this problem on the Conon River system in Scotland, where some water from the River Meig is released from a power station into the River Conon.

Fish in the river below a power station may be subjected to a wide range of flows a number of times in a day. On the River Conon in Ross-shire the water level may rise to flood conditions and fall away to low summer flows as often as three times in the 24 hours. These rapidly fluctuating water levels: (1) may affect sport fishing by unsettling the fish; (2) may affect commercial fishing by decreasing netting efficiency at high flows and making netting too effective for a satisfactory upstream escapement at reduced flows; (3) may result in exposure and drying out of redds constructed along river margins at high flows, and (4) may result in large losses of juvenile salmon stranded as flows are reduced and water levels drop, as Hvidsten (1985) recorded in the regulated River Nidelva in central Norway.

### Descent of downstream migrants

*Smolts.* Young fish, particularly the seaward migrating smolts, may be delayed in the reservoirs either through not finding the entrance to the fish pass at the dam face or through being diverted into the power station tunnel. Although most power station tunnel intakes on Scottish hydroelectric schemes were initially screened to prevent smolts and parr passing through the turbines, the screening was not always completely effective and smolts have been recorded passing through and under the screens and being killed on them. The dimensions of these screens are given in Table 9.1.

**Table 9.1**  Mechanical fish screens installed at North of Scotland Hydro-electric Board installations: the permissible clear spaces and velocities*

|  | Clear space between vertical bars (in) | Velocity (ft/s) |
|---|---|---|
| For ascending salmon | 1.625 | no limit |
| For ascending sea trout | 1.25–1.5 | no limit |
| For descending salmon kelts | 2 | 2.5–3 |
| For descending sea trout | 1.5 | 2.5–3 |

| | Mesh screens: Clear space between | | |
|---|---|---|---|
| | Vertical wires (in) | Horizontal wires (in) | Velocity (ft/s) |
| For descending smolts | 1 | 0.5 | 1 |
| For descending parr | 0.5 | 0.5 | 1 |

*Source: Aitken, Dickerson and Menzies (1966).

Turnpenny (1981) determined the mesh-size requirements for fish screens placed at water intakes. He produced curves relating fish length to the mesh-size requirements for 24 species of marine and freshwater fish including juvenile salmon. He also presented a model for predicting mesh-size requirements as a function of fish shape and size.

The mortality of smolts passing through the turbines may vary widely depending upon the type of turbine, the 'head' of the power station and the turbine operating conditions. According to Ruggles (1980), Carlin estimated that 80–90% of Atlantic salmon smolts survived passage through Kaplan turbines and 50–70% through Francis turbines. Bell (1974) reported survival rates of 90% and over at low-head installations and 85% at high-head installations. Tests on the effects on fish of passage through turbines have been carried out at a number of power stations operated by the North of Scotland

Hydro-electric Board, using salmon smolts, parr and trout of smolt size. Test fish were introduced into the turbines either by releasing them into the tunnel intake or by injecting them under pressure into the pipe-line, and were recovered by nets attached to the tail-race screens. Munro (1965b) found that the mortality of smolts passing through Francis turbines at Clunie Power Station (gross head = 53 m) on the River Tummel was about 27% under normal operating conditions. At Invergarry Power Station (gross head = 53 m), where Kaplan turbines are installed, the mortality under normal running conditions was less than 20% but when the turbines were running at speed but producing no electricity, the mortality was as high as 60%. At Cashlie Power Station, in Glen Lyon, which has vertical Francis turbines and a much higher gross head (145 m), the mortality was much higher and varied from around 55% at the higher loads to over 80% at the lowest load tested. American work has shown that mortality rate is often closely related to turbine efficiency; Munro compared the efficiency of the Cashlie turbine at normal head with the average percentage survival (no. of survivors × 100 total recovered) at various loads and showed that there was a similar relationship in this case. The mortality rates recorded in these tests, which were based on the number of dead fish recovered expressed as a percentage of the total number recovered, were considered to be over-estimates of the actual mortality because, although all the released fish were not recovered, the gear was shown to favour the recovery of dead fish and parts of fish. Control tests indicated that neither the process of injection nor the presence of tail-race screens, nor the method of recovery contributed significantly to observed mortality.

Montén (1955) suggested that the factors likely to cause injury to the smolts were (1) water speed, (2) turbulence, (3) pressure, (4) cavitation and (5) collision with the machinery, particularly the runner vanes. He considered that because of the very short period of time that the smolt was subjected to factors (1), (3) and (4) it was less likely to be injured by them. In relation to pressure this held good for water heads up to 32 m and Calderwood (1945) concluded that smolts would not be injured by a pressure equivalent to a head of about 30 m. Montén considered that mortality is caused by a combination of factors (2) and (5) and principally (5). This mortality was found to depend on the probability of collision, the force of impact and the possibility of the fish being struck in a vital spot. More recently a number of investigators have considered the effects of cavitation to be more serious than collision with the machinery.

During the tests carried out by Munro all dead fish were examined and the types of damage were classified. Broadly, the dead fish could be sorted into three classes: 'whole fish' which were complete, although often severely injured; 'headless fish' in which the head had been severed from the body as if by tearing, leaving the body complete and often with one or two gill arches attached, and 'parts' which varied from almost-complete bodies to quite small sections of fish.

Only 'whole fish' were subjected to further examination; in them two types of damage were distinguished, external damage which could be seen without dissection and internal damage which was visible only on dissection.

The most common types of external damage were:

1. 'Descaling', in which a significant number of scales had been lost, usually in one or more patches;
2. 'Eye damage', which included haemorrhage, abrasion or rupture of the cornea and complete loss of one or both eyes;
3. 'Gashes', which varied from a small cut to almost complete severance of the body: most were inflicted diagonally and the presence of more than one on the same fish was rare;
4. 'Head damage', which included torn opercula, crushed heads and loss of one side of the head;
5. 'Head almost severed', which was characterized by the head being separated from the body ventrally: this is probably a less severe result of the condition that produces 'headless' fish and which is attributed by some American workers to a shearing action caused by two currents of water moving in opposite directions.

These external injuries were also recorded by Mills (unpublished) in an examination of living, moribund and dead fish washed onto a smolt trap sited below a dam on the River Meig and were attributed to the fish having passed through a compensation turbine sited in the Borland fish pass (Pyefinch and Mills, 1963).

The most common types of internal injury were:

1. 'Body cavity damage', which included bleeding in the body cavity and collapse of the swim bladder;
2. 'Internal bruising' of the musculature, which was most frequently associated with external evidence of injury but occasionally occurred in its absence;
3. 'Fractured backbone', which was occasionally associated with the deep penetration of a 'gash' but occurred most frequently in fish which showed no sign of external injury;
4. 'Severed nerve cords', which were always associated with fractured backbones, but were less numerous than the latter because in some cases where the backbone was fractured, the nerve cord remained intact.

Munro (1965b) found that although there was a general increase in injuries at low loads where the mortality rates were high, preliminary analysis of the data did not reveal any clear-cut relationship between turbine conditions and the incidence of any particular type of injury.

If smolts cannot find their way out of an impoundment they may remain a further year in fresh water; large, old smolts have been recorded from a number of Scottish reservoirs, although Koch, Evans and Bergstrom (1959), among others, record that there is a heavy mortality among smolts retained in fresh water due to the impairment of the osmotic capacity in fresh water at the time of transformation from parr to smolt. Predation is a common occurrence in these reservoirs, the main predators being pike and trout.

*Kelts.* It has been found that kelts may be delayed by dams, and they are frequently to be seen swimming in the impoundment along the dam face; Pyefinch and Mills (1963) have described the delay at dams on the Conon River system. On the Tay–Tummel system kelts have been observed passing downstream at the Faskally dam at the normal time (i.e. March to May).

## Damage to, or elimination of spawning and nursery areas

Frequently large spawning and nursery areas are either eliminated by reservoir formation or are reduced by diversion of their water supply to a reservoir. There may also be some damage to other areas through rapid fluctuations in water level below a power station resulting in exposure of redds during periods of frost and stranding both of spawning adults and of young fish. In addition reduced flows may cut down the area available to fish.

## Effects of impoundment on lakes and reservoirs

After impoundment, resulting either in reservoir formation or in raising of the level of an existing lake, there is usually an increase in the general biological productivity due to leaching of salts from newly-inundated ground. Frequently the production of planktonic and semi-planktonic crustacea increases as a result of the leached nutrient salts and decaying terrestrial vegetation, and some of the important food sources for fish during the early impoundment period will be terrestrial invertebrates such as earthworms and terrestrial insect larvae. The forage area of fish is usually greatly increased and therefore their population density is temporarily reduced. Immediately after impoundment the growth rates of fish such as trout, charr and perch have been shown to improve substantially, but in almost all cases it has been found that these improved growth rates only last for a few years. However, if the area of shallow water is increased after impoundment and water levels remain relatively stable the initial increase in fish production may be sustained; Campbell (1963) suggested that this might be the case with trout in Loch Garry, Inverness-shire.

Elder (1966) has pointed out the effects of fluctuating lake levels on the littoral vegetation and fauna. Those species closely associated with the littoral vegetation will be greatly reduced or even eliminated, notably many of the larger insect larvae and crustaceans, while chironomid larvae may increase. However, in terms of the production of fish food the net results of these changes are loss of the most valuable food organisms and survival of types which tend to be less available to fish.

### Pumped storage

Pumped-storage schemes have little effect on migratory fish although the intakes to the generating station require smolt screens if young migratory fish pass through the lower reservoir on their way to sea.

There may be some limnological effects where there are wide ranges in the water levels of both reservoirs and some stocks of indigenous fish species may be affected.

## 9.2   METHODS TO OVERCOME ADVERSE EFFECTS

### Facilities to assist fish migration

On any hydroelectric scheme the river flows have been changed to some extent but provision is nearly always made to ensure that the flows are sufficient to enable migratory fish to ascend. Where spawning areas for salmon and sea trout remain above the dams constructed for hydroelectric purposes it is usually considered economical to provide fish passes to enable them to complete their upstream journey and breed.

*Fish passes.* Some of the earliest fish passes in use at dams were what are known as pool passes. These consist of a series of pools so that the rise from water level below the dam to water level above is broken up into a number of steps which can be negotiated by salmon or sea trout by either swimming or jumping. The pool passes are of two general types, one where the water passes from one pool to the next by falling over a weir and one where the water passes through an orifice in the bottom of the dividing wall between two pools. A development of the normal pool type pass was the construction of pools spirally inside towers close to the face of the dam. Examples of these are to be found at the Loch Doon dam of the Galloway hydroelectric scheme in south-west Scotland and at the Tromie Dam of the Grampian scheme (Aitken, Dickerson and Menzies, 1966).

In the pool-and-overfall type of pass fish have to expend effort in jumping from pool to pool; in the orifice type they have to swim against the velocity of the water in the orifice pipes. In a long pass of 12 or more pools, it is generally accepted that the maximum rise between pools should be restricted to 46 cm (18 in). If a pass exceeds 12 or 15 pools, a resting pool about double the size of a normal pool should be provided at intervals of 8 or 10 pools. In shorter passes rises of 61 cm (2 ft) may be acceptable unless fish ascend late in the season when 46 cm or less may have to be adopted.

Pool passes are relatively expensive and, owing to site conditions, may present design difficulties in relation to the main dam structure. A pass working on the principle of a canal lock and designed by Borland reduced construction costs considerably. The pass, or fish lift, provided a design which is readily adaptable and proves to be very effective. The Borland pass consists of two pools, one totally enclosed at river level at the foot of the dam and the other at the level of the impoundment above. The pools are joined by a sloping shaft located in the dam structure. The fish are attracted into the pool at the foot of the shaft. The outlet to the pool is then closed. As the water continues to pour in from the reservoir via the upper pool (Fig. 9.1), the level rises and the fish rise with it until they reach the top pool and then jump or swim over the sluice into the reservoir. This type of pass is designed to work automatically on a 2 hour or 4 hour cycle, but at most of the dams where they are installed in Scotland they have also been worked manually, as some adjustments to the flow over the top sluice are often found necessary in order to stimulate the fish to jump or swim out of the reservoir.

Since in impoundments the water level is often liable to great variations it is necessary to ensure that a pass of any type can be fed with water at any upstream level to enable fish to escape from, or to enter, the pass. For this reason some of the Borland fish passes have two shafts, one coming into

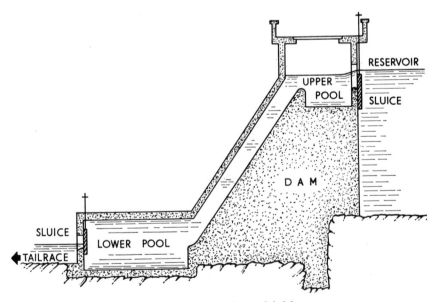

**Fig. 9.1**  Borland type fish lift.

operation when the water in the impoundment drops below a certain level. In the Orrin Dam in Ross-shire there are four steel-lined vertical shafts to cater for the seasonal draw-down of this storage reservoir.

One of the chief difficulties experienced with fish passes is that of ensuring that the entrance will be found readily by the fish and the flow will be attractive enough to induce them to enter in preference to passing on to other more attractive flows close by. This problem has been discussed at some length by McGrath (1959) who considered that it stemmed from the fact that the unidirectional flow of the river downstream from the dam exerts a directive influence on the fish, then is replaced by a many-directional flow caused by the discharge from the turbines. The outflow from the fish pass, which in many cases forms a very small proportion of the total discharge, has to be found and be such that the fish are encouraged to move against it into the pass. Because of this it has been found desirable to introduce extra water to form a more attractive flow to the bottom of the pass. This is done by passing an auxiliary flow through a small turbine to use the energy in the water; the flow from the draft tube is then directed upwards through the floor of the bottom pool of the pool type passes or towards the outflow of the Borland passes. Because of these arrangements there have been few problems in getting fish to ascend fish passes at Scottish hydroelectric installations. Where problems have arisen solutions have soon been found. Mills (1965b) found that more of the salmon passing upstream of a trap on the River Meig in Ross-shire ascended the Borland pass after pools had been constructed below the pass. These allowed the fish to remain in the vicinity of the entrance to the pass until they were inclined to move upstream. Experience has shown that fish do not ascend the fish pass at all times of the year with equal readiness. Sometimes fish will run freely and ascend a pass continuously. At other times, for reasons seemingly unconnected with the arrangements, few will ascend for a week or more. Where there is a series of dams in the course of a river, fish may ascend one fish pass but not for the time being the next, so that there is a temporary accumulation between them. McGrath (1959) made an interesting point when he said that reports of the first year's working of fish passes at hydroelectric dams were not very favourable, whereas the reports of later years were quite favourable. He suggested that some factor in a new pass deters fish until it has been in operation for some time.

In a fish pass at Cathaleen Falls power station at the head of the tidal water on the River Erne (Republic of Ireland), Jackson and Howie (1967) noticed that the salmon exhibited a more or less fixed period of daily activity, which in June and July was about 18 hours, contracting to about 14 hours in November. The start of daily activity appeared to be linked to dawn, but the nightly cessation of movement was not so closely linked to dusk and in October and November the fish continued to run through the upper pools of the pass for several hours after nightfall, although migration stopped shortly after dusk in June and July.

The greatest problem associated with fish passes has been in encouraging smolts and kelts to descend, and again much depends on the correct siting of the pass and the provision of a surface exit. For example, Mills (1965b) showed showed that at Meig Dam in Ross-shire, where the pass had been built at one end of the dam, close to the shore, there was little delay of smolts; but at Luichart Dam, where the fish pass lies to one side of a structure which projects about 23 m into the reservoir, delay was considerable. At some Scottish hydroelectric installations alternative means for smolt and kelt descent have been provided, such as chutes constructed down the face of the dam, spillways and even bag nets set in the reservoir at the dam face.

*Screens.* Fish have to be excluded from the turbines and this is done with screens or hecks. Ascending adults are excluded from the tail-races to turbines while smolts and kelts are excluded from intakes to turbines or from diversion aqueducts. For ascending fish the screens may be mechanical, providing an actual physical barrier, or electrical, providing a field with intermittent pulses which fish avoid. Aitken, Dickerson and Menzies (1966) suggest that where screens are used to exclude fish from a tail-race channel, the alignment should be such as to lead the fish up the main channel. It has been found that screens are seldom required where turbine draft tubes discharge either directly into the river channel or through a very short tail-race. Where screens are not provided, fish may be able to get into the draft tubes of the turbines while they are starting or operating at light load. The best way to avoid this is to run the turbines at flows that will give adequate deterrent velocities. The permissible clear spaces between the vertical bars of the screens, the mesh sizes and velocities through them for installations at Scottish hydroelectric works are given in Table 9.1.

Because of their mesh construction and the small clearances, smolt screens cannot be cleaned *in situ.* Two sets of guide channels are therefore provided so that a spare set of clean screens can be placed in the downstream guide channels before the upstream dirty screens are removed. At large intakes cleaning work has been mechanized by the provision of lifting and washing gantries which deal with complete bays of panels.

There is now ample evidence (Pyefinch and Mills, 1963; Mills, 1965b) that smolts, unlike kelts which move away from an obstruction, are extremely persistent in trying to find a way through or around a screen. It is therefore essential that all screens fit tightly on the sill and in the guides. The maximum clearance in the guides should be 0.6 cm. This small clearance may make the movement of frames difficult and can best be effected by a rubber seal. Particular care must always be taken in replacing frames to ensure that they fit tightly to the sill. The presence of an obstruction, large or small, can prevent the frames resting properly on the sill and so provide a gap through which the smolts can pass. It is of assistance if the bottom of the screen frame is fitted with a sharp edge to cut through any soft debris. The sill should be set above the river bed to allow debris to fall away from it. Screens should be kept clean at all times, particularly the period of smolt migration. Severe smolt mortalities have occurred when the screens have become clogged with debris with a resultant increase in water velocity through those areas of screen that are relatively clean, the smolts being held against the screens by the high water velocity.

Because a high proportion of smolts survive the passage through turbines (Munro, 1965b; Bell, 1974; Ruggles, 1980) smolt screens have been removed from some installations in the North of Scotland Hydro-electric Board area. Struthers (1984) suggested that removal of smolt screens at the Clunie tunnel intake on the River Tummel system in Perthshire would aid migration of smolts out of Loch Tummel. He also considered it reasonable to assume that by reducing delays in migration and the number of smolts failing to migrate, mortality due to predation, physiological stress and disease would also be reduced.

One type of screen which has been used successfully to divert juvenile Pacific salmon from intakes is the louver screen. This consists of a row of vertical louvers through which water passes, inducing small turbulent eddies by the angle at which they are set, and through which small fish will not apparently pass. Although these screens are not in use at Scottish hydroelectric installations Munro (1965c) has tested them in an experimental flume in Scotland. The results were encouraging and suggested that, in suitable situations, diversion efficiencies of more than 90% can be expected at velocities of 0.7–1.1 m/s with gaps between louvers of up to 15 cm, and that even with 30 cm gaps the efficiency may be as high as 90%. The screens were equally effective in daylight and darkness. Ducharme (1972) used louver deflectors for guiding smolts away from turbines at East River, Sheet Harbour, Nova Scotia. Guiding-efficiency studies showed that a minimum approach:bypass velocity ratio of 1.0:1.5 was a prerequisite to high guiding efficiency. From 1967 to 1971 average guiding efficiency was increased from 57% to 80% through modifications which increased velocity and reduced flow turbulence in the bypass.

Electric fish screens for upstream migrants merely require to dissipate sufficient power to prevent fish swimming against the water flow. For this reason alternating current or rectified alternating current can safely be used, as even if fish are tetanized they are immediately washed downstream to safety and recover at once; in general, Hartley and Simpson (1967) have found that the fish avoid the screen without being incapacitated at all.

The situation is not so simple where an electric screen is required to keep descending smolts away from the water flow into a power station, as any interference with their swimming ability will cause them to be washed further into the electric field and thus prevented from escaping from the danger against which the screen is meant to guard. A pulsed current should be used to avoid interfering with swimming ability, and the screen must be located where it can guide the fish into a safe bypass channel.

*Transportation.* Instead of constructing fish passes at some dams, facilities for the trapping and transporting of migrants have been installed. The transportation may in some cases involve no more than lifting the trapped adults over the dam and releasing them in the reservoir, while in other cases it may involve the 'trucking' of the trapped adults some distance and releasing them many miles upstream of the installations. For example, at the Mactaquac Dam and Beechwood Dam on the Saint John River in New Brunswick, the ascending salmon are led into trapping or collection pools and guided into submerged hoppers. They are then transferred to large tank trucks and either transported overland to release points above the dam site or taken to the Mactaquac hatchery.

In Newfoundland, adult salmon are transferred successfully each year at Great Rattling Brook, the Terra Nova River and the Torrent River. The most successful operation is that carried on at Great Rattling Brook (Pratt and Rietveld, 1973) which has opened up 40 000 rearing units (100 m²/unit) and is presently reaching its seeding requirements of 240 eggs/unit (Bourgeois, personal communication).

In addition to the transporting of adults upstream, the transporting of downstream migrants has also been attempted with some success. Smolts have been transported from the lower reaches of the River Bran, a tributary of the Conon, and released at a point below all the dams on this river system (Mills, 1966; Mills and Shackley, 1971). The numbers transported ranged from 207 in 1964 to 9090 in 1966. The percentage recapture of adult fish, tagged as smolts, from these transport experiments ranged from 2.2% to 4.0% (Fig. 9.2 and Table 9.2).

Results from the transport of kelts in Scottish waters have not been so encouraging, albeit transport of kelts was tried in only one year (1960). The surprising result of the kelt transport experiment carried out in December in the Inverness-shire Garry was that, although the 280 fish were transported from Loch Poulary, on the upper reaches of the Garry, to the mouth of the River Ness, a distance of some 88 km, some fish were recaptured upstream in Loch Ness, and even in the Garry, a few weeks later. The fish had been stripped of their eggs and milt and this may have had some effect on their behaviour, but even so one of these fish was caught in the Ness as late as May in the following year, which seems to suggest that spent fish may take a considerable time to return to the sea.

### Artificial propagation

It is the usual practice on rivers affected by hydroelectric schemes to provide facilities for the upstream passage of spawning migrants and the downstream movement of their progeny and the spent spawners, so as to ensure that the spawning grounds on the affected river systems are fully utilized and that the

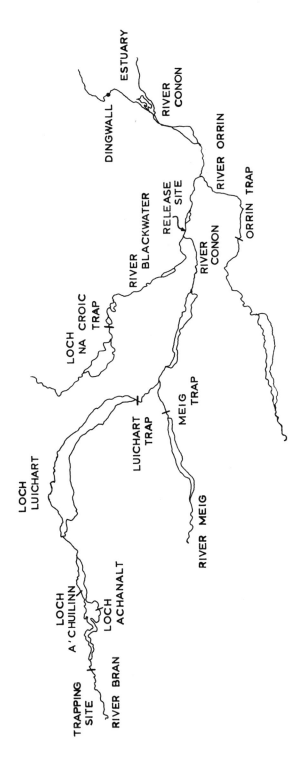

**Fig. 9.2** Sketch map of the Conon river system to show smolt trapping and release sites (reproduced from Mills and Shackley, 1971).

**Table 9.2** Details of transportation experiments, 1963–66, and of adults recaptured in traps at sites illustrated in Fig. 9.2*

| Year | No. of smolts transported | No. tagged | % of smolts recaptured as adult fish† | No. recaptured in: | | | | | | | No. of tagged smolts recaptured in traps as adults: | | | |
|---|---|---|---|---|---|---|---|---|---|---|---|---|---|---|
| | | | | Greenland | Coastal waters | Estuary | River: rod and line | River: kelt nets | River: traps | Site unknown | Luichart | Meig | Loch na Croic | Orrin |
| 1963 | 649 | 649 | 2.8 (18) | 2 | 1 | 2 | 5 | 0 | 7 | 1 | 6 | 0 | 1 | 0 |
| 1964 | 207 | 180 | 2.2 (4) | 2 | 0 | 0 | 2 | 0 | 0 | 0 | 0 | 0 | 0 | 0 |
| 1965 | 536 | 534 | 2.2 (12) | 1 | 1 | 0 | 5 | 0 | 5 | 0 | 3 | 1 | 1 | 0 |
| 1966 | 9090 | 3347 | 4.0 (133) | 14 | 4 | 3 | 29 | 15 | 68 | 0 | 45 | 16 | 7 | 0 |

*Source: Mills and Shackley (1971).
†Numbers in parentheses.

angling is not restricted only to the waters below these schemes. However, in some instances where nursery grounds have been flooded, either alternative areas in the river system have been made available as compensation, by liberating young salmon that were reared in specially-built hatcheries into suitable areas that were previously inaccessible to spawning fish and by making arrangements for their return as adults, or the numbers of young resulting from the reduced spawning stock have been supplemented with hatchery-reared young. These are the types of arrangements that have been made in the United Kingdom and Canada, where salmon angling is so important that all efforts to maintain the sport fishery are considered economically worthwhile. As a consequence, a number of hatcheries have been built at the same time as the hydroelectric installations and provision for the trapping of adult salmon has been made near these installations so as to ensure the collection of brood stock for the hatcheries (Fig. 8.3). Mills (1964, 1965c) has given a detailed account of the smolt production resulting from the stocking of 16 km of previously inaccessible spawning and nursery grounds in the River Bran, Ross-shire. These were made available to fish with the advent of the Conon Basin hydroelectric scheme as compensation for the flooding of traditional spawning grounds on one of the other tributaries of the Conon River.

A plan to re-establish a natural population of salmon was approved for the Point Wolfe River in Fundy National Park (New Brunswick) as a result of the Point Wolfe Dam blocking access to salmon at the river mouth. An investigation suggested that newly accessible portions of the river will produce 6700 two-year smolts annually (Alexander and Galbraith, 1982).

In Sweden, artifical propagation has played a much larger part in compensating for the effects of hydroelectric development. While fishways and transportation facilities were used at first, later, as more and more power plants were built, the natural spawning areas, which in Sweden usually occur in the main river and not in the small tributaries, were either very much reduced or in many rivers completely destroyed. For this reason the few fishways built in later years and many old ones were taken away, and the salmon stock was maintained completely by hatcheries. Natural smolt recruitment to the Baltic area from Swedish rivers is now less than 50% of its original value. However, the greatest part of this loss is compensated for by releasing smolts from these hatcheries (Montén, 1969).

### Spawning channels

Where natural spawning areas have been lost through either impoundment or water diversion alternative spawning sites have to be found for the returning fish, or else the fish have to be trapped, held and stripped at spawning time and the fertilized eggs transferred to a hatchery. An alternative method to hatchery facilities which has been introduced widely on the Pacific side of North America is the construction of spawning channels into which fish are diverted at spawning time.

In order to replace several miles of natural spawning grounds lost due to water diversion on the Indian River, Newfoundland, the Canadian Department of Fisheries built a salmon spawning channel. Controlled-flow spawning channels are used extensively for Pacific salmon but were, until this occasion, untried for Atlantic salmon. The channel, constructed in 1962–63, is designed to provide $930 \text{ m}^2$ of spawning area, capable of accommodating about 300 to 400 adult salmon. Since its construction favourable incubation conditions resulted initially in an annual egg to fry survival rate of 40% to 50%. This is now much higher and the problem of eggs being smothered by a fine suspension of silt has been completely overcome because these channels have now the required hydraulic characteristics of spawning beds described by Stuart (1953).

Since that time additional spawning channels have been set up in other rivers of Newfoundland such as Noel Paul's Brook, a tributary of the Exploits River, and have proved most successful.

## Statutory controls

In a number of countries the development of hydro power is strictly controlled by the government and legislation is enacted which has the security of the environment in mind, but unfortunately not every country is so minded and some hydro schemes have been constructed which have had severe effects on the salmon stocks – this is particularly true of France and Spain. In Scotland the *Hydro-electric Development (Scotland) Act*, 1943, makes it a duty of the Electricity Boards to 'have regard to the desirability . . . of avoiding as far as possible injury to fisheries and to the stock of fish in any waters'. The Secretary of State for Scotland is required by the Act to appoint a Fisheries Committee to give advice and assistance to the Electricity Boards and to himself. The Committee consists of a small group of members who between them contribute expert knowledge of fisheries, water engineering, electrical engineering and administration. Electricity Boards are obliged to consult the Fisheries Committee before and during the preparation of a constructional scheme and the Committee may, upon being consulted, or at any other time, make recommendations to the Board, which transmits copies to the Secretary of State and says whether or not it is prepared to accept the recommendations. The decision whether or not a disputed recommendation should be implemented rests with the Secretary of State. The Board with which the Committee has been chiefly concerned is the North of Scotland Hydro-electric Board. This Board furnishes all information about the proposed scheme; the information about the fisheries has to be obtained by discussion with proprietors, Salmon Fishery District Boards, where they exist, and others having knowledge of the waters affected. Often only a few catch statistics are available and the Committee is further hampered by having no investigating staff. Although the Committee has a fund of experience, its field work is limited to on-the-spot inspections and so its assessments, by force of circumstance, may be speculative.

The proposals for hydroelectric schemes are normally made known to the Fisheries Committee at an early stage, and the North of Scotland Hydro-electric Board begins negotiations with District Boards and proprietors concerned. The scheme is later published and time allowed for objections. If an objection is taken to the stage of an inquiry, the views of the Fisheries Committee, which have been confidential to the Board and to the Secretary of State, are placed before the inquiry, and have often been stated in the press notice announcing it. If there is no inquiry, the recommendations of the Fisheries Committee are first made public when the Secretary of State announces his decision and lays an explanatory memorandum before Parliament (Anon., 1965: *Scottish Salmon and Trout Fisheries.* Cmnd. 2691, 1965, p. 72).

In order to fulfil its obligations under the Act to avoid possible injury to fisheries, the North of Scotland Hydro-electric Board built salmon hatcheries in connection with certain schemes where spawning grounds were due to be flooded, and installed fish passes and fish lifts where fish migrations would be hindered by dams. The Fisheries Committee informed the Secretary of State in May 1956 that, in the light of the information available to it, it was not satisfied that fish passes and lifts in operation at that time were allowing smolts and kelts to descend freely. It felt that the matter was of such importance in the interests of fish preservation that an independent investigation should be made. At that time a committee, the Salmon Research Committee, was already in existence to design, keep under review and have general direction of the census of ascending adult fish and descending smolts to be undertaken on the River Conon and its tributaries by the Scottish Home Department and North of Scotland Hydro-electric Board and to take cognizance of the related programme of salmon research in the same area. It was therefore decided to appoint a Pass Investigation Sub-Committee of the Salmon Research Committee to carry out an investigation into the descent of smolts and kelts at the fish passes and lifts in operation and this Sub-Committee was appointed in August 1956. A report of the Sub-Committee on a preliminary inquiry into this question was published by Her Majesty's Stationery Office just over a year later entitled *The Passage of Smolts and Kelts through Fish Passes* (Anon., 1957). In its report it recommended that a programme of research should be designed to cover: (a) factors influencing smolt behaviour, (b) experimental modifica-tions of the fish passes and (c) a further study of the environmental conditions of parr and smolts. These recommendations were incorporated into an existing research scheme on the River Conon and reported in later publications (Pyefinch and Mills, 1963; Mills, 1964).

In Sweden the Water Law is administered by a Water Court. The country is divided into six areas, each having a Water Court consisting of a chairman, who is a lawyer with the standing of a judge, assisted by two engineers and two lay members. Any sizeable development proposed which is likely to affect a river or lake must be submitted to the local Water Court who not only considers the promoter's case and any objections thereto, but may also initiate investigations on its own account. In this way independent expert evidence on fisheries may be obtained. The Water Court considers the case against the background of the Water Law, which is a comprehensive code describing in detail the circumstances in which development may be allowed, the compensation payable and other requirements. If a hydroelectric scheme is going to harm property, the Water Court assesses in monetary terms the benefits and disadvantages of the scheme and applies a formula given in the Water Law. The decision regarding the development is determined by the results of this assessment and calculation. There is also provision for appeals against decisions of local Water Courts.

## 9.3   PIPELINE CONSTRUCTION

The recent development of North Sea gas and oil resources has resulted in the construction of a number of pipelines through Scotland. The majority of the piping used is of a substantial size, being 1 m in diameter.

Pipeline construction involves considerable negotiations before work can start and includes the initial plotting of routes, agreements with landowners and local authorities and arrangements for compensation, particularly to farmers whose crops and field drains may be affected. Constant liaison with landowners and authorities through liaison officers is a feature of construction work at all stages.

On-site work for the laying of the pipeline starts with the opening-up of the right of way (often referred to as the spread) 30 m wide by removing the topsoil to one side and fencing either side to prevent the straying of livestock. Double-fencing is used where brucellosis-free herds are present. The pipeline is then laid in position and a trench is excavated to a minimum depth of 2.5 m. The indivdual sections of pipe are then welded together and laid in the trench which is then covered. Reinstatement involves replacing the subsoil and topsoil, repairing any damaged field drains and re-seeding.

River crossings involve an initial survey and drawing of a depth profile of the river with notes on the nature of the river bed. The pipeline is prepared beforehand by encasement in concrete. A trench, again to an agreed depth, is excavated and the pipeline is laid (Fig. 9.3). Reinstatement involves returning the river to its previous condition and reinstating the banks. Where bedrock is encountered while river excavation is in progress blasting is usually necessary.

**Fig. 9.3** Laying a gas pipeline, encased in concrete, into a trench excavated in the river bed (photo courtesy of British Gas).

Smaller streams are crossed in the same way but when construction work is in progress these small watercourses may be flumed or bridged to allow vehicle access along the spread.

It will be obvious from such a description of construction work that there can be some temporary effect on the aquatic environment and angling during river excavation, and during land excavation in wet weather. The former would be due to increased suspended-solid loads from disturbance of the river bed, the latter to high silt loads caused by surface drainage from the spread itself or by water pumped out of the excavated trench. The silt loads in the pumped water often find their way to the main river indirectly, via small drains and streams. These increased suspended solids are most likely to have an effect on:

1. The survival of salmon and trout eggs in the gravel and the invertebrate fauna through heavy silt deposition;
2. The survival of young fish through gill damage from sediment particles;
3. The well-being of farmed trout and salmon supplied with water from the affected river;
4. The efficiency of angling due to high turbidity.

In addition, however, material such as gravel, either dislodged during excavation or made unstable after reinstatement of the excavation trench, may be swept downstream at high flows with the consequent in-filling of holding pools for adult salmon and a reduction in angling quality and netting success.

Before any length of pipeline is covered it is pressure tested with water. The water is then discharged into a watercourse. This water has been tested for traces of heavy metals and these have only been found at very low concentrations: zinc, 0.06; copper, 0.01; lead, 0.00; nickel, 0.01; cadmium, 0.01; chromium, 0.02 (all in parts per million).

The values of 0.01 ppm are at the lowest levels of detection. None of the metals are present in sufficiently high concentrations to cause any harm to aquatic life and after dilution in river water are unlikely to be detectable.

As a result of experiences encountered during the laying of the first two British Gas pipelines in 1975/76 during a most severe winter and spring conditions of high rainfall a number of precautions have now been incorporated into construction procedure. These include:

1. A check for any fish farms downstream of pipeline crossings during initial routing plans;
2. Discussion with fishery authorities to identify spawning and nursery areas in area of pipeline crossings during initial routing plans;
3. Arrangements for timing of river crossings, (a) to avoid angling disturbance (e.g. between major runs of migrating fish or during weekly close season) and (b) to avoid disturbance of spawning fish;
4. Erection of a fence of boarding or palings on either side of the stream to prevent surface drainage from the spread in wet weather, which can also be prevented by (5) below;
5. Early reinstatement of the spread for a short distance back on either side of the stream;
6. Reinstatement of banks to original condition or, where previously in poor condition, their improvement by installing gabions or piling;
7. Reinstatement of the river bed to original condition;
8. Frequent liaison with local Salmon District Fishery Board and notification of imminent river crossings to the above and to angling clubs and fish farmers, and also notification to district fishery boards of any blasting operations;
9. Familiarization of construction personnel with need to prevent pollution;
10. Any water lying in pipeline trench to be pumped into settlement tanks and not to watercourses;
11. Bridging rather than fluming of small watercourses;
12. No vehicles to drive through watercourses.

During pipeline construction it is most important that there is constant liaison between construction personnel, the contractors and the fishery interests, including fishery boards, river purification boards, fishing proprietors and angling clubs, and fish farmers. It has not always been realized that fishing interests may well be affected some miles downstream of the actual construction work.

# Water abstraction and transfer

The demands on water resources for industrial and domestic use increase each year. Sometimes the demand in a particular area rises dramatically as a result of new industrial development, and demographers' predictions of likely increases in water demand fall short of actual requirements. Such a situation occurred in north-east Scotland with the advent of the North Sea oil boom. Inevitably water abstraction may affect the river environment through reduced river flows caused either by impoundment and reservoir formation or by direct river abstraction, but the consequences will depend on the amount abstracted and when. It is usually the salmonid rivers that are selected for abstraction schemes because they originate in areas of high rainfall and are of the required purity. As a result there is inevitably a conflict between the water and fishery interests. However, we all need water and it is in the interest of the whole community that these conflicts are resolved sensibly without either the fisheries interests delaying needful developments and making unreasonable claims on the public purse or water bodies riding roughshod over anglers and river proprietors.

It is worth summarizing briefly the various methods of abstraction and what effects these have had on the environment and its fish fauna. One can then consider ways of ameliorating these effects.

## 10.1 METHODS OF ABSTRACTION

1. The simplest method of abstraction simply involves placing a pipe in a stream and diverting some of the water down the pipe under gravity to the supply point. This method is still frequently used in rural areas. Such a method has little or no effect on the aquatic environment.
2. Where a bigger community is to be supplied with water a lake is frequently tapped and a sluice or dam is built at the lake outflow in order to control water levels. On a migratory-fish river this may impede the movement of fish unless a fish pass is incorporated.
3. If there is no convenient lake or pond, reservoir formation is usually

necessary. In its simplest form, water draining from a small catchment area in a hilly region may be trapped behind a small dam and diverted for supply, with the exception of a compensation flow which is allowed to pass downstream to maintain the river environment. In this type of scheme there are few environmental problems that affect the salmon fishery manager.

4. The formation of a large reservoir often entails impounding the upper reaches of a river in an area of high rainfall and diverting the water directly to the demand area. Such a reservoir is known as a direct supply reservoir. It is often the case that the water is piped a great distance and is not returned to that river system after use. For example, in mid-Wales the Elan Valley scheme on the Wye river system supplies Birmingham and in the Scottish border country the Fruid, Talla and Meggat reservoirs on tributaries of the Tweed supply Edinburgh. In some cases the water may be used within the catchment area and is returned to the river further downstream, but usually in a reduced quality. There are more environmental problems associated with this type of scheme and these can include changes in flow, water temperature and water quality, obstruction and delay to migratory fish, and flooding of spawning and nursery areas.

Gudjonsson (1965) gives a detailed account of the effect of water abstraction on the salmon stocks in the River Úlfarsa in Iceland. A dam was built across the Úlfarsa in 1953 and from the reservoir thus formed water was piped at a continuous rate of 220–30 l/s to a fertilizer factory. The average flow of the river lies between 800 and 1000 l/s, so an appreciable amount of the water was being abstracted. The effect of this abstraction resulted in an estimated average annual loss of 281 salmon (61.5% of the predicted average catch). The explanations Gudjonsson gave for these losses were (i) impaired living conditions in the river caused by the removal of the water, (ii) young salmon entering the pipes leading to the fertilizer factory and thus being lost to stock recruitment and (iii) the sudden drying-out of the river channel below the dam during periods of snow and frost.

5. A reservoir may be sited close to a river and kept full by pumping water directly from the river at times when flow is adequate. The reservoir water may then be used to supply a neighbouring town. If the supply is used close to the reservoir and effluent is returned to the river there may be little effect downstream, provided that the effluent has been adequately treated. Where the supply is used outside the catchment area there may be problems, as with (4).

6. Another type of reservoir, which is of greater value to the river system on which it is sited, is a regulating reservoir. Lake Vyrnwy and Clyweddog Reservoir on tributaries of the River Severn and Llyn Brianne on the River

Towy are three such examples from Wales. In this case water is released from the reservoir during periods of low river flow and abstracted downstream at the point of demand. In other words, the river flow is regulated: flood flows are reduced due to some of the water being impounded in the reservoir, and drought flows are increased due to augmentation of flow during dry weather. When water is not required for abstraction a compensation flow is discharged to maintain the 'health' of the river. Environmental problems still occur even with this type of reservoir and these include unusually large fluctuations in river level, a steady compensation flow which may be insufficient to scour the river bed of silt and weed growth and assist ascending migratory fish, and reduced flows below the point of abstraction.

7. Another method of abstraction, where there is no need for a reservoir on the river, is where the water is pumped from the lower reaches of the river either directly into supply or into an existing storage reservoir either close to the river or some distance away. In this type of situation the river is left in its natural state to the 'very last minute' and water is only abstracted after other water users (farmers, anglers, etc.) have benefited from it. Such a scheme can only operate if the water is reasonably pure or where adequate water treatment facilities are available. Aberdeen takes its water from the neighbouring River Dee in this way.

8. In chalk and limestone districts, water is held in the porous rocks and emerges as springs which feed the rivers. An inexpensive way of obtaining water for supply is to sink boreholes and pump away the water. By reducing or stopping the spring supply to nearby streams and rivers this may have catastrophic effects on their ecology. In the 1980s a system was developed of pumping from boreholes but putting the water into rivers and using these as aqueducts to carry the water to the towns that need it; for example the rivers Lambourn and Kennet eventually supply water to metropolitan London. The pumping augments summer flow and so may be beneficial provided that the boreholes are not over-pumped leading eventually to a decline in total river flows.

9. One method of abstraction which does not involve taking water directly from the river, and is unlikely to affect either the river regime or the movements of migratory fish, is to sink wells into the gravel beds bordering the river and pump water from these wellfields. This method of abstraction has been proposed for the River Spey, a few miles from its mouth, and also for the River Lochy near Fort William in Scotland.

10. All the above abstraction schemes are relatively simple and involve single rivers. However, for England and Wales a more integrated strategy of water resource development is required to meet the estimated water deficit by 2001; this strategy will involve transfers between rivers and river regulation. In the transfer of water from one river (the donor) to another

(the recipient) there are likely to be a number of physical, chemical and biological effects on both rivers.


## 10.2   EFFECTS OF ABSTRACTION

In considering the effects abstraction might have on the river environment and the salmon stocks it is necessary to take account of (a) changes in the river flow and the movements of salmon, (b) the aquatic fauna, including the juvenile stages of fish, (c) angling and (d) commercial fishing.


### Changes in flow and the movements of salmon

There has been long-standing concern over the effect of reduced river flow on the entry of salmon into rivers and the consequences this might have on angling success. In addition, there have been fears that fisheries might suffer from the reduced flows. Alabaster (1970) looked at flows utilized by fish by examining available river-flow data and the counts of fish entering traps or ascending fish passes. From his study he concluded that flows utilized by fish are higher than those generally available, but it was evident that neither within nor between rivers is there any consistent relationship between these two flow parameters. However, he stressed that this general observation (that the median flow utilized by fish at a fixed point in a river over the year tends to be higher than the median of the actual river flow) could be made, not because fish do not move at low flows, but because there are coincidental seasonal differences in flow and in the availability of fish downstream.

Alabaster (1970) analysed the data for monthly catches at a trap on the River Coquet (Northumberland). Medians were estimated graphically for each month in each year when most of the fish were running (June to November); from these figures 6-year geometric means for each month were calculated. The analysis demonstrated a tendency for fish to be trapped at median flows higher than those prevailing in the river. There was no tendency for the flow utilized by the fish to be constant throughout the year but it seemed to follow the available flow fairly closely. Data obtained by Stewart (1968) for the rivers Leven and Lune (Lancashire) show a similar consistent trend throughout the fishing season (Table 10.1). Alabaster did point out though that since there does not appear to be any particular flow which is equally associated with fish movement throughout the year, it seems doubtful whether flow *per se* is the stimulating factor, though it does seem likely that factors associated with higher-than-average flows are important – perhaps short-term changes in flow or freshets, together with accompanying changes in concentrations of dissolved substances.

There is one important point which should be borne in mind in accepting the

**Table 10.1** Median values of available water level and flow rate in two rivers at different times of the year, with median values selected by salmon*

|  | River Lune: level 1964–66 (ft) | | | River Leven: flow 1965 (ft³/s)† | | |
|---|---|---|---|---|---|---|
|  | April–May | June–Aug | Sept–Oct | April–May | June–Aug | Sept–Oct |
| Available | 0.54 | 0.37 | 0.56 | 340 | 280 | 360 |
| Used by salmon | 0.60 | 0.47 | 0.86 | 340 | 370 | 540 |

*Source: Stewart (1968).
†100 ft³/s = 2.83 m³/s.

findings of both Alabaster and Stewart, and that is that these are '. . . the median flows at which salmon move into traps . . .' (Alabaster, 1970). Hellawell (1976) considers that relationships based on counting fish over falls or traps introduces uncertainty as to whether the observed pattern is influenced by the obstruction. Stewart in a later paper (1969) reported greater movements and catches of salmon on falling river levels and less movement on steady flows. The findings of Alabaster (1970) and Stewart (1969) were not supported by Hellawell *et al.* (1974) in a study of salmonids of the River Frome, Dorset, where unimpeded movements were monitored at an automatic fish-counting station (Hellawell, 1973). In the Frome, salmonids tended to move at flows lower than generally available and this was attributed to the more equable flow pattern of chalk rivers, which leads us to the conclusion that one cannot make generalities and that prevailing conditions in each river, or river type, must be considered separately. Certainly Cragg-Hine (1985) observed, from data obtained from the operation of resistivity fish counters over several years in north-west England, that during the summer months most fish movement occurs in the higher range of the available flows, but the migration flow range varies from year to year depending on prevailing river levels.

Hellawell (1976) drew attention to one important factor in migratory behaviour of salmon which had received little attention, the extent to which seasonal pattern of movement is constant from year to year, from which one could conclude that the primary factor in salmonid migration is season. The secondary importance of discharge is confirmed from observations of the fixed, seasonal patterns of movements either in fish passes (Gardner, 1976) or with constant, regulated flows (Pyefinch and Mills, 1963; Mills, 1968).

Most water abstraction schemes are designed to take only a small fraction of the daily flow of the river, and in many instances abstraction only takes place when the river flow is greater than a predetermined minimum and then only as a percentage of the excess flow above the minimum. This applies to schemes described in Section 10.1 at 2., 3., 4., 5., 6. and 10. In these a decision has to be reached on a minimum acceptable flow and the amount of water that can be abstracted. Before it is possible to decide the minimum acceptable flow in any river certain basic information is required. For example, one needs to know the yearly river flow pattern, the frequency, size and duration of peak floods, the frequency and length of droughts and the average daily flow. It is also essential that this information is collected over a fairly long period of time. Then there are a number of other factors to be taken into consideration when deciding what is an acceptable flow and these include: (1) existing abstractions and returns of surface and ground water, including the effects of land drainage and afforestation and land use over the whole catchment area, (2) water quality, (3) fisheries, (4) navigational uses and (5) the amenity of the river and its recreational uses.

The procedure for fixing a minimum acceptable flow in England and Wales is laid down in Section 19 of the *Water Resources Act, 1963*, and its purpose is to ensure that consideration is given to all these factors. From a fishery point of view it is essential to know, in terms of water supply, the minimum needs of the fisheries. It is the migratory species particularly for which this information is required, as while a certain discharge may be sufficient to maintain the survival of non-migratory species it may be insufficient to encourage the movement of salmon and sea trout and facilitate their capture with rod and line. However, the minimum acceptable flow for these requirements is not needed for the whole of the year and a smaller flow may be sufficient at other times for spawning requirements and the survival of the progeny.

Millichamp (1976) makes the point that where abstraction occurs immediately above the tidal influence, as it may in scheme 7., and there are no major fisheries downstream, the concept of 'no abstraction at low flows' may be unduly restricting. If critical periods of dry weather occur it is at such times that the abstraction of water from the natural flow of the river is of most importance. Therefore, if it can be shown that upstream movement of fish is negligible or non-existent below a certain flow, then provided enough water is left in the residual flow to meet requirements for the dilution of any estuary discharges, the difference between these two flows can be abstracted. Similarly, Millichamp and Lambert (1967) have shown that above a certain flow additional water plays little part in encouraging greater fish catchability.

Thus it would appear that there is a 'gateway' in the flow pattern which is important for the movement and catching of fish, and that if the range of this gateway can be determined then outside that range little regard needs to be paid to the requirements of fish. Such an arrangement would provide additional water during times of low flow. However, Millichamp (1976) stresses that this proposition will apply only where the abstraction is immediately above the tidal influence. Inevitably there would be objections from the salmon anglers to this arrangement and they would be concerned in any case that this scheme would make more salmon available to the estuary nets. Hellawell (1976) considered that there was little evidence for a gateway for fish movements, although it had to be recognized that research in this area is fraught with difficulties. Without knowing the availability of fish within the estuary it is difficult to interpret apparent responses to discharge variation and thereby to derive values for the gateway. This problem was approached with some success by modelling (Radford *et al.*, 1972) using discharge to derive the model and taking account of the likely availability of fish from data on their movements within the river (Peters *et al.*, 1973). However, some assumptions had to be made regarding the behaviour of fish.

It has been shown (Chapter 4, pp. 69–70) that the relative sea and river water temperatures also influence the movement of fish into the river. During low flow periods in the summer river water temperatures may become much higher than the sea temperature and may consequently deter fish from entering the river.

On the River Towy scheme in south-west Wales water can only be abstracted (about $50 \times 10^6$ gal/day (227 Ml/day)) below the minimum prescribed flow of $150 \times 10^6$ gal/day (682 Ml/day) if the equivalent quantity, plus an allowance for evaporation *en route*, is released from Llyn Brianne (Howells and Jones, 1972). The Water Order allows for a 'maintained' flow of $30 \times 10^6$ gal/day (136 Ml/day) downstream of the abstraction point; the river flow is not allowed to fall below this value. In fact the prescribed flow is not entirely relevant to fish movement and should not be equated to the minimum acceptable flow but only to the limited abstraction concerned and the authors state that it should not be implied that the river could without damage be reduced to this level by bigger abstractions. It was noticed that no daytime salmon movement occurred in flows less than $300 \times 10^6$ gal/day (1364 Ml/day). Low flows on the Towy in summer are, as in many water abstraction schemes, supplemented by reservoir releases, and a 'bank' of water is maintained in the reservoir for this purpose.

Attempts are made on rivers where water abstraction schemes exist to induce fish to move upstream by means of artificial floods or 'freshets'. This ploy has been shown to be successful in at least one case on a river unaffected by water abstraction, the Grimersta River in the Outer Hebrides. A small impounding dam was removed so as to create an artificial spate in order to bring up salmon which had gathered in the tidal waters because of drought conditions in the river. This was so successful that three anglers caught over 400 salmon in the following 10 days. However, not all artificial freshets are so successful.

The works of Harriman (1961) on the Narraguagus, Maine and Hayes (1953) on the La Have River, Nova Scotia, have probably supplied most information on the effects of artificial freshets on the upstream migration of salmon, and the following conclusions were reached by Hayes:

1. Large or small freshets are capable of moving fish when other factors like wind and tide are favourable, otherwise they have no effect;
2. Major runs can occur without the aid of natural or artificial freshets and can be maintained by a steady flow of water during the 'run' season;
3. Artificial freshets can move fish, that happen to be at the head of tide into fresh water, but are unable by themselves to move fish into the estuary, although if they are timed with wind and tides they could probably bring fish into the estuary as well;
4. The reverse of a freshet, that is, cutting down the river level and then increasing it again, may also act as an effective stimulus in moving fish;
5. Temperature appears to have little effect in initiating runs;
6. Fish move out of tidal waters into fresh water at dusk; change in light could be the operating factor;
7. Strong onshore winds, approaching 20 mph (32 km/h), induce salmon to concentrate in the river estuary and eventually ascend;
8. Peaks in the tidal cycles representing daily increasing difference between high and low tides seem to be effective in concentrating salmon in the estuary and initiating a run into fresh water.

Baxter (1961) examined the water requirements for migratory fish on a number of British rivers and produced a plan of water control which took account of the likely needs of the fish at all stages in their life history. He strongly advocates the use of freshets in any river system that has been regulated by man.

From a number of considerations Baxter produced a schedule of flows (Table 10.2) as a guide which could be changed to meet the needs of individual rivers. For small rivers this schedule represents an annual mean of 18.5% of the average daily flow and for larger rivers 15%. This basic schedule is intended to provide adequate flow and bottom coverage, for example at times when these are needed for spawning and during the early summer when large areas of water-covered river bottom will allow greater food production during the growing season of the parr. This schedule does not provide adequate conditions for the ascent of migratory fish, but it is intended that sufficient stored compensation water should be available to provide freshets.

On rivers where a dam is well downstream, so that there will be little natural augmentation to the compensation water, Baxter considered that weekly freshets should be provided from the time that fish are expected to enter the river until spawning time. Where the dam is well upstream a few freshets in summer to bring fish through the fish pass may be all that is needed if there is adequate spate water entering below the dam.

Banks (1969) produced a very good review of the literature on the upstream migration of adult salmonids and considered that for British rivers the general conclusions of Baxter (1961) regarding the volume and number of freshets,

**Table 10.2**   Schedule of flows, exclusive of freshets*

| Month | Smaller rivers (% a.d.f.)† | Larger rivers (% a.d.f.)† | Remarks |
|---|---|---|---|
| October | 15 to 12.5 | 15 to 12.5 | in alternate weeks |
| November | 25 | 15 | |
| December | 25 to 12.5 | 15 to 10 | 25 and 15 normally only in first 2 weeks |
| January | 12.5 | 10 | |
| February | 12.5 | 10 | |
| March | 20 | 15 | |
| April | 25 | 20 | |
| May | 25 | 20 | |
| June | 25 to 20 | 20 to 15 | in alternate weeks |
| July | 20 to 15 | 15 to 12.5 | in alternate weeks |
| August | 15 | 15 to 12.5 | in alternate weeks |
| September | 15 to 12.5 | 15 to 12.5 | in alternate weeks |

*Source: Baxter (1961).*
†*Values are expressed as percentages of average daily flow.*

and of Hayes (1953) regarding their timing, would seem a reasonable working basis. However, subsequent observations on fish movements in rivers on which abstraction schemes have been developed since 1969 would suggest that an update review is necessary.

Freshets are not always successful in stimulating fish to move upstream. Mills (1968) found that artificial freshets over a limited range of water flows had little effect on upstream movements of fish, and the factor that appeared to stimulate more fish to move upstream was rainfall, but without the usually associated increase in river level.

### The aquatic fauna

The effects of abstraction on the invertebrate and resident fish fauna will depend on both the rate at which water is abstracted and the amount. If the natural river channel remains covered no damage to the invertebrate fauna will occur, although there may be some change in the species composition if the water velocity is permanently reduced and the water temperature regime is changed. While young fish will have less water above them they will not be left stranded. If large amounts of water are withdrawn and the margins of the river channel are exposed the invertebrate fauna will die and any young fish that have not retreated with the receding water level will be left stranded in pools and will either be eaten by predators or die from exposure as the pools dry up. The size of the minimum acceptable flow has to take account of these factors.

The effects of reductions or increases in flow and water velocity will be much greater in water transfer schemes as described in Section 10.1 at 10., such as the Kielder scheme connecting the Rivers Tyne, Wear and Tees. In this type of scheme conditions in the donor river will be almost the opposite of the conditions occurring in the recipient river. In recipient rivers one effect of seasonal transfers will be to maintain the flows in the dry-weather flow periods at levels above those previously occurring. This is likely to be beneficial also to fisheries and to fishing. The rates at which a transferred flow is introduced into a recipient river and at which such flow is stopped are important. Sudden deepening of the water may endanger anglers, while a sudden reduction in flow may lead to the stranding of fish in shallow pools. Fluctuations in transfer rates could be beneficial provided that the changes in flow are not abrupt. Seasonal dry weather transfers to even out the annual flow pattern will tend to preserve the 'wetted' perimeter and thus the food production potential. Changes in flow velocity will affect the river bed stability and siltation, the survival of invertebrates and the suitability of the habitat for young fish. The flow velocities may affect the invertebrate fauna by shifting the bed material, leading to destruction of the fauna, or by occluding the bed with silt. The effects on fish may include the scouring of salmon redds and the washing away of alevins. The effects on the donor river of water being transferred will be those associated with water abstraction: a minimum flow would have to be left in the donor river.

One effect of regulated releases of water is a change in the water temperature regime. A study of the effects of such releases of water from Kielder reservoir was made by the Freshwater Biological Association (Crisp, 1984). This temperature change may affect the upper 10 km of the River North Tyne immediately downstream of the reservoir, after which an influence is exerted by incoming unregulated tributaries. The principal effect has been to make the North Tyne warmer in late autumn and winter and cooler in spring and early summer.

It is suggested that an increase in autumn temperatures by several degrees would lead salmon ova to hatch 50–60 days earlier than previously. Lower temperatures in spring mean that it might take a further 40 days before the temperature rises to a level (7 °C) at which salmon fry start to feed. Thus, ready-to-feed fry would emerge when water temperatures were too low for them to feed and they could consequently starve and die.

Cave (1985) points out that, as smolts usually start to migrate when water temperatures rise above 10 °C, the changed water temperature regime in the North Tyne could delay migration by as much as 40 days and smolts could miss the limited time they have to pass through the estuary to the sea. This time, referred to as the 'window' period, is all the more noticeable in the Tyne estuary where dissolved oxygen levels drop after the spring floods have passed to less than 40% in some reaches and thus prevent smolt movement. Cave also suggests that delays in descent to the sea may also affect the sea feeding pattern and the timing of return of adult fish.

An additional consequence of some abstraction schemes is reservoir formation. If the reservoir is situated on the main river or one of its tributaries it is more than likely that it will inundate some of the salmon spawning and nursery areas. Should this happen there has to be some compensation in the form of either opening up new spawning areas, which may be available above insurmountable falls, or re-stocking in suitable areas with eggs or fry originating from local stock.

## Angling

There are considerable data on flows at which salmon are caught by rod and line. Information is available for the Usk (Millichamp and Lambert, 1967), the Avon (Brayshaw, 1967), the Towy (Jones, 1968), the Coquet (Alabaster, 1970) and the Wye (Gee, 1980). Alabaster showed that for the first four rivers the median daily flow associated with angling success, like that associated with the movements of fish into traps and fish passes, is higher than the median flow available in the river over the same period. However, Alabaster stresses that the relationship between river flow and angling success must be treated with some caution because the size of the stock at risk and the fishing effort of the anglers are also important in this context; so while it is apparent in Jones' data for the Towy that the total number of fish caught increases with increase in seasonal daily flow, there is no means of confirming the hypothesis that this is in part due to more fish being available in seasons of high flow. In fact, Alabaster concludes his paper on this subject by saying that no definite conclusions can yet be reached on the effect of flow either on the size of the run passing through a counter or on the total numbers of fish being caught by anglers.

Gee (1980) found on the River Wye that the highest salmon catch rates coincided with a falling hydrograph. Although he found no clear relationship between water temperature and angling success he thought it may be significant that in the fishery furthest upstream salmon were generally caught when temperatures were in the range 5.5–15.6 °C, which according to Banks (1969) and Brayshaw (1967) is the favoured range for migration. Gee considered that the availability of salmon in the upper reaches of the river during July and August may have been limited by temperatures too high ($>16$ °C) for migration and this effect may have been exacerbated by concurrent low flows. Gee (1980) admits that angling success is dependent on several factors which he had not considered and these included availability of fish and skill of individual anglers – two factors which no authors included in their studies of flow and upstream movement and catch of fish, and yet are important considerations.

## Commercial fishing

In any abstraction scheme on a river where commercial salmon netting occurs, consideration has to be given to the size of the minimum acceptable flow, because the level of abstraction during low flow may affect both the entry of salmon and the efficiency of netting. If, during periods of drought, the river flow after abstraction is too low it could be alleged that fish are being held up off the river mouth and the netsmen are not earning a living. On the other hand, if the flow is sufficient for fish to enter the river, assuming that flow and not water temperature is the operating factor, then anglers upstream may allege that the abstraction scheme is benefiting the nets to the detriment of the rods. Some compromise has to be reached, and this may involve either paying the netsmen not to fish during periods of low flow or abstracting over a limited period of the 24 hours, perhaps to coincide with the flood tides. These arrangements are most crucial where the abstraction point is low down the river near the tidal limits.

CHAPTER ELEVEN

# Pollution and acidification

*The river that floods with inspiration*
*Painters and photographers*
*The darling of the calendars!*
*To us is a funeral procession –*
  *Without a fish its cascades toll*
  *A death within the human soul.*

Ted Hughes, 1985
*(unpublished)*

In negotiations over exploitation levels and quota agreements the subject of pollution control is frequently raised. During early discussions with Greenlanders and Faroese on quotas the accusing finger was often pointed at the salmon-producing countries: 'You talk to us about taking your salmon and yet you allow pollution of your rivers to continue.' It is not easy to reject such an accusation as it has an element of truth. There is little doubt that many of our salmon rivers are cleaner today than they were some decades ago. Some of our industrial rivers such as the Clyde, Connecticut, Merrimack, Meuse, Nivelle and Trent have reached or soon will reach a state of purity suitable for salmon restoration. However, pollution continues and the acidification problem increases. Every salmon-producing nation has its pollution legislation but not all have found it easy to enforce; in any case, accidental pollution can cause massive fish mortalities resulting in reduced recruitment and stock decline. Often recently-enhanced rivers with improved salmon runs revert to their previous poor condition as a result of industrialization and economic growth – industrial strikes, vandalism or carelessness. It is no wonder that some of the nations harvesting 'our' salmon on the open seas are sometimes at a loss to understand our concern over fishing mortality when we seem to be indifferent to the state of our rivers. This is not true, of course, but there is no denying that our rivers are still exposed to varying and continuous pollution from numerous sources and the penalties inflicted on the offenders, if identified, are derisorily inadequate to deter.

## 11.1   POLLUTION

Pollution appears in many guises, and the physical, chemical and biological effects of pollution can, from an ecological point of view, be divided into seven major categories, one or more of which may be characteristic of any one effluent. Sewage, for example, is capable of producing most of the above effects. The major types of pollution result from: chemicals, suspended solids, deoxygenation, non-toxic salts, thermal water, oil and radioactive wastes.

### Toxic chemicals

Poisonous chemicals in solution occur in waste waters from many industries. They include (a) acids and alkalis, (b) chromium salts from tanning and electroplating and copper and zinc from base-metal mining and galvanizing, (c) phenols and cyanides from chemical industries and mines, and (d) insecticides, herbicides and other sprays and agricultural chemicals. The commonest inorganic substances are free chlorine, ammonia, hydrogen sulphide and salts of many heavy metals (e.g. copper, lead, zinc, chromium, silver and mercury). Any appreciable amounts of these compounds may kill fish or other aquatic life. Copper and zinc affect the gills of fish and cause respiration troubles. Phosphorus causes haemolysis and rapid death. Some of these substances are rapidly precipitated in the waters into which they flow, but others are very persistent. A few, such as ammonia, are destroyed fairly rapidly by oxidation, while others such as phenolic and cyanide compounds are similarly destroyed, but much more slowly. Streams polluted by the heavy metals zinc, lead and copper in concentrations measured in parts per million or less can be rendered practically devoid of all animal life. The toxicity of lead, zinc and copper is linked to the alkaline content of the water and where this is low the concentrations of these metals required to cause death are greatly reduced. From studies of lead pollution in Wales and copper–zinc pollution in eastern Canada it has been shown that biological conditions in streams can be closely connected with the metallic content of water. Poisons usually decrease steadily in concentration. This is partly because the volume of diluting water in any river increases as more tributaries join it, and partly because many poisons such as metals are precipitated by chemical action, while others, particularly organic compounds, are oxidized and changed into non-toxic materials. A number of toxic discharges also originate from agricultural chemicals such as insecticides, herbicides, fungicides, sheep dip and chemicals used for destroying vermin (Holden, 1964; Holden and Marsden, 1964).

The list of toxic chemicals is alarmingly long. It would be impracticable to itemize these in this chapter and there are many general texts which do this adequately including Hellawell (1986), Klein (1962), Alabaster and Lloyd (1980), Solbé (1986) and Muirhead-Thomson (1971, 1987). However, it is worth selecting a number of examples of chemical pollution which most frequently affect Atlantic salmon stocks.

### Heavy metals

The effects on salmon of extensive development in New Brunswick of mines for the extraction of copper, zinc and associated heavy metals have been studied by Elson (1974), Elson *et al.* (1973), Sprague *et al.* (1965), Sprague (1968) and Saunders and Sprague (1967). The first impact of these mining developments was seen in the unusual behaviour of adult salmon: in some instances, after passing upstream of a counting fence on the Northwest Miramichi, the fish immediately returned downstream. This was found to be an avoidance reaction when cupric and zinc ions reached or exceeded lethal concentrations. The lethal threshold was considered to be 1 toxic unit. This avoidance behaviour was observed whenever the cupric and zinc ion concentration reached or exceeded 0.35–0.43 toxic units. At 0.8 toxic units migration upstream was completely blocked. The downstream movement of salmon under these pollution conditions represented a serious loss in spawning escapement to the river, some two-thirds of downstream migrants not being seen again. Estimated losses to the river above the counting fence were 8–15% of the total run. It was also postulated that the extra stress load imposed by summer copper–zinc pollution and high summer water temperatures made the fish vulnerable to epidemic attack by an indigenous and ubiquitous pathogen (*Aeromonas liquefaciens*) (Pippy and Hare, 1969).

Lethal thresholds for salmon parr were found to be 48 $\mu$g/l for copper and 600 $\mu$g/l for zinc (water hardness about 20 mg/l). In combination the effect of the two heavy metal ions was additive. Resident populations of juvenile salmon dropped to about one-fifth of the previous 10-year level after heavy pollution began in 1960 (Sprague *et al.*, 1965). This was partly due to mortality of the young in the lower, polluted reaches and partly because of avoidance of the upper reaches by spawners. The food of the young salmon, in the form of aquatic insects, was similarly reduced in the lower reaches in 1960.

Significant amounts of humic compounds substantially decrease the acute toxicity of cupric, but not zinc, ions to juvenile salmon (Carson and Carson, 1972). It has also been demonstrated that nitrilotriacetic acid (NTA) protects fish from the acute toxicity of both cupric and zinc ions. However, excess of NTA could have its own deleterious effects as it has been shown that NTA in concentrations as low as 1.0 mg/l releases cupric, zinc and ferric ions from aquatic sediments.

Zinc and lead can be long-lasting contaminants of fresh water and may continue to contaminate rivers many years after mining operations have finished. In west Wales the rivers Ystwyth and Rheidol are subject to lead and zinc pollution from the runoff from disused lead mines in the upper reaches of these rivers. On the river Rheidol lime filters were installed to intercept and successfully treat the lead- and zinc-laden waters draining from lead mines (Jones and Howells, 1969, 1975), but no such treatment has been applied to the river Ystwyth, which is consequently unsuitable for migratory salmonids except in the very lowest part of the river system.

An interesting and worrying effect of copper is that sublethal exposures to copper eliminated the ability of Pacific salmon and steelhead to adapt to ocean water by eliminating their ability to tolerate salt water at typical ocean salinities (Lorz and McPherson, 1976). This indicates that safe limits for many pollutants may depend less on their outright toxicity, and more on subtle physiological or behavioural responses which can affect the fish.

### Organic compounds
There are two main groups of synthetic pesticides, the chlorinated hydrocarbons and the organo-phosphorus compounds. In addition to these the organo-mercuries and certain organic herbicides are also toxic to fish.

*Chlorinated hydrocarbons.* The chlorinated hydrocarbons or organo-chlorines are generally regarded as the group of organic chemicals most toxic to fish. This group includes benzene hexachloride (BHC), DDT, aldrin, dieldrin, endrin and heptachlor. Some of these chemicals present an added danger in that they are resistant to breakdown by the digestive processes of mammals, birds or fish and are concentrated in the food chain. In the USA, recommended levels in fish for the protection of piscivores are that total DDT should not exceed 1 mg per kg wet weight of whole fish and that aldrin, dieldrin, endrin, heptachlor, chlordane, lindane, benzene hexachloride, toxaphene and endosulfan should not exceed 0.1 mg per kg wet weight of whole fish, either singly or in combination (Environmental Protection Agency, 1973). Residues of DDT, dieldrin and heptachlor have been found in various forms of wildlife, mainly in fatty tissues. An example of the contamination of a brown trout population in a lake by a discharge of dieldrin from an industrial establishment is provided by Loch Leven, Kinross-shire. This discharge, which had continued for several years, ceased in 1964. The actual amount discharged into the lake is not known, but dieldrin was found in fish long before it was realized that the source was primarily industrial rather than agricultural (Holden, 1966). Holden (1966) also found concentrations of dieldrin (0.01–0.06 ppm) and DDE (0.01–0.06 ppm) in the muscle of salmon parr in an area of the Highlands of Scotland where sheep dip was the only known source of insecticides. The presence of DDE may have been the result of a partial metabolism of DDT by the fish, or probably was produced at an earlier stage in the food chain.

Large-scale spraying of forest areas with DDT in Canada and the United

States has caused severe fish mortalities. In northern New Brunswick, Quebec and Maine these spraying operations were directed against the spruce budworm (*Choristoneura fumiferana*). In Newfoundland the hemlock looper (*Lambdina fiscellaria*) was the defoliator of the fir and spruce trees. Each spring large forest areas were sprayed. Kerswill (1967) gives an account of the early forest spraying in New Brunswick. Some areas were sprayed at intervals of 1, 2 or 3 years. In spite of this the budworm population continued to expand, until in 1957 over 5 M acres of New Brunswick forest were sprayed, and nine years later, in 1966, 8.5 M acres or 56% of the province's forest were sprayed. In 1954 the effects of spraying one watershed were clearly seen and not one salmon fry was found in that year; the parr were also reduced. In 1954 salmon parr were held in cages in several parts of the Northwest Miramichi and 63–91% of those held within the spray area were dead in 21 days, while only 2% died in an unsprayed control stream during the same period. Fish poisoned by DDT are first excited and then exhibit ataxia and paralysis. The first symptom of DDT poisoning is tremor of the skeletal muscles. Elson *et al.* (1973) gave a detailed account of the effects on juvenile salmon of spraying with DDT at various concentrations. The organo-phosphorus compound phosphami- don, which is less toxic to fish, was tried either on its own or with low dosages of DDT; the effects were less harmful to fish but because of difficulties and costs in its application, as well as its damage to bird life, phosphamidon was not widely used as a forest spray.

DDT and related persistent chlorinated hydrocarbons once introduced into a river basin may remain there for years, either in original form or as degradation products. Dimond *et al.* (1971) reported that DDT persisted in Maine streams for at least 10 years following aerial application of 1.12 kg/ha; it was found in mud, plants, invertebrates, fish and fish-eating birds. However, in some areas the concentrations of DDT some years after spraying are only very low. It is gratifying to know from the work of Sprague and Duffy (1971) that DDT residues are much reduced in salmon that grow to a large size at sea.

Elson *et al.* (1973) point out that it would be a mistake to assume that the small amounts of chlorinated hydrocarbon residues available in the stream environment long after initial application have no ecological significance. They illustrate this warning in citing the work of Anderson (1971) who, with colleagues, found that exposures of young salmon to doses as low as 10–100 $\mu$g/l (parts per billion) resulted in changes in temperature responses and other behaviour, such as decreased reaction to stimuli causing avoidance and/or shelter-seeking behaviour, which lowered survivability under adverse conditions. A finding which caused some concern was that recorded by Anderson and Elson (1971) who obtained a reduced return rate of adult fish exposed to sub-acute DDT poisoning as smolts. They found that sub-acute poisoning of tagged wild smolts resulted in only just over half as many (57%) adult returns as from similarly handled fish not exposed to DDT.

Hamilton (1985) traced the source of aldrin and dieldrin poisoning in salmonid fry in a hatchery on Exmoor to an area in the upper catchment of the River Mole near the site of a disused sheep dip. As there has been a ban on the agricultural use of dieldrin for many years and there was no industrial use of this chemical locally it was obvious that residues of the substance were still available in the environment long after its final use. Hamilton also attributed the absence of salmon fry in the upper reaches of the River Mole to the presence of these pesticides.

Saunders (1969) recorded a mass mortality of brook trout and young salmon in a Prince Edward Island stream after accidental spillage of a spray mixture containing the fungicide nabam (disodium ethylene bisdithiocarbamate) and the chlorinated hydrocarbon endrin. The interesting feature of this pollution was that surviving trout and salmon showed abnormal behaviour, including unseasonal downstream movements in summer. Saunders suggested that this abnormal behaviour could provide a useful biological indicator of pollution by these pesticides.

DDT usage was reduced fairly widely as a result of its adverse effect on wildlife. Dieldrin was no longer used in sheep dips after 1966 and was replaced by organo-phosphorus compounds, although hexachlorocyclohexane (HCH), an organo-chlorine, is still used in dips.

Another group of organo-chlorine compounds, the polychlorinated biphenyls (PCBs), are extensively used in industry as hydraulic fluids, transformer oils and plasticizers, in the manufacture of paints, and for many other purposes. Distributions of PCBs in fish have been recorded by Elson *et al.* (1973) and Holden (1973a, 1987). Holden (1987) records no adverse effects on these on fish. Residue concentrations in fish have sometimes exceeded 1 mg/kg fresh weight as total PCB, but background levels are usually one-hundredth of this. However, fish-eating birds accumulate much higher concentrations and mortalities of some sea birds have been attributed to PCB poisoning.

*Organo-phosphorus compounds.* In this group are included malathion, parathion, phosphamidon and fenitrothion. Fenitrothion largely replaced DDT in forest spraying operations in Canada from 1968. It is not very lethal to fish unless the dosage is unusually high. Wildish *et al.* (1971) recorded 24-hour LC50 (median lethal concentration) of 7.4 mg/l, and an incipient lethal level of about 1 mg/l was recorded by Zitko *et al.* (1970). Normally the concentration in stream water after one application of 0.14 kg/ha at the usual forest spraying operation would be about 0.045 mg/l. Fenitrothion is designed to kill arthropods, therefore lower stream densities of aquatic insects occur after spraying (Penney, 1971), thus reducing the food supply of young fish with a consequent reduction in growth and in numbers. However, it was also found that after exposure to fenitrothion at 1.0 mg/l for 24 hours salmon parr were significantly more vulnerable to capture by large brook trout than those untreated; at 0.1 mg/l there was no noticeable effect.

In Scotland fenitrothion is used for the control of the pine beauty moth (*Panolis flammea*) on lodgepole pine. Holden and Bevan (1979) summarize the results of monitoring its use on lodgepole pine plantations in northern Scotland. The general assessment of the effects of the spraying on fish and wildlife is that, within the limits of the observations made, these were small or unimportant. Provided single treatments are made at long intervals, it seems unlikely that serious damage would be caused to non-target species. Repeated application could be less acceptable where fresh waters are used for commercial purposes (e.g. fish farms).

One organo-phosphorus compound whose use in marine fish farming is causing some concern is dichlorvos, the active ingredient in the chemical Nuvan used in the treatment of sea lice infestation of farmed salmon (Anon., 1988a, b). Although it is not toxic to fish at the normal concentration (1 ppm for 1 h) used for sea louse control, it is poisonous to marine invertebrates such as shellfish. A biological substitute could be 'cleaner fish' to remove lice.

*Organo-mercury compounds.* The organo-mercury compounds are also very toxic to fish and humans. These include methyl mercury dicyandiamide and other alkyl mercurys. These compounds are used as fungicides to dress seeds. Phenyl mercury (phenyl mercuric acetate) may enter the water from pulp mills and from mercury electrodes in the chlorine–alkaline industry and may eventually be taken up by fish. Holden (1973b, c) reviews the use of mercury and its presence in fish and shellfish. Attention was drawn to the organic mercury problem in the 1970s when concentrations regarded as unacceptably high for human consumption were reported in Pacific tuna (*Thunnus* spp.) and swordfish (*Xiphias gladius* L.). The working limit of acceptance of 0.5 ppm imposed in Canada and the United States resulted in the closure of a number of fisheries, and regular monitoring of fish tissue for mercury content was introduced throughout North America, Europe and Japan. The results of a survey of mercury in food were published in 1971 by the Ministry of Agriculture, Fisheries and Food (HMSO). Atlantic salmon were found to have a mean mercury concentration of 0.08 mg/kg (range 0.04–0.13 mg/kg). Zitko *et al.* (1971) also found only small concentrations (0.1 mg/kg) of methyl mercury in salmonid fish in New Brunswick.

*Herbicides.* The main group of herbicides includes Asulam, 2,4-D amine, dalapon, diquat, atrazine glyphosate, mallic hydrazide and terbutryne. They are generally less toxic to fish, but impurities associated with 2,4,5-T (e.g. TCDD, limited by registration in Canada to less than 0.5 ppm in 2,4,5-T) can have a very high toxicity (Elson *et al.*, 1973). This chemical (TCDD) is not one of the approved herbicides for use in the United Kingdom and its use in other countries may have been banned by the late 1980s. Herbicides cleared for aquatic use are restricted to those that are harmless to fish. However, some herbicides used for terrestrial plants have, through carelessness, entered the water and caused fish deaths. In addition, the active ingredients of some weedkillers are toxic to fish. One of these is pendimethalin which was found by chance to be present in the River Mole on Exmoor (Hamilton, 1985).

*Pyrethroids.* Pyrethrins are natural insecticides originating from pyrethrum which is extracted from flowers of *Chrysanthemum cinerariaefolium.* Although it is harmless to mammals it is extremely toxic to fish and aquatic invertebrates. As well as the natural pyrethrum, a number of synthetic pyrethroids are also used, particularly as moth-proofing agents in the carpet industry, and of these permethrin is less toxic than many of the other analogues. Zitko *et al.* (1977) found permethrin to have a 96 h lethal threshold of 8.8 $\mu$g/l. These synthetic pyrethroids have been a problem in the 1980s in some Scottish rivers such as the Clyde and the Tweed and hence have led to major declines in the numbers and types of aquatic insects downstream of points where these agents were entering the river in the sewage effluent.

A number of other types of fungicide used in agriculture from time to time result in fish kills. One, sodium pentachlorophenate, used in mushroom farms, has caused fish deaths as a result of being discharged inadvertently into rivers.

*Other chemicals.* A number of chemicals used in fish farming frequently spread into the natural aquatic environment and become a threat to the indigenous fish populations. These include (a) anti-foulants on nets and cages which until its ban in the mid 1980s was usually tributyl tin (TBT), (b) disinfectants, such as formalin and malachite green, used to combat parasites and diseases, and (c) food additives, including vitamins, minerals, pigments and hormones (Anon., 1988a, b).

Chemical pollution may at times cause some unusual mortalities. In the 1980s 'golden' or pigmented salmon have been recorded in large numbers in the River Don, Aberdeenshire, and in 1983 more than 380 pigmented fish were found dead. The pigmentation varies from a 'yellow' to a 'red' condition. This condition has been identified as haemolytic anaemia and jaundice. A research project headed by Dr D. Groman of the Marine Laboratory, Aberdeen, has been looking at the problem for a few years. The categories of chemicals that seem most likely to be responsible for this condition, and which are all potentially haemolytic to fish blood cells, are pressure washing fluids, emulsifying degreasers, penetration and dewatering fluids, safety solvents, hard surface cleaners, and concrete/rust removers. One common chemical link between all of these cleaning agents was the presence of non-ionic, cationic and/or anionic surfactants, which have been identified elsewhere as haemolytic agents (Groman, personal communication, 1988). Research into this phenomenon is continuing.

## Suspended solids

The effect of inert suspended solids is twofold. If they are light or very finely divided, as are some mine slurries, the waste water from china clay works and coal-washing effluents, they do not settle rapidly but make the river opaque and prevent the penetration of sunlight, so prohibiting plant growth.

When particles are large the deposits smother all algal growth, kill rooted plants and mosses and alter the nature of the substrate. Quantities of silt-like material destroy plants, and quite small amounts, such as those produced by gravel-washing plants or by soil erosion or the regular washing of farm implements or root crops, may change the nature of the stream bed sufficiently to alter the flora and fauna. The coarser sand particles may have a scrubbing effect on the rocks and gravel of the stream; this tends to remove algal growth as well as the bottom fauna. Coarser rock particles may plug up the spaces in the gravel and hence reduce the habitat of the bottom fauna. If salmonid eggs are already in the gravel when pollution occurs the compaction of the gravel with tailings will reduce circulation of the water through the redds and cause the eggs to suffocate. Fish eggs can also become burried by suspended solids and the pressure caused by the weight of solids may even cause the less resistant eggs to burst. Fine silt and other sediments are said to cause the death of alevins by accumulating on the gill membranes.

Hamilton (1961) and others have found that the bottom fauna is unaltered by the presence of sand and silt in suspension except where the river bed is completely covered with sand and silt. Where the stones are partially free from the deposit animals typical of the unaffected part of the river are present. However, in the River Ouvèze, Rivier and Seguier (1985) have shown that the biomass of benthic invertebrates decreases by 62 to 96% downstream from gravel works, and that the effects are particularly noticeable on habitats along the edges, where the deposits of fine material are greater.

Suspended solids decline in amount as one proceeds downstream from the source of pollution because they settle out of the water. The rate of settling depends on the density and size of the particles and the turbulence of the water, and is particularly rapid above weirs and in pools or where the current is slack. If the solids are completely inert, as are the wastes from sand and gravel washing and china clay works, the amount of deposit on the river bed slowly builds up and extends furthers and further downstream as it is stirred up and carried on by floods. Oxidizable solids on the other hand, such as those in sewage, dairy and pulp-mill wastes, are steadily broken down by bacteria; a balance therefore results between the rates of settling and decomposition, and the deposits slowly tail off downstream. In the case of pulp waste, which is broken down more slowly, large deposits of pulp fibre accumulate in the slower-flowing parts of the river. Methane and hydrogen sulphide gases build up underneath and eventually large mats of the decomposing material are lifted from the river bed and float downstream and the gases are liberated.

## Deoxygenation

This is usually caused by bacterial breakdown of organic matter but may be due to other reducing agents. Organic residues include the effluents from a great variety of sources including dairies, silage, manure heaps and cattle yards, slaughter houses, sugar beet factories, textile manufacture, canning plants, laundries, breweries, tanneries, fish-meal factories, paper mills, domestic sewage and leachates from refuse tips. Residues from all these sources contain complex organic compounds in solution and suspension, often together with toxic substances and various salts. The oxidation of sewage effluent uses up a considerable amount of dissolved oxygen: the concentration can decrease below the necessary minimum required by fish, particularly at high water temperatures when there is less dissolved oxygen and the oxygen requirements of the fish are higher. This can be serious in rivers where food-processing plants and other manufacturers use the city sewers for releasing their wastes. This situation can reach very serious proportions in the lower reaches of a river, so much so that seaward-migrating smolts may not be able to negotiate a belt of pollution at the river mouth.

Inorganic reducing agents such as sulphides and sulphites occur as constituents of the effluents of several types of industry. These substances use up the oxygen in the river water, and important among them are the ferrous salts which are present in many underground waters. These often reach the rivers quite naturally, but large volumes are pumped up from mines and can produce serious pollution. Ferrous waters are usually acid, but as the acid becomes neutralized, usually by loss of carbon dioxide to the atmosphere, the ferrous salts become oxidized, often by bacterial action, and ferric hydroxide ('ochre') is precipitated. This then takes on the role of an inert suspension which covers the bed of the river, blanketing all the bottom fauna (see page 235).

The polluting effect of organic materials is correlated with the amount of oxygen taken up by micro-organisms that bring about the decomposition of the material. If large quantities of dissolved oxygen in the water are 'removed' as a result of this decomposition, conditions tend to become anaerobic causing foul smells and the death of all forms of plant and animal life. The intensity of pollution is estimated by determining the amount of oxygen taken up by 1 l of water or effluent at 20 °C for 5 days, and is designated the biochemical oxygen demand (BOD). This is stated as mg/l (also called parts per million, ppm) and a BOD of 20 is considered a satisfactory level for effluent entering a watercourse. In addition to satisfying the BOD standard, effluents in the British Isles must not contain more than 30 mg/l of suspended solids (SS). If the effluent on entering the watercourse is not diluted at least eightfold then a correspondingly lower BOD and SS standard would be required if satisfactory conditions are to be maintained. Crude domestic sewage may have a BOD of about 400 mg/l. In agricultural effluents BOD values can be much higher. The BOD of dairy effluent, including byre washings and equipment cleaning, can vary between 450 and 4000. Piggeries produce an effluent with a much higher BOD in the region of 1200 to 13 000. Silage is the strongest type of polluting material produced on a farm with a BOD varying between 12 000 and 60 000. Up to 40 gallons of effluent may be produced per ton of silage (165 l/tonne), and on this basis the effluent from 300 tons of silage has a polluting power equivalent to the domestic sewage of a town with a population of 60 000. In the paper industry pulp-mill wastes consist of sulphite pulp wastes, kraft pulp wastes, bleach plant wastes and groundwood, woodroom and paper-machine wastes. Spent sulphite liquor (SSL) comes from the sulphite process. It has high oxygen-consuming properties and, on a population-equivalent basis, the oxygen consumption of effluent from a 500 ton/day sulphite mill may be equivalent to that of sewage from 2 M people. Kraft mill and bleach plant effluents have not such a high BOD as spent sulphite liquor. Wastes from mechanical pulping and other non-chemical wood processing are harmful to the aquatic environment because of the high concentrations of suspended particulate materials. There is a nominal BOD associated with groundwood wastes arising from decomposition of raw organic constituents leached from the wood.

The rate at which a particular type of effluent is able, in the presence of ample oxygen, to satisfy its oxygen demand depends on what it contains. Industrial effluents that contain only chemical reducing agents, such as ferrous salts or sulphides, take up oxygen by purely chemical action; they do this very rapidly, exerting what is sometimes known as immediate oxygen demand. Organic substances such as starch, sewage and milk waste become oxidized only by the activities of bacteria. The rate at which they were broken down therefore depends at first on the presence of suitable bacteria, and secondly on how satisfactory and balanced a food they are for microorganisms. Sterile effluents such as phenols take some time to build up a suitable bacterial flora and, if they are very uniform in composition, they may contain inadequate amounts of some substances needed for bacterial growth, such as phosphates, even after they have been mixed with river water. Sewage of course is well inoculated with bacteria and is adequately supplied with a wide range of compounds, so it gets broken down relatively easily. But some materials such as wood pulp are very poor bacterial foods and are decomposed very slowly. They therefore exert a lower oxygen demand but for a long time, and in the aggregate it may be very great.

The oxygen can only be returned to the water by aeration at the surface or by the photosynthetic activities of green plants. This reoxygenation of the water may be slowed by the presence of a thin film of oil on the water surface; a thick film may prevent it. Synthetic detergents also affect the uptake of oxygen by creating foam blankets on the water surface. The same is true of foaming in effluents from chemical pulping.

Hynes (1960) has pointed out that weirs that isolate artificial bypasses, and which allow water to pass only at times of flood, may exert devastating effect on the oxygen regime of the river below them at certain times. The isolated reach may become filled with water at flood time, and this water is often more polluted than usual, because at times of heavy rainfall many sewage works are unable to handle the extra runoff from roads and roof drains and so pass untreated sewage out through 'storm overflows'. Normally this has little effect because the discharge is at a time of high water and maximum dilution, but if such water is then impounded and left to stagnate it rapidly putrefies. Because of the absence of flow and turbulence its rate of oxygen uptake is low and the water becomes totally deoxygenated; anaerobic bacteria then take over and reduce the nitrates to ammonia and then the sulphates to sulphides. Thus a mass of water is formed which is not only deoxygenated but which contains poisons and has a heavy oxygen debt; when a sudden flood such as a summer thunderstorm occurs it is suddenly pushed into the river and passes downstream as a more or less discrete 'plug'. The sudden death of thousands of fish, particularly in hot weather, can often be attributed to this sort of cause, and it may appear as if there has been a 'spill' or some other failure at a treatment plant when in fact everything is functioning normally.

Where conditions are so extreme that there is hardly any oxygen there may be no organisms present except bacteria, but generally the river bed is carpeted with sewage fungus and colonized by small red worms known as Tubificidae and red midge larvae (Chironomidae). As conditions become less severe algae grow among the sewage fungus and eventually replace it; leeches, water slaters and snails are present. As the effects of pollution diminish, a fauna and flora similar to that of the unpolluted stream will reappear and eventually replace the pollution-tolerant organisms. This is the normal succession as one passes downstream from the source of pollution provided new sources do not occur on the way, and it indicates recovery of the river. A bad effluent allows only sewage fungus and worms to exist; a better effluent or greater dilution may produce algal growths, leeches and water slaters; a good effluent or considerable dilution may do no more than increase the productivity, in animal and plant life, of the stream into which it is discharged.

### Farm wastes

One of the main causes of deoxygenation in some rivers is farm waste in the form of slurry from dairy farms and piggeries and silage liquor, and this source of pollution appears to be increasing. In 1986, dairy farms in England and

Wales made up the bulk of offenders with 2400 incidents out of a total of 3427. In one area of Wales, Howells and Merriman (1986) refer to the death of at least 110 000 salmonids in 1983 from farm waste discharges. James (1986) lists a number of fish mortalities resulting from farm wastes in all parts of Wales: (a) in 1982 one slurry discharge affected 12 km of river, killing 5000 juvenile salmon, 120 adult sea trout and 17 000 brown trout; (b) in 1983, when an estimated 110 000 fish were killed by farm wastes in west Wales alone, there were 22 incidents affecting 71.6 km of river, killing about 2500 adult salmon and sea trout, 47 300 juveniles, 281 000 brown trout and 38 000 fry; (c) in 1984 the River Ystwyth, recovering from the effects of zinc and lead pollution, suffered a kill of 5000 fish from a discharge of farm slurry.

In south-west England, Merry (1985) also refers to increases in fish kills caused by farm wastes. In one incident in 1982, 32 km of the River Axe were affected and in 1983 50 000 fish were killed in two separate incidents on the River Torridge. Salmonid spawning areas have been rendered useless, so that even cattle will not drink from those parts of the stream, and surveys have shown salmonid fry to be absent from large areas in headwaters where they were previously widespread and abundant.

However, Kennedy (1987) considers that Northern Ireland is proportionately the worst area in Britain for silage pollution offences. He investigated (1985) the cost of fish kills from silage pollution incidents and estimated the mean cost per silage incident in the River Bush in 1983 at £1820 in terms of replacing the fish; the mean potential loss was approximately £15 510.

These pollution incidents usually result from the inadequate storage of farm slurry in tanks and lagoons. Often the pollution occurs after heavy rain or thunderstorms when slurry ponds or lagoons burst their banks and tanks overflow. Silage liquor is a very corrosive liquid and will often leak from clamps and towers into streams. Taylor and Brownlie (1982), in a survey of 100 silos/clamps in Scotland, found that all had some fault that caused leakage.

One way of overcoming the farm waste problem is greater publicity and awareness among the farming community and more available advice. To this end, the South-west Water Authority in England has produced explanatory leaflets for the farmers and visits are arranged to explain the situation. This is no mean task as there are more than 15 000 farms in the water authority's area. So a pilot scheme was started to deal with small parts of the Taw, Torridge, Axe and other catchments with known farm drainage problems. The scheme was supported fully by agricultural interests such as the Country Landowners' Association, the Agricultural Development Advisory Service (ADAS), the National Farmers' Union and the Farming, Forestry and Wildlife Advisory Group (FFWAG).

Howells and Merriman (1986) put forward the following remedies which, if these objectives were achieved, would result in a better appreciation by the farmers of the need for proper handling and storage of wastes and better installation of suitable systems at the outset of any improvement scheme; (a) full consultation at the planning stage, (b) farmers should be fully informed of the polluting nature of farm wastes, including chemicals, and the best ways to contain, dispose of, or treat these wastes to minimize pollution, (c) measures to store and dispose of waste materials on farms should be eligible for grant aid.

In a report on *Water Pollution from Farm Wastes* (Anon., 1987b) published by the Water Authorities Association and the Ministry of Agriculture, Fisheries and Food, reference is made to the very low fines that are generally given by magistrates for pollution offences. It draws attention to advice to magistrates from former Lord Chancellor Lord Hailsham, who suggested they regard the maximum fine of £2000 as a starting point for farm pollution offences. Fines for pollution by farmers during 1986 ranged from £50 to £1600 (Anon., 1987c).

However, to be more constructive one should be considering how to reduce the volume of farm wastes to be stored or treated. One approach is the recycling of these wastes for animal feed and Lowman, Henderson and Lewis (1983) have investigated feeding silage effluent to farm animals. They found the silage effluent can be fed successfully to cattle, and 20 l have a similar feed value to 1 kg of barley. Silage effluent can also be avoided almost completely by the baler wrapping of silage in 'cling film' type material.

### Fish farm effluents
Fish farms can affect fisheries by causing changes in water quality which may influence the composition of the invertebrate fauna. Solbé (1982) recorded a number of changes which occurred to water during its passage through a fish farm. On average, the dissolved oxygen concentration fell by 1.6 mg/l and there were increases in biochemical oxygen demand of 1.5 mg/l. Although these are relatively small changes the mass flows from the farms he sampled were large enough to change the concentration in the receiving waters. A decrease in dissolved oxygen of 0.3 mg/l occurred in the river and there were increases in BOD of 0.7 mg/l. Suspended-solid loads also increased significantly and the net mass outflow of suspended solids per tonne of fish produced has ranged from 1.35 t in 1980 to 0.55 t in 1987 (Solbé, 1987).

### Iron-bearing mine waters
Discharges of acid ferruginous waters to a number of Scottish rivers have been responsible for leaving them fishless and beyond immediate restoration. In some instances these discharges, which frequently emanate from disused mines, have led to mass mortalities of adult salmon.

When ferruginous water reaches a watercourse the rise in pH and the presence of atmospheric oxygen bring about a hydrolysis, with the production of the typical orange precipitate known as 'iron ochre' which is mainly amorphous ferric hydroxide. Much of the precipitation of iron is brought about by a purely chemical process of oxidation but the deposits on stones and boulders also result from the activity of enormous growths of the sheath bacterium *Leptothrix ochraceae.*

Hammerton (1986) describes a serious pollution incident resulting when acid mine water from the Dalquharran Colliery in Ayrshire broke out from the old mineshaft 2 years after the mine was closed and effectively ruined the River Girvan, one of the best salmon rivers in Ayrshire. Within 24 hours all fish in the 16 km stretch of the river downstream to the sea were killed, including many salmon up to 6.8 kg in weight. After lengthy negotiations between the Clyde River Purification Board and the National Coal Board, which after a long legal battle was held responsible for the pollution, a solution to the problem was reached. This consisted of (a) a dam at the mine outlet with control works to regulate the flow from the mine, (b) injection of lime and sodium hydroxide to precipitate the iron deep inside the old workings, and (c) diversion of all surface waters which were entering the mine. The result has been a success and the Girvan is once more a productive salmon river.

## Oil

Oil spills may cause fish mortalities, but usually they do no more than contaminate or taint the flesh of fish. Elson *et al.* (1973) refer to frequent oil spills in the Miramichi estuary and mention periodic complaints of oil-tainted salmon. Similar observations have been made about the condition of salmon caught in the Forth estuary in Scotland, which is not surprising with the large Grangemouth oil refinery being sited on its shores.

Occasionally large fish mortalities do occur from oil spills. An accident to a storage tank containing flux oil (a mixture of creosote and diesel oil) resulted in 4000 gallons of the liquid entering the River Tees in north-east England and killing all fish in its path as it was carried down to the sea. Unlike other oils, which can be contained by floating booms, flux oil does not float on the surface but disperses in water and becomes invisible. The estimates of dead fish included 48 000 brown trout, 300 adult salmon, 250 juveniles and 200 sea trout. In addition, it was estimated that about 5 M brown trout ova, 1.5 M salmon ova and 0.25 M sea trout ova were destroyed.

## Radioactive waste

The problem of pollution of the aquatic environment with radioactive waste, usually in the form of fission and activation products, is not one of fish mortalities, but of the accumulation of these products in the flesh of the fish. On the River Meuse in Belgium, where two nuclear power stations are sited and where salmon restoration is being planned, caesium-137 ($^{137}Cs$) is concentrated in the muscles, skeleton and internal organs of the indigenous fish species – roach, houting (*Coregonus oxyrinchus*), chub, bream and perch (Genin-Meurisse and Micha, 1981).

Hunt (1983) in a survey of radioactivity in the surface and coastal waters of the British Isles recorded the mean radioactivity concentration in a number of fish species. The mean radioactivity concentration (wet) for salmon in the vicinity of Chapelcross Nuclear Power Station, Dumfriesshire, in 1981 was 2.6 Bq/kg (Becquerels per kilogram) of $^{137}$Cs. This is a low value when one compares it with the values obtained from rainbow trout (68 Bq/kg $^{137}$CS) and brown trout (610 Bq/kg $^{137}$Cs) near Trawsfynydd Nuclear Power Station on the shore of Llyn Trawsfynydd in North Wales.

R. Scott (personal communication) measured the concentrations of caesium-137 in salmon and sea trout from the Border Esk which flows into the Solway Firth and obtained values of 12.1 and 7.7 picocuries (pCi)/g respectively. The values obtained from sea trout from the River Tweed (on the opposite side of Scotland) were only 0.45 pCi/g. These values are low and would be unlikely to affect the health of human beings.

As a result of the Chernobyl disaster, levels of radioactivity in salmonids in parts of north-west England and south-west Scotland have increased. In 1986 the average value for total caesium ($^{134}$Cs and $^{137}$Cs) for 20 brown trout in Loweswater (Lake District) was 1130 Bq/kg and for 28 brown trout in Ennerdale 730 Bq/kg. In south-west Scotland the values for samples of trout from Loch Doon and Loch Dee were 580 Bq/kg and 1890 Bq/kg. Many other sites in the west of Scotland gave values of 300–1000 Bq/kg. Values for adult salmon were very much lower and were of the order of 10 Bq/kg. Not many salmon parr were analysed, but a sample of parr from the River Nith in south-west Scotland gave values of between 107 and 121 Bq/kg.

The acceptable limit in lamb in Britain is 1000 Bq/kg, but the EEC limit is 600 Bq/kg and in Sweden 300 Bq/kg. Some figures for Loch Dee trout in 1987 not yet published officially show averages of 2400 and 2770 Bq/kg, with one fish as high as 4030 Bq/kg, a year after Chernobyl! (Anon., 1988c).

## 11.2    ACIDIFICATION

The acidification of lakes and rivers is caused mainly by acid precipitation in the form of what is referred to as acid rain, and also as 'dry' deposition. Salmon and trout are particularly sensitive to acidic water and it has been shown to have a detrimental effect on stocks of both salmon and trout (Jensen and Snekvik, 1972; Schofield, 1976; Leivestad *et al.*, 1976; Sevaldrud *et al.*, 1980; Muniz, 1981; Rosseland *et al.*, 1986a). Atlantic salmon in the rivers of southern Norway were probably the first to be affected by such acid deposition (Huitefeldt-Kaas, 1922; Dahl, 1927) (Fig. 11.1). Although Smith recorded its damaging effects on plants in 1872, the decline in salmon stocks in Norway's

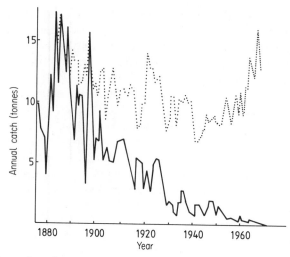

**Fig. 11.1**   Annual catches of salmon from the acidic Tøvdal River in Sorlandet (solid curve) compared with the total from 79 other Norwegian salmon rivers (broken curve) (reproduced with permission from Wright *et al.*, 1975).

southernmost rivers probably started before the end of the last century (Hesthagen and Mjdell-Larsen, 1987). The estimate of sulphur dioxide emissions based on consumption of fossil fuels in Europe was already relatively high in 1900, compared with the next 50 years (Dovland and Semb, 1980) and Hesthagen and Larsen (1988) consider that this indicates that effects on Atlantic salmon due to acidification was in progress in river systems in southernmost Norway before the beginning of this century. For example, in the autumn of 1920, there was a high mortality of adult salmon and trout in three rivers in southern Norway. Subsequently, acidification has been recorded affecting salmonid stocks in Sweden (Dickson, 1978), Canada (Watt, 1981), the United States (Haines, 1981) and the United Kingdom (Harriman and Morrison, 1982; Stoner, Gee and Wade, 1984).

   The main causes of acid deposition are the emissions of the gaseous oxides of sulphur and nitrogen. Sulphur oxides are produced by the burning of fossil fuels and emanate chiefly from the tall chimney stacks of power stations, smelters, refineries and chemical works. The oxides of nitrogen are produced by the oxidation of atmospheric nitrogen at high temperatures in the stacks. The 'dry' deposition consists of sulphate particles which settle on such substrates as the needles of coniferous trees and snowfields. When this dry deposition reaches the soil and lakes and rivers in solution when snow melts and after heavy rain following a prolonged drought, the pH values drop dramatically. Acidity of rain has also been shown to be greatly altered within the coniferous forests: the water flowing down the trunks (stemflow) is increased on average by a factor of eight. It has also been found that when liquid manure is sprayed on fields much of the nitrogen disappears in the air and is transformed by combining with sulphur dioxide in the air into a rain of dilute sulphate of ammonia. This may also be deposited on trees in a dry form, later to be washed onto the ground.

The primary water-quality changes resulting from acidification are (a) a change in the capacity of the soil to buffer or neutralize the acid and (b) a decreased pH and an increased mobility of toxic metals. When the pH drops below 5.0 a different buffering system in the soil becomes activated and deposits of aluminium become more soluble and are leached into the water. It is the inorganic monomeric aluminium which is particularly toxic to fish. So, in addition to the direct effects of pH on fish physiology, one has the toxic effects of aluminium which is especially toxic to fish and other aquatic organisms at levels of pH which on their own would not be harmful. Several studies have shown that young stages of salmon are very sensitive to acid aluminium-rich water low in calcium (Rosseland *et al.*, 1986a). In North America however, many salmon rivers are relatively high in dissolved organic carbon, with concentrations of 5 to 15 mg/l or more. As a result, virtually all of the total aluminium in the water is in the organically bound, non-toxic form. Therefore aluminium toxicity is probably negligible and most toxicity is the result of hydrogen ion stress alone.

The eggs and alevins are highly sensitive to acidification and cannot tolerate a pH of much less than 4.5. Low pH affects the reproductive function of fish, their gill performance and respiration and also the regulation of body salts. Fertilization and water hardening are the most sensitive stages in early egg development. Hatching of eggs can be delayed and inhibited by depressed pH conditions. In field experiments hatching has been shown to be positively correlated with the pH of redd interstitial water (LaCroix, 1985). Four study sites with mean pH of 4.92, 4.77, 4.72 and 4.64 had mean percentage survivals of 77.8, 53.5, 53.3 and 45.5% respectively. The threshold for direct alevin mortality lies between pH levels of 5.0, where mortalities are negligible and 4.5, where mortalities are near 30% (Peterson and Martin-Robichaud, 1986). Salmon alevins also show reduced rates of yolk utilization and reduced conversion efficiencies so that they are smaller at swim-up stage and may take longer to reach this stage (Peterson and Martin-Robichaud, 1986).

The later juvenile stages are all sensitive to acidic water. Short-term pH depressions of a few days during snow melt have caused high mortalities of overwintering parr in southern and western Norwegian rivers (Hesthagen, 1986; Hesthagen and Larsen, 1988) (Fig. 11.2). Production of salmon fry in the Högvadsen River on the Swedish west coast was normal during the 1970s. However, mortalities of overwintering parr and pre-smolts were high and the smolt migration was nearly eliminated during this period (Edman and Fleicher, 1980).

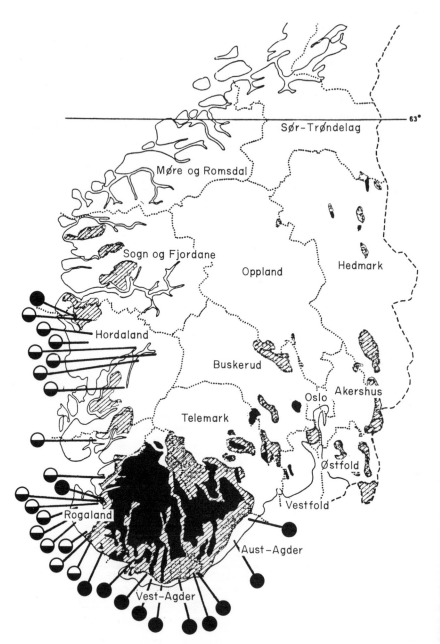

**Fig. 11.2** Location of rivers in Agder, Rogaland and Hordaland counties (Norway) which have lost or reduced salmon stocks according to official catch statistics. Black areas and filled circles indicate lost fish stocks; shaded areas and half-filled circles indicate reduced stocks (reproduced with permission from Sevaldrud and Muniz, 1980).

Adult salmon are also affected by acidification. An increased mortality of overwintering adults may occur in rivers with pH depressions during spring snow melt; dead salmon have been recorded at this time from the Vikedal River in Norway. Even if no adults are killed acidification has been recorded as having an effect on their physiology. Wild male salmon captured at the Westfield River, Nova Scotia, counting fence had much lower 11-keto-testosterone levels than fish in a neighbouring hatchery (Freeman *et al.*, 1983). Salmon held in cages at this acidic river (pH 5.14–4.83) produced fewer and smaller eggs, had higher egg mortalities and had abnormal male sex hormone metabolism, all compared to fish held under similar conditions in a more neutral river (Freeman and Sangalang, 1985).

The countries whose salmon are most under threat from acidification are Norway and Sweden and Hesthagen and Larsen (1988) have estimated the annual loss of adult Atlantic salmon in Norway due to acidification (Table 11.1). The estimated annual loss in weight ranged from 153 000 to 918 000 kg. In Scotland, only two or three salmon rivers in south-west and central Scotland have reached pH levels which could affect existing stocks, while in Wales it is mainly the upland areas that have been affected. In these latter two countries, the trout populations in the lakes in these regions have declined dramatically and in some instances have become extinct. (Maitland *et al.*, 1987; Stoner, Gee and Wade, 1984; Harriman and Morrison, 1982; Harriman and Wells, 1985). A survey of water chemistry in the Atlantic salmon rivers of Canada's Maritime Provinces (Watt, 1981) revealed that the only severely acidified areas in the Maritimes were in the Southern Upland zone of Nova Scotia. In the United States, the majority of the accessible Atlantic salmon habitat is not vulnerable to damage from atmospheric acid deposition at present loading rates. However, Haines (1981) has pointed out that there are some tributary streams, most not presently accessible to returning adult fish, that may reach pH levels during periods of high discharge that are critical for survival of sensitive Atlantic salmon stages. These streams are tributaries of the Narraguagus River and the Connecticut River.

**Table 11.1** Estimated loss of Atlantic salmon in Norway, due to acidification in Norway, by number and weight (kg), based on production values of 4, 6 and 8 smolts per 100 m² and at three different survival levels*

| Smolt loss | 10% survival | | 20% survival | | 30% survival | |
|---|---|---|---|---|---|---|
| | Number | Weight (kg) | Number | Weight (kg) | Number | Weight (kg) |
| 408 000 | 40 800 | 153 000 | 81 600 | 306 000 | 122 400 | 465 000 |
| 612 000 | 61 200 | 229 500 | 122 400 | 459 000 | 183 600 | 688 500 |
| 816 000 | 81 600 | 306 000 | 163 200 | 612 000 | 244 800 | 918 000 |

*Source: Hesthagen and Larsen (1988).*

Liming of acidified waters, both streams and lakes, is now carried out in Scandinavia, Scotland and North America. In Sweden, liming was used to increase fish survival in acid lakes from the early 1960s. A 5-year governmental liming programme was started in 1977 and a national liming programme commenced in 1982 with government subsidies being as much as 100% in the case of salmon and sea trout rivers. The main liming agent was finely ground limestone. The best biological response after liming of rivers was obtained when headwater lakes were treated to avoid acid episodes (Andersson *et al.*, 1984).

Limestone filters were installed in salmon hatcheries in southern Norway as long ago as the early 1920s to counteract acidity. In 1979 a liming project was initiated in order to investigate the biological effects, technical possibilities and economical considerations for liming lakes and rivers in Norway (Abrahamsen and Matzow, 1984). Limestone slurry proved to be an effective substance for reducing physiological stress and increasing survival of salmon fry, parr and smolts. The addition of the limestone slurry increased pH from 4.6 to 6.9, increased calcium from 0.6 to 2.6 mg/l, and reduced the labile aluminium concentration from 59 to 35 $\mu$g/l immediately downstream of the liming site (20 m after 30 s) (Rosseland *et al.*, 1986b). A liming project is presently being carried out in the River Audna in southern Norway, where the natural salmon stock has been exterminated by acidification. This project uses dry pulverized calcium carbonate, which is mixed with water before release into the river. A similar project started in the River Vikedal in early 1987. Hesthagen and Mjdell-Larsen (1987), although recognizing that the period during spring snow melt is the most critical with regard to survival of the young stages of the salmon and that liming is most important during these episodes with increased and high river discharges, point out that acid episodes may also occur during the late autumn (Henriksen *et al.*, 1984).

In Scotland, liming has been carried out on Loch Fleet (Howells, 1986) and Loch Dee (Tervet and Harriman, 1988) with a consequent increase in calcium levels. However, Tervet and Harriman (1988) noted that in Loch Dee 50% of the limestone, added as powder to Loch Dee via the major inflow stream, was lost at the loch outflow. Within two years calcium concentrations and pH had returned to pre-liming levels. These results suggest that, in sensitive rapid-turnover lochs, the addition of limestone will be at least an annual requirement if water quality is to be maintained at levels desirable for a viable fishery. The better procedure is, as was carried out on Loch Fleet, to put the limestone on the surrounding land, including the neighbouring bogs. This has been most successful and has maintained the calcium levels which, in fact, rise during periods of heavy rain.

There has been no liming of salmon rivers in the United States but in Canada investigations using limestone to restore salmon production in acidified rivers were first started in the early 1980s in Nova Scotia. The two methods employed were (a) *in situ* gravel deposits in rivers and (b) the addition of powdered limestone to headwater lakes to protect downstream habitat. A liming project began on the East River system in Nova Scotia in the late 1980s.

An evaluation of techniques for limestone application to acid river systems in both Europe and North America indicates that the best liming techniques are applications to headwater lakes. If the river system has few lakes, then limestone application to wetlands and direct dosing of the river water are the best methods.

Liming is an expensive temporary measure to counteract the effects of acidification. The only permanent solution is to get to the root cause and either to reduce the level of sulphur and nitrogen oxide emissions by incorporating expensive 'scrubbers' or 'washers' to clean the emissions, or reducing the number of coal-burning plants. All three of these options raise economic and political problems. Fortunately a number of countries are taking their emission-control programmes seriously.

It is worth stressing at this point that changes in the environment can affect the genetics of wild populations. First, by depressing the effective size of the population, which causes a loss of genetic diversity; and secondly by natural selection for increased fitness in the new environment. Kapuscinski and Jacobson (1987) point out that depression of effective population size (leading to increased inbreeding, increased genetic drift and loss of genetic diversity) is a certain consequence of environmental changes that reduce habitat size (e.g. obstruction of spawning streams), kill fish (e.g. pollution) or limit reproductive success (e.g. acid rain). Population fitness may be reduced by a major change in habitat because characteristics that maximize fitness in the old environment may not maximize fitness in the new environment. Natural selection for increased fitness in the new environment is, for this reason, a certain consequence of major habitat alterations. However, as Kapuscinski and Jacobson (1987) state, a number of related consequences should be kept in mind. Fish adapted to a new environment (e.g. tolerant of polluted water) may not be desirable for human consumption. Productivity of the population may remain low even after elapses before the population adapts to the new environment.

# CHAPTER TWELVE

# Afforestation and land drainage

The upland areas of many salmon-producing countries have been extensively afforested and continued expansion in afforestation over the next few decades is expected. It is in these upland areas that many salmon rivers begin, arising from an extensive network of small fast-flowing tributaries which serve as the spawning and nursery areas. These upland areas are invaluable to the river system, and the degradation of their abundant, clean, cool, well-aerated and silt-free waters would lead to the loss of much of the area upon which salmon depend for the survival of their young. It is not always realized that even the smallest of these streams, some little more than 1 m wide, can be important. Often salmon will penetrate these channels to spawn. It is therefore important to appreciate how delicate the natural balance is when considering forest management practices which could affect the aquatic environment.

## 12.1   EFFECTS OF FOREST MANAGEMENT AND THEIR CONTROL

### Ploughing and drainage

Sedimentation from the erosion of plough furrows, drainage channels and roads on steep hillsides has detrimental effects on the salmon and its habitat. (a) The ova in the gravel may be smothered and killed due to lack of dissolved oxygen in the interstitial water. For example, Mills (1967) recorded a 50% mortality of eyed ova planted out in plastic-slatted Vibert boxes in a forest stream and Hall and Lantz (1968) noted that about 30% of coho salmon (*Oncorhynchus kisutch*) ova and fry died in redds containing 15% sand and silt and all died when levels reach 32%. (b) Sediment can fill in the spaces among the gravel and stones reducing the amount of cover for small fish and (c) sand, silt and heavier eroded material carried downstream can fill in pools thus reducing their depth and making them unsuitable as holding pools for adult fish and (d) the blanketing of the stony substrate with silt reduces the invertebrate population upon which the young fish feed. (e) Suspended solids can affect fish at high concentrations (Alabaster and Lloyd, 1980) and it has been estimated that 20 mg/l of suspended solids would cause 25% mortality of sockeye salmon (*Oncorhynchus nerka*) ova and fry in redds and 200 mg/l would cause 100% mortality.

Although drainage channels may at first prevent flooding by reducing surface runoff they will, during periods of heavy or continuous rain and when the surrounding land is saturated, produce very sudden floods of a short duration resulting in serious erosion.

Sediment yield is increased by drainage ditches that discharge into natural watercourses from ploughed areas. This is not a temporary phenomenon, because the banks of overplanted watercourses become devoid of vegetation, thus increasing bank erosion. Erosion and sedimentation are also increased by damage to stream banks by machinery during forestry operations, and by the inevitable build-up of brash or 'lop and top' and other debris in streams after thinning and clear-felling.

Alignment of ploughing along the contour was once favoured and is still occasionally practised. It is now felt that this is inappropriate in wetland situations, since each furrow tends to 'pond' surface runoff and gives rise to lines of stagnant conditions. Alignments are now made to run roughly up and down the slope to improve runoff and to provide pathways for downhill seepage when the furrows become filled with plant litter. The risk of severe erosion has been shown to be small, provided that cut-off drains are used and that individual furrows are not used to carry water drainage from large areas lying above. The current policy of varying the lines of ploughing for landscape reasons or interrupting them on fragile areas further diminishes the risk from erosion. The alignment of the deep drains intended to collect water from the superficial furrows and from the subsoil should be nearly parallel with the contour, consistent with maintaining a suitable drain gradient (Taylor, 1970). A drain with a gentle gradient of no more than 2° is ideal and generally accords with normal forest practice. Except at the start of the drain, gradients steeper than 3° should be avoided to prevent severe erosion. The alignment of the drain should be designed to achieve the maximum interception effect with the minimum drain length. In order to catch silt where drains are leading to streams or small watercourses, they should either be tapered in depth and stopped 15–20 m short in order that the water discharging from these drains has to filter through the ground vegetation or, in areas of higher rainfall, a sump should be taken out just before the drain opens into the watercourse. On the very steep slopes where it is not possible to put in the cut-off drain, it is suggested that a large V-type sump drain should be cut along the bottom of the slope to trap debris carried down the plough furrows (Graesser, 1979). At no time should plough furrows intercept natural drains and small watercourses as this could lead to ponding and diversion of the watercourse down the furrows, resulting in accelerated erosion.

From time to time it may be necessary to clean out certain drains within the forest if waterlogging is evident. This operation should be very carefully timed so that little silt enters the watercourses to affect the stream bed and bank habitats. For this reason it is important not to clean out drains during the period mid-October to mid-May, if possible, as during this time the eggs, and latterly the alevins, are in the gravel and would be suffocated by the silt. The time of the early autumn floods would be the most suitable for cleaning drains, but care should be taken to remove as much of the silt and leaf litter as possible from the drain and deposit it on dry land some distance away from any watercourse.

## Road construction

Road building may initially cause erosion, sometimes severe, until the exposed soil and tracks have become stabilized. Even then there may be considerable surface runoff in very wet weather and the only solution is to have a road with an asphalt surface. Missing or badly-positioned culverts may hinder or prohibit fish ascent. Proper drainage should be incorporated into the road construction to minimize erosion on the road surface, on the slopes and in the ditches. In order to achieve this the following steps are usually necessary:

1. Water from roadside drains should be discharged into watercourses at frequent intervals, culverts being provided where necessary;
2. Drainage structures should be big enough to accommodate runoff from the drainage areas;
3. Where ditches drain directly into permanent watercourses, a sump to trap silt and debris may be necessary;
4. Special erosion-control measures may be required on roadside banks including such measures as intercepting trenches or terracing: bare earth embankments and cuttings should be left at the natural angle of repose to encourage the establishment of vegetation;
5. Culverts should be rip-rapped as necessary, to prevent erosion at both inflow and outflow ends: this is done by reinforcing the substrate at each end and reducing flow velocities;
6. The outflow ends of hanging culverts should be provided with flumes or other suitable drains where necessary; rock or concrete aprons should be provided as stilling areas to decrease water velocity and prevent stream-bed erosion;
7. Culverts or other drainage devices should be placed so as to attain a maximum drainage efficiency;
8. Whenever possible culverts should be installed so as to allow passage of fish on all watercourses frequented by them;
9. The inverts (ends) of culverts should be laid to be self-cleansing and properly bedded to avoid settlement. The size of the culvert will depend on

**Fig. 12.1**     A series of pools created on a steep slope leading up to a culvert facilitate the passage of fish (reproduced with permission from Lugmayr, 1984).

the characteristics of the catchment area and the natural watercourses. Lugmayr (1984) describes an excellent structure to incorporate in the floor of culverts and any steep slope leading up to the culverts, to produce a series of pools to facilitate the passage of fish (Fig. 12.1).

Water crossings for heavy vehicles and forest machinery should not be used at high flows and care must always be taken to avoid oil spillage. Fords are sometimes used as spawning grounds by salmon.

Where it is necessary to extract gravel from a watercourse it is essential that this is done in amounts and at a period which will minimize damage to fish, especially migratory fish. Consultations with the river authority, the riparian owner and tenants are advisable. It is essential that the stability of the stream bed is subsequently restored.

If any construction work is planned which involves the use of concrete – such as in road-works, bank reinforcement and bridge building – care must be taken to ensure that no cement flour or raw concrete enters the watercourse. A number of serious fish mortalities have resulted from the careless use of cement, which is toxic to fish.

### Planting

Changes in the flow regime of streams, as well as being affected by drainage, are further accentuated by higher water use by a forest through transpiration;

it has been shown that trees can, under certain conditions, intercept substantially more water than open moorland in areas of high rainfall (Gash *et al.*, 1978).

Planting of conifers close to the edges of streams has seriously affected the streams' productivity. Planting has led to a paucity of insect life and fish in streams which flow through mature forest because a dense tree canopy prevents the growth of ground vegetation (Mills, 1967; Smith, 1980). Basically, the protection of stream banks requires the establishment of permanent reserve strips of vegetation. Valley topography, soil and aesthetic factors will usually help to define the area and shape of reserve strip required. Before considering the scale and the nature of the bank vegetation the importance of streamside vegetation should be stressed, as it (a) shades water, stream bed and stream bank from the sun's heat, (b) provides energy to the stream through leaf fall, terrestrial insect drop and dissolved nutrients, (c) gives protective cover for fish, (d) protects the stream banks from channel erosion, erosion from overland runoff, and the erosive effects of precipitation impact, (e) acts as a buffer against debris from overland runoff, and (f) intercepts toxic materials from spraying (Burns, 1970). Removal of streamside vegetation can facilitate increases in the temperature of streams which may then reach a lethal point for salmon and trout (Brown, 1971; Hall and Lantz, 1968).

Terrestrial insects have been shown to make up 5–65% of the diet of trout and salmon in some streams. Most of these insects come from streamside vegetation and its removal reduces the number available to trout and salmon, as well as to birds and some other animals.

Cover is important in providing hiding places for fish and it has been shown that the removal of bank vegetation and other shelter can destroy trout streams (Warner and Porter, 1960). It has been found that larger brown trout were 27% more numerous and weighed 44% more in a sheltered section of stream than in a non-sheltered section (Gunderson, 1968), while trout were found to be 78% more abundant in well-covered mountain streams than in an area where cover had been removed.

Vegetation on the stream banks also helps to maintain deep pools by preventing lateral erosion, which results in a wider but shallower stream channel (Johnson, 1953). Adverse effects can be reversed or minimized by the introduction of reserve strips, or unafforested buffer zones, between the plantation and the banks of every natural watercourse. Within the reserve areas tree planting should be kept to the minimum required for landscape reasons; in addition, heavy machinery should be confined as far as possible to defined roads and tracks. The widths of the reserve areas of vegetation will vary with the land form, but as a rough guide the overall width (sum of both sides) could be ten times the width of the stream, up to a maximum of 30 m overall. These areas may seem unnecessarily large but they will also help to counteract the effects of precipitation interception. Furthermore, they give easy access for anglers, walkers and forestry staff.

Drakeford (1981) determined the width of areas on the basis of their functions, as follows:

1. To prevent direct fall of coniferous litter into watercourses;
2. To allow sunlight to penetrate to the stream and its banks;
3. To prevent damage to stream banks by machinery and felling operations;
4. To allow the colonization of the banks by natural vegetation (deciduous scrub) and so enhance food supply;
5. To prevent direct discharge of ditches into streams, thus reducing sediment input and any acid pulse;
6. To allow liming of streams, stream banks and ditch discharges, should this prove necessary.

It was considered that conditions (1) and (4) could normally be fulfilled by a zone of 5 m width on each bank. However, for (1) and (2), the extent of the zone would depend on the height of the crop, which is determined by the windthrow hazard (i.e. the risk of being uprooted by wind). In areas of low windthrow hazard the zone width was doubled. The fulfilment of condition (5) meant the blocking of ditch entries at the stream banks. This causes flooding back from the blockage which can damage roots and so induce windthrow. The cropless buffer zone therefore has to extend as far as the flood, which depends upon topography (Table 12.1).

Streamside vegetation can be encouraged to provide shade as a source of food for both fish and aquatic invertebrates. This can consist of ordinary ground vegetation and small deciduous tree species such as birch (*Betula* spp.),

**Table 12.1**   The extent of flooding backing up blocked ditches on sloping ground

| Slope (degrees) | Ditch depth (m) | Extent of flood (m) |
|---|---|---|
| 1 | 1 | 57.3 |
| 2 | 1 | 28.6 |
| 3 | 1 | 19.1 |
| 4 | 1 | 14.3 |
| 5 | 1 | 11.4 |
| 10 | 1 | 5.8 |
| 1 | 0.5 | 28.6 |
| 2 | 0.5 | 14.3 |
| 3 | 0.5 | 9.5 |
| 4 | 0.5 | 7.2 |
| 5 | 0.5 | 5.7 |
| 10 | 0.5 | 2.8 |

willow (*Salix* spp.), rowan (*Sorbus aucuparia* L.) or alder (*Alnus* spp.). Alders may also contribute substantial amounts of dissolved nutrients such as nitrates to the stream and it has been found that leaf fall from alders contained four times as much nitrogen as that from other deciduous species (Goldman, 1961). Alder grows vigorously on most streamsides and, to prevent excessive shading and to allow access for recreation and stream management, it should be used in well-scattered groups, especially along streams less than 12 m wide. If willows are used they require regular basal pruning. Their root systems are effective in preventing bank erosion. A variety of other species suitable for water margins have also been suggested (Greer, 1979), including common ash (*Fraxinus excelsior* L.) and aspen (*Populus tremula* L.).

It is often advisable to plant only one bank with deciduous trees to allow access to the stream from at least one side. The side to be planted is the one that will give the most shade to the fish.

Fencing may be required to restrict access to the plantation from streamside. Where fences are needed they should be erected well back from the stream bank and above the flood channel so that they will not catch debris or be washed out during high flows. For this reason, too, fences should be well back from the outside banks of the bends as the stream may soon undermine the fence unless bank-protection devices have been constructed. The fences should be far enough back to allow vegetation control and stream improvements and not to interfere with angling. It must be remembered that some grazing animals can stretch their heads through a fence and graze bare the other side to a distance of about 1 m.

Barbed wire may be required on stock fences but, in any event, stiles should be erected at suitable places. Where livestock must have access to the water, their access should be on gently sloping ground where the stream substrate is hard and the water shallow. Their approach paths, which should be wide enough to prevent bunching up and panic, should be fenced on either side (White and Brynildson, 1975).

Where boundary or accommodation fences or drystone walls cross a watercourse, a water-gate is often necessary to prevent stock passage. Water-gates will vary in design but must always be independent of the fence and may require regular cleaning to prevent stream blockage.

### Spraying

The effects on fish and stream insect populations of improperly controlled forest spraying have been well documented. The spraying of spruce budworm with DDT in New Brunswick did considerable damage to the stocks of young salmon in the Miramichi River watershed (Keenleyside, 1959; Elson, 1967). After the banning of the use of DDT in Canadian forests in 1968 Fenitrothion was used instead. Although this had no direct effects on fish it did reduce some of the aquatic invertebrate populations and thus reduced the food supply for the young salmon, whose growth was consequently reduced (Symons, 1978). It is common knowledge that spraying over watercourses should be avoided if at all possible, and that the correct spray dosages should be used to minimize the damage to fish and wildlife. When agricultural chemicals are used at recommended rates and with due care, the risk to fisheries is relatively small and is limited to certain types of chemicals (Holden, 1964). In the event of accidental spillage or careless disposal of concentrated chemicals, however, the problem is more serious. Exposure of fish for only a few minutes to high concentrations can result in a rapid absorption of the toxicant via the gills and death follows quickly (Frederikson *et al.*, 1975). For this reason no spraying equipment or empty, or partially empty, tins or drums of chemical should be washed out in or near any watercourse, however small, nor should empty containers be punctured and buried. Advice should be sought from the appropriate authority on the safe disposal of unwanted chemicals.

At no time should the roots or foliage of planting stock (such as young trees ready to be planted out) which have been treated with Gammacol be soaked in a watercourse just prior to planting, even if they show signs of distress in hot weather. Gammacol is extremely toxic to fish.

### Application of fertilizers

Leaching of fertilizers into streams in forested catchments has been well recorded (Anderson *et al.*, 1976; Harriman, 1978; Moore, 1974). In some cases this leaching has had little effect on water quality, and in other instances it has been suggested that it could beneficially increase stream productivity. However, leaching into streams running into closed areas of water such as lakes and reservoirs could produce undesirable conditions of eutrophication and for this reason fertilizer programmes should be discussed with water authorities if domestic-supply reservoirs are likely to be affected.

### Fire

In order to provide a ready supply of water for fire-fighting purposes, it is sometimes the practice where the land configuration is suitable to impound small streams and form what are known as 'fire dams'. This purpose can be achieved with less damage to the stream environment if water is diverted into an excavated pond. In this way the stream is kept open along its length and the passage of fish is consequently unhindered. Furthermore, the silt load in the stream is not trapped in the fire dam to lower the dam's capacity and value.

**Thinning, felling and extraction**

There has been considerable research into the effects of these operations on fish and their stream environment, and the probable effects of logging on stream quality; salmon and trout populations in North America have received the most attention (Gibbons and Salo, 1973; Meehan, 1974; Meehan *et al.*, 1969; Ramberg, 1974). The major effects of these activities can be changes in stream flow and water temperature, sedimentation, loss of nutrients, damage to spawning grounds, blockage of streams, prevention of the movement of migratory fish, and bacterial decomposition of any bark and wood debris smothering the stream bed.

Preventing the fall of 'lop and top' into streams is the best way to control the last three mentioned effects. It is vital that trees should be felled away from streams wherever possible. If tree tops and branches do enter a stream they should be removed as soon as possible, certainly no later than when the logs are extracted. Before felling teams move away the stream should be checked to ensure that the 'lop and top' is neither in the stream nor likely to enter the stream on high flows..

When logs are to be moved care should be taken not to break the soil surface of the forest floor unduly, resulting in stream sedimentation. This can be done by avoiding the use of long skid-roads on steep slopes, stacking logs well away from watercourses and not operating heavy equipment in or near streams.

## 12.2 CONCLUSIONS FOR FOREST MANAGEMENT

As Ramberg (1974) points out, the majority of the above-mentioned forestry operations have complex effects upon aquatic environments, and this is particularly marked for clear-felling. This operation alone produces (a) a decrease in transpiration and interception resulting in a change in the flow regime, (b) increased solar radiation leading to higher water temperatures and increased primary production, and (c) nitrification resulting in increased primary production and eutrophication.

Drainage, too, produces a complex combination of effects not all of which are predictable. For example, there is evidence that drainage from some afforested areas is making the neighbouring water more acid and there is considerable proof (Jensen and Snekvik, 1972; Last, 1982) that this increase in their acidity is being hastened by acid rain produced from sulphur dioxide carried with the wind from industrial areas; this is a phenomenon which has already had serious repercussions in salmon rivers in southern Norway and eastern Canada.

If the salmon frequenting afforested areas are to be protected, the types of management practice outlined above must be observed and, in addition, every step must be taken to consider additional stream improvements (Mills, 1980b) which will help increase the numbers of fish.

## 12.3 LAND DRAINAGE

Land drainage, often involving river channel works or channelization, affects many salmon spawning and nursery areas. In these areas land drainage is undertaken to improve farmland by land reclamation and to assist in flood control. For these reasons many streams being modified or 'improved' are straightened to reduce meanders and are dredged to deepen the stream channel so as to accommodate the predicted increased flow.

As a result, there is a reduction in the size and diversity of stream habitat. In-stream cover in the form of boulders and large stones is removed, the pattern of alternating riffles and pools is drastically altered and the substrate is modified. Furthermore, riparian and bank habitat is changed with the loss of vegetation. As a consequence, the initial effect on the stream is to reduce the size of the fish populations and the size and diversity of invertebrate communities. Frequently there is subsequent erosion due to the shape and nature of the realigned banks, and increased water turbidity occurs at high flows, resulting in sedimentation of the stream with similar effects to those occurring in forest streams.

Stewart (1963) refers to the drainage of the fells in the upper reaches of the Ribble in Lancashire. In 1947 small open channels 30.5 cm wide and 23 cm deep were cut in the hills in a herring-bone pattern. By 1963 the main channels had eroded into large drainage channels varying in width from 1.8 m to 3.6 m with depths greater than 1.2 m. Stewart found that the suspended silt flowing down the River Lune during a January spate amounted to 1.5 tons for each 250 000 gallons (1.2 tonnes per million litres).

Wolf (1961) has also shown in the case of the Kävlinge River system in Sweden that, through ditching, canalizing and cultivation of bad as well as good farm land over 150 years, the greater part of the surface water has disappeared. The intensive cultivation of the area has caused every possible bit of land to be drained, ditched and ploughed. Wolf also estimated the amount of topsoil in the catchment area of the Kävlinge River system carried away by flood water. He found that 1 m³ of water contains about 50 g of humus material and about 100 g of minerals. This means that a stream carrying 60 m³ of water per second also carried with it 3 kg of humus material and 6 kg of mineral matter. So in 24 hours about 780 000 kg of soil would be carried downstream.

In the early 1980s a number of farms in the south of Scotland carried out extensive land reclamation involving straightening and deepening of stream channels. On one tributary of the River Tweed, 162 ha of land were reclaimed. An electrofishing survey of this modified section of stream where salmon used to spawn, revealed a total absence of young salmon (Mills and Tomison, 1985). A later survey in 1987 showed that salmon were beginning to recolonize this area. A similar situation occurred on the River Camowen in Co. Tyrone, Northern Ireland, where dredging operations initially reduced densities of young salmon but where there was a subsequent progressive downstream recovery, with fry densities taking up to 6 years to improve at the most downstream site surveyed. However, yearling and older fish recovered to pre-drainage scheme levels more rapidly than fry (Kennedy *et al.*, 1983). The effect of arterial drainage on the Trimblestown River on the Boyne catchment was a change in fish species from predominantly salmonids to small riverine coarse fish species (McCarthy, 1983). Recovery of pre-channelized level of fish stocks may take up to 40 years (Toner, O'Riordan and Twomey, 1965). Dredging of streams can have much more drastic effects. In Finland, for example, dredging for timber floating has altered the natural structure of the river bed of many northern rivers by removing the coarser bottom material and by changing the water flow in the rapids. This has caused extensive damage to the salmon spawning areas. Jutila (1985) recorded mean densities of 1–4 salmon parr per $100 \text{ m}^2$ in the dredged rapids but 6–9 parr per $100 \text{ m}^2$ in the natural areas. He calculated that this resulted in a loss of 10–20 tonnes in the annual salmon catches.

It is not only the juvenile salmon that are affected by these schemes: where stream channelization has been carried out in spawning tributaries of the River Tweed in southern Scotland, many holding pools for adult fish have been filled in with gravel washed downstream due to the unstable conditions arising from dredging.

McCarthy (1985) reviewed the adverse effects of channelization and made recommendations for ameliorating these effects. These remedial measures included:

1. Desedimentation with water jets (raking of the gravel is also effective);
2. Installation of in-stream structures such as random rock clusters, jetties, low dams, weirs, current deflectors and artificial cover structures;
3. Stabilization of the riparian zone through removal of spoil banks and revegetation schemes;
4. Replacement of gravel in riffle habitats;
5. Restocking with fish.

Kennedy (1984b) looked at the ecology of salmonid habitat reinstatement following river drainage schemes in Ireland, and McGrath (1985) considered the rehabilitation works and post drainage activity of arterial drainage schemes in that country and commented on their efficacy.

Although not strictly land drainage, the subject of stream sedimentation from other sources should be mentioned here, as it occurs as a result of other agricultural practices, namely sheep grazing, muir burn and peat working.

In Scotland sheep cause a great deal of erosion by destroying the ground vegetation by grazing. They also contribute to the instability of hill ground and river banks by creating innumerable tracks and narrow paths and by using small knolls and irregularities in the ground and river banks for protection from the weather; these places are gradually worn down until a shallow soil profile is exposed which later increases in width and depth. Fairbairn (1967) and McVean and Lockie (1969) mention just how dangerous this erosion can be by drawing attention to the damage done in the south-east Scotland floods of 1948 and floods in the White Esk, Ettrick, Dulnain and Lochaber areas in 1953.

Muir burn may contribute to erosion and to landslides in certain types of terrain. Muir burn is an age-long practice of rotational firing of heath land, used particularly on hill land to prevent tree regeneration and especially to promote new growth of ling heather (*Calluna vulgaris*) which provides part of the diet of sheep and grouse. The firing is usually carried out in the spring as a basic part of moorland management; as Fairbairn (1967) points out, repeated burning at close intervals may result in the disappearance of herbaceous species, which in turn has an adverse effect on the soil, destroying the organic horizon, whereupon erosion is inevitable and becomes accelerated.

Peat workings on peat mosses and moors can also lead to adverse effects. The Peat Silt Research Group in Ireland have found that high concentrations of peat silt in a river reduce the bottom fauna density. The silt may also eliminate certain invertebrate species by altering the habitat, increase the mortality of fish ova, and affect the growth rate of young fish. It was noticed that larger fish were not affected by the presence of peat silt except where concentrations were very high.

# CHAPTER THIRTEEN

# Strangers in the house

Ever since man has travelled around the world and set up house in other countries he has been inclined to introduce plants and animals alien to the country in which he has settled. Often the reasons have been simply sentimental and the acclimatization societies in New Zealand, for example, have been responsible for the release of many European songbirds into their country (Thomson, 1922). Other introductions have been for increasing the number of species that can be used for food or for the biological control of pests. Fish are no exception to this practice and the usual reason why they have been transferred outside their natural range is to attempt to establish natural self-sustaining populations for sport or commercial fisheries. However, they are now also frequently imported to countries in which they are not indigenous by fish farmers who want to extend the range of fish species for cultivation. Of all the fish, the salmonids have probably been moved around the globe more than most.

## 13.1  AUSTRALIA AND NEW ZEALAND

The first introductions of both Atlantic and Pacific salmon were attempted over 100 years ago when shipments of eggs of Atlantic salmon and quinnat (*Oncorhynchus tshawytscha*) were sent to both Tasmania (Allport, 1870) and New Zealand (Nicols, 1882; Thomson, 1922; Godby, 1925; McDowall, 1968; Flain, 1981). Neither the Atlantic salmon nor the quinnat salmon introductions to Tasmania were successful. The introductions to New Zealand were much more productive, although the Atlantic salmon releases in the Waiau system only resulted in non-migratory populations becoming established. Sockeye salmon (*Oncorhynchus nerka* (Walbaum)) only produced non-migratory populations on the Waitaki system, but the chinook or quinnat salmon established both migratory and resident populations in South Island.

## 13.2  EUROPE

In Europe early attempts were made to establish various Pacific salmon species. Davidson and Hutchinson (1938) record introductions of chinook salmon to the United Kingdom between 1872 and 1880, to France (1872–1900), Germany (1872–1900), Ireland (1891–1900), The Netherlands (1872–1930) and Finland (1930s). Sockeye salmon have been released into lakes in the USSR and Sweden, but no information is available on recaptures. The two most popular species of Pacific salmon both for release into European waters and for cultivation have been the pink salmon (*O. gorbuscha* (Walbaum)) and the coho (*O. kisutch* (Walbaum)). In addition the chum salmon (*O. keta* (Walbaum)) has been introduced to rivers in the Murmansk region of the USSR.

### Pink salmon

Between 1956 and 1971 large numbers (up to 36 M a year) of pink salmon ova were transferred from the Pacific to the Kola Peninsula (Berg, 1961, 1977b). A total of over 220 M ova was involved, resulting in the release of 187 M fry. Varying numbers of adults were caught each year after these releases. In the USSR the numbers of adult salmon returning increased each year and some natural spawning populations developed (Grinyuk *et al.*, 1978a,b). These fish not only returned to the rivers in which they had been released but also spread into Norwegian rivers, and by 1954 there were reports of their presence in more than 40 rivers in North Norway, and a number of spawning fish were observed in many rivers in this part of the country. They subsequently entered many Norwegian rivers as far south as Bergen (Fig. 13.1) and were also recorded from Spitsbergen (Berg, 1977b), Iceland (Gudjonsson, 1961) and Scotland and England (Shearer and Trevawas, 1960; Shearer, 1961; Williamson, 1974). Berg considered that the reason why the pinks ascend so many different rivers may be that their homing instinct does not function as efficiently in the new surroundings as in the natural habitat. In 1976 some pink salmon were caught in southern Norway and these may have been stray fish from USSR plantings in the Bay of Riga in the Baltic since 1972. Some 20 pink salmon were also caught along the Swedish coast.

A firm in Norway imported in 1976 100 000 pink salmon eyed ova from the University of Washington, USA. They hatched well but after transfer to sea water the young fish died of vibriosis. Further more successful attempts at culture were carried out elsewhere in Norway (Ingebrigsten, 1976; Berg, 1977b). As pink salmon spawn in the lower reaches of the rivers, almost in estuarial waters, Berg considered that the pink salmon might serve a useful role in southern Norwegian rivers which had become too acidified to support Atlantic salmon. Ten thousand fed pink salmon fry were planted in the River Søgne in 1976 and the first results were promising. However, these experiments have been discontinued, as has the cage culture of pink salmon in Norway.

For some time the UK government considered the possibility of developing

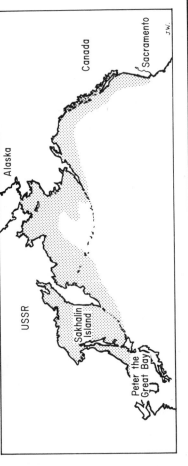

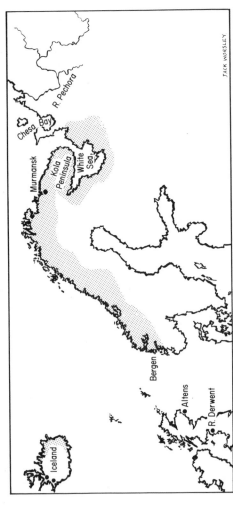

**Fig. 13.1** Distribution of the pink salmon. Shaded areas show (above) natural distribution, (below) areas and places where pink salmon from Russian experiments have been caught. Recaptures in Iceland have been in the rivers, while in Norway, Russia and the United Kingdom they have been in rivers and on the coast (reproduced with permission from Shearer, 1961).

pink salmon ranching in UK waters. The proposals were to investigate the feasibility of establishing a pink salmon broodstock in UK waters and of obtaining an all-female line of pink salmon for the purpose of eventual ranching. The aim of the proposals was not to provide a viable commercial fishery open to the public but, in the words of the Ministry of Agriculture, Fisheries and Food (Anon., 1983):

To establish the feasibility of maintaining localised runs of pink salmon, entirely by hatchery releases, where they can provide the basis for a new fishery to add to the range of resources available to local communities without ecological conflict with existing resources, and which can be harvested in a cost and energy efficient, and readily controlled manner without conflict with other local fisheries.

There has been no more word of these proposals since 1985 so it is to be hoped that they have been shelved for good.

### Coho salmon

Coho salmon have been introduced to a number of countries in Europe for cage culture, and Munro (1979) and Solomon (1980) refer to introductions in the Federal Republic of Germany, Spain, Latvian SSR, France and the United Kingdom. Little seems to be documented about the fate of those introduced to the first three countries named, except that in cage-rearing experiments in Latvia many thousands escaped during storms. Cage rearing of coho in Brittany and France has been described by Harache and Novotny (1976) and Harache (1979a, b). There have been a number of escapes from the freshwater hatcheries and the sea cages as well as intentional introductions by a sport-fishing association on the Sienne River. A number of the escapees returned, successfully spawned in the rivers and produced viable juveniles. One of the first attempts to rear coho in Normandy took place on the River Risle and the same hatchery owner set up an additional project on the River Varenne where considerable escapes occurred. These amounted to 50 000 yearlings in one instance in 1974 and 10 000 underyearlings on another occasion in 1975. The escapes in Normandy rivers and their consequences have been recorded in detail by Euzenat and Fournel (1981). Coho failed to become established in the River Varenne and Euzenat and Fournel (1981) consider that the number of fish involved (a few tens of thousands) was too small and the sheltered rearing of the coho up to the time of release would have led to a lower survival rate in the wild. Furthermore, the marine environment is unsuitable, as both salinity and summer water temperature in the eastern Channel and North Sea reach levels not normally tolerated by coho.

The proposal by a commercial salmon farming company to rear coho salmon in sea cages off the west coast of Scotland was fiercely resisted by salmon angling and conservation bodies for fear of them introducing disease and competing with Atlantic salmon for spawning areas. This stimulated the passing of an Act (*Import of Live Fish (Scotland) Act*, 1978) restricting in Scotland the import, keeping or release of live fish or shellfish or the live eggs or milt of fish or shellfish of certain species. Twenty thousand coho salmon eggs were imported into Scotland by the aforesaid company to evaluate their cultivation potential (Solomon, 1980). They were reared under strict conditions of quarantine and confinement and the resulting fry were also confined and the effluent from the rearing tanks was sterilized. There have been no further imports.

### Chum salmon

During the period 1933–39 the Soviets transferred approximately 9 M chum salmon eggs from the Far East to rivers in the Murmansk region without any practical success. The experiment was resumed in 1956, and between 1956 and 1959 the Soviets flew 13 M chum salmon eggs from Sakhalin Island, north of Japan, to the rivers of the Kola Peninsula (Fig. 13.1). Only a few adults were recaptured (Grinyuk *et al.*, 1978b). In a personal communication Dr Magnus Berg said there was little known about the occurrence of the chum salmon as the fishermen cannot distinguish them from Atlantic salmon. The first chum salmon to be caught in Norway was taken at Soroya in Finnmark in 1963, and in 1965 eight chums were caught in the lower part of the River Tana, Finnmark and one was caught in the Mandalselve in Troms.

### Rainbow trout

The rainbow trout (*Salmo gairdneri*, Richardson) has been introduced widely over Europe both for the purpose of angling and for fish culture. It has become established in the wild in some countries; in Great Britain self-sustaining populations occur in the Derbyshire Wye. Because there are both escapes from farms and releases of stock fish into rivers and lakes it is difficult to know for certain whether or not other smaller wild populations exist. What is interesting is the incidence of numbers of sea-run or steelhead trout resulting from farm escapes or releases of fish by angling clubs. Shearer (1975) recorded a number of sea-run rainbow trout caught in salmon nets off the Scottish east coast. The weights of these fish ranged from 1 kg to 3 kg. The scales of some of the fish examined by Shearer indicated that they had probably spawned previously. Sea-run rainbow trout have also been observed ascending the fish pass on the River Awe into Loch Awe in west Scotland where the cage rearing of rainbow trout has been in operation for some years.

In Norway sea-run rainbow trout, previous escapees from cages, enter a number of rivers. Each autumn 75–150 adult sea-run rainbow trout ascend the Imsa and spawn, but no juveniles have been recorded (Hansen, personal communication, 1987).

## 13.3   NORTH AMERICA

Davidson and Hutchinson (1938) and Ricker and Loftus (1968) give accounts of the introductions of Pacific salmon to the US Atlantic and Gulf States, the Great Lakes and eastern Canada. Chinook salmon were introduced into the Great Lakes and the US Atlantic coast and New Brunswick in the 1870s, and from 1919 to 1925 the Canadian Department of Fisheries planted numbers of chinook salmon eggs into Lake Ontario streams. None of these introductions resulted in populations becoming established.

However, renewed attempts since the 1960s have resulted in some natural spawning. In addition, chinook strays have been reported spawning in the St Lawrence River near Montreal (NASCO, 1987) and two mature chinook salmon have been captured in the Annapolis River in the Bay of Fundy.

Ricker (1954a), in discussing the failure of chinook salmon introductions in New Brunswick rivers, suggested two desirable characteristics for any transplantation programme: (a) relatively large plantings should be made to one or a few sites at first, so that there will be an adequate expendable surplus while the selection process is weeding out genes whose effects are in poor adjustment to the new situation; (b) donor stocks should be carefully selected in order to match up the freshwater and marine conditions of existence of the old and new sites as closely as possible.

Another characteristic to consider is (c) genetic resistance of the introduced stock to native diseases or parasites. For example, when a stock of summer steelhead trout from the Siletz River, a coastal river in Oregon, was introduced to the Willamette River it failed to become established, while three strains of steelhead from the Columbia river system, of which the Willamette is part, released into this river became established successfully. The key to success was genetic resistance of Columbia stock to a myxosporidian parasite *Ceratomyxa shasta* which was absent from the Siletz stock. Almost the same thing happened when fall chinook salmon from Elk River and Trask River (both coastal streams) were released into the Willamette, and both these stocks were much more susceptible to *Ceratomyxa*. The performance of stock-specific differences in different environments is well documented in the *Proceedings of the Stock Concept International Symposium* published in the *Canadian Journal of Fisheries and Aquatic Sciences* (**38** (12), December 1981).

Harache (1979b) considers that to be successful, the transplantation of any Pacific salmon species to new geographic areas must satisfy two basic conditions: (a) there must be a marine environment that matches the preferendum or tolerable range of the species considered, allows normal behaviour, permits active feeding and respect of the timing of the homing migration; (b) there must be a freshwater environment corresponding to the stenothermic character of Pacific salmon and allowing normal reproduction and freshwater life of juveniles to create a self-sustaining smolt production.

From 1941 to 1951 unsuccessful attempts were made to establish sockeye salmon in Maine. More success was achieved with introductions of kokanee (i.e. 'land-locked' sockeye) salmon to the Great Lakes in the late 1960s. Natural spawning occurred for several generations but populations declined and are now at a low level.

The most successful introductions, as in Europe, have been with pink and coho salmon.

### Pink salmon

Attempts to introduce pink salmon to the North Atlantic have continued since the early 1900s. These included sites in Maine from 1906 to 1926 where, while not entirely successful, there were returns for a number of years, and Goose Creek, Hudson Bay in 1956 where no returns were recorded.

Five transplants of eyed pink salmon ova were made between streams in southern British Columbia and North Harbour River, Newfoundland in the early and mid 1960s. Quantities transplanted were 0.25 M in 1959, 2.5 M in 1962, 3.4 M in 1964, 3.3 M in 1965 and 5.9 M in 1966. Adult returns from the transplants were 1, 49, 638, 8500 and 2426 during 1961, 1964, 1966, 1967 and 1968 respectively. Since 1969 returns have been the progeny of naturally spawning fish and have steadily declined in numbers. Lear (1975) could not be sure of the reasons for the failure of the transplants, but the possibilities he suggested included: predation on the fry by brook trout (*Salvelinus fontinalis*, Mitchill) and possibly eels in North Harbour Pond and estuary, unfavourable surface water temperatures in the river during the fry run, predation by herring on fry in St Mary's Bay, year-class failure of the even-year stocks that were introduced, unsuitability of donor stocks with respect to migration patterns and homing behaviour, and inadequate numbers of eggs were transplanted to produce populations required to maintain runs in anything below optimum environmental conditions. The evaluation of this introduction of a Pacific salmon species is probably the best documented of any.

Pink salmon have also been introduced to the Great Lakes (Lake Superior) and, as a result of straying, spawning populations have been established in Lakes Huron, Michigan, Erie and Ontario (Dermott and Timmins, 1986).

### Coho salmon

The largest introductions of coho salmon to the North Atlantic area have been in the Great Lakes and in the New England states of New Hampshire, Massachusetts, Rhode Island and Connecticut (Stolte, 1974). These introductions in the New England rivers have been relatively successful; there has been some natural spawning and a small sport fishery has developed (Netboy, 1976). However, there has been some straying and small breeding populations of coho have appeared in New Brunswick and Nova Scotia. Symons and Martin (1978) describe a population of juvenile fish in Frost Fish Creek on the

Digdeguash River in New Brunswick, and mature adult cohos were first reported in the Cornwallis River, Nova Scotia, in 1976, with juveniles being found in 1978. Successful reproduction has been observed in subsequent years by Dr S. Barbour of the Department of Fisheries and Oceans in Halifax. Dr Barbour considers that the population may be self sustaining. Coho have also been recorded as spawning in other streams in the Bay of Fundy (Martin and Dadswell, 1983) but it is not known whether or not self-sustaining populations have been established.

The renewed stocking of the Great Lakes with coho, which has continued since the mid-1960s, has resulted in limited spawning populations, but the populations are otherwise almost entirely maintained by stocking. There is some evidence to suggest that natural spawning of coho, probably originating from these plantings, has occurred in the St Lawrence River near Montreal.

### Rainbow trout

MacCrimmon (1971) has reviewed the world distribution of the rainbow trout. It was introduced into the north-eastern United States and Canada in the late 1800s and early 1900s and self-sustaining populations have developed in the New England states, the Great Lakes and the Maritime Provinces of Canada. They have probably extended their range as a result of further releases and escapes from hatcheries and cage-rearing projects.

## 13.4 POTENTIAL DANGERS TO ATLANTIC SALMON OF INTRODUCTIONS OF PACIFIC SALMON

There are potential dangers in introducing any of the Pacific salmon species to waters draining into the Atlantic, as there could be an unforeseen change in their behaviour which might seriously affect Atlantic salmon stocks. Harache (1979b) considers that transplantation of a given species to a new and different environment often results in changes in the natural processes, especially in cold-blooded animals which are strictly dependent upon the ambient water temperatures. In referring to the introduction of coho salmon to France he points out that the US Pacific North-west states and north-western France, although on the same latitude, present important climatic and hydrological differences which seem to modify the natural biological rhythms of coho salmon.

Unfortunately there has been little research to determine the likely adverse effects on Atlantic salmon of the introduction of Pacific salmon species. The prediction of what these effects might be is therefore to some extent speculative. Most studies have centred on the coho salmon, as this species, of all the Pacific salmon species, has a life history closest to that of the Atlantic salmon. These studies have concentrated on (a) competition with the indigenous species and (b) disease factors.

### Competition with indigenous species

One of the first considerations must be the spawning requirements of the introduced species and whether these overlap with or are the same as those of indigenous or other introduced species already established (McDowall, 1968). Probably the classic example of this is the introduction of brown trout and rainbow trout to North Island, New Zealand. The brown trout, which were introduced first (1867), spawn in the autumn while the rainbow trout, introduced later (1883), spawn in the spring. As both species have similar spawning requirements, it was the brown trout that suffered, as its redds were disturbed by the later-spawning rainbow trout and the brown trout eggs were dislodged.

One of the reasons pink and chum salmon introductions were said to be harmless to Atlantic salmon was that as pink and chum salmon spawn in the lower reaches of the river system they would not compete with Atlantic salmon for spawning area. However, Atlantic salmon are also known to spawn just above the tidal influence (Saunders, 1966; Mills and Graesser, 1981, p. 80) and consequently there could be competition for spawning space in certain situations.

Harache (1979b) asked two questions regarding the spawning of coho. (a) Will coho spawn first and have their redds partially destroyed by the later-spawning Atlantic salmon? In this case, cohos emerging earlier will select the best habitats. (b) Will Atlantic salmon spawn first and emerge from the gravel before the coho? This brings us on to the problem of interspecific competition between the juveniles.

Another of the reasons for supporting pink and chum salmon transplants was that, as the fry of these species go to sea straight after emerging from the gravel, they would not compete with juvenile Atlantic salmon for either habitat or food (Solomon, 1979). There has been little research on the interactions of juvenile Pacific and Atlantic salmon, but the work of Gibson (1981) suggests that while Atlantic salmon parr will displace coho parr from riffle areas of streams, coho appear to dominate in pools and will displace Atlantic salmon parr there. Coho salmon fry emerge earlier than Atlantic salmon fry and grow faster; Hunter (1959) has shown that they are voracious feeders and prey on small salmonids. In a *Report on Salmonid Introductions and Transfers* by the Bilateral Scientific Working Group of the North American Commission of the North Atlantic Salmon Conservation Organisation (NASCO, 1987) it was pointed out that in Newfoundland, Labrador and the North Shore of the St Lawrence, Quebec, where competition and predatory species are scarce, Atlantic salmon parr are abundant in pools and shallow lakes. If coho became established they could have substantial deleterious effects on Atlantic salmon. Dr S. Barbour is cited (NASCO, 1987) as considering that good habitat and climatic conditions for coho occur in Cape Breton Island and Newfoundland. He postulated that the 'coho niche' contributes up to 50% of the Atlantic salmon production in many Newfoundland rivers. Coho and chinook spawn later than Atlantic salmon and as the three species spawn in similar-size substrate, so superimposition of the redds could occur where spawning substrate is limited.

Gibson (1981) also suggested, from his behavioural studies of juvenile rainbow trout and juvenile Atlantic salmon, that competitive interactions occur between this species also, and the Atlantic salmon could be displaced from some habitats. Furthermore, it has been found that stocked rainbow trout may travel many miles. For example, they have been recorded migrating up to 500 miles (804 km) in the Great Lakes (Hansen and Stauffer, 1971) and, as steelhead trout, over 800 miles (1287 km) in the eastern Pacific (Pearcy and Masuda, 1982). This provides ample opportunity for escaped rainbow trout to interact with indigenous fish species. It is the consensus of the Bilateral Scientific Working Group of the North American Commission in NASCO (NASCO, 1987), set up to study salmonid introductions and transfers, that the steelhead rainbow trout (and domestic rainbow trout having anadromous tendencies), due to its life history, has the potential to pose a severe ecological threat to Atlantic salmon management in North America.

### Disease

One of the main fears expressed about introductions is the threat of disease, and yet there is little documented evidence of disease outbreaks from salmonid introductions. The introduction of parasites is a different matter and *Gyrodactylus salaris* will remain a classic example of how a parasite can spread in the wild with disastrous effects after introduction on hatchery stock. Harache (1979b) refers to coho salmon being more resistant to bacterial diseases such as furunculosis and vibriosis than Atlantic salmon or rainbow trout, but more sensitive to bacterial kidney disease (*Corynebacterium* sp.). One viral disease which could be damaging, particularly to hatchery stocks, if introduced to Great Britain is infectious haematopoietic necrosis (IHN).

So far, this chapter has been concerned with the introduction to the Atlantic area of species originating in north-west America. It should be mentioned that similar concern is voiced by steelhead anglers in the Pacific region who are concerned at the possible consequences of cage rearing Atlantic salmon in British Columbia waters.

## 13.5  RECOMMENDATIONS

In 1969 the International Council for the Exploration of the Sea set up a Working Group on Introductions and Transfers of Marine Organisms 'to consider the principles which might govern the introduction and acclimatisation of non-indigenous marine organisms, especially shellfish and anadromous and catadromous fish species.' The Working Group is still continuing its excellent work and in 1973 produced a *Code of Practice to Reduce the Risks of Adverse Effects Arising from the Introductions of Non-indigenous Marine Species*. A revised code was produced in 1979. At the moment this Working Group is preparing a 'protocol' document, in conjunction with the European Inland Fisheries Advisory Commission, to provide specific details on quarantine, inspection and certification procedures as well as on pathological, ecological, genetic and behavioural considerations (Anon., 1987d).

The Bilateral Scientific Working Group of the North American Commission on Salmonid Introductions and Transfers of NASCO made the following recommendations for inclusion in a policy statement:

1. Develop legislative authority and regulations to control the introduction or transfer of fish which may affect the genetic integrity or productivity of Atlantic salmon stocks;
2. Submit proposed introductions and transfers of non-indigenous stocks of salmonids to the NAC Bilateral Scientific Study Working Group on Introductions and Transfers of Salmonids for review of their potential for adversely affecting Atlantic salmon populations;
3. Discourage the introduction or transfers of salmonids which may have an adverse effect on wild stocks if they should escape into rivers supporting Atlantic salmon populations.

# CHAPTER FOURTEEN

# Wild or domesticated?

## 14.1 SALMON FARMING AND RANCHING

The rearing of salmon to the adult stage first started in the early 1960s in the fjords of Norway, beginning with a venture by the Vik brothers who held and fed adult salmon in a sea-water pool in Sykkylven Fjord after they had been stripped of their eggs, at the same time acclimating the young salmon to increasing salinities until they could be introduced to net enclosures in the fjord (Vik, 1962). From the beginning salmon farming developed rapidly in Norway (Møller, 1973) and by 1975 the annual production had risen to 1000 tonnes. Eleven years later, in 1986, the production of Norwegian farmed salmon had soared to 45 494 t and is expected to reach 80 000 t in the not-too-distant future.

Scotland began salmon farming in the late 1960s when Marine Harvest Ltd used the 'Vik process' to acclimatize juvenile fish to the saline water in cages moored in a Scottish sea loch, Loch Ailort. Since that time Scottish salmon farms, as in Norway, have proliferated (J. Mills, 1985) and by the late 1980s the annual production of Scottish farmed salmon from over 170 farms was more than 15 000 worth over £60 M. The Faroe Islands, too, although arriving later on the salmon-farming scene, are expected to achieve an annual production of 12 000 t by 1989 and Ireland about half that amount. Iceland, although one of the first countries to develop the ranching of Atlantic salmon successfully, has been hindered by climatic conditions in her development of cage rearing of salmon. However, later onshore tank developments now promise to produce a significant contribution to the world production of farmed Atlantic salmon. On the eastern seaboard of Canada salmon farming is also developing rapidly in the sheltered waters around Passamaquoddy Bay and the Bay of Fundy. The world production of farmed Atlantic salmon has exceeded 60 000 t (Fig. 14.1), which is almost seven times the total landings of wild Atlantic salmon in 1986 (Shaw and Muir, 1987).

The advent of salmon farming has resulted in an impact on both the economy of wild salmon harvesting and the well-being and future of wild salmon stocks in addition to effects on the environment which are discussed elsewhere (Chapter 11).

As more and more farmed salmon have entered the market the price of wild

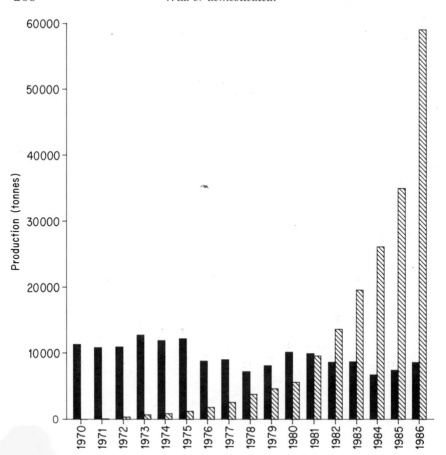

Worldwide total annual production of Atlantic salmon. Solid columns, wild fish; shaded columns, farmed fish (reproduced with permission from NASCO).

salmon has been increasingly affected (Table 14.1). Briefly, the position has been that prior to the presence of farmed salmon on the market the price of wild salmon fluctuated according to periods of scarcity and abundance. During periods of scarcity the salmon netsmen made their profits through selling their fish at high prices, so their poor catches were compensated for by the high selling prices. Now, at times when wild salmon are scarce, the salmon farmers can supply the market with farmed fish, which are available throughout the year, so reducing the market price of salmon and thus affecting the netsmen's profits. The change in marketing patterns has affected commercial salmon harvesting and some Scottish salmon companies have reduced their fishing effort by closing some of their marginal netting stations and working other

**Table 14.1** Average prices of wild and farmed Atlantic salmon in Scotland 1978–85*

| Year | Average price of wild salmon and grilse (£/kg) | Average price of farmed salmon and grilse (£/kg) |
|------|------|------|
| 1978 | 3.97 | 3.30 |
| 1979 | 5.53 | 3.77 |
| 1980 | 4.83 | 4.04 |
| 1981 | 4.06 | 3.15 |
| 1982 | 4.47 | 3.56 |
| 1983 | 4.18 | 4.06 |
| 1984 | 4.65 | 4.28 |
| 1985 | 5.64 | 4.84 |

*Source: Stansfeld (1986).

stations for a shorter season. The effect of the competition of farmed salmon in the market place on the state of Scottish commercial salmon fisheries has been admirably described by Stansfeld (1986) who takes the opposite view to Tuomi (1986) who considers that 'salmon farming points to the end of traditional commercial fishing for salmon', in Canada at any rate.

Salmon ranching, which has been practised for a much longer time than salmon farming, involves rearing the juvenile fish to the smolt stage, releasing them into rivers (usually the lower reaches) or estuaries to go to sea to feed naturally, and harvesting them on their return as adult fish. Salmon ranching is often referred to as sea ranching. In order to ensure ease of harvesting and the maximum recapture rate the release of the smolts is by means of release ponds, enclosures or channels to which they home on maturation. Those countries therefore most suitable for salmon ranching are those which have no or little coastal salmon fishing to intercept the returning fish. For this reason, countries such as Iceland, the Faroes and Spain should have the best return rates. However, the ranching of Atlantic salmon is undertaken also in Norway (Hansen, 1982), the Republic of Ireland, on the west coast of Scotland, in the Maritime Provinces of Canada, in France and in the Baltic (Thorpe, 1980; Eriksson, Ferranti and Larsson, 1982), and there are plans for salmon ranching in Portugal (Ramos, 1982) and on a larger scale in Norway.

## 14.2 EFFECTS ON WILD STOCKS

Of greater concern are the increasing effects the salmon farming industry is likely to have on wild salmon stocks. The first of these effects arises from:

### Escapes of adult fish from sea cages

Many salmon escape from sea cages along the Norwegian and Scottish coasts as a result of damage to the cages by seals, storms, ship collisions and vandalism. There are no data on the proportion of salmon that escape from fish farms, but Hansen, Lund and Hindar (1987) record single accidents in which up to 20–30 tonnes of salmon have escaped. These authors state that if only 1% of the annual Norwegian production escapes then 500 t and 740 t of farmed salmon entered salt water in 1987 and 1988 respectively. A tagging experiment with a group of escapees demonstrated that these fish were homeless and did not select any particular river in which to spawn (Hansen, Døving and Jonsson, 1987). Immature fish migrated to the feeding areas in the Northern Atlantic and if not caught in the fishery, the mature individuals entered fresh water. The survival and migration pattern of escapees depended on a number of factors such as the size and developmental stage of the fish, and the site and seasonal time of escape.

Artificially reared fish have been identified among salmon taken in the high seas fishery north of the Faroes (Craik *et al.*, 1987). These fish were identified by pectoral and dorsal fin abrasion and deformity, scale reading and muscle pigment analysis based on the detection of the carotenoid canthaxanthin (used in farm diets). While fin and scale characters may identify salmon which have been reared for some period of their life, pigment analysis identifies some of those fish which have been held on marine farms after smolting and fed with commercial canthaxanthin-containing diets. Others could conceivably escape prior to being fed with 'pigmented' pellets, as the time at which farmers start feeding these to their caged fish depends on when they are to be marketed and which manufacturer's pellets they are using.

What effect these reared fish may have on the wild fish on their entering the rivers is not know for certain. It is assumed that in strong natural populations a moderate number of reared fish will not have a significant genetic impact on the population with which they breed. However, if a weak population is invaded by reared fish the isolation mechanisms may break down if interbreeding between the 'strays' and wild fish occurs, and as a result the genetic integrity of the natural populations will no longer be maintained. This is because reared salmon have a decreased genetic variability and different genetic profiles from the wild stocks from which they have originated (Ståhl, 1983; McElligott, Maguire and Cross, 1987). Dilution of the local stock with strays may therefore upset the process of local adaptation by disrupting the accumulation of suitable genotypes (Wilkins, 1985). This being so, farm escapees could be a very considerable source of 'genetic pollution'.

### Transfer and restocking with surplus fish from hatcheries

The total genetic make-up of the salmon in a local stock is known as the gene pool and it is unique to that stock (Cross and Healy, 1983; Ryman, 1983). It is also inherited from generation to generation. The inherited characteristics may include growth rate, resistance to disease, ocean migration patterns and timing of return to the river and area of spawning. The pressures of natural selection probably differ among rivers and the genetic composition of the salmon in one river differs from that in the next (Ståhl, 1981, 1987). Such a close match between genotype and environment would be preserved through high homing precision, so that these stocks remain discrete (Gjedrem, 1979; Gunnes, 1980; Thorpe and Mitchell, 1981). The implications of such a close genetic adaptation for restocking would be very important, partly because of the introduction of life stages from the hatchery which have not been subject to the rigours of natural selection pressures which might have affected their survival. Accordingly hatchery populations are particularly susceptible to genetic changes because of modified environments and controlled reproduction. Consequently any restocking, unless it utilizes native stock suitably reared, may erode genetic variability and will change genetic profiles in wild populations, resulting in the possible breakdown of adaptive gene complexes. Even when using native parents, hatchery procedures can alter genetic composition if insufficient broodstock are used; Cross and King (1983), Ståhl (1987) and McElligott *et al.* (1987) confirm that few hatchery strains are similar genetically to the wild stocks from which they were derived. Therefore loss of genetically determined stock characteristics by unintentional hybridization of different gene pools in hatchery operations might result in the disappearance of local adaptations reflected by population characteristics such as time of return and homing precision.

Restocking of salmon rivers with hatchery stock from elsewhere has been carried out for a considerable number of years (Harris, 1978), in some cases with apparent success, particularly in rivers where stocks were either lost or reduced to a very low level. Wilkins (1985) considers that the use of hatchery-reared juveniles in stocking programmes is of value in these situations and he cites the River Lee in Ireland in which river over 95% of the fish returning to the fish counters are hatchery reared. Other examples could include the Thames, which had lost its entire stock of salmon and which is now undergoing restoration with introductions of eggs and fry from some Scottish rivers, and the Connecticut River. On the other hand, Ritter (1975) has shown lower survival rates for hatchery-reared Atlantic salmon released in various rivers than those stocked in their native streams. Nevertheless, Thorpe (1988a) feels that there is a scarcity of evidence for adverse effects and that long-term success of augmentation has not been measured.

Saunders (1981) pointed out that the restoration of vanished populations had been difficult and suggested that important genetically-based behavioural traits had been lost, especially in relation to run-timing of smolting and spawning fish, and Bailey (1987) also mentioned the loss of navigational control. Ikonen (1987) has found that the timing of spawning migration of salmon in the Baltic Sea differs between wild and hatchery-reared salmon, the salmon of wild origin migrating earlier than hatchery-reared ones. It is also believed, although not proven, that not all hatchery fish migrate for spawning and it has further been suggested that their migration routes differ so much from those of the wild fish, which are known to the fishermen, that the hatchery fish are difficult to catch. Struthers and Stewart (1986) also recorded differences on the River Tummel in Scotland between the timing of the migration of smolts that were the progeny of wild fish and that of smolts that had been stocked as fry. The differences were so great that the migration periods of the two groups were almost completely separate. The authors attribute the delay among stocked fish to a difference in developmental timing implying differences in adaptation between the local and planted stocks. Thorpe (1988a) points out, using the above example, that timing of events such as emigration from rivers must relate to optimal protection from predators, optimal physical conditions for downstream transport, and optimal physical and biological conditions for entering the sea. In large southern systems like the Connecticut River this would include arrival in the ocean before inshore temperatures reached lethally high levels. He points out that such a timetable will be specific not only to individual river systems, but to separate regions thereof. With respect to geographical regions, there is some evidence (Léaniz, personal communication) to suggest that salmon originating from eggs introduced to Spain from a northern Scottish river (the Conon) are not so able to tolerate the high summer water temperatures prevailing in the isolated pools of some Spanish rivers as are the native stocks. The consequences of the interbreeding of these two stocks are perhaps obvious.

Thorpe (1988a) considers that much 'foreign' material would be useless for stocking into a river since it might fail to return or might be of value only once, if after return it failed to breed at all. He suggests that some could be useful as long as its breeding behaviour and occupancy of the river environment complemented but did not interfere with those of existing stocks, so that there was no reduction or dilution of the 'essential genetic information' within the populations.

However, Reisenbichler and McIntyre (1977) demonstrated decreased stream survival rates in hybrids between hatchery and native steelhead trout and predicted a long-term decrease in the stock–recruitment relationship in such a stock. Furthermore, Altukhov (1981) attributed a catastrophic decline in population size of chum salmon, *Oncorhynchus keta* (Walbaum), in the Naiba River to 'disturbance of genetic structure' of the native population, resulting from several years' introduction of eggs from a neighbouring river, the Kalininka. Before the transfer, the Naiba River carried a spawning population of about 650 000 chum salmon. By 1969–70 the genetic characteristics of the stock returning to the Naiba had shifted towards those of the Kalininka fish, and by 1980 the returning population had decreased to 30 000 to 40 000 spawners. By 1985 the population was virtually extinct (Thorpe, 1988a). Altukhov (1981) concluded that this local disaster was the result of massive genetic migration of non-adapted genotypes.

Until the advent of salmon farming and ranching, stocking was relatively well controlled and the numbers of eggs and juvenile fish released were usually carefully recorded. Certainly there were transfers between rivers, but often these were of eggs or unfed fry which had had a limited hatchery existence or none at all. There are many anecdotal accounts of the success of these transfers in improving the stock and size of the fish in the river to which they were introduced. Since salmon farming and ranching have increased, releases of discards of unwanted or poor-grade juvenile fish have been both massive and random. In addition escapes of juvenile fish from large freshwater cage units and during transit at sea have been extensive and have involved, as with sea cage units, large numbers of fish. Some of these units rear up to 300 000 smolts annually and escapes of up to 30 000 fish have been recorded from units damaged by ice and storms (Mills, 1987b), and a recent loss of 100 000 smolts was recorded when a ship transporting smolts went aground on the Orkneys. Young fish are also released from freshwater cages during grading operations and the smaller, slower-growing fish or potential S2 smolts (i.e. fish which will become smolts at the end of their second year) are either released or offered to salmon proprietors for restocking of neighbouring or distant river systems. By restocking with potential S2s one may be selecting for slow growth. This could influence the age composition of adult stocks in the river in which they have been released.

Although considerable concern has been shown regarding the introduction of disease with hatchery stock and the possible transfer of disease, there is little record of wild fish being affected by farm stock. Munro et al. (1976) showed that while IPN (infectious pancreatic necrosis) had been transferred from a rainbow trout farm to native Atlantic salmon, brown trout and other freshwater fish in Loch Awe, fewer than 2.5% of each of the indigenous species were infected. BKD (bacterial kidney disease) had also occurred in some rainbow trout cage units, particularly in Central Scotland where the disease is considered endemic. This disease has not yet been recorded from Scottish smolt cage-rearing units, but it has proved a problem in some Icelandic smolt-rearing units linked to ranching schemes. However, most fish farmers would claim that the greatest threat of disease transfer is from wild fish to farmed fish rather than the reverse. This is not always the case, and Egidius (1987) records that furunculosis appeared in Norway with an importation of Scottish salmon smolts.

The skin parasite *Gyrodactylus salaris* too was introduced to Norwegian salmon farms, probably from resistant stock from Sweden (Johnels, 1984) and subsequently to wild salmon stocks in Norwegian rivers where it has considerably reduced the numbers of young salmon in many river systems (Heggberget and Johnsen, 1982; Johnsen and Jensen, 1986) (pp. 88–90).

Transfers of hatchery stock have wider implications for the survival of distinct races. In Europe there exist at least two major races of salmon – 'celtic' and 'boreal' (pp. 17–20) – and within both these races there exist genetically distinct river stocks. However, both Cross and Healy (1983) and Ståhl (1987) have failed to demonstrate any differences between these groups using enzyme loci. Nevertheless, with increasing numbers of transfers within the British Isles and between Scandinavia and the British Isles for farming and restocking purposes these races, if they exist, may be at risk, and indeed their genetic structure may have been affected already. As Wilkins (1985) states:

The further studies on British and Irish populations are urgently needed. The populations of these islands constitute the largest elements of the European stock of salmon and they are under significant threat from over-exploitation. Once wild stocks decline quantitatively, qualitative changes occur in their genetic make-up by a process called genetic drift. This phenomenon causes a decrease in genetic variability and can hasten the extinction of wild stocks.

The added threat from misguided introductions of hatchery stock is obvious. More-distant transfers between the continents of North America and Europe, which are occurring now, could have serious effects on the genetic structure of the two major continental races which have been suggested to be separate subspecies (p. 18).


## 14.3   PRECAUTIONS

The International Council for the Exploration of the Sea is aware of these problems and the Report of its Working Group on Introductions and Transfers of Marine Organisms (Anon., 1987c) expresses continuing concern over the trans-Atlantic and other transfers of Atlantic salmon relative to the genetic and ecological implications of stock mixing, and urges that studies be encouraged by member countries to determine means of stock identification and to examine the effects of these movements.

A number of programmes are being implemented to determine these effects more accurately including such studies as (1) field trials to gauge the success of 'foreign' introduced material at the freshwater stage, (2) an examination of the reproductive physiology of escapees, particularly in relation to the possibility of hybridization between these and indigenous spawning stocks, and (3) DNA 'fingerprinting' using mitochondrial DNA (mtDNA) (Hartley, 1987).

In addition to such scientific studies, in view of the threat to natural genetic resources from the escapes of farmed salmon, the Norwegian Directorate for Nature Management has established a national sperm bank for wild salmon.

The main purpose of the sperm bank is to preserve genetic variation and the following strategy has been adopted:

1. Sperm from at least 50 individuals from each stock is deep frozen by a method known as cryopreservation (Stoss and Refstie, 1983);
2. Emphasis is placed on sampling from stocks representing a wide geographical and ecological range;
3. Stocks threatened by extinction are given priority over other stocks;
4. Stocks which are of particular scientific value or are valuable for fishing purposes are also given priority.

Helle (1981), Maitland (1985, 1986, 1987) and Wilkins (1985) suggest a number of guidelines for those involved in the management of salmonids and their handling in captivity, which include:

1. Some pristine stocks should be maintained and conserved in each geographical area: stocking and hatching in these areas should be strictly controlled;
2. Broodstock for hatcheries used for stock enhancement should be obtained regularly from the wild and where possible broodstock should not be kept in captivity for more than one generation;
3. Surplus hatchery-reared juveniles should not be used for stocking in the wild simply because they are available;
4. Large numbers of adults should be used as broodstock to avoid 'bottleneck' effects and genetic drift (indeed Franklin (1980) considers that a minimum of 500 is needed to preserve useful genetic variation within any stock, but this may not be practical).

Nyman and Norman (1987) have also produced a basic list of recommendations for 'breeding methodology and management'. Their list includes the following:

1. Use river-specific stocks;
2. Collection of potential spawners should encompass the entire spawning migration period;
3. At least 25 pairs of parental fish, chosen at random, should be used as broodstock;
4. The progeny from all pairs should be mixed;
5. Rivers that have a potential to support populations of salmon should serve as gene banks;
6. Population genetic tags should be employed to test stock characteristics and evaluate the proposed breeding methodology.

Control should also be stricter by having a system of monitoring as recommended by Allendorf *et al.* (1987) who point out that, with electrophoretic monitoring, genetic stability or change can be measured directly. They feel that a need for monitoring exists within all hatchery populations. They also consider that monitoring of totally wild populations is equally feasible and desirable to measure their genetic stability in the absence of the influences of hatchery fish. Monitoring can also provide a valuable updating of genetic information on wild and hatchery populations if these populations are to be included in analyses of stock mixtures. To this end, a consultancy service in genetics and fisheries management has been set up by both the Queen's University Business and Industrial Services in Belfast, Northern Ireland and the Zoology Department at University College, Cork.

The Bilateral Scientific Working Group of the North American Commission on Salmonid Introductions and Transfers set up by the North Atlantic Salmon Conservation Organisation (NASCO, 1987) recommended that a policy statement should state the desire:

To strive to maintain the genetic diversity and productivity of wild Atlantic salmon stocks (as well as strains currently being utilised for the development of such stocks) by encouraging each affiliated agency to:

1. Develop legislative authority and regulations to control the introduction or transfer of fish which may adversely affect the genetic integrity or productivity of Atlantic salmon stocks;
2. Encourage the use of local-origin salmonid stocks in aquaculture and restoration projects;
3. Encourage the protection of selected wild stocks from hybridization with hatchery-cultured fish or foreign stock and over-fishing, thus ensuring total protection of genetic integrity of such stocks.

The use of sterile triploid female fish could be another solution to the problem. Experimental trials with triploid salmon smolts are being carried out already at Howietoun hatchery near Stirling in Scotland (Anon., 1986). The advantage of these sterile non-mating triploids, besides being a boon to the farming industry by eliminating the need for grading and ensuring more predictable growth, would be their inability to breed with wild fish. However, one cannot be sure what other interactions there might be between them and the wild stocks if these hormone treated females were to enter the rivers.

Wilkins (1985) summarizes the situation realistically when he says:

Artificial production of salmon, whether for stocking, cage-culture or ranching operations, can be expected to increase in future years. Provided that broodstock numbers are sufficiently large, an increase in the number of hatcheries and a greater spread of their locations, will ultimately be of benefit. Locally-produced fry or smolts are more likely to be suitable for local introductions than more distant stock. The increased number of distinct broodstock lines derived from different founder stocks which is implicit in the strategy of multiple dispersed hatcheries, will facilitate the maintenance of genetic diversity which can be exploited through cross-breeding. Perhaps it is only as salmon production becomes increasingly harnessed to commercial development that the intrinsic value of the wild salmon stocks and their genetic diversity will be appreciated. Whether there will still be wild stocks in existence by then is entirely a matter of how we act now.

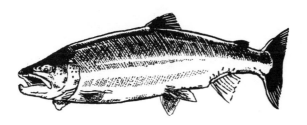

# PART FOUR

# Conservation

# CHAPTER FIFTEEN

# Improvement, restoration and conservation

As salmon stocks decline in various rivers for one reason or another, salmon fishery managers and proprietors, government fishery agencies, local fishery boards and water authorities attempt to rectify the situation. Improvement measures include either planting out eggs or releasing fry, parr or smolts in streams and lakes and/or opening up areas of river systems previously inaccessible to the salmon. In addition, steps are taken to control predators and enhance the nursery habitat by providing more shelter for the young stages and deeper pools for adult fish waiting to spawn and by reinstating spawning gravel. Needless to say, none of these measures is worthwhile unless the various effects of land and water use described in the earlier chapters are ameliorated, poaching is controlled and legislation is adequate.

Stocking of the various juvenile stages of salmon has been practised for many years: Harris (1978) and Kennedy (1988) have reviewed the current state of the art and give a full account of the many results obtained from the numerous plantings of eggs, fry, parr and smolts in the various Atlantic-salmon-producing countries. Kennedy (1988) gives a detailed summary of stocking activities in the nine water authority areas in England and Wales, and in Scotland, Northern Ireland and the Republic of Ireland, Canada, Faroes, France, Iceland and Norway. The results of his survey of the extent of these stocking programmes indicate that over 38 M juvenile Atlantic salmon may be stocked annually. The success of these programmes in terms of improvement is open to doubt in some instances and its value will be discussed in a general context later in this chapter. It should be stressed that there are certain principles to be observed before engaging in any restocking programme and these are set out in detail by Egglishaw et al. (1984) and Mills and Raynor (1987).

A number of stocking programmes have been undertaken in conjunction with major restoration and improvement schemes. For example fish passes, the transfer of adult fish and controlled-flow spawning channels are being used to extend the distribution of Atlantic salmon within Newfoundland watersheds. Pratt and Rietveld (1973) describe the construction of fish passes (fishways) in both the Upper Terra Nova River, permitting a gradual extension of adult fish into the head waters, and Great Rattling Brook which, with concurrent adult fish transfers, has resulted also in rapid increases in the adult salmon population. The other means of making efficient use of broodstock investigated by these authors was the construction of controlled-flow spawning channels on Noel Paul's Brook. These provide holding and spawning areas for adult fish. The adults initially remain in the holding pools and then move to adjacent spawning beds. These beds consist of clean round gravel with water-velocity depth profiles similar to those of natural spawning beds in Newfoundland. The emerging fry are collected from the beds and distributed to various sections of the main river and tributaries.

The practice of transporting adult fish either upstream or to other rivers is carried out on a number of other rivers in Newfoundland including the Exploits River (Taylor and Bauld, 1973; Davis and Scott, 1983) and the Biscay Bay River.

Major salmon-restoration projects have been undertaken in a number of countries in recent years. In Canada, a plan to re-establish a natural spawning population in the Point Wolfe River, Nova Scotia, was instigated in 1981 (Alexander and Galbraith, 1982), while in Quebec the restoration of salmon runs to the Jacques Cartier River commenced in 1979 (Frenette, Dulude and Beaurivage, 1988). A significant salmon-restoration programme, which has been continuing for some years, is progressing on the Connecticut and Merrimack rivers in the New England states of Connecticut, Massachusetts, New Hampshire and Vermont (Stolte, 1980; Jones, 1988) and the Penobscot River in Maine (Cutting, 1963).

Many restoration schemes have been undertaken where stocks have been lost as a result of the effects of pollution or hydroelectric development. In Europe, advantage has been taken of the improved water-quality status of a number of rivers to reintroduce salmon. One of the greatest success stories in this respect is the return of the salmon to the Thames (Fig. 15.1). From an annual average stocking of 61 000 parr and 14 000 smolts in a number of the Thames tributaries the recapture rate has been of the order of 100 adults per year between 1982 and 1985 from partial trapping, electrofishing and angling, and 176 in 1986. It has been estimated that this represents an actual return of 300 adults annually (Anon., 1985c; Gough, 1982, 1983, 1987). Although salmon have spawned successfully within the Thames catchment each year since 1983 it is not thought that the minimal spawning activity observed has contributed significantly to the run of fish. In order to increase the return rate of fish, larger numbers of parr and smolts are now being released annually.

Another English river in which the level of pollution has been greatly reduced in recent years is the Trent. Here too there are plans to restore the salmon runs. A preliminary survey of the Trent river system revealed that the

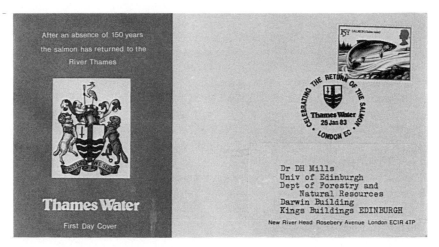

**Fig. 15.1**    After an absence of 150 years the salmon has returned to the River Thames. Thames Water Authority first day cover, taking advantage of a new issue (26 January 1983) of fish stamps to celebrate the event.

two tributaries having the most-suitable spawning and nursery areas are the Dove and the Derwent. It was estimated that the Dove could support a minimum home run of 1000 adults and the Derwent 500, without exploitation, assuming that all obstructions could be overcome. There are a considerable number of obstructions, mostly weirs, on both the Derwent and the Trent and 100 of these were examined with a view to determining the cost of making them surmountable. Bottomley (1986), in describing the proposals, mentions catches of over 3000 salmon occurring in the Trent Fisheries District in the 1880s but declining rapidly after then. There was a slight recovery in the 1930s when catches of about 200 fish were recorded. After then only a few distressed or dead fish were seen in the tidal reach of the Trent. In 1982, however, a small run resulting in a catch of 22 fish was recorded. So the possibility of the Trent returning to its former glory as a salmon river is good.

In Scotland, too, there have been a number of promising prospects, with salmon returning to the River Clyde after an absence of some 80 years. The numbers of salmon now seen at Blantyre weir are so encouraging that a Clyde Fisheries Management Trust has been set up to supervise and co-ordinate the future development of the River Clyde salmon fishing rights (Holden and Struthers, 1987). Gardiner (1987) estimates that the Clyde and its tributaries could eventually yield 30 000 adult salmon a year. Conditions in the Clyde estuary have been improving for some time, so much so that salmon started to reappear in the late 1970s in the once salmon-productive River Gryfe which flows into this estuary.

Another of central Scotland's industrial rivers which may once again become a salmon river is the Carron, which flows into the Forth estuary, the site of a large oil refinery. In 1987, as a result of a recession in the paper-making industry, which was the main culprit in pollution of this river, and of the provision of effluent treatment, 60 000 salmon parr and 750 smolts were released at various points on the river.

The River Akerselv, flowing through Norway's capital city of Oslo, has been heavily polluted for more than 100 years, but the water quality has improved so much that in 1981 and 1984 a total of 5775 tagged salmon smolts were released in this river. A total of 236 adults were recaptured, but only 29 in the Akerselv. However, Hansen (1986b) feels that the results were sufficiently promising and that releases of smolts in this river might be a useful strategy in order to develop a recreational fishery both in the river and in Oslofjord. This is a promising development when so many of the rivers in southern Norway are too acid to support salmon.

The French salmon rivers have suffered badly in the past from pollution, but the situation has improved significantly in recent years; with the successful restoration of salmon to the Bresle River in Normandy (Arrignon, 1973a, b, 1988) many large rivers, such as the Loire and Allier, are now being restored (Arrignon, 1988).

There is hope, too, for rivers in other countries in Europe from which salmon have long since disappeared as a result of navigation locks, pollution and damage to spawning grounds (Philippart, 1987). One of these is the River Meuse flowing through the French Ardennes, Belgium and The Netherlands. A research project is being developed by the University of Liège in the Laboratory of Fish Demography and Experimental Fish Culture, with the aim of reintroducing salmon to this river to which sea trout have already returned (Philippart, 1985; Philippart *et al.*, 1987). It would be a tremendous achievement if this were successful, it would add another country to the list of those to which Atlantic salmon have been either restored or introduced, and, who knows, salmon could also return to the Rhine (Anonyme, 1984).

One should not overlook those areas in the Northern Hemisphere to which Atlantic salmon have been introduced for the first time. The most significant introduction of this sort has been to the Faroes. Until 1957 no salmon were recorded in the rivers of the Faroe Islands although one small river on Eysturoy, called the Laksa or 'salmon' river may have held salmon a long time ago. There had been attempts 10 years earlier to establish a run by importing 10 000 eggs from Iceland and releasing the subsequent fry in the Fjardara, but there were no records of returning adults from these early plantings, although the first record in 1957 is almost certainly attributable to these early attempts. Some of the fish seen in 1957 were caught and formed the basis of all subsequent plantings in the Faroes. Over the last 25 years salmon have become established in five rivers through the efforts of the Fisheries Research Institute and the Faroes Sport Fishing Association who have released fry and smolts from their hatcheries. The rivers are the Leynara, Dalsa or Saksun and Stora on Streymoy, the Fjardara on Eysturoy and the Sanda on Sandoy. The Leynara has two lakes on its course in which salmon tend to stay until spawning time. The Stora and Fjardara have no natural lakes on their course, although there have been plans to construct small man-made lakes to serve as holding areas for salmon because the rivers have few good holding pools. Fish passes have been constructed on the lower reaches of the Leynara to enable salmon to negotiate a series of steep falls (Fig. 15.2).

Attempts have been made to introduce salmon into West Greenland rivers, but low water temperatures have prevented their success (Jonas, 1974). However, Greenland is still considering ways of increasing its contribution to the salmon stocks in its coastal waters. One possibility is salmon ranching using its one salmon river, the Kapisigdlit, as a natural point of return.

**Fig. 15.2** The Lower Leynara – one of the best salmon rivers in the Faroes. (Photo **by** Derek Mills.)

**Fig. 15.3**  The 50 kroner Greenland stamp, issued on 27 January 1983, is of particular interest, as is the first day cancellation depicting a salmon alevin.

Greenland's interest in salmon conservation is apparent from its issue in 1983 of a postage stamp portraying a salmon and a first day cancellation depicting a salmon alevin (Fig. 15.3).

The question is often raised as to whether or not the cost of salmon restoration is worth it. The immediate answer from those who want to see salmon back in their rivers at any cost would be 'yes'. However, those who are responsible for allocating funds for such projects may wish to have a cost–benefit analysis made. Then one may have to weigh the value to the community of having salmon return to the river against the additional costs, imposed on the community indirectly by taxation, rates or even an increase in the price of electricity, of having to improve effluent treatment and/or install fishways and fish screens and construct hatcheries. Kay *et al.* (1988) refer to the efforts to restore Atlantic salmon to about 20 rivers in New England since the late 1940s and point out that during that time over $74 M has been spent on restoration activities. They mention estimates provided by the Fish and Wildlife Service that indicate that restoration efforts during the next 50 years will require over $100 M of additional investment in upstream and downstream fish-passage facilities. The authors show, however, that fairly conservative estimates of the benefits of the Atlantic salmon restoration scheme set benefit levels for the New England public at just over $100 M. These estimates are derived from the public's willingness to pay increased taxes or other fees and also to purchase a licence to fish.

In Canada, consideration of the economic management of the Atlantic salmon resource, and assessment of the cost–benefit implications of management and improvement of salmon stocks to various users, have been made for the Saint John River (New Brunswick) by Morse and DeWolf (1973, 1979). Full assessments of the potential additional salmon returns from enhancement schemes in eastern Canada are calculated from habitat surveys, production potentials and rates of survival and exploitation (Anon., 1978). Within eastern Canada the potential for improvement was identified in 175 of the 350 watersheds, and the additional adult production was estimated at 562 000 adults. The total projected costs for a large-scale improvement programme in the Maritime Provinces and Newfoundland were about $250 M in 1978.

On the River Thames, the costs of the salmon rehabilitation scheme were running at about £65 000 a year in 1988, giving a production cost of £163–325 for each returning adult. In addition, the estimated cost of providing fish-passage facilities in the lower half of the Thames is £280 000.

Restoration schemes can, of course, be funded by conservation trusts: these obtain their funds from subscriptions, deeds of covenant, bequests, donations and grants. The Committee of the Restoration of the Jacques Cartier River benefited from a number of grant programmes which provided almost $2 M. The Quebec government itself contributed some $700 000 and the Federal government just over $1 M. The local communities along the river felt the scheme sufficiently worthwhile and donated almost $150 000. In addition many people provided voluntary help with the manual work.

A number of charitable trusts have been set up in the United Kingdom to provide funds for salmon improvement and conservation schemes on specific rivers. The funds come from private and public benefactors and, sometimes, levies on anglers and angling clubs and proprietors. Such trusts include the Thames Salmon Trust, the Tweed Foundation, the Spey Trust, the Dee Salmon Improvement Association, the Forth Fishery Conservation Trust and the Tay Foundation.

National and international organizations have also been founded, the four most important being the North Atlantic Salmon Conservation Organisation (NASCO), the Atlantic Salmon Trust, the Atlantic Salmon Federation and l'Association Internationale de Défense du Saumon Atlantique. Others include the Restoration of Atlantic Salmon in America, Inc., the Salmon and Trout Association and the Scandinavian Atlantic Salmon Group. Other important salmon conservation bodies are included in the list given in Appendix B.

The North Atlantic Salmon Conservation Organisation was set up by the Convention for the Conservation of Salmon in the North Atlantic, which came into force on 1 October 1983 following ratification by six parties (Windsor and Hutchinson, 1988). This organization was conceived partly as a result of a resolution proposed at the Second International Atlantic Salmon Symposium held in Edinburgh in 1978. Since its formation NASCO has met at its headquarters in Edinburgh each year until 1988, when it met in Reykjavik where the Treaty was initially signed in 1983. The three regional commissions have worked effectively and have already achieved significant results, not only in reducing the quotas in the Greenland and Faroese fisheries, but also in considering the impact of introductions and transfers of various salmonids.

As a result of increasing threats to Atlantic salmon stocks from the escalating high seas fisheries in the early 1960s, the Atlantic Salmon Research Trust (now the Atlantic Salmon Trust) was formed in 1967 to help with salmon conservation both at national and international level. It was successful, along with the International Atlantic Salmon Foundation (its North American counterpart) and the Restoration of Atlantic Salmon in North America, Inc., in putting pressure on various governments, through a specially-formed Committee for the Atlantic Salmon Emergency (CASE), to control the Greenland fishery. This control was achieved through US Senate Bill 2191 ('The Pelley Bill') signed by President Nixon on Christmas Eve 1971. This gave the President power to restrict the import of fish products from countries 'conducting fishing operations in a manner or under circumstances which diminishes the effectiveness of an international fishery conservation programme'. A Danish delegation agreed with the US government that their offshore netting should be reduced each year from 1972 to 1975 and cease altogether in 1976. The agreement was presented to the International Commission for the Northwest Atlantic Fisheries (ICNAF) (now replaced by the North Atlantic Fisheries Organisation, NAFO) in the following year for their approval.

The Trust now liaises with all Atlantic-salmon-producing nations in continuing endeavours to protect salmon from over-exploitation in the open seas off Greenland, the Faroes and inshore waters close to countries of origin. It is particularly concerned over the rate of exploitation of the legal (licensed) and illegal drift-net fisheries off north-west Ireland and north-east England. It sponsored jointly with the International Atlantic Salmon Foundation (now the Atlantic Salmon Federation) an expedition of salmon experts to Greenland to inspect the fishery in 1980 (Kreiberg, 1981) and similarly to the Faroes in 1982 (Mills and Smart, 1982). It subsequently invited Greenland and Faroese fishermen to the United Kingdom to see at first hand the salmon conservation measures being undertaken.

The Trust is also alert to environmental problems and developments which may adversely affect the survival of the young stages of the salmon. It is particularly aware of the deleterious effects of pollution, acidification and afforestation. It also keeps itself informed of the problems of the conflicting interests of animal conservation bodies and fisheries organizations, particularly with regard to fish-eating birds and grey seals. The Trust has also drawn attention to the effects of salmon farming and the possible introductions of specific diseases and parasites associated with this industry. Other activities include the organization of workshops on various aspects of salmon ecology and management, with the proceedings being published in the form of booklets (now popularly referred to as 'blue books').

Through its scientific advisory panel, the AST considers research and management projects and and has sponsored a number of studies. These have recently included the sonic tracking of adult salmon and a study of the genetic variations in salmon stocks. The Director of the Trust liaises regularly with the government and research laboratories and nature conservation bodies and he and delegated members of the Trust's Council or Committee of Management attend as observers at meetings of both NASCO and the International Council for the Exploration of the Sea (ICES).

An activity which the Trust sponsored with their co-sponsor l'Association Internationale de Défense du Saumon Atlantique (AIDSA) was the successful Third International Atlantic Salmon Symposium held in Biarritz in 1986. A significant resolution agreed at the end of the conference called on all salmon-producing nations to reduce harvesting of salmon and to encourage greater effort in using this valuable resource for sport fishing.

The AST is a charitable trust and obtains a large part of its funds as donations from companies, private individuals and sponsors. However, further money is obtained from its successful annual 'postal fishing auction' which attracts a lot of attention from anglers in Britain and abroad.

The International Atlantic Salmon Foundation (now the Atlantic Salmon Federation) was formed in 1968 and works closely with the Atlantic Salmon Trust. Like the AST, the ASF organizes workshops and publishes the proceedings. In 1972 it organized the First International Atlantic Salmon Symposium which was held in St Andrew's, New Brunswick. In 1982 it amalgamated with the Atlantic Salmon Association to become the Atlantic Salmon Federation. In 1988 in Portland, Maine, it organized a symposium on Future Atlantic Salmon Management. Among its other activities it is encouraging the Canadian government to proceed with the buy-back of commercial salmon fishing licences, being prepared to subscribe \$2 M to the buy-back fund. Along with the AST, the ASF offers travelling fellowships through the Bensinger–Liddell Fund and also has an active education programme for schoolchildren.

Another trust, set up in Scotland in 1985, is the Atlantic Salmon Conservation Trust (Scotland) whose main purpose is to purchase commercial salmon fishing rights, both around the Scottish coast and in the rivers. So far, a significant number of fishings have been bought by the Trust, including many coastal netting stations in the Moray Firth. River nets have also been purchased and removed by the Trust from the rivers Conon, Don, Aberdeenshire Dee and Tweed. It is not the intention of the Trust to curtail commercial fishing for ever, and should it consider that stocks have reached a commercially exploitable level in any area it would resume commercial fishing on a limited scale. However, it has not indicated how it assesses whether or not a stock has reached an exploitable level.

Many salmon managers are concerned that with reduced commercial fishing effort, poaching and illegal fishing will increase. At the moment governments operate efficient surveillance systems using helicopters, aircraft and patrol boats to restrict illegal fishing. Offenders are given extremely heavy fines which seem to be some deterrent to further offences (Crawford, 1988). Fishery Boards, too, have their own anti-poaching patrols and in Scotland the Association of Scottish District Salmon Fishery Boards has produced a video to train bailiffs in identifying and apprehending poachers, but more bailiffs are urgently needed. In addition, the UK government is now introducing a salmon dealer licensing scheme using the powers contained in the *Salmon Act*, 1986. In Canada, France and Spain the tagging of all landed fish is a statutory requirement (Fig. 15.4).

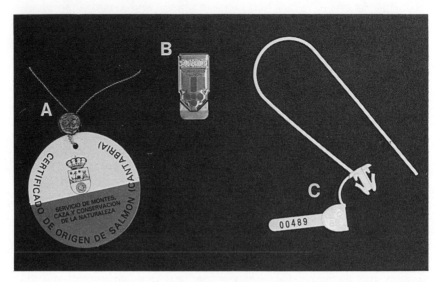

**Fig. 15.4** Tags attached to adult salmon after capture: (A) in Spain, a circular cardboard tag is attached to the fish with a lead seal; (B) tag clipped to the gill cover of a Norwegian farmed salmon before being sent to market; (C) Canadian Department of Fisheries and Oceans tag – when locked it would be around the jaw of the fish.

The salmon's future lies also in the hands of the general public, and a greater public awareness (Fig. 15.5) of the various threats to the salmon fostered through the media, school projects and the written word, will, it is hoped, help to ensure its survival – so providing us all with endless pleasure.

**Fig. 15.5** A greater public awareness – salmon held up in Loch Fleet during drought conditions in the River Fleet, Sutherland. (Photo by C. Mylne.)

# World catches of Atlantic salmon

**Table A1** Atlantic salmon catches for the North Atlantic (tonnes)*

| Where caught | 1975 | 1976 | 1977 | 1978 | 1979 | 1980 | 1981 | 1982 | 1983 | 1984 | 1985 | 1986 | 1987† |
|---|---|---|---|---|---|---|---|---|---|---|---|---|---|
| France | 25 | 9 | 19 | 20 | 10 | 30 | 20 | 20 | 16 | 25 | 22 | 28 | 27 |
| England and Wales | 447 | 208 | 345 | 349 | 261 | 360 | 493 | 286 | 432 | 345 | 361 | 430 | 291 |
| Scotland | 1561 | 1010 | 1131 | 1323 | 1075 | 1134 | 1233 | 1092 | 1221 | 1013 | 913 | 1271 | 910 |
| Northern Ireland | 164 | 113 | 110 | 148 | 99 | 122 | 101 | 132 | 187 | 78 | 98 | 109 | 48 |
| Republic of Ireland | 2216 | 1561 | 1372 | 1230 | 1097 | 947 | 685 | 993 | 1656 | 829 | 1595 | 1730 | 1239 |
| Norway | 1537 | 1530 | 1488 | 1050 | 1831 | 1830 | 1656 | 1348 | 1550 | 1623 | 1561 | 1598 | 1389 |
| Sweden (west coast) | 26 | 20 | 10 | 10 | 12 | 17 | 26 | 25 | 28 | 40 | 45 | 54 | 47 |
| USSR | 811 | N/A | N/A | N/A | 430 | 631 | 450 | 311 | 436 | 354 | 652 | 608 | 559 |
| Spain | 25 | 20 | 18 | 30 | 28 | N/A | N/A | N/A | N/A | N/A | N/A | N/A | N/A |
| Iceland | 266 | 225 | 230 | 291 | 225 | 249 | 163 | 147 | 198 | 159 | 217 | 330 | 220 |
| Canada | 2485 | 2506 | 2545 | 1545 | 1287 | 2680 | 2437 | 1798 | 1434 | 1112 | 1133 | 1559 | 1731 |
| USA | 1.7 | 0.8 | 2.4 | 4.1 | 2.5 | 5.5 | 6.0 | 6.4 | 1.3 | 2.0 | 2.1 | 1.9 | 1.1 |
| Faroes‡ | 28 | 40 | 40 | 51 | 194 | 718 | 1125 | 680 | 753 | 697 | 672 | 530 | 510 |
| Greenland§ | 2030 | 1175 | 1420 | 984 | 1395 | 1194 | 1264 | 1077 | 310 | 297 | 864 | 960 | 966 |

*Source: International Council for the Exploration of the Sea (N/A denotes unavailable data).

†Provisional figures.

‡The 1980 seasonal catch is reported to have been 968 tonnes (gutted weight); by agreement with the EEC the Faroes accepted catch quotas of 750 tonnes for 1981 and 625 tonnes for 1982; later the quota was agreed for 1985 as 550 tonnes.

§The internationally agreed quota was 1190 tonnes until 1982 when it became 1270 tonnes but related to a later opening of the season; later quotas were 1983:1190; 1984:870; 1985:852; 1986:909, and 1987:935 tonnes.

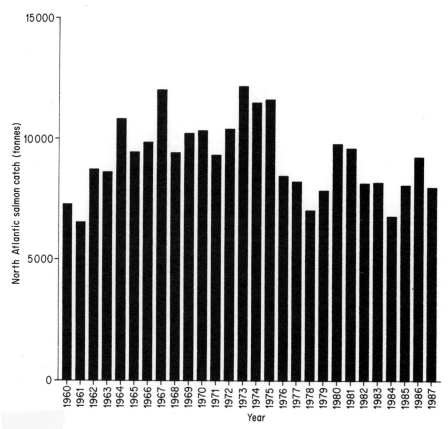

Total annual North Atlantic salmon catch, 1960–86 (reproduced with permission from NASCO).

# APPENDIX B

# Atlantic salmon conservation organizations

Asociación Asturiana de Pesca,
  Covadonga 17 – 1,
  Oviedo,
  Spain.

Association Internationale de Défense du Saumon Atlantique,
  214 Boulevard St. Germain,
  75007 Paris,
  France.

Atlantic Salmon Conservation Trust (Scotland),
  121 High Street,
  Forres,
  Moray IV36 0AB,
  Scotland.

Atlantic Salmon Federation,
  P.O. Box 429,
  St. Andrew's,
  New Brunswick,
  Canada, E0G 2X0.

Atlantic Salmon Federation,
  1435 Saint-Alexandre,
  Suite 1030,
  Montreal,
  Quebec,
  Canada, H3A 2G4.

Atlantic Salmon Trust,
  Moulin,
  Pitlochry,
  Perthshire, PH16 5JQ,
  Scotland.

Belgian Salmon Club,
Avenue de Mercure 9,
  1190 Brussels,
  Belgium.

Corporation de Restauration de la Jacques Cartier,
  C.P. 36,
  St. Catherine,
  Quebec,
  Canada, G0A 3M0.

Federation Québecoise pour la Saumon Atlantique,
  1900, Boulevard Charest Ouest,
  Suite 225,
  Sainte-Foy,
  Québec,
  Canada, G1N 4K8.

North Atlantic Salmon Conservation Organisation,
  11 Rutland Square,
  Edinburgh, EH1 2AS,
  Scotland.

Restoration of Atlantic Salmon in America, Inc.,
  Box 164,
  Hancock,
  New Hampshire, 03449,
  USA.

Salmon Conservancy,
  22 East Lennox Drive,
  Helensburgh,
  Dunbartonshire, G84 9JD,
  Scotland.

Salmon and Trout Association,
  Fishmongers Hall,
  London Bridge,
  London, EC4R 9EL,
  England.

Scandinavian Atlantic Salmon Group,
  Box 7328,
  103 90 Stockholm,
  Sweden.

Thames Salmon Trust,
  34 Smith Square,
  London, SW1P 3HE,
  England.

# References

Abrahamsen, H. and Matzow, D. (1984) Use of lime slurry for deacidification of running water. *Verh. Internat. Verein. Limnol.*, **22**, 1981–5.

Acheson, J.H. (1975) Fisheries management and social context: the case of the Maine lobster fishery. *Trans. Amer. Fish. Soc.*, **104** (4), 653–68.

Aitken, P.L., Dickerson, L.H. and Menzies, W.J.M. (1966) Fish passes and screens at water power works. *Proc. Instn Civ. Engrs*, **35**, 29–57.

Alabaster, J.S. (1970) River flow and upstream movement and catch of migratory salmonids. *J. Fish Biol.*, **2**, 1–13.

Alabaster, J.S. and Lloyd, R. (1980) *Water Quality Criteria for Freshwater Fish*, Butterworth, London.

Alexander, D.R. and Galbraith, P. (1982). A plan to re-establish a natural population of Atlantic salmon in the Point Wolfe River, Fundy National Park. Canadian Manuscript Report of Fisheries and Aquatic Sciences no. 1667, 8 pp.

Allan, I.R.H. (1965) Counting fences for salmon and sea trout and what can be learned from them. Salmon and Trout Association, London Conference, 1965, 1–16.

Allan, I.R.H. and Ritter, J A. (1975) Salmonid terminology. *J. Cons. Perm. Int. Explor. Mer*, **37**, 293–9.

Allen, K.R. (1940) Studies on the biology of the early stages of the salmon (*Salmo salar*). 1. Growth in the River Eden. *J. Anim. Ecol.*, **9**, 1–23.

Allen, K.R. (1941) Studies on the biology of the early stages of the salmon (*Salmo salar*). 2. Feeding habits. *J. Anim. Ecol.*, **10**, 47–76.

Allen, K.R. (1944) Studies on the biology of the early stages of the salmon (*Salmo salar*). 4. The smolt migration in the Thurso river in 1938. *J. Anim. Ecol.*, **13**, 63–85.

Allendorf, F.W., Ryman, N. and Utter, F.M. (1987) Genetics and fishery management. In *Population Genetics and Fishery Management* (eds N. Ryman and F. Utter), University of Washington Press, Seattle, pp. 1–19.

Allport, M. (1870) Brief history of the introduction of salmon (*S. salar*) and other Salmonidae to the waters of Tasmania. *Proc. Zool. Soc. London*, 1870, 14–30, 750–2.

Alm, G. (1955) Artificial hybridisation between the different species of the salmon family. *Rep. Inst. Freshwat. Res., Drottningholm*, **36**, 13–56.

Altukhov, Yu.P. (1981) The stock concept from the viewpoint of population genetics. *Can. J. Fish. Aquat. Sci.*, **38**, 1523–8.

Andersen, K.P., Horsted, Sv. Aa. and Møller Jensen, J. (1980) Analysis of recaptures from the West Greenland tagging experiments. *Rapp. Proc. Verb. Réun. Cons. Perm. Int. Explor. Mer*, **176**, 136–47.

Anderson, H.W., Hoover, M.D. and Reinhart, K.G. (1976) *Forests and Water: effects of forest management on floods, sedimentation and water supply*. USDA Forest Service General Technical Report, PSW 18, 115 pp.

Anderson, J.M. (1971) Sublethal effects and changes in ecosystems. Assessment of the effects of pollutants on physiology and behaviour. *Proc. R. Soc.*, **B, 177**, 307–20.

Anderson, J.M. (1986) Merganser predation and its impact on Atlantic salmon stocks in the Restigouche River System, 1982–1985. *Atlantic Salmon Federation Special Publication Series*, no. 13, 66 pp.

Anderson, J.M. and Elson, P.F. (1971) Effect on adult returns of exposure of native wild smolt to sub-lethal DDT. *International Council for the Exploration of the Sea*, C.M.1971/M:7.

Andersson, B.I., Alenäs, I. and Hultberg, H. (1984) Liming of a small acidified river (River Anråseån) in southwestern Sweden, promoting successful reproduction of sea trout (*Salmo trutta* L.). *Rep. Inst. Freshwat. Res., Drottningholm*, 61, 16.

Anon. (1957) *The Passage of Smolts and Kelts through Fish Passes*, Scottish Home Department, Her Majesty's Stationery Office, London.

Anon. (1961) *Report of Committee on Salmon and Freshwater Fisheries*, (The Bledisloe Report), Her Majesty's Stationery Office, London, Cmnd. 1350.

Anon. (1963) *Scottish Salmon and Trout Fisheries*. Her Majesty's Stationery Office, London, Cmnd. 2096. (First Hunter Committee Report.)

Anon. (1965) *Scottish Salmon and Trout Fisheries*. Her Majesty's Stationery Office, London, Cmnd. 2691. (Second Hunter Committee Report.)

Anon. (1967) Salmon disease in Irish rivers. *Salmon Net*, 111, 44–9.

Anon. (1978) Atlantic salmon review, *Government of Canada, Fisheries and Oceans Resource Development Sub-Committee Report*, November 1978, 55 pp.

Anon. (1982a) Report of Meeting of the Working Group on North Atlantic Salmon. *International Council for the Exploration of the Sea*, C.M. 1982/Assess. 19.

Anon. (1982b) Salmon control: tagging along. *Water Bulletin.*, no. 19, 6 August.

Anon. (1983) Introduction of pink salmon to United Kingdom water. *Atlantic Salmon Trust Progress Report*, October, pp. 11–12.

Anon. (1985a) *Atlantic Salmon Scale Reading*. Report of the Atlantic Salmon Scale Reading Workshop. International Council for the Exploration of the Sea.

Anon. (1985b) Report of Meeting of the Working Group on North Atlantic Salmon. *International Council for the Exploration of the Sea*, C.M.1985/Assess. 11.

Anon. (1985c) Salmon rehabilitation scheme. Phase 1. Review. *Thames Water, Rivers Division, Special Publication*, 46 pp.

Anon. (1986) First triploid smolts leave Howietoun. *Aquaculture News*, vol. I.

Anon. (1987a) Report of the North Atlantic Salmon Working Group. *International Council for the Exploration of the Sea.*

Anon. (1987b) *Water Pollution from Farm Wastes*. Water Authorities Association/Ministry of Agriculture, Fisheries and Food, WAA Publications, Sheffield.

Anon. (1987c) *Report of the Salmon Review Group*. Framework for the development of Ireland's salmon fishery. Stationery Office, Dublin, 103 pp.

Anon. (1987d) *Codes of Practice and Manual of Procedures for Consideration of Introductions and Transfers of Marine and Freshwater Organism*. Prepared by the Working Group on Introduction and Transfer of Marine Organisms of the International Council for the Exploration of the Sea and by the Working Party on Introductions of the European Inland Fisheries Advisory Commission. (ed. G.E. Turner), ICES Doc. No. F:35A, 42 pp.

Anon. (1988a) *Marine Fishfarming in Scotland*. A discussion paper prepared by the Scottish Wildlife and Countryside Link, Perth, Scotland.

Anon. (1988b) *The reduction of the impact of fish farming on the natural marine environment*, A report prepared for the Nature Conservancy Council by the Institute of Aquaculture, University of Stirling, pp. 167.

Anon. (1988c) Chernobyl and trout, In FISH, January, 9, 30–1.

Anonyne (1984) Schon bald wieder Lachs im Rhein. *Fliegenfischen*, 1, 24–7.

Arrignon, J. (1973a) Tentative de réacclimation de *Salmo salar* dans la bassĭn de la Bresle. *Bulletin Français Pêche Pisciculture*, **248**, 91–190.

Arrignon, J. (1973b) An attempt at *Salmo salar* acclimatization in the Bresle River Basin, Normandy, France. In *International Atlantic Salmon Symposium, St Andrew's* (eds M.W. Smith and W.M. Carter), *International Atlantic Salmon Foundation Special Publication Series*, **4** (1), 463–74.

Arrignon, J. (1988) Exploitation of the resource in France. In *Atlantic Salmon: Planning for the Future* (eds D. Mills and D. Piggins), Croom Helm, London, pp. 29–68.

Bailey, J.K. (1987) Canadian sea ranching program (East Coast). In *EIFAC/FAO Symposium on Selection, Hybridisation and Genetic Engineering in Aquaculture*, (ed. K. Tiews), Heinemann, Berlin.

Bailey, N.T.J. (1951) On estimating the size of mobile populations from recapture data. *Biometrika*, **38**, 293–306.

Balmain, K.H. and Shearer, W.M. (1956) Records of salmon and sea trout caught at sea. *Freshwat. Salm. Fish. Res., Scotland*, 11, 12 pp.

Balon, E.K. (1968) Notes to the origin and evolution of trouts and salmons with special reference to the Danubian trouts. *Vest. Csl. spol. zool.*, **32**, 1–21.

Banks, J.W. (1969) A review of the literature on the upstream migration of adult salmonids. *J. Fish Biol.*, **1**, 85–136.

Barton, J. Kingston (1902) *Salmo salar*: the digestive tract in kelts. *J. Anat. Physiol.*, n.s. **16**, 142–6.

Baxter, G. (1961) River utilisation and the preservation of migratory fish life. *Proc. Instn Civ. Engrs*, **18**, 225–44.

Behnke, R.J. (1972) The systematics of salmonid fishes of recently glaciated lakes. *J. Fish. Res. Bd Can.*, **29**, 639–71.

Beland, K.F., Jordan, R.M. and Meister, A.L. (1982) Water depth and velocity preferences of spawning Atlantic salmon in Maine rivers. *North Am. J. Fish. Mgmt*, **2**, 11–13.

Belding, D.L. (1934b) The cause of the high mortality in the Atlantic salmon after spawning. *Trans. Amer. Fish. Soc.*, **64**, 219–24.

Belding, D. L. (1934a) The spawning habits of the Atlantic salmon. *Trans. Amer. Fish. Soc.*, **64**, 211–8.

Bell, M.C. (1974) Fish passage through turbines, conduits and spillway gates. *Proceedings of the Second Workshop on Entrainment and Intake Screenings* (ed. L.D. Jensen), Reprint 15, Electric Power Research Institute, Palo Alto, California, pp. 251–61.

Berg, L.S. (1935) Evidence on the biology of *Salmo salar*. Izv. VNIORKH, 20.

Berg, M. (1953) A relict salmon, *Salmo salar* L., called 'smablank' from the River Namsen, North Trondelag. *Acta Borealia*, **6**, 1–17.

Berg, M. (1961) Pink salmon (*Oncorhynchus gorbuscha*) in Northern Norway in the year 1960. *Acta Borealia*, A. Scientia, 17, 24 pp.

Berg, M. (1964) *Nord-Norske Lakseelver*, Johan Grundt Tanum Forlag, Oslo, 300 pp.

Berg, M. (1977a) Tagging of migrating smolts (*Salmo salar*, L.) in the Vardnes River, Troms, Northern Norway. *Rep. Inst. Freshwat. Res., Drottningholm*, **56**, 5–11.

Berg, M. (1977b) Pink salmon (*Oncorhynchus gorbuscha* (Walbaum)) in Norway. *Rep. Inst. Freshwat. Res., Drottningholm*, **56**, 12–17.

Berg, M., Abrahamsen, B. and Berg, O.K. (1986) Spawning of injured compared to uninjured female Atlantic salmon, *Salmo salar*, L. *Aquaculture and Fisheries Management*, **17**, 195–200.

Berry, J. (1932) Report of an investigation of smolts in the River Tay during Spring, 1931. *Fisheries Scotland, Salmon Fisheries*, 1931, **IV**, 21 pp.

Berry, J. (1933) Notes on the migration of smolts from Loch Ness, summer, 1932. *Fisheries Scotland, Salmon Fisheries*, 1933, **I**, 12 pp.

Bertram, C. and Holst, J. (eds) (1977) *New Strategic Factors in the North Atlantic*, IPC Science and Technology Press Ltd, Guildford.

Bielak, A.T. and Power, G.G. (1988) Catch-records – facts or myths? In *Atlantic Salmon: Planning for the Future* (eds D. Mills and D. Piggins), Croom Helm, London, pp. 235–55.

Bledisloe Committee: *see* Anon. (1961).

Boece, H. (1527) A History of Scotland (*Scotorum Historiae: Scotorum Regni Descriptio*, folio XII), Paris.

Bottomley, P.E. (1986) Re-introduction of salmon into the River Trent. Atlantic Salmon Trust Progress Report, May 1986, 30–31.

Brannon, E.L. (1965) The influence of physical factors on the development and weight of sockeye salmon embryos and alevins. *Internat. Pacif. Salmon Fish. Comm*, Prog. Rep., **12**, 1–26.

Brannon, E.L. (1972) Mechanisms controlling migration of sockeye salmon fry. *Internat. Pacif. Salmon Fish. Comm. Bull.*, 21, 86 pp.

Brayshaw, J.D. (1967) The effects of river discharge on inland fisheries. In *River Management* (ed. P.C.G. Isaac), Proceedings of a symposium of the Department of Civil Engineering, University of Newcastle-upon-Tyne, London, pp. 102–18.

Brett, J.R. (1957) Salmon research and hydro-electric power development. *Bull. Fish. Res. Bd Can.*, 114, 26 pp.

Brooker, M.P., Morris, D.L. and Hemsworth, R.J. (1977) Mass mortalities of adult salmon (*Salmo salar*) in the R. Wye, 1976. *J. Appl. Ecol.*, **14**, 409–17.

Brown, G.W. (1971) Water temperature in small streams as influenced by environmental factors and logging. *Proceedings of a Symposium – Forest Land Uses and Stream Environment*, Oregon State University, Corvallis, pp. 175–81.

Brown, W.G., Singh, A. and Castle, E.N. (1964) *An Economic Evaluation of the Oregon Salmon and Steelhead Sport Fishery*, Technical Bulletin 78, Agricultural Experimental Station, Corvallis, Oregon, 46 pp.

Browne, J. (1986) The data available for analysis on the Irish salmon stock. In *The Status of the Atlantic Salmon in Scotland* (eds D. Jenkins and W.M. Shearer) ITE Symposium no. 15, Institute of Terrestrial Ecology, Abbots Ripton, pp. 84–90.

Browne, J. (1988) The use of Leslie Matrices to assess the salmon population of the River Corrib. In *Atlantic Salmon: Planning for the Future* (eds D. Mills and D. Piggins), Croom Helm, London, pp. 275–300.

Browne, J. and Gallagher, P. (1981) Population estimates of juvenile salmonids in the Corrib system 1981. *Fishery Leaflet*, Department of Fisheries and Forestry, **115**, 1–6.

Browne, J. and Gallagher, P. (1987) Population estimates of juvenile salmon in the Corrib system from 1982–1984. *Fishery Leaflet*, 135, Department of Tourism, Fisheries and Forestry, 14 pp.

Browne, J., Eriksson, C., Hansen, L.-P. *et al.* (1983) COST Project 46/4 on ocean ranching of Atlantic salmon: Final Report, 16–91. In Anon. Action cost 46: Rapport 1980–1983. Commission des Communautés Européennes, Brussels.

Buck, R.J.G. and Hay, D.W. (1984) The relation between stock size and progeny of Atlantic salmon (*Salmo salar* L.) in a Scottish stream. *J. Fish Biol.*, **24**, 1–11.

Buckland, F. (1880) *Natural History of British Fishes*, SPCK, Unwin Bros, London.

Bullock, A.M. and Roberts, R.J. (1979) Introduction of UDN-like lesions in salmonid fish by exposure to ultra-violet light in the presence of phototoxic agents. *Journal of Fish Diseases*, **2** (5), 439–41.

Burczynski, J. (1979) Introduction to the use of sonar systems for estimating fish biomass. FAO Technical Paper no. 191.

Burns, J.E. (1970) The importance of streamside vegetation to trout and salmon in British Columbia, *Fisheries Technical Circular* No. 1. Vancouver Island Region, Fish and Wildlife Branch, Department of Recreation and Conservation, Nanaimo, British Columbia.

Calderwood, W.L. (1903a) Water temperature in relation to the early annual migration of salmon from the sea to the rivers in Scotland. *21st Annual Report of the Fishery Board for Scotland*, **II**, 71–6.

Calderwood, W.L. (1903b) The temperature of the River Tay and its tributaries in relation to the ascent of salmon. *21st Annual Report of the Fishery Board for Scotland*, **III**, 77–82.

Calderwood, W.L. (1904) The bull trout of the Tay and Tweed. *Proc. R. Soc. Edin.*, **XXV** (Pt. 1), 27–38.

Calderwood, W.L. (1906a) Autumn migration of smolts in Scotland. *Report for the Fishery Board of Scotland*, 1905, Part II, 70–74.

Calderwood, W.L. (1906b) The white spot disease in salmon in the Island of Lewis. *24th Annual Report of the Fishery Board for Scotland*, Appendix 5, 78–9.

Calderwood, W.L. (1907) *The Life of the Salmon*, Edward Arnold, London.

Calderwood, W.L. (1909, 1921) *The Salmon Rivers and Lochs of Scotland*, Edward Arnold, London.

Calderwood, W.L. (1925) The relation of sea growth and spawning frequency in *Salmo salar*. *Proc. R. Soc. Edin.*, **45**, 142–8.

Calderwood, W.L. (1930) *Salmon and Sea Trout*, Edward Arnold, London.

Calderwood, W.L. (1940) Thirty years of salmon marking. *Salmon and Trout Magazine*, no. 88, 207–13.

Calderwood, W.L. (1945) Passage of smolts through turbines: effect of high pressures. *Salmon and Trout Magazine*, no. 115, 214–21.

Campbell, R.N. (1963) Some effects of impoundment on the environment and growth of brown trout (*Salmo trutta* L.) in Loch Garry (Inverness-shire). *Freshwat. Salm. Fish. Res.*, **30**, 37 pp.

Carberry, J.T. and Strickland, K.L. (1968) Resistance of rainbow trout to ulcerative dermal necrosis. *Nature*, **217** (5134), 1158.

Carlin, B. (1969) The migration of salmon. *Swedish Salmon Research Institute*, LFI Meddelande 4, 14–21.

Caron, F. (1983) Migration vers l'Atlantique des post saumoneaux (*Salmo salar*) du Golfe du Saint-Laurent. *Naturaliste Can.* (Quebec), **110**, 223–7.

Carson, W.G. and Carson, W.V. (1972) Toxicity of copper and zinc to Atlantic juvenile salmon in the presence of humic acid and lignosulfonates. *Fish. Res. Bd Can.*, MS Report, Series 1181, 10 pp.

Carter, W.M. (1964) Quebec's salmon rivers. A glance at the past. A plan for the future. *The Atlantic Salmon Journal*, Winter 64/65, 18–22, 36–7.

Carter, W.M. (1985) The Atlantic salmon – a social welfare species. In *Transactions of the 1984 Canadian Sport Fisheries Conference – Canada's Sport Fisheries: Getting Ready for the 1990's* (ed. A.L.W. Tuomi). *Canadian Special Publications of Fisheries and Aquatic Sciences*, 82, 338 pp.

Cave, J.D. (1985) The effects of the Kielder scheme on fisheries. *J. Fish Biol.*, **27** (Suppl. A), 109–21.

Chadwick, E.M.P. (1982a) Stock recruitment relationships for Atlantic salmon (*Salmo salar*) in Newfoundland. *Can. J. Fish. Aquat. Sci.*, **39**, 1496–1501.

Chadwick, E.M.P. (1982b) Dynamics of an Atlantic salmon stock (*Salmo salar*) in a small Newfoundland river. PhD Thesis, Memorial University of Newfoundland, 267 pp.

Chadwick, E.M.P. (1982c) Recreational catch as an index of Atlantic salmon spawning escapement. *International Coouncil for the Exploration of the Sea*, C.M.1982/M:43.

Chadwick, E.M.P. (1982d) 1 SW Atlantic salmon harvests predicted one year in advance. *International Council for the Exploration of the Sea*, C.M.1982/M:20.

Chadwick, E.M.P. (1985a) Atlantic salmon production (*Salmo salar* L.) in a largely lacustrine Newfoundland watershed. *Ver. Internat. Verein. Limnol.*, **22**, 2509–15.

Chadwick, E.M.P. (1985b) The influence of spawning stock on production and yield of Atlantic salmon (*Salmo salar* L.) in Canadian rivers. *Aquaculture and Fisheries Management*, **16** (1), 111–19.

Chadwick, E.M.P. (1985c) Fundamental research problems in the management of Atlantic salmon, *Salmo salar*, in Atlantic Canada. *J. Fish Biol.*, **27** (Suppl. A), 9–25.

Chadwick, E.M.P. (1988) Relation between Atlantic salmon smolts and adults in Canadian rivers. In *Atlantic Salmon: Planning for the Future* (eds D. Mills and D. Piggins), Croom Helm, London, pp. 301–24.

Chadwick, E.M.P. and Randall, R.G. (1986) A stock–recruitment relationship for Atlantic salmon in the Miramichi River, New Brunswick. *North Am. J. Fish. Mgmt*, **6**, 200–203.

Chapman, A. (1924) *The Borders and Beyond*, Gurney and Jackson, Edinburgh.

Chidester, F.E. (1924) A critical examination of the evidence for physical and chemical influences on fish migration. *J. Exp. Biol.*, **2**, 79–118.

Child, A.R., Burnell, A.M. and Wilkins, N.P. (1976) The existence of two races of Atlantic salmon (*Salmo salar* L.) in the British Isles. *J. Fish Biol.*, **8**, 35–43.

Clavel, P., Cuinat, R., Hamon, Y. and Romaneix, C. (1978) Effets des extractions de materiaux alluvionaires sur l'environnement aquatique dans les cours supérieurs de la Loire et de l'Allier. *Bulletin Français de Pisciculture*, **268**, 121–54.

Clawson, M. (1959) *Methods of Measuring the Demand for and the Value of Outdoor Resources*, Reprint no. 10, Resources for the Future Inc., Washington, D.C., 36 pp.

Cook, B. and Mc Gaw, R. (1988) The economic performance of the commercial salmon fishery in New Brunswick. *Technical Report of the Canadian Journal of Fisheries and Aquatic Sciences* (in the press).

Copes, P. (1977) The law of the sea and management of anadromous fish stocks. In *Ocean Development and International Law, J. Mar. Affairs*, **4**, 233–59.

Copes, P. and Knetsch, J.L. (1981) Recreational fisheries analysis: management modes and benefit implications. *Can. J. Fish. Aquat. Sci.*, **38**, 559–70.

Cousens, N.B.F., Thomas, G.A., Swann, G.G. and Healey, M.C. (1982) A review of salmon escapement estimation techniques. *Can. Tech. Rep. Fish. Aquat. Sci.*, 1108, 112 pp.

Cragg-Hine, D. (1985) The assessment of the flow requirements for upstream migration of salmonids in some rivers of north-west England. In *Habitat Modification and Freshwater Fisheries* (ed. J. Alabaster), Butterworth, London, pp. 209–15.

Craik, J.C.A., Harvey, S.M., Jakupsstovu, S.H.i. and Shearer, W.M. (1987) Identification of farmed and artificially reared Atlantic salmon among the catch of the wild salmon fishery of the Faroes. *International Council for the Exploration of the Sea*, C.M. 1987/M:26.

Crawford, W.G. (1988) The impact of illegal fishing on salmon stocks in the Foyle area. In *Atlantic Salmon: Planning for the Future* (eds D. Mills and D. Piggins), Croom Helm, London, pp. 424–34.

Crichton, M.J. (1935) Scale absorption in salmon and sea trout. *Fisheries, Scotland, Salmon Fisheries*, **IV**, 8 pp.

Crisp, D.T. (1984) Water temperature studies in the River North Tyne after impoundment by Kielder dam. Freshwater Biological Association, Teesdale Unit, Unpublished report.

Cross, T.F. and Healy, J.A. (1983) The use of biochemical genetics to distinguish populations of Atlantic salmon, *Salmo salar*. In *Advances in Fish Biology in Ireland* (ed. C. Moriarty), Irish Fisheries Investigations, Series A, no. 23, pp. 61–6.

Cross, T.F. and King, J. (1983) Genetic effects of hatchery rearing in Atlantic salmon. *Aquaculture*, **33**, 333–40.

Crutchfield, J.A. (1979) Economic and social implications of the main policy alternatives for controlling fishing effort. *J. Fish. Res. Bd Can.*, **36**, 742–52.

Crutchfield, J.A. and MacFarlane, D. (1968) *Economic Valuation of the 1965–1966 Salt-Water Fisheries of Washington*, State of Washington, Department of Fisheries, Seattle, Research Bulletin no. 8, 44 pp.

Cuinat, R. (1988) Atlantic salmon in an extensive French river system: the Loire–Allier. In *Atlantic Salmon: Planning for the Future* (eds D. Mills and D. Piggins) Croom Helm, London, pp. 389–99.

Cushing, D. (1983) *Climate and Fisheries*, Academic Press, London.

Cutting, R.E. (1963) *Penobscot River Salmon Restoration*. Maine Atlantic Sea-Run Salmon Commission, Bangor, Me., 162 pp.

Dahl, K. (1910) *The Age and Growth of Salmon and Trout in Norway as Shown by their Scales* (translated by I. Baillie, eds J.A. Hutton and H.T. Sheringham), Salmon and Trout Association, London.

Dahl, K. (1927) The effects of acid water on trout fry. *Salmon and Trout Magazine*, no. 46, 35–43.

Dalley, E.L., Andrews, C. and Green, J.M. (1983) Precocious male Atlantic salmon parr (*Salmo salar*) in Newfoundland. *Can. J. Fish. Aquat. Sci.*, **40**, 647–62.

Dam, A. (1988) Interception fisheries – the Faroese point of view. In *Future Atlantic Salmon Management* (in press).

Davidson, F.A. and Hutchinson, S.J. (1938) The geographic distribution and environmental limitations of the Pacific salmon (genus *Oncorhynchus*). *Bull. Bureau Fish.*, Washington State, **48**, 667–92.

Davis, J.P. and Scott, D.C. (1983) Exploits River Atlantic salmon development program 1978, 1979 and 1980. Freshwater and Anadromous Fisheries Management Program, Dept. of Fisheries and Oceans.

Davy, H. (1832) *Salmonia*, Murray, London.

Day, F. (1887) *British and Irish Salmonidae*, Williams and Norgate, London.

Delvingt, W. (1985) Reintroduction du saumon atlantique dans le bassin de la Meuse. Compte rendu du colloque tenu à Namur le 28 mars 1985, Service de la pêche de la Région Wallonne, 144 pp.

Dempson, J.B. (1980) Application of a stock recruitment model to assess the Labrador Atlantic salmon fishery. *International Council for the Exploration of the Sea*, CM 1980/M: 28, 15 pp.

Dermott, C.A. and Timmins, C.A. (1986) Occurrence and spawning of pink salmon, *Oncorhynchus gorbuscha* in Lake Ontario tributaries. *Canadian Field Naturalist*, **100** (1), 131–3.

Dickson, W. (1978) Some effects of the acidification of Swedish lakes. *Verh. Internat. Verein. Limnol.*, **20**, 851–6.

Dill, L.M. (1969) The sub-gravel behaviour of Pacific salmon larvae. In *Symposium on Salmon and Trout in Streams* (ed. T.G. Northcote), H.R. MacMillan Lectures in Fisheries, 1968, University of British Columbia, Vancouver, pp. 89–99.

Dill, P.A. (1977) Development behaviour in alevins of Atlantic salmon (*Salmo salar*) and rainbow trout (*S. gairdneri*). *Animal Behaviour*, **25**, 116–21.

Dimond, J.B., Getchell, A.S. and Blease, J.A. (1971) Accumulation and persistence of DDT in a lotic ecosystem. *J. Fish. Res. Bd Can.*, **28**, 1872–82.

Dogiel, V. and Petrushevski, G. (1935) An ecological study of the parasites of the salmon. (In Russian.) *Publ. Ecol. Biocenol. Leningrad*, **2**, 137–69.

Dolmen, D. (1987) *Gyrodactylus salaris* (Monogenea) in Norway: infestations and management. *Proceedings of the Symposium on Parasites and Diseases in Natural Waters and Aquaculture in Nordic countries* (eds A. Stenmark and G. Malmberg), Stockholm, Dec. 1986. Zoo-taax, Naturhistoriska riksmuseet, University of Stockholm, 63–9.

Døving, K.B., Jonsson, B. and Hansen, L.P. (1984) The effect of anosmia on the migration of Atlantic salmon smolts (*Salmo salar* L.) in fresh water. *Aquaculture*, **38**, 383–6.

Dovland, H. and Semb, A. (1980) Atmospheric transport of pollutants. In *Ecological Impact of Acid Precipitation*. Proceedings of an International Conference (eds D. Drablos and A. Tollan), Sandefjord, pp. 14–21.

Drakeford, T. (1981) Management of upland streams. (An experimental fisheries management project on the afforested headwaters of the River Fleet, Kirkcudbrightshire). In *Proceedings of the 12th Annual Study Course of the Institute of Fisheries Management*, University of Durham, pp. 86–92.

Ducharme, L.J.A. (1969) Atlantic salmon returning for their fifth and sixth consecutive spawning trips. *J. Fish. Res. Bd Can.*, **26**, 1661–4.

Ducharme, L.J.A. (1972) An application of louver deflectors for guiding Atlantic salmon (*Salmo salar*) smolts from power turbines. *J. Fish. Res. Bd Can.*, **29** (10), 1397–1404.

Dunbar, M.J. (1958) Physical oceanographic results of the 'Calanus' expeditions in Ungava Bay, Frobisher Bay, Cumberland Sound, Hudson Strait and Northern Hudson Bay, 1949–1955. *J. Fish. Res. Bd Can.*, **15**, 155–201.

Dunbar, M.J. (1981) Twentieth century marine climatic change in the northwest Atlantic and subarctic regions. In *Symposium on Environmental Conditions in the northwest Atlantic during 1970-79*, NAFO Scientific Council Studies 5, Dartmouth, Nova Scotia, Canada, pp. 7–15.

Dunbar, M.J. and Thomson, D.H. (1979) West Greenland salmon and climatic change. *Meddelelser om Grønland*, 2022, 1–19.

Dunkley, D.A. (1986) Changes in the biology and timing of salmon runs. In *The Status of the Atlantic Salmon in Scotland* (eds D. Jenkins and W.M. Shearer), ITE Symposium no. 15, Institute of Terrestrial Ecology, Abbots Ripton, pp. 20–27.

Dunkley, D.A. and Shearer, W.M. (1982) An assessment of the performance of a resistivity fish counter. *J. Fish Biol.*, **20**, 717–37.

Dunkley, D.A. and Shearer, W.M. (1983) The reliability of population data obtained from the use of a resistivity counter in a major salmon river. *International Council for the Exploration of the Sea*, C.M.1983/M:25.

Dymond, J.R. (1961) Fishes of the Western North Atlantic. *Memoirs Sears Foundation for Marine Research*, **1**, 460–98.

Earp, B.J., Ellis, C.H. and Ordal, E.J. (1953) Kidney disease in young salmon. *State of Washington, Department of Fisheries*, Special Report Series no. 1, 74 pp.

Edman, G. and Fleicher, S. (1980) The river Högvadsån liming project – a presentation. In *Ecological Impact of Acid Precipitation* (eds D. Drablos and A. Tollan), International Conference SNSF-project, Sandefjord, Norway, pp. 300–301.

Egglishaw, H.J. (1967) The food, growth and population structure of salmon and trout in two streams in the Scottish Highlands. *Freshwat. Salm. Fish. Res., Scotland*, **38**, 32 pp.

Egglishaw, H.J. (1970) Production of salmon and trout in a stream in Scotland. *J. Fish Biol.*, **2**, 117–236.

Egglishaw, H.J. (1983) The Tummel Valley salmon smolt stock augmentation project. *Proc. 3rd British Freshwater Fish Conf.*, 1983, 20–29.

Egglishaw, H.J. and Shackley, P.E. (1977) Growth, survival and production of juvenile salmon and trout in a Scottish stream, 1966–1975. *J. Fish Biol.*, **11**, 647–72.

Egglinshaw, H.J. and Shackley, P.F. (1980) Survival and growth of salmon, *Salmo salar* L., planted in a Scottish stream. *J. Fish. Biol.*, **16**, 564–84.

Egglishaw, H.J. and Shackley, P.E. (1982) Influence of water depth on dispersion of juvenile salmonids, *Salmo salar* and *S. trutta* L. in a Scottish stream. *J. Fish Biol.*, **21**, 141–55.

Egglishaw, H.J. and Shackley, P.E. (1985) Factors governing the production of juvenile Atlantic salmon in Scottish streams. *J. Fish Biol.*, **27** (Suppl. A), 27–33.

Egglishaw, H.J., Gardiner, W.R., Shackley, P.E. and Struthers, G. (1984) *Principles and practice of stocking streams with salmon eggs and fry.* Information Pamphlet 10, Department of Agriculture and Fisheries for Scotland, Aberdeen, 22 pp.

Egidius, E. (1987) Import of furunculosis to Norway with Atlantic salmon smolts from Scotland. *International Council for the Exploration of the Sea*, C.M.1987/S:8.

Einarsson, S.M. (1987) Utilisation of Fluvial and Lacustrine Habitat by a Wild Stock of Anadromous Atlantic Salmon (*Salmo salar* L.) in an Icelandic Watershed. MPhil Thesis, University of Edinburgh, 187 pp.

Elder, H.Y. (1966) Biological effects of water utilisation by hydro-electric schemes in relation to fisheries, with special reference to Scotland. *Proc. R. Soc. Edin.*, **B, LXIX**, iii/iv, 246–71.

Elson, K.R. (1968a) Salmon disease in Scotland. *Salmon Net*, **4**, 9–17.

Elson, K.R. (1968b) Salmon disease in Scotland. *Scott. Fish. Bull.*, **30**, 8–16.

Elson, P.F. (1957) The importance of size in the change from parr to smolt in Atlantic salmon. *Can. Fish Cult.*, **21**, 1–6.

Elson, P.F. (1962) Predator-prey relationship between fish-eating birds and Atlantic salmon. *Bull. Fish. Res. Bd Can.*, 133, 87 pp.

Elson, P.F. (1967) Effects on wild young salmon of spraying DDT over New Brunswick forests. *J. Fish. Res. Bd Can.*, **24**, 731–67.

Elson, P.F. (1974) Impact of recent economic growth and industrial development on the ecology of Northwest Miramichi Atlantic salmon (*Salmo salar*). *J. Fish. Res. Bd Can.*, **31** (5), 521–44.

Elson, P.F. (1975) Atlantic salmon rivers smolt production and optimal spawning: an overview of natural production. *International Atlantic Salmon Foundation Special Publication Series*, **6**, 96–119.

Elson, P.F. and Tuomi, A.L.W. (1975) *The Foyle Fisheries: New Bases for Rational Management*, The Foyle Fisheries Commission, Londonderry, Northern Ireland.

Elson, P.F., Meister, A.L., Saunders, J.W., Saunders, R.L. and Zitko, V. (1973) Impact of chemical pollution on Atlantic salmon in North America. In *International Atlantic Salmon Symposium, St Andrew's* (eds M.W. Smith and W.M. Carter), *International Atlantic Salmon Foundation, Special Publication Series*, **4** (1), 83–109.

Environmental Protection Agency (1973) *Ecological Research Series, Water Quality Criteria*, 1972, Washington, DC.

Eriksson, C., Ferranti, M.P. and Larsson, P.O. (eds) (1982). *Sea Ranching of Atlantic Salmon*, Cost 46/4. Workshop Proceedings. Commission of the European Communities.

Euzenat, G. and Fournel, F. (1981) L'introduction des saumons de Pacifique en France. Ministére de l'environnement et du cadre de vie, Conseil supérieur de la pêche. Delegation Regionale No. 1. Compiegne, 111 pp.

Fairbairn, W.A. (1967) Erosion in the River Findhorn valley. *Scottish Geographical Magazine*, **83** (1), 46–52.

Fisher, R. (1969) *Basic Negotiating Strategy*, Allen Lane, The Penguin Press, London.

Flain, M. (1981) The history of New Zealand's salmon fishery. In *Proceedings of the Salmon Symposium* (compiler, C.L. Hopkins). NZ Ministry of Agriculture and Fisheries, Fisheries Research Division Occasional Publication, no. 30, 8–10.

Flowerdew, H. (1871) *The Parr and Salmon Controversy*, with authentic reports of the legal judgements and judge's notes in the various lawsuits on the parr question, and also a brief sketch of some incidents connected with the dissemination of the modern parr theory, Clark, Edinburgh, 147 pp.

Fontaine, M. (1951) Rémarques sur certain comportements due saumon. *Bulletin Français de Pisciculture*, no . 160, 85–8.

Fox, P. (1982) The usefulness of redd counts for salmon stock assessment. In *Workshop on The Acquisition and Use of Salmon Data for Management Purposes* (ed. G.D.F. Hadoke), Atlantic Salmon Trust, Farnham, pp. 6–8.

Franklin, I.A. (1980) Evolutionary change in small populations. In *Conservation Biology: an Evolutionary Ecological Perspective*, Sinaeur Association, Sunderland, pp. 11–34.

Fraser, P.J. (1987) Atlantic salmon feed in Scottish coastal waters. *Aquaculture and Fisheries Management*, **18** (3), 243–7.

Frederikson, R.L., Moor, R.G. and Norris, L.A. (1975) The impact of timber harvest, fertilisation and herbicide treatment on stream water quality in Western Oregon and Washington. In *Forest Soils and Forest Land Management, Proceedings of the Fourth North American Forest Soils Conference* (eds L. Bernier and C.H. Winget).

Freeman, H.C. and Sangalang, G.B. (1985) The effects of an acidic river on weight gain, steroid geneses and reproduction in the Atlantic salmon (*Salmo salar*). *International Council for the Exploration of the Sea*, C.M.1985/E:45.

Freeman, H.C., Sangalang, G.B., Burns, G. and McMenemy, M. (1983) The blood sex hormone levels in sexually mature male Atlantic salmon (*Salmo salar*) in the Westfield River (pH 4.7) and Medway River (pH 5.6), Nova Scotia. *The Science of the Total Environment*, **32**, 87–91.

Frenette, M., Dulude, P. and Beaurivage, M. (1988) The restoration of the Jacques-Cartier: a major challenge and a collective pride. In *Atlantic Salmon: Planning for the Future* (eds D. Mills and D. Piggins), Croom Helm, London, pp. 400–14.

Friend, G.F. (1941) The life history and ecology of the salmon gill maggot *Salmincola salmonea* (L.) (Copepod crustacean). *Trans. R. Soc. Edinb.*, **60**, 503–41.

• Frost, W.E. and Brown, M.E. (1967) *The Trout*, Collins, London.

Furunculosis Committee (1933) *Second Interim Report* (June, 1933). Her Majesty's Stationery Office, London, 81 pp.

Gardiner, W.R. (1987) The potential of the Clyde as a salmon producing river. In *The Return of Salmon to the Clyde* (eds A.V. Holden and G. Struthers), Institute of Fisheries Management (Scottish Branch), Pitlochry, pp. 21–5.

Gardiner, W.R. and Geddes, P. (1980) The influence of body composition on the survival of juvenile salmon. *Hydrobiologia*, **69**, 67–72.

Gardner, M.L.G. (1976) A review of factors which may influence the sea-age of maturation of Atlantic salmon *Salmo salar* L. *J. Fish Biol.*, **9**, 289–327.

Garnås, E. and Hvidsten, N.A. (1985) Density of Atlantic salmon (*Salmo salar* L.) smolts in Örkla, a large river in central Norway. *Aquaculture and Fisheries Management*, **16**, 369–76.

Gash, J.H.C., Oliver, H.R., Shuttleworth, W.J. and Stewart, J.B. (1978) Evaporation from forests. *J. Instn Wat. Engrs Scient.*, **32** (2), 104–10.

Gee, A.S. (1980) Angling success for Atlantic salmon (*Salmo salar*) in the River Wye in relation to effort and river flows. *J. Fish Biol.*, **11** (3), 131–8.

Gee, A. S. and Edwards, R.W. (1981) Recreational exploitation of the Atlantic salmon in the River Wye. In *Allocation of Fishery Resources* (ed. J.H. Groves), Proceedings of the Technical Consultation in Fishery Resources, Vichy, France, FAO, Rome, pp. 129–37.

Gee, A.S. and Milner, N.J. (1980) Analysis of 70-year catch statistics for Atlantic salmon (*Salmo salar*) in the River Wye and its implications for management of stocks. *J. Appl. Ecol..*, **17**, 41–57.

Gee, A.S., Milner, N.J. and Hemsworth, R.J. (1978) The effect of density on mortality in juvenile Atlantic salmon (*Salmo salar*). *J. Anim. Ecol.*, **47**, 495–505.

Genin-Meurisse, M. and Micha, J.-C. (1981) Impacts des rejets radioactifs provenant d'une centrale nucléaire de type PWR sur les poissons de la Meuse. In *Allocation of Fishery Resources* (ed. J.H. Groves), Proceedings of the Technical Consultation in Fishery Resources, Vichy, France, FAO, Rome, pp. 138–45.

George, A.F. (1982) Cyclical Variations in the Return Migration of Scottish Salmon by Sea-age c. 1790–1976. MPhil Thesis, Open University, Milton Keynes, 365 pp.

Gibbons, D.R. and Salo, E.R. (1973) *An annotated bibliography of the effects of logging on fish of the western United States and Canada.* USDA Forest Service General Technical Report PNW 10, 145 pp.

Gibson, R.J. (1978) Recent changes in the population of juvenile Atlantic salmon in the Matamek River, Quebec, Canada. *J. Cons. Perm. Int. Explor. Mer*, **38** (2), 201–7.

Gibson, R.J. (1981) Behavioural interactions between coho salmon (*Oncorhynchus kisutch*), brook trout (*Salvelinus fontinalis*) and steelhead trout (*Salmo gairdneri*) at the juvenile stage. *Can. Tech. Rep. Fish. Aquat. Sci.*, no. 1029, 116 pp.

Gibson, R.J. and Côté, Y. (1982) Production de saumoneaux et récaptures de saumons adults étiquetés à la rivière, Matamec, Côte-Nord, Golfe du Saint-Laurent, Quebec. *Naturaliste Can.*, **109**, 13–25.

Gibson, R.J. and Cunjak, R.A. (1986) An investigation of competitive interactions between brown trout (*Salmo trutta* L.) and juvenile Atlantic salmon (*Salmo salar* L.) in rivers of the Avalon Peninsula, Newfoundland. *Can. Tech. Rep. Fish. Aquat. Sci.*, no. 1472, 82 pp.

Gibson, R.J. and Dickson, T.A. (1984) The effects of competition on the growth of juvenile Atlantic salmon. *Naturaliste Can.*, (*Revue Ecologie Systematique*), **111**, 175–91.

Gilchrist, A. (1977) *Cod Wars and How to Lose Them*, Q Press, Edinburgh.

Gjedrem, T. (1979) Selection for growth rate and domestication in Atlantic salmon. *Z. Tierz. Zuchtungsbiol.* **96**, 56–9.

Godby, M.H. (1925) '*Salmo salar*': at home and abroad. History of its acclimatisation in New Zealand. *N. Z. J. Sci. Technol.* **8**, 19–27.

Goldman, C.R. (1961) The contribution of alder trees (*Alnus terrui folia*) to the primary productivity of Castle Lake, California. *Ecology*, **42**, 282–7.

Gordon, H. Scott (1954) The economic theory of a common property: the fishery. *J. Political Economy*, **62** (2), 124–43.

Gough, P.J. (1982) Salmon rehabilitation scheme report. Thames Water, Directorate of Scientific Services.

Gough, P.J. (1983) Salmon rehabilitation scheme report. Juvenile salmon production in the Thames catchment, 1981–1982. *Proc. Ann. Study Course Inst. Fish. Mgmt*, City University, London.

Gough, P.J. (1987) Thames salmon rehabilitation – the next steps. Atlantic Salmon Trust Progress Report, December 1987, 23–24.

Graesser, N.G. (1979) How land improvements can damage Scottish fisheries. *Salmon and Trout Magazine*, no. 215, 39–43.

Grasberg, E. (1956) Economic benefits of the Atlantic salmon to the Province of New Brunswick. Department of Economics and Political Sciences, University of New Brunswick, Fredericton, N.B.

Gray, R.W., Cameron, J.D. and Jefferson, E.M.J. (1986) Stream characteristics and assessment of Atlantic salmon spawning and nursery habitat in the Le Have River, N.S. *Can. Tech. Rep. Fish. Aquat. Sci.*

Gray, R.W., Cameron, J.D. and McLennan, A.D. (1987) Artificial reconditioning, spawning and survival of Atlantic salmon, *Salmo salar* L., kelts in salt water and survival of their F1 progeny. *Aquaculture and Fisheries Management*, **18**, 93–110.

Greer, R.B. (1979) A tree planting trial at Loch Garry (Tayside Region) aimed at habitat improvement for fish. *Scott. For.*, **33** (1), 37–44.

Grey, and Tosh, J.R. (1894) *14th Annual Report of the Fishery Board for Scotland*, Part II, Note 2.

Grimble, A. (1902) *The Salmon Rivers of Scotland*, Kegan Paul, London.

Grimble, A. (1903, 1913) *The Salmon Rivers of Ireland*, Kegan Paul, London.

Grimble, A. (1904, 1913) *The Salmon Rivers of England and Wales*, Kegan Paul, London.

Grimble, A. (1913) *The Salmon Rivers of Scotland*, Kegan Paul, London.

Grinyuk, I.N., Kanep, S.V., Salmov, V.Z. and Yakovenko, M.Ya. (1978a) Effects of ecological factors upon pink salmon population in basins of the White and Barents Seas. *International Council for the Exploration of the Sea*, C.M.1978/M: 6.

Grinyuk, I.N., Kanep, S.V. and Yakovenko, M.Ya. (1978b) On the acclimitisation of the Pacific salmon *Oncorhynchus* in the White and Barents Seas. *VIth Soviet-Japanese Symposium on Questions of Aquaculture and Raising the Bioproductivity of the Worldwide Ocean*, Moscow, 1977, 124–8.

Groves, A.B., Collins, G.B. and Trefethen, P.S. (1968) Roles of olfaction and vision in choice of spawning site by homing adult chinook salmon (*Oncorhynchus tshawytscha*) *J. Fish. Res. Bd Can.*, **25**, 867–76.

Gruchy, C.G. (1971) Salmon nomenclature. *Nature*, **234**, 360.

Gudbergsson, G. and Gudjonsson, S. (1986) Rannsoknir a fiskistofnum Blondu. Manuscript, Reykjavik, 40 pp.

Gudjonsson, T. (1961) Occurrence of pink salmon (*Oncorhynchus gorbuscha*) in Iceland in 1960 and 1961. *International Council for the Exploration of the Sea*, 1961, Anacat Committee.

Gudjonsson, T. (1965) The effect of water removal on the catch of salmon in the River Ulfarsa, Iceland. *International Council for the Exploration of the Sea*, C.M.1965/M: 171.

Gudjonsson, T. (1988) Exploitation of salmon in Iceland. In *Atlantic Salmon: Planning for the Future* (eds D. Mills and D. Piggins), Croom Helm, London, pp. 162–78.

Gudjonsson, T. and Mills, D.H. (1982) *Salmon in Iceland*, Atlantic Salmon Trust, Farnham.

Gulland, J.A. (1969) Manuel des méthodes d'évaluation des stocks d'animaux aquations. Première partie – Analyse des populations. *Manuel FAO de Science halieutique*, **4**, 160 pp.

Gulland, J.A. (ed.) (1970) *The Fish Resources of the Ocean*, Fishing News Books, Farnham.

Gunderson, D.R. (1968) Floodplain use related to stream morphology and fish populations. *J. Wildl. Mgmt*, **32**, 507–14.

❢ Gunnes, K. (1980) Genetic variation in production traits between strains of Atlantic salmon. In *Atlantic Salmon: its Future* (ed. A.E.J. Went), Fishing News Books, Farnham, pp. 165–72.

Gunther, A. (1864) *Catalogue of Fishes in the British Museum*, Taylor and Francis, London.

Hadoke, G.D.F. (1967) An examination of the fishing effort of a selected number of anglers during the 1966 season. *Salmon and Trout Magazine*, no. 181, 245–9.

Hadoke, G.D.F. (1972) *The Salmon Fisheries of the Foyle Area*. Foyle Fisheries Commission, 128 pp.

Haines, T.A. (1981) Effects of acid rain on Atlantic salmon rivers and restoration efforts in the United States. In *Acid Rain and the Atlantic Salmon* (ed. L. Sochasky), International Atlantic Salmon Foundation Special Publication Series, no. 10, pp. 57–64.

Hall, J.D. and Lantz, R.L. (1968) *Effects of logging on the habitat of coho salmon and cutthroat trout in coastal streams*. Oregon Agricultural Experiment Station, Technical Paper 2570.

Hamilton, J.D. (1961) The effect of sand-pit washings on a stream fauna. *Verh. Internat. Verein. Limnol.*, **XIV**, 435–9.

Hamilton, R. M. (1985) Discharges of pesticides to the Rivers Mole and Taw, their accumulation in fish flesh and possible effects on fish stocks. *J. Fish Biol.*, 27 (Suppl. A), 139–48.

Hammerton, D. (1986) Mineral extraction and water quality in Scotland. In *Effects of Land Use on Fresh Waters* (ed. J.F. Solbé), Ellis Horwood, Chichester, pp. 127–46.

Hansen, L.P. (1982) Salmon ranching in Norway. In *Sea Ranching of Atlantic Salmon*, (eds. C. Eriksson, M. Ferranti and P.O. Larsson), Cost 46/4 Workshop Proceedings, Commission of the European Communities, Brussels, pp. 95–108.

Hansen, L.P. (1986a) The data on salmon catches available for analysis in Norway. In *The Status of the Atlantic Salmon in Scotland* (eds D. Jenkins and W.M. Shearer), ITE Symposium no. 15, Institute of Terrestrial Ecology, Abbots Ripton, pp. 79–83.

Hansen L.P. (1986b) Introduction of Atlantic salmon *Salmo salar* L. to the river Akerselv, Oslo. *Fauna Norvegica*, Series A, 7, 27–32.

Hansen, L.P. (1988) Status of exploitation of Atlantic salmon in Norway. In *Atlantic Salmon: Planning for the Future* (eds D. Mills and D. Piggins), Croom Helm, London, pp. 143–61.

Hansen, L.P. and Pethon, P. (1985) The food of the Atlantic salmon, *Salmo salar* L., caught by long-line in northern Norwegian waters. *J. Fish Biol.*, 26, 553–62.

Hansen, L.P., Døving, K.B. and Jonsson, B. (1987) Migration of farmed adult Atlantic salmon with and without olfactory sense, released on the Norwegian coast. *J. Fish Biol.*, 30 (6), 713–21.

Hansen, L.P., Jonsson, B. and Andersen, R. (1988) Salmon ranching experiments in the River Imsa: is homing dependent on sequential imprinting of the smolts? In *Proceedings of the Second International Symposium on Salmon and Trout Migratory Behaviour*, Trondheim, June 1987 (eds. E. Brannon and B. Jonsson), (in press).

Hansen, L.P., Lund, R.A. and Hindar, K. (1987) Possible interaction between wild and reared Atlantic salmon in Norway, *International Council for the Exploration of the Sea*, C.M.1987/M:14.

Hansen, L.P., Naesje, T.F. and Garnås, E. (1986) Stock assessment and exploitation of Atlantic salmon *Salmo salar* L. in the river Drammenselv. *Fauna Norvegica*, Series A, 7, 23–6.

Hansen, M.J. and Stauffer, T.M. (1971) Comparative recovery to the creel, movement and growth of rainbow trout stocked in the Great Lakes. *Trans. Amer. Fish. Soc.*, 100, 336–49.

Harache, Y. (1979a) Coho salmon farming in France. Part I. The reasons for the choice. Part II. Technical aspects and results. *Fish Farmer*, **2** (1), 66–7; **2** (3), 40–44.

Harache, Y. (1979b) Coho salmon and environment in Brittany. *Proceedings of the 10th Annual Study Course, Institute of Fisheries Management*, University of Nottingham, 272–89.

Harache, Y. and Novotny, A.J. (1976) Coho salmon farming in France. *Mar. Fish. Rev.*, **38** (8), 1–8.

Harden Jones, F.R. (1968) *Fish Migration*, Edward Arnold, London.

Hardin, G. (1968) The tragedy of the commons. *Science*, **162**, 1243–8.

Harriman, P. (1960) The black salmon controversy. *Maine Atlantic Salmon Federation*, Document no. 1, 8 pp.

Harriman, P. (1961) Water control + artificial freshets = Atlantic salmon. *Maine Atlantic Salmon Federation*, Document no. 2, 14 pp.

Harriman, R. (1978) Nutrient leaching from fertilised watersheds in Scotland. *J. Appl. Ecol.*, **15**, 933–42.

Harriman, R. and Morrison, B.R.S. (1982) Ecology of streams draining forested and non-forested catchments in an area of central Scotland subject to acid precipitation. *Hydrobiologia*, **88**, 251–63.

Harriman, R. and Wells, D.E. (1985) Causes and effects of surface water acidification in Scotland. *Journal of Water Pollution Control*, **84**, 215–41.

Harris, G.S. (1978) Salmon propagation in England and Wales. A Report by the Association of River Authorities/National Water Council Working Party. National Water Council, London.

Harris, G.S. (1988) The status of exploitation of salmon in England and Wales. In *Atlantic Salmon: Planning for the Future* (eds D. Mills and D. Piggins), Croom Helm, London, pp. 169–90.

Hart, J.A. (1976) *The Anglo–Icelandic Cod War of 1972–73*. Institute of International Studies, University of California, Berkeley Research Series no. 29.

Hartley, Sheila E. (1987) A potential new method for stock identification. Atlantic Salmon Trust, Progress Report, June 1987, 34–6.

Hartley, W. G. and Simpson, D. (1967) Electric fish screens in the United Kingdom. In *Fishing with Electricity – its Applications to Biology and Management* (ed. R. Vibert), Fishing News Books, London, pp. 183–97.

Hasler, A.D. (1954) Odor perception and orientation in fishes. *J. Fish. Res. Bd Can.*, **11**, 107–29.

Hasler, A.D. (1966) *Underwater Guideposts: Homing of Salmon*, University of Wisconsin Press, Madison.

Hasler, A.D. and Wisby, W.J. (1951) Discrimination of stream odors by fishes and its relation to parent stream behaviour. *Amer. Nat.*, **85**, 223–38.

Hasler, A.D., Scholz, A.T. and Horrall, R.M. (1978) Olfactory imprinting and homing in salmon. *American Science*, **66**, 347–55.

Haukbø, T. (1983) Guidelines regarding: the salmon parasite *Gyrodactylus salaris*. Plans of action for combating the parasite in the rivers round Isfjord, in the Rauma district. Memo from the Chief Administrative Officer for More and Romsdal, County Buildings, 6400 Molde, Norway, 17 pp.

Hawkins, A.D. (1988) Factors affecting the timing of entry and upstream movement of Atlantic salmon in the Aberdeenshire Dee. In *Proceedings of the Second International Symposium on Salmon and Trout Migratory Behaviour, Trondheim, June 1987*, (eds E.L. Brannon and B. Jonsson) (in press).

Hawkins, A.D. and Smith, G.W. (1986) Radio-tracking observations on Atlantic salmon ascending the Aberdeenshire Dee. *Scottish Fisheries Research Report* no. 36, 24 pp.

Hawkins, A.D., Urquhart, G.G. and Shearer, W.M. (1979) The coastal movements of returning Atlantic salmon, *Salmo salar* L. *Scottish Fisheries Research Report* no. 15, p. 15.

Hay, D. (1984) The relationship between redd counts and the numbers of spawning salmon in the Girnock Burn. *International Council for the Exploitation of the Sea*, C.M.1984/M: 22.

Hayes, F.R. (1953) Artificial freshets and other factors controlling the ascent and population of Atlantic salmon in the La Have River, Nova Scotia. *Bull. Fish. Res. Bd Can.*, 99, 47 pp.

Hazell, S. (1988) The indian Atlantic salmon fishery on the Restigouche river: illegal fishing or aboriginal right? In *Atlantic Salmon: Planning for the Future* (eds D. Mills and D. Piggins), Croom Helm, London, pp. 535–56.

Hector, J. (1966) The bag net. *Salmon Net*, 2, 27–9.

Heggberget, T.G. and Johnsen, B.O. (1982) Infestations by *Gyrodactylus* sp. of Atlantic salmon, *Salmo salar* L. in Norwegian rivers. *J. Fish Biol.*, 21, 15–26.

Heggberget, T.G., Lund, R.A., Ryman, N. and Stahl, G. (1986) Growth and genetic variation of Atlantic salmon (*Salmo salar*) from different sections of the River Alta, North Norway. *Can. J. Fish. Aquat. Sci.*, 43, 1828–35.

Heitz, A. (1918) *Salmo salar*, seine Parasitenfauna und seine Ernahrung im Meer und im Susserwasse. *Archive Hydrobiologie*, XII, 2–3.

Hellawell, J.M. (1973) Automatic methods of monitoring salmon populations. In *International Atlantic Salmon Symposium, St Andrew's* (eds M.W. Smith and W.M. Carter), *International Atlantic Salmon Foundation, Special Publication Series*, 4 (1), 317–37.

Hellawell, J.M. (1976) River management and the migratory behaviour of salmonids. *Fish. Mgmt*, 7 (3), 57–60.

Hellawell, J.M. (1986) *Biological Indicators of Freshwater Pollution and Environmental Management*, Elsevier, London.

Hellawell, J.M., Leatham, H. and Williams, G.I. (1974) The upstream migratory behaviour of salmonids in the River Frome, Dorset. *J. Fish Biol.*, 6, 729–44.

Helle, J.H. (1981) Significance of the stock concept in artificial propagation of salmonids in Alaska. *Can. J. Fish. Aquat. Sci.*, 38, 1665–71.

Henriksen, A., Skogheim, O.K. and Rosseland, B.O. (1984) Episodic changes in pH and aluminium–speciation kill fish in a Norwegian salmon river. *Valten*, 40, 255–60.

Hesthagen, T. (1986) Fish kills of Atlantic salmon (*Salmo salar*) and brown trout (*Salmo trutta*) in an acidified river of SW Norway. *Water, Air and Soil Polln*, 30, 619–28.

Hesthagen, T. and Mjdell-Larsen, B. (1987) Acidification and Atlantic salmon in Norway. *International Council for the Exploration of the Sea*, C.M.1987/M: 28.

Hesthagen, T. and Larsen, L.P. (1988) Estimates of the annual loss of Atlantic salmon (*Salmo salar*) in Norway due to acidification. *International Council for the Exploration of the Sea*, Working Paper, 1988. Study Group on Acid Rain.

Hewetson, A. (1962a) Furunculosis in salmon kelts. *Nature*, 194, 312.

Hewetson, A. (1962b) Furunculosis in salmon kelts. *Nature*, 196, 1009.

Hislop, J.R.G. and Youngson, A.F. (1984) A note on the stomach contents of salmon caught by longline north of the Faroes Islands in March, 1983. *International Council for the Exploration of the Sea*, C.M.1984/M: 12.

Hoar, W. S. (1976) Smolt transformation: evolution, behaviour and physiology. *J. Fish. Res. Bd Can.*, 33, 1233–52.

Hoek, P.P.C. (1910) On the age of salmon to be derived from the structure of its scales. Proceedings of a Meeting, 30 October 1909 of Koninklijke Akademie van Wetenschappen Te Amsterdam.

Hoffman, G.L. (1967) *Parasites of North American Fishes*. University of California Press, Berkley.

Holden, A.V. (1964) The possible effects on fish of chemicals used in agriculture. *J. Proc. Inst. Sew. Purif.*, Part 4, 10 pp.

Holden, A.V. (1966) Organochlorine insecticide residues in salmonid fish. *J. Appl. Ecol.*, 3 (Suppl.), 45–53.

Holden, A.V. (1973a) Monitoring PCB in water and wildlife. PCB Conference II, National Swedish Environment Protection Board.

Holden, A.V. (1973b) Mercury and organo-chlorine residue analysis of fish and aquatic mammals. *Pesticide Sci.*, 4, 399–408.

Holden, A.V. (1973c) Mercury in fish and shellfish. *J. Food Technol.*, 8, 1–25.

Holden, A.V. (1987) Changes in water quality in Scottish river systems. In *Developments in Fisheries Research in Scotland* (eds R. Bailey and B.B. Parrish), Fishing News Books Ltd, Farnham, pp. 220–31.

Holden, A.V. and Bevan, D. (eds) (1979) *Control of the Pine Beauty Moth by Fenitrothion in Scotland in 1978*. Forestry Commission Report, Edinburgh, 176 pp.

Holden, A.V. and Marsden, K. (1964) Cyanide in salmon and brown trout. *Freshwater and Salmon Fisheries Research, Scotland*, 33, 12.

Holden, A.V. and Struthers, G. (eds) (1987) *The Return of Salmon to the Clyde*, Institute of Fisheries Management (Scottish Branch), Pitlochry, 39 pp.

Howells, G. (ed.) (1986) Loch Fleet Report. A report of the pre-intervention phase 1984–86. CEGB, SSEB, NSHEB and British Coal.

Howells, W.R. and Jones, A.N. (1972) The River Towy regulating reservoir and fishery protection scheme. *Fish. Mgmt*, 3, 5–19.

Howells, W.R. and Merriman, R. (1986) Pollution from agriculture in the area of the Welsh Water Authority. In *Effects of Land Use on Fresh Waters* (ed. J.F. Solbé), Ellis Horwood, Chichester, pp. 267–82.

Hoydal, K. (1988) Sea mortality of Atlantic salmon. In *Future Atlantic Salmon Management* (in press).

Hughes, Ted. (1985) *The Best Worker in Europe*. Atlantic Salmon Trust, 7 pp.

Huitefeldt-Kaas, H. (1922) Om aarsaken til massedod av laks og orret i Frofjordelven, Helleelven og Dirdalsalven i Ryfylke hosten, 1920. *Nork Jaeger-og Fiskefor.*, tidsskrift, 37–44 (in Norwegian).

Hunt, G.J. (1983) Radioactivity in surface and coastal waters of the British Isles, 1981. Ministry of Agriculture, Fisheries and Food, Lowestoft, Aquatic Environment Monitoring Report no. 9, 36 pp.

Hunter Committee: *see* Anon (1963).

Hunter, J.G. (1959) Survival and production of pink and chum salmon in a coastal stream. *J. Fish. Res. Bd Can.*, 16, 835–86.

Huntsman, A.G. (1931) The maritime salmon of Canada. *Bull. Biol. Bd Can.*, no. 21, 99 pp.

Huntsman, A.G. (1937) The cause of periodic scarcity in Atlantic salmon. *Trans. R. Soc. Can.* (v), 31, 17–27.

Huntsman, A.G. (1942) Death of salmon and trout with high temperature. *J. Fish. Res. Bd Can.*, 5, 485–501.

Huntsman, A.G. (1952) Wandering versus homing in salmon. *Salmon and Trout Magazine*, no. 130, 227–30.

Huntsman, A.G. and Hoar, W.S. (1939) Resistance of Atlantic salmon to sea water. *J. Fish. Res. Bd Can.*, 4 (5), 409–11.

Hutchings, J. and Myers, R.A. (1985) Mating between anadromous and non-anadromous Atlantic salmon, *Salmo salar*. *Can. J. Zool.*, 63, 2219–21.

314

References

Hutton, J.A. (1909) *Salmon Scales as Indicative of the Life History of the Fish*, Sherratt and Hughes, London.

Hutton, J.A. (1910) *Salmon Scale Examination and Its Practical Utility*, Sherratt and Hughes, London.

Hutton, J.A. (1923) The parasites of salmon. *Salmon and Trout Magazine*, no. 34, 302–12.

Hutton, J.A. (1924) *The Life History of the Salmon*, Aberdeen University Press, Aberdeen.

Hutton, J.A. (1937) The inverse ratio theory of river and sea life. *Salmon and Trout Magazine*, no. 87, 3–7.

Hutton, J.A. (1947) Salmon scarcity. An attempt to get the real facts. *Salmon and Trout Magazine*, Advance Report, 1–8.

Huxley, T. (1882) Saprolegnia in relation to salmon disease. *Q. J. Microsc. Sci.*

Hvidsten, N.A. (1985) Mortality of pre-smolt Atlantic salmon, *Salmo salar* L., and brown trout, *Salmo trutta* L., caused by fluctuating water levels in the regulated River Nidelva, central Norway. *J. Fish Biol.*, **27**, 711–18.

Hvidsten, N.A. and Møkkelgjerd, P.I. (1987) Predation on salmon smolts, *Salmo salar* L., in the estuary of the River Surna, Norway. *J. Fish Biol.*, **30**, 273–80.

Hynd, I.J.R. (1964) Large sea trout from the Tweed District. *Salmon and Trout Magazine*, September, 151–4.

Hynes, H.B.N. (1960) *The Biology of Polluted Waters*, University Press, Liverpool.

Ikonen, E. (1986) Spawning migration of salmon (*Salmo salar* L.) in the coastal waters of the Gulf of Bothnia. *International Council for the Exploration of the Sea*, C.M.1986/M:24.

Ikonen, E. (1987) Mixing of wild and hatchery-reared salmon during migration in the Baltic Sea. *International Council for the Exploration of the Sea*, C.M. 1987/M:10.

Ingebrigtsen, O. (1976) Produsjon av porsjonsssfisker pukkellaks losningen? *Norsk fiskeoppdrett*, Bergen, **2**, 4–5, 17.

Iremonger, D.J. (1981) England profits and Scotland pays. The Northumbrian drift-net fishery. *Salmon Net*, **XIV**, 29–36.

Jackson, P.A. and Howie, D.I.D. (1967) The movement of salmon (*Salmo salar*) through an estuary and a fish pass. *Irish Fisheries Investigations*, Series A, No. 2, 28 pp.

Jákupsstovu, S.H.i. (1988) Exploitation and migration of salmon in Faroese waters. In *Atlantic Salmon: Planning for the Future* (eds D. Mills and D. Piggins), Croom Helm, London, pp. 458–82.

Jákupsstovu, S.H.i., Jorgensen, P.T., Mouritsen, R. and Nicolajsen, A. (1985) Biological data on preliminary observations on the spatial distribution of salmon within the Faroese fishing zone in February, 1985. *International Council for the Exploration of the Sea*, C.M.1985/M:30.

James, G.T. (1986) Pollution from farms in Wales. Atlantic Salmon Trust Progress Report, May 1986, 27–29.

Jefferts, K.B., Bergman, P.K. and Fiscus, H.F. (1963) A coded wire identification system for macro-organisms. *Nature*, **198** (487), 460–2.

Jensen, A.J. and Johnsen, B.O. (1986) Different adaptation strategies of Atlantic salmon (*Salmo salar*) populations to extreme climates with special reference to some cold Norwegian rivers. *Can. J. Fish. Aquat. Sci.*, **43**, 980–4.

Jensen, J.M. (1967) Atlantic salmon caught in the Irminger Sea. *J. Fish. Res. Bd Can.*, **24** (12), 2639–40.

Jensen, K.W. (1979) Lakseundersokelser i Eira. In *Vassdragsregulingers biologiske virkninger i magasiner og lakseelver* (eds T.B. Gunnerod and P. Mellquist), Norge Vassdrags og Elektrisitetsvesen, Direktoratet for vilt og ferskvannsfisk (in Norwegian), 165–71.

Jensen, K.W. (1981) On the rate of exploitation of salmon from two Norwegian rivers. *International Council for the Exploration of the Sea*, C.M.1981/M: 11.

Jensen, K.W. and Snekvik, E. (1972) Low pH levels wipe out salmon and trout populations in southwestern Norway. *Ambio*, **1**, 223–5.

Jessop, B.M. (1975) Investigation of the salmon (*Salmo salar*) smolt migration of the Big Salmon River, New Brunswick, 1966–72. Canadian Fisheries and Marine Service, Ottawa, Technical Report Series Mar/T-75-1, 57 pp.

Johansson, N., Svensson, K.M. and Fridberg, G. (1982) Studies on the pathology of ulcerative dermal necrosis (UDN) in Swedish salmon, *Salmo salar* L. and sea trout, *Salmo trutta* L., population. *Journal of Fish Diseases*, **5** (4), 293–308.

Johnels, A.G. (1984) Masken som hotar laxen (*Gyrodactylus salaris*), a parasite threatening the Atlantic salmon. *Svenskt Fiske* 9/84, 42–4 (in Swedish).

Johnsen, B.O. (1978) The effect of an attack by the parasite *Gyrodactylus salaris* on the population of salmon parr in the river Lakselva, Misvaer in northern Norway. *Astarte*, **11**, 7–9.

Johnsen, B.O. and Jensen, A.J. (1986) Infestations of Atlantic salmon, *Salmo salar*, by *Gyrodactylus salaris* in Norwegian rivers. *J. Fish Biol.*, **29** (2), 233–41.

Johnson, F.W. (1953) Forests and trout. *Journal of Forestry*, **51** (8), 551–4.

Johnston, H.W. (1904) The scales of Tay salmon as indicative of age, growth and spawning habit. *23rd Annual Report of the Fishery Board of Scotland*, Appendix II.

Jonas, R.F. (1974) *Prospect for the establishment of stocks of Atlantic and Pacific salmon in south-west Greenland; a survey with emphasis upon an evaluation of potentials for significant natural production*. Grønlands Fiskerundersogelser, Charlottenlund, 114.

Jones, A.N. (1968) *The relationship of river flow and salmon angling success in the River Towy*. South West Wales River Authority Report.

Jones, A.N. (1970) A study of salmonid populations of the River Teifi and tributaries near Tregaron. *J. Fish Biol.* **2**, 183–97.

Jones, A.N. and Howells, W.R. (1969) Recovery of the River Rheidol. *Effluent Water Treat. Journal*, November 1969, 605–10.

Jones, A.N. and Howells, W.R. (1975) The partial recovery of the metal polluted River Rheidol. In *The Ecology of Resource Degradation* (eds M.J. Chadwick and G.T. Goodman), 15th Symposium of the British Ecological Society, Blackwell, Oxford, pp. 443–59.

Jones, J.W. (1949) Studies of the scales of young salmon *Salmo salar* L. (juv.) in relation to growth, migration and spawning. *Fishery Invest., Lond.*, Ser. I, **5** (1), 23 pp.

Jones, J.W. (1959) *The Salmon*, Collins, London.

Jones, J.W. and King, G.M. (1949) Experimental observations on the spawning behaviour of the Atlantic salmon (*Salmo salar* Linn.) *Proc. R. Soc.*, **119**, 33–48.

Jones, R. (1985) *Manual on Population Dynamics*, Kuwait Institute for Scientific Research, Kuwait.

Jones, R.A. (1988) Atlantic salmon restoration in the Connecticut River. In *Atlantic Salmon: Planning for the Future* (eds D. Mills and D. Piggins), Croom Helm, London, pp. 415–26.

Jonsson, B. and Ruud-Hansen, J. (1985) Water temperature as the primary influence on timing of seaward migration of Atlantic salmon (*Salmo salar*) smolts. *Can. J. Fish, Aquat. Sci.*, **42** (3), 593–5.

Jutila, E. (1985) Dredging of rapids for timber-floating and its effects on river-spawning fish stocks. In *Habitat Modification and Freshwater Fisheries* (ed. J. Alabaster), Butterworth, London, pp. 104–8.

Jutila, E. and Toivonen, J. (1985) Food composition of post smolts (*Salmo salar* L.) in the northern part of the Gulf of Bothnia. *International Council for the Exploration of the Sea*, C.M.1985/M:21.

Kalleberg, H. (1958) Observations in a stream tank of territoriality and competition in juvenile salmon and trout (*Salmo salar* L. and *S. trutta*). *Report of the Institute of Freshwater Research, Drottningholm*, **39**, 55–98.

Kapuscinski, A.R. and Jacobson, L.D. (1987) *Genetic Guidelines for Fisheries Management*, Minnesota Sea Grant Publications, University of Minnesota, 66 pp.

Kay, D.L., Allee, D.J. and Brown, T. (1988) Atlantic salmon restoration – is it worth it? In *Future Atlantic Salmon Management* (in press).

Keenleyside, M.H.A. (1959) Effects of spruce budworm control on salmon and other fishes in New Brunswick. *Can. Fish Cult.*, **24**, 17–22.

Keenleyside, M.H.A. and Yamamoto, F.T. (1962) Territorial behaviour of juvenile Atlantic salmon (*Salmo salar* L.). *Behaviour*, **19** (1), 139–69.

Kennedy, G.J.A. (1984a) Evaluation of techniques for classifying habitats for juvenile Atlantic salmon (*Salmo salar* L.). *Atlantic Salmon Trust Workshop on Stock Enhancement*, University of Surrey.

Kennedy, G.J.A. (1984b) The ecology of salmonid habitat re-instatement following river drainage schemes. *Institute of Fisheries Management* (N. Ireland Branch), Fisheries Conference Proceedings.

Kennedy, G.J.A. (1985) River pollution – how much does it cost fisheries? *Advisers' and Lecturers' Conference*, Loughry College of Agriculture and Food Technology, 15 pp.

Kennedy, G.J.A. (1987) Silage effluent pollution – costs and prevention. *Agriculture North. Ire.*, **60** (12), 5 pp.

Kennedy, G.J.A. (1988) Stock enhancement of Atlantic salmon (*Salmo salar* L.). In *Atlantic Salmon: Planning for the Future* (eds D. Mills and D. Piggins), Croom Helm, London, pp. 345–72.

Kennedy, G.J.A. and Greer, J.E. (1988) Predation by cormorants (*Phalacrocorax carbo* (L.)) on the salmonid populations of the River Bush. *Aquaculture and Fisheries Management*, **19** (2), 159–70.

Kennedy, G.J.A. and Strange, C.D. (1980) Population changes after two years of salmon (*Salmo salar* L.) stocking in upland trout (*Salmo trutta* L.) streams. *J. Fish Biol.*, **17**, 577–86.

Kennedy, G.J.A., Cragg-Hine, D., Strange, C.D. and Stewart, D.A. (1983) The effects of a land-drainage scheme on the salmonid populations of the River Camowen, Co. Tyrone. *Fish. Mgmt*, **14** (1), 1–16.

Kennedy, M. (1954) *The Sea Anglers' Fishes*, Hutchinson, London.

Kerswill, C.J. (1955a) Effects of black salmon angling on Miramichi salmon stocks. *The Atlantic Salmon Journal*, January, 30–31.

Kerswill, C.J. (1955b) Recent developments in Atlantic salmon research. *The Atlantic Salmon Journal*, January, 26–30.

Kerswill, C.J. (1967) Studies on effects of forest spraying with insecticides, 1952–63, on fish and aquatic invertebrates in New Brunswick streams: Introduction and summary. *J. Fish. Res. Bd Can.*, **24**, 709–29.

King-Webster, W.A. (1969) The Galloway Dee – a short history of a salmon river. *Salmon Net*, **V**, 38–47.

Klein, L. (1962) *River Pollution 2: Causes and Effects*, Butterworth, London.

Koch, H.J., Evans, J.C. and Bergstrom, E. (1959) Sodium regulation in the blood of parr and smolt stages of Atlantic salmon. *Nature*, **184**, 283.

Kozhin, N.I. (1964) Atlantic salmon in the U.S.S.R. *Atlantic Salmon Journal*, **2**, 3–7.

Kreiberg, H. (1981) *Report of the Joint Greenland Expedition (1980)*, Atlantic Salmon Trust, Farnham, 47 pp.

Kristinsson, B. and Alexandersdottir, M. (1978) Design and calibration of a salmon counter. *J. Agr. Res. Iceland*, **10**, 57–66.

Lack, D. (1966) *Population Studies of Birds*, Oxford University Press, Oxford.

LaCroix, G.L. (1985) Survival of eggs and alevins of Atlantic salmon (*Salmo salar*) in relation to the chemistry of interstitial water in redds in some acidic streams of Atlantic Canada. *Can. J. Fish. Aquat. Sci.*, **42**, 292.

Larsson, P.-O. (1984) Effects of reduced fishing for feeding salmon (*Salmo salar* L.) in the Baltic on home water fisheries according to simulations with the Carlin–Larsson population model. *Fish. Mgmt*, **15** (3), 97–105.

Lassen, H. (1978) An assessment model applied to the Baltic salmon. *International Council for the Exploration of the Sea*, C.M.1978/M:25.

Last, F. (1982) Effects of atmospheric sulphur compounds on natural and man-made terrestrial and aquatic ecosystems. *Agr. Environ.*, **7**, 299–387.

Lawson, K.M. (1974) The electronic monitoring of salmon in Lancashire, England. *European Inland Fisheries Advisory Commission* 74/1 Symposium, 15, 11 pp.

Léaniz, C.G. de (1988) Site fidelity and homing of Atlantic salmon parr in a small Scottish stream. In *Proceedings of the Second International Symposium on Salmon and Trout Migratory Behaviour*, Trondheim, June 1987 (eds E. Brannon and B. Jonsson), (in press).

Léaniz, C.G. de, Hawkins, A.D., Hay, D. and Martinez, J.J. (1987) *The Atlantic Salmon in Spain*, Atlantic Salmon Trust, Pitlochry.

Léaniz, C.G. de and Martinez, J.J. (1988) The Atlantic salmon in the rivers of Spain with particular reference to Cantabria. In *Atlantic Salmon: Planning for the Future* (eds D. Mills and D. Piggins), Croom Helm, London, pp. 179–209.

Léaniz, C.G. de and Verspoor, E. (in press) Natural hybridisation between Atlantic salmon (*Salmo salar*) and brown trout (*Salmo trutta*) in northern Spain. *J. Fish Biol.*

Lear, W.H. (1972a) Scale characteristics of Atlantic salmon from various areas in the North Atlantic. *International Council for the Exploration of the Sea*, C.M.1972/M:10.

Lear, W.H. (1972b) Food and feeding of Atlantic salmon in coastal areas and over oceanic depths. *ICNAF Res. Bull.*, **9**, 27–39.

Lear, W.H. (1975) Evaluation of the transplant of Pacific pink salmon (*Oncorhynchus gorbuscha*) from British Columbia to Newfoundland. *J. Fish. Res. Bd Can.*, **32**, 2343–56.

Lear, W.H. and Christensen, O. (1980) Selectivity and relative efficiency of salmon drift nets. *Rapp. P.-V. Réun. Cons. Perm. Int. Explor. Mer*, **176**, 36–42.

Lear, W.H. and Sandeman, P. (1974) Use of scale characters and a discriminant function for identifying continental origin of Atlantic salmon. *International Commission for the Northwest Atlantic Fisheries*, ICNAF Research Document 74/40, 12 pp.

Leivestad, H., Hendrey, G., Muniz, T.P. and Snekvik, E. (1976) Effects of acid precipitation on freshwater organisms. In *Impact of Acid Precipitation on Forest and Freshwater Ecosystems in Norway* (ed. F.H. Braekke), SNSP–project, FR6/76.

Lerner, L.J. (1962). Quantitative indices of recreational values. In *Economics of Outdoor Policy*, Report No. 11, Conference Proceedings, Western Agricultural Economics Research Council, Committee on the Economics of Water Resources Development, Reno, 55–80.

Leslie, P.H. (1945) On the use of matrices in certain population mathematics. *Biometrika*, **33**, 183–212.

Lind, E.A. (1981) Long-term trends in river and offshore exploitation of the salmon, *Salmo salar*, in Finland. In *Allocation of Fishery Resources* (ed. J.H. Groves), Proceedings of the Technical Consultation in Fishery Resources, Vichy, France, FAO, Rome, pp. 249–54.

Lindroth, A. (1950) Fluctuations of the salmon stock in the rivers of northern Sweden. (English summary.) *Svenska Vatenkraft Foren.* no. 415, 99–224.

Lindroth, A. (1952) Salmon tagging experiments in Sundsvall Bay of the Baltic in 1950. *Rep. Inst. Freshwat. Res., Drottningholm*, **44**, 105–12.

Lindroth, A. (1961) Sea food of Baltic smolts. *International Council for the Exploration of the Sea*, C.M.1961/M: 8.

Lindroth, A. (1965) The Baltic salmon stock. *Mittelungen Internationalis Vereiningen Limnologae*, **13**, 163–92.

Lorz, H.W. and McPherson, B.P. (1976) Effects of copper or zinc in fresh water on the adaptation to sea water and ATPase activity and the effects of copper on migratory disposition of coho salmon (*Oncorhynchus kisutch*). *J. Fish. Res. Bd Can.*, **33** (9), 2023–30.

Lowman, B.G., Henderson, A.R. and Lewis, M. (1983) Feeding silage effluent to farm animals – an alternative method of effluent disposal. ESCA (East of Scotland College of Agriculture) Technical Note 321A, May 1983, 5 pp.

Ludwig, D. and Walters, C.J. (1981) Measurement errors and uncertainty in parameter estimates for stock and recruitment. *Can. J. Fish. Aquat. Sci.*, **38**, 711–20.

Lugmayr, F. (1984) Regulierung von Fliessgewassern Vorschlage uber fischereifreundliche Einbauten. *Österreich Fischerei*, **37** (7), 179–83.

McCarthy, D.T. (1983) The impact of arterial drainage on fish stocks in the Trimblestown River. *Advances in Fish Biology in Ireland* (ed. C. Moriarty), Irish Fisheries Investigations, Series A, no. 23, 16–19.

McCarthy, D.T. (1985) The adverse effects of channelisation and their amelioration. In *Habitat Modification and Freshwater Fisheries* (ed. J. Alabaster), Butterworth, London, pp. 83–97.

MacCrimmon, H.R. (1971) World distribution of rainbow trout (*Salmo gairdneri*). *J. Fish. Res. Bd Can.*, **28**, 663–704.

MacCrimmon, H.R. and Claytor, R.R. (1986) Possible uses of taxonomic characters to identify Newfoundland and Scottish stocks of Atlantic salmon, *Salmo salar* L. *Aquaculture and Fisheries Management*, **17** (1), 1–17.

MacCrimmon, H.R. and Gots, B.L. (1979) World distribution of Atlantic salmon, *Salmo salar*. *J. Fish. Res. Bd Can.*, **33**, 2616–21.

MacCrimmon, H.R., Dickson, T.A. and Gibson, R.J. (1983) Implications of differences in emergent times on growth and behaviour of juvenile Atlantic salmon (*Salmo salar*) and brook charr (*Salvelinus fontinalis*) in sympatric stream populations. *Naturaliste Can.*, **110**, 379–84.

McDowall, R.M. (1968) Interactions of the native and alien fauna of New Zealand and the problem of fish introductions. *Trans. Am. Fish. Soc.*, **97** (1), 1–12.

McElligott, E.A., Maguire, T.M.F. and Cross, T.F. (1987) The amount and nature of electrophoretically-detectable genetic polymorphism in hatchery-reared Atlantic salmon (*Salmo salar* L.) in Ireland. *International Council for the Exploration of the Sea*, C.M.1987/M: 13 ref. E.

McGrath, C.J. (1959) Dams as barriers or deterrents to the migration of fish. *Proceedings of the IUCN Technical Meetings, Athens*, Vol. IV, 81–92.

McGrath, C.J. (1975) A report on fish counting installations in Ireland. *European Inland Fisheries Advisory Commission Technical Report*, **23**, 447–65.

McGrath, C.J. (1985) The role of the fisheries engineer in the design and execution of arterial drainage schemes. In *Habitat Modification and Freshwater Fisheries* (ed J. Alabaster), Butterworth, London, pp. 98–103.

McGrath, C.J. and Murphy, D.F. (1965) Engineering investigations into the effects of the harnessing of the River Lee, Co. Cork, Ireland, for hydro-electric purposes on the habitat and migration of salmonid stocks in that river system. *International Council for the Exploration of the Sea*, C.M.1965/M: 41.

McVean, D.N. and Lockie, J.D. (1969) *Ecology and Land Use in Upland Scotland*, University Press, Edinburgh.

Maheux, G. (1956) Le saumon de l'Atlantique dans l'économie de la province de Québec, Canada. Laval University Forest Research Foundation, Quebec, 30 pp.

Maitland, P.S. (1985) Criteria for the selection of important sites for freshwater fish in the British Isles. *Biol. Conserv.*, **31**, 335–53.

Maitland, P.S. (1986) The potential impact of fish culture on wild stocks of Atlantic salmon in Scotland. In *The Status of the Atlantic Salmon in Scotland* (eds D. Jenkins and W.M. Shearer), ITE Symposium no. 15, Institute of Terrestrial Ecology, Abbots Ripton, pp. 73–8.

Maitland, P. S. (1987) Genetic impact of farmed Atlantic salmon on wild populations. *Nature Conservancy Council OGD 87/1*.

Maitland, P.S., Lyle, A.A. and Campbell, R.N.B. (1987) *Acidification and Fish in Scottish Lochs*, Institute of Terrestrial Ecology, Grange over Sands, 71 pp.

Malloch, P.D.H. (1910) *Life History of the Salmon, Trout and Other Freshwater Fish*, A. and C. Black, London.

Mann, R.H.K., Hellawell, J.M., Beamont, W.R.C. and Williams, G.J. (1983) Records from the automatic fish counter on the river Frome, Dorset, 1970–81. *Freshwater Biological Association, Occasional Publications*, no. 19, 100 pp.

Marr, D.H.A. (1966) Factors affecting the growth of salmon alevins and their survival and growth during the fry stage. Association of River Authorities Yearbook 1965, 133–41.

Marshall, T.L. (1984) Status of Saint John River, N.B., Atlantic salmon in 1984 and forecast of returns in 1985. CAFSAC Research Document 84/84.

Marshall, T.L. (1988) Harvest and recent management of Atlantic salmon in Canada. In *Atlantic Salmon: Planning for the Future* (eds D. Mills and D. Piggins), Croom Helm, London, pp. 117–42.

Martin, J.D. and Dadswell, M.J. (1983) Records of coho salmon (*Oncorhynchus kisutch* (Walbaum, 1792)), in the Bay of Fundy and its tributary drainage. *Can. Tech. Rep. Fish. Aquat. Sci.*, 1204, 6 pp.

Martin, J.H.A. and Mitchell, K.A. (1985) Influence of sea temperature upon the numbers of grilse and multi-sea winter Atlantic salmon (*Salmo salar*) caught in the vicinity of the River Dee (Aberdeenshire). *Can. J. Fish. Aquat. Sci.*, **42**, 1513–21.

Mason, J.C. (1976) Some features of coho salmon *Oncorhynchus kisutch* fry emerging from simulated redds, and concurrent changes in photobehaviour. *Fish. Bull. Fish Wildl. Serv. U.S.*, **74**, 167–75.

Masterman, A.T. (1913) Report on the investigations on the salmon with special reference to age determination by study of scales. *Fishery Invest. Lond.*, Ser. I, Vol. 1, Part 1.

May, A.W. (1973) Distribution and migrations of salmon in the northwest Atlantic. In *International Atlantic Salmon Symposium*, St. Andrews (eds. M.V. Smith and W.M. Carter), *International Atlantic Salmon Foundation Special Publication Series*, **4**, 373–82.

Meagher, D. (1981) New Brunswick commercial Atlantic salmon fishery (1981): observations, comments and recommendations. *International Atlantic Salmon Foundation*, St Andrew's, N.B., 53 pp.

Meehan, W.R. (1974) *The Forest Ecosystem of south-east Alaska 3. Fish habitats.* USDA Forest Service General Technical Report, PNW 15, 41 pp.

Meehan, W.R., Farr, W.A., Bishop, D.M. and Patrie, J.H. (1969) *Some effects of clearcutting on salmon habitat of two southern Alaska streams.* USDA Forest Service Research Paper, PNW 82, 45 pp.

Meister, A.L. (1962) Atlantic salmon production in Cove Brook, Maine. *Trans. Amer. Fish. Soc.*, **91**, 208–12.

Meister, A.L. (1984) The marine migrations of tagged Atlantic salmon (*Salmo salar* L.) of U.S.A. region. *International Council for the Exploration of the Sea*, C.M.1984/M: 27.

Menzies, W.J.M. (1931) *The Salmon*, 2nd edn, Blackwood, Edinburgh.

Menzies, W.J.M. (1949) *The Stock of Salmon, its Migration, Preservation and Improvement*, Edward Arnold, London.

Menzies, W.J.M. and Shearer, W.M. (1957) Long-distance migration of salmon. *Nature*, **179**, 790.

Merican, Z.O. and Phillips, M.J. (1985) Solid waste production from rainbow trout, *Salmo gairdneri* Richardson, cage culture. *Aquaculture and Fisheries Management*, **16** (1), 55–70.

Merry, E.R. (1985) Pollution from farms. Atlantic Salmon Trust, Progress Report, September, p. 25.

Metcalfe, N.B., Huntingford, F. and Thorpe, J.E. (1986) Seasonal changes in feeding motivation of juvenile Atlantic salmon (*Salmo salar*). *Can. J. Zool.*, **64**, 2439–46.

Metcalfe, N.B., Huntingford, F. and Thorpe, J.E. (1987) The influence of predation risk on the feeding motivation and foraging strategy of juvenile Atlantic salmon. *Animal Behaviour*, **35**, 901–11.

Millichamp, R.I. (1976) Some thoughts on water abstraction on migratory fish rivers. *Fish. Mgmt*, **7** (1), 1–3.

Millichamp, R.I. and Lambert, A.O. (1967) An investigation into the relationship between salmon catch and flow on the River Usk during the 1965 season. In *River Management* (ed. P.C.G. Isaac), MacLaren, London, pp. 119–123.

Mills, C.P.R., Mahon, G.A.T. and Piggins, D.J. (1986) Influence of stock levels, fishing effort and environmental factors on anglers' catches of Atlantic salmon, *Salmo salar* L., and sea trout, *Salmo trutta* L. *Aquaculture and Fisheries Management*, **17** (4), 289–97.

Mills, D.H. (1962) The goosander and red-breasted merganser as predators of salmon in Scottish waters. *Freshwat. Salm. Fish. Res., Scotland*, 29, 10 pp.

Mills, D.H. (1964) The ecology of the young stages of the Atlantic salmon in the River Bran, Ross-shire. *Freshwat. Salm. Fish. Res., Scotland*, 32, 58 pp.

Mills, D.H. (1965a) The distribution and food of the cormorant in Scottish inland waters. *Freshwat. Salm. Fish. Res., Scotland*, 35, 16 pp.

Mills, D.H. (1965b) Observations on the effects of hydro-electric developments on salmon migration in a river system. *International Council for the Exploration of the Sea*, C.M.1965/M: 32.

Mills, D.H. (1965c) Smolt production and hydro-electric schemes. *International Council for the Exploration of the Sea*, C.M.1965/M: 3.

Mills, D.H. (1966) Smolt transport. *Salmon and Trout Magazine*, no. 177, 138–41.

Mills, D.H. (1967) The occurrence of the fish leech (*Piscicola geometra* L.) on salmonid fish in the River Tweed and its tributaries. *Salmon and Trout Magazine*, no. 181, 234–5.

Mills, D.H. (1967) A study of trout and young salmon populations in forest streams with a view to management. *Forestry*, **40** (1), Suppl., 85–90.

Mills, D.H. (1968) Some observations on the upstream movements of adult Atlantic salmon in the River Conon and River Meig, Ross-shire. *International Council for the Exploration of the Sea*, C.M.1968/M: 10.

Mills, D.H. (1969a) The survival of juvenile Atlantic salmon and brown trout in some

Scottish streams. In *Symposium on Salmon and Trout in Streams* (ed. T.G. Northcote), H.R. MacMillan Lectures in Fisheries, 1968, University of British Columbia, Vancouver, pp. 217–28.

Mills, D.H. (1969b) The survival of hatchery-reared salmon fry in some Scottish streams. *Freshwat. Salm. Fish. Res., Scotland*, 39, 10 pp.

Mills, D.H. (1970) Preliminary observations on fish populations in some Tweed tributaries. Annual Report to the River Tweed Commissioners, Appendix III, 24 pp.

Mills, D.H. (1971) *Salmon and Trout: A Resource, its Ecology, Conservation and Management*, Oliver and Boyd, Edinburgh.

Mills, D.H. (1973) Preliminary assessment of the characteristics of spawning tributaries of the River Tweed with a view to management. In *International Atlantic Salmon Symposium*, St Andrew's (eds M.W. Smith and W.M. Carter), *International Atlantic Salmon Foundation Special Publication Series*, 4 (1), 145–55.

Mills, D.H. (1978) *Fisheries Management*, Training Course, Diploma, Section 2. Institute of Fisheries Management.

Mills, D.H. (1980a) The people from the sea. *Blackwoods Magazine*, 328 (1982), 508–15.

Mills, D.H. (1980b) *The Management of Forest Streams*, Forestry Commission Leaflet no. 78, Her Majesty's Stationery Office, London, 19 pp.

Mills, D.H. (1981) Iceland's salmon in the clear. *The Field*, no. 6721, 1044–6.

Mills, D.H. (1983) Veidin i Dimmu stangaveidimann James Maitland Burnett. *Veidimadurinn*, 112, 5–10 (in Icelandic).

Mills, D.H. (1986) The biology of Scottish salmon. In *The Status of the Atlantic Salmon in Scotland* (ed. D. Jenkins and W.M. Shearer), ITE Symposium no. 15, Institute of Terrestrial Ecology, Abbots Ripton, pp. 10–19.

Mills, D.H. (1987a) Atlantic salmon management. In *Developments in Fisheries Research in Scotland* (eds R. Bailey and B.B. Parrish), Fishing News Books, Farnham, pp. 207–19.

Mills, D.H. (1987b) Consideration of scientific problems associated with possible cage-rearing of salmon smolts in Scottish lochs and hydroelectric reservoirs. *International Council for the Exploration of the Sea*, C.M.1987/M: 5 Ref. F.

Mills, D.H. (1988) Summary and Recommendations. In *Atlantic Salmon: Planning for the Future* (eds D. Mills and D. Piggins), Croom Helm, London, pp. 569–76.

Mills, D. H. and Graesser, N.W. (1981) *The Salmon Rivers of Scotland*, Cassell, London.

Mills, D.H. and Piggins, D. (eds) (1988) *Atlantic Salmon: Planning for the Future*, Croom Helm, London.

Mills, D.H. and Raynor, R. (1987) *A Biological Survey of Tweed Tributaries*, Tweed Foundation, Kelso, 34 pp.

Mills, D.H. and Shackley, P.E. (1971) Salmon smolt transportation experiments on the Conon river system, Ross-shire. *Freshwat. Salm. Fish. Res., Scotland*, 40, 8 pp.

Mills, D.H. and Smart, N. (1982) *Report on a Visit to the Faroes*, Atlantic Salmon Trust, Farnham, 52 pp.

Mills, D.H. and Tomison, A.T. (1985) *A Survey of the Salmon and Trout Stocks of the Tweed Basin*, Tweed Foundation, Kelso, 39 pp.

Mills, D.H., Griffiths, D. and Parfitt, A. (1978) *A Survey of the Fresh Water Fish Fauna of the Tweed Basin*, Nature Conservancy Council, Edinburgh, 100 pp.

Mills, Jennifer (1985) The Development, Marketing, Organisation and Future of Scottish Farmed Salmon. Thesis for BA degree in Home Economics, Queen Margaret College, Edinburgh, 61 pp.

Mills, S. (1982) Salmon: demise of the landlord's fish. *New Scient.*, **93** (1292), 354–67.

Mitans, A.R. (1973) Dwarf males and the sex structure of a Baltic salmon (*Salmo salar*) population. *J. Ichthyology*, **13**, 192–7.

Mitchell, I. (1985) North-east England drift-net fishery. *Salmon Net*, **XVIII**, 23–8.

Møller, D. (1970a) Transferrin polymorphism in Atlantic salmon (*Salmo salar*). *J. Fish. Res. Bd Can.*, **27**, 1617–25.

Møller, D. (1970b) Genetic diversity in Atlantic salmon management in relation to genetic factors. *International Atlantic Salmon Foundation Special Publication Series*, **1** (1), 7–29.

Møller, D. (1973) Norwegian salmon farming. In *International Atlantic Salmon Symposium*, St. Andrew's (eds M.W. Smith and W.M. Carter), International Atlantic Salmon Foundation, Special Publication Series, **4** (1), 259–63.

Møller Jensen, J. and Lear, W.H. (1980) Atlantic salmon caught in the Irminger Sea and at East Greenland. *J. Northwest Atlantic Fish. Sci.*, **1**, 55–64.

Montén, E. (1955) *Om utvandrande laxungen moj-ligheter alt oskadda passera genour kraftverksturbiner.* Vandringfiskrutredningen, Meddelande sr. 13, Stockholm.

Montén, E. (1969) *Vattenfalls fiskodlingsverksamket 1950—1968. (Fish culturing with the Swedish State Power Board 1950–1968.)* Swedish Salmon Research Institute Report, LFI Medd. 11/1969, 28 pp.

Moore, D.G. (1974) Impact of forest fertilisation on water quality in the Douglas fir region – a summary of monitoring studies. *Proceedings, 1974 National Convention, Society of American Foresters.*

Morgan, R.I.G., Greenstreet, S.P.R. and Thorpe, J.E. (1986) First observations on distribution, food and fish predators of post-smolt Atlantic salmon, *Salmo salar*, in the outer Firth of Clyde. *International Council for the Exploration of the Sea*, C.M./M: 27.

Morse, N.H. (1965) *The Economic Value of the Atlantic Salmon Fishery in Nova Scotia*, Acadia University Institute, Wolfville, N.S., 31 pp.

Morse, N.H. and DeWolf, A.G. (1973) Economic principles for the management of Atlantic salmon – St. John River system. In *International Atlantic Salmon Symposium, St Andrew's* (eds M.W. Smith and W.M. Carter), *International Atlantic Salmon Foundation Special Publication Series*, **4** (1), 355–64.

Morse, N.H. and De Wolf, A.G. (1979) Options for the management of the Atlantic salmon fisheries of the Saint John River, New Brunswick, *Fisheries and Marine Service Technical Report*, no. 819, 57 pp.

Muirhead-Thomson, R.C. (1971) *Pesticides and the Freshwater Fauna*, Academic Press, London.

Muirhead-Thomson, R.C. (1987) *Pesticide Impact on Stream Fauna with Special Reference to Macroinvertebrates*, Cambridge University Press, Cambridge.

Muniz, J.P. (1981) Acidification and the Norwegian salmon. SNSF – contribution Fa 120/80. In *Acid Rain and the Atlantic Salmon* (proceedings of a conference, 22–3 November 1980), *International Atlantic Salmon Foundation Special Publication Series*, **10**, 65–72.

Munro, A.L.S. (1970) Ulcerative dermal necrosis, a disease of migratory salmonid fishes in the rivers of the British Isles. *Biol. Conserv.*, **2** (2), 129–32.

Munro, A.L.S. (1979) Introduction of Pacific salmon to Europe. *International Council for the Exploration of the Sea*, C.M./F: 28.

Munro, A.L.S., Liversidge, J. and Elson, K.G.R. (1976) The distribution and prevalence of infectious pancreatic necrosis virus in wild fish in Loch Awe. *Proc. Roy. Soc. Edin.* B.75, 223–32.

Munro, W.R. (1965a) Observations on the migration of salmonids in the River Tummel

(Perthshire, Scotland). *International Council for the Exploration of the Sea,* C.M.1965/M: 30.

Munro, W.R. (1965b) Effects of passage through hydro-electric turbines on salmonids. *International Council for the Exploration of the Sea,* C.M.1965/M: 57.

Munro, W.R. (1965c) The use of louver screens as a means of diverting salmon smolts. *International Council for the Exploration of the Sea,* C.M.1965/M: 33.

Munro, W.R. (1969) The occurrence of salmon in the sea off the Faroes. *Scott. Fish. Bull.,* **32,** 11–13.

Murray, A.R. (1968) Numbers of Atlantic salmon and brook trout captured and marked at the Little Codroy River, Newfoundland, counting fence and auxiliary traps, 1954–63. *Fish. Res. Bd Can. Tech. Rep.,* 84, 135 pp.

Myers, R.A. (1983) Evolutionary change in the proportion of precocious parr and its effect on yield in Atlantic salmon. *International Council for the Exploration of the Sea,* C.M.1983/M: 14.

Myers, R.A. (1984) Demographic consequences of precocious maturation of Atlantic salmon (*Salmo salar*). *Can. J. Fish. Aquat. Sci.,* **41,** 1349–53.

Myers, R.A. and Hutchings, J.A. (1987) Mating of anadromous Atlantic salmon, *Salmo salar* L. with mature male parr. *J. Fish Biol.,* **31** (2), 143–6.

Nall, G.H. (1930) Sea trout of the River Tweed. *Fishery Board for Scotland, Salmon Fisheries,* 1929, V, 59 pp.

Nall, G.H. (1933) Salmon of the River Ewe and Loch Maree. *Fishery Board for Scotland, Salmon Fisheries,* 1932, V.

NASCO (1987) Report of the Activities of the Bilateral Scientific Working Group of the North American Commission on Salmonid Introductions and Transfers. Annex 13 to NAC (87) 20, 72 pp.

Neave, F. (1958) The origin and speciation of *Oncorhynchus. Trans. R. Soc. Can.,* Ser. 3, **52,** 25–39.

Netboy, A. (1968) *The Atlantic Salmon: A Vanishing Species,* Faber and Faber, London.

Netboy, A. (1976) Coho versus Atlantic. *Trout and Salmon,* **258,** 39–40.

Nicols, A. (1882) *The Acclimatisation of the Salmonidae at the Antipodes,* Sampson Low, London.

Niemela, E., McComas, R.L. and Niemela, M. (1985) Salmon (*Salmo salar*) parr densities in the Teno River (Finland). *International Council for the Exploration of the Sea,* C.M.1985/M: 23.

Nikolsky, G.V. (1969) *Theory of Fish Population Dynamics,* Oliver and Boyd, Edinburgh.

Norden, C.R. (1961) Comparative osteology of representative salmonid fishes with particular reference to the grayling (*Thymallus thymallus*) and its phylogeny. *J. Fish. Res. Bd Can.,* **18,** 679–791.

Nordeng, H. (1971) Is the local orientation of anadromous fishes determined by pheromones? *Nature,* **233,** 411–13.

Nordeng, H. (1977) A pheromone hypothesis for homeward migration in anadromous salmonids. *Oikos,* **28,** 155–9.

North, C. (1840) Shaw on salmon fry. *Blackwoods Edinburgh Magazine,* **47** (294), 531–43.

Nott, F.H. and Bielby, G.H. (1966) *River Erme Fisheries Survey, 1965,* Devon River Authority Report.

Nyman, O.L. (1966) Geographic variation in Atlantic salmon (*Salmo salar* L.). Swedish Salmon Research Institute Report, LFI Medd. 3, 6 pp.

Nyman, O.L. (1967) Protein variation in various populations of Atlantic salmon. Swedish Salmon Research Institute Report, LFI Medd. 8, 11 pp.

Nyman, O.L. (1970) Electrophoretic analysis of hybrids between salmon (*Salmo salar* L.) and trout (*Salmo trutta* L.). *Trans. Amer. Fish. Soc.* **99** (1), 229–36.

Nyman, O.L. and Norman, L. (1987) Genetiska aspekter pa odling av lax och havsoring utplantering: Riktlinjer for avelsmetalik och fiskevard. *Swedish Salmon Research Institute Report*, LFI Medd. 4, 20 pp.

Nyman, O.L. and Pippy, J.H.C. (1972) Differences in Atlantic salmon, *Salmo salar*, from North America and Europe. *J. Fish. Res. Bd Can.*, **29** (2), 179–85.

O'Connor, R. (1983) An economic evaluation of salmon fishing in Ireland in 1982. Paper to South Western Regional Fisheries Board Seminar, Kenmore, 12 pp.

O'Connor, R., Whelan, B.J. and McCashin, A. (1973–4) An economic evaluation of Irish salmon fishing. Parts I–III. *The Economic and Social Research Institute* Papers 68, 75 and 78.

Österdahl, L. (1969) The smolt run of a small Swedish river. In *Symposium on Salmon and Trout in Streams* (ed. T.G. Northcote), H.R. MacMillan Lectures in Fisheries, 1968, University of British Columbia, Vancouver, pp. 205–21.

Otterström, C.V. (1938) Salmon from west Jutland. *Medd. Komm. Havundersog., kibh.*, **9** (10), 3–20.

Palmer, C.H. (1928) *The Salmon Rivers of Newfoundland*, Farrington Printing Co., Boston.

Parnell, R. (1840) Account of a new species of British bream and of an undescribed species of skate: to which is added a list of fishes of the Frith of Forth and its tributary streams, with observations. *Trans. R. Soc. Edinb.*, **14**, 143–57.

Patterson, J.H. (1903) The cause of salmon disease. *Fishery Board for Scotland, Salmon Fisheries*, 1–52.

Payne, R.H., Child, A.R. and Forrest, A. (1971) Geographical variation in the Atlantic salmon. *Nature*, **231**, 250–52.

Payne, R.H., Child, A.R. and Forrest, A. (1972) The existence of natural hybrids between the European trout and the Atlantic salmon. *J. Fish Biol.*, **4**, 233–6.

Pearcy, W.G. and Masuda, K. (1982) Tagged steelhead trout (*Salmo gairdneri* Richardson) collected in the North Pacific on the Oshoro-Maru, 1980–1981. *Bulletin of the Faculty of Fisheries*, Hokkaido University, **33**, 249–54.

Pearson, K. (1982) On a method of ascertaining limits to the actual number of marked members of a population of a given size from a sample. *Biometrika*, **20**, 149–74.

Pennant, T. (1761) *British Zoology*. Vol. 3.

Penney, G.H. (1971) Summary report on the effects of forest spraying in New Brunswick in 1971, on juvenile Atlantic salmon and aquatic insects. Appendix 4 in 1971. Report of the Interdepartmental Committee on Forest Spraying Operations, Ottawa, 22 November 1971, 7 pp.

Peppar, J.L. (1977) Angling survey, Crown Open Water, Little Main Restigouche River, New Brunswick. *Fisheries and Environment, Canada, Fisheries and Marine Service Manuscript Report*, no. 1441.

Peppar, J.L. and Pickard, P.R. (1978) Angling survey of the Cairns River, Miramichi river system, New Brunswick, 1976. *Fisheries and Environment, Canada, Fisheries and Marine Service Manuscript Report*, no. 144.

Pepper, V.A. (1976) Lacustrine nursery areas for Atlantic salmon in insular Newfoundland. *Fisheries and Environment, Canada, Fisheries and Marine Service Technical Report*, no. 671. 61 pp.

Peters, J.C., Farmer, H.R. and Radford, P.J. (1973) A simulation model of the upstream movement of anadromous salmonid fish. *Water Resources Board Publication* no. 21, 76 pp.

Peterson, R.H. (1978) Physical characteristics of Atlantic salmon spawning gravel in some New Brunswick streams. *Fisheries and Environment, Canada, Fisheries and Marine Service Technical Report*, no. 785, 28 pp.

Peterson, R.H. and Martin-Robichaud, D.J. (1986) Growth and major inorganic cation budgets of Atlantic salmon alevins at three ambient acidities. *Trans. Amer. Fish. Soc.*, **115**, 220–6.

Phélipot, P. (1982) *Rivières à saumons de Bretagne et de Basse-Normandie.* Published by the author, Quimperlé, 197 pp.

Philippart, J.C. (1985) Reverrons-nous des saumons dans la Meuse? *Cahiers d'Ethologie Appliquée*, **5** (3), 189–226.

Phillippart, J.C. (1987) Histoire de l'extinction et problématique de la restauration des Salmonides migrateurs dans la Meuse. In *La Restauration des Rivières à Saumons* (eds M. Thibault and R. Billard), Collection Hydrobiologie et Agriculture, INRA, Paris, pp. 125–37.

Phillippart, J.C., Gillet, A. and Micha, J.-C. (1987) *Fish and Their Environment in Large European River Ecosystems. The River Meuse.* Network of Scientific and Technical Co-operation on the Management of Water Resources. Topic 1 – Water Management in the alluvial valleys of large rivers, research theme no. 5. Workshop held in Liège, 21–22 November 1986.

Piggins, D.J. (1959) Investigations on predators of salmon smolts and parr. *Salmon Research Trust of Ireland, Inc.* Report and Statement of Accounts for year ended 31st December, 1958. Appendix no. 1, 12 pp.

Piggins, D.J. (1961) Salmon × sea-trout hybrids. In *Salmon Research Trust of Ireland, Inc.* Report and Statement of Account for year ended 31st December, 1960, pp. 5–6.

Piggins, D.J. (1962) Salmon × sea-trout hybrids. In *Salmon Research Trust of Ireland, Inc.* Report and Statement of Accounts for year ended 31st December, 1961, pp. 5–6.

Piggins, D.J. (1963) Salmon × sea-trout hybrids. In *Salmon Research Trust of Ireland, Inc.* Report and Statement of Accounts for year ended 31st December, 1962, pp. 7–8.

Piggins, D.J. (1964) Salmon × sea-trout hybrids. In Salmon Research Trust of Ireland, Inc., Report and Statement of Accounts for year ended 31st December, 1963, pp. 7–10.

Piggins, D.J. (1965a) Appendix III Salmon × Sea Trout Hybrids. In *Salmon Research Trust of Ireland, Inc.*, Report and Statement of Accounts for year ended 31st December, 1964, pp. 27–37.

Piggins, D.J. (1965b) Salmon and sea trout hybrids. *Atlantic Salmon Journal*, Autumn, 3–5.

Piggins, D.J. (1974) The results of selective breeding from known grilse and salmon parents. Report for 1973. *Salmon Research Trust of Ireland, Incorporated*, Appendix 1, 35–9.

Piggins, D.J. (1976) Exploitation of grilse stocks by rod fishing in a lake system and subsequent spawning escapements, smolt productions and adult returns, 1970–75. *International Council for the Exploration of the Sea*, C.M.1976/M: 10.

Piggins, D.J. (1987) Summary of selective breeding programme. In *Salmon Research Trust for Ireland, Inc.*, Report and Statement of Accounts for year ended 31st December, 1986, p. 31.

Pippy, J.H.C. and Hare, G.M. (1969) Relationship of river pollution to bacterial infection in salmon (*Salmo salar*) and suckers (*Catostomus commersoni*). *Trans. Amer. Fish. Soc.*, **98**, 685–90.

Pomerleau, C., Côté, Y. and Migneault, J.G. (1980) Répertoire de donnés relatives aux populations de saumon Atlantique (*Salmo salar*) des rivières de la région du Bas Saint-Laurent et de la Gaspésie. 1. Guide méthodologique. Direction de la Recherche Faunique. Ministère du Loisir, et de la Chasse et de la Pêche.

Pontual, H. de and Prouzet, P. (1987) Atlantic salmon, *Salmo salar*, stock discrimination by scale-shape analysis. *Aquaculture and Fisheries Management,* **18** (3), 277–89.

Pope, J.A., Mills, D.H. and Shearer, W.M. (1961) The fecundity of Atlantic salmon (*Salmo salar* L.). *Freshwat. Salm. Fish. Res., Scotland,* 26, 12 pp.

Porter, T.R., Riche, L.G. and Traverse, G.R. (1974) Catalogue of rivers in insular Newfoundland. Vols. A–D. *Research Development Branch, Newfoundland Region, Data Record Series,* NEW/D – 74–9.

Potter, E.C.E. (1982) Assessment of North Atlantic salmon stocks. *International Council for the Exploration of the Sea,* Working Group on North Atlantic Salmon, 1982.

Potter, E.C.E. and Swain, A. (1982) Effects of the English north-east coast salmon fisheries on Scottish salmon catches. *Fisheries Research Technical Report,* No. 67, Ministry of Agriculture, Fisheries and Food, Lowestoft, 8 pp.

Power, G. (1969) The salmon of Ungava Bay. *Arctic Institute of North America,* Technical Paper 22, 72 pp.

Power, G. (1976) History of the Hudson's Bay Company salmon fisheries in the Ungava Bay region. *Polar Record,* **18**, 151–61.

Power, G. (1981) Stock characteristics and catches of Atlantic salmon (*Salmo salar*) in Quebec and Newfoundland and Labrador in relation to environmental variables. *Can. J. Fish. Aquat. Sci.,* **38** (12), 1601–11.

Pratt, J.D. and Rietveld, H.J. (1973) Atlantic salmon development techniques used in Newfoundland. *Environment Canada, Fisheries and Marine Service, Technical Report Series* no. NEW/T–73–1, 19 pp.

Prouzet, P. (1978) Relationship between density and growth of Atlantic salmon reared in nursery streams in natural conditions. *International Council for the Exploration of the Sea,* C.M.1978/M: 13.

Prouzet, P. (1981) Observation d'une femelle de tacon de saumon Atlantique (*Salmo salar* L.) parvenue à maturité sexuelle en rivière. *Bulletin Français de Pisciculture,* **282**, 16–19.

Prouzet, P. and Dumas, J. (1988) Measurement of Atlantic salmon spawning escapement. In *Atlantic Salmon: Planning for the Future* (eds D. Mills and D. Piggins), Croom Helm, London, pp. 325–43.

Pyefinch, K.A. (1952) Capture of the pre-grilse stage of salmon. *Scott. Nat.,* **64**, 47.

Pyefinch, K.A. and Elson, K.R. (1967) Salmon disease in Irish rivers. *Scott. Fish. Bull.,* **26**, 21–3.

Pyefinch, K.A. and Mills, D.H. (1963) Observations on the movements of Atlantic salmon (*Salmo salar* L.) in the River Conon and the River Meig, Ross-shire. I. *Freshwat. Salm. Fish. Res., Scotland,* **31**, 24 pp.

Pyefinch, K.A. and Woodward, W.B. (1955) The movements of salmon tagged in the sea, Montrose, 1948, 1950, 1951. *Freshwat. Salm. Fish. Res., Scotland,* **8**, 15 pp.

Radcliffe, W. (1921) *Fishing from the Earliest Times,* John Murray, London.

Radford, A. (1984) The economics and value of recreational salmon fisheries in England and Wales: An analysis of the rivers Wye, Mawddach, Tamar and Lune. *Marine Resources Research Unit, Portsmouth Polytechnic,* 250 pp.

Radford, P.J., Peters, J.C. and Farmer, H.R. (1972) Digital simulation of the upstream movement of migratory salmonids. In *Proceedings of the International Symposium on Modelling Techniques in Water Resources Systems* (ed. A.K. Biwas), Ottawa, May 1972, **1**, 21–38.

Rae, B.B. (1960) Seals and Scottish fisheries. *Marine Research Series, Scotland,* 2, 39 pp.

Rae, B.B. and Shearer, W.M. (1965) Seal damage to salmon fisheries. *Marine Research Series, Scotland,* **2**, 39 pp.

Ramberg, L. (1974) Effects of forestry operations on aquatic ecosystems. *Ecol. Bull.*, **21**, 143–9.

Ramos, M.A. (1982) Atlantic salmon ranching in Portugal. In *Sea Ranching of Atlantic Salmon* (eds C. Eriksson, M. Ferranti and P.O. Larsson), Cost 46/4 Workshop Proceedings, Commission of the European Communities, Brussels, pp. 109–25.

Randall, R.G. (1982) Emergence, population densities and growth of salmon and trout fry in two New Brunswick streams. *Can. J. Zool.*, **60**, 2239–44.

Randall, R.G. (1984) Number of salmon required for spawning in the Restigouche River, N.B., pp. 15. CAFSAC Res. Doc. 84/16.

Randall, R.G. and Paim, U. (1982) Growth, biomass and production of juvenile Atlantic salmon (*Salmo salar*, L.) in two Miramichi River, New Brunswick, tributary streams. *Can. J. Zool.*, **60**, 1647–59.

Rantz, S.E. (1964) Stream hydrology related to the optimum discharge of king salmon spawning in the northern California coast ranges. (Water Supply paper 1779-AA.) United States Geological Survey, California Dept. of Fish and Game, 16 pp.

Rasmuson, M. (1968) Populationgenetiska synpunkter pa laxodlingsverksaamheten i Sverige. *Swedish Salmon Research Institute*, LFI Medd. 3/1968, 18 pp.

Ray, J. and Willughby, F. (1686) *De Historia Piscium*, Oxford.

Reddin, D.G. (1982) Some general information on discriminant functions and accuracy for identifying North American and European Atlantic salmon caught at West Greenland. *International Council for the Exploration of the Sea*, C.M.1982/M: 15.

Reddin, D.G. (1985) Atlantic salmon (*Salmo salar* L.) on and east of the Grand Bank. *Journal of Northwest Atlantic Fisheries*, **6**, 157–64.

Reddin, D.G. (1988) Ocean life of Atlantic salmon (*Salmo salar* L.) in the northwest Atlantic. In *Atlantic Salmon: Planning for the Future* (eds D. Mills and D. Piggins), Croom Helm, London, pp. 483–511.

Reddin, D.G. and Burfitt, R.F. (1983) An update: the use of scale characters and multivariate analysis to discriminate between Atlantic salmon (*Salmo salar* L.) of North American and European origin caught at West Greenland. *International Council for the Exploration of the Sea*, C.M.1983/M: 11.

Reddin, D.G. and Burfitt, R.F. (1984) A new feeding area for Atlantic salmon (*Salmo salar* L.) to the east of the Newfoundland continental shelf. *International Council for the Exploration of the Sea*, C.M.1984/M: 13.

Reddin, D.G. and Carscadden, J.E. (1982) Salmon–capelin interactions. *International Council for the Exploration of the Sea*, C.M.1982/M: 17.

Reddin, D.G. and Dempson, J.B. (1986) Origin of Atlantic salmon (*Salmo salar* L.) caught at sea near Nain, Labrador. *Naturaliste Can.*, **113**, 211–18.

Reddin, D.G. and Murray, J.J. (1985) Environmental conditions in the northwest Atlantic in relation to salmon catches at West Greenland. *International Council for the Exploration of the Sea*, C.M.1985/M: 10.

Reddin, D.G. and Shearer, W.M. (1987) Sea-surface temperature and distribution of Atlantic salmon (*Salmo salar* L.) in the northwest Atlantic. *American Fisheries Society Symposium 1*, 262–75.

Reddin, D.G., Shearer, W.M. and Burfitt, R.F. (1984) Intercontinental migrations of Atlantic salmon (*Salmo salar* L.). *International Council for the Exploration of the Sea*, C.M.1984/M: 11.

Regan, C. Tate (1911) *The Freshwater Fishes of the British Isles*, Methuen, London.

Regan, C. Tate (1914) Systematic arrangement of Salmonidae. *Ann. Mag. Nat. Hist.*

Reisenbichler, R.R. and McIntyre, J.D. (1977) Genetic differences in growth and survival of juvenile hatchery and wild steelhead trout, *Salmo gairdneri. J. Fish. Res. Bd Can.*, **34**, 123–8.

Ricker, W.E. (1954a) Pacific salmon for Atlantic waters. *Can. Fish Cult.*, **16**, 6–14.

Ricker, W.E. (1954b) Stock and recruitment. *J. Fish. Res. Bd Can.*, **11**, 559–623.

Ricker, W.E. (1975) Computation and interpretation of biological statistics of fish populations. *Bull. Fish. Res. Bd Can.*, no. 191, 382 pp.

Ricker, W.E. and Loftus, K.N. (1968) Pacific salmon moves east. *Fisheries Council of Canada Ann. Rev. 1968*: 37–43.

Rimmer, D.M., Paim, U. and Saunders, R.L. (1984) Changes in the selection of microhabitat by juvenile Atlantic salmon (*Salmo salar*) at the summer–autumn transition in a small river. *Can. J. Fish. Aquat. Sci.*, **41**, 469–75.

Ritchie, J. (1920) *The Influence of Man on Animal Life in Scotland*, Cambridge University Press, Cambridge.

Ritter, J.A. (1975) Lower ocean survival rates for hatchery-reared Atlantic salmon (*Salmo salar*) stocks released in rivers other than their native streams. *J. Cons. Perm. Int. Explor. Mer*, **26**, 1–10.

Ritter, J.A. and Porter, T.R. (1980) Issues and processes for Atlantic salmon management in Canada. In *Atlantic Salmon: its Future* (ed. A.E.J. Went), Fishing News Books, Farnham, pp. 108–27.

Rivier, B. and Seguier, J. (1985) Physical and biological effects of gravel extraction in river beds. In *Habitat Modification and Freshwater Fisheries* (ed. J. Alabaster), Butterworth, London, pp. 131–46.

Roberts, R.J. (1969) The pathology of salmon disease. *Salmon Net*, V, 48–51.

Roberts, R.J. (1978) Miscellaneous non-infectious diseases. In *Fish Pathology* (ed. R.J. Roberts), Bailliere Tindall, London, pp. 227–34.

Roberts, R.J., Shearer, W.M. and Elson, K.R. (1969) The pathology of ulcerative dermal necrosis of Scottish salmon. *J. Pathology*, **97** (3), 563–5.

Robitaille, J.A., Côté, Y., Shooner, G. and Hayeur, G. (1986) Growth and maturation patterns of Atlantic salmon *Salmo salar* in the Kilsoak River, Ungava, Quebec. In *Salmonid Age at Maturity* (ed. D.J. Meerburg). *Can. Spec. Publ. Fish. Aquat. Sci.*, pp. 62–9.

Rolland, L. (1987) Report from Canada. *Progress Report of the Atlantic Salmon Trust, 1986*, 26–9.

Rommel, S.A. Jr and McLeave, J.D. (1973) Sensitivity of American eels (*Anguilla rostrata*) and Atlantic salmon (*Salmo salar*) to weak electric and magnetic fields. *J. Fish. Res. Bd Can.*, **30**, 657–63.

Rosseland, B.O., Skogheim, O.K. and Sevaldrud, J.N. (1986a) Acid deposition and effects in nordic Europe. Damage to fish populations continue to apace. *Water, Air and Soil Pollution*, **30**, 65–74.

Rosseland, B.O., Skogheim, O.K., Abrahamsen, H. and Matzow, D. (1986b) Limestone slurry reduces physiological stress and increases survival of Atlantic salmon (*Salmo salar*) in an acidic Norwegian river. *Can. J. Fish. Aquat. Sci.*, **43**, 1888–93.

Rosseland, L. (1979) Litt om bestand og beskatning av laksen fra Laerdalselva. In *Vassdragsregulingers bilogiskee virkninger i magasiner og lakseelver* (eds T.B. Gunnerod and P. Mellquist), Norges Vassdrags og Elektrisitetsvesen, Direktoratet for vilt og ferskvannsfisk, pp. 174–86 (in Norwegian).

Ruggles, C.P. (1974) The use of fish passes, traps and weirs in eastern Canada for assessing populations of anadromous fishes. *European Inland Fisheries Advisory Commission*, 74/1/Symposium – 56.

Ruggles, C.P. (1980) A review of the downstream migration of Atlantic salmon. *Can. Tech. Rep. Fish. Aquat. Sci.*, no. 952, 39 pp.

Ruggles, C.P. and Turner, G.E. (1973) Recent changes in stock composition of Atlantic salmon (*Salmo salar* L.) in the Miramichi River, New Brunswick. *J. Fish. Res. Bd Can.*, **30** (6), 779–86.

Russel, A. (1864) *The Salmon*, Edmonston and Douglas, Edinburgh.

Ryman, N. (1970) A genetic analysis of recapture frequencies of released young salmon (*Salmo salar* L.) *Hereditas* **65**, 159–60.

Ryman, N. (1983) Patterns of distribution of biochemical genetic variation in salmonids: differences between species. *Aquaculture*, **33**, 1–21.

Saunders, J.W. (1966) Estuarine spawning of Atlantic salmon. *J. Fish. Res. Bd Can.*, **23** (11), 1803–4.

Saunders, J.W. (1969) Mass mortalities and behaviour of brook trout and juvenile Atlantic salmon in a stream polluted by agricultural pesticides. *J. Fish. Res. Bd Can.*, **26** (3), 695–9.

Saunders, R.L. (1981) Atlantic salmon (*Salmo salar*) stocks and management implications in the Canadian Atlantic salmon Provinces and New England, USA. *Can. J. Fish. Aquat. Sci.*, **38**, 1612–25.

Saunders, R.L. and Bailey, J.K. (1980) The role of genetics in Atlantic salmon management. In *Atlantic Salmon: its Future* (ed. A.E.J. Went), Fishing News Books, Farnham, pp. 182–200.

Saunders, R.L. and Sprague, J.B. (1967) Effects of copper–zinc pollution on a spawning migration of Atlantic salmon. *Wat. Res.*, **1**, 419–32.

Saunders, R.L. and Sreedharan, A. (1977) The incidence and genetic implications of sexual maturity in male Atlantic salmon parr. *International Council for the Exploration of the Sea*, C.M.1977/M:21.

Saunders, R.L., Henderson, E.B., Glebe, B.D. and Loudenslager, E.I. (1983) Evidence of a major environmental component in the determination of grilse:salmon ratio in the Atlantic salmon (*Salmo salar*). *Aquaculture*, **33**, 107–18.

Scarnecchia, D.L. (1984a) Climatic and oceanic variations affecting yield of Icelandic stocks of Atlantic salmon (*Salmo salar*). *Can. J. Fish. Aquat. Sci.*, **41**, 917–35.

Scarnecchia, D.L. (1984b) Forecasting yields of two-sea-winter Atlantic salmon (*Salmo salar*) from Icelandic rivers. *Can. J. Fish. Aquat. Sci.*, **41**, 1234–40.

Schaefer, M.B. (1951) Estimates of the size of animal populations by marking experiments. *Fishery Bull.*, Fish Wildl. Serv. U.S., **52**, 189–203.

Schofield, G.L. (1976) Acid precipitation: effects on fish. *Ambio*, **5**, 228–30.

Scholz, A.T., Horrall, R.M., Cooper, J.C. and Hasler, A.D. (1976) Imprinting to chemical cues: the basis for homestream selection in salmon. *Science*, **196**, 1247–2149.

Scott, A.D. (1965) The Valuation of Game Resources: Some Theoretical Aspects. *Proceedings of the Symposium on the Economic Aspects of Sport Fishing* (Canadian Fisheries Report No. 4), Department of Fisheries of Canada, Ottawa.

Scott, M. (1968) The pathogenicity of *Aeromonas salmonicida* (Griffin) in sea and brackish waters. *J. Gen. Microbiol.*, **50**, 321–7.

Selset, R. and Døving, K.B. (1980) Behaviour of mature anadromous char (*Salvelinus alpinus* L.) towards odorants produced by smolts of their own population. *Acta Physiol. Scand.*, 14–23.

Semple, G. (1967) Mythical profits of the fishing proprietors. *The Financial Scotsman*, 23 August, p. 17.

Sevaldrud, I.H. and Muniz, I.P. (1980) Sure vatn og innlandsfisket i Norge. Resultater fra intervjuundersokelsene 1974–1979. SNSF – prosjektet IR 77/80. 95s (in Norwegian, English summary).

Sevaldrud, I.H., Muniz, I.P. and Kalvenes, S. (1980) Loss of fish populations in Southern Norway. Dynamics and magnitude of the problem. In *Ecological Impact of Acid Precipitation* (eds D. Drablos and A. Tollan), Proceedings of an International Conference, Trykkeri Sandefjord, Norway, pp. 350–1.

Sewell, W.R.D. and Rostron, J. (1970) *Recreational Fishing Evaluation*, Department of Fisheries and Forestry, Ottawa, 133 pp.

Shaw, J. (1836) An account of some experiments and observations on the parr and on the ova of the salmon, proving the parr to be the young of the salmon. *Edinburgh Philosophical Journal*, **21**, 99–116.

Shaw, J. (1840) Account of experimental observations on the development and growth of salmon fry, from the exclusion of the ova to the age of 2 years. *Trans. R. Soc. Edinb.*, **14**, 547–66.

Shaw, S.E. and Muir, J.F. (1987) *Salmon: Economics and Marketing*, Croom Helm, London, 270 pp.

Shearer, W.M. (1961) Pacific salmon in the North Sea. *New Scientist*, **10**, 184–6.

Shearer, W.M. (1972) A Study of the Atlantic Salmon Population in the North Esk, 1961–70. MSc Thesis, University of Edinburgh, 437 pp.

Shearer, W.M. (1975) Sea-going rainbow trout. *Scott. Fish. Bull.*, **42**, 17–18.

Shearer, W.M. (1983) The use of scale characteristics and multi-variate analysis to distinguish between stocks of fish. *International Council for the Exploration of the Sea*, C.M.1983/M:21.

Shearer, W.M. (1984a) The natural mortality at sea for North Esk salmon. *International Council for the Exploration of the Sea*, C.M.1984/M:23.

Shearer, W.M. (1984b) The relationship between both river and sea-age return to homewaters in Atlantic salmon. *International Council for the Exploration of the Sea*, C.M.1984/M:24.

Shearer, W.M. (1985) Salmon catch statistics for the River Dee, 1952–83. In *The Biology and Management of the River Dee* (ed. D. Jenkins), Institute of Terrestrial Ecology, Abbots Ripton, pp. 127–41.

Shearer, W.M. (1986a) The exploitation of the Atlantic salmon in Scottish home water fisheries in 1952–83. In *The Status of the Atlantic Salmon in Scotland* (eds D. Jenkins and W.M. Shearer), ITE Symposium no. 15, Institute of Terrestrial Ecology, Abbots Ripton, pp. 37–49.

Shearer, W.M. (1986b) The relationship between catches and stocks in Scottish salmon rivers with particular reference to the River North Esk. *International Council for the Exploration of the Sea*, C.M.1986/M:5.

Shearer, W.M. (1988) Relating catch records to stocks. In *Atlantic Salmon: Planning for the Future* (eds D. Mills and D. Piggins), Croom Helm, London, pp. 256–74.

Shearer, W.M. and Balmain, K.H. (1967) Greenland salmon. *Salmon Net*, **III**, 19–24.

Shearer, W.M. and Trevawas, E. (1960). A Pacific salmon (*Oncorhynchus gorbuscha*) in Scottish waters. *Nature*, **188** (4753), 868.

Shearer, W.M., Cook, R.M., Dunkley, D.A., *et al.* (1987) A model to assess the effect of predation by sawbill ducks on the salmon stock of the River North Esk. *Scottish Fisheries Research Report* no. 37, 12 pp.

Shelton, R.G.J. (1984) The state of salmon stocks. In *The Atlantic salmon and its economic importance*, Highlands and Islands Development Board, Inverness, pp. 5–7.

Shelton, R.G.J. (1986) Aspects of open sea exploitation of Atlantic salmon and the problems of assessing the effects on Scottish home water stocks. In *The Status of the Atlantic Salmon in Scotland* (eds D. Jenkins and W.M. Shearer), ITE Symposium no. 15, Institute of Terrestrial Ecology, Abbots Ripton, pp. 28–36.

Shepherd, J.G., Pope, J.G. and Cousens, R.V. (1982) Variations in fish stocks and hypotheses concerning their links with climate. *International Council for the Exploration of the Sea*, C.M.1982/GEN.6.

Smart, G.N.J. (1986) Recent changes in fishing methods. In *The Status of the Atlantic Salmon in Scotland* (eds D. Jenkins and W.M. Shearer), ITE Symposium no. 15, Institute of Terrestrial Ecology, Abbots Ripton, pp. 50–54.

Smirnov, Y.A. (1971) Salmon of Lake Onega. *Fish. Res. Bd Can. Transl. Ser.*, (2137), 212 pp.

Smith, B.D. (1980) The effects of afforestation on the trout of a small stream in southern Scotland. *Fish. Mgmt,* **11** (2), 39–58.

Smith, I.W. (1960) Furunculosis in salmon kelts. *Nature,* **186,** 733–4.

Smith, I.W. (1962) Furunculosis in kelts. *Freshwat. Salm. Fish. Res., Scotland,* **27,** 12 pp.

Smith, I.W. (1963) The classification of 'Bacterium salmonicida.' *J. Gen. Microbiol.,* **33,** 263–74.

Smith, I.W. (1964) The occurrence and pathology of Dee disease. *Freshwat. Salm. Fish. Res., Scotland,* **34,** 12 pp.

Smith, R.A. (1872) *Air and Rain. The Beginnings of a Chemical Climatology,* Longmans Green, London.

Snieszko, S.F. and Griffin, P.J. (1955) Kidney disease in brook trout and its treatment. *Progve Fish Cult.,* **17,** 3–13.

Solbé, J.F. (1982) Fish farm effluents – cause for concern? *Water,* March 1982, 22–5.

Solbé, J.F. (ed.) (1986) *Effects of Land Use on Fresh Waters,* Ellis Horwood, Chichester.

Solbé, J.F. (1987) European Inland Fisheries Advisory Commission working party on fish-farm effluents. *Water Research Centre Environment,* Medmenham.

Solomon, D.J. (1973) Evidence for pheromone-influenced homing by migratory Atlantic salmon, *Salmo salar,* L. *Nature,* **224,** 231–2.

Solomon, D.J. (1978) Some observations on salmon smolt migration in a chalk stream. *J. Fish Biol.,* **12,** 571–4.

Solomon, D.J. (1979) *Coho Salmon in Northwest Europe. Possible Effects on Native Salmonids.* Ministry of Agriculture, Fisheries and Food, Directorate of Fisheries Research, Lowestoft, Laboratory Leaflet no. 49, 21 pp.

Solomon, D.J. (1980) Pacific salmon in the North Atlantic: A history and assessment of current status. *International Council for the Exploration of the Sea,* C.M.1980/M: 15.

Solomon, D.J. (1985) Salmon stock and recruitment, and stock enhancement. *J. Fish Biol.,* **27** (Suppl. A), 45–57.

Sømme, S. (1941) On the high age of smolts at migration in Northern Norway. A preliminary report. Norske Vidensk. Akademie, Oslo. I. Mat. – Naturvklasse No. 16, 5 pp.

South West Wales River Authority (1968) Fishing effort report for the 1967 season (unpublished).

Spencer, J. (1988) The Community's approach to international salmon management. In *Atlantic Salmon: Planning for the Future* (eds D. Mills and D. Piggins), Croom Helm, London, pp. 12–20.

Sprague, J.B. (1968) Promising anti-pollutant: chelating agent NTA protects fish from copper and zinc. *Nature,* **220,** 1345–6.

Sprague, J.B. and Duffy, J.R. (1971) DDT residues in Canadian Atlantic fishes and shellfishes in 1967. *J. Fish. Res. Bd Can.,* **28,** 59–64.

Sprague, J.B., Elson, P.F. and Saunders, R.L. (1965) Sublethal copper–zinc pollution in a salmon river – a field and laboratory study. *Int. J. Air Wat. Pollut.,* **9,** 531–43.

Stabell, O.B. (1984) Homing and olfaction in salmonids: a critical review with special reference to the Atlantic salmon. *Biol.Rev.,* **59,** 333–88.

Stabler, M. J. (1982) Estimation of the economic benefits of fishing: a review note. In *Allocation of Fishery Resources* (ed. J. H. Groves), Proceedings of the Technical Consultation in Fishery Resources, Vichy, France, FAO, Rome, pp. 356–65.

Ståhl, G. (1981) Genetic differentiation among natural populations of Atlantic salmon (*Salmo salar*) in northern Sweden. In *Fish Gene Pools* (ed. N. Ryman), *Ecological Bulletins (Stockholm)* **34,** 95–105.

Ståhl, G. (1983) Differences in the amount and distribution of genetic variation between natural populations and hatchery stocks of Atlantic salmon. *Aquaculture,* **33,** 23–32.

Ståhl, G. (1987) Genetic population structure of Atlantic salmon. In *Population Genetics and Fishery Management* (eds N. Ryman and F. Utter), University of Washington Press, Seattle, pp. 121–40.

Stansfeld, J.R.W. (1986) The effects of the competition of farmed salmon in the market on the present state of commercial salmon fisheries. In *The Status of the Atlantic Salmon in Scotland* (eds D. Jenkins and W.M. Shearer), ITE Symposium no. 15, Institute of Terrestrial Ecology, Abbots Ripton, pp. 60–65.

Stasko, A.B. (1975) Progress of migrating Atlantic salmon (*Salmo salar*) along an estuary, observed by ultrasonic tracking. *J. Fish Biol.*, 7, 329–38.

Stasko, A.B., Sutterlin, A.M., Rommel, S.A. and Elson, P.F. (1973) Migration-orientation of Atlantic salmon (*Salmo salar* L.). In *International Atlantic Salmon Symposium, St Andrew's*, (eds M.W. Smith and W.M. Carter), *International Atlantic Salmon Foundation Special Publication Series*, 4 (1), 119–37.

Stewart, L. (1963) *Investigations into Migratory Fish Propagation in the Area of the Lancashire River Board*, Barber, Lancaster, 80 pp.

Stewart, L. (1968) The water requirements of salmon in the River Lune; the water requirements of salmon in the River Leven. *Lancashire River Authority Report*, Fisheries Department, Lancaster.

Stewart, L. (1969) Criteria for safeguarding fisheries, fish migration and angling in rivers. *Yearbook of the Association of River Authorities*, 1969: 134–49.

Stewart, L. (1973) Environmental engineering and monitoring in relation to salmon management. In *International Atlantic Salmon Symposium, St Andrew's* (eds M.W. Smith and W.M. Carter), *International Atlantic Salmon Foundation Special Publication Series*, 4 (1). 297–316.

Stewart, L. (1978) Why no southern hemisphere salmon? The gyre theory. *Salmon and Trout Magazine*, no. 213, 46–50.

Stewart, R.N. (1949) *Experiments in Angling and Some Essays*, Northern Chronicle Press, Inverness.

Stewart, R.N. (1950) *Rivers of Iceland*, Iceland Tourist Bureau, Reykjavik.

Stoddart, T.T. (1831) *The Scottish Angler*, The Edinburgh Printing Company, Edinburgh.

Stolte, L.W. (1974) Introductin of coho salmon into coastal waters of New Hampshire. *Progve Fish Cult.*, 36, 29–32.

Stolte, L.W. (1980) Planning as related to the restoration of Atlantic salmon in New England. In *Atlantic Salmon: Its Future* (ed. A.E.J. Went), Fishing News Books, Farnham, pp. 133–45.

Stoner, J.H., Gee, A.S. and Wade, K.R. (1984) The effects of acidification on the ecology of streams in the upper Tywi catchment in West Wales. *Environ. Pollut.*, 35, 125–57.

Stoss, J. and Refstie, T. (1983) Short-term storage and cryopreservation of milt from Atlantic salmon and sea trout. *Aquaculture*, 30, 229–36.

Stradmeyer, L. and Thorpe, J.E. (1987) Feeding behaviour of wild Atlantic salmon, *Salmo salar*, L., parr in mid- to late summer in a Scottish river. *Aquaculture and Fisheries Management*, 18, 33–49.

Struthers, G. (1970) A report on a salmon long-lining cruise off the Faroes during April, 1970. Freshwater Fisheries Laboratory, Pitlochry, Report 54, FW 70.

Struthers, G. (1971) A report on the 1971 long-lining cruise off the Faroes. Freshwater Fisheries Laboratory, Pitlochry, Report 33, FW 71.

Struthers, G. (1984) Comparison of survival rates of Atlantic salmon smolts which by-pass or migrate through a high-head hydro-electric power station (30 m). *International Council for the Exploration of the Sea*, C.M.1984/M:19.

Struthers, G. and Stewart, D. (1984) A report on the composition of the adult salmon stock on the upper River Tummel, Scotland and the evaluation of the accuracy of a closed channel resistivity counter. *International Council for the Exploration of the Sea*, C.M.1984/M: 20.

Struthers, G. and Stewart, D. (1985) The composition and migration of the adult salmon stock in the upper River Tummel, Scotland, in 1984, with observations of the accuracy of the resistivity counters at two fish passes. *International Council for the Exploration of the Sea*, C.M.1985/M: 14.

Struthers, G. and Stewart, D. (1986) Observations on the timing of migration of smolts from natural and introduced juvenile salmon on the upper River Tummel, Scotland. *International Council for the Exploration of the Sea*, C.M. 1986/M:4.

Stuart, M.R. and Fuller, H.T. (1968) Mycological aspects of diseased Atlantic salmon. *Nature*, **217**, 90–2.

Stuart, T.E. (1953) Water currents through permeable gravels and their significance to spawning salmonids. *Nature*, **172**, 407–8.

Stuart, T.E. (1962) The leaping behaviour of salmon and trout at falls and obstructions. *Freshwat. Salm. Fish. Res., Scotland*, 28, 46 pp.

Symons, P.E.K. (1978) Assessing and predicting effects of the fenitrothion spray program on aquatic fauna. In *Proceedings of the Symposium on Fenitrothion: The Long-term Effects of its Use in Forest Ecosystems*, National Research Council of Canada, Ottawa, NRCC 16073, 391–414.

Symons, P.E.K. (1979) Estimated escapement of Atlantic salmon (*Salmo salar*) for maximum smolt production in rivers of different productivity. *J. Fish. Res. Bd Can.*, **36**, 132–40.

Symons, P.E.K. and Martin, J.D. (1978) Discovery of juvenile Pacific salmon (coho) in a small coastal stream of New Brunswick. *Fishery Bull., Fish Wildl. Serv. U.S.*, **76**, 487–9.

Taylor, G.G.M. (1970) *Ploughing Practice in the Forestry Commission*, Forest Record no. 73, Her Majesty's Stationery Office, London, 44 pp.

Taylor, G.R. (1968) *The Biological Timebomb*, Thames and Hudson, London.

Taylor, N. and Brownlie, T.G. (1982) *Report on Survey of Fodder Silos.* Department of Agriculture and Fisheries for Scotland.

Taylor, P.B. (1986) Experimental evidence for geomagnetic orientation in juvenile salmon, *Oncorhynchus tschawytscha* Walbaum. *J. Fish Biol.*, **28**, 607–23.

Taylor, P.B. (1988) Effect of anaesthetic MS 222 on the orientation of juvenile salmon, *Oncorhynchus tschawytscha* Walbaum. *J. Fish Biol.*, **32**, 161–8.

Taylor, V.R. and Bauld, B.R. (1973) A program for increased Atlantic salmon (*Salmo salar*) production on a major Newfoundland river. In *International Atlantic Salmon Symposium, St. Andrew's*, (eds M.W. Smith and W.M. Carter), *International Atlantic Salmon Foundation Special Publication Series*, **4** (1), 339–54.

Tchernavin, V. (1938) The absorption of bones in the skull of salmon during their migration to rivers. *Fisheries, Scotland, Salmon Fisheries*, **VI**, 4 pp.

Tchernavin, V. (1939) The origin of salmon: is its ancestry marine or freshwater. *Salmon and Trout Magazine*, no. 95, 120–40.

Templeman, W. (1968) Distribution and characteristics of Atlantic salmon over oceanic depths and on the bank and shelf slope areas off Newfoundland, March–May 1966. *Res. Bull. int. Comm. NW Atlant. Fish.*, **5**, 62–85.

Templeton, R.G. (1987) An assessment of freshwater fish stocks by hydroacoustic instrumentation techniques. *Severn-Trent Water 1987 Travelling Scholarship*, Nottingham, 31 pp.

Tervet, D.J. and Harriman, R. (1988) Changes in pH and calcium after selective liming in the catchment of Loch Dee, a sensitive and rapid-turnover loch in south-west Scotland. *Aquaculture and Fisheries Management* **19** (2), 73–95.

Tetreault, B. (1967) The salmon rivers of the Province of Quebec. *Report of the Swedish Salmon Research Institute*, LFI Medd. 6, 15 pp.

Thomson, G.M. (1922) *The Naturalisation of Animals and Plants in New Zealand*, Cambridge University Press, Cambridge.

Thorpe, J.E. (ed.) (1980) *Salmon Ranching*, Academic Press, London.

Thorpe, J.E. (1981) Migration in salmonids, with special reference to juvenile movements in fresh water. In *Salmon and Trout Migratory Behaviour Symposium* (eds E.L. Brannon and E.O. Salo), School of Fisheries, University of Washington, Seattle, pp. 86–97.

Thorpe, J.E. (1984) Downstream movements of juvenile salmonids: a forward speculative view. In *Mechanism of Migration in Fishes* (eds J.D. McCleave, G.P. Arnold, J.J. Dodson and W.H. Neill), Plenum Publishing Corporation, New York, pp. 387–96

Thorpe, J.E. (1988a) Salmon enhancement: stock discreteness and choice of material for stocking. In *Atlantic Salmon: Planning for the Future* (eds D. Mills and D. Piggins), Croom Helm, London, pp. 373–88.

Thorpe, J.E. (1988b) Salmon migration, *Science Progress* (in press.)

Thorpe, J.E. and Mitchell, K.A. (1981) Stocks of Atlantic salmon (*Salmo salar*) in Britain and Ireland: discreteness and current management. *Can. J. Fish. Aquat. Sci.*, **38** (12), 1576–90.

Thorpe, J.E. and Morgan, R.I.G. (1978) Parental influence on growth rate, smolting rate and survival in hatchery-reared juvenile Atlantic salmon, *Salmo salar* L. *J. Fish Biol.*, **13**, 549–56.

Thorpe, J.E., Miles, M.S. and Keay, D.S. (1984) Developmental rate, fecundity and egg size in Alantic salmon, *Salmo salar* L. *Aquaculture*, **43**, 289–305.

Thorsteinsson, G. and Gudjonsson, T. (1986) Experimental salmon fishing at east Greenland in summer 1985 and recaptures of tagged fish. *International Council for the Exploration of the Sea*, C.M.1986/M: 25 (Ref. B).

Thurow, F. (1968) On food, behaviour and population mechanisms of Baltic salmon. *Swedish Salmon Research Institute Report* (LFI Medd.) **4**, 16 pp.

Toner, E.D., O'Riordan, A. and Twomey, E. (1965) The effects of arterial drainage works on the salmon stock of a tributary of the River Moy. *Irish Fisheries Investigations* Ser. A, **1**, 36–55.

Trefethen, P.S. and Collins, G.B. (1974) Techniques for appraising adult salmon and trout populations in the Columbia River Basin. *European Inland Fisheries Advisory Commission* (EIFAC)/74/1/Symp.

TRRU (1984) *A study of the economic value of sporting salmon fishing in three areas of Scotland*. Tourism and Recreation Research Unit, University of Edinburgh, 21 pp.

Tuomi, A.L.W. (1980) *Canadian Atlantic Salmon: An Economic Evaluation of the New Brunswick Salmon Sport Fishery*, International Atlantic Salmon Foundation, St. Andrew's, New Brunswick.

Tuomi, A.L.W. (1986) *Canada's Atlantic Salmon Recreational Fisheries and their Future: An Economic Overview*. Report for the Alantic Salmon Federation, St. Andrew's, 41 pp.

Turnpenny, A.W.H. (1981) An analysis of mesh sizes for screening fishes at water intakes. *Estuaries*, **4** (4), 363–8.

Tytler, P., Thorpe, J.E. and Shearer, W.M. (1978) Ultrasonic tracking of the movements of Atlantic salmon smolts (*Salmo salar* L.) in the estuaries of two Scottish rivers. *J. Fish Biol.*, **12**, 575–86.

Valle, E. (1985) Predation of birds on salmon and sea trout smolts and post smolts. *International Council for the Exploration of the Sea*, C.M.1985/M: 22.

van Someren, V.D. (1937) A preliminary investigation into the causes of scale absorption in salmon (*Salmo salar* L.). *Fishery Board for Scotland, Salmon Fisheries*, 11, 11 pp.

Ventura, J.A.M. (1988) The Atlantic salmon in Asturias, Spain; Analysis of catches, 1985–86. Inventory of juvenile densities. In *Atlantic Salmon: Planning for the Future* (eds D. Mills and D. Piggins), Croom Helm, London, pp. 210–27.

Verspoor, E. (1986) Genetic discrimination of European and North American Atlantic salmon using multiple polymorphic protein loci: potential for stock separation in the West Greenland fishery. *International Council for the Exploration of the Sea*, C.M.1986/M:10.

Verspoor, E. (in press) Widespread hybridisation between native Atlantic salmon, *Salmo salar*, and introduced brown trout, *S. trutta*, in eastern Newfoundland. *J. Fish Biol.*

Vik, K.-O. (1962) Fish cultivation. *Salmon and Trout Magazine*, no. 169, 203–8.

Waddington, I.I. (1957) The development of *Cladophora* in the River Tweed and its tributaries. *Third Annual Report of the Tweed River Purification Board for Year Ending 15 May 1957. Appendix III*, Galashiels, p. 52.

Walker, A. (1988) A record around the corner? *Trout and Salmon*, April, **47**.

Wallin, O. (1957) On the growth structure and developmental physiology of the scale of fishes. *Report of the Institute of Freshwater Fisheries, Drottningholm*, **38**, 385–447.

Walton, Izaak (1653) *The Compleat Angler*, Marriott, London.

Wankowski, J.W.J. and Thorpe, J.E. (1979) Spatial distribution and feeding in Atlantic salmon, *Salmo salar* L. juveniles. *J. Fish Biol.*, **14**, 239–47

Warner, K. and Porter, F.R. (1960) Experimental improvement of a bulldozed trout stream in northern Maine. *Trans. Amer. Fish. Soc.*, **89** (1), 59–63.

Watt, W.D. (1981) Present and potential effects of acid precipitation on the Atlantic salmon in eastern Canada. In *Acid Rain and the Atlantic Salmon* (ed. L. Sochasky), *International Atlantic Salmon Foundation Special Publication Series* no. 10, pp. 39–45.

Went, A.E.J. (1956) The Irish drift net fishery for salmon. *J. Dept. Agriculture*, **52**, 131–45.

Went, A.E.J. (1964a) Irish salmon a review of investigations up to 1963. *Scient. Proc. R. Dubl. Soc.*, Ser. A, **1** (15), 365–412.

Went, A.E.J. (1964b) The pursuit of salmon in Ireland. *Proc. R. Ir. Acad.*, **63** (C) 6, 191–244.

Went, A.E.J. and Piggins, D.J. (1965) Long-distance migration of Atlantic salmon. *Nature*, **205** (4972), 723.

Westerberg, H. (1984) The orientation of fish and vertical stratification at fine- and micro-structure scales. In *Mechanisms of Migration in Fishes* (eds J.D. McCleave, G.P. Arnold, J.J. Dodson and W.H. Neill), Plenum Publishing Corporation, New York, pp. 179–204.

Wheeler, A. and Gardner, D. (1974) Survey of the literature of marine predators on salmon in the north-east Atlantic. *Fish. Mgmt*, **5** (3), 63–6.

Whelan, B.J. and Whelan, K.F. (1987) The economics of salmon fishing in the Republic of Ireland: Present and potential. In *Proceedings of the 17th Annual Study Course of the Institute of Fisheries Management*, University of Ulster, Coleraine, 1986, pp. 191–207.

White, H.C. (1936) The homing of salmon in Apple River, N.S. *J. Fish. Res. Bd Can.*, **2** (4), 391–400.

White, H.C. (1940) Sea lice (*Lepeophtheirus*) and death of salmon. *J. Fish. Res. Bd Can.*, **5**, 172–5.

White, H.C. (1942) Life history of *Lepeophtheirus salmonis*. *J. Fish. Res. Bd Can.*, **6**, 24–9.

White, H.C. (1957) Food and natural history of mergansers on salmon waters in the Maritime Provinces of Canada. *Bull. Fish. Res. Bd Can.*, no. 116, 63 pp.

White, H.C. and Huntsman, A.G. (1938) Is local behaviour in salmon heritable? *J. Fish. Res. Bd Can.*, **4**, 1–18.

White, H.C. and Medcof, J.C. (1968) Atlantic salmon scales as records of spawning history. *J. Fish. Res. Bd Can.*, **25** (11), 2439–41.

White, R.J. and Brynildson, O.M. (1975) *Guidelines for Management of Trout Stream Habitat in Wisconsin.* Department of Natural Resources, Madison, Wisconsin, Technical Bulletin no. 39, 64 pp.

Wilder, D.G. (1947) A comparative study of the Atlantic salmon, *Salmo salar* Linnaeus, and the Lake salmon, *Salmo salar sebago* (Girard). *Can. J. Res.*, **25D** (6), 175–89.

Wildish, D.J., Carson, W.G., Cunningham, T. and Lister, N.J. (1971) Toxicological effects of some organophosphate insecticides to Atlantic salmon. *Fish. Res. Bd Can. MS Rep. Ser.*, 1157, 22 pp.

Wilkins, N.P. (1971) Biochemical and serological studies on Atlantic salmon (*Salmo salar* L.). *Rapp. P.-V. Réun. Cons. Perm. Int. Explor. Mer*, **161**, 91–5.

Wilkins, N.P. (1985) *Salmon Stocks: A Genetic Perspective*, Atlantic Salmon Trust, Pitlochry, 30 pp.

Williamson, D.S. (1843) *The Statistical Account of Tongland.*

Williamson, R.B. (1974) Further captures of Pacific salmon in Scottish waters. *Scott. Fish. Bull.*, no. 41, 28–30.

Williamson, R.B. (1988) Status of exploitation of Atlantic salmon in Scotland. In *Atlantic Salmon: Planning for the Future* (eds D. Mills and D. Piggins), Croom Helm, London, pp. 91–116.

Windsor, M.L. and Hutchinson, P. (1988) International co-operation through NASCO. In *Alantic Salmon: Planning for the Future* (eds D. Mills and D. Piggins), Croom Helm, London, pp. 1–11.

Wisby, W.J. and Hasler, A.D. (1954) Effect of olfactory occlusion on migrating silver salmon (*O. kisutch*). *J. Fish. Res. Bd Can.*, **11**, 472–8.

Wolf, P.H. (1961) Land drainage and its dangers as experienced in Sweden – II, IV and V. *Salmon and Trout Magazine*, no. 161, 24–30; no. 162, 95–100; no. 163, 145–50.

Wooten, R., Smith, W. and Needham, E. (1982) Aspects of the biology of the parasitic copepods *Lepeophtheirus salmonis* and *Caligus elongatus* on farmed salmonids and their treatment. *Proc. R. Soc. Edinb.*, **81 (B)**, 185–97.

Wright, R.F., Dale, T., Gjessing, E.T., *et al.* (1975) *Impact of Acid Precipitation on Freshwater Ecosystems in Norway.* Research Report (3), SNSF Project, NISK, 1432 ÅS-NLH, Norway, 16 pp.

Yarrell, W. (1836). *British Fishes*, Vol. 2, Van Voorst, London.

Yarrell, W. (1839) *British Fishes*, Supplement, Van Voorst, London.

Young, A. (1843) On the growth of grilse and salmon. *Trans. R. Soc. Edinb.*, **15**, 343–8.

Zarnecki, S. (1956) Summer and winter-races of salmon and sea trout from the Vistula river. *International Council for the Exploration of the Sea*, C.M.1956/M: 142.

Zitko, V., Carson, W.G. and Finlayson, B.J. (1970) The inhibition of fish brain acetylcholinesterase activity by fenitrothion, Bay 77488 and Dylox, and by the 1969 aerial spraying of fenitrothion in New Brunswick. *Fish. Res. Bd Can.*, MS Report Ser. no. 1108, 11 pp.

Zitko, V., Carson, W.G. and Metcalfe, C.D. (1977) Toxicity of pyrethroids to juvenile Atlantic salmon. *Bull. Environ. Contam. Toxicol.*, **18**, 35–41.

Zitko, V., Finlayson, B.J., Wildish, P.I., Anderson, J.M. and Kohler, A.C. (1971) Methylmercury in freshwater and marine fishes in New Brunswick, in the Bay of Fundy, and on the Nova Scotia Banks. *J. Fish. Res. Bd Can.*, **28**, 1285–91.

Zitko, V., McLeese, D.W., Metcalfe, C.D. and Carson, W.G. (1979) Toxicity of permethrin, decamethrin and related pyrethroids to salmon and lobster. *Bull. Environ. Contam. Toxicol.*, **21**, 338–43.

# Index